JOHN LOCKE
SELECTED CORRESPON

C000063205

 Toleration

Democracy

 Revolution

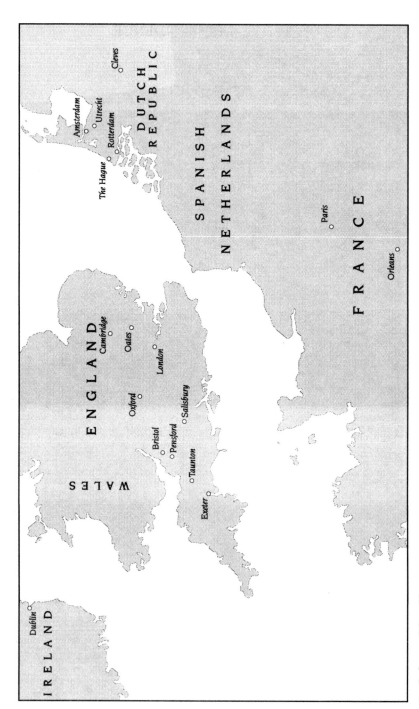

Locke's republic of letters

John Locke
Selected Correspondence

edited by

MARK GOLDIE

from the Clarendon Edition by E. S. de Beer

OXFORD
UNIVERSITY PRESS

OXFORD
UNIVERSITY PRESS

Great Clarendon Street, Oxford OX2 6DP

Oxford University Press is a department of the University of Oxford.
It furthers the University's objective of excellence in research, scholarship,
and education by publishing worldwide in

Oxford New York

Auckland Cape Town Dar es Salaam Hong Kong Karachi Kuala Lumpur
Madrid Melbourne Mexico City Nairobi New Delhi Shanghai Taipei Toronto

With offices in

Argentina Austria Brazil Chile Czech Republic France Greece
Guatemala Hungary Italy Japan Poland Portugal Singapore
South Korea Switzerland Thailand Turkey Ukraine Vietnam

Oxford is a registered trade mark of Oxford University Press
in the UK and in certain other countries

Published in the United States
by Oxford University Press Inc., New York

First published 2002
First published in paperback 2007

British Library Cataloguing in Publication Data

Data available

Library of Congress Cataloging in Publication Data

Data available

ISBN 978-0-19-823542-2 (Hbk.) 978-0-19-920430-4 (Pbk.)

Typeset in Minion by Graphicraft Limited, Hong Kong
Printed in Great Britain
on acid-free paper by
Biddles Ltd., King's Lynn, Norfolk

Contents

Acknowledgements

This book stands on the shoulders of a magnificent achievement in modern scholarly editing. Locke's complete correspondence, published by Oxford University Press between 1976 and 1989, fills 6,000 pages in eight volumes. It was the work of Esmond de Beer, who was a 'virtuoso' of a rare sort. He never held a university post, being the beneficiary of a New Zealand chain store fortune. Born in Dunedin in 1895, he took a degree at New College, Oxford, and settled in England after the First World War. Until after the Second War the front door of his London home was opened by a uniformed parlourmaid. He never possessed a gramophone, radio, television, or motor car, but he had 8,000 books, a Monet, and some Rembrandt drawings. Only sturdy walking holidays in Dr Johnson's Hebrides, the acquisition of rare books, and the committees of half a dozen learned societies—the Antiquaries, the Hakluyt, the Historical Association—distracted him from scholarship. In the 1920s he began an edition of John Evelyn's *Diary*. That took him until 1955, when it appeared in six volumes, establishing him as the 'prince of textual editors'. Then he turned to Locke's correspondence, which occupied him for the next thirty years. With iron determination and infinite patience, he transcribed in longhand all 3,600 letters and supplied thousands of erudite footnotes. He was ninety-five when he died in 1990.

De Beer's list of acknowledgements extended to four pages, and I owe renewed thanks to the army of scholars and librarians who helped him. These included John Simmons, who proofread all eight volumes. I have accumulated my own debts. The board of the Clarendon Edition of the Works of John Locke (Michael Ayers, Jonquil Bevan, John Dunn, the late Peter Laslett, John Milton, Robin Robbins, John Rogers, Sandy Stewart, and James Tully), which I joined in 1998, looked benignly on the project. Several people made suggestions about what to include: Justin Champion, Michael Hunter, Sarah Hutton, Matthew Kramer, John Marshall, and John Rogers. John and Jean Yolton, John Milton, and Sandy Stewart put their deep knowledge of Locke at my disposal. So did Elizabeth Short, who has prepared the index for the long awaited ninth volume of the complete correspondence, which will unlock de Beer's great repository. Clare Jackson was indefatigable: she advised, polished prose, solved puzzles, and collated. She and Jane Spencer created the index. John Milton, Philip Milton, Sami-Juhani Savonius, Hannah Smith, and Jane Spencer helped to improve the introduction and headnotes. Una McCormack and Susan Sadler provided editorial assistance. Melissa Percival made translations from the French. At Oxford University Press, Peter Momtchiloff has been an astute and patient editor. Finally, although they have not had a direct hand in this volume, I pay tribute to the constant support of two colleagues, John Morrill and Quentin Skinner.

Esmond de Beer's tenacity was indomitable. His text doubtless has flaws; no editor is free from them; but his standards were impeccable. I hope that this book does not bring his ghost upon me to repeat what he said of an earlier editor of Locke's letters: 'incompetent and irresponsible'.

Churchill College,
Cambridge,
September 2001

Introduction

Few people before John Locke's time left so much correspondence behind them. There are 3,637 surviving letters written by him and to him. Certainly some of his contemporaries, such as Leibniz and Mersenne, exceed this total. And, of course, his successors did so: Goethe with about 13,000, Voltaire and Darwin with some 15,000 each. But private correspondence on a large scale is a phenomenon of the seventeenth century and scarcely before. The most famous letter-writers of the ancient world, Cicero and Augustine, left only a few hundred each, though Erasmus, the epistolary genius of the Renaissance, bequeathed over 3,000. The tally for Locke's great philosophical contemporary, Thomas Hobbes, is just 211.

Locke is widely known for his books, but deserves to be better known by his letters. He conducted a life of prodigious intellectual activity, yet also one of political and personal engagement. He corresponded with such luminaries as Isaac Newton and Robert Boyle and with such leading politicians as the Earl of Shaftesbury and Lord Somers, though many of his correspondents were people little remembered today. Some were friends over whose children's nurture he took immense pains, or men of business who told him the price of East India Company stock, or women who engaged him in philosophical enquiry. Others were noble patrons whom he advised, protégés whose careers he sponsored, polemicists who defended or attacked his writings, strangers who sought assurance on the evidence for a godhead or support for a piece of reforming legislation, publishers who produced his books, and physicians with whom he swapped diagnoses. There were plutocrats and philanthropists, tailors and sailors, watchmakers and gardeners. Locke's correspondence not only illuminates the thinking of a great philosopher, but also provides an unsurpassed entrée to the social, cultural, political, and scientific world of the second half of the seventeenth century. Accordingly, one aim of this book is to make Locke as familiar to readers of history as he is already to readers of philosophy and political theory.

Locke wrote a philosophical work which gave the basis for modern epistemology, *An Essay Concerning Human Understanding*, and a political work which is a canonical text in the making of modern liberalism, the *Two Treatises of Government*. The first he put his name to, the second remained anonymous in his lifetime. Consequently it was pre-eminently the *Essay*, enquiring into 'the original, certainty, and extent of human knowledge',[1] which captivated his contemporaries, some applauding, others aghast. Here Locke argued that knowledge was not innate, not planted by the hand of God. What we can know

---

[1] Locke, *An Essay Concerning Human Understanding*, I. i. 2.

with any confidence derives from the experience of the senses, ordered by reason. 'Let us then suppose the mind to be, as we say, white paper, void of all characters, without any ideas; how comes it to be furnished? . . . Whence has it all the materials of reason and knowledge? To this I answer, in one word, from experience.'[2] Locke urged that our faculties are best exercised by observation of, and action within, the natural and social world about us. This was a scheme for humankind's purposes which banished speculative metaphysics, religious dogma, and the wisdom of the ancients.

In the *Two Treatises* Locke continued his self-appointed task of clearing aside the obstacles in the way of rational thought. Here, he set out to eradicate from English minds the poison of the Tory doctrine of monarchical absolutism. He believed that the sycophantic preachers of the divine right of kings, and of 'passive obedience and non-resistance', had underwritten the growth of tyranny. He aimed to show that governments exist to preserve our natural rights to 'life, liberty, and estate'.[3] Consequently, no government could be legitimate unless it was grounded in the consent of the governed. Any regime that betrayed its trust could be overthrown, if necessary by revolution. In his final sentence, Locke wrote that when rulers become tyrants, 'the people have a right to act as supreme' and to 'erect a new form' of government, or 'under the old form place it in new hands, as they think good'.[4]

Locke worked on the *Essay* from about 1671 and on the *Two Treatises* from about 1679, but it was not until 1689 that he published them. In the same year there also appeared, at the instigation of his friends, his eloquent *Letter Concerning Toleration*. It proved a pivotal year not only in his own life but also in the history of the British Isles. England in the 1680s witnessed a political regime of considerable brutality, marked by a Tory backlash against the Whig movement to which Locke belonged. Locke had become an adviser to the Whig leader, the Earl of Shaftesbury, who had challenged the regime of King Charles II and been crushed. Colleagues in the movement were executed for treason or jailed on suspicion of sedition. Locke had been spied upon, had feared for his life, and had fled into exile in the Dutch Republic. When Charles II died in 1685, the brief reign of his Roman Catholic brother James II ensued. Domestic resistance against both monarchs failed, but in the winter of 1688–9 England was successfully invaded by a Dutch army, led by Prince William of Orange. For the second time in forty years a Stuart monarch was deposed. James II fled and King William III was installed. After spending five years in exile, Locke now returned to England.

Aged fifty-six when he came home, Locke had published almost nothing and was virtually unknown. But soon the *Essay* brought him to the attention of the public. By the middle of the 1690s his *Thoughts Concerning Education* (1693) and his tracts on money (1691–5) had added to his renown, and his authorship of the *Two Treatises* and of *The Reasonableness of Christianity* (1695)

---

[2] Ibid. II. i. 2.   [3] Locke, *Two Treatises of Government*, II, para. 87.   [4] Ibid., para. 243.

began to be suspected. Though Locke lived discreetly, his life ended in 1704 amid the din of those who hailed him as 'the Socrates of the age'[5] and of those who accused him of holding heretical and seditious opinions.

Locke's letters provide a record of both the private and the public man, a man who was not only a philosopher, but also a physician, educationist, theologian, economist, civil servant, counsellor, and Fellow of the Royal Society. They are letters which encompass a remarkable range of topics. They touch, for example, on the medical efficacy of bloodletting and purging; on child-beating and the respective merits of schools and private tutors; on the date of the Creation, the threat of 'popery', the nature of clerical bigotry, and the spread of 'free-thinking'; on the relief of poverty and the means of preventing currency speculation; on the resentments of Ireland and the provisioning of Virginia; on the measurement of longitude and the nature of comets. They seek information about the Indian mogul Aurangzib and about the natural produce of North America. It is a diversity that is the measure of a polymath of insatiable curiosity.

This book contains just 7 per cent of Locke's vast surviving correspondence. Later something will be said about the criteria of selection. But first, it is worth exploring further the character of the letters taken as a whole. This we can do by considering when, where, and by whom they were written.[6]

From Puritanism to the Enlightenment

The correspondence spans fifty-two years. It begins in a society lacerated by civil war, rebellion, and religious strife, and ends in an era of parliamentary parties, religious toleration, and a flourishing worldwide commercial empire. The earliest datable letter, of May 1652, was written when Locke was nineteen years old. England was a republic, King Charles I had been executed, and the House of Lords and the bishops had been abolished. Puritan godly commonwealths, and sectarian animosities, were planted in towns and villages. Popish rebellion in Ireland and Covenanting rebellion in Scotland had been bloodily subdued by Oliver Cromwell's army. The final letter dates from October 1704, in the reign of Queen Anne, Protestant daughter of the Catholic James II who had been deposed in 1688. It was the year the Duke of Marlborough fought the battle of Blenheim against Louis XIV, in which the Navy captured Gibraltar, in which Jonathan Swift published *A Tale of a Tub* and Isaac Newton his *Opticks*. England was a parliamentary monarchy, in which the sovereignty once claimed exclusively for the crown was now exercised by the crown-in-parliament. The contest between Whig and Tory remained fierce, but had been

---

[5] L3346. Throughout the footnotes in this book, 'L' stands for 'Letter number'. The numeration was established by E. S. de Beer in his *Correspondence of John Locke* (8 vols., Oxford, 1976–89).

[6] In this Introduction I take examples from throughout Locke's correspondence. The letters selected for inclusion in this book are all introduced in the headnotes to individual chapters.

successfully contained within electoral politics. The removal of Catholics from access to power, and an Act of Toleration, which allowed freedom of worship for Protestant Dissenters, had relaxed religious tensions. Yet this was also an England in which state power, both fiscal and military, had grown immensely. A great navy stood guardian over the traffic of empire, and a slave economy was entrenched in North America and the Caribbean.

Locke's letters begin during the Puritan Revolution and end in the dawn of the Enlightenment. They provide a microcosm of the remarkable shift in English civilization from an era of godly zeal, in which men and women engaged in religious violence and utopian experiment, to an age that was suspicious of 'reformation' and 'enthusiasm' (as fanaticism was called), and which valued latitude, 'politeness', and 'improvement'. Equally, the letters mark England's transition from a marginal position in international affairs to world-power status, recording as they do the humiliation of Charles II's navy by the Dutch in 1667, and, in the 1690s, Locke's personal involvement in imperial policy-making as a member of the Board of Trade and Plantations.

From Somerset to Amsterdam

Most of Locke's correspondence has its provenance in three countries, England, France, and the Netherlands. Within England, it chiefly centres on four places, the West Country, Oxford, London, and a manor house called Oates in west Essex. Locke seems only once to have travelled further north than Cambridge: to Belvoir Castle in Leicestershire, where he negotiated the marriage of the future second Earl of Shaftesbury to the daughter of the Earl of Rutland.

Locke's childhood was spent in Somerset. He inherited a small estate from his father, but after his father's death in 1661 he rarely returned. His affairs were conducted by estate stewards, who collected rents, negotiated tenancies, paid local taxes, and saw to repairs. The dozens of letters between Locke and his stewards, Cornelius Lyde and William Stratton, are revealing of the lives of tenant farmers and of Locke's attitudes to economic justice and poverty.

The counties of Somerset and Devon were strongholds of Whiggery and Dissent. When the Duke of Monmouth staged his disastrous rising against James II in 1685, they provided him with his makeshift army of yeomen and artisans. Locke's gentry friends, though conspicuously absent from Monmouth's army, were immediately suspect and their homes searched for arms. From the 1670s onward Locke developed close friendships with the Clarke, Yonge, and Duke families. He called them 'the Row', because their houses ran north to south from Taunton down to the Devon coast. They in turn knew Locke's cousins among the merchant families of Exeter, including the future Lord Chancellor Peter King, who would be his literary executor. The Clarkes,

Yonges, and Dukes intermarried, they served as Members of Parliament, and they protected the interests of Dissenters and of the woollen textile industry. In the 1690s Clarke was the key man in the group known as the 'College', who acted as Locke's spokesmen in the House of Commons. It was for the upbringing of Clarke's eldest son that Locke drafted *Some Thoughts Concerning Education*.

The second of Locke's English locales was Oxford, where he studied and taught in early adulthood. There are letters reflecting on the turmoil as England's Republic fell in 1659–60, and letters to his pupils and their parents. It was at Oxford, later, in 1681, that Charles II summarily dismissed a Whig-dominated parliament, which set in train the Tory purges. In 1684 Locke's colleagues at Christ Church succumbed to a royal demand to expel him. In the 1690s the Tory and High Church dons pronounced condemnations of his heresies. But even there, finally, his *Essay* began to enter the curriculum. Near Oxford lived James Tyrrell, a lifelong friend, a Whig lawyer and historian, who, like Locke, wrote anonymously in the early 1680s against the absolutist doctrine of Sir Robert Filmer, and who in 1681 helped Locke write a defence of religious toleration. Later, Tyrrell was an invaluable conduit for news of English affairs when Locke was in Holland, and, after the Revolution, of Oxford affairs when Locke was in London and at Oates.

After Oxford came London, where Locke resided from 1667 to 1675, and periodically thereafter. The Earl of Shaftesbury drew him there, to Exeter House in the Strand, to serve as secretary, adviser, and tutor. It was to London that Locke returned after his exile, taking lodgings first in Westminster and then in Lincoln's Inn Fields. He continued to visit on business throughout the 1690s. London was the home of the Royal Society, which, in the hands of its secretaries Henry Oldenburg and Hans Sloane, provided a clearing house for the dissemination of new knowledge of the natural world. London was also the centre of printing and bookselling, and Locke had constant dealings with his publisher, Awnsham Churchill, whose shop was at 'the sign of the Black Swan in Paternoster Row', by St Paul's Cathedral. After the Revolution, London was the seat of a parliament that now became a permanent institution, sitting for several months every year. At Richard's Coffee House in Fleet Street, Locke's colleagues gathered to hear the news and plan parliamentary tactics.

Coal smog and asthma drove Locke from London in 1691. Damaris Masham invited him to Oates, in the village of High Laver, twenty miles to the north. There he settled for the remainder of his life, receiving a stream of visitors, Isaac Newton among them. Masham was the daughter of the Cambridge Platonist Ralph Cudworth, and was perhaps the only woman whom Locke took entirely seriously intellectually. They were devoted to each other, though there is no evidence that their love was other than Platonic. Her husband, Sir Francis Masham, was Whig MP for Essex. Theirs was a substantial household, with ten servants besides a large family. Locke paid rent for his chamber, servant, and horse.

To these four English locales, we can add two on the Continent of Europe, where Locke's correspondence is the legacy of two periods when he lived abroad. He was in France from 1675 to 1679. In Paris he came to know Nicolas Toinard, with whom he discussed astronomy, scientific instruments, and the consistency of the Gospel narratives, a correspondence frustrated in the 1690s by warfare between England and France. From 1683 to 1689 Locke resided in Holland. In Amsterdam he met Jean Le Clerc, a Swiss theologian, who edited a learned journal, the *Bibliothèque universelle*, in which Locke published a summary of his *Essay* in 1688. Locke also encountered Philip van Limborch, a pillar of the Remonstrants, the moderate party in the Dutch Reformed Church, who was striving to complete an encyclopaedic history of religious persecution. In Rotterdam, Locke lodged with Benjamin Furly, a prosperous cloth merchant, host to passing Englishmen of unorthodox intellectual tastes, and owner of a substantial library. The Dutch Republic, more tolerant than its neighbours and a haven for refugees, was the intellectual *entrepôt* of western Europe.

From shopkeepers to earls

With what 'ranks' and 'qualities' of person did Locke correspond? He was himself a gentleman, and the demarcation between him and his aristocratic patrons on the one hand, and his artisan and tradesmen acquaintances on the other is palpable. But, though he owned some land, he did not live as a landed squire, and his paternal estate placed him barely on the margins of gentility. His grandfather was a tanner and his cousins included yeomen and shopkeepers. He owed his first advancement to a local squire, who got him to school and university, and his later advancement to aristocrats who valued his talents. In the mid-1690s he acquired a handsome state salary, though his growing wealth came chiefly from shrewd investment in one of the world's first stock markets.

Taking Locke's correspondence as a whole, there is a total of 378 identifiable people who exchanged letters with him. The size of their surviving correspondence ranges from, in many cases, only a single letter, to 374 in the case of Edward Clarke. Five people account for one-third of the total extant correspondence and fourteen for one-half. In the case of letters written by Locke himself, the concentration is even greater. Two recipients, Clarke and Peter King, account for 453 out of the 1,051 surviving letters written by Locke. Others for whom there are large survivals include Furly, Le Clerc, Limborch, Sloane, Toinard, Tyrrell, the deist Anthony Collins, and William Molyneux, the Dublin philosopher. Also among these are Edward Clarke's wife Mary, Locke's youthful flame Elinor Parry, a clergyman friend John Mapletoft, the stewards Lyde and Strachey, his cousin John Bonville, and Damaris Masham's young stepdaughter Esther.

Locke was well connected with the principal politicians and savants of the age. His correspondents include sixteen peers, forty-one MPs (including three in the Irish and Scottish parliaments), and thirty-seven Fellows of the Royal Society. A striking characteristic is the predominance of the professions and servants of the state. There are forty physicians, thirty lawyers, nearly seventy clergymen, more than two dozen civil servants and colonial administrators, and eight booksellers and publishers. Most of the peers were new or recent creations, weighty by virtue of service to the state rather than rural acreage: in French parlance they were *noblesse de robe* rather than *noblesse d'épée*. John Somers—son of a Worcestershire attorney—who rose to be Lord Chancellor, is a salient case. There are two dozen merchants and financiers, such as Samuel Heathcote, a founder of the Bank of England, and John Cary, a West Indies sugar merchant. By his later years, Locke moved in circles which were predominantly metropolitan, commercial, governmental, and imperial. These were people at the heart of what historians have called the 'fiscal-military' state of post-Revolution England, and the 'gentlemanly capitalism' of the first British empire.[7]

Forty-four women are known to have corresponded with Locke. Three of them published works of philosophy or divinity: Elizabeth Berkeley (Mrs Burnet), Damaris Masham, and Catherine Trotter (Mrs Cockburn). Some were the wives and daughters of aristocrats, such as Margaret Ashley Cooper, Countess of Shaftesbury, to whom Locke dedicated his translation of Pierre Nicole's moral essays. Others were courtiers, such as Martha Lockhart, lady-in-waiting to Queen Mary II; another was Rabsy Smithsby, an expert shopper for Locke and the Clarkes.

Fifty-three of the sixty-eight clerical correspondents were ministers of the Church of England, including several bishops. There is a tendency in some modern scholarship to identify Locke's religious affinities as more Dissenting than Anglican. This claim looks odd in the light of this figure. Certainly Locke defended Dissenters' rights, but just five of his clergymen correspondents were Dissenters, though it is true that lay Dissenters figure importantly, such as the Quaker Furly and the Presbyterian John Shute. Surprisingly, for so committed an anti-papist as Locke, there are six French Roman Catholic *abbés*, though perhaps they scarcely count, so secularized had such positions become. As many as fourteen clerical and lay Huguenots appear, driven from France and often seeking tutorships or secretaryships in English households; their cultural presence is as tangible as their economic desperation. One of them, Pierre Coste, who came to live at Oates, was crucial in the transmission of Locke's philosophy to the French-speaking world.[8]

---

[7] John Brewer, *The Sinews of Power: War, Money and the English State, 1688–1783* (London, 1989); P. J. Cain and A. G. Hopkins, *British Imperialism: Innovation and Expansion, 1688–1914* (London, 1993).

[8] A fuller analysis of Locke's correspondents will appear in vol. 9 of the complete *Correspondence of John Locke* (Oxford, forthcoming).

The philosopher in his letters

The character of the man revealed by his letters provokes admiration rather than endearment. Locke was reserved and aloof, anxious and evasive, secretive in his literary and financial dealings. His record-keeping was meticulous to the point of obsessional, though he was scarcely ever confessional and never autobiographical. He could be testy and peremptory, and, for all his scoffing at scholastic disputation, could be a wrangler and a bludgeoning polemicist. His sense of justice was apt to overbalance his sense of charity, and in the midst of condolence he was capable of reminding a widow of money that was owed him. He schooled his time and his tongue, and was moved more by propriety than by spontaneity. This is not to say that he was pompous or ceremonious, for, even when famous, he was unshowy. He expected moral and intellectual seriousness, though he warned against excessive scrupulosity and puritanical moroseness. He probably spent more time in coffee houses and inns than he pretended, if only because, when in town, it was a necessity for doing business and being informed. On one occasion he wrote to Edward Clarke's wife, Mary, from 'the tavern with your husband'.[9] He was not above fashion, splashing out on a new beaver hat after his return from exile. He enjoyed satire and banter, and could be skittish: youthful letters find amusement in bodily malfunction and poke fun at people he thought absurd, such as baroque poets and popish monks; in old age he recollected a tedious Oxford practical joke involving a college porter's beard. His humour, complained a Victorian prude, 'exhibited more vivacity than good taste'.[10] Throughout his life Locke's sharpest wit took the form of sarcasm, and even close friends feared the sharpness of his quill.

Locke unbent especially with children and he loved to watch them growing up, doting on Betty Clarke and Esther and Frank Masham. He reserved his warmth and confidences for a small chosen circle. He was not promiscuous in friendship, admission to Locke's friendship being elaborately choreographed, while acquaintances beyond this circle were kept at bay with evasive pleasantries. He took pains to produce lengthy, mannered missives that praised a patron or flattered an aristocratic lady. Locke never married, though apparently came close to it more than once. Nothing in his surviving writings suggests that he was troubled by sexual desire. Perhaps only once does he mention a woman as being physically attractive: a pretty maidservant at a French inn.[11] Flirtation and flattery were of course expected. Lady Mordaunt, a veteran of Charles II's libidinous court, flirted with him, and he colluded; while, conversely, Lady Calverley told him to dispense with his tiresome gallantries.[12]

---

[9] L1220.
[10] Anon., Introduction to John Locke, *The Reasonableness of Christianity* (London, 1836), p. x.
[11] L310.   [12] L1099; L1305.

If always a man of discretion, Locke did become more expansive with age, and less intellectually and emotionally straitened. In young adulthood he came to feel constrained by the academic and intellectual orthodoxies of Oxford. In her memoir of him, Masham recorded that it was by writing letters that he began to liberate himself. Discontent with Oxford

put him upon seeking the company of pleasant, and witty men; with whom he likewise took great delight in corresponding by letters. And in conversation, and these correspondences, he (according to his own account of himself) spent for some years much of his time. It is scarce to be thought he writ so well then as after he had lived more in the world, and been advantaged by the politer conversation of great men: else it would be pity that those letters should be lost.[13]

Fortunately, many are not lost.

The epistolic age

From the mid-seventeenth century letter-writing became a practice central to English culture. The Verney family of Claydon in Buckinghamshire, for whom 30,000 letters survive from the 1630s to the mid-eighteenth century, inducted each generation into devotion to, and the protocols of, corresponding: letters were docketed, endorsed, reviewed.[14] Rates of literacy and education had improved. By the late seventeenth century, most of the gentry and professional classes had attended university or the Inns of Court, and around three-quarters of urban tradesmen were literate. *The Young Secretary's Guide* of 1687 was the first handbook to provide model letters for maidservants. A handful of Locke's correspondents were marginally literate, such as his cousin, the pewterer John Bonville. Despite her being a courtier, Lady Mordaunt's letters are markedly defective in punctuation and spelling, though this does not inhibit her from writing acutely and persuasively.[15]

During the seventeenth century the growth of letter-writing had a significant impact on political literacy, on the flow of information about parliamentary debates, court faction, and the fate of the Reformed religion abroad. A metropolitan political diarist like Roger Morrice, writing in the 1680s, relied heavily on letters for news. A typical entry begins, 'we are credibly informed by a letter out of Ireland'.[16] Likewise, letters kept Locke informed

---

[13] Remonstrants Library, Amsterdam, MS J57a: Damaris Masham to Jean Le Clerc, 12 Jan. 1705.

[14] Susan E. Whyman, *Sociability and Power in Late Stuart England: The Cultural World of the Verneys, 1660–1720* (Oxford, 1999). More generally, see Rebecca Earle (ed.), *Epistolary Selves: Letters and Letter-Writers, 1600–1945* (Aldershot, 1999); W. H. Irving, *The Providence of Wit in the English Letter Writers* (Durham, NC, 1955); H. Anderson, P. B. Dahglian, and I. Ehrenpreis (eds.), *The Familiar Letter in the Eighteenth Century* (Lawrence, KS, 1966).

[15] Her words were quoted verbatim, and she was given a central role, in David Edgar's British television drama, *Citizen Locke*, broadcast on Channel Four in 1994.

[16] Roger Morrice's unpublished 'Entring Book' is at Dr Williams's Library, London. An edition is in preparation.

of political developments. John Freke wrote from a London coffee house, quickly scribbling down what he had just heard about Lord Monmouth's disgrace.[17] Mary Clarke sent a prediction of the outcome of the general election of 1690 in Somerset constituencies.[18] The emerging newspapers were heavily indebted to epistolary form. London scriveners produced multiple copies of manuscript newsletters for despatch to provincial gentlemen. After the 1690s these were displaced by the rapid growth of printed newspapers, but these in turn relied upon the simple device of printing letters sent by correspondents. In the 1690s the *Athenian Mercury* was the first newspaper to print letters to the editor (real or concocted), together with practical and homely replies from the editorial staff. Hundreds of political pamphlets had titles like *A Letter to a Friend*. During the eighteenth century, the letter became a presiding literary genre. Novels, like those of Samuel Richardson, were written in epistolary form, and printed editions of collected letters were published in abundance. Lady Mary Wortley Montagu, Lord Chesterfield, and Horace Walpole are remembered chiefly for their letters.

Among scholars and intellectuals, the last quarter of the seventeenth century saw the emergence of the 'Republic of Letters': the regular exchange of ideas and information, and of 'news of the works of the learned'. This chiefly occurred in the triangle demarcated by London, Amsterdam, and Paris. For some, like the Royal Society's first secretary, Henry Oldenburg, this became a profession, driven by ideals of 'pansophism', the effort at an encyclopaedic record of all knowledge of the natural world. New learned journals, like the Society's *Philosophical Transactions*, and Le Clerc's *Bibliothèque universelle*, relied on 'philosophical letters' for copy, and Locke contributed to them both.[19]

Letter writing had a pervasive presence in the world of the literate. Travel was slow and difficult. Through correspondence people at a distance from each other could continue to live in each others' imaginations. After Locke returned to England from exile he never again met the friends he made in Holland, but he preserved the intimacies of those friendships by correspondence which continued until his death. In Amsterdam, Locke's letters were circulated among his friends and read out loud.[20] Locke read letters aloud to children and he encouraged them to strike up their own penfriendships.[21] Letters often expressed a longing for a future personal meeting, or nostalgic recollection of past encounters. Correspondence also served to rescue people from intellectual and personal isolation. Samuel Bold, a scholarly cleric in a dull Dorset parish and victim of local Tory dislike of his tolerant religious views, was elated that the great Locke should deign to strike up a correspondence

---

[17] L2183, to be printed in vol. 9 of the *Correspondence*.   [18] L1253.

[19] Maarten Ultee, 'The Republic of Letters: Learned Correspondence, 1680–1720', *The Seventeenth Century*, 2 (1987), 95–112; Anne Goldgar, *Impolite Learning: Conduct and Community in the Republic of Letters, 1680–1750* (New Haven, 1995).

[20] L1124.

[21] L1966 (in a missing paragraph, to be restored in vol. 9 of the *Correspondence*).

with him.[22] Conversely, by correspondence, Locke could preserve the distinctly cool authority of an absentee landlord over cottagers who may never have set eyes on him. Correspondence also opened windows upon a rapidly expanding world. He could hear of the problems of New England colonizers in confronting native Americans, and could feed his anthropological curiosity about non-European cultures. Locke was one of the first people to receive letters from many far-flung places, from Charleston in Carolina, from Jamaica in the West Indies, from Bengal in India, and Amoy in China.[23]

In the growth of letter writing we should not overlook a major practical innovation: a reliable, frequent postal service. The General Post Office was founded in 1657 and created a national network of inns, shops, and coffee houses designated as receiving places, and soon called 'post offices'. Epistolary output rose dramatically, especially in London after William Dockwra created a penny post for the metropolis in 1680. When Locke was living in Essex, letters were sent to him care of a shopkeeper in Bishops Stortford or the innkeeper at the Crown in Harlow. It became habitual to set aside time to catch the mail. Elinor Hawkshaw, 'at the post office' in Anglesey, wrote to Locke in haste, for 'the post horse is pressing'.[24] The post became predictable. James Houblon wrote to Samuel Pepys at 3 p.m. on 9 July 1689, suggesting a meeting the next day at 7 p.m., and asking that he confirm the arrangement by 'penny post letter'.[25] John Somers could calculate his expectations exactly: on Wednesday 5 March 1690 he wrote to Locke from Oxford, hoping that Locke would reply by Saturday's post, and expecting to receive the reply at Worcester on Monday the 10th; he did.[26] Only rarely is there complaint that a letter had gone astray, and even then the explanation might be ready to hand. In the 1690s England was at war with France, and on one occasion a postbag that included two of Locke's letters to the Netherlands was flung overboard to prevent capture by French privateers.[27]

Letter writing occupied considerable amounts of time. There are several occasions when three letters by Locke survive which were written on the same day. He wrote to Peter King on 4, 5, 13, 15, 16, 23, 24, 25, and 28 November 1702. Ensconced at Oates during the 1690s, the ageing philosopher, struggling with his asthmatic cough, sat in the 'chimney corner' by the fire, writing letter after letter.[28] Fame carried its price, for now he received letters from people he did not know, but who had read his books and wanted him to explain a logical lacuna or to reassure them he had not slipped into heresy. Others arrived from friends and acquaintances who pressed him to put in a word so that a son might acquire a vicarage in the gift of a great lord, or a clerkship in the

---

[22] L2232.
[23] Letters from outside Europe included in this volume are: L253, L275, L279, L305, L2545, L2614, L3046, L3136.
[24] L1209, L1210.
[25] R. G. Howarth (ed.), *Letters and the Second Diary of Samuel Pepys* (London, 1933), 202.
[26] L1255.   [27] L1325.   [28] L2719.

civil service. He lamented in 1696 that because 'I had play'd the fool to print' about the coinage crisis, there was 'scarce a post wherein somebody or other did not give me fresh trouble'.[29]

The accidents of survival

About 70 per cent of Locke's surviving correspondence comprises letters *to* him. The surprise is that as many as 1,051 letters *by* him survive. The acceleration of letter writing does not of itself explain the peculiarities of survival into modern archives. It had long been the practice of governments and businesses to keep letterbooks—scribal copies of outgoing letters—as an administrative record. When Locke served on an embassy to Cleves in 1665–6 he wrote up the ambassador's letterbook. As secretary to the Proprietors of Carolina he transcribed and summarized incoming letters for his busy employers. Generally, he did not keep a letterbook of his personal letters, but he often kept drafts, carefully working over the texts of important or delicate letters. About 140 out of the 1,051 letters survive as drafts. Nearly all the extant early letters, down to 1663, are in this category, and we cannot always be sure that they were in fact posted, or that the fair copy was not further amended.

Two-fifths of Locke's own letters have survived because two friends kept their papers and their descendants remained in their ancestral homes until modern times. Edward Clarke kept all his papers, and his descendants are still at Chipley near Taunton, although the papers are now in the Bodleian Library in Oxford and the Somerset Record Office. The letters to Peter King, Locke's executor, survived in the hands of the Earls of Lovelace, though they were scarcely accessible to scholars until they were also deposited in the Bodleian, in 1942. Just over half of Locke's extant letters are today in Oxford. The others are scattered far and wide: from Lambeth Palace and the Bank of England to New York, Boston, Austin, Chicago, Santa Barbara, Berlin, Paris, Copenhagen, Uppsala, Venice, and Moscow.

The disappearance of letters wreaks invisible havoc on perceptions of a life. We scarcely detect relationships that happen not to be visible to us on paper. Locke's relationship with the Earl of Pembroke, to whom he dedicated the *Essay*, and to whose dinner table he was often invited, is shrouded in mystery. We have only snippets of information and those mainly from independent sources: John Aubrey, in a letter to Anthony Wood in 1694, tells of a conversation he had with Locke in the company of Pembroke.[30] There is only one surviving letter from Locke to Pembroke, an often quoted one of 1684 which disingenuously denies that he had been politically active. Only three letters survive to Lord Somers, the Whig leader to whom Locke was close in the 1690s, but whose papers were destroyed by fire in 1752. In the earliest letter, of

---

[29] L2059. [30] *Notes and Queries*, 195 (1950), 553.

September 1689, we learn that Somers was already Locke's 'honoured friend', but we cannot reconstruct their political relationship during the crucial months of the Revolution.[31] Since no letters remain between John Evelyn and Locke, what are we to make of Evelyn's reference to 'our friend' Locke in a letter to Pepys in 1694?[32] Or, again, there are no extant letters between Locke and Christopher Wren or the classicist Richard Bentley, but we know independently that Locke was named as belonging to a discussion group comprising Newton, Evelyn, Wren, and Bentley.[33]

Sometimes letters were deliberately destroyed. There can be no doubt that during the Tory purges of the 1680s letters were suppressed to avoid political incrimination.[34] The mails were opened by government officials, and Locke and Clarke used code names. Political risks probably explain the paucity of letters with the Earl of Shaftesbury. For the politically crucial years of 1681–2, all but two of the twenty-five surviving letters by Locke are to the French virtuoso Toinard, but these say almost nothing about politics.

Gaps also arise because letter-writing depends upon absence. The early letters between Locke and Damaris Masham are poignant and revealing; letters cease when Locke came to live in her house, and we are tantalized by their life at Oates. Conversely, the simplest of contingencies have left us with richly revelatory letters. Our picture of Locke in the immediate aftermath of the Revolution is immeasurably enhanced because Lord Mordaunt was not at home when he called on the morning of 21 February 1689, and he had to write him a letter instead.[35]

Self-fashioning?

Letters cannot be assumed to be artless and unselfconscious productions. It is not only published treatises which merit examination for their rhetorical strategies, but also 'private' writing. Scholars of the Renaissance have recently drawn attention to the process of 'self-fashioning': the deliberate shaping of a life project, the witting construction of a persona, through crafted narratives of the self.[36] It has been argued that Erasmus used his letters to sculpt an image of the quintessential humanist intellectual.[37] Locke's case is more problematic. Unlike Erasmus, he did not orchestrate the publication of his

[31] L1186.   [32] Howarth (ed.), *Letters of Pepys*, 242.

[33] John and Christopher Wordsworth (eds.), *The Correspondence of Richard Bentley* (2 vols., London, 1842), i. 152.

[34] L816 and L820 (Mar.–Apr. 1685) are mutilated, probably because Locke was alarmed at this time. English agents were not above abducting exiles on the streets of Holland.

[35] L116.

[36] Stephen J. Greenblatt, *Renaissance Self-Fashioning from More to Shakespeare* (Chicago, 1980).

[37] Lisa Jardine, *Erasmus, Man of Letters: The Construction of Charisma in Print* (Princeton, 1993). Locke's friend Le Clerc included many of Erasmus's letters in his edition of Erasmus's *Works* (10 vols., Leiden, 1703–6).

own letters, and weight must be given to his intense sense of privacy and self-effacement.[38] He wanted his legacy to be his published books, and his labours were chiefly lavished upon trying to make sure that his publisher produced accurate editions. To this end, he corrected and augmented his *Essay* through successive editions, and the second and subsequent editions carried his portrait. Locke became an iconic philosopher of the Enlightenment, but overwhelmingly because of his books. Knowledge of his life and letters remained limited.

Even so, letters that were not intended for publication were nonetheless crafted. 'There is', wrote Samuel Johnson in his *Life of Pope*, 'no transaction which offers stronger temptations to fallacy and sophistication than epistolary intercourse': a letter is a 'deliberate performance'.[39] Scholars today are especially cautious about supposing that private correspondence is more 'authentic' than what is said in print. What are we to make, for instance, of Locke's frequent protestations of ill health? He was 'a decayed shell . . . a breathless skeleton'.[40] It is hard to doubt that he was tortured by asthma, but it is equally evident that it provided him with excuses to resist distractions from study. Moreover, the notion of the entrapment of the soul and mind in the rotting carcass of the earthly body is a familiar trope in the Platonist and Christian traditions, indicating an elevated yearning by the philosopher to escape the toils of materiality.[41]

Nobody has critically examined Locke's letters for their rhetorical structures. It is certain that his contemporaries understood that there were protocols to be observed. Letters were often written formulaically, their framework culled from influential instructional handbooks and model letter collections, inherited from the elaborate traditions of the humanist *ars dictaminis*. We can be sure of at least three models that impressed Locke at various times. In his youth, there was a vogue for the letters of Jean Louis Guez de Balzac, which appeared in 1624 and in English translation in 1634. In 1659 Locke wrote to a friend that it was 'impossible to return an answer' to his letter without 'the genius or letters of Balzac'.[42] Balzac's influence gave to Locke's early letters, when youthful shyness is added, and especially when addressing women he admired, a stifling air of baroque mannerism, laced with hyperbolic compliments and arcane allusions to Platonic love. The two models he preferred in maturity were the letters of another contemporary Frenchman, Vincent Voiture (first translated into English in 1657), and of the acknowledged classical master of letters, Cicero. In *Some Thoughts Concerning Education* Locke recommended them both, and pointed out the reasons why the epistolary arts required discipline and care. Children should be given

[38] In 1690, apropos recent editions of letters of Vossius and Grotius, Limborch complained to Locke of the unnecessary industry of editors who publish private and domestic letters: L1262.
[39] Samuel Johnson, *The Lives of Dryden, Pope, and Addison* (Oxford, 1877), 103.   [40] L3475.
[41] See Steven Shapin, *A Social History of Truth: Civility and Science in Seventeenth-Century England* (Chicago, 1994), 152–6, for Robert Boyle's frailty as his 'badge of spirituality'.
[42] L66.

the example of Voiture for the entertainment of their friends at a distance, with letters of compliment, mirth, raillery or diversion; and Tully's [Cicero's] epistles, as the best pattern, whether for business or conversation. The writing of letters has so much to do in all the occurrences of human life, that no gentleman can avoid showing himself in this kind of writing. Occasions will daily force him to make this use of his pen, which besides the consequences that, in his affairs, his well or ill-managing of it often draws after it, always lays him open to a severer examination of his breeding, sense, and abilities, than oral discourses; whose transient faults dying for the most part with the sound that gives them life, and so not subject to a strict review, more easily [e]scape observation and censure.[43]

By the end of Locke's life, convention dictated greater informality. The new world of 'politeness' entailed a repudiation of the mannered and metaphorical in preference for candid plain speaking. This was accompanied by a rejection of 'courtly' style, as being an inauthentic sycophancy typical of absolutist regimes, in contrast to the honest conversation of free citizens. Locke expatiated on the value of free discourse among friends, asserting that 'no one anywhere exists who is readier to fulfill all the duties of friendship'.[44] Friendship binds with a 'stronger tie' than 'blood or nationality'.[45] Yet this cult of friendship and informality was a self-conscious design. Locke's affirmations of his quest for unbiased truth, and his contempt for flummery, hackery, 'Billingsgate' invective, and courtly affectation, are assertions of the ground rules of the 'polite' discourse his world was now seeking to adopt.

Moreover, the cultivation of a 'friendship levelling all inequalities'[46] did not readily transcend the large distances in the social hierarchy visible in his correspondence. Locke was both client and patron. Here it was not so much Cicero or Voiture who provided guidance, but rather Seneca in *De beneficiis*. Locke's was a world in which power relations—those relations that were not conducted by the rules of formal political institutions or governed by the marketplace—were conducted according to the protocols of the giving and receiving of benefits. The patron had the means of liberality, the client the power of service and the obligation of gratitude. 'My service to his lordship' is a frequent Lockean valediction. Correspondingly, the language of benefit and gratitude is to be found in many letters Locke received from supplicants, who sought a college place, a church living, or a clerkship in the revenue.[47]

The uncertain boundary between manuscript and print

Occasionally Locke published a letter. One example is his account to Boyle of a barometric experiment in the Mendip mines, which appeared in Boyle's

---

[43] John Locke, *Some Thoughts Concerning Education*, ed. John W. Yolton and Jean S. Yolton (Oxford, 1989), 243. On the influence of Balzac and Voiture see Irving, *Providence of Wit*. Locke's friend J. G. Graevius published an edition of Cicero's letters in 1677.

[44] L1127 (*omnia amicitiae officitia*).   [45] L1117 (*sanguis vel civitas*).   [46] L3301.

[47] John Marshall, *John Locke: Resistance, Religion and Responsibility* (Cambridge, 1994), 161 ff.

General History of the Air (1692) prepared for the press by Locke after Boyle's death.[48] On another occasion, Locke used the preface to one of his own treatises to write an open letter to a stranger, Samuel Bold, who had recently published a tract in his defence.[49] This prompted a private correspondence and a warm friendship. In other ways too, Locke bridged the boundary between manuscript and print, especially in the case of his long correspondence with Edward Clarke about his son's upbringing, which constituted the first draft for *Thoughts Concerning Education*.

Another ambiguity of genres lies in the dedicatory epistles which prefaced so many printed books in Locke's era. Locke published half-a-dozen dedicatory epistles in the front of his tracts and treatises, and wrote half-a-dozen more for works not published in his lifetime, to people who were also his private correspondents. There are, in turn, books carrying dedicatory letters to Locke by friends and admirers. Dedicatory epistles are generally excluded from modern editions of correspondence, including those of Locke and Hobbes, though they are included in the calendar of Richard Baxter's correspondence.[50] The case for inclusion is that they are often inseparable from the sequence of items in a private exchange. Moreover, treatises often circulated in manuscript, and the word 'published' did not necessarily mean 'printed'.[51]

There are yet further softenings of boundaries between genres. There is an overlap between some of Locke's letters and the philosophical memoranda he wrote in his notebooks. Locke's opinion of the Cambridge Platonist, John Smith, occurs in his journal and carries over into a letter to Damaris Masham.[52] His essays on conduct in the 1670s were drafted in his journal before being sent as letters to Dennis Grenville.[53] The description in his journal of a deformed child encountered at the hospital in Paris was copied into a letter to Boyle and later printed in the *Philosophical Transactions*.[54] All in all, 'private' and 'public' writing often intermingled.

The publication of Locke's correspondence

Such exceptions aside, it was not Locke but his successors who put his letters into print. Shortly after his death, his publisher Awnsham Churchill issued *Some Familiar Letters between Mr Locke and his Friends* (1708). The editor's preface announced that the letters 'contain not only such civil and polite conversation as friendship produces among men of parts, learning, and candour; but several matters relating to literature, and more particularly Mr Locke's

---

[48] L197. [49] *A Second Vindication of The Reasonableness of Christianity* (London, 1697).

[50] The point is discussed by Noel Malcolm in his edition of *The Correspondence of Thomas Hobbes* (2 vols., Oxford, 1994), p. xlv. See also N. H. Keeble and Geoffrey F. Nuttall, *Calendar of the Correspondence of Richard Baxter* (2 vols., Oxford, 1991). Dedicatory epistles by and to Locke will be included in vol. 9 of the *Correspondence*.

[51] Harold Love, *Scribal Publication in Seventeenth-Century England* (Oxford, 1993).   [52] L696.

[53] L327, L328, L374, L426.   [54] L478.

notions'. Philosophy was here called a part of literature, implying that it had been rescued from cloistered pedantry. In the eighteenth century, the philosopher in his letters became the textual equivalent of the philosopher pictured in portraits, dressed informally in loose cravat and gown—by contrast with the starched collars of seventeenth-century divines.

This first collection chiefly contained the exchanges with the Dublin 'virtuoso' (polymath), William Molyneux, and the Dutch theologian, Limborch. The former of these was philosophically the most important exchange Locke had, for through discussion with Molyneux he honed the revisions he made to successive editions of his *Essay*. In the eighteenth century these were the best known of Locke's letters. They provided ammunition in controversies ranging from Unitarianism to Ireland's claim to legislative autonomy. Locke's remarks on the compatibility of man's freedom and God's omnipotence appeared in a sermon to the House of Lords in 1784.[55] Especially combustible was Molyneux's provocative query to Locke, apropos Ireland's subordination to England: 'How justly [parliaments] can bind us without our consent and representatives, I leave the author of the *Two Treatises* to consider.'[56] This was grist to the mill of the Tory, George Hickes, who charged that it demonstrated that Whigs believed that 'all government is the people's servant', which is 're-bellion and regicide in the seed'.[57] In 1784 a defender of American independence, John Dickinson, blithely ignored the inconclusiveness of Locke's response to Molyneux's query, and insisted that both men had affirmed the rights of Ireland, and therefore, by implication, of America.[58] Correspondingly, the anti-Lockean Josiah Tucker denounced the two men for inciting the Irish to 'intemperate heats by those very notions of unalienable rights and independence': 'see the whole correspondence carried on between them'.[59]

In 1714 the opportunist publisher, Edmund Curll, transmuted five of Locke's letters into essays, presented as if they were newly discovered works by the master. Thus a letter to Humfry Smith about the Arabist scholar, Edward Pococke, becomes 'Some Memoirs of the Life and Character of Dr Edward Pococke', and brief opinions articulated in a letter to Richard King become 'Sentiments Concerning the Society for Promoting Christian Knowledge'.[60] In 1720 Pierre Desmaizeaux published the exchange with Anthony Collins in *A Collection of Several Pieces of Mr John Locke*. It is possible that the young Collins, who struck up a friendship with Locke in the closing months of his life, set out to seduce the elderly philosopher into engaging in a publishable

---

[55] Richard Watson, *Sermons on Public Occasions* (London, 1788), 142.

[56] L2407. See L2414 below.

[57] George Hickes, Introduction to William Carroll, *Spinoza Reviv'd* (London, 1709), sig. d4ʳ–d5ʳ.

[58] John Dickinson, *A New Essay on the Constitutional Power of Great Britain over the Colonies in America* (Philadelphia, 1774), 103–4.

[59] Josiah Tucker, *A Treatise Concerning Civil Government* (London, 1781), repr. in Mark Goldie (ed.), *The Reception of Locke's Politics* (6 vols., London, 1999), iv. 16.

[60] L3321, L2846.

exchange, one which so carefully instructed the new century in modern codes of civility.

By the end of the eighteenth century about 200 letters to or from Locke were in the public domain. Lord King's *Life of Locke* (1828) included further letters, especially of his ancestor Peter King. Early scholarship on Boyle's and Newton's works and lives brought their exchanges with Locke to light.[61] In 1833 Henry Acton remarked that 'there are few passages of personal history more interesting and affecting' than the quarrel and reconciliation between Newton and Locke.[62] Thomas Forster's *Original Letters of Locke, Algernon Sidney, and Anthony Lord Shaftesbury* (1830) included correspondence with Furly and Clarke. The depositing of the Shaftesbury papers in the Public Record Office made possible the inclusion of further material in W. D. Christie's *Life of Anthony Ashley Cooper, First Earl of Shaftesbury* (1871) and in H. R. Fox Bourne's *Life of John Locke* (1876). Fox Bourne reckoned there to be some 350 letters previously in print and a further 220 newly available to him. Benjamin Rand published a large new collection in his *Correspondence of John Locke and Edward Clarke* (1927), some of which have subsequently crumbled to dust, so that we rely on his transcriptions. Henry Ollion's *Lettres inédites de John Locke* (1912) contained letters to Toinard, Clarke, and Limborch. The transfer of the Lovelace Collection to the Bodleian Library made available a large amount of Lockeana, and a good many new letters were quoted in Maurice Cranston's biography of 1957. It was left to Esmond de Beer to bring off the extraordinary achievement of collecting and publishing the whole of Locke's correspondence in eight volumes between 1976 and 1989.

More than a dozen letters have been discovered since de Beer completed his labours. One turned up in the Somerset Record Office, neatly folded into a strip and serving for three centuries as a bookmark in one of the Clarkes' Chipley account books. It concerns training little Betty Clarke in the art of letter writing, and it warns against her tutor's penchant for making children write 'high unnatural compliments . . . as if it could be civility in any one to say what could not be believed', for it is better to 'make them write their own thoughts'.[63]

The selection

This book contains 244 of the 3,637 surviving letters. Making the selection has been a painful pleasure, for it has involved discarding so much I wished

---

[61] Robert Boyle, *Works* (London, 1744). Locke–Newton letters were published by Dugald Stewart in his 'Dissertation on the Progress of Philosophy', prefixed to *Encyclopaedia Metropolitana* (London, 1821).

[62] Henry Acton, *Religious Opinions and Example of Milton, Locke, and Newton* (London, 1833), 45.

[63] Somerset Record Office, Taunton, Sanford (Clarke) Papers, DD/SF 3304. The new letters will appear in vol. 9 of the *Correspondence*.

to include. There is a corpus of some three dozen letters which were easily chosen: they are the best known to Locke scholars and the most often cited. For example, the anxious 'letter to Tom' in the year of anarchy 1659; John Aubrey's tantalizing hint of an acquaintance between Locke and Hobbes in 1673; Locke's judgement upon the revolutionary parliament in February 1689; the posing to Locke of the 'Molyneux Problem'; and the prescriptions for a gentleman's reading in ethics and politics of 1697.[64] It ought, perhaps, to be added that for Locke there is no single pre-eminent letter that attaches to him by common scholarly fame. In Plato's case, it is the seventh letter about his attempt to educate Dionysius, the ruler of Syracuse; in Augustine's, the letter to the Roman proconsul urging that the Christian ruler should compel heretics to return to the church; in Machiavelli's, that to Vettori explaining his relish at the opportunity to write a little book about princes.

After the three dozen, the difficulties of selection begin, accompanied by the risks of arbitrary choice. The temptation to a personal and perhaps whimsical choice has been kept in check by keeping a close eye on the pattern of citations of letters made by modern scholars of Locke, and on those letters which Locke thought important enough to prepare in draft.

The problem of selection is compounded by having to disrupt the flow of philosophical conversations that unfolded through long correspondence. This is acute in the case of the major philosophical series between Locke and Molyneux. With twenty selected from sixty-seven, this exchange has been better represented than any other, but damage has still been done to its continuities. Beside Molyneux, six people stand out as the most prominent correspondents in this selection: the politician Edward Clarke, the polemicist and historian James Tyrrell, the rising lawyer Peter King, the Dutch theologian Philip van Limborch, the Platonic love of Locke's later life, Damaris Masham, and (hampered though one is by his loquacity) the rumbustious anticler-ical Quaker merchant of Rotterdam, Benjamin Furly. These seven comprise 41 per cent of the letters here, compared with 32 per cent in the complete correspondence. However, since I have also tried to represent the diversity of people with whom Locke corresponded, ninety-three (one quarter) of the 378 known correspondents are included. Nineteen of the forty-four women are represented.

Two radical adjustments have been made by which the selection does not reflect the correspondence *in toto*, the reasons for which hardly need spelling out. In the whole correspondence, letters *by* Locke account for 29 per cent of the total, whereas in this book they constitute 51 per cent. Put another way, I have included 12 per cent of Locke's own letters and 5 per cent of letters to him. The other adjustment concerns chronological spread. Most modern scholar-ship on Locke is devoted to the period prior to the Glorious Revolution. Scholars have been concerned with the evolution and the contexts of the *Essay*, the

---

[64] L82, L268, L1102, L1609, L2320.

Two Treatises, and the *Letter Concerning Toleration*, which had long gestations in his developing intellectual life. Yet the bulk of the surviving correspondence—70 per cent—belongs to the last sixteen years of his life, after the Revolution. In this selection, I have reduced the post-Revolution representation to 58 per cent. But, even so, it is arguably the case that scholars should pay more attention to 'late Locke', to the public savant and public servant, who had suddenly emerged into the limelight.

In order to put aside 3,400 letters, just a handful of examples have been taken from genres which each absorb hundreds of letters. These include medical and educational letters, pupils' and parents' letters from his time as a tutor at Christ Church, supplications for his patronage, letters concerning tenants and investments, on monetary reform, and of compliment and condolence. One systematic exclusion has been the series on education written to Clarke between 1684 and 1691: they are very long and reappeared almost verbatim in *Thoughts Concerning Education*. It is more regrettable that two further genres have had to be almost wholly suppressed, thereby distorting our picture of Locke's preoccupations. To have captured the extent of his discussions about the latest learned productions of the Republic of Letters would have overloaded the text and footnotes with details of obscure books and vanished erudition, while to have conveyed his absorption in the minute explication of ambiguous biblical verses would try the patience of most modern readers. In short, we partially lose the bibliophile and the exegete. The historian's obligation to defer to the priorities in the mental life of people in the past struggles with the principle that history is what the present finds interesting in the past.

Letters about politics, philosophy, and religious toleration are well represented as compared with their presence in the correspondence as a whole, a presence that is often surprisingly thin. There is a frustrating paucity of letters about politics and political theory, and scholars greedily grasp at what little there is. It is also striking how little discussion of philosophical questions occurs in the twenty years during which the *Essay* was in preparation; evidently Locke did not feel the need to test his ideas on others, at least not in the surviving correspondence. I have given special weight to letters that refer to the political crises of the 1680s. Every reference to the *Two Treatises*—there are extremely few—is included. Early responses to the *Essay* are quite well represented, though less so the rapidly ramifying quarrel with Bishop Stillingfleet and other divines after 1695. The correspondence with Limborch about toleration has been given prominence. More generally, I have included letters which refer directly to Locke's writings, from the early, conservative, *Tracts on Government* to the late *Essay on the Poor Law*. Letters sent from beyond Europe—from the Americas and Asia—have been given a more than proportionate share of space.

I have tried to include the more reflective and considered letters. This will lend to the philosopher a reassuringly philosophical air, by hiding from the reader many hundreds of letters which are by turns mundane, arcane, mercenary, dutiful, gossipy, fractious, or fawning. I have, however, striven to make space for letters which capture the broader humanity of seventeenth-century life—a child's letter, an impoverished cousin's plea for money, an account of an awful coach journey, a menu for a feast, a complaint about parking problems in Oxford, and a recommendation of the good effects of drinking 'Bath water'. These are emphatically not intended as mere colour or *jeux d'esprit*. This is a correspondence unparalleled in what it tells us about the texture of seventeenth-century life: it is not only a correspondence about philosophy.

The vicissitudes of reputation

At the start of the twenty-first century, Locke is not quite a public figure, not a name well known outside academic study. His portrait hangs in the National Portrait Gallery, but you cannot buy a postcard of it. Locke would have been content that his friend Isaac Newton is more secure in the pantheon of England's intellectual heritage, for he described himself as an 'under-labourer in clearing ground' for the great 'master-builders, whose mighty designs, in advancing the sciences, will leave lasting monuments'.[65]

Yet England did not always neglect Locke. He became a secular saint of the Enlightenment, apostrophized in poetry and statuary, his works republished in scores of editions, his name a cynosure for doctrines and causes, although he personally deplored the dragooning of arguments by the authority of dead mentors. In the 1740s Lord Cobham placed Locke's bust in the Temple of British Worthies at Stowe. The inscription reads:

LOCKE

Who, best of all philosophers, understood the powers of the human mind; the nature, end, and bounds of civil government; and, with equal courage and sagacity, refuted the slavish systems of usurped authority over the rights, the consciences, and the reason of mankind.[66]

The nineteenth-century Romantics dimmed Locke's reputation, thinking him the sponsor of a soulless materialism and a narrow utilitarianism. Anglo-Catholics and Evangelicals alike detested his piety as anaemic and his theology as suspect. Socialists and Marxists thought him the ideologist of nascent capitalism, who legitimized the exploitative system of the rising bourgeoisie. It was not until the second half of the twentieth century that Locke recovered his standing, admired by practitioners of analytical philosophy and by theorists of political liberalism, and newly discovered by intellectuals in nations liberated from fascist and communist totalitarianism. In 1996, one newspaper

---

[65] *An Essay Concerning Human Understanding*, Epistle to the Reader.
[66] Still *in situ*. Stowe Gardens, near Buckingham, is a National Trust property open to the public.

columnist wrote that the Cold War had been about 'whether the ideas attributed to Karl Marx or those attributed to John Locke should rule the world'.[67] It is true, however, that Locke's credit today stands low among postmodern and postcolonial doubters of the Enlightenment 'project'. They argue that the Enlightenment's claim to rationalist universalism was, at best, spurious and, at worst, oppressive, for it was the ideological instrument of a world that was European, white, and male. Whether or not we think the Enlightenment 'project' was a worthwhile episode in human history, Locke was indubitably one of its quintessential voices.

[67] Peregrine Worsthorne, the *Guardian*, 14 Sept. 1996.

Note on the text

The texts of the letters have been reset from Esmond de Beer's edition of the complete correspondence. His numeration of the letters has been followed.

Reading the letters may sometimes need a little effort. Seventeenth-century English is not generally difficult, but private correspondence is more problematic than printed books. The lack of settled conventions in spelling, the private knowledge and allusions between friends, the classical and biblical learning taken for granted, the casual informality in some cases and the mannered formality in others, can all present obstacles to the modern reader. Sometimes only one side of an exchange survives, so that it is not always clear what is being alluded to in the surviving side. I have tried to provide explanations, but sometimes puzzles remain.

The presentation of the letters has been driven by two scarcely compatible concerns: to explain whatever may be perplexing, and to save space so that as many letters as possible could be included. At the head of each chapter there is a headnote describing the contexts of the letters grouped in that chapter. Other supporting information will be found in the introduction, footnotes, and biographical register. Life dates for people mentioned in the text and footnotes are, where known, given in the index. There are occasional repetitions of information between the introduction, headnotes, and footnotes: it became apparent that each element needed to stand on its own feet, since readers will often wish to browse or just look up a particular letter.

The letters selected for this volume have been abridged. About 30 per cent of their bulk has been excised. What has usually been lost is the opening and closing passages, typically salutations to family and friends, affirmations of affection, minor practical arrangements, and apologies for tardy letter writing. Rarely has material been lost from the middle of letters, and I have striven to avoid filleting them. In a minority of cases more drastic cutting of multi-faceted letters has been resorted to, in order to extract discussion of one particular topic. All omissions, except for salutations, valedictions, and postscripts, are marked by ellipses. The decision to abridge has been the hardest. An editor thereby not only interjects contestable judgements about which passages are significant, but also disrupts something of the flavour and intimacy of the originals. But the overriding priority has been to maximize the number of letters that could be included. Moreover, the complete correspondence is available in print for readers who wish to explore further.

The only amendments to de Beer's texts are as follows. Angle brackets have been replaced by square brackets: these denote interventions by de Beer or earlier editors, for example to supply conjectural readings of damaged originals, or amendments of minor authorial slips; I have added a few such interjections of my own. Small spaces in the original manuscripts, reproduced by de Beer, have been closed up, but paragraphing has not been tampered with. Where appropriate, I have silently changed 'then' to 'than', since seventeenth-century usage can needlessly trip up the modern reader.

De Beer provided an elaborate editorial apparatus, including headnotes to every letter and two tiers of footnotes, textual and substantive. This has all gone. In supplying footnotes I initially expected simply to abridge de Beer's. I have of course relied heavily upon him, but I found I needed to supply many new notes. He took for granted a demanding level of erudition on the part of his readers: they were expected to know words that have changed their meanings or have disappeared; to know the classics and the scriptures; and to know a good deal of seventeenth-century history. I have pared notes to the minimum compatible with providing essential information. All names of persons are footnoted, except where they can be found in the biographical register of correspondents.

All letters are given in English. In the case of letters in Latin the translation is that provided for de Beer by W. M. Edwards (250, 394, 974, 1100, 1101, 1120, 1122, 1127, 1147, 1158, 1182, 1791, 1804, 1901, 2395, 2413, 2498, 2925, 2935, 2979). In the case of letters in French the translations have been made by Melissa Percival of Exeter University (605, 2107, 2340, 2673, 2748, 3232).

For good or ill, I have relied upon the accuracy of de Beer's transcriptions. To have returned to all the manuscripts would have involved a prohibitive prolongation of this project. In two cases de Beer did not provide the text of letters and here I have used the manuscripts (108, 687).

Letters that crossed the English Channel are dated Old and New Style. England was ten days (eleven after 1700) behind the Continent of Europe, which had adopted the Gregorian calendar.

In Locke's time English currency was divided into pounds, shillings, and pence, there being twenty shillings in a pound, and twelve pence in a shilling. Thus 15s means 15 shillings. 20l means £20.

Throughout the footnotes, 'L' stands for 'letter number'; *Essay* for *An Essay Concerning Human Understanding* (1689); *Two Treatises* for the *Two Treatises of Government* (1689); *Education* for *Some Thoughts Concerning Education* (1693); *Political Essays* for my edition of Locke's *Political Essays*, published by Cambridge University Press (1997); and *Works* for *The Works of John Locke* (10th edn., 10 vols., London, 1801). Citations of particular paragraphs or sections of Locke's major works follow the numeration in the standard modern editions: of the *Essay* by P. H. Nidditch (Oxford, 1975); of the *Two Treatises* by Peter Laslett (Cambridge, 1960); and of *Education* by John and Jean Yolton (Oxford, 1989). Cross-references to other letters in this volume appear in the form 'L851', without the phrases 'see above' or 'see below'. All colleges mentioned are those of Oxford University, unless otherwise stated. For brevity, and with apologies to the Scottish nation, I refer to James II rather than to James II and VII.

Chronology

1688   Glorious Revolution: invasion of England by Prince William of Orange; overthrow and flight of James II
1689   Accession of William III and Mary II (son-in-law and daughter of James II)
        War against Louis XIV of France (to 1697, and again 1702–13)
        Toleration Act: freedom of worship for Protestants Bill of Rights
1690   Battle of the Boyne: defeat of James II in Ireland
1694   Bank of England founded
        Triennial Act, requiring regular elections
        Death of Mary II
1695   End of press censorship
1697   Treaty of Ryswick: temporary peace with France
1701   Act of Settlement, ensuring Protestant (Hanoverian) succession
1702   Death of William III; accession of his sister-in-law Queen Anne
        First daily newspaper
1704   Battle of Blenheim: Marlborough's victory over France
1707   Union of England and Scotland
1714   Hanoverian succession: accession of George I

Philosophy, literature, and science

1625   Hugo Grotius, *On the Laws of War and Peace*
1632   Galileo Galilei, *The System of the World*
1637   René Descartes, *Discourse on Method*
1651   Thomas Hobbes, *Leviathan*
1653   Henry More, *Antidote against Atheism*
1656   James Harrington, *Oceana*
1661   Joseph Glanvill, *The Vanity of Dogmatizing*
1662   Antoine Arnaud and Pierre Nicole, *The Art of Thinking*
        Samuel Butler, *Hudibras*
1665   François de la Rochefoucauld, *Maximes*
1666   Margaret Cavendish, *Description of a New World*
1667   John Milton, *Paradise Lost*
        Blaise Pascal, *Pensées*
1670   Baruch (Benedict) Spinoza, *Tractatus Theologico-Politicus*
1672   Samuel Pufendorf, *On the Law of Nature and Nations*
1673   Samuel Pufendorf, *On the Duty of Man and Citizen*
1674   Nicolas Malebranche, *Search after Truth*
1677   Baruch (Benedict) Spinoza, *Ethics*
        Andrew Marvell, *Account of the Growth of Popery*
1678   Ralph Cudworth, *True Intellectual System of the Universe*
        John Bunyan, *Pilgrim's Progress*
1680   Robert Filmer, *Patriarcha, or the Natural Power of Kings*

Locke's life and works

1671   Secretary to the Lords Proprietors of Carolina (until 1675)
        Begins writing *An Essay Concerning Human Understanding*

1672   First visit to France, October–November
        Ashley created Earl of Shaftesbury and Lord Chancellor

1673–4 Secretary to the Council of Trade and Plantations

1673   Shaftesbury ousted from office, and begins to lead parliamentary opposition to Charles II

1675   The Shaftesburian manifesto published: *A Letter from a Person of Quality to his Friend in the Country*; perhaps part authored by Locke
        Graduates MB
        Goes to France, chiefly resident in Montpellier until 1677; then mainly in Paris

1679   Returns to England

1679–83 Resides in Oxford, London, and Oakley (James Tyrrell's home in Buckinghamshire)
        Writes *Two Treatises of Government*

1681   Writes a defence of toleration against Edward Stillingfleet
        Shaftesbury charged with treason; charge dismissed by a Whig grand jury

1682   Flight of Shaftesbury to Holland

1683   Flight to Holland; in exile until 1689, mainly in Utrecht and Amsterdam until early 1687, then in Rotterdam

1684   Expelled *in absentia* from Studentship of Christ Church
        Writes his first letter to Edward Clarke concerning education

1685   In hiding in Amsterdam
        Writes the *Epistola de Tolerantia* (*Letter Concerning Toleration*)

1686   *An Essay Concerning Human Understanding* substantially finished

1688   Publishes an *Abrégé* (summary) of the *Essay*

1689   Returns to England in February
        Declines an ambassadorship; appointed Commissioner of Appeals in Excise
        Publication in the autumn of *Two Treatises of Government*, *An Essay Concerning Human Understanding* (though both carry the date 1690), and *A Letter Concerning Toleration*

1690   Publication of *A Second Letter for Toleration*

1691   Settles at Oates in Essex in Damaris Masham's household
        Publication of *Some Considerations of the Consequences of the Lowering of Interest and Raising the Value of Money* (dated 1692)

1692   Publication of *A Third Letter for Toleration*

1693   Publication of *Some Thoughts Concerning Education*

1694   Subscribes £500 to the Bank of England

1695   Advises on the ending of press censorship and the recoinage
        Publication of *The Reasonableness of Christianity* and its first *Vindication*, and of *Further Considerations Concerning Raising the Value of Money*.

Letters

1

Revolutionary England, 1656–1660

Locke was born in Wrington, Somerset, in 1632, and brought up in the village of Pensford, a few miles south of Bristol. The mainstays of the local economy were farming, woollen textiles, and, in the Mendip Hills, coal mining. Although Locke was eventually to die a wealthy man, his close relations included yeoman farmers and tanners. His grandfather was a clothier, and his father a minor gentleman and attorney of puritan persuasion. Locke's education depended upon the benevolence of Colonel Alexander Popham, MP, under whose command his father fought in the Parliamentarian army during the Civil Wars. Locke studied at Westminster, the most famous school in England, where the headmaster, Richard Busby, provided a combination of classical erudition and beatings. In 1649 King Charles I was executed nearby.

Locke went up to Christ Church, Oxford, in 1652 and remained there as a scholar and teacher until 1667. His college and his fellow students became permanently woven into the fabric of his life. After graduating in 1656, Locke went to London to seek admission to the Inns of Court, but he decided not to pursue a legal career. In the first letter in this book, Locke provides his father with an account of a coach journey from Bath to London in October of that year (L29). It is a piece of youthful mirth about an obese fellow passenger. Here, and in later letters, Locke is scornful of the recently founded sect of mystical and levelling puritans, known as the Quakers. Again to his father, he writes about the famous case of James Nayler, savagely punished by parliament for blasphemy, and also about a student riot against Quakers in Oxford (L30, L59).

Locke never married, although in Oxford he encountered several stylish women at Black Hall in St Giles, including a bishop's daughter, Elinor Parry, with whom he was probably in love (L72). Another resident of Black Hall was Anne Evelegh—whose letters made early use of the word 'Romantick'. She writes an affectionate encomium to comfort Locke in rural exile on a visit to his father at Pensford (L83). In the West Country, Locke had another female friend, Sarah Edwards, whose husband provides occasion for a remarkable piece of scatological ribaldry (L64).

From 1653 until his death in 1658, Oliver Cromwell ruled the English republic as Lord Protector. Thereafter the country slid towards anarchy as the army and its civilian rivals struggled for power. In April and May 1659 there was a showdown between Lord Protector Richard Cromwell (Oliver's ineffectual son) and the army; the army won, Richard was dismissed, and the remnants of the regicidal Rump Parliament of 1648–53 were recalled. Republicans and adherents of the 'Good Old Cause' briefly assumed power once again, while moderate Parliamentarians plotted with Royalists to restore the Stuart monarchy. In October 1659, General John Lambert evicted the Rump, but this coup was opposed by General George Monk, who was the commander in Scotland. Monk may already have decided to attempt to secure the restoration of Charles II, who had been in exile since his father's execution.

Locke contemplates this political world with foreboding. Denouncing the 'hot headed men' of both sides (L59), he complains that the world has abandoned reason in favour of brutish passion, frenzy, and fanatical sophistry (L81). Resolving to remain 'Stoick' in the face of the buffetings of worldly fortune, he comments pessimistically on affairs during the tumultuous months before the Restoration (L82, L91). Behind the 'religious pretenders' and 'promisers of liberty' he perceives only ambition, tyranny, and bloodshed.

Fearing that he might be forced to take arms in a renewed civil war, Locke sought quietness above all. In a commentary on Henry Stubbe's tolerationist *Essay in Defence of the Good Old Cause* (L75), Locke appears to support toleration, saying that people can live in peace, 'though they take different way[s] towards heaven'. Perhaps however, he is writing ironically, for he indicates that the experience of history is not that of peaceful coexistence but of sectarian violence. This letter is puzzling, since not only is there no other sign of a tolerationist stance before 1667, but Locke emphatically rejected toleration in his conservative *Two Tracts on Government*, which he wrote soon afterwards. In the same letter, he criticizes Stubbe's suggestion of toleration for Roman Catholics, on the grounds that papists support a foreign power and do not feel obliged to keep engagements with heretics.

Corresponding with his schoolfriend, William Godolphin, he discusses well-known texts of utopian and non-utopian political theory (L60, L66). By way of metaphorical depictions of Godolphin's character, Locke offers a mannered panegyric, suggesting that if everyone were a model citizen like Godolphin, there would be no need of the utopias of Thomas More and James Harrington.

29. Locke to John Locke, sen., Westminster, 25 October 1656

The next morning after I sent home Tom: Watts[1] I tooke coach at Bathe, which brought to London three persons besides my self of the English size and one woman of the race of the Anakime,[2] soe that in all I may count six in our company, for that mountaine of flesh that cald herself a merchants wife, by her tongue and her body may well be taken for two, shee was soe grosse that shee turnd my stomack and made me sick the two first mornings and the third[3] I was like to be buried, for had the coach (as it might) overturnd and shee fell upon me I should have been dead and buried at a time, but I thank god after that and a thousand squeeses which my place some time alotted me to I came safe to London and tooke up my quarters at Mr Knights.[4] and the next morning saw our Senators enter the house which a stranger would have mistaken for a fenceing schoole there were soe many swords worne into it.[5] I beleeve this councell is not to be parraleld in Europe if you compare either their ages or faces. What is beyond that was not obvious to my eys. but noe more, The news of Digby is contradicted[6] and that of the prize either not come hither yet, for perhaps it keeps its native Spanish pace or else dead before I came hither.[7] the most remarkable thing I have met with since I came hither was a company of quakers in Westminster hall this afternoone, one whereof being brought the last terme to the chancery to give testimony there, refuseing to put of his hat, had it strooke of,[8] for a marke of which persecution he hath gonne ever since bare, and this day came to complaine to the Lords Commissioners and to have redresse for the injury, I saw him walke bare headed in the Hall which he might well doe haveing come soe out of Yorkshire, The rest of his breathren may doe well to immitate him, the keepeing the head to hott being dangerous for mad folks . . .

30. Locke to John Locke, sen., Westminster, 15 November 1656

. . . I came just now from heareing the examination of Nayler[1] and his Proselites who haveing before the Committee upon reexamination own'd what

---

[1] Perhaps a servant of the Lockes.　　[2] Old Testament giants: Numbers 13:33.
[3] Bath is 110 mls. from London.　　[4] Unidentified.
[5] Oliver Cromwell's second parliament, which opened on 17 Sept., included many soldiers. Senators: MPs.
[6] Presumably Sir Kenelm Digby, author, sometime Catholic, former courtier of Charles I, now a confidential diplomat for Cromwell.
[7] Spain and England were briefly at war. A Spanish ship was captured off Cadiz on 9 Sept.
[8] Believing that everyone is equal in Christ, Quakers refused to respect 'hat honour' (doffing of hats in the presence of social superiors). They were regarded as dangerous hotheads. The law courts sat in Westminster Hall.

[1] The Quaker James Nayler entered Bristol in imitation of Christ's entry into Jerusalem, heralded by women crying hosannas. Parliament found him guilty of blasphemy and he was savagely punished.

he receivd and they what they gave him as Christ, after all being askd what he had to say made this evasion (which I pickd as well as I could out of his uncouth and unusuall expression, whose canting language with that of his disciples I made an hard shift some times to understand) That Christ being the same to day and for ever what honour was given to him at Jerusalem might be given to him where and in whomesoever he is manifested from god. His owning of the name of Jesus of the sonne of god, of the prophet of the most high god, of haveing him his father whome we call our god and his disciples owing the attributeing of these to him, Sir the shortnesse of my paper and the consideration of the presse which I beleeve will shortly better informe you,[2] adviseth me to leave out. only this, after their examination I went to the roome by the painted chamber whether[3] the committee orderd them to retire where I found Nailer one man more and 3 or 4 women of the tribe all with white gloves and the womens heads in white baggs. their carriage was strange to me, one of the women made a continued humming noise longer then the reach of an ordinari breath without motion either of lips or breath that I who stood next her could perceive, shee ceaseing another sung holy holy holy with the addition of some other words, then the other (her song being donne) gave some of their ordinary exhortacon with their common mixture of judgment and threatning and after a little pause they went over the same round, without answering any questions which by the standers by were proposd, and those which by the committee were urgd. I observd they either not answerd or did it with a great deale of suttlety besides the cover and cunning of that language which others and I beleeve they them selves scarce understand, but I am weary of the Quakers . . .

59. Locke to John Locke, sen., 22 June [1659]

Yours by Sancho[1] with all its retinue came safely to my hand and brought me noe small satisfaction in the account it gave me of your health and quiet which is a blessing this tumbling world is very spareing of, though I cannot remember any days of my life wherein I have injoyd more. and all these tossings have servd but to rock me into a pleasant slumber, whilst others dreame, (for our life is noething else) of noe thing but fire sword and ruine, but you may easily guesse what sort of hott headed men they are whose brains are troubld with such distempers. I hope I shall not be thought unsensible for

---

[2] Several accounts were published, including James Deacon's *Nayler's Blasphemies Discovered* (1657).

[3] Whither.

[1] Unidentified. Sancho is a nickname derived from Cervantes's *Don Quixote* (1605), apparently Locke's favourite novel.

this serenity which I thinke ought to be the endeavour of every one that remembers there is a god to rest on, and an other world to retire into. I have taught my hopes to overlooke my fears and suppresse those troublers, and as I doe not credit all the glorious promises and pretences of the one side. soe neither am I scared with those threats of danger and destruction which are soe perremptorily asserted by a sort of men which would perswade us that the cause of god suffers when ever they are disappointed of their ambitious and coviteous ends. I hope I am to be pardond on both sides if I am not quick sighted enough to see either that glorious fabrick of liberty and happinesse, or those goblins of warre and bloud which either side would perswade us they behold over our heads ready to drop downe on us, that which I looke to is the hand that governs all things, that manages our Chaos and will bring out of it what will be best for us and what we ought to acquiesce in, I have long since learnd not to rely on men. These bubles however swolne and glittering, soft and inviteing are not yet fit to be lean'd on and who ever shall make them his support shall finde them noething but a little guilded aire, But I wander beyond my intention, which designd something that you did not know not what you are well acquainted with allready, and a comment on these times is as dangerous as to you uselesse, and therefor fitt for noething but the fire. . . . We have beene long since acquainted with the Railery of the Quakers and it would be strange if we alone[2] of all the people in England should not be sported with, for I looke on such papers as noething but a sceane of mirth, if there were any such people and such usage here in some particulars it comes very short of their story and aggravations and if such people (who cannot in their carrage and raptures be thought any other than madd or jugglers[3]) fall into the hands of young men that have not yet learned of them a personated sobriety what can be expected but some such usage,[4] or what accusation will arise hence against the university from the extravigancys of youth, not authorizd nor countenanced by the governors or goverment of the place. . . .

60. William Godolphin to Locke, London, 7 July 1659

I receiv'd long ago both your letters with as much joy and Satisfaction, as I doe now with shame reflect on their date: And if at that time I blush'd to see my-selfe Commended by a Pen which seemes fashion'd to illustrate the Noblest Theames, how much more am I provok'd therunto by considering my Negligence in not sooner thanking you for the honour you have done mee.

---

[2] i.e. Oxford University. The Quakers published attacks on the universities as seminaries of corrupt clergy devoted to vain and useless learning.
[3] Charlatans, tricksters.   [4] The Quakers suffered assaults by students.

I hope you have a better opinion of mee then to beleive that I consent by my Silence to those high Expressions you give mee, which I never consider'd otherwise than as your modest way of instructing mee; the benefit wherof I shall bee better able to acknowledge, when I have in any measure attain'd the least of those qualityes you attribute to mee, which I can by no better title claime than that I have not Vanity enough to own them. In the mean time I give you leave to make such use of mee, as Sir Tho: More did of (what never was) his Utopia, which hee made the Subject of those Excellent formes of Government his brain had contriv'd, therby teaching the World not what really was, but what ought to bee[1] I shall bee as litle angry, as any of the Utopians, for being the Name of your Romance, and shall lend my-selfe at any time to so good purpose, as is the receiving your Precepts, and the Characters which you make of Virtue. But I am very sorry that I am not able to returne to you Conceptions of the same Nature, unlesse I would make some other Person the Subject therof, since to describe you is not so much the Worke of Invention as of Memory, and needs only to recollect what I have known and Observ'd concerning You. But such an Undertaking would render this not a Letter, but History, and I should therin doe like Sir Tho: Smith who being well acquainted with the Country hee lov'd, and preferring the Reality of its Policy before the Imaginations of Others, made an Exact description therof to Posterity, either out of Gratitude, or designe to give a Pattern to the rest of the World of an Exact Government.[2] Wheras you have chosen to imitate Mr Harrington, who having fancy'd a Modell borrow'd a Name to bee a title to his Conceptions.[3] . . .

64. Locke to Sarah Edwards, Oxford, 21 July 1659

I am sorry you had not the clouts[1] I promisd you sooner since I heare you had lately soe much need of'em. But who could guesse that you should be soe soone brought to bed with a youngster[2] that should want diteing[3] and indanger your linin? but god give you joy on't tis a chopping boy god blesse it, and though its loosnesse may sometimes offend the sheets, and it be troubld with the usuall infirmity of children yet age and whiping may mend that, and tis not to be despaird but by that time it comes to be threescore it may grow cleanly espetially if it feed on dry meate, and beware of soluble[4] ale. Had I knowne the babe your bedfellow had wanted wipers at Stanton[5] I

---

[1] Sir Thomas More, *Utopia* (1516).
[2] Sir Thomas Smith, *De Republica Anglorum* (*The Commonwealth of England*) (1583).
[3] James Harrington, *The Commonwealth of Oceana* (1656), the principal English republican treatise.

[1] Pieces of cloth.   [2] Locke is teasing; he means her husband.   [3] Wiping clean.
[4] Laxative.   [5] Stanton Drew, 1½ mls. west of Pensford.

doubt not but my interest could have prevaild with Captain Burges[6] for his saile cloth rather then he should have been destitute. What pitty 'twas that Jack Constable[7] had not made use of his authority to prevent such mischeef, undoubtedly the cheif man of a whole hundred had power enough to restraine such miscarrages, and keepe in offenders from breakeing prison at such a time as that, were it not to be feard that the man of worship himself were guilty of the scape. Had such a thinge been donne at Westbury[8] assuredly the cleanly officers of that place had severly punishd such a loose companion and your quick sented husband would have smelt out the Transgressor, and the stocks and whiping post he soe much talkd on had beene his guerdon.[9] But poore man his authority reachd not soe far as Stanton, and he that at Westbury usd to scourge the hinder parts of others had not there the command of his owne. The truth is being lately in the country I wonderd to finde him returnd to the necessity of clouts and swathbands, and could scarce beleeve that those infirmitys should hang on him at his full age with all his honours and offices about him which uses to leave children before seven. They should have conceald it from me had it been possible but murder and—will out, besids it was too manifest in its ill consequences my Cosin Besse[10] and some of the family haveing been ill ever since he was there, whose distempers must needs be oweing to the infection and fowlenesse of the aire, which how it was occasiond I leave him to guesse. well! should any of them miscarry pray god he be not found guilty, I feare it would lye heavy on his conscience should the Jury acquitt him. If he scape 'twill be noe small advantage to your corporation, who when they choose Burgeses next need not be troubld to seeke far for a Parliament man,[11] since they have at home a grave man of office and one of a free utterance, he will be very fitt to make a member of Parliament, but what member lett any one judg, I shall not name it. He and his brother alderman Atkins[12] will make sweet worke in the house when they come to hold forth before the assembly, and undoubtedly we shall have a fruitfull and flourishing land under their manureing. Pray tell Mr Constable 'twas noe ill grounded conjecture that I told him when I saw him last that he was in the way to preferment: I then smelt advancement in his breeches and his luck was sure to be good according to the proverb.[13] . . .

---

[6] Unidentified.

[7] A nickname; apparently Sarah's husband was a high (hundredal) constable.

[8] Probably Westbury, Wiltshire, 20 mls. from Pensford (though there are two other Westburys in the district).

[9] Reward.

[10] Perhaps Elizabeth Locke of Cerne Abbas, Dorset, who later married the vicar of Broadmayne, Dorset.

[11] Westbury was an incorporated borough, sending MPs to parliament.

[12] Thomas Atkin (Atkins, Atkyn), radical Puritan MP, Lord Mayor of London 1644–5; 'an unpleasant mishap subjected him to much royalist ridicule'.

[13] 'Shitten luck is good luck'.

66. Locke to G W [William Godolphin], [*c.* August 1659?]

When I lately revisd[1] your letter which I carried into the country as a spell against Barbarisme and a fence against the incroachments of rusticity I wish'd for the Genius or letters of Balzac[2] without one of which it is impossible to returne an answer, certainely had I had his volume by me I had thence transcribd an answer since it is fitt that I should borrow or pilfer from anothers treasure than returne you my owne brasse for your gold. and I may be permitted rather to be carelesse of my owne credit than to be insensible of your favour or not indeavour make some returne. as often as I reade your letter I examine my self what great things I have donne whether I ever yet releivd cittys and conquerd armys, whether I ever yet made the Turk tremble, and made some other place out sound Lepanto,[3] for methinks tis requisite that I should have worne laurells and rode at least 3 times in triumph all [as] preparations and gradations to your panagyricks, and I very much doubt if fortune should have raisd me to such a greatnesse whether yet your complements would not be to large for me. Sir these are the recreations of your pen when ever you please to sport your self with your owne eloquence, and frame a world better peopld than that you dwele in, and since this age is not able to entertaine you with persons of equall worth you are faine to retire into your owne thoughts, and to fashon to your self fitt companions. and you would converse with things excellent it must be either your self or your owne workemanship. I cannot but be sensible of this great honour that you will take the pains to disguise me under one of these handsome [shapes], and make choise of me to weare soe glorious a livery, and to mak me a fitt objet for your thoughts, this is like the sun to guild every thing you cast your eye on, and with your reflection to clothe dull earth with flowers and gayety. After this I cannot wonder to finde my self ranke with Harrington and More,[4] I know you are able to fashon me into what shape you please, and as if you were Deucalion[5] like to new people the world what would be but a shapeless [lump] in anothers hand prooves a compleat and accomplishd man when it parts from yours. but you have not only compard me to them but taught me [a way] to exceed those Politick contrivers whose curious modells though they may impale some part of the wide world yet leave the inhabitants wild still noe! I could easily frame a happier Utopia then either only by makeing you the patterne of my citizens. Such a country would want noe more law than we are now governed by. But I feare it is not the way to make us a glorious Oceana. I cannot hope that we shall ever be able to trace your steps and therefor shall need some other rule to guide us besides every mans private moralls. . . .

---

[1] Reread. [2] Jean-Louis Guez de Balzac, *Letters* (1624; Eng. trans. 1634).
[3] A great naval battle in which the Christians beat the Turks, 1571. [4] L60.
[5] Son of Prometheus, husband of Pyrrhe; after a great flood they began humankind anew.

72. Locke to P E [Elinor Parry?], [Pensford], [early September 1659?]

Tis certaine that the Genious of the University flourishes and is more vigerous and sprightly now then ever and tis with injustice that some complaine of the decay of learning there such confident censurers would be silencd had they but read those two letters I lately receivd from thence and would soone be of another minde when they did see that there be ladys in Oxford that write things now which the Doctors of former ages would have envid, such evidences as these would easily perswade the most obstinate that the Muses dwell still in Oxford and that B[lack] H[all]¹ holds at least two of them. and I should not at all nick name things if I cald your mount, Parnassus.² Well my faire Urania.³ must noething be wanting to your perfection and must rhetorick be added to all your other accomplishments, is it not enough that you have a minde above the ordinary rate of mortalls, that vertue stamps grandure on all your actions, that your eys cary authority in them and can looke us into subjection, But must every part have the priviledg to command and be ordaind for empire. who would not be proud to be guided by that hand which soe easily converts a pen into a scepter. tis you that justify the dareing fictions of the Poets which will now begin to appeare true history and the tale of Orpheus⁴ shall noe more be reckond amongst the fabulous. since your quill⁵ strikes an harmony whose soveraignety doth greater wonders wherewith you absolutely command the wilde and savage part of man that pays noe homage to Laws and reason. those unruly affections that rebell against all other commands readily obey yours we hope and feare are merry or sad just as you please to order us, and have noe other passions but those that you please to imploy, and tis you that can reach out comfort to on[e] that is two days journy from his happinesse.

I wonder with what spell it is that you convert your inke into soe efficacious a balsame. that when I thought myself in a condition destind to misery beyond remedy and beyond comfort behold two or three drops have revivd me. Is it not strang[e] that when my minde was over cast with sadnesse and all my joys darkend and dampd with melancholy day should breake to me but M[adam] twas from your standish,⁶ who could produce light and sune shine out of such a place but you, and that which in an other hand would be but blots and blacknesse in yours becomes rays and splendor. thus you and Nature are able to raise the brightnesse and beautys of the morning out of

---

¹ In St Giles, a street in central Oxford, where Elinor Parry and Anne Evelegh lived. Now Queen Elizabeth House.

² Home of the muses, source of inspiration.

³ Plato turned Aphrodite, goddess of sexual love, into Urania, 'heavenly dweller', goddess of intellectual love. Perhaps a reference to Lady Mary Wroth's romance, *Urania* (1621).

⁴ Mythic hero with superhuman musical skills.

⁵ Both a pen and a plectrum.   ⁶ Inkstand.

night obscurity. I could loose my self in these thoughts and look my self blinde in this dazleing radiancy. but there is something else that more affects me, is it not a strange priviledg and such as I ought to be satisfide with that the sun should shine on me alone when those that are round about me live in darkenesse, but you can doe more then this when you please to exercise your bounty. tis time I admire the gallantry and composure of your expressions, but tis that veine of goodnesse that runs throug it that I take my self to be concearnd in. and tis this that makes me adore the Graces of your letter that they are kinde as well as handsome, and that you have made them smile upon me. . . .

75. Locke to S H [Henry Stubbe], [Pensford], [mid-September? 1659]

The same messengar that carryd my letter the last weeke to Bristoll returnd with your booke[1] which I have read with very much satisfaction and the only pauses I made in my hasty perusal were to reflect with admiration the strength and vigor of your stile checkerd embelishd seasond with many poinant passages of witt and sharp sallys, and that clearnesse of reason and plenty of matter wherewith every part is stuffd. . . . If I may be permitted to complaine after satisfaction, which I doe not that I thinke your weapon less sharpe if you doe not every where shew where the point lys . . . But because that party you more particulary designe it against[2] are soe blinded with prejudice and [ignorance] that they will not be able to discover them unlesse a figure or hand in the margent[3] direct their purblind observation. . . . I am sorry that you continued not your history of toleration downe to these times, and given us an account of Holland France Poland[4] etc. since nearest examples have the greatest influence and we are most easily perswaded to tread in those fresh steps which time hath least defacd and men will travell in that road which is most beaten though Carriers only be their guides, when you have added the authority of dayly experience that men of different professions may quietly unite (antiquity the testimony) under the same government and unanimously cary the same civill intrest and hand in hand march to the same end of peace and mutuall society though they take different way towards heaven you will adde noe small strength to your cause and be very convinceing to those to whome what you have already said hath left noething to doubt but wither it be now practicable. But this I expect from the promise of a second edition, however you must be sure to reserve me one more of this, for I beleeve the importunity of many here will not lett me bring back this to Oxford.

---

[1] Henry Stubbe, *An Essay in Defence of the Good Old Cause; or a discourse concerning the rise and extent of the power of the civil magistrate in reference to spiritual affairs* (1659).
[2] Those who are for strict religious uniformity.   [3] Margin.
[4] Countries in this period conspicuous for religious toleration.

The only scruple I have is how the liberty you grant the Papists can consist with the security of the Nation (the end of goverment) since I cannot see how they can at the same time obey two different authoritys carrying on contrary intrest[5] espetially where that which is destructive to ours [is] backd with an opinion of infalibility and holinesse supposd by them to be immediatly derivd from god founded in the scripture and their owne equally sacred tradition, not limitted by any contract and therefor not accountable to any body, and you know how easy it is under pretence of spirituall jurisdiction to hooke in all secular affairs since in a commonwealth wholy Christian it is noe small difficulty to set limits to each and to define exactly where on[e] be gins and the other ends. Besids I cannot apprehend, where they have soe neare a dependency, what security you can take of their fidelity and obedience from all their oaths and protestation, when that other soverainty they pay homage to is acknowledgd by them to be owner of a power that can acquitt them of all perfidy and perjury,[6] and that will [be] ready to pardon and court them to it with dispensations and rewards; and you will have but small reason to repose trust in one who when ever it shall be his interest (which it will always be) shall by deceiveing you not only obteine the name of Inocent but meritorious, who by throwing of[f] his obligations (whereof he will always keep the key himself) shall not only possesse himself of your portion of earth but purchasse aditionall a title to heaven and be Canonized saint at the charge of your life and liberty. and seeing you your self (if I remember aright) make the apprehensions of intrest and the justice of the cause the rule and measure of, constancy to, activity for and obedience under any goverment you can never hope that they should cordially concur with you to any establishment whose consciens. and concearments both for this world and the other shall always biasse them another way. these are those tares started up in my thoughts amongst those better seeds you have sowne there, and possibly are only oweing to the temper of the soile and must grow or wither as you please to order them. Thus you see how I make use of the liberty you allow me out of a beleef that you have as much ingenuity as learning, and tis in this confidence that I appeare perhaps in the head of your assailants but not with the thoughts of a duelist but doubter being resolvd not to be an opponent but your Admirer.

81. Locke to Tom [Thomas Westrowe?], Pensford, 20 October 1659

. . . tis Phansye that rules us all under the title of reason, this is the great guide both of the wise and the fooleish, only the former have the good lucke to

---

[5] Catholics were held to owe civil as well as spiritual allegiance to the pope.

[6] Catholics were believed to consider themselves exempt from ordinary moral obligations when dealing with heretics.

light upon opinions that are most plausible or most advantageous. Where is that Great Diana[1] of the world Reason, every one thinkes he alone imbraces this Juno,[2] whilst others graspe noething but clouds, we are all Quakers here and there is not a man but thinks he alone hath this light within and all besids stumble in the darke. Tis our passions that bruiteish part that dispose of our thoughts and actions, we are all Centaurs[3] and tis the beast that carrys us, and every ones Recta ratio[4] is but the traverses of his owne steps. When did ever any truth settle it self in any ones minde by the strength and authority of its owne evidence? Truths gaine admittance to our thoughts as the philosopher did to the Tyrant by their handsome dresse and pleaseing aspect,[5] they enter us by composition, and are entertaind as they suite with our affections, and as they demeane themselves towards our imperious passions, when an opinion hath wrought its self into our approbation and is gott under the protection of our likeing tis not all the assaults of argument, and the battery of dispute shall dislodge it? Men live upon trust and their knowledg is noething but opinion moulded up betweene custome and Interest, the two great Luminarys of the world, the only lights they walke by. Since therefor we are left to the uncertainty of two such fickle guids, lett the examples of the bravest men direct our opinions and actions; if custome must guide us let us tread in those steps that lead to virtue and honour. Let us make it our Interest to honour our maker and be usefull to our fellows, and content with our selves. This, if it will not secure us from error, will keepe us from loseing our selves, if we walke not directly straite we shall not be alltogeather in a maze, and since tis not agreed where and what reason is, let us content our selves with the most beautifull and usefull opinions. . . .

82. Locke to [Thomas Westrowe?], Pensford, 8 November [1659?]

I did not guesse that you would finde a prophesye of these new stirs[1] in my last midnights meditations, that was the hower of their birth you might easily finde by the drowsinesse of them and did not this mad world too much justifye them they might well be accounted a melancholy dreame, and conceivd at that time when at least my reason was dormant, But this age is soe

---

[1] 'Great goddess Diana': Acts 19:34–5.   [2] Chief Roman goddess.
[3] A mythical monster, half man, half horse.   [4] Right reason.
[5] Perhaps Simonides and King Hiero of Syracuse (Xenophon, *Hiero*); alternatively, Plato and King Dionysius of Syracuse.

[1] General Lambert expelled the Rump Parliament on 13 Oct. Military confrontation with General Monk was expected.

frantick that it will make good what ever can be said against it, and I cannot repent the troubleing you with any thoughts of mine which may help to make you slight that world which fosters scarce any reasonable creaturs. I would not have it thought that I arrogantly extoll my self by condemning all others. I am one of the mad men too of this great Bedlam England, and shall thinke my self happy enough if I can but order my fits and frenzys any way to the advantage of my freinds, if my extravagancys can be improvd to your caution or my talkeing idle your pastime, which is the best use you can make of the world its self which with all its frippery is scarce worth a serious thought. he that pays downe any part of his quiet or content for it hath a hard bargaine, I wonder what evill Genius possesse men now that they are enamourd of this maukin,[2] that they will venture their blood for mire and scramble soe much for dirt, I thinke a very small portion of it is requird to the composition of happinesse, tis a scurvy dull ingredient and at best doth rather clog then cure the stomach, they that feed on it often surfett are never [satisfyd]. I thought to have said some thing else to you but being upon this chapter of the world I could not easily leave it. and pray now how doth this phylosophie become a rustick? doe I not grow Stoick apace? me thinkes I finde my self hard and half Iron already and can turne a churlish insensible outside to the world, though my warme affections will still keepe my heart neald[3] soft and pliant to all your commands and ready to receive any impressions from you. tis this tendernesse makes me inquisitive after our affairs, and I cannot but be concearnd for that ship in which you as well as I venter all [our] fortunes with which we must either sinke or swim; a ship me thinks is noe improper name for this Iland for surely it hath noe foundation, it is not firme land but hath been floateing these many years and is now puting forth into a new storme ill victuald ill tackld and the passengers striveing for the helme. Oh for a Pilot that would steare the tossed ship of this state to the haven of happinesse! doe not laugh at this expression for I assure you I have learnt it out of the pulpit from whence I heare it every Sunday. you must not misse the next post, nor leave out any tittle of authentick news but tell me what's past present and to come, this you'l say is a hard taske, but tis for a freind, for whome you ought to doe more then every pamphleteer[4] doth for a penny a sheet, here in you will favour not soe much my curiosity as my credit I being the prime Statesman of the place, and the Dictator of intelligence. You would laugh to see how attentive the gray-heads be to my reports (of more credit and concear[n]ment than Cook's)[5] and how they blesse them selves at my relations, and goe home and tell wonders and prophesye of next years affairs. The Royalists and . . .[6] with all their subdevided interest looke merry . . .

---

[2] Malkin: slut.   [3] Tempered by heat.   [4] The word was coined in 1642.
[5] Sir Edward Coke's revered law reports.   [6] Page torn.

83. Anne Evelegh to Locke, Oxford, 8 November 1659

[T]hose generouse expressions and markes of your frindshipe which you have with so much zeale lavished away upon me: makes my dull genious at length produce this ill shaped letter: no Sir I should not thus long have hazared the loss of your good opinion by my silence: had I not feared that my last letter: hath given you new discoveries of my folly and weakenesse: for when I reflect on your genious: and one of so cleare a judgment and quick sighted which can acquiesse in the harts and soon find out there infirmityes: therfore I give you a more plainer way: that I durst adventur to write to one of so cleare intellects: but I have had suficient experience of your worth or else I shuld not thus have exposed my folly to the view of so compleat a Person: no—no mr Lock it is not for want of true respect that I have for you that I have been speechlesse all this while: [it] is still beleiveing that you would not have let us bin mourning for your absence: and I was unwilling to expose those commands which I have to lay on you to the thinnes of a sheet paper: no you need not feare of any supplanting you for it is not possible to finde one in the universe of more merrit than your selfe, but I being conscious to my selfe of my owne unworthynesse: I may justly feare you are willing to be free from such a mistress: but stay Sir I will not part with my hapinesse at so cheape a rate: as to give you your fredome to loose you for ever: for could I once claime that title of being soveraigne my ambition weare at the highest pitch and my thought should be at rest and never thinke of aspiring no farther: I could wish I had that Power over you which you faine would make me beleive: I have I would then indevour to accomplish my desires: that is you should soone be at black hall[1] againe: for I will say with the wise man that the desires accomplished is sweet to the soule:[2] therefore the conclusion is the want of your vertuous conversation is sorrow and bitternesse: for did you really know the resentment of my soule you would there find ingraven the Characters of true frindshipe and high esteem for you and to supply the defect of my unhapinesse, that wee cannot injoy your companie here: I am forced to veiw and reveiw your letter over againe: wherein I find such a grandure of goodnesse and such sweet obliging expressions: which puts me in an extasy: and makes me sigh and that Somersetshire will outvie oxford in ingrosing so exquisite and so vertuous a soule all to themselves: but I cannot blame there prudence but rather aplaud and commend there ingenuity: for being ambitious of a person which can challeng[3] from all the world: nay more, than it is able to bestow: but the heavens will doe justice to your merit: and do more than mortals are able to imagine: as for your happinesse weare it any to be in my thoughts: you need not then feare to be ruined for time nor abscence shall never make me forget the delights of your ingenious conversation: nor there is none more propitious stars which can challeng a greatter esteeme in my

---

[1] L72, n. 1.   [2] Proverbs 13:19.   [3] Claim.

thoughts, than your selfe: therefore I beseech you doe not make an ill exposition on a hart which dayly wishes you both spirituall and temporall blesings: and I could wish that would come and make those tedious houres which paseth away with sad and melancholy actions become more pleasant: for those little cupids which you mention flie from me and returne to som beautifull objects which are able to read lectures of love with more ingenuity than I can: for I am not verst in that science therfor I cannot instruct others: I feare I have committed a crime which will not be veniall, in suffering the extravagancy of my pen to be so tedious: . . .

91. Locke to John Locke, sen., [Oxford], [*c*.9 January 1660]

I finde noe disapointment at all in the delay of your treaty with Dr I[1] since I shall not willingly be drawne from hence whilst things are in these uncertaine hurrys, nor thinke to enter upon a steady course of life whilest the whole nation is reeleing. What face soever affaires may weare there it appeares to me here altogether lowering and cloudy and I feare a storme will follow. Divisions are as wide, factions as violent and designes as pernicious as ever and those woven soe intricately, that there are few know what probably to hope or desire, and the best and wisest are faine to wish for the generall thing settlement without seeing the way to it. In this time when there is noe other security against mens passion and reveng but what strength and steell yeelds I have a long time thougt the safest condition to bee in armes could I be but resolvd from whome I ought to receive them and for whome to imploy them, or could be but securd that I should not spend my bloud to swell the tide of other mens fortune or make myself a c[ar]kas for their ambition to advance its self on. Armes is the last and worst of refuges, and tis the great misery of this shatterd and giddy nation that warrs have producd noething but warrs and the sword cut out worke for the sword, and I can scarce thinke that the drum was ever intended to lull this nation into quiet. I must confesse in this posture of affairs I know not what to thinke what to say. I would be quiet and I would be safe, but if I cannot injoy them togeather the last certainely must be had at any rate. I know it will not become either my condition nor inexperience to offer at advice only I wish that you may not venture your rest, health or estate for ingratefull men as all ambitious are, nor deceitfull, as religious pretenders are, nor tyrants such as are the promisers of liberty. nor giddy such as I had almost said all English men are, You are too well acquainted with the publick faith to lett it run in your debt, and you have had too much experience of their gratitude to be willing to obleige them at your owne cost. I must begg your pardon for this boldnesse, which possibly doth better bespeake my affection

---

[1] Dr Ayliffe Ivye, one of Locke's father's physicians.

than discretion, But this is a time when few men injoy the priviledg of being sober, and I am something excuseable if I cannot consider you steping again into danger without some emotion. If the sword be drawne againe I hope the nation and you too will reape greater advantages by it then either hath donne hither to. The most Authentick news here is, that the Rump hath voted out all the secluded members and made them incapable of being chosen into those vacancys which they intend to fill againe with qualified elections. Lambert is come to London with about forty horse and Munck is sent for whose good affections to the Rump is suspected. Fairfax in armes in the North for a free Parlament and the Citty not very well satisfyd. What you can spell from this medly I know not, to me it hath noe pleasant meaneing.[2] . . .

---

[2] General Lambert strove to preserve army rule. The Rump Parliament, which reassembled on 26 Dec., refused to sanction him, and invited General George Monk, army commander in Scotland, to march on London. Monk arrived in February, recalled the 'secluded' MPs, purged in 1648, thus restoring the Long Parliament that had tried (in 1646–8) to negotiate with Charles I, the king they had defeated. The restored Long Parliament dissolved itself in March. After new elections a Convention (a 'free parliament') met, which, in May, proclaimed Charles's son king as Charles II. General Thomas Fairfax: commander of the Parliamentary army in the Civil War.

2

Restoration Oxford and the Embassy to Cleves, 1660–1666

At the Restoration of King Charles II in May 1660, the House of Lords and the Anglican church were returned to their former status. On the eve of the Restoration, Locke offered to assist a Christ Church pupil, Francis Popham, son of his own patron Alexander Popham. As Locke explains to Popham senior (L96), he was offering his services in honour of the personal generosity shown to himself, and as a tribute to Popham's national standing as a member of the Council of State and of the Convention which recalled Charles II. Popham was typical of the Parliamentarians and Presbyterians in Locke's background who accepted the Restoration and conformed to the re-established Church of England, while retaining some of their puritan sentiments and loyalties. The old puritan movement had fragmented, some people remaining within the fold of the official church, others—the Nonconformists or Dissenters—forming denominations outside.

At the close of 1660 Locke writes a last letter to his dying father (L110). Shortly afterwards, he became a tutor at Christ Church, lecturing in Greek, rhetoric, and moral philosophy. Over the next seven years, he supervised a score of Christ Church pupils. One of his charges was John Alford, later a moderate Tory MP, from whose mother Locke receives a letter of limited literacy, expressing anxiety about her son's recklessness with money (L171). One of the most revealing of these early letters is Locke's parting advice to young Alford upon his leaving Christ Church (L200). The phonetic spelling in the mother's letter incidentally reveals the drawled 'e' in Restoration pronunciation ('desarve', 'sarvent').

At Oxford, Locke befriended another member of the 'club' at Black Hall, a Fellow of All Souls called Gabriel Towerson. Discussion with Towerson on the law of nature helps Locke formulate his lectures on the subject (L106). These lectures were not published until 1954, when they appeared under the title *Essays on the Law of Nature*. The two men also discussed Locke's other early essays (published in 1967 with the title *Two Tracts on Government*), which, in their defence of the magistrate's right to enforce religious uniformity, foreshadowed the Act of Uniformity of 1662. Locke had penned these essays to attack the views of his Christ Church colleague, Edward Bagshaw, who had denied the right of civil or ecclesiastical authorities to impose forms of religious worship. This Bagshaw did in his *Great Question Concerning Things Indifferent in Religious Worship* (1660). Towerson urges Locke to publish his reply and Locke seriously considers doing so. He prepares a dedicatory epistle to Towerson (L108), who continues to provide his friend with news of Bagshaw's controversial preaching in the university church (L118).

At Oxford Locke acquired his lifelong interest in science—or 'natural philosophy' as it was then called—frequenting Robert Boyle's experimental club in the High Street.

Locke provides Boyle with an account of a barometric experiment undertaken in the Mendip lead mines (L197). Locke acquired immense regard for Boyle, later esteeming him, in the Epistle to the Reader in his *Essay Concerning Human Understanding*, as one of the 'master builders' in the advancement of science, alongside Isaac Newton, Thomas Sydenham, and Christiaan Huygens.

The natural progression for a Christ Church tutor, such as Locke, would have been to become a clergyman, in Oxford or in a country parsonage, and he received several offers of clerical preferment during this period. However, in 1663, his child-hood friend, the barrister John Strachey, advises Locke against taking holy orders, pointing to the poverty of country parsons and the demeaning search for preferment (L163). The same topic recurs in 1666 when Locke was offered preferment by John Parry, Dean of Christ Church, Dublin, and brother of Elinor, whom we encountered in the previous chapter. Parry was confident of securing for Locke not only a chap-laincy with the Duke of Ormonde, but also a 'dignity' in the cathedral, 'handsomely provided for . . . without being a constant preacher'. Notwithstanding the attractions of this offer, Locke declines (L219). This resolve not to be ordained jeopardized his tenure at Christ Church, but he subsequently managed to secure a royal dispensation from taking holy orders.

In the previous year, Locke evidently decided to take the advice of his friend, Strachey, to spend some time abroad. England was at war with the Dutch Republic, and, between November 1665 and February 1666, Locke served as secretary to Sir Walter Vane's embassy to Cleves (Kleve) in the Rhineland. The purpose of Vane's embassy was to canvass the support of Prince Frederick William of Hohenzollern, the Elector of Brandenburg. The prince proved to be non-committal. Three of Locke's remarkable letters describing Cleves are included here. One to Boyle comments upon the unusual extent of religious toleration in the duchy (L175). Some picaresque observa-tions reveal Locke's distaste for Aristotelian philosophy, fruitless disputation, and Catholic monkishness. He sends satirical accounts of dinner at a friary, a Lutheran church service, and an encounter with an absurdly vain poetaster (L177, L182).

96. Locke to P A [Alexander Popham],
[Oxford], [*c*. April 1660?]

The greatest advantage I demand of my studys is an ability to serve you with them, and I shall thinke those years I have spent in Oxford not lost when I perceive they have renderd me any way usefull to him that first placd me there. The Muses deserve better of me than that by my negligence I should disgrace them to their best Patron and make them seeme ungratefull, and I would not willingly give you a reason to thinke that your care of Learning is a fruitlesse thing and such as from whence you must expect noe returne. This mak[e]s me diligently eye all occasions that may beccon me to your service, which should I oversee or be lesse carefull to observe it might justly be thought that in a place where all others improve their knowledg and become quicksighted I alone grew blinde and stupid or at least that all the light I have gaind from philosophie hath beene noe other than that of the Quakers which leads men from the sense of curtesy and gratitude. Sir to say that I am obleigd to you is noe more then to professe my self an English man and it cannot passe for a peculiar acknowledgement at a time when the whole nation lookes on you as a defender of their laws and libertys, but besides my share in the common benefit I have receivd many particular favours and owe you not only for my safety and prosperity but my knowledg and reason too, and my private obligations as far exceed the publick (though they be such as the good of 3 nations depends on) as the minde doth the body. if then I have made any acquisitions in learning tis fitt I dedicate them to you as their first author, which I cannot any way better doe, then by offering them to the assistance to your sonne. . . .

106. Gabriel Towerson to Locke, [Oxford],
[*c*.3 November 1660?]

The papers that have past between us being now growne so voluminous that I conceive it more difficult to informe our selves of the state of the controversie[1] between us, than to refell[2] what either of us hath said; I shall crave leave for my owne ease and because I would willingly be Mr. Ailmer's Auditor this 5th. of November[3] to respite my answer till the next week, in the which intervall I intend (God willing) to peruse all that hath past between us upon this head, and then on mine owne part to put a period to this

---

[1] Concerning the law of nature.   [2] Refute.
[3] i.e. attend the Gunpowder Day sermon by John Aylmer, Fellow of New College.

controversie, if I find you inclinable therto. Which I no way doubt but you will be, if you consider but these two things which I have now to propose to you. 1. Whether (it being agreed upon between us that there is such a thing as a law of nature and one of those arguments which I produc'd for it admitted without any scruple) it were not much more for our advantage to proceed in our enquiry touching the law of nature, than to contend any longer about a second argument 2. I would willingly know of you whether you thinke the being of the law of nature can be evinc'd from the force of conscience in those men who have no other divine law to square theire actions by.[4] If you doe (as for my owne part I doe because I thinke it to be St. Pauls owne argument)[5] I shall then thinke it incumbent upon you, who have engag'd in the same designe with your servant,[6] to answer in short your owne objections. If not, I shall despaire of perswading you, if what I have already said and shall in my next (which will I beleive be all that I can say for it) be not of force so to doe.

108. Locke to [Gabriel Towerson?], [Pensford or Oxford], 11 December 1660

In obedience to your commands I here send you my thoughts[1] of that treatise which we not long since discoursed of,[2] which if they convince you of nothing else, yet I am confident will of this, that I can refuse you nothing that is within the reach of my power. I know not what entertainment they will deserve from you, yet I am sure that you have this reason to use them favourably, that they owe their original to you. Let not the errors [which] may appear to you in their perusal, meet with too severe a censure, since I was neither led to them by the beaten track of writers, nor the temptation of interest, but they are, if any, the wanderings of one in pursuit of truth, whose footsteps are not always so clear as to leave us a certain direction or render our mistakes unpardonable, but very often so obscure and intricate that the quickest sighted cannot secure themselves from deviations. This candour I may

---

[4] Towerson's two arguments were that the law of nature may be inferred from the existence of a God who legislates for his creatures, and from the existence of a conscience that passes judgement on our actions. Locke took up these points in the first of his *Essays on the Law of Nature* (*Political Essays*, 81 ff.).

[5] Apparently Romans 2:14–15.   [6] Locke.

[1] The *First Tract on Government* (*Political Essays*, 3–53). This letter is a dedicatory epistle to the tract, but it was struck through and replaced by a preface.

[2] Edward Bagshaw, *The Great Question Concerning Things Indifferent in Religious Worship* (1660), to which Locke's tract is a reply.

with justice expect from you since I should never have gone out of my way had not you engaged me in the journey. Whatsoever you shall find in these papers was entertained by me only under the appearance of truth, and I was careful to sequester my thoughts both from books and the times, that they might only attend those arguments that were warranted by reason, without taking any upon trust from the vogue or fashion. My greatest fear is for those places of Scripture that fall in my way, whereof I am very cautious to be an over-confident interpreter, as on the other side I think it too servile wholly to pin my faith upon the not seldom wrested expositions of commentators, whom, therefore, in the haste I make to satisfy you I have not been much encouraged to consult on this occasion being only content with that light which the Scripture affords itself, which is commonly the clearest discoverer of its own meaning. I[3] have chose to draw a great part of my discourse from the supposition of the magistrate's power, derived from, or conveyed to him by, the consent of people, as a way best suited to those patrons of liberty, and most likely to obviate their objections, the foundation of their plea being usually an opinion of their natural freedom, which they are apt to think too much intrenched upon by impositions in indifferent things.[4] Not that I intend to meddle with that question whether the magistrate's crown drops down on his head immediately from heaven or be placed there by the hands of his subjects, it being sufficient to my purpose that the supreme magistrate of every nation what way soever created, must necessarily have an absolute and arbitrary power over all the indifferent actions of his people. And if his authority must needs be of so large an extent in the lowest and narrowest way of its original (that can be supposed) when derived from the scanty allowance of the people, who are never forward to part with more of their liberty than needs must, I think it will clearly follow, that if he receive his commission immediately from God the people will have little reason thereupon to think it more confined than if he received it from them until they can produce the charter of their own liberty, or the limitation of the legislator's authority, from the same God that gave it. Otherwise no doubt, those indifferent things that God doth not forbid or command his vicegerent[5] may, having no other rule to direct his commands than every single person hath for his actions, *viz:* the law of God. And it will be granted that the people have but a poor pretence to liberty in indifferent things in a condition where in they have no liberty at all, but by the appointment of the great sovereign of heaven and earth are born subjects to the will and pleasure of another. But I shall stop here . . .

---

[3] The remainder of the letter is reproduced in Locke's preface.

[4] 'Things indifferent' to salvation (or 'adiaphora') are those aspects of worship (or doctrine, or discipline) that have not been commanded or prohibited by God, as opposed to 'things necessary', which God has prescribed.

[5] Deputy, one who acts with delegated authority.

110. Locke to John Locke, sen.,
[Oxford], 20 December [1660?]

I did not doubt but that the noise of a very dangerous sicknesse here[1] would reach you, but I am alarmd with a more dangerous desease from Pensford and were I as secure of your health as (I thanke god) I am of my owne, I should not thinke my self in much danger, but I cannot be safe soe long as I heare of your weakenesse, and the increase of your malady upon you, which I begge that you would by the timely application of remedys indeavour to remoove, Dr Meara[2] hath more then once putt a stop to its incroachments. the same skill, the same means, and the same god to blesse them is left still, doe not I beseech you by that care you ought to have of your self, by that tendernesse I'm sure you have of us, neglect your owne and our safety too. doe not by a too pressing a care for your children endanger the only comfort they have left.[3] I cannot distrust that providence which hath conducted me thus far. and if either your disapointments or Necessitys shall reduce us to narrower conditions than you could wish, content shall enlarge it, therefor lett not those thoughts deject you, there is noe thing that I have which can be soe well imployd as to his use from whome I first receivd it, and if your convenience can leave me noething else, I shall have a head, and hands and Industry still left me, which alone have beene able to raise sufficient fortunes. Pray Sir therefor make your life as comfortable and lasting as you can, lett not any consideration of us cast you into the least despondency, if I have any refletions on or desires of a free and competent subsistence, it is more in reference to another (whome you may guesse) to whome I am very much obleigd,[4] than for my self, but noe thoughts how importunate soever shall make me forgett my duty, and a father is more then all other relations and the greatest satisfaction I can propose to my self in this world is my hopes that you may yet live to receive the returne of some comfort for all that care and Indulgence you have placd on Sir your most obedient sonne

118. Gabriel Towerson to Locke, All Souls,
Oxford, 9 April 1661

... This day fortnight your freind Mr. B.[1] preach'd at St. Maries and in the close of his sermon insisted upon his old theme, and though he prayed for

[1] An epidemic of smallpox.

[2] Dr Edmund Meara, physician in Bristol. In Jan. 1661 he wrote that Locke's father's liver and intestines were 'so much out of order that there are little hopes of repayreing them' (L111). Locke senior died in February.

[3] Locke had a brother, Thomas.

[4] Perhaps Locke's father; possibly Alexander Popham or Elinor Parry.

[1] Edward Bagshaw; 'freind' is ironical (L108).

Archbishops and Bishops yet he tooke away theire power and made it a marke of AntiChrist to impose ceremonies. He had a fling or two at Tho: Peirce[2] for so all interpreted it but I suppose he is not much troubled at it though all the church look'd upon him. for he only said and that too ἐν παρόδῳ[3] where it might very well have bin spar'd could he have but supprest his anger, that the elect could not fall from grace let Devils doe and men say what they would. . . . This I thought good to informe you of partly that I might not want matter for a letter and partly too that you might know there may be some necessity that your papers should see the light. . . .

163. John Strachey to Locke, 18 November 1663

Whilst you accuse mee of a litle complement, you have putt the greatest upon mee imaginable, in asking my advise in this concerne of yours,[1] certainly your owne strength is greate enough not to neede any forreine succours, and those small auxiliaries I can bringe may possibly share in the glory, not contribute the least in your aid, but since you are pleased to call for my assistance, I will chuse rather to manifest my owne weaknesse than not appeare forward to serve you. And since I must confine my thoughts to this paper, I will not state your case, but suppose that your Genius and Studies doe now crosse your present Interest, and you must necessarily declare your selfe for one; as to your studies (I hope I may speake without flattery) I beleive you and your parts such, that you may bee well said to bee *homo versatilis ingenii*,[2] and fitted for whatever you shall undertake, but to deale freely I have alwaies lookt on you as one of a higher head then to take covert under a Cottage, and in my opinion the best Country Parsonage is noe more, and although our holy Mother[3] makes better provision for some of her children and bestows titles and preferments on them, yett the expectation is soe tedious, and the observance soe base besides the uncertainty, that it will tire the patience of an ingenious spiritt to wait on such an old doting Grandame, not to meddle with your owne Genius and inclination which is as bad as Helmonts Archeus[4] if once thwarted and one were as good hange as contradict it, for what is a restraint but a strangling of nature. This is such a trade as may be tooke to at any time and as longe as there are dunces in the world a man of parts, lett him study but complyance,

---

[2] Thomas Pierce, President of Magdalen College, later Dean of Salisbury. Bagshaw fiercely upheld Calvinist predestination; Pierce fiercely opposed it. Bagshaw was expelled for nonconformity in 1662; Pierce had been expelled for royalism in 1648.

[3] 'In passing'.

[1] Whether to become a clergyman.

[2] 'A man of versatile mind' (Livy, *History of Rome*, XXXIX. lx. 5).   [3] The Church of England.

[4] Jan Baptista van Helmont, chemist and physician: his 'archeus' is the life force, which, when disturbed, causes diseases.

hee need want noe preferment. The onely thing you can well stagger at is the present losse, but surely you are not of the Simpletons mind in the Gospell that would not lend out his money for feare of loosing it,[5] not forgoe a Colledge Pension out of distrust that you shall neere meete with the like againe, prithee leave that leare shore[6] and putt to sea, Neptune is not soe mercilesse as most men fancy, and if you returne not in a yeare or two with as rich a Cargoe as the best, Ile neere cast figure more, and the Sea putts mee in mind that a litle outlandish[7] aire would doe mighty well if not for health yett for reputation, and sure as longe as I had [land] I would not want money for such a purpose, and if you dont redeeme it againe in a short space, the world would bee a hard Stepdame . . .

171. Lady Anne Alford to Locke, 23 May 1665

At the recait of your letter I [was so] weak as not able tow wright tow you tow [give] you my many thanks for your letter which was as a Cordiall tow me in heareing so good a Carracter of my son which I hop he will desarve from you and all that knows him. Sir I shall thinke my selfe much obliged tow you if you doe still continu your care over him As tow read tow him and give him all such instroductions which you shall thinke fitt tow make him a religious honest good man which I pray dayly for I have looked over his quarters expences both in your bill as in his own and trouly I doe find things very high as tow his batlings[1] I doe very will like of your preposall to give him a sartaine alowance which I hop will make him a better husband[2] and more thrifty of his mony and then it will doe him good tow set down what he lays out tow mak him parfict in keeping accounts when he coms tow his estat. So if you please tow pay your selfe of what you have layd out in this bill above the 20l sent the remainder of that 5–18–6 which was left in your hands at first I pray pay unto my son and the naxt mounth I shall returne him 10 pounds more which will I hop discharge all his expences untill August when I intend tow send for him hom the next yeare I intend to alowe him a 100 a yeare so he shall pay all and by all his Clothes and living himselfe which is a very grat allowance out of his estat. when he coms tow keep house he will find he cannot live tow spend so much upon himselfe I perceive he is removed tow an other Chamber more conveniant and chaper, which I lik very well of he must be a good husband for he hath a great Charg of Brothers and a Sister tow provid for and noe grat estat tow doe it if god should take me which is more likly then tow hop of recovery his Car[3] will be the gratter so as I doubt

---

[5] Matthew 25:14–30.   [6] Lee shore.   [7] Foreign.

[1] Battels: kitchen and buttery bills.   [2] Economical manager.   [3] Care, responsibility.

not of your discration in advising him for his good and tow soport his poore famely when I am in my grave which if you pleas tow doe me that faver you will furder oblig me tow be Your sarvent

175. Locke to Robert Boyle, Cleves, 12/22 December 1665

... We are here in a place very little considerable for any thing but its antiquity, which to me seems neither to commend things nor opinions; and I should scarce prefer an old ruinous and incommodious house, to a new and more convenient, though Julius Cæsar built it, as they say he did this the Elector[1] dwells in, which opinion the situation, just on the edge of a precipice, and the oldness of the building seems to favour. The town is little, and not very strong or handsom; the buildings and streets irregular; nor is there a greater uniformity in their religion, three professions being publickly allowed: the Calvinists are more than the Lutherans, and the Catholicks more than both (but no papist bears any office) besides some few Anabaptists,[2] who are not publickly tolerated. But yet this distance in their churches gets not into their houses. They quietly permit one another to choose their way to heaven, for I cannot observe any quarrels or animosities amongst them upon the account of religion. This good correspondence is owing partly to the power of the magistrate, and partly to the prudence and good nature of the people, who (as I find by enquiry) entertain different opinions, without any secret hatred or rancour. I have not yet heard of any person here eminently learned. There is one Dr. Scardius,[3] who, I am told, is not altogether a stranger to chemistry.[4] I intend to visit him as soon as I can get an handsom opportunity. The rest of their physicians go the old road, I am told, and also easily guess by their apothecary's shops, which are unacquainted with chemical remedies. This, I suppose, makes this town so ill furnished with books of that kind, there being few here curious enough to enquire after chemistry or experimental learning. And as I once heard you say, I find it true here, as well as in other places, that the great cry is ends of gold and silver. A catalogue of those books I have met with, some at Antwerp, and some in this town, I here inclosed send you, and am told by the only bookseller of this place, that he expects others daily from Francfort.[5] The weather is here exceedingly mild, and I have not seen any frost or snow since my coming; but it is an unusual clemency of the air, and the heavens seem to cherish the heat men are in to destroy one another. I suppose it no news to tell you, that the Dutch have forced a surrender of Lochem;

[1] Frederick William of Hohenzollern, Elector of Brandenburg.
[2] Mennonites, a Dutch sect which rejected infant baptism.
[3] J. Schard, physician of Cleves: later he sent medical prescriptions to Locke at Oxford.
[4] Medical chemistry (iatrochemistry), sponsored by the followers of J. B. van Helmont.
[5] Frankfurt was the centre of the German book trade.

there marched out of it two hundred and fifty of the bishop's men.[6] In another rencounter the bishop's men killed and took four hundred Dutch horse: so that this has only shaked the scales, not much inclined them to either side. The States of Cleve and March[7] are met here to raise money for the Elector, and he with that intends to raise men, but as yet declares for neither side: whether he be willing, or will be able to keep that neutrality I doubt, since methinks war too is now become infectious, and spreads itself like a contagion, and I fear threatens a great mortality the next summer, The plague has been very hot at Cologne; there have died there within this quarter of a year above eight thousand. A gentleman, that passed by that town last week, told me, that the week before there died there three hundred and forty eight. I know these little trivial things are as far distant from what I ought to send you, as I am from England: for this I do not only blame my own present poverty, but despair of the future, since your great riches in all manner of knowledge forbid me the hopes of ever presenting you with any thing new or unknown. . . .

177. Locke to John Strachey, [Cleves], 14/24 December 1665

. . . Dec. 9 I was invited and dind at a monastary with the Franciscan Friers, who had before brought a Latin Epistle to us for releife, for they live upon others charity, or more truly, live Idly upon others labours. But to my diner. For my mouth waters to be at it: and noe doubt you will long for such another enterteinment when you know this. After something instead of grace or Musick, choose you whether, for I could make neither of it. For though what was sung were Latin, yet the tone was such that I neither understood the Latin nor the Harmony. The begining of the Lords prayer to the 1st petition they repeated aloud, but went on silently to, sed libera nos[1] etc and there broke out into a loud Chorus which continued to the end, dureing their silence they stoopd forwards and held their heads as if they had been listening to one anothers whispers. After this præludium downe we sat. The cheife of the Monks, (I suppose the Prior) in the inside of the table just in the middle and all his breathren on each side of him. I was placd just opposite to him, as if I had designd to bid battle to them all. But we were all very quiet and after some silence, in marchd a solem procession of pease porredg every one his dish. I could not tell by the looks what it was. till puting my spoone in for discovery, some few pease in the bottom peepd up, lookd pittifully, and divd again. I had pitty on them, and was willing enough to spare them, but was forcd by

---

[6] The Bishop of Münster was at war with the Dutch: he had captured Lochem in September but now surrendered it.

[7] The estates (assembly) of Cleves and Mark.

[1] 'Deliver us (from evil).'

good manners, though against my nature and appetite, to destroy some of them, and soe on I fell. All this while not a word, I could not tell whether to impute this silence to the eagernesse of their stomachs, which allowd their mouths noe other imployment but to fill them, or any other reason: I was confident it was not in admiration of their late musick. At last the Oracle of the place spoke, and told them he gave them leave to speake to enterteine me. I returnd my complement, and then to discourse we went hilter skilter, as hard as our bad Latin and worse pronuntiation on each side would let us: But noe matter we car[e]d not for Priscian, whose head sufferd that day not a little.[2] However this savd me from the pease pottage and the pease pottage from me, for now I had something else to doe. Our next course was every one his cut of fish, and butter to boot. but whether it were intended for fresh or salt fish, I cannot tell and I beleive tis a question as hard as any Thomas[3] ever disputed, our third service was cheese and butter, and the cheese had this peculiar in it which I never saw any where else, that it had Caraway seeds in it. The Prior had upon the table by him, a little bell which he rang when he wanted anything, and those that waited never brought him anything or tooke away, but they bowd with much reverence, and kisd the table, The Prior was a good plump fellow, that had more belly than brains, and me thought was very fit to be reverencd, and not much unlike some head of a Colleg. I liked him well for an entertainment, for if we had had a good dinner, he would not have disturbd me much with his discourse. The first that kisd the table did it soe leasurely, that I thought he had held his head there, that the Prior dureing our silence, might have writt something on his bald crowne, and made it sinke that way into his understanding. Their beer was pretty good, but their countenances bespoke better, their bread browne and their table linnin neat enough. After dinner we had the second part of the same tune, and after that I departed. The truth is they were very civill and courteous and seemd good naturd. It was their time of fast in Order to Christmas. If I have another feast there you shall be my guest. You will, perhaps, have reason to thinke, that what ever becomes of the rest, I shall bring home my belly well improvd, since all I tell you is of eateing and drinking. But you must know that Knights Errant, doe not choose their adventures; and those who sometimes live pleasantly in brave Castles, amidst feasting and Ladys, are at other times in battles and wildernesses and you must take them as they come

Dec 10 I went to the Lutheran church, I found them all merrily singing with their hats on. Soe that by the posture they were in and the fashon of the building, not altogether unlike a theater, I was ready to feare that I had mistooke the place. I thought they had met only to exercise their voices, for after a long stay they still continued on their melody, and I veryly beleive they sung 119 psalme, noething else could be soe long, that that made it a little

---

[2] Roman grammarian: 'to break Priscian's head' was to break the rules of grammar.
[3] St Thomas Aquinas, 13th-cent. Scholastic theologian.

tolerable was that they sing better than we doe in our churches and are assisted by an organ. The musick being donne up went the preacher and praid and then they sung again and then after a little prayer, at which they all stood up (and as I understand since was the Lords prayer) read some of the bible, and then laying by his booke preachd to them memoriter.[4] His sermon I thinke was in blank verse, for by the modulation of his voyce, which was not very pleasant, his periods seemd to be all neare the same length, but if his matter were noe better then his delivery those that slept had noe great losse and might have snord as harmoniously. after sermon a prayer and then the organ and voices again, and to conclude all up stood another minister at a little deske above the Communion table (for in the Lutheran and Calvinist churches here there are noe Chancells) gave the benediction, which I was told was this Ite in nomine domini,[5] crosd himself and soe dismisd them. In this church I observd two pictures one a crucifix, the other I could not well discerne, but in the Calvinist church noe pictures at all. Here are besides Catholicks, Calvinists and Lutherans (which 3 are allowd) Jews Anabaptists[6] and Quakers[7] . . .

182. Locke to [John Strachey?], [Cleves], [early January 1666?]

The old opinion that every man had his particular Genius, that ruled and directed his course of life, hath made me sometimes laugh, to thinke, what a pleasant thing it would be, if we could see little Sprites[1] bestride men, (as plainely as I see here women bestride horses) ride them about, and spur them on in that way, which they ignorantly thinke they choose themselves. And would you not smile to observe that they make use of us, as we doe of our palfrys,[2] to trot up and downe, for their pleasure and not our owne? To what purpose this from Cleve? I'll tell you; if there be any such thing (as I can not vouch the contrary) certainly mine is an Academick goblin. When I left Oxford I thought for a while to take leave of all university affairs. And should have least expected to have found any thing of that nature here at Cleve of any part of the world. But doe what I can I am still kept in that tract. I noe sooner was got here, but I was welcomd with a divinity disputation, which I gave you an account of in my last.[3] I was noe sooner rid of that, but I found my self up to the ears in poetry, and overwhelmed in Helicon.[4] I had almost as rathe[r] have beene soused in the Reyne[5] as frozen as it was, for it could not have beene

---

[4] From memory.   [5] 'Go in the name of the Lord.'   [6] Mennonites. L175, n. 2.
[7] Presumably a Quaker-like sect.

[1] Goblins.   [2] Saddle-horses.
[3] '[A] young sucking Divine . . . accosted me . . . I found my self assaulted most furiously, and heavy loads of arguments fell upon me. . . . noething but some rubish of divinity, as uselesse and incoherent as the ruins the Greeks left behinde them' (L180).
[4] In Boeotia (Greece): favoured seat of the Muses.   [5] River Rhine.

more cold and intollerable, than the poetry I met with . . . My invisible master therefor haveing mounted me rod[e] me out to a place where I must needs meet a learned Bard, in a thread bare coat . . . After a little discourse wherein he sprinkled some bays[6] on our British Druid Owen,[7] out he drew from under his coat a folio of Verses, and that you may be sure they were excellent: I must tell you that they were Achrosticks[8] upon the name and titles of the Elector of Brandenburg. I could not scape readeing of them. When I had donne I endeavourd to play the poet a little in commending them, but in that he out did me clearly, praised faster than I could, preferred them to Lucan and Virgill, shewed me where his Muse flew high, squeesed out all the very juce of all his conceits and there was not a secret Conumdrum which he laid not open to me: and in that little talke I had with him afterwards, he quoted his owne verses a dozen times and Gloried in his works. This poem was designed as a present to the El[ector]: but I being Owens country man had the honour to see them before the Elector, which he made me understand was a singular courtesie, though I belieue 100 others had beene equally favoured. . . . I applauded his Generosity and great minde, thanked him for the favour he had donne me and at last got out of his hands. but my University goblin left me not soe, for the next day when I thought I had beene rod[e] out only to aireing, I was had to a fodering of chopped hay or Logick forsooth,[9] poore materia prima[10] was canvessed cruelly, stripped of all the gay dresses of her formes and shewne naked to us, though I must confesse I had not ey[e]s good enough to see her, however the dispute was good sport and would have made a horse laugh, and truly I was like to have broke my bridle. The young Munks[11] (which one would not guesse by their lookes) are subtile people, and dispute as eagerly for materia prima, as if they were to make their diner on it, and perhaps sometimes tis all their meale, for which others charity is more to be blamed than their stomacks. The professor of Philosophy and moderator of the disputation, was more acute at it than father Hudebrasse,[12] he was top full of distinctions, which he produced with soe much gravity and applyed with soe good a grace, that ignorant I began to admire Logick again, and could not have thought that simpliciter and secundum quid, materialiter. and formaliter,[13] had beene such gallant things, which with the right stroking of his whiskers, the setling of his hood, and his stately walke made him seeme to himself and me something more then Aristotle and Democritus.[14] But he

---

[6] Laurels.   [7] John Owen, epigrammatist.

[8] Acrostic: a poem in which the first letter of each line spells a word or phrase; fashionable in the 17th cent.

[9] Logic chopping: useless contentious argument.

[10] In Aristotelian metaphysics, prime matter is the indeterminate stuff of the universe, before it is given positive form or qualities, such that it becomes actually existing substance. The notion was ridiculed by the proponents of the new philosophies.

[11] Probably Franciscan friars rather than strictly monks.

[12] *Hudibras* (1663): popular satirical poem by Samuel Butler, which, *inter alia*, ridiculed pedantry.

[13] Technical terms in Scholastic philosophy.   [14] i.e. more than the great philosophers.

was soe hotly charged by one of the Seniors of the fraternity, that I was affraid sometimes what it would produce, and feared there would be noe other way to decide the controversy betweene them but by cuffs, but a subtile destinction devided the matter betweene them and soe they parted good freinds. The truth is here hogsheering[15] is much in its glory, and our disputeing in Oxford comes as short of it, as the Rhetorick of Carfax does that of Belings gate.[16] But it behoves the Moncks to cherish this art of wrangleing in its declineing age, which they first nursed and sent abroad into the world to give it a troublesome idle imployment . . .

197. Locke to Robert Boyle, Christ Church, Oxford, 5 May 1666

. . . The Barometer I had from you was conveyed safe into the Country, and as soon as it came to my Hands, I rode to Minedeep,[1] with an Intention to make use of it there, in one of the deepest Gruffs[2] (for so they call their Pits) I could find: the deepest I could hear of was about 30 Fathom, but the Descent so far either from easy, safe, or perpendicular, that I was discouraged from venturing on it. They do not, as in Wells, sink their Pits strait down, but, as the Cranies of the Rocks, give them the easiest Passage; neither are they let down by a Rope, but taking the Rope under their Arm, by setting their Hands and Legs against the sides of the narrow Passage, clamber up and down, which is not very easy for one not used to it, and almost impossible to carry down the Barometer, both the Hands being imployed. This Information I should have suspected to come from their Fear, had not an intelligent Gentleman, Neighbour to the Hill, assured me 'twas their usual way of getting up and down. For the Sight of the Engine, and my Desire of going down into some of their Gruffs, gave them terrible Apprehensions, and I could not perswade them but that I had some Design: So that I and a Gentleman that bore me Company, had a pleasant Scene, whilst their Fear to be undermined by us, made them disbelieve all we told them; and do what we could, they would think us craftier Fellows than we were. But, Sir, I will not trouble you with the Particulars of this Adventure: but certain it is the Women too were alarm'd, and think us still either Projectors or Conjurers. Since I could not get down into their Gruffs, I made it my Business to inquire what I could concerning them: The Workmen could give me very little Account of any thing, but what Profit made them seek after; they could apprehend no other Minerals but Lead Oar, and believed the Earth held nothing else worth seeking for: besides, they were not forward to be too communicative to one, they thought they had Reason to

---

[15] 'A great cry and little wool, quoth the devil when he sheared the hog' (proverb).
[16] Carfax: central crossroads in Oxford. Billingsgate: fish-market in London, a byword for foul-mouthed talk.

[1] Mendip Hills, Somerset: probably around Chewton Mendip and Priddy.   [2] Mineshafts.

be afraid of. But at my Return, calling at a Gentleman's House, who lives under Minedeep-Hills, and who had sent out his Son to invite me in; amongst other things he told me this, that sometimes the Damps catch them, and then if they cannot get out soon enough, they fall into a Swound, and die in it, if they are not speedily got out; and as soon as they have them above ground, they dig a Hole in the Earth, and there put in their Faces, and cover them close up with Turfs; and this is the surest Remedy they have yet found to recover them. In deep Pits they convey down Air by the side of the Gruff, in a little Passage from the Top; and that the Air may circulate the better, they set up some Turfs on the Lee side of the Hole, to catch, and so force down the fresh Air: But if these Turfs be removed to the windy side, or laid close over the Mouth of the Hole, those below find it immediately, by want of Breath, Indisposition, and Fainting: and if they chance to have any sweet Flowers with them, they do not only lose their pleasant Smell immediately, but stink as bad as Carrion. Notwithstanding this ill Success, I had attempted some Trials once more, had not the spreading of the Contagion[3] made it less safe to venture abroad, and hastened me out of the Country sooner than I intended. But I have some Hopes, the next Journey I make into those Parts, to give you a better Account than this that follows. Near the House where I sometimes abode, was a pretty steep and high Hill. *April. 3. hora inter 8 et 9. Matutin.*[4] the Wind West, and pretty high, the Day warm, the Mercury was at 29 Inches and $\frac{1}{8}$, being carried up to the Top of the Hill, it fell to 28 Inches $\frac{3}{4}$, (or thereabouts, for I think it was a little above 28 Inches $\frac{3}{4}$:) Both going up and coming down, I observed that proportionably as I was higher or lower on the Hill, the Mercury fell or rose. At my return to the bottom of the Hill, the Mercury wanted of ascending to its former Height $\frac{1}{32}$ of an Inch, which I impute to the Sun's rarifying some Particles of Air that remained in the upper Part of the Tube, rather than to any other Change in the Air; for I find it harder to clear the Tube of Air perfectly, than at first I thought, or of Water, if that have been put in with the Mercury. and I fear liable to the same Inconvenience with Air inclosed. I know this is far short of what you might have expected, and has, I fear, but little answered your Desires, since I guess it was the perpendicular Height of the Place I made the Experiment in, that you would have had, and perhaps other Considerations of Air, inclosed, and liable to mineral Steams, would have made a Trial in one of the Gruffs more acceptable to you. I do not think any thing in this Letter worthy of you, or fit for the Publick. But since I find by the two last Philosophical Transactions, that Observations on the Torricellian Experiment are much look'd after, and desired to be compared; if for want of better, this should be thought fit to fill an empty Space in the Philosophical NewsBook, I shall desire to have my Name concealed.[5] But I fear that this

---

[3] Plague.   [4] Between 8 and 9 a.m.

[5] The *Philosophical Transactions of the Royal Society* began in 1665. Locke's account was in fact published in Boyle's *General History of the Air* (1692). Evangelista Torricelli devised the mercury barometer in 1643.

very Caution of being in Print, where there is no Danger of it, has too much of Vanity in it. I'm sure 'tis Boldness enough, though allaid with Obedience, to venture such slight things to your Sight. . . .

200. Locke to John Alford, Christ Church, Oxford, 12 June 1666

I have not yet quite parted with you. and though you have put off your gowne, and taken lea[ve] of the University. you are not yet got beyond my affection or concernment for you. Tis true, you are now past Masters and Tutors, and it is now therefor that you ought to have the greater care of your self: since those mistakes or miscarriages, which heretofore would have beene charged upon them, will now, if any, light wholy upon you. and you your self must be accountable for all your actions; nor will any longer any one else share in the praise or censure they may deserv[e.] 'Twill be time therefor, that you now begin to thinke your self a man. and necessary that you take the courage of one. I meane not such a courage, as may name you one of those daring galla[nts] that stick at noe thing. but a courage that may defend and secure your virtue and religion. for in the world you are now lanching into, you will finde perhaps more onsets made upon your innocence then you can imagine. and there are more dangerous theeves, than those that lay wait for your purse, who will endeavour to rob you of that virtue which they care not for themselves. I could wish you that happynesse, as never to fall into such company. But I consider you are to live in the world and whilst either the service of your country, or your owne businesse makes your conversation with men necessary, perhaps this caution will be needfull. But you may with hold your heart where you cannot deny your company. and you may allow those your civility, who possibly will not deserve your affecti[on.] I thinke it needlesse and impertin- ent to dissuade you from vices I never observed you incline[d] to. I write this to strengthen your resolutions Not to give you new ones. But let not the importunitys or examples of others, prevaile against the dictates of your owne reason and education: I doe not in this advise you to be either a Munke, or Morose: to avoid company, or not enjoy it. One may certainly with innocence use all the enjoyments of life. and I have beene always of opinion, that a virtuous life is best disposed to be the most pleasant. For certainly amidst the troubles and vanitys of this world, there are but two things, that bring a reall satisfaction with them, that is, Virtue and Knowledg. What progresse you have made [in the latter] you will doe well not to loose. your spare howers from devotion, businesse, or recreation, (for that too I can allow, where imploy- ment not idlenesse gives a title to it) will be well bestowd in reviveing or im- proveing your University notions, and if at this distance I could afford your st[ud]ys any direction or assistance I should be glad and you need only but let me know it. Though your anc[e]stors have left you a condition above the

ordinary rank, yet tis your self alone that can advance your self to it: For
tis not either the goeing upon two legs, or the liveing in a greate house, or
possessing many acres: that gives one advantage over beasts or other men: but
the being wiser and better. I speake not this to make you carelesse of your
estate, for though riches be not vertue, tis a great instrument of it, wherein
lyes a great part of the usefullnesse and comfort of life. In the right management of this lyes a great part of prudence. and about mony is the great
mistake of men; whilst they are either too covetous, or too carelesse of it. If
you throw it away idlely, you loose your great support, and best freind. If you
hugge it too closely, you loose it, and your self too. To be thought prudent
and liberall, provident and good naturd, are things worth your endeavour to
obtei[n,] which perhaps you will better doe, by avoiding the occasions of
expences, than by a frugall limiting them when any occasion hath made them
necessary. But I forget you are neere your Lady Mother, whilst I give you these
advises. and doe not observe that what I meant for a letter begins to grow
into a treatise. . . .

219. Locke to [John Parry], [Oxford], [*c.*15 December 1666]

The letter I sent by your Sister[1] I perceive came to you by a wellcome hand,
which it could not otherwise have deservd soe kind a returne, with which
I pay you my thanks and acknowledgment you cannot doubt but I have
Inclination enough to be in Dublin without considering the beauty and
largenesse of the towne. It being the conversations of those I love and company of my freinds (and how much you are soe your letter shews) that makes
any place desirable to me. But Sir he must needs be a very quick sighted or
very inconsiderat person that can between the comeing of one post and
goeing of the next peremptoryly resolve to transplant himself from a country affairs and studys he has been bread in into all these very distant. upon
probability, which though perhaps your interest there may make you look
on as certain, yet my want of fitnesse may possibly disapoint, for certainly
something is requird on my side, it is not enough for such places barely to
be in orders,[2] and I cannot thinke that preferments of that nature will be throwne
upon a man that hath never given any proofs of him self nor ever tried the
pulpit
   would you not thinke it a strange question if I should aske you whether
I must be first in those places or in orders, yet if you will consider with
me it will not prhaps seeme altogeather irrationall; for should I put my
self into order[3] and yet by the meanesse of my abilitys prove unworthy such

---

[1] Elinor Parry, then in Dublin.   [2] i.e. in holy orders, ordained a clergyman.
[3] Be ordained.

expectation, (for you doe not thinke that Divines are now made as formerly by inspiration and on a suddain,[4] nor learning caused by laying on of hands)[5] I unavoidably loose all my former studys and put my self into a calling that will not leave me nor keep me, were it a profession from whenc there were any return,[6] (and that amongst all the occurrences of life may happn to be very convenient if not necessary) you would finde me with as much forwardnesse imbrace your proposals, as I now acknowledg them with gratitude.

You cannot then thinke it strange if these reasons, the difference of my studys, with a just feare, sure sight of myself, and the misfortune of altogether, suffer me not at least soe much on a suddain to resolve on so waity an undertaking, since the same considerations have made me a long time refuse very advantageous offers of severall considerable freinds in England. I am apt [to] flatter my self that the reason of this your kindenesse is yet a very much greater. and which above all things in the world I should be glad to meet in a way wherin I should [be] not unworthy of it, and shall be infinitely indebted to any one that shall open such a one to me. but I can not be forward [to] disgrace you or any body else by being listed into a place which perhaps I cannot fill and from whence there is noe desending without tumbleing. (If any shame or misfortune attend me it shall be only mine and if I am covetous of any good fortune tis that one I love[7] may share it with me.) . . .

---

[4] A reference to the irregular making of Puritan ministers during the Civil Wars and Interregnum.
[5] At the ordination of clergy the bishop lays his hands on the ordinand's head.
[6] Anglican clergy could not relinquish their orders before 1870.
[7] Presumably Elinor Parry.

3

Lord Ashley's Servant and the 'New World', 1667–1675

In 1666 Locke met Anthony Ashley Cooper, Lord Ashley, the king's Chancellor of the Exchequer. The two got on well, and the following spring Locke accepted an invitation to live in Ashley's household at Exeter House in the Strand, London, where he served as adviser and secretary for the next eight years. There he mingled with the stewards, attorneys, chaplains, and other servants of one of the great magnates and statesmen of the age. In 1667 Ashley's influence significantly increased following the fall of Lord Chancellor Clarendon, who was made the scapegoat for the disastrously humiliating attack by the Dutch on the Royal Navy in the River Medway (L226). Created Earl of Shaftesbury in 1672, Ashley served briefly as Lord Chancellor, although he subsequently exerted his greatest influence as the leader of the Whig opposition which challenged Charles II's regime between 1675 and 1683.

Through Shaftesbury's extensive interests in the Americas, Locke became involved in England's burgeoning commercial empire. As well as serving as secretary to the Lords Proprietors of Carolina and to Charles II's Council of Trade and Plantations, Locke also became one of a syndicate of eleven 'adventurers to the Bahamas' under contract from the Carolina Proprietors. One of those Proprietors was Sir Peter Colleton, deputy governor of Barbados, who writes to Locke discussing trade between the West Indies and England, the plight of the Carolina settlers, and the medicinal properties of American plants (L275, L279). Describing the advantages of Carolina over England, Colleton petitions for supplies, and notes Locke's role in drafting for Shaftesbury *The Fundamental Constitutions of Carolina* (1669). Locke's involvement with slave-owning and slave-trading enterprises does not seem to have presented itself to him as posing a moral or intellectual dilemma.

Letters from his correspondents often answered to Locke's botanical and anthropological curiosities. Henry Woodward, a surgeon and explorer in Carolina, provides Locke with an account of the religious and medical practices of the native Americans (L305). Elsewhere, in Syria, the Levant Company's chaplain discusses the unsolved problem of measuring longitude and the declining condition of the Ottoman lands (L253).

Having studied medicine at Oxford, Locke throughout his life advised friends on their health. In 1668, Shaftesbury almost died of a ruptured liver cyst and believed he owed his life to Locke's direction of an operation which drained the cyst—undertaken of course without anaesthetic or antiseptic (L250). The operation involved the permanent insertion of a silver pipe to drain matter from the abscess. In that era of merciless political satire, Tory journalists sported with 'Count Tapski' and the Cooper who had a cooper's tap. Locke met the greatest physician of the age, Thomas Sydenham, with whom he discussed a host of medical matters. Sydenham advises about an illness Locke suffered while 'broken with business'—Locke fears he is consumptive (L295).

Locke became increasingly interested in financial and fiscal matters. In 1668 he drafted a tract on economics which is of greater scope than is suggested by the title under which it eventually appeared in 1692, *Some Considerations of the Consequences of the Lowering of Interest*. To ease cash flow during the Third Dutch War, Charles II stunned the financial markets in 1672 by the Stop of the Exchequer which suspended payments on government debt. As a leading minister, Shaftesbury was implicated in this imprudent measure. Vindicating his role, Shaftesbury places responsibility on Lord Clifford, who had attacked him, and who was apparently acting on behalf of angry, but avaricious, bankers (L297). Shaftesbury also alludes to the relationship between banking, trade, and land, foreshadowing the controversies which developed after the Glorious Revolution about the relative fiscal burden borne by land and trade. An earlier letter from John Strachey comments on Locke's views on various forms of taxation, including the newly emerging excise duties (L261).

As Shaftesbury's political secretary, Locke kept up with a large variety of contemporary issues, ranging from ideas articulated in the popular press to recent philosophical treatises. In 1673 John Aubrey recommends some of Thomas Hobbes's works to Locke and Shaftesbury (L268). This important letter is the only document which implies an acquaintance between Locke and Hobbes. Locke's intellectual relationship with Hobbes remains a disputed topic; Locke mentioned Hobbes on only a handful of occasions in his writings.

In the autumn of 1672 Locke travelled to France for the first time, as the companion of the 26-year-old, newly widowed, Countess of Northumberland. He had been a frequent visitor to Northumberland House, in the Strand. English aristocratic circles were besotted with French fashions and manners, and Locke's first experiences of Paris and of the French are recounted with delicate wit and sardonic distaste; his hostility to the tyranny of Louis XIV is already apparent (L264).

226. Locke to John Strachey, [London], 15 June [1667]

I beleive report hath increasd the ill news we have here. therefor to abate what possibly feare may have rumord I send you what is vouchd here for nearest the truth. The Dutch have burnd 7 of our ships in Chatham. (viz) the Royal James. Royal oake, London. Unity St Matthias. Charles 5th. and the Royal Charles which some say they have towed off, others that they have burnd.[1] One man of warre of theirs was blown up and 3 others they say are stuck on the sands, the rest of their fleet is fallen downe out of the Medway into the Thames. Twas neither excesse of courage in them, nor want of courage in us that brought this losse upon us, (for when the English had powder and shott they fought like them selves and made the Dutch feele them) but whether it were fortune or fate or any thing else let time and tongues tell you. . . .

250. Locke to Abbé René de Briolay de Beaupreau, 20 January 1671

It is now the second year since that remarkable abscess and humoral trouble of the illustrious Lord Ashley, Baron of Wimborne St. Giles,[1] was brought to a state of healthiness which one could not call altogether complete, but which leaves the noble lord with nothing to complain of. There is moderate exudation and discharge from the ulcer, which gives him no trouble; by this means any noxious humours that arise anywhere in the body are forthwith got rid of through this open drain, designed as it were by nature, so providing an excellent precaution against future ailments. The state of things has in fact remained the same up to the present day as it was when I wrote to you, excellent Sir, two years ago. For at one time an over-hasty closure of the approach was resulting in a recrudescence of the internal trouble, and there was a fear that if the ulcer were allowed to heal up and the external orifice to become closed there might be some very slight trace of corruption left inside, supposing that some very small part were not yet sound, and that this might produce a fresh collection of pus and corrupt matter, which might not easily find such a fortunate outlet; it therefore seemed wiser to secure access to the actual source of the trouble with a silver tube, and thus to provide a permanent passage for any foul matter that might collect or arise there; this plan proved reasonable and successful. The silver tube, an inch and a half long, which was

[1] On 12 and 13 June the Dutch sailed up the River Medway, burnt eight ships, and towed away the *Royal Charles.*

[1] The Ashley family seat in Dorset.

inserted in the ulcer about the middle of September 1668, has been worn ever since then without trouble or inconvenience; all that is done is to withdraw it every other day in order to clear it of any foul matter, after which it is washed out with hot wine and replaced. This ulcer differs in no way from a simple contusion except for its position and depth, owing to which it appears to threaten the healthy flesh lying beneath it; yet the noble patient has experienced no inconvenience during these two years, except that last summer, as a result of excessive movement or perhaps an undue bending of the body whilst playing tennis or possibly some fall which escaped observation, the tube was shifted in its seating and slightly twisted round; the point of it, which is usually inclined downwards, was turned upwards, and being thus bent it injured the tender internal flesh; this was followed by pain, and the watery discharge was stained with one or two drops of blood. But the silver pipe was soon restored to its position, and the patient's suffering and our own fears were immediately relieved. The noble lord has only once suffered this inconvenience, such as it is, in the course of two years, and that by accident, though he walks, rides, plays tennis, and performs all the functions of daily life as usual in a brisk and active manner. These kind of injuries, which are to be expected only from displacement of the pipe, we hope can be guarded against for the future. This ulcer seems, in fact, simply like a fontanel[2] in an unusual situation; it gives hardly as much trouble as those commonly inserted in the arms and discharges very little more, whilst it far surpasses them in its useful and beneficial effects. For ever since the malady was first checked and the evacuation of the putrid humour collected internally gave hopes of a cure he has suffered no ill health at all; on the contrary, vigour has gradually returned to his expression and his eyes, his muscles have recovered their strength, and he has become far more brisk and active than he had been for many years before the inimical onset of the disease. He is no longer frightened or afflicted by weakness of the stomach, or attacks of indigestion, or jaundice with periods of lassitude, but has enjoyed such good and sound health that he has not once needed to use even the mildest purgative or any other medicine. Such has been the end of this humoral affection and of a case as remarkable as any in medical practice. . . .

253. Robert Huntington to Locke, Aleppo, Syria, 1 April 1671

. . . Though wee sayld much in sight of Land, yet sometimes wee had sea-roume enough, to discover how usefull it must needs be in Navigation, to find out the Longitude of the place exactly, in which a ship at any time chanceth to sayle; a Probleme by some suppos'd very easy, allthough I never yet found it

---

[2] An opening for discharge.

attempted with right good and certain successe; And really the advantages of it when known will recompense the labour of any ingenious Person that shall travaile therein.[1] The Variation of the Compass observable in severall places more or lesse, but wee took notice of it nowhere so much as between Rhodes and Cyprus, is a riddle of Nature, and deserveth the search of Curious men to find out a satisfactory reason;[2] notwithstanding the Skill of our mariners, and their Rationall method generally preventeth the inconveniences it might occasion. Indeed I saw not anything more remarquable by Land: As for the flax-stones[3] which once made the Linumvivum or Asbestinum, and might doe so still, they can be no rarity in Europe, since there are rocks of them in Cyprus, out of which the Inhabitants make lint upon occasion for their wounds; which seemeth feaseable enough to be carded and spun and fitted for the loome. The Great Cities once famous through the world, are now fallen into small Townes or Villages, or else quite buryed in their Ruines; and by the crumbling and hollow soyle (as at Ephesus and Antioch)[4] it appeareth that Earthquakes, the deadly Falling-sicknesse of These Places, might very well help on their Destruction. The Country is miserably decay'd, and hath lost the Reputation of its Name, and mighty stock of Credit it once had for Eastern Wisedome and learning: It hath followed the Motion of the Sun, and is Universally gone Westward. May it never sett there: I am still an Englishman; and consequently, to wish all happiness to the Land of my Nativity, and my Friends there, is no more than my Duty . . .

261. John Strachey to Locke, 19 January 1672

I must confesse that I have taken too much time to answer your letter, but I hope the Holydays and Xmas Gambolls may bee my excuse, which delights although the[y] come very short of a correspondence with you, yett tis a hard matter to shake of Custome, video meliora etc.[1] As to your 3 first reasons[2] why taxes should bee laid on Land, as I write not for dispute but satisfaction, soe I acknowledg myselfe convinc'd, but as to your fourth that all taxes terminate at last on the land,[3] I cannot soe readily subscribe, for methinks your instances doe not reach it, the Excise on Ale not making barley cheaper, but only less Ale is sold for the money and thereby the Drinkers and not the

---

[1] John Harrison devised a chronometer to determine longitude in 1735. L3499.

[2] Compasses are affected by the varying magnetism of iron-bearing rocks.

[3] A variety of asbestos with flax-like fibres.

[4] Ancient Greek cities (now in Turkey) known to Bible readers as sites of St Paul's missionary journeys.

---

[1] 'I see the better (but follow the worse)' (Ovid, *Metamorphoses*, vii. 20).

[2] Locke's comments to Strachey do not survive.

[3] Locke's remark, in *Some Considerations of the Consequences of the Lowering of Interest* (1691), that 'taxes . . . for the most part terminate upon land' was much commented upon in the 18th cent.

Countriman pay the Tax, indeed if the Statute was putt in Execution which commands such a quantity to bee sold for a penny, then Barley must bee sold cheaper, else the Brewer would not buy it to bee a Looser by the bargaine, but since as the Excise doth rise hee may lessen the quantity of his Ale, I can't see why it should fall on Barley. Soe for the Rest, and although you speake never soe rationally on this subject, the Country will hardly be brought to yeild, I could wish I had your thoughts on a Free Port,[4] for I doubt not but they are very ingenious. . . .

264. Locke to John Strachey, [Paris], [mid October 1672]

If you are as you ought to be at leisure to hearken to the words of a gentleman and a traveller, and which is more thought of a Monsieur, the time is now come that you are to be beatified by the refined conversation of a man that knows the difference between a black and white feather, and who can tell you which side of his two-handed hat ought to be turned up, and which only supported with an audace. I fear you have the unpardonable ignorance not to know what an audace is; to oblige you then, know that what an untravelled Englishman would take to be a piece of ordinary loop lace made use of to support the overgrown brims of a flapping hat has by the virtuosos and accomplished gallants of Paris, when I was there, been decreed to be an audace. And thus you may reap the benefit of what cost me many a step. O the advantage of travel! You see what a blessing it is to visit foreign countries and improve in the knowledge of men and manners. When could you have found out this by living at Sutton Court[1] and eating crammed capons and apple pies? But now I have communicated this to you and enriched your understanding with the notice of a new fashionable French word, let it not make you proud, that belongs to us only that have taken pains and gone a great way for it. If I thought it would not, and being embellished by some scatterings of those jewels I have lately picked up in France you would not be elevated in your own thoughts and at the next sessions laugh at those of the worshipful quorum,[2] which you are not to do till you have been refined with French air and conversation, I would tell you yet better things, and you should (as Don Quixote saw Dulcinea by hear say)[3] see the Louvre, the Seine and Pont Neuf over it, Paris, and, what is the perfection and glory of all, the King of France himself. And is not this do you think well worth a journey of 5 or 600 miles, and are not our people wise when they admire and run even mad after these things and

[4] A port that permits the duty-free entry of goods for re-export.

[1] Strachey's home, 3 mls. south-west of Pensford.

[2] The quorum of county magistrates at the quarter sessions.

[3] Cervantes, *Don Quixote* (1605).

several others, whereof I care not if I give you a little taste, viz., There I saw
vast and magnificent buildings as big almost as others dominions preparing
only for one man, and yet there be a great many other two legged creatures,
but 'tis not the way of that country much to consider them, and so let them
go who are in such perpetual motions that they will not much need mansions
till they come to their long home. [I saw] there men that had forsaken the
world and women that professed retirement and poverty[4] have yet in the ornaments of their buildings and the hatchments of their trinkets all the mighty
riches exquisite art could produce of convenience, beauty or curiosity. This I
saw and what is more believed that this was to forsake the world and I take
it may be allowed to be a heavenly life to have all things with ease and security in a place where labour and vexation enter not. I saw too infinite gay things
and gewgaws, feathers and [frippery], and to come to you I saw Westminster
Hall in epitome,[5] which exceeds ours (how wide mouthed soever it be) a
thousand times, in the noise and din. How much it came short in honesty I
had not occasion to know, I thank my stars, but the hum and buzzing of those
busy hornets made me suspect the laborious bee did not keep all his honeys
to himself. . . .

Perhaps your mouth will water after other matters, but to stop your longing I am to tell you that the great happiness of this heaven upon earth, Paris,
lies wholly in vision too. Eating, drinking, sleeping and the entertainment of
the other senses are not there altogether so voluptuous; but those are earthly
pleasures for clodpate[6] mortals, and we [ayry] men contemn them. And I think
a man that hath once tasted the dirty water of the Seine, and smelled the
variety of stinks that set off Paris, is thereby privileged to contemn you men
of toast and ale and powdered beef, which salt keeps from due haut gout.
If the air of the country hath given me but half so much health as it hath
vanity, I shall quickly be as strong as I am now conceited. I only wish this puffing
up would make me in truth more bulky. But if it do not, 'tis yet a piece of
greatness to have been amongst a sort of men that look down on all the world,
and to have seen him that tramples on them who undervalues us.[7] To get this
gift of undervaluing all on this side the water is (as experience shows) one of
the best qualities one can learn amongst them, and therefore do but think
how your quondam[8] friend John,[9] now fashionable Monsieur John, abomin-
ated damned roastbeef and the other gross meats of England, when his mouth
watered at the sweet grapes and insipid or sour bread that those brave men
make meals and feast on, and how did he a night's laugh at the drowsy English
men when the *punaise*[10] and other creepers tickled him. This accomplishment
[you will permit] a man that hath gone so many miles for it, and you will
not deny me this privilege of my travels to bring home with me the contempt
of my country. I wish you were but here to see how I could cock my hat,

---

[4] Monks and nuns.   [5] The Palais (now Palais de Justice).   [6] Stupid.
[7] Presumably the French king, Louis XIV.   [8] Former.   [9] Locke himself.   [10] Insect.

strut and shake my garniture,[11] talk fast, loud, confidently and nothing to the purpose, slight you and everybody . . .

268. John Aubrey to [Locke?], 11 February 1673

I cannot but present you my thankes for your great Humanity and kindnes to me; as also for the honour you doe me to peruse my Scriblings. I was at your lodgeing twice to have kiss't your hands before I came out of Towne— to have recommended a MSS or two (worthy of your perusall) of my old friend Mr Th: Hobbes. One is a Treatise concerning the Lawe,[1] which I importun'd him to undertake about 8 yeares since and then in order thereto presented him with my L. Ch: Bacons Elements of the Lawe.[2] All men will give the old Gentleman that right as to acknowledge his great felicity in well defining: and all know that the lawyers especially the common (omnium Doctorum genus indoctissimum)[3] superstruct on their old fashion'd Axioms, right or wrong; for great practisers have not the leisure to be analytiques. Mr H. seem'd then something doubtfull he should not have dayes enough left to goe about such a worke. In this treatise he is highly for the Kings Prerogative: Ch: Just: Hales haz read it,[4] and very much mislikes it; is his enemy and will not license it. Judge Vaughan[5] haz perusd it and very much commends it, but is afrayd to license for feare of giving displeasure. 'Tis pitty fire should consume it, or that it should miscarry as I have known some excellent things. I never expect to see it printed, and intended to have a copy, which the bookeseller will let me have for 50s; and God willing I will have one at my returne. He writes short and therfore the fitter for your reading, being so full of Businesse. When you goe by the Palsgrave-head Taverne[6] be pleasd to call on mr W: Crooke[7] at the green dragon[8] and remember me to him by the same token I desired Mr Hobbes to give his Workes to Magd: hall[9] and he will shew it to you. I have a conceit that if your Lord[10] sawe it he would like it. You may there see likewise his History of England from 1640 to 1660[11] about a quire of paper, which the King haz read and likes extremely, but tells him there is so much truth in it

---

[11] Trimmings, apparel.

[1] Hobbes, *A Dialogue between a Philosopher and a Student of the Common Laws of England* (1681).
[2] Lord Chancellor Francis Bacon, *The Elements of the Common Lawes of England* (1630).
[3] 'The most unlearned type of all learned men.'
[4] Sir Matthew Hale, Chief Justice of King's Bench, who licensed law books. He wrote a critique of Hobbes on law.
[5] Sir John Vaughan, Chief Justice of Common Pleas. A friend of Hobbes.
[6] In the Strand near Temple Bar.   [7] William Crooke, Hobbes's publisher.
[8] Street numbering was not common before the late 18th cent.; businesses were located by iconic signs (which today survive in pub signs).
[9] Magdalen Hall, which Hobbes had attended.   [10] Presumably Shaftesbury.
[11] *Behemoth, or The Long Parliament* (1679).

he dares not license for feare of displeasing the Bishops. The old gent is still strangely vigorous (85) if you see him (which he would take kindly) pray my service to him . . .

275. Sir Peter Colleton to Locke, Barbados, 12 August 1673

I wrote you by his Majestys Ship the St: David[1] which Letter I hope came safe to your hands. Since then wee have had newes from Carolina of the 28th of May where the poor people had been exposed to very great misery and hardship's for want of supplyes one vessel by which they expected them was 7 months on a voyage that might have been performed in two Months, the other was taken by a Caper,[2] they have sent home Mr Christopher Portman[3] to make their condition known to the proprietors,[4] and they must be fair spoken at this Instant or they may chance to quitt the Collony in a humour and wee loose all the money wee have been out, In this nick it hath gone hard even with those that are best able, for fraught[5] being here at 12 l. per tonn wee could not get a vessel to goe there, to carry the supplys that were ready in this place to be sent, Inclosed is, a Letter from Mr Owen[6] by which you may perceive what tune the people sing, they have now launched two vessells there, and I have bought another to ply there which will be a help to them, if wee can but make them stand untill the warr be over,[7] wee need not doubt the comeing to them of most of the people Northward of them, they should presently have a supply of tools cloathes and amunition sent them.

By the last Fleet I sent you a parcell of Carolina China Root,[8] which was directed to Colonel Thornburgh[9] for you, by this I send you a Jarr of this countrey Tarr, which I think is Oyl of Bitumen of whose sanative quallity some here talke wonders, I have Known the Oyl of it helpe the sciatica, and it with white lilly root hath cured the Glanders in severall of my horses, I also send you a pott of Tarara root,[10] which is the root which cures the wounds made by the Indians poysoned Arrows, which was first discovered by Major Walker a Kinsman of mine, and now a Captain in the princes Regiment of Dragoons,[11] an Indian that had accidentally prick'd his Thumb with an arrow

---

[1] 646 tons, 54 guns.   [2] Privateer.

[3] Portman was a member of the Carolina parliament and council; he sailed in June on the *Blessing*.

[4] Shaftesbury and Colleton were two of the eight Proprietors of Carolina; Locke was secretary to them.

[5] Freight.

[6] William Owen, a leading colonist, with a house at Charleston and plantation on the Ashley river.

[7] The Third Dutch War (1672–4).   [8] Cinchona bark: quinine.

[9] Edward Thornburgh, agent for Barbados in England.

[10] Arrowroot: its rhizome is an antidote to poison.

[11] Probably James Walker of Prince Rupert's Barbados Regiment of Dragoons.

being at Sea, and having none of this root gave him self over for dead, and his hand swell'd extreamly, Major Walker being with him found a mongst his things a small piece of the root at the sight of which the Indian rejoyced extreamly, and chewing and applying some of it to the wound and swallowing another part put a stop to the swelling, and when he came on shore being brought to a garden where Walker had formerly planted some, by the fresh Juce of that root quite cured his Thumb in a very short time, I find amongst the people it hath an extream hygh reputation, but our Doctors who think it not for their proffit that any should have the power of healing but themselves, are Infidells, yet some have confessed to me that the sediment of the Juce dried and powdred is a most forcible diaphoretick,[12] Colonel Codrington[13] my Lord Willoughbys[14] deputy in this place, hath assured mee that he hath by giveing the Juce inwardly cured gonorheas in his Negros so virulent, and Coroding, that bloud hath Issued mingled with the usual Flux of that distemper, nor hath any accidents hapned upon the suddan stopping of that flux, it cures the yawes[15] in our negroes. which I think is a disease between the Leprosy and the pox, a grave Gentleman a Judge and neighbour of mine tells me that a Negroe of his hath had a sore legg 17 years, which was so bad the Surgeons would have cutt it off, which the Negroe refuseing to suffer they left him as Incureable, this Gentleman hath caused the arrow root to be tryed on his negroe, of the Juce of which he drinks and hath it applyed outwardly to his legg also, which hath almost brought the ulcer to a perfect cure, and tells me he doth not doubt it will make him quite well ...

279. Sir Peter Colleton to Locke, [Barbados], [c. October 1673]

... Since then is arrived here the Bahama Merchant[1] whom Captain Dorrell[2] hath luckily sent here to seek a fraught[3] and I hope he will make upwards of 1000ld: fraught of what he takes in here, I find the people in providence[4] did not well brook the adventurers[5] being jealous they would turn to a company like that of Bermuda[6] at first but being satisfied of the contrary have at length

---

[12] Sudorific: causing sweat.
[13] Christopher Codrington, Colleton's predecessor as deputy governor of Barbados.
[14] William, Baron Willoughby of Parham, governor.   [15] Yaws: contagious disease of the skin.

[1] A ship of that name.
[2] John Dorrell (Darrell) of Bermuda: with Locke, one of the eleven Bahamas adventurers. The eleven also included John Mapletoft (L360, L417), Thomas Stringer (L478, n. 1), and Edward Thornburgh (L275, n. 9). Adventurer: one who undertakes a hazardous or speculative enterprise.
[3] Freight.
[4] New Providence Island, Bahamas. The Bahamas at this time had about 1,000 inhabitants, including 400 slaves.
[5] The Bahamas adventurers.
[6] Probably referring to a failed attempt to settle the Bahamas from Bermuda in the 1640s.

submitted, but what great proffitt this trade will bring unto us I must confesse I cannot see unlesse you can set up the whale fishing. and that turn to accompt or that by haveing all the Brasiletto wood[7] in your hands you can raise the price of that and whether that will doe it you may easily be informed, if you Inquire amongst the Dyers whether Brasiletto be of absolute necessity for the dying of any couller, or whether onely to helpe when Logwood[8] is deare, for if it be onely used in that case, or as I am Informed ground and mingled with Log-wood by the Salter[9] to cheat the dyer, the price is not like to rise for the English haveing found the way to cutt Logwood themselves which was formerly onely done by the Spaniard in the uninhabited places about the Bey of Campeache[10] have reduced the price of that wood from 60l: per tonn to under 20ld: as I am Informed it ought also to be inquired whether their comes no Brasiletto wood but from the Bahama Islands for if there doe, you shall no sooner rise your price but the markett will be cloyd with that wood from other places, I am Informed that Braseletto is not now worth in England above 10ld: per tonn It cost you 5ld and that Ship that shall fetch it from the Bahamas for under 7ld: per tonn will not save by the voyage so that at this rate you will loose 40s: per tonn. as to Ambergrice[11] the quantity found is not much nor can you be at certainty to have all that is found Nor will the Seader[12] turn to any great accompt, it will helpe to save the charge of a Ship when nothing else offers, this what I write Dorrell Knowes well enough therefore wisely sent the Ship hither with not much more Brasiletto in her then will serve for dunnage[13] for the sugar taken in . . . [I]f you fall upon a plantation its my opinion you will loose your stock for besides the disadvantage that country hath by the nature of its Soyle compared with the other English settlements, I never yet knew any man that setled a plantation by the management of any other but himself that ever saw his money again, If I judge right in what I have written I shall have the reputation to have foreseen what came to passe, if I mistake and the trade prove proffitable I shall get my share, Dorrell hath the reputation of a cunning Snap[14] amongst his countrymen and you ought to have a strict eye upon him.

    The want of the supply of cloathes and tooles I desired might be sent to Carolina when I left England, hath been much felt there, to which hath been added a great want of victualls, occasioned by miscarriage of their supplyes from a broad, which hath made them suffer much misery, In so much that two of the councell and the Surveyor generall are run away, by which you may see what great reason the Lords Proprietors have to strive who shall have the disposure of the Offices since men run from them, I doe Intend to Perswade Andrew Norwood[15] of Bermudas to goe theire and take the office upon him

---

[7] A dye-wood, inferior to Brazil-wood.   [8] Another dye-wood.
[9] Drysalter: trader in dye-stuffs.   [10] Bay of Campeche, Gulf of Mexico.
[11] Ambergris: a secretion from sperm whales, used in cookery and medicine.
[12] Presumably cedar.   [13] Materials stowed among or beneath the main cargo.   [14] Swindler.
[15] Son of the surveyor of Bermuda.

he is an Ingenious man and I shall endeavour to make him understand the drift of the Lords as to lyeing out of the countrey, I finde all men that are come from thence to agree, that the country is extream healthy and pleasant, and the understanding planters say its very fertill, but better further up than where they are Setled, which is soe near the barren sands of the Sea shore, I am very sure that if we overcome the want of Victuall, all the English planted northward will come into us for in new England the greatest [part] of the summer labour of the husbandman, is spent to p[rovide] fother[16] to Keep his cattle alive in the winter, Its the same at new Yorke, and in Virginia and Mary-land where they are not soe carefull in doeing it, they lost above two thirds of their cattle the last winter, whereas the cattle of Carolina were beef all the while, and will never need to be fothered, which advantage added to our being able to produce many commodityes that they cannot, and all their owne cheaper then they can, must force them in time all to come to us, and that this hopefull countrey may not be lost and that that excellent forme of Government in the composure of which you had soe great a hand may speedily come to be put in practice[17] I earnestly desire you to solicit my Lord Chancellor[18] that the supply of cloathes and tooles may be sent them togather with the 1,000 bushells of pease I have writt about which may put them past want of Victuall any more and about 600ld: will effect it . . .

295. Dr Thomas Sydenham to Locke, [*c*. November 1674?]

[Y]our age, ill habitt of body, and approach of winter concurring, it comes to pass that the distemper you complaine of yealds not so soone to remidies as it would doe under contrary circumstances. However you may not in the least doubt but that a steddy persisting in the use of the following directions (grounded not on opinion but uninterrupted experience) will at last effect your desired cure. First therfore in order to the diverting and subducting[1] allso the ichorose[2] matter, 'twill be requisitt to take your pills twice a weeke as for example every Thursday and Sonday about 4 a clocke in the morning, and your Clyster[3] in the intermitting dayes about 6, constantly till you are well. In the next place forasmuch as there is wanting in bodyes broaken with business and dispirited upon the before mentioned accounts, that stock of naturall heat which should bring the matter quickly to digestion 'twill be highly necessary that you cherish your selfe as much as possibly you can by going to bed very early at night even at 8 a clocke, which next to keeping bed that

---

[16] Fodder.   [17] *The Fundamental Constitutions of Carolina* (1669): *Political Essays*, 160–81.
[18] Shaftesbury.

[1] Abstracting: drawing out.   [2] A watery discharge from a wound or sore.
[3] A purgative. Purging and bloodletting were the favoured treatments in 17th-cent. medicine.

is unpracticable will contributt more to your reliefe than can be imagined. As to diett all meats of easy digestion and that nourish well may be allowed, provided they be not salt sweet or spiced and allso excepting fruits, roots and such like. For wine a totall forbearance therof if it could possibly be and in its steede the use of very mild small beer such as our lesser houses doe afford, would as neare as I can guess be most expedient, for therby your body would be kept coole and consequently all accidents proceeding from hott and sharpe humors grating upon the part, kept off. As to injections,[4] in your case these things disswade the use of them. First your more than ordinary both naturall tenderness and delicacy of sence. Then the blood that twice allready hath bin fetched by this operation, which if we are not positively certaine (as how can we be) that it proceeded not from the hurt of the instrument, will (if often repeted) endanger the excoriating the part[5] and making it liable to accidents. Besides they have bin allready used (perhapps as often is wont to be don) and this is not a remidy to be long persisted in by the confession of every body. Sure I am as I have over and over sayd to you and you know it to be true by my written observations which you have long since seen, that I never use any, where I am concerned alone, there being noe danger nor less certainty of cure in the omitting; and in relation to this business I have now asked myselfe the question what I would doe, and have resolved that I would lett them alone. . . .

297. Sir Anthony Ashley Cooper, First Earl of Shaftesbury, to Locke, Wimborne St Giles, Dorset, 23 November [1674]

. . . You guesse very right at the designe of the Pamphelet you sent me,[1] tis Certainely designed to throw dirt at me, but is like the great Promoters of it, foolish as well as false, it labours onely to asperse the Originall Authour of the Councell, which it will have to be one person and therefore seemes to know; and never Considers that it is impossible that any stats man[2] should be soe Mad as to give a Counsel of that Consequence to a juncto[3] or Number of Men, or to any but the king Himselfe who tis not to be imagined will ever be come a Witnes against any Man in such a Case, especially when he hath approved the Counsell so far as to Continue the stop[4] ever since by a new great seale every yeare, besides I am very well armed to Cleare my selfe, for tis not impossible for me to prove what my opinion was of it when it was first proposed

---

[4] Presumably here meaning bloodletting by venesection.   [5] Stripping the skin.

[1] Unidentified, perhaps a manuscript 'publication', apparently blaming the Stop of the Exchequer upon Shaftesbury. The later *Plain Dealing* (1682), a Tory tract defending Charles II from the charge of arbitrary government, made Shaftesbury responsible for advising the Stop: 'was there ever so high a violation of property?'.

[2] Statesman.   [3] Junto: junta, cabal, faction.   [4] Stop of the Exchequer.

to the Councill. and if any man Consider the Circumstance of time when
it was done, that it was the prologue of makeing the Lord Clifford[5] Lord
Treasurer, he will not suspect me of the Councill for that busines, unles he
thinkes me at the same time out of my witts; besides if any of the Banckers
doe enquire at the Clerckes of the Treasurie with whom they are well
acquainted, they will find that Sir John Duncome[6] and I were so little satisfied
with that way of proceeding as from the time of the stop we instantlie quitted
all paying and borrowing of Money and the whole transaction of that part of
the affaire to the Lord Clifford, by whom from that time forward it was onely
Managed, I shall not deney but that I knew earlier of the Counsel and foresaw
what necessarily must produce it sooner than other Men haveing the advantage of being more verst in the Kings secret affaires, but I hope it will not be
expected by any that doe in the least know me that I should have discovered[7]
the kings secrets or betrayed his busines whatever my thoughts were of it. This
worthy scribler if his law be true or his quotations to the purpose should have
taken notice of the Combination of the banckers who take the protection of
the Court and doe not take the remedie of the law against those upon whom
they had assignements, by which they might have been enabled to pay their
Creditors, for it is not to be thought that the king will put a stop to their
legall proceedings in a Court of justice. besids if the Writer had been really
concerned for the Banckers He would have spoken a little freelier against the
continueing of the stop in a time of peace as well as against the first makeing
of it in a time of War,[8] for as I remember there were some reasons offered for
the first that had their weight viz that the Banckers were growne destructive
to the Nation especially to the Country Gentleman and farmer and their
interest. that under the pretence and by the advantage of lending the king Money
upon very great use they got all the ready money of the kingdome into
their hands so that no Gentleman Farmer or Merchant Could without great
difficulty Compasse money for their occasions unlesse at almost double the
rates the law allowed to be taken:[9] that as to the kings affaires they were growne
to that passe that twelve in the Hundred did not Content them but they bought
up all the kings assignements at 20 or 30 per Cent. profit.[10] so that the king
was at a fifth part losse in all the issues of his whole Revennue, besids in support of this Councill, I remember it was alleaged, by those that Favoured it
without dores[11] for I speake onely of them that the king Mought[12] without
any dammage to the subject or unreasonable oppressure upon the Bancker
pay them six in the hundred interest dureing the war and three hundred
thousand pound each yeare of their principall assoon as there was peace, which

---

[5] Sir Thomas Clifford, made Baron Clifford and Lord Treasurer, 1672. A Catholic.
[6] Sir John Duncombe, Chancellor of the Exchequer, 1672–6. He, Ashley, and Clifford were
Treasury commissioners at the time of the Stop.
[7] Revealed.   [8] The Third Dutch War (1672–4).   [9] The law set a standard interest rate of 6%.
[10] Bankers purchased government debt at high rates of discount.
[11] Outside the council chamber or parliament.   [12] Might.

why it is not now don the learned writer I believe hath friends can best tell Him. this I write that you may shew my friends or any body else, the Messenger staying for me I have written it in hast and not kept a Copy therefor I pray loose not the letter

I am sorry you are like to fair soe ill in your place,[13] but you know to whom your company is ever most disirable and acceptable pray lett me see you speedily and I shall be ready to accomodate you in your annuity at seaven yeares purchase if you gett not elswhere a better bargain for I would have you free from care and thinke of living long and at ease[14] . . .

305. Dr Henry Woodward to Locke, Westo, [Georgia], 12 November 1675

I have made the best inquiry that I can concerneing the religion and worship. Originall, and customes of our natives. especeally among the Port Royall Indians[1] amongst whom I am best accquainted. they worship the Sun and say they have knowledge of Spirits who appeare often to them. and one sort there is who abuses their women when he meets them opportunely in the woods, the which women never after conceive. they acknowledge the sun to bee the immedeate cause of the groth and increse of all things whom likewise they suppose to be the cause of all deseases. to whom every year they have severall feast and dances particularly appointed. they have some notions of the deluge,[2] and say that two onely were saved in a cave, who after the flood found a red bird dead: the which as they pulled of his feathers between their fingers they blew them from them of which came Indians. each time a severall tribe and of a severall speech. which they severally named as they still were formed. and they say these two knew the waters to bee dried up by the singing of the said red bird. and to my knowledg let them bee in the woods at any distance from the river they can by the varying of the said birds note tell whether the water ebbeth or floweth. they seeme to acknowledge the immortality of the soul in alloweing to those that live morally honest a place of rest, pleasure and plenty: and contrary wise to the others a place were it is very cold and they are fed with nothing but nuts and acornes setting upright in their graves. they say they had knowledge of our comeing into these parts severall yeares before wee arrived, and some of them in the night have heard great noise and as it were falling of trees. one sort of them pretend to cure deseases by sucking the part affected which is but a Fallacy they makeing their owne mouths bleed pretend to have

---

[13] Presumably Locke's secretaryship of the Council of Trade: the Council was abolished in December.
[14] Shaftesbury awarded Locke an annuity of £100.

[1] On the coast of South Carolina, south of Charleston.   [2] Noah's Flood.

sucked the said blood from their patients. another sort doe accquire great knowledge in hearbs and roots, which they impart onely to the next akin. had I not bin upp in the maine[3] I should have sent some now, but shall by the next oppertunity. another sort have power over the ratle snakes soe farr as to send one severall miles over rivers and brooks to bite a particular Indian which has bin don since our being here. and the said doctor kild by the relations of the other at whose death severall snakes came and liked up his blood. the westoes[4] amongst whom I now am worship the [de]vel in a carved image of wood. they are seated in a most fruitfull soyle and are a farre more ingeneous people then our coast indians . . .

[3] Mainland: inland.   [4] Westo, on the Savannah river, now near Augusta, Georgia.

4

France, 1675–1679

Between 1675 and 1679 Locke lived in France. His reasons for leaving England are unclear. It may have been because of his association with a seditious tract from the Shaftesbury circle entitled *A Letter from a Person of Quality*, although this remains unproven. He spent most of the period residing in Montpellier, on the Mediterranean coast and his decision may, alternatively, have been made for health reasons. Locke was a lifelong asthmatic and often pleaded his delicate health for his actions—and his evasions—though sometimes this plea surely belonged to the cultivation of the image of the fragile philosopher, living on the brink of another world. During his stay abroad, Locke spent several months touring France, as well as spending time in Paris. His journals for this period are particularly full, mingling observations on French society with philosophical meditations preparatory to his *Essay Concerning Human Understanding*. The first letter in this chapter tells of the travails of the journey from Calais to Paris and is full of ironic wit at the expense of the French (L310).

In Montpellier Locke encountered a clergymen, driven there by debt, Dr Denis Grenville, who pestered him for advice about how he should conduct his life, and specifically how to balance the various demands of business, study, religious devotion, conversation, and recreation. Just one of Grenville's half-dozen ingratiating letters is included here (L327). Locke's replies to Grenville were so expansive that they transcend the boundary between 'letters' and 'essays' and were, in fact, included among the collections of 'set piece' letters subsequently seized upon by enterprising publishers as newly discovered tracts by the master moral philosopher. Commencing his advice with a disquisition on recreation (L328), Locke proceeds to instruct Grenville on scrupulosity and ethical latitude, while ostensibly covering the topics of business, study, and conversation (L374). Holding that it is a mistake to suppose that there is only one absolutely right action in every human circumstance, Locke argues that to raise every possible moral doubt will tend to inhibit the possibility of action. Furthermore, he urges that, as 'born members of commonwealths', we have a duty to attend to worldly business and ought not always to be engaged in private meditation or prayer (L426). Grenville gives an impression of interminably anxious importunity, yet the recent suggestion that he was spying on Locke for political reasons is probably fanciful, even though his later politics were diametrically opposite to those of Locke. As Dean of Durham in 1688, Grenville would vigorously defend King James II in the midst of the Glorious Revolution, before fleeing into Jacobite exile in France.

Apparently at the Earl of Shaftesbury's request, another task undertaken by Locke was to act as tutor and guardian to Caleb Banks, who had been sent on an extended French sojourn by his parents. Sir John Banks was a wealthy East India Company merchant and a government creditor, who, despite being a Court supporter, managed to retain an association with Shaftesbury. One sample of Locke's reports to Sir John on his son's progress offers an endorsement of the benefits of foreign travel (L352).

Another person concerned to enquire of Locke after young Caleb was the diarist Samuel Pepys—although this sole surviving letter between Pepys and Locke is not included here. Despite Locke's influence, Caleb later followed in his father's footsteps and sat as a Tory MP.

By December 1677 Locke was in Paris and was summoned to attend the Countess of Northumberland, suffering agonizingly from trigeminal neuralgia (L360). The countess had now married the English ambassador, Ralph Montagu, who was currently acting as the conduit for King Louis XIV's secret subsidies to Charles II, as well as for payments to members of the English opposition. A century later the discovery that the Whig guardians of English liberties—as well as the tyrant monarch Charles II—had received money from Louis XIV was to appal the Whigs' political descendants. It is highly unlikely that Locke had any inkling of Montagu's dealings.

In Paris Locke befriended a scholar from Orleans, Nicolas Toinard, whose interests included scientific experiment, mechanical invention, and scriptural hermeneutics. A sample of their correspondence, sustained over many years, discusses microscopy, hygrometry, and phonetic orthography, as well as touching on several current preoccupations such as the search for a perpetual motion machine and the desirability of a simplified language (L394). In addition to jokes about Parisian fashions, Locke enthuses about the gatherings of 'virtuosi' in the city and seeks a letter of recommendation to their company from Robert Boyle (L335).

While abroad, Locke continues to receive medical advice concerning his own health from Sydenham (L337). Shortly before his return to England, he expresses regret at being prevented from visiting Rome (L417).

310. Locke to ?, Montpellier, 1 March 1676

... 2 Dec.[1] The Ambasador[2] resolveing to goe by Amiens, our Governor the messenger[3] was willing to goe the ordinary rode by Poy,[4] which we,[5] who went to seek adventures beyond Paris, easily consented to, we therefor plodded on the carriers rode and pace our 9 leagues[6] to Poy, and though that way of travailing tires an Englishman sufficiently, yet we were noe sooner got into our chambers, but we thought we were come there too soone, for the highway seemd the much sweeter cleaner and more desireable place. had I not been of old acquainted with this memorable lodging, I should have suspected that General Messenger had been leading us against the Germans, and that now we had been just on those frontires which both armys had pilaged at the end of the last campagne,[7] and had left this castle garisond not with horse, but an other sort of 6 legd creature[8] to defend it against the next comers. It being decreed we must stay there al night, I cald, intreated, and swaggerd a good while, (for necessity multiplys ones French mightily) for a pair of slippers, at last they were brought, and I sat me down on the only seat we had in our apartment, which at present was a forme,[9] but I beleive had been heretofore a wooden horse,[10] but the legs being cut shorter and the ridg of the back taken down to the bredth of ones hand it made a considerable part of the furniture of our chamber. my boots being off I thought to ease my self of my seat by standing, but I assure you with noe very good sucsesse, for the soles of my Pantofles[11] being sturdy timber had very litle compliance for my feet. and soe made it some what uncomfortable for me to keepe my self (as the French call standing) on one end.[12] This smal tast of Sabots,[13] gave me a surfet of them and left such an aversion to them in my stomach, that I shall never make choise of a country to passe my pilgrimage in, where they are in fashion. Tis possible they may be very necessary to the aiery people of this country, who being able to run, skip, and dance in these, would certainly mount into the aire, and take most wonderfull frisks, were there not some such clogs at their heels,

---

[1] The account was written up later as a travel journal.

[2] The English ambassador to France (and a Proprietor of Carolina), Lord Berkeley of Stratton.

[3] *Messager*: a guide and travel agent (as well as courier).   [4] Poix, 85 mls. south of Calais.

[5] Locke was travelling with his Christ Church friend, George Walls, a clergyman.

[6] The length of a French league varied. Abbeville, the previous night's stop, is 25 mls. from Poix.

[7] The French campaigns in 1675 were chiefly in Alsace and along the Moselle. Louis XIV expanded the frontiers of France.

[8] Fleas, this being a filthy lodging.   [9] Bench.   [10] An instrument of punishment.

[11] Slippers.   [12] *Se tenir debout.*

[13] Wooden shoes, clogs, worn by French peasants. Locke's extended ridicule of them is striking. Soon, and for decades afterwards, the English would use the phrase 'wooden shoes'—or 'popery and wooden shoes'—in contempt for the miserable condition of the benighted French. In Oct. 1673 a wooden shoe was found on the Speaker's chair in the House of Commons as a warning against the tendency of Charles II's government.

but I beleive a dul heavy Englishman might be as soon brought, to dance a jig with a pair of stocks about his ankles, as to walke the streets in such brogues as these, though they were never soe curiosly carved as I have seen some of them. Of these crabtree soled slippers we had two pair between three of us, and there could never happen a nicer case in breeding, than there was then between us three, to know whether one were bound by the rules of civility, to take ones self, or offer to an other, or refuse the offer of a pair of these slippers, it being still a doubt to this day, and like to remain soe, whether barefoot in a ragged brick floore, or these slippers on, were the better posture. However to shew that we profited by our travails, and were willing to improve our manners into the courtlynesse of the country, we made it a matter of complement. many good things, I assure you, were spoke on the occasion, we had shuffled favour, civility, obligacon, honour, and many other the like words (very usefull in travaild and well bred company) forwards and backwards in severall obleigeing repartees: and this fashionable conversation had lasted longer had not supper come in and interrupted us. Here the barefoot gent thought to finde comfort in his humility, and the others in the stocks to divert their pain, but we quickly found that a supper of ill meat, and worse cookery, was but an insignificant sound, and served ill to fill ones belly. soup and ragoo and such other words of good savour, lost here their relish quite, and out of 5 or 6 dishes were served up to us, we patchd up a very untoward supper, but be it as rascally as it will and meane, it must not faile in the most material part to be fashionable, we had the ceremony of first and second course besides a disert in the close, for were your whole bill of fare noe thing but some cabbage and a frog that was caught in it, and some haws[14] of the last season, you would have a treat in all its formalitys, and would not faile of three courses, the first would make a soope, the second a good fricasie (of which I have eaten) and twas not long since that preserved haws were served up for a disert to me and some others of my country men, who could not tell what to make of this new sort of fruit, they being some thing biger then ordinary, and disguised under the fine name of pomet de Paradise,[15] till the next day on the road our Voiturin[16] shewd us, upon what sort of tree this, that made soe fine a wett sweetmeat[17] grew. After supper we retreated to the place that usually gives redresse to all sorts of moderate calamitys, but our beds served but to compleat our vexation and seemd to be ordeind for antidotes against sleepe. I will not complain of their hardnesse, because tis a quality I like, but the thinnesse of what lay upon me and the tangible qualitys of what was next me, and the savour of all about me, made me quite forget my slippers and supper, and twas impossible I should have lasted in that strong perfume till morning, had not a large convenient hole in the wall at my beds head powerd in plenty of fresh aire. As good luck would have it, we had a long journey of twelve leagues to goe

[14] Hawthorn fruit.   [15] On 4 Mar. Locke was given *pommette*, a fruit larger than a haw.
[16] A *voiturin* hired out horses and served as a guide.   [17] Fruits preserved in syrup.

next day,[18] which made our stay here the shorter; we were rousd before day, and I heard nobody complain of it; we were glad to be released from this prison (for tis impossible to beleive, freemen should stay themselves here) and willingly left it to those miserable soules were to succeed us. If Paris be heaven (for the French with their usuall justice extol it above al things on earth) Poy certainly is purgatory in the way to it . . .

327. Dr Denis Grenville to Locke, [Montpellier], [c.6/16–8/18 March 1677]

I cannot Content myselfe (Sir) to loose one of those few dayes you intend to stay, without making some Improvement of your Freindly Compliance with my desires. And therefore without any more adoe, (having received, both *in scriptis*, and *vivâ voce*,[1] noe small Incouragement) shall begin to set you to Worke. But least you may bee scared at my Importunity, I doe declare that I shall not presse to bee allowed more than one houre, of your pretious time, each day, for the penning downe your thoughts on such particular things, as I shall present you with in Writing, in which Method I shall desire, (if you please to give me leave,) to proceed; first for the better securing your thoughts, secondly for the helpe of my Infirmity in not being able otherwise easily, and clearly to expresse mine. The subjects concerning which I shall in order write, and desire you to discourse, are five. *1.* Recreation. *2.* Buisnesse. *3.* Conversation. *4.* Study. *5.* Exercise of Devotion. I begin with the first, and shall thinke my selfe very happy if wee can but fully discourse that one point before wee part, it being of noe small importance to mee (as you will finde when I have said all) to bee set right, but, in this particular; soe far am I, poor fellow, from being advanced above your good Counsell and advice in other matters of greater moment. It is since I entred into holy Orders about 16. yeares, (which obliged mee to bee a Guide to Others,) during which time I cannot deny but that I have been buisy about discharging my Office (how Imperfectly soever I have performed itt) and may have been usefull possibly (through Gods Blessing) to some, as to Counsell, in those very matters concerning which I have needed it myselfe, having in my nature, sometimes, somewhat of the Infirmitie of the Great Dr. Reynolds, who, when hee had convinced his adversary, could not Confirme himselfe.[2] To Indulge to so

---

[18] To Tillard, near Beauvais, 30 mls. from Poix, of which Locke comments: 'Good mutton and a good supper here, cleane sheets of the country, and a pretty girle to lay them on (who was an angell compard to the Feinds of poy) made us some amends for the past nights sufferings.'

[1] In writing and verbally.

[2] John Reynolds (Rainolds), President of Corpus Christi College. There was a popular story that Reynolds and his brother started out as Catholic and Protestant, but argued each other into the opposite camp.

much thoughtfullnesse as my Temper Inclines mee to, may perchance hurt my Body or Braine; and to Divert this Temper with the ordinary Recreations which some Christians, and Divines (nay I might add) Bishops) use, as Hunting, Shooting, Angling, chesse, cards, or Tables[3] etc. is dangerous, (as I finde) and often hurtfull to my spirit. I have therefore thought it the safest way to quit these and all such Recreations for many yeares together, nay most of my seculars Buisnesse too (for the same Reason) and give my selfe up to Solitude and Contemplation, according to the desires and necessities of my Minde, and which, I Blesse God, is still soe pleasing to mee, that I could with great Delight Continue soe to doe my whole life. But having seen some sad Consequence thereof in Others, of stronger heads and constitutions (in all appearance) than my selfe, (tho. I was never sensible of any inconvenience of my owne Course) have returned for some while to some of the former Divertisements as Chesse, or Angling, the most Innocent that I could pick out abroad, or at home, till I found my boyish temper Revive in mee, which made mee too intent upon them, and some times Immoderate in Consumption of time; which hath made mee with fresh Force and Resolution recoyle back to my studies and Retirements, feeling the Truth of Honest Tho. a Kempis his beloved Motto vizt. *In omnibus Requiem quæsivi, et nusquam Inveni nisi Angello cum libello.*[4]

From which pleasing Course I have been againe soon pulled of by the Importunities of Freinds, who have thought it Injurious to mee, and that it might bee of ill Consequence. Thus have I long been, and am still, tossed between the Feares and Inconveniences accompanying one Extreame or the other, and can not tell how to establish myselfe, tho I often afford some freinds assistance in these particulars. I humbly beg your Judgement, in this particular, where to set Bounds to my Retired studies, and Divertisements abroad. I am of the minde that it is the best and wisest Course to leane to the Excesse of study, and Devotion, rather than that of Recreation; It being more eligible, methinks, to *hazard the hurting* the mind by Imployment soe good and acceptable to God, than *certainly hurting* itt with Recreation, or at least Indisposing itt for Spirituall Imployment thereby. I would faigne hit the Meane if I could tell how. It is my earnest prayer to the Wise God, that I, at last, may. Which prayer is in some sort heard, by Directing mee to soe discreet a Freind, (when I was in search of one) as your selfe, whoe doe Evidence by your discourse and Carriage that you are above the poor difficulties I struggle with and soe very well quallified to assist mee. . . .

---

[3] Backgammon.
[4] 'I have sought repose in all things and nowhere found it except in a little nook with a little book'. Thomas à Kempis, 15th-cent. mystical devotionalist, popular with Protestants as well as Catholics.

328. Locke to Dr Denis Grenville, [Montpellier], [c.9/19–11/21 March 1677]

As for my Recreation thus I thinke[1]

That Recreation being a thing ordeind not for it self but for a certain end. That end is to be the rule and measure of it

Recreation then seemeing to me to be the doeing of some easy or at least delightfull thing to restore the minde or body tired with labour, to its former strength and vigor and thereby fit it for new labour it seems to me

1   That there can be noe generall rule set to *divers persons* concerning the time, manner, duration or sort of recreation that is to be used, but only that it be such that their experience tells them is suited to them and proper to refresh the part tired

2   That if it be applied to the minde it ought certainly to be delightfull because it being to restore and enliven that which is don by relaxing and composeing the agitation of the spirits, that which delights it without imploying it much is not only the fitest to doe soe, but also the contrary i e what is ungratefull[2] does certainly most discompose and tire it

3   That it is impossible to set a standing rule of recreation to ones self, because not only the unsteady fleeting condition of our bodys and spirits require more at one time than another, which is plain in other more fixd refreshments as food and sleepe, and likewise requires very different according to the imployment that hath preceded, the present temper of our bodys and inclination of our mindes, but also because variety in most constitutions is soe necessary to delight, and the minde is soe naturally tender of its freedome, that the pleasantest diversions become nauseous and troublesome to us when we are forced to repeat them in a continued fixd round

It is farther to be considerd

1   That in things not absolutely commanded or forbiden by the law of god, such as is the materiall part of Recreation he in his mercy considering our ignorance and fraile constitution, hath not tied us to an indivisible point, to a way soe narrow that allows noe latitude at all In things in their owne nature indifferent there is the liberty of great choise great variety within the bounds of innocence

2   That god delights not to have us miserable either in this or the other world, but haveing given us all things richly and to enjoy[3] we cannot imagin that in our recreations we should be denied delight which is the only necessary and usefull part of it

---

[1] Answers L327.   [2] Unpleasing.
[3] 1 Timothy 6:17. Later cited in *Two Treatises*, I, § 40; II, § 31.

This supposd I imagin

1   That recreation supposes labour and wearynesse and therefor that he that labours not hath noe title to it

2   That it very seldome happens that our constitutions (though there be some tender ones that require a great deale) require more time to be spent in recreation than in labour

3   That we must beware that custome and the fashon of the world or some other by interest doth not make that passe with us for recreation which is indeed labour to us though it be not our businesse, as playing at cards for example though noe otherwise allowable but as a recreation is soe far from fiting some men for their businesse and giveing them refreshment, that it more discomposes them then their ordinary labour

Soe that god not tieing us up to exact nicetys of time, place, kinde etc in our recreations, if we secure our main duty which is in sincerity to doe our dutys in our calling as far as the frailty of our bodys or mindes will allow us (beyond which we cannot thinke any thing should be requird of us) and that we in truth designe our diversions to put us in a condition to doe our dutys we need not perplex our selves with too scrupulous an enquiry into the precise bounds of them, for we cannot be suppos'd to be obleiged to rules which we cannot know. for I doubt first whether there be any such exact proportion of recreation to our present state of body and minde. that soe much is exactly enough and what soever is under is too litle what soever is over is too much. but be it soe or noe this I am very confident of, that noe body can say in his owne or an other mans case, that thus much is the precise dose hither you must goe and noe farther. Soe that it is not only our priviledg but we are under a necessity of useing a latitude, and where we can discover noe determined precise rule it is unavoidable for us to goe sometimes beyond, and sometimes stop short of that which is, I will not say, the exact but nearest proportion, and in such cases we can only governe our selves by the discoverable bounds on one hand or other, which is only when by sensible effects we finde our recreation either by excess or defect serves not to the proper end for which we are to use it. Only with this caution, that we are to suspect our selves most on that side to which we finde our selves most inclined. The cautious devoute studious man is to feare that he allows not himself enough. the gay, carelesse and idle that he takes too much.

To which I can only adde the following directions as to some particulars

1   That the properest time for recreateing the minde is when it feels it self weary and flaging, it may be wearied with a thing when it is not yet weary of it

2   That the properest recreation of studyous sedentary persons whose labour is of the thought is bodyly exercise. To those of bustleing imployment sedentary recreations

3   That in all bodily exercise those in the open aire are best for health
4   It may often be soe orderd that one business may be made a recreation
to an other, as visiting a freind to study

These are my suddain extempory thoughts upon this subject, which will
deserve to be better considerd when I am in better circumstances of freedome
of thought and leisure.

335. Locke to Robert Boyle, Paris, 25 May / 4 June 1677

... Now I am come to this place, which is one of the great magazines of things
and persons of all sorts, I thought, that perhaps there might be something,
wherein I might be here in a condition to serve you. And though I believe
you are not much concerned to know, whether broad or narrow brim'd hats
be like to carry it this summer, or which is the newest alamode cut of pan-
taloons; yet in this universal mint of new things, there are some others, that
possibly you will think worth your enquiry and knowledge. In something
of this kind I would be glad to have the honour of your commands; and
methinks whilst the press furnishes every day new books to St. Jaques Street,[1]
the observatoire,[2] laboratories, and other officinæ[3] of the virtuosi[4] here are so
busy to produce something new, I should not be without some employment
from you. I dare undertake for myself, that I shall be a very faithful and diligent factor;[5] and you cannot blame me for desiring the employment, since I
may inrich myself in it very honestly, without at all lessening any part of your
returns. And to confess the truth, I have besides this another private interest
of my own in it; for who ever served you in any thing without being an extraordinary gainer by it? I would beg the favour of two or three lines from your
hand, to recommend me to the acquaintance of any one of the virtuosi you
shall think fit here. I know your bare name will open doors, and gain admittance for me, (where otherwise one like me without port[6] and name, that have
little tongue, and less knowledge, shall hardly get entrance. Pardon, I beseech
you, this freedom I take; your goodness hath taught it me, and however faulty
it may be, let it pass under the plausible title of *libertas philosophica*. They
talk here of a little brass globe three or four inches diameter, that being wound
up once a month, shews all the motions of the heavens[7] ...

---

[1]   Near the Sorbonne, full of bookshops.
[2]   The Observatoire Royal, built 1668–72 (today south of the Jardin du Luxembourg), directed by
Giovanni (Jean) Cassini.
[3]   Workshops.   [4]   Savants.   [5]   Agent.   [6]   Social position, grand station.
[7]   An orrery: a clockwork model of the solar system.

337. Dr Thomas Sydenham to Locke, 4 [June] 1677

I am glad to heare that you are advanced so farr on your way homewards that we may hope to see you here shortly,[1] but I stand amased at your taking bloud[2] and as much at the purging[3] you have allready used and that which you further intend after your Ague,[4] which latter would here infallibly returne it upon you or bring on worse mischiefe. I conceave (and I would my selfe take the same course) tis your best course to doe nothing at all. But in point of diett twill be convenient that you drinke somewhat more liberally wine than before and ride as much as possibly you can. The symptoms you complayne of you ought not to be concerned att, for they are noe other than what are usuall after agues, and endeed if you shall so mind them as to obviatt each particulare one you will create to your selfe great danger. they all depending upon one cause viz the weakenesse of your bloud by the ague, which I am sure nothing will reduce but time and exercise, and even a Clyster[5] of milke and sugar will make worse. If you would but ride on horsbacke from Paris to Calis and from Dover to London, upon that and drawing in this aer your symptoms will vanish. Since your going hence I have had multiplied experiences of riding long and persisting journies in England, which hath cured more inveteratt distempers then ever yours was, I meane of the longues. I have bin and am still very ill of the gout, pissing of bloud etc. more than a quarter of an year; and having so many distempers broaken in upon [a] very impayred and ill body I dispaire of being evr well agayne, and yet I am as well content as if I were to live and be well ...

352. Locke to Sir John Banks, [Paris], [18/28 August 1677]

As to the improvements of travell I think they are all comprehended in these four—Knowledge, which is the proper ornament and perfection of the minde: Exercise, which belong to the body: Language and Conversation. Of all these, Exercise only is that which seems to perswade the spending his[1] time in Paris. ... I grant some parts of Mathematiques might be learnt here, but methinks he is not yet ready for those sciences. For to engage one in Mathematiques who is not yet acquainted with the very rudiments of Logique is a method of study I have not known practised, and seems to me not very

---

[1] The letter was addressed to Locke at the English ambassador's residence in Paris. Locke did not return to England till 1679.

[2] Bloodletting, generally by venesection. Locke had a fever in May and tried purging, bloodletting, and enemas.

[3] Cathartic cleansing of the alimentary canal or bowels.   [4] Fever.   [5] Enema.

[1] Caleb Banks, Sir John's son, aged about 18.

reasonable. . . . They who imagine that the improvements of forain conversation are to be sought by making acquaintance and friendships abroad, seeme to me wholy to mistake the matter, and it appears to me quite another thing. The great benefit to be found by travell is by constant changeing of company, and conversing every day with unknown strangers is to get a becomeing confidence and not to be abashed at new faces—to accustome ones self to treat every body civilly, and to learne by experience that that which gets one credit and recommends one to others, is not the fortune one is borne to, but the riches of the minde and the good qualities one possesses. And were it not for this one thing I know not why young gents should not be sent for breeding rather to the Court of England than the Inns and Eating Houses of France.

360. Locke to Dr John Mapletoft, Paris, 24 November / 4 December 1677

I never had a more unwelcome occasion of writing to you than now, believing I can scarce send you more unacceptable news than that of the illnesse of a person whom not only you and I, but all the world have soe just reason to esteeme and admire. On Thursday night last I was sent for to my Lady Ambassadrice,[1] whom I found in a fit of such violent and exquisite torment, that (though she be, as you know, a person of extraordinary temper, and I have seen her even in the course of this distemper endure very great pain with a patience that seemd to feele noe thing) it forced her to such cries and shrieks as you would expect from one upon the rack, to which I beleive her's was an equal torment, which extended itself all over the right side of her face and mouth. When the fit came, there was, to use my Lady's own expression of it, as it were a flash of fire all of a suddaine shot into all those parts, and at every one of those twitches, which made her shreeke out, her mouth was constantly drawn on the right side towards the right eare by repeated convulsive motions, which were constantly accompanied by her cries. This was all that appeard outwards in these fits according to the exactest observation I could make, haveing had but too many oportunitys to doe it. These violent fits terminated on a suddaine, and then my Lady seemd to be perfectly well, excepting only a dull pain which ordinarily remained in her teeth on that side, and an uneasinesse in that side of her tongue which she phansied to be swollen on that side, which yet when I lookd on it, as I often did, had not the least alteration in it in colour, bignesse, or any other way, though it were one of her great complaints that there was a scalding liquor in her fits shot into all that half

---

[1] Elizabeth, Countess of Northumberland, daughter of the Earl of Southampton, wife of the English ambassador, Ralph Montagu.

of her tongue. She had usually a presentation[2] of the fit by a little throbing
upon her gum of the lower jaw, where she had this summer a tooth drawn;
and a like throbing in the upper jaw, just over against it. In all this time of
her being ill she has not found the least pain in all the other side of her face
or teeth, which hath soe wholy possessed the right side that it went even to
the very tip of her tongue, and the last tooth before on that side.—With all
this torment that she endurd, when the fit was over there was not the least
appearance of any alteration any where in her face, nor inflamation or
swelling in her mouth or cheeke; very little defluction of rhewm[3] more then
what the contraction of those parts in those fits might cause. Speaking was
apt to put her into these fits; sometimes opening her mouth to take any thing,
or touching her gums, especially in the places where she used to finde those
throbings: pressing that side of her face by lying on it were also apt to put
her into fits. These fits lasted sometimes longer, sometimes shorter; were more
or less violent, without any regularity, and the intervals between them at the
longest not halfe an hower, commonly much shorter. It being night when I
was cald, I saw noe roome for any thing else to be done but to endeavour to
give her present ease by topical anodyn applications to those parts of her gums
where the first beginnings of her fits appeare, which had soe good an effect
that that night she had two or three howers rest togeather without any fits,
besides some other litle intervalls of sleepe. But the next day the fits returning, tho' not altogeather soe frequent and violent as they had been, yet bad
enough to make us feare they might, I thought it necessary to purge her Honour,
for besides that I saw noe indication for bleeding.[4] My Lady had beene soe
often and soe much bleeded on the like occasion this sommer, without any
reliefe, that there was litle to be hoped from it, and I thought it ought to be
very waryly made use after soe much taken already. The purge wrought seven
or eight times, the fits continuing still by intervalls after her purge; soe at night,
as you know is usuall, she tooke a quieting cordial. The first part of the night
she had her fits very severely, but the latter part hath been more favourable,
and till about nine or ten of the clock that I write this, there remains only an
ordinary tooth acke, the violence of those fits being ceased; but whether we
are not to apprehend their returne in this extraordinary case I cannot be over
confident, two or three days of ordinary tooth acke having preceded them. I
wish with all my heart you were here, both to assist my Lady by your better
skill, and to ease me of a part of that sollicitude I am under, haveing the
care of a person of her consideration wholy upon me; she haveing had soe
litle successe with the French phycitians here this summer, in the like case,
wherein for eight days togeather their applications did her noe good, that
she is resolved to trie them noe more. If I durst interpose my opinion in a
case soe extraordinary as this, I should aske whether you did not thinke this
to proceed from some affections in the nerves in the place where the tooth

was drawn, which draws all the rest into consent and convulsive motions on this side, and that perhaps some sharpness in her blood may contribute to it. I beg your opinion, and of whoever else of the ablest of our phycitians you shall think fit to consult with . . .

374. Locke to Dr Denis Grenville, Paris, 13/23 March 1678

Shall I not passe with you for a great empirick[1] if I offer but one remedy to the three maladies you complain of?[2] Or at least will you not thinke me to use lesse care and application than becomes the name of freind you honour me with if I thinke to make one short answer serve to the three papers you have sent me in matters very different? But yet if it be found as I imagin it will that they all depend on the [same] causes I beleive you will thinke they will not need different cures.

I conceive then that the great difficulty, uncertainty, and perplexity of thought you complain of in those particulars arises in a good measure from this ground, that you thinke that a man is obleiged strictly and precisely at all times to doe that which in it self is absolutely best, and that there is always some action soe incombent upon a man, soe necessary to be donne preferable to all others, that if that be omitted, a man certainly failes in his duty, and all other actions whatsoever otherwise good in themselves, yet comeing in the place of some more important and better that at that time might be donne are tainted with guilt, and can be noe more an acceptable offering to god than a blemished victim under the law.[3]

I confesse our duty is sometimes soe evident, and the rule and circumstances soe determin it to the present performance, that there is noe latitude left, noe thing ought at that time to come in the roome of it. But this I thinke happens seldome. At least I may confidently say it does not in the greatest part of the actions of our lives wherein I thinke god out of his infinite good-nesse considering our ignorance and frailty hath left us a great liberty

Love to god and charity to our selves and neighbours are noe doubt at all times indispensibly necessary. But whilst wee keepe these warme in our hearts, and sincerely practise what they upon occasions suggest to us I cannot but thinke God allows us in the ordinary actions of our lives a great latitude. Soe that two or more things being proposed to be donne, neither of which crosses that fundamentall law but may very well consist with the sincerity wherewith we love god and our neighbour. I conceive tis at our choise to doe either of them

The reasons that make me of this opinion are

---

[1] Quack. [2] The second to fourth of Grenville's topics: business, study, conversation (L327).
[3] Law of Moses: Leviticus 1:3.

1° That I cannot imagin that God who has compassion on our weaknesse and knows how we are made, would put pore man nay the best of men, those that seeke him with sincerity and truth under almost an absolute necessity of sining perpetually against him, which will almost inevitably follow if there be noe latitude alowed us in the occurrences of our lives; But that every instant of our being in this world has always incumbent on it, one certaine determinate action exclusive of all others. For according to this supposition the best being always to be donne, and that being but one it is almost impossible to know which is that one. There being soe many actions which may all have some peculiar and considerable goodnesse, which we are at the same time capeable of doeing: and soe many nice circumstances and considerations to be weighed one against an other before we can come to make any judgment which is best, and after all shall be in danger to be mistaken. The Comparison of those actions that stand in competition togeather with all their grounds motives and consequences as they lye before us being very hard to be made. And which makes the difficulty yet far greater is that a great many of those which are of moment and should come into the reconing always scape us, Our short sight not penetrateing far enough into any action to be able to discover all that is comparatively good or bad in it: Besides that the extent of our thoughts is not able to reach all those actions which at any one time we are capeable of doeing. Soe that at last when we come to choose which is best, we makeing our judgment upon wrong and scanty measures we cannot secure our selves from being in the wrong. This is soe evident in all the consultations of mankinde that should you peeke[4] out any number of the best and wisest men you could thinke of to deliberate in almost any case what were best to be donne, you should finde them make almost all different propositions, wherein one (if one) only lighting on what is best, all the rest acting by the best of their skil and caution would have been sinners, as misseing of that one *Best.* The Apostles themselves were not always of a minde

2° I cannot conceive it to be the designe of god, Nor to consist with either his goodenesse or our businesse in the world, to clog every action of our lives, even the minutest of them (which will follow if one thing that is best be always to be donne), with infinite Consideration before we begin it and unavoidable perplexity and doubt when it is donne. When I sat downe to write you this hasty account, before I set pen to paper I might have considerd whether it were best for me ever to medle with the answering your questions or noe. My want of ability; It being besides[5] my businesse; The difficulty of adviseing any body and the presumpsion of adviseing one soe far above me would suggest doubts enough. Next I might have debated with my self whether it were best to take time to answer your demands or as I doe set presently to it. 3° Whether there were not some what better that I could doe at this time. 4° I might doubt whether it were best to read any books upon those subjects

---

[4] Pick: find.   [5] Beside: beyond.

before I gave you my opinion, or to send you my own naked thoughts. To these a thousand other scruples as considerable might be added which would still beget others, in every one of which there would be noe doubt still a better and a worse, which if I should sit down and with serious considera-tion endeavour to finde and determin clearly and precisely with my self to the minutest differences before I betake my self to give you an answer, perhaps my whole age might be spent in the deliberation about writeing half a sheet of paper to you. And I should perpetually blot out one word and put in another, raze to morrow what I write to day. For it is not an easy matter even when one is resolved to write to know what words, expressions, and arguments are the very best to be made use of. Whereas haveing this single consideration of complying with the lawfull desire of a freind whom I honour and whose desires I thinke ought to weigh with me, and one who perswades me too that I have an oportunity of doeing him some pleasure in it, I cannot thinke I ought to be scrupulous in the point or neglect obeying your commands, though I cannot be sure but I might doe better not to offer you my opinions which may be mistakes, and probably I should doe better to imploy my thoughts how to be able to cure you of a quartan ague[6] or to cure in my self some other and more dangerous faults, which is properly my businesse. But my intention being respect and service to you, and all the designe of my writeing comporting with the love I owe to god and my neighbour I should be very well satisfied with what I write could I but be as well assurd it would be usefull as I am past doubt it is lawfull, and that I have the liberty to doe it, and yet I cannot say, and I beleive you will not thinke it is the best thing I could doe.

If we were never to doe but what is absolutely the best all our lives would goe away in deliberation and we should never come to action

3° I have often thought that our state here in this world is a *State of Mediocrity*[7] which is not capeable of extreams though on one side or other of this mediocrity there might lie great excellency and perfection. Thus we are not capeable of continuall rest nor continuall exercise, though the later has certainly much more of excellency in it. We are not able to labour always with the body nor always with the minde. And to come to our present purpose, we are not capeable of liveing altogeather exactly by a strict rule, nor alto-geather without one. not always retird nor always in company. But this being but [an] odde notion of mine it may suffice only to have mentioned it, my authority being noe great argument in the case. Only give me leave to say, that if it holds true it will be applicable in severall cases and be of use to us in the conduct of our lives and actions. But I have been too longue already to enlarge on this phansy any farther at present

As to our actions in generall this in short I thinke

---

[6] A fever which recurs every third or fourth day.   [7] A middle way.

1° That all negative precepts are always to be obeyd

2° That positive commands only sometimes upon occasions. But we ought to be always furnished with the habits and dispositions to those positive dutys in a readynesse against those occasions

3° That between these two i e Between *Unlawfull* which are always and *necessary* quoad hic et nunc[8] which are but sometimes there is a great latitude, and therein we have our liberty which we may use without scrupulously thinkeing ourselves obleiged to that which in it self may be Best.

If this be soe, as I question not but you will conclude with me it is, the greatest cause of your Scruples and doubts I suppose will be removd and soe the difficultys in the cases proposd will in a good measure be removd too . . .

394. Locke to Nicolas Toinard, Orleans, 16/26 July 1678

. . . As soon as I received your letter of the 22nd I went to see Mr. Perrot;[1] he told me that the glasses you asked for were now ready and promised to send them to you the same day. If I had thought you did not know of the most convenient and finest powder for hour-glasses of that sort, which is made from tin, I would have sent you the method of preparing it. It is certainly an object worth looking at under that microscope you mentioned, for the powder is very fine, its granules being mostly round and smooth, so that it is wonderfully pleasing to study in such a minute mirror a whole window, or indeed a whole house, as it were, in a single spot with the aid of the microscope. What you tell me about the hygrometer is important, and you are doing the best thing both for your friend and for the learned world in advising that it should be made public immediately, in case anyone else with a covetous eye on other people's discoveries should snatch for himself the signal credit of this invention, which is the due reward of the ingenious inventor, who deserves even greater things. If moreover, as I cannot doubt from your description, it is powerful enough to move other weights and is not liable to fail at times through irregular working, the originator will be affording a great relief to human labours and making a contribution to mechanics, for nothing greater can be counted among our long-felt wants than perpetual motion.[2] I am sure, indeed, that those who come after us will discover many things that are not only unknown to us but even seem impossible; yet we need not despair even

---

[8] In the present circumstances.

[1] Bernard Perrot (Bernardino Perotto), Italian glass manufacturer at Orleans; Locke visited his factory.

[2] Abbé Jacques de Hautefeuille attempted to make a self-winding clock that derived its energy from atmospheric changes recorded by a hygrometer.

of the present age, in which we see you and those like you. I congratulate myself and the commonwealth of learning on your recent victory in the courts;[3] good men are badly treated if you are to be involved any longer in the dust of that conflict; but Almighty God, who is concerned for good men, will, I hope, relieve you entirely of these cares and wranglings and will restore you to your learned leisure free from these troubles. I studied your ingeniously constructed mill[4] again and again both inside and outside with great pleasure; I have never yet had the opportunity of seeing so much power, especially for those uses, in such a small body. I have not tested it in any way nor is there any need, for one is certain of it simply by looking at it; why should one want to make any further trial? here too is a product of harmony, and the thing approves itself on sight. You can hardly imagine with what pleasure I read the Abbé Gendron's book,[5] not only for the subject-matter, which includes some remarkable things, but for the spelling of words, which is adapted to their pronunciation; for since I have been here in France I have amused myself by composing some thoughts on that subject. I now feel satisfied with myself about it, as I believe that you are not unsympathetic in this matter; so with your support I may possibly venture some day to give a specimen of heterodox orthography in our own language as well. Why must the propagation of knowledge, which demands easy language and writing, be hindered by such pedantic and useless futilities? But enough of this; I am afraid I am too talkative and a greater nuisance than even the lawyers; . . .

417. Locke to Dr John Mapletoft, Lyon, 29 October / 8 November 1678

If all the world should goe to Rome I thinke I should never, haveing been twice firmely bent upon it, the time set, the company agreed, and as many times defeated. I came hither in all hast from Montpellier (from whence I writ to you) with the same designe: but old father Winter, armed with all his snow and isecles, keeps gard on Montsenny,[1] and will not let me passe. . . . Were I not accustomed to have fortune to dispose of me contrary to my designe and expectation, I should be very angry to be thus turnd out of my way when I imagined myself almost at the suburbs of Rome, and made sure in a few days to mount the Capitol, and trace the footsteps of the Scipios[2] and the Caesars; but I am made to know 'tis a bold thing to be projecting of things for tomorrow, and that it is fit such a slight buble as I am should let itself be

---

[3] Unidentified.   [4] A handmill.
[5] Abbé François Gendron, priest and surgeon of Orleans. Perhaps his *Principaux remedes*, which apparently used phonetic orthography.

[1] Mont Cenis pass.   [2] Roman generals who crushed Carthage in the 3rd and 2nd cents. BC.

carried at the phancy of winde and tide without pretending to direct its own motion. I thinke I shall learne to doe soe hereafter: this is the surest way to be at ease. But hold; I forget you have quitted Galen[3] for Plutarch; and 'tis a litle too confident to talke philosophie to one who converses dayly with Xenophon.[4] I cannot tell how to blame your designe, but must confesse to you I like our calling the worse since you have quitted it; yet I hope it is not to make way for another, which, with more indissoluble changes, has greater cares and sollicitude accompanying it. If it be soe, you need be well prepard with philosophie; and you may finde it necessary sometimes to take a dram of *Tully de Consolatione*.[5] I cannot forbear to touch, *en passant*, the chapter of matrimony, which methinks you are still hankering after;[6] . . .

426. Locke to Dr Denis Grenville, [Paris], 26 November / 6 December 1678

By Yours of 21 Nov you assure me that in my last[1] on this occasion I hit right on the Originall and principall cause of some disquiets you had had in yourself upon the matters under consideration, I should have been glad to have known also, whether the cure, I there offerd at, were any ways effectuall: or wherein the reasons I gave came short of that satisfaction and establishment as to that point. (*viz That We are not obleiged to doe always that which is precisely best*) as was desired

For I thinke it properest to the subdueing of those enemys of our quiet Fears Doubts, and Scruples, to doe as those who designe the conquest of new terretorys, viz cleare the country as we goe and leave behinde us noe enemys unmasterd, noe garisons unreducd, noe lurkeing holes unsearchd which may give occasion to disorders and insurrections or excite new disturbances . . .

For your minde haveing been long accustomed to thinke it true that *The thing absolutely in it self best ought always indispensably to be donne.* you ought, in order to establishing your peace, perfectly examin and cleare up that question, soe as at the end of the debate, to reteine it still for true; or perfectly reject it as a wrong, and mistaken measure, and to setle it as a maxim in your minde, that you are noe more to govern your self or thoughts by that false rule, but wholy lay it aside as condemned without puting your self to the

---

[3] Greek physician, the principal classical medical authority. Mapletoft quitted medicine and was ordained in 1683, but is here depicted as quitting medicine for philosophy.

[4] Locke lent Mapletoft editions of the Greek historians and philosophers, Plutarch and Xenophon.

[5] Cicero's *Consolatio* is lost, but is quoted in later works.

[6] Mapletoft married in 1679. (The postscript of the letter refers to 'our friends', Benjamin Whichcote, Edward Fowler, and Thomas Firmin, indicating Locke's links with latitudinarian churchmen.)

[1] L374.

trouble, every time you reflect on it, to recall into your minde, and weigh again all those reasons upon which you made that conclusion. And soe also in any other opinions or principles you have had when you come once to be convinced of their falshood. . . .

For these reasons it is that I thinke we ought to cleare all as we goe and come to a plenary result in all the propositions that come under debate before we goe any farther. This has been usually my way with my self to which I thinke I owe a great part of my quiet. And I beleive a few good principles well establishd will reach farther and resolve more doubts then at first sight perhaps one would imagin. And the grounds and rules on which the right and wrong of our actions turne and which will generally serve to conduct us in the cases and occurrences of our lives in all states and conditions lie possibly in a narrower compase, and in a lesse number than is ordinarily supposed. But to come to them one must goe by sure and well grounded steps—

This being premised I come to make good my promise to you in mentioning what I guesse may be an other cause of your doubts unsteadynesse and disturbances in the points under consideration. And that I suppose is, that you thinke those things inconsistent that in themselves I judg are not soe. Viz Worldly businesse and Devotion, Study and conversation; and Recreation with all. As if the most material of these soe deserved; or the present and most presseing soe possessed the whole man, that it left noe roome, noe time for any of the other

This if it has had any influence upon your minde to disturb it (as it seems to me by some passages in your papers it has) is not yet of that weight and difficulty as that I before mentioned: And I am apt to think that a few easy and naturall considerations will be sufficient to remove it, And to get quite rid of this, (if any,) ground of disturbance and scrupule, or [unsetlednesse]. And for this we need only reflect a litle upon the state and condition that it hath pleased god to place us in here in this world

1   We are not born in heaven, but in this world, where our being is to be preserved with meat drink and clothing and other necessarys that are not borne with us, but must be got and kept with forecast care and labour: and therefor we cannot be all Devotion, All Prayses and Halilujahs and perpetually in the Vision of things above, that is reserved for another state and place. Had it been otherwise, god would not have put us in a condition, where we are obleiged to use all meanes to preserve our selves, and yet those meanes of preserveing our selves in that condition (i e this life) not to be had without thoughtfulnesse and turmoile; without imploying upon the search of them the greatest part of our time and care. For at a lesse rate the greatest part of mankinde can hardly subsist in this world, Espetially this civilized world wherein you are obleiged to keepe your rank and station, and which if by mismanagement or neglect of your temporall affairs you fall from, you by your own fault put your self out of a condition of doeing that good and performing those offices requird from one in that station.

2   We are not placed in this world to stay here for ever, or without any concernment beyond it. and therefor we are not to lay out all our thoughts, and time upon it, and the concernments of it. The author of our being, and all our good here, and the much greater good of another world, deserves and demands frequent addresses to him of thanks prayer and resignation; and our concernments in an other world make it reason, wisdome and duty soe to doe

3   We are borne with ignorance of those things that concerne the conduct of our lives in this world in order to atteining what we desire, or is usefull to us in this world; or we hope in the next; and therefor enquiry, study, and meditation is necessary, without which a great part of Necessary knowledg is not to be had. espetially in some callings.

4   We are borne with dispositions and desires of Society, we are by nature fited for it, and Religion increases the obligation. We are borne members of common wealths, beset with relations, and in need of freinds, and under a necessity of acquaintance, which requireing of us the mutuall offices of familiarity freindship and charity, we cannot spend all our time in retired devotion or study, nor in ploding or takeing care of our worldly affaires i e that viaticum[2] which is to serve us (or those we are to provide for) through this pilgrimage, or some thing in order to it.

5   We are soe framed, soe constituted that any imployment of minde, any exercise of body, will weary, and unfit us to continue longer in that imployment. The springs by which all our operations are performed are finite and have their utmost extent; and when they approach that, like watches that have gon till their force is spent, we stand still, or move to litle purpose, if not wound up again, and thus after labour of minde or body we have need of Recreation to set us agoeing again with fresh vigor and activity . . .

[2] Provision, means.

5

Popery and Arbitrary Power,
1679–1683

In 1678 a supposed Roman Catholic conspiracy to destroy the government was unmasked, which quickly provoked an anti-Catholic frenzy. In the wake of this 'Popish Plot', members of the Whig opposition, under Shaftesbury, began campaigning to exclude Charles II's brother and heir, James, Duke of York, from succeeding to the throne, on the ground that his conversion to Catholicism was incompatible with Protestant nationhood. The Whigs accompanied this campaign with an assault upon Charles II for presiding over a regime increasingly given to 'arbitrary power', the subversion of English liberties, and the repression of religious nonconformity. The Tories responded by publishing the cardinal text of English absolutist political theory, Sir Robert Filmer's *Patriarcha*. During this crisis the party names Whig and Tory were coined.

Before returning to England in 1679, Locke received news of the first general election of that year from a Christ Church friend, George Walls (L459). Once back in residence at Christ Church, he caught up with news from Shaftesbury's London household (L528). By the beginning of 1680 Shaftesbury's political circumstances were changing rapidly. As one of his aides, John Hoskins, recounts, although the king had attempted to placate the Whigs by including them in the Privy Council, the experiment had proven short-lived, and the Whigs were turned out again. Furthermore, the rivalry had intensified between the Duke of York and Charles II's illegitimate son, the Protestant Duke of Monmouth, whom many Whigs canvassed for the throne.

Hoskins mentions a former governess in the Shaftesbury household, Elizabeth Birch, whose deceased father had conducted an illegal Dissenting academy in Oxfordshire. In discussing whether or not Elizabeth should continue the school, this letter provides evidence of Locke's familiarity with the plight of English Dissenters, constantly harried for worshipping, preaching, and teaching illegally.

In August 1680 it was Locke's turn to furnish Shaftesbury with rumours, optimistic but unfounded, that Charles II might again break with the Tories (L561). Locke hints that the Whig parliament which had been elected in the autumn of 1679 might finally be allowed to sit. It did sit, during the winter, but the Lords threw out the Commons' bill for preserving the Protestant succession. When the king decided to call another parliament to meet in Tory Oxford in 1681, Shaftesbury asked Locke to arrange for a college to be made available to serve as a Whig headquarters. But, as Locke reports, the college heads declared that their colleges were unavailable (L620). Limited accommodation was offered by the Rector of Exeter College, and, through Locke's connection with Monmouth's secretary, lodgings were secured from the mathematician John Wallis.

The dissolution of the Oxford Parliament after only one week marked the triumph of Charles II's prerogative power over the parliamentary opposition. Aware that the

Whigs had now won three general elections since 1679, Charles never again summoned parliament. A savage Tory purge of Whigs and Dissenters ensued, and some leading Whigs turned to conspiracy. Shaftesbury, fearful of charges of treason, fled England and died in exile in Holland. In 1683 efforts to crush the Whigs were redoubled when the Rye House Plot to assassinate Charles II and the Duke of York was uncovered. Lord Russell was executed and the Earl of Essex committed suicide in the Tower of London. Also executed was the republican Algernon Sidney, whose manuscript *Discourses Concerning Government* was used as evidence of treasonable intent. Oxford University meanwhile issued a declaration condemning Whig doctrines and staged a public book-burning. By now Locke had drafted his own assault on absolutist political theory, the *Two Treatises of Government*. His movements were under surveillance. Locke hurriedly arranged his affairs, made a will, and then fled to Holland, unsure if he would ever see England again (L771). He had no family to concern him, although in the previous year he made a loan to a cousin, John Bonville, who was keen to establish himself as a pewterer in London (L692).

In the years before leaving England, Locke had developed a strong bond of affection with Damaris Cudworth, the talented daughter of the Master of Christ's College, Cambridge, Dr Ralph Cudworth, who later published philosophical and theological treatises of her own. Having spent most of her life among 'those metaphysical contemplative people', the Cambridge Platonists, she was disconcerted by Locke's acerbity about their doctrines. Discussing the Platonist John Smith's *Select Discourses*, Locke denounces religious 'enthusiasm', a term resonant with suspicions of the religious hysteria of the Civil War era (L687, L696). In reply, she argues the case for authentic mystical communion with the divine (L699).

Exhibiting his anthropological curiosity, Locke requests information about local customs from Cudworth's brother, Charles, who was in India (L765). He tells Robert Boyle of a strange medical phenomenon and recommends a unique system of decimal measurement (L478). He keeps Toinard up to date with scholarly developments in England, and fantasizes about emigrating to an Edenic world in Carolina (L475). Toinard in turn provides Locke with an account of a comet which he observed in the company of several astronomers, including Edmond Halley, after whom it was later named, and Jean Picard, who made measurements of the earth's size (L605).

459. George Walls to Locke, Christ Church,
Oxford, 22 March [1679]

... [Y]ou shall have what I thinke most like news. the candidates at our Election were Mr Solicitour Finch, Dr Lamphire, and Dr Edisbury (brother to him that liv'd at Vigan) of which Dr Lamphire did not succeed.[1] The bishop of Lyncolne hath reprinted an account (that was not but with great difficultie to bee met with) of the powder plot, with a preface of his owne, and the addition of some papers of Sir Everard Digby's that were found in Warwickeshire about the time of the first discovery of the plot.[2] Mr Oates hath a sermon lately come out.[3] Sir William Robinson (formerly your patient) died not long since in Oxon.[4] My Lord Donegall is deade.[5] This day died our univercitie Oratour (one Mr Cradocke of Magdalene College) of the small pox, and mr Wyatte of Christ Church is likely to succeede him.[6] Dr Boucher is principle of Alban Hall.[7] Serjeant Gregory is speaker of the house of Commons,[8] and 44 Christ Church men members of it. Mr Herbert burgesse for Wilton.[9] the bishop of Peterborough is deade,[10] and wee can spare more. your affaires accordeinge to your pleasure are manag'd by mr Thomas.[11] you have had a constant tenant for your chamber,[12] the vicechancellour[13] has scons'd you 20s. as prior opponent in a phil: disputation.[14] I quarrell'd with him about it; the reason for my soe doeinge you shall know and will approve of hereafter. my Lord Lexington[15] is design'd at his returne from travell to live with us at christ church: and my request to you is that if hee bee in Paris, and you have opportunity that youle please to recommende mee to that relation that some student must customarily have to him.[16] as our affaires now stande the protection of a gentleman seems more eligible than some other uncertaine preferments. twas not in my thoughts to lay any snare for your kindnesse, when I formerly desir'd

---

[1] The Oxford University seat in parliament: Heneage Finch, Solicitor-General, son of the Lord Chancellor, and John Edisbury, civil lawyer, elected; John Lamphire, Principal of Hart Hall, and Thomas Bouchier, defeated; Vigan unidentified.

[2] Thomas Barlow, *The Gunpowder-Treason* (1679). The popish plots of 1605 and 1678 were paralleled, in a litany of Catholic infamy. Digby was a Catholic conspirator, executed in 1606.

[3] Titus Oates, *A Sermon Preached at St Michael's, Wood-Street* (1679). Oates was a hero for uncovering the Popish Plot.

[4] Son of a Lord Mayor of London.

[5] Sir Arthur Chichester, Earl of Donegal, whom Locke apparently met in Montpellier.

[6] Thomas Cradock; William Wyatt, orator until 1712.

[7] Thomas Bouchier, regius professor of civil law. St Alban's Hall no longer exists.

[8] William Gregory, serjeant-at-law, later a judge.

[9] Thomas Herbert, later eighth Earl of Pembroke, dedicatee of Locke's *Essay*. Burgess: MP.

[10] Dr Joseph Henshaw.   [11] Samuel Thomas, chaplain of Christ Church.

[12] Locke's rooms in Christ Church were sublet.   [13] Dr John Nicholas, Warden of New College.

[14] Apparently a fine for absence from a disputation.   [15] Robert Sutton, Baron Lexington.

[16] i.e. his lordship will need a Student (Fellow) of Christ Church for a tutor.

the favour of you to buy mee a table booke;[17] and I cannot certainely now bee suspected to requeste any thinge but the trouble of it, if I begge that youle bringe mee another somewhat larger, when you come over, which I hope will bee very suddenly . . . I am glad to heare of your successe in your designe in goeinge abroad, and wish the greatest improvement (or continuance if it bee perfecte) of your health . . .

475. Locke to Nicolas Toinard, Bexwells, Essex, 6 June 1679

. . . I was told the Talmud[1] is not printed at Cambridge and the man who was to translate it in Cambridge has quarrelled with the University of Cambridge, and is gone from that place to Oxford.[2] When I have learned the details of this affair I shall relate them to you at length. In the meantime I should have told you that when I spoke about this translation of the Talmud with Mr Boyle he told me that the Zoar has been newly translated into Latin in Germany by a very learned man with notes which explain the ancient Cabala of the Jews.[3] He had forgotten the author's name but said that he is at present chancellor to one of the German princes.[4] He had been sent one copy of this book which he greatly feared was lost at the London customs where the captain of the vessel which brought it had stowed it in a place where he could not yet retrieve or even locate it. . . . I have not yet had the time to go to the Royal Society, and so I can say nothing about what is happening among our virtuosos. In a little while I hope to reconcile myself with the Muses, or if the wickedness of our Europeans will not permit us to lead a good and honest life in peace here, I am quite ready to accompany you to the Isle of Bourbon,[5] if you could but bring yourself to leave these wicked people and cross the great ocean[6] which was the limit of the ambition and avarice of their grandfathers, . . . together we will go to Carolina to a very fine island there which they have done me the honour of naming after me,[7] and it is there that you shall be Emperor because I can vouch that everything that is called Locke is ready to obey you and there you will establish an empire of repose and letters. To this end (if

---

[17] A pocket memorandum book.

[1] The authoritative elaboration of the Jewish code of religious and communal law.

[2] Isaac Abendana. He taught Hebrew at both universities and published almanacs. His translation of the Mishnah (part of the Talmud, originally oral teaching and later recorded) was not published.

[3] Cabbala (Kabbalah), the hermetic tradition of the Jews: metaphysical, mystical, magical; the Zohar (13th cent.) is a work of theosophy, dwelling on immediate divine inspiration. Gentile scholars were fascinated by the Kabbalah, believing that it blended Mosaic and Platonic wisdom.

[4] Christian Knorr von Rosenroth (councillor to Christian August of Sulzbach in the Upper Palatinate), *Kabbala Denudata* (1677), a principal source of gentile knowledge of the Cabala until the 20th cent.

[5] Réunion (Indian Ocean).   [6] The Atlantic.

[7] Locke Island, established 1674; today Edisto Island, South Carolina.

you make some journey) I wish you would go with Monsieur St Colombe[8] rather than with another man because I hope that when you are at sea and in the English Channel you will desire to land at Rie[9] or Dover and thus we will have the possibility of talking to each other of this matter and of making plans to establish ourselves there. There are many other reasons why I ardently wish for the honour of seeing you in England which you will know about when you arrive. Among other things I have ordered you a beautiful girl to be your wife. Do not be afraid, do not leave off the plans for your voyage like our good friend Monsieur Bernier[10] did. The condition of men is much better here than in Ethiopia.[11] If you do not like her after you have experimented with her for a while you can sell her and I think at a better price than a man received for his wife last week in London[12] where he sold her for four *sous*[13] a pound; I think that yours will bring you 5 or 6s per pound because she is beautiful, young, and very tender and will fetch a good price in her condition. I beg you to bring Monsieur St Colombe with you whom I think would go to great lengths to see you well married and to even greater ones to be at the market where you sold your wife at so much per pound as I have seen done with the pigs at Montpellier. . . . I hope that in your retreat at Orleans you will finish the notes and everything which relates to your harmony[14] so that it is soon published with all the perfection which such a work deserves. I will inform you by the first post of the opinion on it here. I have had a volume sewn together out of those pages which you gave me in order to show it to some erudite men . . .

478. Locke to Robert Boyle, Bexwells, Essex, 16 June 1679

. . . Being[1] the 24th of May, 1678, at the hospital called La Charité,[2] I was there shewed a lad between nineteen and twenty years old, who had a sort of horns grew out of all his fingers of both hands, and most of his toes. On the two least toes of each foot there were now none, upon three whereof there had never been any, and upon the fourth, which (as I remember) was the little

---

    [8] A friend of Toinard's.   [9] Rye, Sussex, a landing place for boats from Dieppe.
    [10] François Bernier of Montpellier, physician and traveller.
    [11] Bernier reported that if he went to Ethiopia he would be obliged to marry.
    [12] Wife sales did occur: the poor man's divorce.
    [13] French currency. Apparently the woman in question sold for about £2.
    [14] Toinard's life work was to construct a Harmony of the Gospels, a coherent narrative of Christ's life reconciling and integrating the evangelists' accounts. He privately printed and circulated a version in 1678; it was finally published as *Evangeliorum Harmonia Graeco-Latina* (1707).

    [1] The letter is written at Bexwells (Bexfield), near Chelmsford, Essex, home of Thomas Stringer, Shaftesbury's steward.
    [2] L'hôpital de la Salpêtrière (also La Charité), founded by Louis XIV in 1654 'for the homeless and poor' (today near the Gare d' Austerlitz).

toe of the right foot, that, which formerly grew there, was fallen off about six months before, and came no more, but left the nail very little different from natural. On all the rest of his fingers and toes there were of these horny substances, when I saw him, but of very different lengths, some of them having began to sprout a long time after some of the others, and others of them having been broken off by the surgeon, that healed him.

The longest of all was that on the middle finger of the right hand, when I saw him, which was three inches and nine grys[3] long, and one inch seven lines in girt, of which the surgeon broke off a large piece, and gave me, which you may command, when you please. . . .

There grew also horny excrescences, some bigger, some less, on several parts of the backs of his hands, that rose very little above the skin; some of them looked like flat, but very broad warts, but to the touch they felt as hard as horn.

He told me it was about three years before, that this began, first to come upon him after having had the small pox; to the remains of which disease he imputed this accident, he having else enjoyed a health good enough, and kept the ordinary diet of his country, which was Brie.

About a week after, I went to the Charité, to see him again, and then, after having been twice purged, some of the horns of his fingers began to loosen at the roots.

I went thither again to see him, some time after, but he was gone perfectly cured, as they told me; and that the chief things were done to him were, purging and bathing.[4]

Before I conclude, I must not forget to tell you, that the measure I made use of was the philosophical foot, *i.e.* $\frac{1}{3}$ of a pendulum of seconds, which I divided thus: the foot into ten inches, the inch into ten lines, the line into ten grys; so that a gry is $\frac{1}{1000}$ part of PP; which measure, whatever it be for other purposes, I thought the fittest for philosophical communications, and therefore made use of it in this and several other occasions. But I have troubled you too long already to mention here the conveniencies of this foot, and (as I think) of the way of dividing it by decimals.[5] . . .

---

[3] See n. 5.

[4] Locke published his account of the boy with 'horny excrescences' in the *Philosophical Transactions of the Royal Society* in 1697.

[5] Several scientists (including Robert Hooke, Christiaan Huygens, Gabriel Mouton, Jean Picard, John Wilkins, and Christopher Wren) investigated the possibility of a universal natural standard of measurement. It was proposed that the vibrations of a pendulum might provide a standard. Later, the standard chosen, when the metric system was adopted, was a measure of latitude, a metre being intended to be one ten millionth of the distance from the pole to the equator, a system proposed by Mouton. In 1670 Picard made the first measurement of the earth's circumference. The 'gry' is Locke's invention, the smallest unit in a proposed decimal system of measurement; he repeats and recommends his system in the *Essay*, IV. x. 10. PP: *pes philosophicus* (philosophical foot). 'Philosophical': scientific.

528. John Hoskins to Locke, London, 5 February 1680

I have yours of the 1st: and 2d: Instant; togeather with a Book, which I have delivered according as you directed me in the paper wherein 'twas wrapt; my Lord[1] received it with great joy; and bid me give you a thousand thanks, he perused it greedily, and I see him at it very intent last night again, I told him you desired you might know, if there were anything in it, he would have further satisfaction about. how he likes the whole I cannot yet account to you, for I have not spook to him of it. But before I acquainted him with what you writt relating to the Schole at Mrs: Birches.[2] he is well pleased with the offer you make of going over to her, being desirous to know what in her own mind she is most inclind to; whether she had rather keep the boording her self and a Master to teach them; or quitt all to an other that shall be commended to her. and when you have found her own Inclination, to sound likewise what she may be perswaded to, but how this business will comport with your removall from Oxford I cannot tell;[3] ... Publick news I have as little as I have taken time to write it; I perceive by J:Ts:[4] Letter (which he tells me was to come with the book that came from you, but came the day after) all the news I can tell you is what of those things you hear, are fals, or are suspected. 1st: the D: of Y: is not come. nor is there any reconciliation made between him and the D: of M: nor how confidently so ever it is talkd, doe we beleive the former will capacitate himself for Admirall, nor the latter be restored.[5] the report of the Generall Pardon is over, twas said at first it should extend to all but the Lords in the Tower,[6] but tis hush'd. there is no Inditement yet brought in against Sir Ro: Peyton. so that tis expected he shall be baild the last day of the Term;[7] Harris that Publishes the Protestant Intelligence was Indited to day for selling a book calld the Appeale, which was found against him;[8] so we shall see who

---

[1] Shaftesbury. The book is *Observations upon the Growth and Culture of Vines and Olives*, probably written while Locke was in France; publ. 1766. The tract was probably intended as a proposal for developing the Carolina economy.

[2] Elizabeth Birch, who contemplated taking over a Dissenting school from her recently deceased father, Samuel. She continued as governess to Shaftesbury's grandson. 'Mrs' here means 'mistress': Elizabeth was unmarried.

[3] Locke left Oxford for Salisbury on 3 Feb.   [4] Probably James Tyrrell.

[5] The dukes of York and Monmouth, Catholic and Protestant claimants to the throne. In 1673 York resigned as Lord Admiral because the Test Act incapacitated Catholics from holding office. In 1679, in an attempt to defuse the succession crisis, York was sent as viceroy to Scotland and Monmouth sent abroad.

[6] Five Catholic peers awaited trial for treason in the Tower; one, Viscount Stafford, was executed. Twenty Catholic priests were executed 1679–81, the last of the English Catholic martyrs. Some are now saints of the Catholic Church.

[7] Sir Robert Peyton, Whig MP, who tried to go over to York's camp and was under suspicion of treason.

[8] Benjamin Harris, Baptist printer, who published the Whig newspaper, *The Protestant Domestic Intelligence* (1679–81), and the raucous *Appeal from the Country to the City* (1679), probably written by Charles Blount, deist, and Tyrrell's brother-in-law.

will be fined highest the Protestant Pamphleteers or Popish subborners.[9]
Mr: S: Coventrey has leave to sell his Place. we hear tis a great dispute whether
my L: Sunderl: or L: Hide shall be L: high Treasurer. if the former then the
latter and S: Godolphin shall be the 2 Secretarys. confident rumours we have
had that Sir L: Jenkings, or a Bisshop neer you shall have the great Seale; but
Mr: Finch being made first Commissioner of the Admiralty and P[rivy]:
Councillor stounds that report. my Lord Bronkerd, and Sir T: Littleton come
in the places of Sir H: Capell and Mr: Vaughan that have both quitted.[10] There
is a great Alteration making in the Commissions of the Justices of the Peace,
but tis carried very secrettly, and will be so till the whole be finished.[11] these
heads of news J:Ts: Letters puts me in Mind of; I wish I knew or could think
of anything that would make my Letter savory to the D:[12] whose appetite to
news I take to be sharper than yours.

561. Locke to Sir Anthony Ashley Cooper, First Earl of Shaftesbury, [London], 5 August 1680

Though Mr. Percival[1] comes as well furnished with all the current news of
the town as his, Mr. Hoskins's,[2] and my stock put together could amount to,
yet your lordship will pardon me if I take the liberty to trouble you with one
piece of news. I was told to-day by one who had it whispered to him as a
very true and serious secret, viz., that my Lord Sunderland was to go Lord
Lieutenant of Ireland,[3] the Duke[4] to retire thither, and that the white staff[5]
would very speedily be sent to your lordship, and that the Duchess of
Portsmouth[6] was soliciting it with all her endeavours.

This, though it be so extraordinary that it seems fit to be put amongst hunts-
men's stories, and therefore I have desired Mr. Percival to give it to you as
you are returning from the chase, yet it is apt to make one reflect upon what

[9] Catholic witnesses to the Meal Tub Plot, an alleged Presbyterian plot invented by Catholics to counter the (no less invented) Popish Plot.

[10] The king dismissed his Whig privy councillors and installed Tories. Those named are: Henry Coventry, the Earl of Sunderland, Laurence Hyde (later Earl of Rochester), Sidney (later Baron) Godolphin, Sir Leoline Jenkins, Daniel Finch (later Earl of Nottingham), Lord Brouncker, Sir Thomas Littleton, Sir Henry (later Viscount) Capel, and Edward Vaughan. The bishop is perhaps Henry Compton, Bishop of London.

[11] The county magistracies were purged of Whigs.

[12] Dr David Thomas, with whom Locke was staying at Salisbury.

[1] Peter Percival, Shaftesbury's banker.   [2] John Hoskins, Shaftesbury's solicitor.

[3] Robert Spencer, Earl of Sunderland, consummate politician, who traversed Whiggery, Toryism, and, under James II, Catholicism.

[4] James, Duke of York.   [5] The Lord Treasurer's symbol of office.

[6] Louise de Keroualle, the king's mistress, who was plotting a rapprochement with the Whigs.

is very much believed, that there must be a parliament;[7] and in preparation thereunto there is already great striving amongst those who think themselves most in danger who shall be thrown to the dogs. And who can think it other than good court-breeding that might become a duke or a duchess to strain courtesy in the case, and each desire to prefer the other as most deserving? This is agreed, that there is a great ferment working now at court, and 'tis not everybody knows who influences. Mr. Brisbane,[8] who is looked on as none of the most inconsiderable of men in employment, is newly turned out of his judge advocate's place, and nobody knows the hand that hurt him, though it were the commissioners of the admiralty that visibly gave him the blow.

The Duke of Ormond, 'tis believed, will certainly be sent for over.[9] 'Tis hard to conceive it shall be to make way for my Lord of Essex,[10] though he be a man of known merit, and harder that it should be to succeed to the care of Aldersgate[11] upon occasion. 'Tis certain his son's ravings in his fever plainly showed how full his head was with Tangier, and many conclude that sunk him to his grave.[12] But who knows the secrets of fate? Your lordship has seen many a lusty undertaker[13] go before you. My Lord Latimer,[14] 'tis reported, has his bedchamberman's place,[15] as my Lord Lumley[16] that of the Earl of Rochester, whose penitential confessions, I am told, are speedily to be published by Dr. Burnet, who was with him till a little before his death.[17]

If what his Majesty is reported to have said to the Lord Mayor yesterday, when he presented the Common Hall petition to him,[18] be true, 'tis probable that Whitehall is as little dissatisfied as the city overjoyed with Bethel's choice,[19] for 'tis the talk that his Majesty said that he hoped he might prove (as several others who had been represented to him as enemies) a very good servant, and particularly named Lawson, as one who served him faithfully and died in his service.[20] But what expectation he has already raised of himself Mr. Percival will be able to inform your lordship at large.

---

[7] The parliament elected in Aug./Sept. 1679 was not permitted to sit until Oct. 1680.

[8] Unidentified.

[9] i.e. dismissed. James Butler, Duke of Ormonde, prominent Tory, Lord Lieutenant of Ireland.

[10] Arthur Capel, Earl of Essex, Whig, previous Lord Lieutenant of Ireland. He committed suicide in the Tower in 1683, though Whigs suspected murder.

[11] Residence for a displaced statesman.

[12] Thomas Butler, Earl of Ossory, soldier, Tory, who died on 30 July, protesting the inadequacy of the force to be sent under his command to hold Tangier in North Africa.

[13] Probably here meaning one who undertakes a great political task.

[14] Edward Osborne, Viscount Latimer, the Earl of Danby's son, a Tory.

[15] Gentleman of the King's Bedchamber.   [16] Richard Lumley, Viscount Lumley, soldier, a Tory.

[17] John Wilmot, Earl of Rochester, libertine poet. Gilbert Burnet, *Some Passages of the Life and Death of John, Earl of Rochester* (1680).

[18] Lord Mayor: Sir Robert Clayton, Whig financier. The petition was for parliament to sit. Common Hall was the City's citizen assembly.

[19] Slingsby Bethel, elected sheriff in July after a bitter contest; reputedly a republican; he fled to Holland in 1682.

[20] Sir John Lawson, anabaptist and republican in Cromwell's era, but became an admiral in Charles II's service.

My Lord Russell I found not at home when I went to wait on him to-day
from your lordship. My lady was well, and very glad to hear that your lordship
and my lady were so.[21] . . .

605. Nicolas Toinard to Locke, Paris, 18/28 December 1680 and 22 December 1680 / 1 January 1681

The day before yesterday I received all your gifts from Mr Nelson[1] for which
I am most grateful and especially for the portrait of that Lord for whom you
have inspired in me such veneration.[2] I will preserve it with the greatest care.
At the same time I also received a visit from Mr Halley who has been at St
Helena.[3] He has passed on to me a letter from Mr Hooke[4] and the observations of the satellites[5] made by Mr Flamsteed,[6] with a book by Mr Wood[7] like
that which you spoke of so warmly to me. I pray you thank Mr Hooke for
this on my behalf. Yesterday afternoon I took the said observations directly
to the Abbé Picard[8] who sends you his greetings. His measurement of the earth,
his levelling, all his already published observations are to be reprinted in a
quarto volume together with other new things and it is bound to sell this time.[9]
For a long time now I have been tormenting him about this and about the
form of the volume. I will tell you another time about the report of his
latest observations made at Bayonne and at the tower of Cordoba with those
of Mr Flamsteed. We went together to the observatory[10] where I made better
provision for the comet[11] than I have of wood, for I did not think to be in
Paris at this time. We found [it] at 12 minutes after 5, the head measured
10.D.40′ in height and the tail more than 53.D. in length excluding its end
which disappeared into the fog, so that it occupies almost an eighth part of
the sky in height. Otherwise as far as I can judge, since I am not an expert
in these sort of animals any more than I am in stars, this comet shows a resentment of the birds for since it appeared it has wanted to take the crow by the

---

[21] Lord William Russell, and Lady Rachel Russell, half-sister of the Countess of Northumberland. Russell was executed for treason in 1683.

[1] Robert Nelson, travelling companion of Edmond Halley; later a High Church religious writer and philanthropist.

[2] An engraving of the Earl of Shaftesbury.

[3] Edmond Halley, astronomer. He was at St Helena in the South Atlantic, 1676–8, where he mapped the southern constellations, improved the sextent, observed the transit of Mercury, and noted the equatorial retardation of the pendulum.

[4] Robert Hooke, scientist, secretary of the Royal Society.   [5] Of Jupiter.

[6] John Flamsteed, first Astronomer Royal, founder of Greenwich Observatory.

[7] Robert Wood, *A New Al-moon-ac for Ever; or A Rectified Account of Time* (1680).

[8] Abbé Jean Picard, French astronomer (L478, n. 5).

[9] Probably *Traité du Nivellement . . . et un abbrégé de la mesure de la terre* (1684).

[10] L335, n. 2.

[11] In 1705 Halley published his calculation that the comet of 1682 would return in 1758.

tail, and yesterday the swan by the wing. As for the eagle it would have liked to pluck out one of its feathers, but it feared a sharp peck and we saw that it let it pass in front.[12] This is not the only mark it has given of its good conduct, for it has a great desire to be seen, and it heeded the advice it was given on how cold it is down here, so that recognising the error it had made of expecting to be looked upon as early as 4 or 5 in the morning which was not a convenient time for spectators and even less for lady spectators, it prudently resolved to appear at sundown, which was an immense success as regards Paris, for yesterday there was an incredible crowd of both sexes at the observatory. You may well think that the hair-brained or those who wish to become so made up the greatest number, for the whole terrace was covered with people who firmly believed that one cannot see the comet legitimately outside the place which has been built expressly for it. . . .

I wrote the above so that it might be dispatched on Saturday, but the arrival of Mr Romer[13] has delayed this missive which I have not had the time to set right. Since that time I have accompanied Messrs Nelson and Halley to the observatory outside which there is no salvation for astronomers. We noted last Sunday the 29th that it does but grow in size and beauty. Shots were fired at it as was necessary, and its tail was found to measure 62 degrees in length, to the nearest few inches. There is no doubt here that the great length of its tail is the cause of the influences it showers upon us, and as we cannot prevent the comet appearing we think only of how we might tie up this tail very tight in several places so that we might prevent it from shaking it and according to its whims sending a million infirmities thick and thin like dew-fall in May. The Academy is working on this matter and I ask you to invite your Royal Society to do the same. . . .

Yesterday after dinner I had the honour of accompanying Mr Nelson to the Abbé Picard's with the intention of going with him to the vantage point to see the comet, but it has chosen to hide itself until this year[14] and so we stayed at my lord the Abbé's home and drank your health, and Mr Hooke's and that of all astronomy. I read to my lord the Abbé the article concerning the [movement] of the earth by Mr Hooke and the movement of the stars,[15] and Mr Picard who today at midday measured the height of Lyra[16] with a lens so as to compare it in six months with its nocturnal meridian height, as it is the third time he has done this he could tell us that there is not a 20″ difference as Mr Hooke maintains, but only a 10″ one.

I will send you some almanacs as soon as some appear as well as a little speech on the variation of magnets and a tiny scrap on the comet. It has passed through thirty constellations in three months, which shows that it has legs as

---

[12] Constellations: Corvus (the Crow), Cygnus (the Swan), Aquila (the Eagle).
[13] Olaus Roemer (Ole Rømer), Danish astronomer, investigator of the speed of light.
[14] It was now 1 Jan. in France.
[15] *An Attempt to Prove the Motion of the Earth* (1674), which reported his observations of parallax.
[16] Constellation: the Lyre or Harp.

good as its tail is long and its tail was but two degrees wide on Sunday. By all appearances it will not move backwards, and will disappear between Pegasus and the Southern Fish.[17] Its head has never appeared to us bigger than a star of the third degree, and even this was most unclearly. I saw it with 35 and 60 foot lenses. . . .

620. Locke to Sir Anthony Ashley Cooper, First Earl of Shaftesbury, Christ Church, Oxford, 6 February 1681

. . . [B]y the account I received from Mr Vernon,[1] there was litle hopes to compasse your proposalls about a Colledg.[2] However I could not satisfie my self without doeing all was possible for me in what ever your Lordship commanded or had a concerne in. Assoon as I saw Mr Vernon the D of Monmouths secretary he told me that the haveing a colledg being past hopes your Lordship had pitchd upon Dr Wallis's house[3] and that he had direct order from his Grace to take it for your Lordship. The place I judgd as convenient as any in towne, being in the lane between the Schools and new Colledg neare in the midway betwixt them as quiet a place as any in the town. And Mr Vernon haveing not yet been there we went togeather to see the house and found the Doctor very ready to accomodate your Lordship the best he could, and not knowing but that since the designe of being in a Colledg to keepe house togeather was broken your Lordship might returne to the desire of haveing an house for your family[4] (which was in the first letter that bid me speake to Alderman Wright[5] to provide for you) I desired to see all the Doctor could spare you. I asked too where about the price would be but could get noe other answer but that he would leave that to your Lordship though I moved it a second time, But then Mr Vernon saying that it was left soe to the D[uke] his master by Alderman Wright (at whose house he was to lodg) I could not well presse it farther, Espetially not haveing particular instructions how many rooms your Lordship would have need of. Since that by a letter I received from Mr Stringer[6] on Friday night being informed that your Lordship desired only

---

[17] Constellations: Pegasus (the Flying Horse), Pisces (the Fishes).

[1] James Vernon, the Duke of Monmouth's secretary; Secretary of State under William III.

[2] I.e. find accommodation for the Whig leader in an Oxford college for the duration of the forthcoming parliament.

[3] John Wallis, Whig, former Presbyterian and Parliamentarian, professor of geometry. He began the development of calculus, and quarrelled with Hobbes over mathematics.

[4] Family: household. It was commonplace for the term 'family' to include staff and servants; Locke, the critic of patriarchalism, conforms to this usage. L797, n.6; L3400, n.1.

[5] William Wright, goldsmith, Whig MP for Oxford City, sometime mayor; he provided lodgings for Monmouth.

[6] Thomas Stringer, Shaftesbury's steward.

some rooms for your self, and a small . . . I went again yesterday to Dr Wallis's and there measured the ro[om]s and [m]ore particularly observed the furniture whereof I have here inclosed sent your Lordship a particular, and a hasty draught of the ground floore that your Lordship might choose those rooms were fitest for your service.[7] . . . I accepted too of the Cellars and Kitchin below to be offerd to your Lordship as you [might need them] because though your Lordship designed to eate abroad, yet I concluded that would be only dinners, and it would not be inconvenient to have at least a barrell of [ale] or s[m]all beare and bread for the use of your owne self and company at other times, and there must be places for wood etc under Locke and Key. And if your Lordship should make noe other use of the litle Kitchen on the ground floore the Doctor Said there might be a bed set up in it for servants. . . .

As soon as I had taken my first view of Dr. Wallis's house I went to Dr Berry[8] and gave him your Lordships thanks (as you commanded me) for the civility of his offer. He told me there were three of the best rooms togeather in the house[9] if your Lordship pleased to accept of them I answerd that your Lordship had now given order to take lodgings in the towne, after which he again made an offer of those cha[mbe]rs and told me he thought some other conveniencys might be got to them, but that the whole colledg could by noe meanes be had: . . . I was willing they should remaine some time under the offer of your acceptance because they might be serviceable to [the] designe I had of geting you yet a whole college, which I saw would be of mighty use to you and the rest of the Lords. the project I thought fesible, because I'm sure it was very reasonable and I should have thought it to be imbraced as very advantageous had I been in his place to whome it was [made and in whose power it was to have But not to trouble] your Lordship with that which was noe thing but an unsuccesfull contrivance I can only say that we have all here but one sort of reasoning[10] . . .

As to stables Alderman Wright brought me to a great yard in Jesus lane[11] where were severall livery stables, he has one there of his owne for 4 or 5 horses and I shall have an answer the begining of the weeke whether they may be had soe as to have stable roome enough for your Lordships eleven horses (the number sent me) . . . Alderman Wright has very kindely offerd to s[end] his owne horses into the Country to make roome for your Lordships when they c[ome] and if the worst comes to the worst you shall be sure of his and he doubts not to get another stable in some other convenient place to serve your turne. He tells me he will furnish you with hey as good as any in England, and very good oats at 20d. per bushell the rate that he pays his owne tenant for them, there are also conveniencys to be got there by for lodgings for grooms and coach men. But not knowing whether this place which is in the midle of

---

[7] Locke's letter is long: he goes into domestic detail and draws a ground plan.

[8] Dr Arthur Bury, Rector of Exeter College, later expelled for alleged heresy in his *Naked Gospel* (1690).

[9] i.e. at Exeter College.   [10] i.e. Tory reasoning.   [11] Now Market Street.

the town just by Jesus Colledg would altogeather please your Lordship because of an intimation in Mr Stringers letter. I went to seeke a place nearer the feilds and the aire for your horses. At the Dolphin Inne[12] joyning to St Johns Colledg I found stable roome enough untaken up (which is now but in few of them) but the stables not very good. he stands upon 10d. per horse a night for hey and will have the furnishing of oats at 8 groats[13] a bushell. He has promised to keepe stable roome for eleven horses if I give him an answer by the end of this weeke. At Dr Wallis's joyning to the court that is before his house is a coach house a pretious thing now in Oxford this also your Lordship may have. There is never an one at the place where Alderman Wrights stable is, nor at the Dolphin but the fellow haveing a large yard will set up one on purpose if your Lordship thinke it necessary to have your coach and horses stand togeather. . . . [T]hough I designed when I writ to your Lordship from Okeley[14] to come away hither the next day after, yet not [know]ing how I might be able to goe through with it after soe long keepeing my bed and being almost constantly in a breathing sweat I thought it the best way [no]t to be too positive in undertakeing, least your Lordship depending upon me and I should be disabled your Lordship might be disappointed in a businesse that soe nearly[15] concernd you. . . . I am exceeding glad if I have donne your Lordship [a]ny manner of service in it I'm sure I was very much troubled I could not goe [a]bout it the very moment I received your Lordships commands. And I thanke god that slow hast I made [ha]th not had such effects as the freinds where I was, feard. I wrapd my self very war[m]e and gallopd most part of the way and I thanke god have found noe great increase of my cough since. I beg your Lordships pardon for this tedious long letter . . .

687. Locke to Damaris Cudworth, [Christ Church, Oxford], [*c.*21 February 1682]

I[1] have read it again with care,[2] but cannot I confesse reconcile the four heads very well with my expectation which the begining gave me of a *fourfold kinde of Knowledg* whereas those four differences he afterwards enumerates and describes seeme not to me to be soe much four sorts of knowledg but severall degrees of the love of God and practise of vertue.[3] For though I grant

---

[12] Now the Lamb and Flag in St Giles.   [13] Groat: a silver coin worth fourpence.
[14] Oakley, Buckinghamshire, James Tyrrell's home, 10 mls. north-east of Oxford.
[15] Closely.

[1] This letter derives from an entry in Locke's journal.
[2] John Smith (the Cambridge Platonist), *Select Discourses* (1660), First Discourse, on attaining divine knowledge. The book was republished in the 18th and 19th cents.
[3] Smith, in Platonic fashion, depicted a hierarchy of four kinds of knowledge and four kinds of people, ascending to the highest type through progressive transcendence of earthly passions: hence,

it is easily to be imagind that a love and practise of vertue may and naturally doth by imploying his thoughts more on heavenly objects give a man a greater Knowledg of God and his duty, and that reciprocally produce a greater love of them, yet I cannot allow that it is a different sort of knowledg or any know-ledg at all above his reason, for what ever opinions or perswasions are in the minde without any foundation of reason, may indeed by the temper and disposition of some mindes whether naturall or acquired seeme as cleare and operate as strongly as true knowledg, but indeed are not knowledg but if they concerne God and religion deserve the name of Enthusiasme,[4] which however you seeme to plead for and thinke St Paul to a degree allows yet I must still say is noe part of knowledg and the new creature in my sense does not consist soe much in notions nor indeed in any irrationall notions at all, but in a new principle of life and action i.e. the love of God and a desire of being in holyness like unto him. What unassisted reason can or cannot doe I cannot determin since I thinke the faculty its self in its severall degrees of perfection all the helps and improvements of it by education discourse con-templation or otherwise are all assistances from God and to be acknowledg[ed] to the goodnesse of his providence, but I thinke of reason as I doe of the sight [of] an ordinary eye [which] by constant imployment about any object may grow very accute in it [and] the assistance of glasses may make it see things both better and at a greater distance but yet whatever is discerned by the eye however assisted is perceived by and comes under the naturall faculty of seeing, and soe what ever is known, however sublime or spirituall, is known only by the naturall faculty of the understanding and reason, however assisted. Though there may be this difference that one perhaps has got an help to see and discerne heavenly objects which an other never soe much as looked after, and therefor I cannot quit my former division of men (who either thinke as if they were only body and minde not soule or spirit at all, or those who in some cases at least thinke of them selves as all soule seperate from the com-merce of the body and in those instances have only visions or more properly imaginations, and a third sort who considering them selves as made up of body and soule here and in a state of mediocrity[5] make use and follow their reason) untill you tell me what sort of persons those are *who are not included in any part of it.* I hope they will not be his fourth[6] which to deale truly with you seeme to me very much to savour of Enthusiasme and soe will be very litle different from my Visionarys I meane in respect of their opinions and knowledg, for if you take in their Seraphyke love and Heroick vertue those

---

virtue is the path to knowledge. As Locke says, Smith draws no real epistemological distinction between kinds of knowledge.

[4] A term increasingly used at this time, to mean an unbalanced or ungrounded religious exaltation, often equated with the fanaticism of the puritan sects of the Civil War era.

[5] Middle way, balance.

[6] Smith: 'The true metaphysical and contemplative man, ... who running and shooting up above his own logical or self-rational life, pierceth unto the highest life'.

I confesse may give them great degrees of Excellency and perfection but we have noething to doe with those in our present discourse as not lyeing in the speculative but practicall and operative part of the soule wheras we are now enquireing only after the distinction of men in respect of knowledg which I cannot but thinke is all except that of sense comprehended under reason, and whatever strong perswasions we have in matters divine not riseing from nor vouchd by reason I cannot looke on otherwise than perfect Enthusiasme. But I will not now enter into a discourse of that haveing more than enough tired you already which will be to use you worse than your fall[7] did if I breake your brains with my Jargon. The next discourse of Supersition is one of the best I ever read, but as to his third I shall talke more particularly with you when we are got over this first.[8]

692. John Bonville to Locke, London, 18 March 1682

I have Received yours Wherein I understand your Desire is to have one bound with me,[1] I could have Asked my Master Hicks with whome I served my time[2] and I think he would not denied me such A kindnes but I Am very Loath too make my Case knowne because it ware Ever Reported that I had A great deal more of my owne when I Came to him, There for Deare Sir doe not stay your hand In doeing of me this great kindness for In soe doeing you will make A man of me: my Cousin keen[3] will Lett me have As many tools As will come to 14 or 15 [l] which make me Loath to desire Any for there ki[nd]nes, But If I knew my self not In A Copacity Too pay Too whome I Ame Obliged I should think my self wors then Ann Infidell:[4] to desire Either mony or goods, Dear Sir In A word it is well known that Am soe neare Related to such A worthy person as your self And my unkle,[5] shold it be knowne that I have Nothing it wold be such A disparegment to me that it will be my Ruen, Sir I Am now in my new habitation, I am Cumpeld for to Lay Aside That Little In which the Lord have blesed for I Cannot goe noe forether, without your Asistanc. Deare Cousin I now Live The next dore to the signe of the Crowne In Hounsditch,[6] Pray Sir be plesd to Let me heare your Comfortable Answar with speed that time may not be Lost, soe I Rest your Kinsman And very Humble servant.

---

[7] Damaris had almost broken her arm a few days before.
[8] Smith's 2nd Discourse, on Superstition; 3rd, on Atheism; 4th, on Immortality.

[1] Locke wanted somebody to stand security for the loan which Bonville sought.
[2] As apprentice.   [3] John Keene, son of Locke's aunt Frances.   [4] 1 Timothy 5:8.
[5] Their mutual uncle, Peter Locke, tanner of Chew Magna, Somerset.
[6] In the City of London, a street of small traders. L268, n. 8.

696. Locke to Damaris Cudworth, [Christ Church, Oxford], [6 April 1682?]

A[1] strong and firme perswasion of any proposition relateing to religion for which a man hath either noe or not sufficient proofs from reason but receives them as truths wrought in the minde extraordinarily by god him self and influences comeing immediately from him seemes to me to be Enthusiasme,[2] which can be noe evidence or ground of assureance at all nor can by any means be taken for Knowledg.[3] For I finde that Christians, Mahumetans and Bramins all pretend to it (and I am told the Chineses too) But tis certain that contradictions and falshoods cannot come from god, nor can any one that is of the true Religion be assured of any thing by a way whereby those of a false religion may be and are equally confirmed in theirs.[4] For the Turkish Dervises[5] pretend to Revelations Extasies vision Rapture. to be swallowed up and transported with illuminations of god. Discourseing with god. seeing the face of god. v. Ricaut $\overline{216}$ (i e Of the Ottoman Empire folio London $\underline{70}$ 1.2 c. 13 etc)[6] and the Jaugis[7] amongst the Hindous talke of being illuminated and intirely united to god Bernier. $\overline{173}$ (i e memoires Tome 3. 8° London $\underline{72}$) p. 36[8] as well as the most spiritualised Christians

699. Damaris Cudworth to Locke, 20 April [1682]

... The thing I suppose then in question betweene us was whether or no my Author[1] were an Enthusiast (since we are agreed in the Opinion of Enthusiasme to which I hope I am as much an Enemie as you), But as to That, I have nothing more to say onely that when I read his Book I did not at all apprehend him to be soe, but that if I should beleeve him so upon any Body's Authoritie it would assoone be yours as the Churchmans you tell me of,[2] who I suppose without any Disrespect to his Worth or Order was Fallible like other

---

[1] This letter derives from an entry in Locke's journal (*Political Essays*, 289–91).   [2] L687, n. 4.

[3] Added in the margin: 'If such groundlesse thoughts as these concerne ordinary matters and not religion and possesse the minde strongly we call it raveing and every one thinkes it a degree of madnesse, but in religion men accustomed to the thoughts of revelation make a greater allowance to it, though indeed it be a more dangerous madnesse. but men are apt to thinke that in religion they may and ought to quit their reason.'

[4] Added in the margin: 'Enthusiasme is a fault in the minde opposite to bruitish sensuality as far in the other extreme exceeding the just measures of reason as thoughts groveling only in matter and things of sense come short of it.' That is, rational religion is a middle way between mystic enthusiasm and the superstitious idolatry characteristic of paganism and popery.

[5] Dervishes: Muslim ascetics.

[6] Sir Paul Rycaut, *The Present State of the Ottoman Empire* (1667; 3rd edn., 1670).

[7] Yogis: Hindu ascetics.   [8] François Bernier, *A Continuation of the Memoirs* (1672).

[1] John Smith: L687, L696.   [2] Unidentified. There were no published replies to Smith.

men, and that I am no more Oblig'd to beleeve as he does, than to reject for That reason any Opinion that is held by those of the Church of Rome, truth and Falshood being still the same from whom ever they are receiv'd, which I say not because I agree with the Jesuits in that Opinion of theres[3] (if it be so) since I neither well know what they meane, nor think my self a fit judge of these things. But that I may Answeare the Authoritie of your Churchman with another,[4] there is one who giveing reasons why there is no Communication betweene Good Angells and the Vertuous, gives it for one That God Himself affords his Intimacies and Converses to the better Souls that are prepar'd for it, That the Proud and Phantastick Pretences of the conceited Melancholists of this age to Divine Communion had indeed Prejudic'd many very Intelligent Persons against the beleefe of any such thing, They looking upon it but as a High flowne Notion of Warme Immagination as he acknowledges himself formerly to have done, But that haveing since consider'd it he is convinc'd, and does now abundantly beleeve That the Divine Spirit does afford its Sensible Presence and Immediate Beatifick touch to some Persons so and soe Qualify'd. They are his owne words, but whether they amount to what was condemn'd in the Jesuits, or whether it be a Truth and Reallitie or not, is more than I know, and I only tell it you because it was from a Churchman who had the Reputation of Learning as well as yours, and was Esteem'd a more then ordinaryly Ingenious Man. As for my self being not in the number of those fitly Qualify'd Persons I can be no judge of it, Things of inward sense being not to be Deny'd (as Hee says) because wee our selves do not feell them, nor can form any Apprehension of them, Nor are they to be Judg'd of by the noetical[5] exercises of speculative understanding, but by the Sentient and Vital Faculties. whatever therefore another professes to Experience in this kind How should I be able to Deny? and Provided that they Act not nor Admit any thing but what they can give a Rational Account of, That they Pay a Universal Obedience to all the laws of God, and that they beleeve the Holy Scriptures I do not see any Reason why there opinion should be quarrel'd with, or themselves Condemn'd as Persons who let themselves be impos'd upon by there Immaginations and by the Suggestions of unbridled Phancie since thus long they do not quit there Reason; (as the Enthusiast does, who pretends to leave that light for a better (in which I suppose is there great Mistake, there being no suggestions of the Holy Spirrit but what are always agreable to, if not Demonstrable from Reason) But if to any this great Priviledge be Vouchsaf'd I do not know why it may not as well be so, to all who are as Sincere and Devout lovers of God and Vertue, and who do Faithfully adhere to that light which they already have, of which I suppose there are many amongst the most Barbarous Nations and Professors of the Wildest Religions in the World, as

---

[3] Unidentified.

[4] Joseph Glanvill, 'Against Modern Sadducism', in *Essays* (1676), here paraphrased.

[5] Purely intellectual; Glanvill again.

well as reall Enthusiasts every where, as I suppose those Ricaut and Monsieur Berniere[6] speake of might bee, but in the number of whom I did not indeed beleeve Mr S—,[7] looking upon the designe of that whole Discourse in General as no other than to recommend Puritie of Life as the onely true way of attaining to Divine Knowledge in which are made the greater advances by how much the more the Mind is purg'd from all Impuritie, there being a Natural Cohesion of Truth with impolluted Souls, and also, as Dr More says,[8] a Principle Antecedaneous to Reason which he calls Divine Sagacitie which is onely Competible to Persons of Pure and Unspoted Minds and without which Reason is not succesfull in the Contemplation of the Highest matters. . . .

765. Locke to Charles Cudworth, London, 27 April 1683

Though you are got quite to the other side of the world[1] yet you cease not to make new aquisitions here, and the character you have left behinde you makes your acquaintance be sought after to the remotest parts of the earth. There is a commerce of Freindship as well as merchandise and though noe body almost lets his thoughts goe as far as the East Indies without a designe of geting mony and growing rich, yet if you allow my intentions I hope to make a greater advantage by another sort of correspondence with you there. In the conversation I have had the happynesse to have sometimes with your sister[2] here I have observed her often to speake of you with more tendernesse and concerne than all the rest of the world, which has made me conclude it must be something extraordinary in you which has raisd in her (who is soe good a judg,) soe particular an esteeme and affection beyond what is due to the bare ties of nature and bloud. and I cannot but thinke that your soules are akin as well as your bodys and that yours as well as hers is not of the ordinary alloy. I account it none of the least favours she has don me that she has promised me your freindship and you must not thinke it strange if I presume upon her word and trouble you with some enquirys concerning the country you are in, since she incourages me in it and assures me I shall not faile of an answer. Some of those who have traveld and write of those parts, give us strange storys of the tricks donne by some of their Juglers[3] there, which must needs be beyond leger de main and seeme not within the power of art or nature. I would very gladly know whether they are really donne as strange as they are reported, and whether those that practise them are any of them

---

[6] L696, nn. 6, 8.   [7] John Smith.

[8] Henry More, *A Collection of Several Philosophical Writings* (1662).

[1] Cudworth was at Kasimbazar (Cossimbazar) in Bengal, the centre for European textile purchases before the rise of Calcutta.

[2] Damaris.   [3] Magicians.

Mahumetans, or all (which I rather suppose) heathens, and how they are looked on by the Bramins and the other people of the country, whether they have any aparitions amongst them and what thoughts of spirits, and as much of the opinions religion and ceremonys of the Hindos and other heathens of those countrys as comes in your way to learne or enquire. It would be too great kindenesse if you could learne any news of any copys of the old or new testament or any parts of them which they had amongst them, in those easterne countrys, in any language, before the European trade thither by the Cape of good hope. I should trouble you also with enquirys concerning their languages learning government manners and particularly Aurange Zebe[4] the Emperor of Indostan, since I could promise my self a more exact account from you than what we have in printed travells, but I feare I have beene more troublesome than what you will imagin will become a man that does but now begin to beg your acquaintance. . . . One thing which I had forgot give me leave to adde which is a great desire to know how the severall people of the east keepe their account of time as months and years and whether they generally agree in any periods answering to our weeks and whether their arithmatike turns at ten as ours doth.

771. Locke to Edward Clarke, [Salisbury], 26 August 1683

. . . I have herewith sent you many papers. You will know how and how far and in what occasions they are to be made use of better than I. What you dislike you may burn. I have sent amongst them a letter of attorney to Mr. P. P;[1] if you think that a fit place to lodge money in pray give it him, for I thought it convenient to have somebody in London to lodge and return it: if you should leave the town you must be judge whether this be well contrived, and so I pray order it accordingly.

My Lady Shaftesbury[2] has, I suppose, money in one Mr. Prince's[3] or some other hands in Amsterdam. Pray talk with her about it, for that probably may both suit her and my occasions, but mention not me but a friend of yours you will be responsible for, for I would be private at least till you hear from me again. . . .

You remember the word *papers*. This enclosed will guide you to a gentle-woman[4] in whose hands are lodged the writings concerning my annuity. Those I think were best to be sealed up and left with her still. In another paper sealed

---

    [4] Aurangzib, Mogul from 1658.

    [1] Peter Percival, Shaftesbury's banker.
    [2] Lady Dorothy Manners, the new Countess of Shaftesbury, whose marriage and pregnancies Locke had supervised.
    [3] Francis Prince, merchant, Shaftesbury's banker in Amsterdam.
    [4] Unidentified; perhaps Damaris Cudworth.

up you will find a bond of Dr. Thomas's[5] for fifty pounds, which pray deliver him, with other writings of the like kind which dispose of as you think fit, though I think they will be best there till you have occasion to make use of them. There is an other paper also sealed up which what it contains I suppose you will guess by the shape of it from what I have formerly told you. You may consider whether you think it best to lie there or no. There is also a purse of gold, about 100 guineas I suppose in value. The ruby ring in it give her, and all the other pieces that are wrapped up in little papers to keep them for me. The onyx ring with a seal cut in it, if you please, accept from me. This purse with all in it I would also have lie there till you have an opportunity to return the money to me; for if that cannot be done I would have it rest all with her, only the two rings there I would have you take, the one for your self, the other for your Lady.[6] . . .

In the same place as Dr. Thomas's bond you will find a bond of my cousin Bonville's for twenty pounds.[7] I lent it him to help set him up, and design to receive nor use nor to call in the principal till my own necessities force me. And if I die before I call for it, and he behave himself well to me, which you will know from Dr. Thomas, I would have the bond given up to him. I have given order to Mr. [Pawling][8] to send up to you when he sends you your coach glass with a little red trunk of mine, in which you will find my book of accounts, which I put into your hands for two reasons, first that you may see how my moneys stand, and so get in what money you find owing to me where the sums are considerable enough to give you the trouble, and next to let you see therein my method. Pray keep this book as safe as you can. Stands ready cased. Dr. Thomas has paid me now at Salisbury fifty pounds, and therefore pray deliver him up his bond: how our account stands you will see by that book. I have ordered Mr. Pawling to return you some money he has of mine. I think it is not much. What he sends take without asking any account from him, for I am sure he will keep back nothing that is mine. Dr. Thomas, who brings you this, comes almost on purpose about my affairs, whom pray advise in my concernments. What news the Old Bailey affords from time to time I would gladly receive from you.[9] The key of that little red trunk before mentioned Dr. Thomas has: it serves to that and a little leather standish[10] I have in Oxford. I have writ to Mr. Pawling to send you also my hat and clothes, which I should be glad to receive if they can be sent me. . . .

Pray talk with Dr. Thomas about the best way of securing the books and goods in my chamber at Christ Church if there should be any danger. There is a pair of silver candlesticks, too, and a silver standish of mine in Mr. Percivall's hands. When a safe and sure way of returning money to me is found, I would have them also turned into money and returned to me. Upon consideration

---

[5] Dr David Thomas, with whom Locke was staying.   [6] Mrs Mary Clarke.   [7] L692.
[8] Robert Pawling, Whig activist, Oxford merchant, now settled in London.
[9] The treason trials of Whig conspirators. Lord Russell was executed on 21 July.   [10] Inkstand.

I have thought it best to make a will, which you will find amongst the other papers, by which you may be legally entitled to whatsoever I leave; and it being uncertain whether that may be more or less, I can without making another formal will give you new directions to dispose of what I shall leave as occasions and circumstances may vary. I have assigned over my annuity, due from my Lady Shaftesbury, to Dr. Thomas, who has promised to leave the assignment with you and a declaration of trust, and if there be occasion to assign it to Mr. Tyrrell. . . .

All my wearing linen, flannel shirts, waistcoats, stockings, either at Dr. Goodall's[11] or Oxford, I would have sent to me. My old suits and a cloak at London I would have sold forthwith . . .

[11] Dr Charles Goodall, physician in London; Locke sometimes lodged with him after Shaftesbury's flight.

6

Exile in Holland, 1683–1688

Even in exile, Locke's former associations with Shaftesbury rendered him insecure. In 1684 he was expelled *in absentia* from his Studentship at Christ Church. Deliberately playing down his Shaftesburian connection, Locke sought the protection of the moderate Tory peer, the Earl of Pembroke. In one of his most disingenuous, but nevertheless revealing, letters, Locke portrays himself as a withdrawn, consumptive, bookish man, preoccupied with abstract philosophical speculation and forced abroad for health reasons; he denies authorship of any political treatises 'in print' (L797). Despite Pembroke's subsequent assurances that he is no longer under suspicion (L828), Locke is aware that he is spied upon (L974). For a period he went into hiding to escape government agents seeking to arrest and extradite seditious exiles.

In February 1685, Charles II died and was succeeded by James II, England's last Catholic monarch. The power struggle between James and the Protestant Duke of Monmouth ended decisively in James's favour with the crushing defeat of the Monmouth rebellion in July 1685. It has been argued, but not proved, that Locke was among those Whigs who committed themselves to Monmouth's cause. From one Whig gentleman, James Tyrrell, Locke receives detailed accounts of political life under James II. The king, as well as initiating a vigorous press campaign to promote Catholicism (L842), also, paradoxically, solicited the Whigs in an attempt to create a pro-toleration alliance against the persecution conducted by the Anglican church and its Tory supporters. Despite his opposition to James's Catholicizing policies, Tyrrell encourages Locke to publish a treatise supporting toleration, which they had begun together in 1681. In fact, during the winter of 1685–6, Locke had written, though he did not yet publish, a new work on toleration, the *Letter Concerning Toleration*. The tract had a Continental dimension, for Louis XIV had just revoked the Edict of Nantes and commenced a savage onslaught on French Protestants, the Huguenots. After James promulgated an edict of toleration in 1687, Tyrrell returns to the theme of religious accommodation by welcoming the reduced power of the Anglican hierarchy (L932). He also recounts James's project to intrude Catholics into the universities (L973), a policy which subsequently provoked the *cause célèbre* of Protestant civil disobedience against the 'popish king', at Magdalen College, Oxford. Later, Tyrrell mentions James's attempts to reinstate Whigs into political office provided they agree to support a toleration bill in the next parliament (L985). Although some Whigs complied, it was the steadfast opposition of Tories like Pembroke which fortified Whig opinion and forged an increasingly united Protestant common front.

While in exile Locke maintained regular contact with a rising Whig lawyer, Edward Clarke of Chipley, near Taunton in Somerset, to whom he sent the series of letters which later became *Some Thoughts Concerning Education* (1693). Although Locke said little about female education, he advises Mary Clarke about the upbringing of her daughter, Betty (L809). Elsewhere, with guarded irony, Locke remarks upon Whig pamphleteering, before turning to advise Clarke on tree-planting (L776). The suggestion by a modern scholar that Locke's reference to trees and seeds denotes a code for the arms and money needed for rebellion is implausible: Clarke was building a house and garden at Chipley, where the trees still remain. Other letters concern the preparation for publication of Locke's *Essay Concerning Human Understanding* (L801, L886), the origin of which lay in conversations among Locke's friends in 1671. Mutual friends of Locke and of the Clarkes visited Locke: while touring Holland, Richard and Isabella Duke visited him at Utrecht, despite the rigours which such travel involved (L854).

In 1688 Locke produced an abridged version of the *Essay*, the *Abrégé*. Among the friends to whom he sent copies was Lady Guise, who worries that some readers might 'cavil with your philosophy or question your religion'. Although Locke was not seriously attacked for heterodoxy until the mid-1690s, he acknowledges to Guise that 'there are men touchy enough to be put into a heat by my little treatise' (L1056). It was a premonition of future controversies. Another recipient of the *Abrégé* was Damaris Cudworth. Having wanted to become a philosopher herself, her earlier letters reveal her stoical resolve in the face of the constraints upon a woman's life (L779 and 805). Locke was probably in love with her, but failed to commit himself, or else he was rebuffed. Despite having previously baulked at the idea of marriage, in June 1685 Damaris married a widower who had nine children. By November, she is longing for Locke's company, poignantly confessing her frustration at housewifely immurement in the dreary Essex countryside (L837). Two years later, she remains bitterly convinced that she is 'placed in the wretchedest neighbourhood in the whole world' (L896). Having read the *Abrégé*, she challenges Locke's epistemology—his insistence that all knowledge derives from sense experience—reverting instead to the innatist doctrines of the Cambridge Platonists (L1040).

In exile, Locke sustained his interest in matters scientific, commenting on Thomas Burnet's *Sacred Theory of the Earth*, one of an increasing number of attempts to provide scientific explanations for biblical phenomena (L911). Following the fashion for collecting exotica from around the world, Locke recounts his acquisition of unusual plant seeds and drawings of native peoples, including Brazilian cannibals (L951).

776. Locke to Edward Clarke, Amsterdam, 7/17 March [1684]

... If I should contrary to my custom write news, I should tell you that I think that an evil spirit possesses people everywhere. Here, too, people are writing against one another as hot as may be,[1] and there are every day pamphlets published here that deserve as well to be burnt[2] as the *History of the Growth of Popery*,[3] or *No Protestant Plot*,[4] or the like, in other places. Tares and divisions sowing everywhere, and methinks the tares take root and spread apace. Whether the late great conjunction in the heavens make these divisions on earth I know not astrology enough to resolve, but I wish King James's maxim were more in credit on this side the water, and beati pacifici[5] would pass among Christians for good gospel, as I think it would be good policy in defence of Christendom against the great event of war with the Turk[6] But you know I have little skill in politics and therefore may mistake, and so I leave these matters *quae supra nos*———.[7]

I have since my last inquired most particularly of a very skilful man concerning abele[8] and lime trees. He tells me of the abele trees there is but one sort, and in them you cannot be mistaken. Of lime trees there be two sorts, but the best is that which they call the female lime tree. It is that which bears the flowers, and the bark looks a little reddish and is not altogether so sad as the other. The offsets from the roots will grow. If I can light of any here in time enough I will send you some by a ship that is going hence for Exeter, which I conclude will be much more convenient than London and all the long cartage by land. I have not yet got the lime seeds which were promised me, for our highways, that is rivers and canals, are scarce yet quite open. And now I consider you in the country I can not but be talking to you of those innocent designs of building houses and planning walks: the latter is my theme at present. I desire you to make your walks broad enough, that is, let the bodies of the trees stand in two lines twenty foot in each side wider than the outside walls of your house, and then another row on the outside of those twenty further. On the front I think lime trees would do best, on the east side

---

[1] The French fomented quarrels between the Dutch republicans and the stadholder, Prince William of Orange.

[2] Locke is being ironical.

[3] Probably Andrew Marvell, *An Account of the Growth of Popery* (1677), rather than Henry Care, *The History of Popery* (1682).

[4] Probably by Robert Ferguson (1681), though Locke was also accused of its authorship (L797, n. 10).

[5] 'Blessed are the peacemakers': King James I, *The Peace-Maker* (1618).

[6] The Turks besieged Vienna in 1683, their furthest advance into Europe.

[7] 'Which are above our heads.'   [8] White poplar.

elms, and on the north witch elms, which is a better sort of trees than we commonly imagine. So much at present for walks.[9] . . .

779. Damaris Cudworth to Locke, [London], 16 June [1684]

. . . I am now I hope Absolutely Cur'd of Promiseing my self any great Pleasure in this World, tho it depended upon so many Contingences before, that I think I deserv'd to be Punish'd for but Flattering my self with an Imagination that it may be it might bee.

If I ever did Act any Part upon the Stage of this Earth in the Anti-diluvian State of it, that Golden Age,[1] I wish it were Possible for me now to Remember it, that I might have no Temptation to Quarrel with Providence for giveing me Inclinations so little Sutable to this, and so unlike ever to be Gratify'd; Tho if I could have Faith enough to beleeve Helmonts Opinion,[2] and Could with as strong a Fancie conceit my self to have beene Methuselah (as its said a great Philosopher did Him self to have beene One who was Slaine at the Seige of Troy)[3] I think it might do all [but] as well, and I could not sure then want Patience to Compleate my Thousand Yeares either now, Or in any other Age of the World; The Truth is, with the Present I have beene much more out of Conceite for these Ten Days, and feare I shall continue so, than when I had the Designe that you Know of turning Stoick; I see more than ever, that it is a Base, False, Foolish World; and that Vertue, Honour, and Friendship, are but Names in it, Whilst People sell theire Honestie for Imaginarie Profit, and theire Happiness for the Senceless Reputation of being Wise. But this is our World, and as it Appears to me in the Discontented Humour that I am in; I should be very glad to heare a Better Account of yours; which if you cannot give, Pray inform me a little about your Neighbors in Frieze Land, the L'abadies,[4] Since tho I be ever so far Distant from them, it would much Reconcile me to the World to know that there were but somewhere in it a better sort of People than those where I am; I desire therefore that you will tell me what theire Manner of liveing is; and Whether it be that, or any Peculiar Principle, or Opinion, in theire Religion which Unites them together; What that is; Whether they be Learn'd, or Unlearn'd; and whether in theire Lives, and Conversation one amongst Another they do really differ from the rest of the World, and do appeare to have more true Honestie amongst them. . . .

---

[9] Edward Clarke's landscaping at Chipley, near Taunton, Somerset, remains today substantially intact.

[1] Thomas Burnet's *Theory of the Earth* (1684) equated the antediluvian era with the Golden Age.
[2] Francis Mercury van Helmont's *Two Hundred Queries Concerning the Doctrine of Humane Souls* (1684) argued for a version of metempsychosis: we live for a thousand years, in successive lives.
[3] Pythagoras.
[4] The Labadists, a Quaker-like quietist and communistic community in Friesland, North Holland, founded by Jean de Labadie: Locke visited them on 22 Aug. (*Political Essays*, 293–6).

797. Locke to Thomas Herbert, Eighth Earl of Pembroke, Amsterdam, 28 November / 8 December 1684

In my passage through this town from Leyden (where I had been for some time at an auction) to Utrecht (where I designed to passe this winter) I was surprised with the news of a moneo,[1] summoning me to appear at Ch: Ch:[2] by the first of January. The occasion, and circumstances of it, I suppose, your Lordship may have heard; and therefor I shall not trouble your Honour with the recitall of them. When I was prepareing to comport my self to that citation as became me, the next post brings the news, that I am actually expeld;[3] but with it brings also the notice of your [Lordships] generous concerne for an unfortunate and exposed innocence. My Lord I have had the honour to be known to your Lordship these many years, both at home and abroad; and I appeale to your Lordship, whether in all my conversation (which if it trespassed any way I am sure it was not in being over reserved) your Lordship ever observed the least appeareance of any thing in me of the kinde I am charged with; but quite the contrary. I appeale likewise to my Lord Bishop of Oxford[4] whether my cariage in the colledg, for soe long a time, caryed in it any the least mark of undutifull against the government either of the church, state, or Colledg it self; or whether there were any appearance of turbulency, faction, or sedition in my nature. Afterwards when chance, and not my owne seekeing (as your neighbour Dr Thomas[5] can informe your Lordship at large) threw me into my Lord Shaftsburys acquaintance and family,[6] I chalenge any one to say my behaviour was otherwise. If it had been, it would have belyd my minde and temper; and therefor I cannot but thinke it hard, that any imputation that lyes upon him should draw suspitions upon me. For though either through attention, or good luck, I happend to doe him some acceptable service in that great, and strange disease, when he was opend,[7] soe that he was afterwards pleased to own, that he owed his life to my care; and possibly the memory of that, might make him treat me ever after (as I confesse he did) with great civility and kindenesse; Yet some of my freinds, when they considerd, how small an advancement of my fortune I had made, in soe long an attendance have thought, that I had noe great reason to brag of the effects of that Kindenesse. I say not this, my Lord, to complain of my dead master, it will be noe way decent in me, But in this extremity, I cannot but complain of it as an hard case, that haveing reaped soe litle advantage from my service to

---

[1] 'I warn': Oxford usage for a formal instruction. The summons was issued on 8/18 Nov.

[2] Christ Church.

[3] From his Studentship (Fellowship) of Christ Church. The government ordered Locke's immediate deprivation on 11/21 Nov.; it was carried out on 15/25 Nov.

[4] John Fell, Dean of Christ Church, as well as Bishop of Oxford.

[5] Dr David Thomas of Salisbury, 2 mls. from Pembroke's seat at Wilton.

[6] Note the equation of 'family' with 'household'. L620, n. 4.

[7] The operation on Shaftesbury's liver cyst in 1668. L250.

him whilst liveing, I should suffer soe much on that account now he is dead. For if I had spent those years I lived with him, in the publique practise of physique,[8] I beleive, I may say without boasting, that I might have made my self an other maner of establishment, than now I have; at least I should have been rich still in my students place,[9] which I always soe valued, as the highest convenience for a retired single life, that the keepeing of it (which was always my great care) was what most satisfied me in the not geting other things: and I imagin had I spent my time, just as I did, in any but my Lord Shaftsburys house, I might now search my health, and injoy my pittance, and privacy any where, quietly without being suspected of libells,[10] or any other miscariages,[11] though in every thing else, but barely liveing in his family, my actions had been all exactly the same they have been now. For I never did any thing undutifully against his Majestie or the government: I know noe thing in my life scandalous, or am conscious of any thing that ought to give any offence; I have never been of any suspected clubs or caballs, I have made litle acquaintance, and kept litle company in an house where soe much came, and for that litle my choyse was of bookish not busy men. All this my Lord is known to be soe, and the constant course of soe many years cannot but be visible. And indeed such a course was the natural product of my unmedleing temper, which always sought quiet and inspired me with noe other desires, noe other aimes than to passe silently through this world with the company of a few good freinds and books. And therefor to remove my self as far as might be from any publique concernes, I in the late unhappy times pitchd upon the study of physique. But my Lord one accident of my life (my falling into a great mans family) and one fault in my health (a consumptive indisposition which forbad me a setled abode to looke after others health and gave me worke enough to take care of my owne) have (I know not by what witchcraft) confounded the quiet, I always sought; and the more I endeavour to get into some quiet retreat, the more still I finde my self in a storme. For now, when with some degree of health (which has improved here beyond my expectation) I hoped to enjoy some repose, in a separation from almost all conversation, I am suspected to write divers scandalous and seditious libells. I have often wonderd in the way that I lived, and the make I knew my self of, how it could come to passe, that I was made the author of soe many pamphlets, unlesse it was because I of all my Lords family happend to have been most bred amongst books. This opinion of me I thought time and the contradictions it caryed with it would have cured, and that the most suspitious would at last have been weary of imputeing to me writeings whose matter, and stile have I beleive (for pamphlets have been laid to me which I have never seen) been soe very different, that

---

[8] Medicine.   [9] His Studentship at Christ Church.

[10] Locke was suspected of writing *No Protestant Plot* (1681), *An Enquiry into the Barbarous Murder of the Late Earl of Essex* (1684), and *An Impartial Enquiry into the Administration of Affairs in England* (1684).

[11] Misdemeanours.

it was hard to thinke they should have the same author, though a much abler man than me. This suspition however follows me, it seems, here, where I hoped to be out of the way of all publique concernes, for that made some part of my satisfaction in those many solitary howers I spent alone, industriously avoiding company, to that degree, that it was reproachd to me here, that I was a man by my self. And it is a very odde fate, that I should get the reputation of noe small writer, without haveing donne any thing for it. For I thinke two or three copys of verses of mine, published with my name to them,[12] have not gaind me that reputation. Bateing[13] those I here solemnly protest in the presence of god, that I am not the author, not only of any libell, but not of any pamphlet or treatise whatsoever in print good bad or indifferent.[14] The apprehension and backwardnesse I have ever had to be in print even in matters very remote from any thing of Libellous or seditious, is soe well known to my freinds, that I am sure I can in this have many compurgators.[15] As to the company I am said to keepe at Coffee houses, the honour of your Lordships acquaintance flatters me, that your Lordship beleives me not a natural foole, which I must needs be, if I should come hither to make acquaintanc[e] now, and keepe company with men, whom every one that would be safe shuns, and who were never any of my associates in England, when they were under much better circumstances. Those who are particularly named for my Companions, I assure your Lordship with the truth I would speake my last breath, I never saw out of England, nor in a long time before I left it.[16] Coffee houses it is well known I loved and frequented litle in England, lesse here. I speake much within compasse when I say I have not been in a Coffee house as many times as I have been months here, haveing noe great delight either in the conversation or the liquor, and when I went there, which I remember I was once forced to doe three or fower times in one weeke, it was only to speake with some merchant I had businesse with. My time was most spent alone, at home by my fires side, where I confesse I writ a good deale, I thinke I may say, more than ever I did in soe much time in my life, but noe libells, unlesse perhaps it may be a libell against all mankinde to give some account of the weaknesse and shortnesse of humane understanding, for upon that my old theme de Intellectu humano (on which your Lordship knows I have been a good while a hammering),[17] has my head been beating, and my pen scribleing all the time I have been here except what I have spent

---

[12] Locke had published congratulatory verses to Cromwell (1654), Charles II (1660), Queen Catherine (1662), and Thomas Sydenham (1668). *Political Essays*, pp. 201, 203–4, 209–11.

[13] Excepting.

[14] 'In print' is a saving clause: Locke had by now drafted the *Two Treatises of Government*. He has been suspected of a role in composing the Shaftesburian manifesto, *A Letter from a Person of Quality* (1675), and did have a hand in *The Fundamental Constitutions of Carolina* (1669).

[15] Testifiers.

[16] The king's agents in the Netherlands, Thomas Chudleigh and Bevil Skelton, reported that Locke was associating with such Whig conspirators as Robert Ferguson and Ford, Lord Grey.

[17] *An Essay Concerning Human Understanding*, begun 1671, publ. 1689.

in travelling about to see the country. It has been asked too, why I chose
Holland, and not France for change of aire (For this consumptive poor shadow
of a man moves noe where without a noise) The reasons in short were, I
had tried France and it would not prove a cure, it only kept my cough at a
pretty tolerable abatement, but silenced it not quite. And this country I had
not tried, which I now finde more effectuall, and I have reason to hope in
time a perfect cure. Besides wine always sensibly hurts my lungs, and water
since my last sicknesse gives me the colique, and there is but litle beare in
France, none in the southern parts, These considerations made this choise
necessary

My Lord though this be the second letter I have given my self the honour
to write your Lordship since I left England, yet when I consider the length
of this, I am apt to feare, I am more than a dayly importuner. It was my duty
and designe to return your Honour my most humble thanks for your
Lordships most generous continuation of your favour and kindenesse to me
in this my disgrace. But instead of it I see I have troubled your Lordship with
a tedious account of my self, and am falne into such a stile as I was not wont
to use with your Lordship. Tis a great part of the misfortune of the unhappy
that they are full of noething but their own misery. And those who thinke
they have not merited the hardships they lye under would willingly finde a
patron to tell the story of their innocence to, I perswade my self I might have
spared my long one to your Lordship, and that your owne knowledg of me
would have justified me in your Lordships thoughts. But your Lordships good
opinion and favour is of soe mighty a value and comfort to me that my
concerne to preserve it could not expresse it self in fewer words; And when
I cease to be a loyall subject, or an honest man, may I (as the last of miserys)
loose that too.

801. Locke to Edward Clarke, Utrecht,
22 December 1684 / 1 January 1685

I have been very unfortunate and other people very malitious to raise
Suspitions upon me without any ground but their owne misinterpretations
of my most innocent actions. For I am more and more confirmed in my
opinion that my being much in my chamber alone the last winter and
busy there for the most part about my enquiry concerneing *Humane
Understanding* a subject which I had for a good while backwards thought on
by catches and set downe without method severall thoughts upon as they
had at distinct times and on severall occasions come in my way and which I
was now willing in this retreat to forme into a lesse confused and coherent
discourse and adde what was wanting to make my designe intelligible to some
of my freinds who had desired it of me and to whom I had promised a sight

of it when it was a litle out of the rubish,[1] and to that purpose had brought those papers along with me into this country, and I was glad I did soe since they not only gave me an innocent and (as I thought) a safe imployment for my solitary howers here, but I was also satisfied I should scarce any where else, where I had had the company of my freinds, and where soe much time had not lain upon my hands, ever have had the patience to have revised and new formed my old scatterd notions it takeing up more time and pains with lesse pleasure and profit than the pursuit of new ones. This however innocently it then helped me to passe away my time with some satisfaction in the absence of my freinds and almost all company I am confident has been the occasion of my misfortune. The more I consider it the more I am confirmed in this opinion, and I phansy I could guesse pretty neare the very person who tooke an oportunity from my being constantly almost writeing to give a rise to that suspition which has soe much ruined me.[2] For why should I thinke those that I have known busy in other peoples affairs and free of their misrepresentations and wrong reports should be more civil to me, Into the acquaintance with some such unavoidable accidents brought me here. But a [man] that thinkes noe ill is apt to feare none, and therefor knowing my actions and intentions cleare I had noe apprehensions of any thing like what has befallen me. I know not whether this may bring my prudence in question I am sure it cannot my innocence: He that had designed to write libells would have been more [cautious and not] put himself into a house where he knew he should meet with such as would not [be backwards to give information.] I wish all that I have writ here were seen by those that most suspect me or wish ill to me (if there be any such for I deserve it from noe body) they would then see my [head was] imploid about speculations remote enough from any publique [or] politique concern and was not teemeing with any thing for the presse here. For I tell you again with that truth which should be sacred betwixt freinds that I am not the Author of any treatise or pamphlet in print good bad or indifferent and therefor you may be sure how I am used when people talke of libells. Two or three copys of verses indeed there are of mine in print as I have formerly told you [but] those have my name to them.[3] But as for libells I am soe far from writeing any that I take care not to read any thing that lookes that way, I avoid all commerce about them and if a letter from a freind should have in it but the title or mention of any libell, I should thinke it a sufficient reason to burne it immediately what ever else of concernement there might be in it, and to quarrell with him that writ it and I desire noe other usage for my letters or my self from my freinds. But to keepe myself far enough from that I have never any commerce of news with any absent acquaintance,

---

[1] In the Epistle to the Reader of the *Essay* Locke described himself as 'an Under-Labourer in clearing Ground a little, and removing some of the Rubbish, that lies in the way to Knowledge'.

[2] Locke was spied upon in Holland (L797, n. 16); and also in Oxford, before he fled England, by Humphrey Prideaux, for the Under Secretary of State, John Ellis.

[3] L797, n. 12.

and inquire not after it amongst those I am with, I have scarce read soe much as half a dozen gazet[4] since I have been here and those only when other people have put them into my hands, not that I thinke it a fault, but haveing resolved not to medle in the least with any publique affairs, I decline as much as I can the discourse of them and the rather because forainers (for with those I choose rather to converse than with my countrymen) being apt to aske an English man concerning English news I may truly tell them I know not any.

Though all I said in my long letter to E:P[5] be all true yet it is not all I have to say for my self. For to mention but one thing more to you. Can any one thinke I should lay out soe much mony in books as I have since I came hither (above 50l and should have donne more) which would be an intolerable burden to a wanderer, and at the same time by libels and other miscariages have shut up the way to my returne into England and forfeit my place at Ch: ch:[6] which I knew any displeasure might take from me, and now that it is gon I know not what to doe with my books haveing noe where to place them. Before this calamity I considerd my purchase of them with pleasure but now with regreat, It displeases me as often as I thinke on them, and if my innocence did not give me some hopes of my place again I thinke I should disburthen my self of them presently. But though the consideration of his Majesties *great clemency* and of my own innocence give me reason to hope a restoration, yet I doe not thinke it convenient to move [in it yet. Great men doe not love to have] innocence pleaded in the first heat of their [suspition, however raised by misinformation] when I am satisfied that it is a proper time to stir in it I will [in] another long letter to him make my innocence yet clearer, but [neither is it fit to load him with such a letter, nor is it] yet a proper time to move, at present there is no remedy but patience, and therefor pray manage his forward kindenesse soe as dexterously to put it off from stiring in it till a fiter season, least by too much hast the businesse be sp[oi]led and I loose the benefit of his assistance afterwards at a more proper time. For [you may] let him know I have a great deale more to say for my self but that I cannot thinke it reasonable to tire him with long storys haveing soe lately offended that way already. . . .

805. Damaris Cudworth to Locke, [London], 15 January [1685]

. . . It is so long since the 8th of Oct:[1] that I know not now what it was that I then said to you, nor what my Thoughts were. But I assure you since then,

---

[4] Newspapers.   [5] The Earl of Pembroke. L797.
[6] His Studentship at Christ Church. L797.

[1] When she last wrote: a letter similar to L779.

whatever you may think, I have beene much more a Stoick than you ever knew me, and have now such a Zeal for the Sect I have embrac'd, that I never was so sorry as since I had your letter that I am neither Handsome nor Witty; since you think such an Example would do so much Good in the World. But it is not my fault I am sure and so I indeavour to sattisfie my self, who tho I am now altogether a Stoick as to my Philosophy Yet may I Hope be a Labadist[2] too if I see it Convenient, there being no Inconsistencie I think, but a very Good Agreement betweene them. Should I ever resolve for Matrimonie,[3] You have so far improv'd my Reasons and Arguments for it that I should Certainly then go into Freezeland,[4] But should I do the Contrary I beleeve you will think it best that I stay where I am, especially since if Men should ever become my Aversion, or that I should grow extraordinarie Devout and Religious, things that sometimes Happen in that case, Here is a Friend of yours who doubts not in a little time but that she shall see her selfe an Abbess,[5] With whom I Question not but you have sufficient Interest to Procure that I may be one of Her Nuns. The Difficultie therefore lyes in makeing this Choise, and since it seemes I have so far alreadie Trusted you as to Confess to You that I am but Half Arm'd against Matrimonie I cannot fancie that I can Pitch upon any Body better, to Advise me by which of my Halfs it is that I ought to be Determin'd which till you have done I meane to Converse indeed in this Present Evill world, but with such a Stoical sort of Indifference that the Brethren in Freezeland shall have no Reason to say that Damaris has forsaken them and to Convince you that there is alreadie a very great Change wrought in me I assure you I cannot remember that any discourse of Mine since I came to Towne has beene able to tend at all to Mr Clarks Edification Concerning the fasions Or that Mrs Clarke[6] and I or any other Lady have once sat in Councell about that Matter. Tis true, I am not yet got into a Tammy Petticoat and Wastcoate, nor a Say Apron,[7] But the Reason is that if I should continue onely to be a Plaine Stoick I cannot yet Determine my self whether it may not be as agreable, or more so, to the Severitie of our Sect to go without any Cloaths at all,[8] since Certainly They are a Part of, at lest Depend upon the Goods of Fortune. I Hope therefore you will be Convinc'd now that I am true to my Principles, and that a Proselite is not Lost, Also since My Quarrel with the World is so Lasting, that it is more likelie it was occasion'd for want of a Servant,[9]

---

[2] L779, n. 4.

[3] Damaris married Sir Francis Masham in June. In her previous letter she wondered 'if ever I [would] come to be Perfectly reconcil'd to Matrimonie' (L787).

[4] Friesland in north Holland, where the Labadists lived. L779, n. 4.

[5] Probably Anne Grigg, a High Church Anglican with conventual tendencies. (Damaris's future philosophical rival, Mary Astell, proposed a Protestant nunnery as an alternative to married life, in her *Serious Proposals to the Ladies* (1694).)

[6] Edward and Mary Clarke, who sometimes sojourned in London.

[7] Tammy: a worsted. Say: light woollen. Cudworth implies Quaker plain dress.

[8] The supposed sect of Adamites, who went naked.   [9] Lover.

than through any falling out with any that I Had. You know I have Liv'd Lately a great while in a Place[10] where it has been a Complaint (as you may remember) that there was no Occasion for a Heart, and therefore the thing is not at all Unlikely. However since perhaps it may not be so much for my Honour to have it thought so, I think I am Concern'd if it were but on that Score to Continue the same Here that I use to be in that Duller Aire, which for a Thousand New Reasons I was not a little glad to Quitt at this time, but should have beene much more so could I have had any Hopes of Meeting you Here. . . .

809. Locke to Mary Clarke, [Utrecht], [28 January / 7 February 1685?]

. . . '[T]is fit I acquit myself of my promise to you in reference to my little mistress[1] . . . [and] you will think that speaking with [the sincere] affection I have for the softer sex I shall not think of any rougher usage than only what [her sex] requires. Since therefore I acknowledge no difference of sex in your mind relating . . . to truth, virtue and obedience, I think well to have no thing altered in it from what is [writ for the son]. And since I should rather desire in my wife[2] a healthy constitution, a stomach able to digest ordinary food, and a body that could endure upon occasion both wind and sun, rather than a puling,[3] weak, sickly wretch, that every breath of wind or least hardship puts in danger, I think the meat drink and lodging and clothing should be ordered after the same manner for the girls as for the boys. There is only one or two things whereof I think distinct consideration is to be had. You know my opinion is that the boys should be much abroad in the air at all times and in all weathers, and if they play in the sun and in the wind without hats and gloves so much the better. But since in your girls care is to be taken too of their beauty as much as health will permit, this in them must have some restriction, the more they exercise and the more they are in the air the better health they will have, that I am sure: but yet 'tis fit their tender skins should be fenced against the busy sunbeams, especially when they are very hot and piercing: to avoid this and yet to give them exercise in the air, some little shady grove near the house would be convenient for them to play in, and a large airy room in ill weather: and if all the year you make them rise as soon as it is light and walk a mile or two and play abroad before sun-rising, you will by that

---

[10] Probably Cambridge. Damaris's father, Ralph, was Master of Christ's College.

[1] The Clarkes' daughter, Elizabeth (Betty), aged about 7.

[2] Locke's epithet for Betty. Martha Lockhart, one of Queen Mary II's Ladies of the Bedchamber, called little Francis Cudworth Masham 'my husband' (L1314).

[3] Whining.

custom obtain more good effects than one; and it will make them not only fresh and healthy, but good housewives too. But that they may have sleep enough, which whilst they are young must not be scanty, they must be early to bed too.

Another thing is, that of washing their feet every night in cold water and exposing them to the wet in the day.[4] Though my reason is satisfied that it is both the healthiest and safest way, yet since it is not fit that girls should be dabbling in water as your boys will be, and since perhaps it will be thought both an odd and new thing, I cannot tell how to enjoin it. This I am sure I have seen many a little healthy [child do in] winter, and I think that had I a daughter I should order water to be put in her [shoes] when she put them on, and have her feet well washed in cold water. . . . But since I affect not to go out of the ordinary road, and there are many healthy women without it, I do not advise it for my pretty little Mis[s], though if there should be any inconvenience in it, the very leaving of it off would remove it.

Their heads, I think, should never be covered, nor their necks within doors, and when they go abroad the covering of these should be more against the sun than the cold. And herein you may take notice how much it is use that makes us either tender or hardy, for there is scarce a young lady so weak and tender who will not go bare in her neck without suffering any harm at a season when if a hardy strong man not used to it should imitate her it would be intolerable to him, and he would be sure to get a cold if not a fever.

Girls should have a dancing master at home early: it gives them fashion and easy comely motion betimes which is very convenient, and they, usually staying at home with their mothers, do not lose it again, whereas the boys commonly going to school, they lose what they learn of a dancing master at home amongst their ill-fashioned schoolfellows, which makes it often less necessary because less useful for the boys to learn to dance at home when little: though if they were always to play at home in good company I should advise it for them too. If the girls are also by nature very bashful, it would be good that they should go also to dance publicly in the dancing schools[5] when little till their sheepishness were cured; but too much of the public schools may not perhaps do well, for of the two, too much shamefacedness better becomes a girl than too much confidence, but having more admired than considered your sex I may perhaps be out in these matters, which you must pardon me.

This is all I can think of at present, wherein the treatment of your girls should be different from that I have proposed for the boys. Only I think the father [ought] to strike very seldom, if at all to chide his daughters. Their governing and correcting, I think, properly belongs to the mother. . . .

---

[4] *Education*, § 7.

[5] In 1691 a friend recommended to Mary Clarke Josias Priest's school for ladies in Chelsea, which had recently staged Henry Purcell's opera *Dido and Aeneas*.

828. Thomas Herbert, Eighth Earl of Pembroke to Locke, London, 20 August [1685]

I have often writt to you with great satisfaction in hopes of an answer, you will easily therfore conclude with how much more I write now since it will be the occasion of injoying your Company here in England: I need not tell you that I have omitted no oppertunety of contradicting all false reports to the King,[1] and (as in so good a cause none can but succeed) I have so satisfied the King that he has assurd me he will never believe any ill reports of you, he bid me write to you to come over, I told him I would then bring you to kiss his hand and he was fully satisfied I should: pray for my sake let me see you before this summer be over, I believe you will not mistrust me I am sure none can the Kings word; you having so many friends least you should mistake who I am I must subscribe my self

Your friend
PEMBROKE.

837. Lady Damaris Masham [née Cudworth] to Locke, [Oates, Essex], 14 November [1685]

I have several times begun to write to You since I received Yours But the Necessitie of Household Affaires[1] will have it so that I could never Yet finish one Letter; what the Fate of This will be I Know not, But I have in my designe set apart this Day to Discharge my self to my Friends of All Obligations of this Kind; In the first Rank of whom I Hope you doubt not but you stand It being Altogether impossible for any thing whatever to incroach upon the Place You have theire, whilst I may Beleeve I have any in Yours, And yet I cannot but Acknowledge that as to some Things Matrimonie and Familie Cares have Alter'd me very much. Though I was Always Dull, I find that I am now a Thousand times more so than formerly; And the little Knowledge that I once had, is now exchangd for Absolute Ignorance; I am taken off of All that I once did Know, and Understand; and Have nothing at All in lieu of it; Tis in Vain that you bid me Preserve my Poetry; Household Affaires are the Opium of the Soul[2] and it is impossible for me to make use of that Preservative unless I can Recover first from this Lethargie that am now in. Which that you may

---

[1] L797. James II was now king; Charles II died in February.

[1] In June Damaris had married Sir Francis Masham. Oates was at High Laver, Essex, 20 mls. north of London.

[2] 'The Soul seeming not to be Thoroughly Awake here [on earth], but as it were Soporated, with the Dull Streams and Opiatick Vapours of this gross Body' (Ralph Cudworth, *True Intellectual System* (1677), 795).

have some Hopes of However, Know that I am at Present All alone in that Place I told you of except the Gentleman you Kno of,[3] a Young Man of 16,[4] a Child of 5,[5] and a Girl between both that speakes not yet a Word of English;[6] For These last you may judge what conversation They are; and for the first the Business of this World Almost wholly imploys him when he is at Home, so that I have very little of His Company. All my Friends and Relations have just left me, and the Badness of the Season Permits not now any Visits from the Neighborhood which However are not very Desireable. These things with the consideration of finding every Thing New About me may perhaps be some excuse for the Present, and afford some Hopes that when some of them are remov'd, and that I am Accustom'd to the rest I may returne to my self againe, which I heartilie wish; since whatever Value I in my last set upon the Accomplishment of being a Countrey Housewife, I owne I slight it as much now; which is however Perhaps but the last Shift of Prudence in me who may be (as Davenant has it) What I would Prize

When I find I can't get, seeme to Dispise.[7]

But I find I am geting into Poetry alreadie before I Have thought of it, I cannot therefore but Hope well of my self Though Certainly nothing but the Aire of Essex would have brought this Poet to my Mind. That, where You are, has had a Much better effect sure upon You, tho I should not have Hop'd for so much from it, since how it comes about otherwise I Know not, but you are methinks of late growne a most Wonderfull Platonist Tho by your leave you greatly mistake in your Accusation of the Platonique you mention,[8] if you think she has any Way Profan'd those Misteries, or Degenerated from theire Principles; Souls are not fetch'd from those Happy Abodes, before they have forfeited Them; Nor clad in Clay, whilst they are Capable of Acting in any better Vehicle.[9] The former, is but the meanes to restore them againe to the latter, and she is so far therefore from being any way guiltie upon that score, that it is indeed the greatest Act of Platonique Charitie that she was Capable of Performing, and The Omission of it so long, the greatest thing she ought to Repent of; But it is not a yeare yet since she writt her Recantation, and Promis'd Amendment, (which I would now send you, since you desire Verse,[10] but that it is too long) and she has so Honestly Kept Her Word since, that I hope she has sufficiently Merrited her Pardon for that Sin of Ignorance.[11]

---

[3] Her new husband.   [4] Probably Henry Masham.

[5] Probably Samuel Masham, later Baron Masham, husband of Abigail Hill, Queen Anne's confidante.

[6] Esther Masham, of whom Locke became especially fond.

[7] Apparently citing Sir William Davenant's play *The Siege of Rhodes* (1656), pt. 2, II. i. 153–4.

[8] Damaris herself.

[9] Alluding to transmigration of souls, perhaps echoing Henry More's *The Immortality of the Soul*, II. xii. 8.

[10] Several times she and Locke wrote poems to each other.

[11] The passage is unclear, but perhaps relates to Locke's hurt and reproaches at her marriage to Masham.

But how shall I do to forgive all your Abuse of me, as well as Her, Since I can neither make any Verses at this Time, nor remember any to the Purpose. But be Assur'd your Punishment is but Defer'd, since if ever that Humour come on me againe You shall Wish for Finis a Thousand times before you find it; I will set the Affronted Countrey Ladies too upon you, and They shall Abuse you Ten times more than I can, for All your Contempt of Theire Sublime Ideas of Goose Pye, and Bag Puding. This would bring me again now to the Chapter of Household Affaires, and my imployments; but that I am awearie; However for All my quarrel with you I cannot help telling you that there is scarse any thing I would not give to see you Here in my Closet where I am now writeing to You; I can but Think how you would smile to see Cowley[12] and my Surfeit Waters[13] Jumbled together; with Dr More[14] and my Gally Potts of Mithridate and Dioscordium;[15] My Receits and Account Books with Antoninus's his Meditations,[16] and Des Cartes Principles;[17] with my Globes, and my Spining Wheel; for just in this order They at presently, and tis not without Reason I think that I designe to Draw Curtains over this Fantastical Furniture. Neither is it so, that I may beleeve you Tyr'd by this Time as well as my self; who you see cannot forbeare writeing long letters where ever I am ...

842. James Tyrrell to Locke, Cam[berwell, Surrey], 20 January [1686]

... I thank you for the account of the bookes you sent me;[1] and if those of Controversy would please you I would send you over the papist misrepresented with the answere, replications, and replye.[2] very well worth the readeing for those who desire a true state of that controversye: I could allso send you some papers lately here published under the name of the late Dutchesse of Y:[3] and those attested by his present Majesty and said to be found in the late Kings box and Closet after their decease conteining their reasons for their leaveing the church of E. and turneing to the R.C.C[4] but these are of too great bulk and weight to be trusted by the Post, and unlesse you desire them and could

---

[12] Abraham Cowley, poet.   [13] Medicinal drink for the cure of indigestion.
[14] Henry More, Cambridge Platonist.
[15] Gallipot: earthenware bowl used by apothecaries. Mithridate: medicine of many ingredients. Dioscordium: possibly dioscoreia: an impure substance.
[16] Marcus Aurelius Antoninus, *Meditations*.   [17] René Descartes, *Principles of Philosophy* (1644).

[1] Unidentified.
[2] John Gother, *A Papist Misrepresented and Represented* (1686), the most prominent defence of Catholicism published in James II's reign; there were many replies.
[3] *Copies of Two Papers Written by the Late King Charles II* (1686), which included a paper by Anne Hyde, Duchess of York, James's first wife.
[4] Church of England; Roman Catholic Church.

direct me to a private hand to send them by are not to be ventured. as for my Lord Ps: life,[5] or the letters: they are now got into Sir R.L.s hands for a License;[6] and when they will be got out againe I know not: if you desire to know how things are like to goe here I recommend his observatour,[7] to your reading: and you will by that see what heresyes in Politicks are most prevalent here. . . .

854. Isabella Duke to Locke, Spa, [Spanish Netherlands], 9/19 July 1686

. . . [I]n obedience to the obliging command you laid on me to give you an account of my Journey,[1] I must tell you that I endured it much better than I could have imagined, for though the Utrecht Chariots[2] made us all weary enough, and is without dispute the worst Carriage in the World, yet I was much better at the end of the Journey, than when I sate out in the morning, and had the Courage to leave Bois le Duc[3] the next day after dinner in a large Brabant Waggon which held us all, and our Baggage, and undertook to bring us into Mastricht the next day in good season; but we suffered many hardships before we got thither, for we were wretchedly lodged the first Night in a German Town call'd Enthoven,[4] whither we came extream late, and could get nothing good or wholsome to eat or drink, beds we had, such as they were, but our Waggoner allowed us but little time in them, but called us up at two a Clock that we might reach Mastricht in good season; but after a hard dayes Journey we were forced to lye upon straw a Mile short of it, the Rogue pretending to be sick stopt at noon two or three hours, so that 'twas nine a Clock before we got thither and then the gates had been shut an hour, that Town being kept very strictly by a Garison of about 8000 men. However we were told that our Inn was the best in all that country, we met with good Milk and Eggs, and a room tolerably clean, Just large enough to hold us, where we lay all together till sun rising, and then got into the Town and went to bed; and tarried several days till we were well recruited;[5] and then came hither in one day in a Brabant Waggon, which is a way of travelling that we are very well pleased with, and I beleive you would have endured very well; but when

---

[5] 'Primate's': Richard Parr, *Life of James Ussher* (1688), primate of Ireland. Parr was vicar of Camberwell, from where this letter was written.

[6] Sir Roger L'Estrange, notorious Tory journalist, censor, and magistrate. Under the Licensing Act, books had to be approved by the censor. One of the letters in the *Life* caused a two-year delay in publication.

[7] *The Observator*, L'Estrange's raucous Tory newspaper (1681–7), which thundered against the seditious doctrines of the Whigs and Dissenters.

[1] Utrecht to 's-Hertogenbosch, 30 mls.; 's-Hertogenbosch to Maastricht (via Eindhoven), 70 mls.; Maastricht to Spa, 30 mls.

[2] Wagons.   [3] 's-Hertogenbosch.   [4] Eindhoven, in fact Dutch.   [5] Refreshed.

any cross accidents occurr'd we drank your health, and rejoyced that you were at your ease in Amsterdam, and that our importunity's had not exposed you to those inconveniencies; though we want your company extreamly; this is the dullest place that ever I came into; I was never so disappointed in my expectations of which it fals infinitely short. 'tis a poor Village that lyes at the foot of 2. or 3. great hills that surround it somewhat like Bath, but 'tis a little contemptible place that bears no proportion to it, where we have no walk, nor conveniencyes of any sort; and very little company. Mr Forester his Lady[6] and Family came this after noon, and I beleave will make a much greater figure then any of the company here, and I beleeve will quickly be weary of the place, as I shall be, unless the waters do wonders for us; but I cannot yet say any thing of their nature, or use, having only tasted them, but had neither time, or opportunity of informing my self concerning them. Mr Duke[7] took 21. of his Pils[8] at Mastricht which wrought about 6. times, he has begun his Waters[9] this day, and is much pleased with them; and confident of good success. . . .

886. Locke to Edward Clarke, [Amsterdam], 21/31 December 1686

You have here at length the [four]th and last book of my scattered thoughts concerning the *Understanding*,[1] and I see now more than ever that I have reason to call them scattered, since never having looked them over all together till since this last part was done, I find the ill effects of writing in patches and at distant times as this whole essay has been. For there are so many repetitions in it, and so many things still misplaced, that though I venture it confused as it is to your friendship, yet I cannot think these papers in a condition to be showed anyone else, till by another review[2] I have reduced them into yet better order. Though bateing[3] that, and the negligence of the style, you will find very little in the argument itself, that I think for the matter of it needs altering. Of what use it may be to any other I cannot tell, but, if I flatter not myself, it has been of great help to [our first enquiry], and the search of knowledge ever since has been in my thoughts, which is now five or six years.[4] For so long ago is it since some friends upon an accidental discourse [started me] upon this enquiry, which I am not sorry for. And if it

---

[6] Probably William Forrester, former Whig MP and conspirator, put in the Tower in 1685, now in exile, and his wife Lady Mary, daughter of the Earl of Salisbury.
[7] Isabella's husband, Richard Duke, former Whig MP.   [8] Presumably purgatives.
[9] Drinking the spa water.

[1] *Essay*, IV, 'Of Knowledge and Opinion'.   [2] Revision.   [3] Excepting.
[4] Probably an error for 'fifteen or sixteen'; Locke began the *Essay* in 1671. Tyrrell tells us that the *Essay* germinated in a discussion among five or six friends about 'the Principles of morality, and reveald Religion'.

has cost me some pains in thinking, it has rewarded me by the light I imagine I have received from it, as well as by the pleasure of discovering certain truths, which to me at least were new. For being resolved to examine *Humane Understanding*, and the ways of our knowledge, not by others' opinions, but by what I could from my own observations collect myself, I have purposely avoided the reading of all books that treated any way of the subject, that so I might have nothing to bias me any way, but might leave my thought free to entertain only what the matter itself suggested to my meditations. So that, if they at any time jump with others, 'twas not that I followed them; and if they differ 'twas not out of contradiction, or a mind to be singular. My aim has been only truth so far as my shortsightedness could reach it, and where I have misstated it in part or in the whole I shall be glad to be set right. Read it, therefore, as a friend's act, judge of it as a stranger's, and let me have your opinion with . . . the greatest freedom . . .

896. Lady Damaris Masham [née Cudworth] to Locke, Oates, Essex, 17 January [1687]

. . . To what Purpose should you know that I am in an Ill Humor (since in short that is the thing which I would tell you) when perhaps before This comes to you I may be Return'd to a good One Or if I be not tis not in your Power to help it? Yet Could I certainlie tell [at] what Moment you received This it would at that verie time I fancie, bring your Idea so livelie into my Mind when you were wont to Chide me out of Vaine troubles that I verylie think it would have almost the same effect as if you your self were Present. But this Cannot be and therefore I must be Content to waite till a Better Temper dos of its self or assisted by some other Happy Accident take Place and Dispell those Clouds of Melancholy that Represent everie thing either as Sad and Displeaseing, or at best Emptie and Insipid; and Onelie serve to Obscure the Light of Reason, and All good Understanding

Were I ever Capable of Philosophizing I beleeve I might find some Solid Argument now against Materialists since I clearlie perceive in my self that a Disturb'd Mind and Disorder'd Body such as will not permit the free Exercise of Reason in Any thing else besides, dos the more Indispose to those Spiritual Speculations which sometimes so well serve to beare up the Mind in such a due decree of Tranquilitie as is necessarie Both to the Injoyment of Life and performing the Duties of it as one ought. But I suspect you might not Allow of This whatever I thought; for that Reason therefore I shall not Attempt it, tho I assure you I am in so Dull and Earthy a Dispensation at This time that I am not Capable of Any Discourse of Reason upon anie subject whatsoever Neither do I now Know whether I express what I would say so as to be Intelligible But you have had this Complaint so often from me that I ought to feare wearying you with it, and I should do so did I not think you would beleeve I would not make it so often were not the very Complaining its self some releife to the Humor that Causes it, and then I cannot doubt but you will have the Charitie to allow of it. . . . I am Certainlie Plac'd in the Wretchedest Neighborhood in the whole World and never had so Violent a Desire in my life as now to good Companie. Tis in Vaine that I think (and therefore Pray say nothing of it) of Suiting my Mind to my Condition, for Business and the Impertinent Concernes of a Mistress of a Familie will never have Anie Place in my Heart, and I can at most do no more than submit to Them. I wish I could do otherwise with All my Heart but tis in Vaine to strive against the streame. You will perhaps Advise me to Converse with the Dead since Here are so few Liveing that are Worth it; I am indeed forc'd to do so more then I have of a long time done before But besides that I do not Naturally Love Reading My Eyes will not permit me to do it very much. The most Comfortable thing that you can say to me that I can Think of, is, still to Assure me you have some Esteeme for me. That Alone would make me think Life not Altogether Insignificant were there yet fewer things Pleasing in it to me than there Is; and Besides it will Continue in me some Value for my self which as Proud as I sometimes seeme I think I do at Others a little Want. . . .

911. Locke to James Tyrrell, [Rotterdam], [14/24 February 1687?]

The New Theory of the Earth[1] I have read in English, and cannot but like the style and way of writing upon thoughts wholly a man's own; but since you desire my opinion, as to the treatise itself, though it be a good while since I read it, and that but cursorily; yet there sticks with me still some of those objections, which rose in my way as I perused it, and which offered themselves against the truth or probability of his hypothesis, which made me not able then to reconcile it either to philosophy,[2] scripture, or itself. In the first part (as I remember) he makes the globe of the earth round, both by its schemes and hypothesis of its formation; and in the second part oval, without giving (as I remember) any reason for it. He makes the circulation of the water[3] to be drawn up by the sun as now, but all the clouds to go and empty themselves at the poles only. How he makes out the physical reason of this motion, I do not well remember, but this I am sure of, by this means there could be no rivers; for all the water that should fall in those parts he designs for it, must needs in that state he puts the world in (the sun being constantly in the

---

[1] Thomas Burnet, *The Theory of the Earth* (1684), which argued that the earth began as a perfect sphere, that at the Flood the surface cracked, releasing inner waters, which created the oceans, and that the fragments of the broken shell formed mountains. Tyrrell passed Locke's letter to Boyle.

[2] Natural philosophy: science.   [3] At the beginning of the world.

equator,) must needs have fallen frozen, and so remained in mountains of snow. But granting water, though without a sea, where lived the whales mentioned in the creation?[4] But that, which seems to be the principle of his design, to make out (*viz.*) the history of the Flood, is that methinks, which he hath least succeeded in: for when this crust of earth broke, what hindered the broken pieces from sinking down into the abyss, and so being quite lost under water? And if the middle of the world, which lay under the sun, was that, which first failed, how comes it, that we find so much of the torrid zone above water? But if we may judge by the Andes (one of the highest and longest tracts of hills in the world) the crack (if there were any) seems to run the other way: but that which seems most incomprehensible of all is, how the water, that is now in the world, and was in his account no more then, could cover the tops of the highest hills, and remain above them so long a time as Moses mentions; for the flashing[5] of it, upon the falling in of the earth, (which is the cause he assigns) will be found (if considered) impossible to raise them[6] so high, much less to continue them there so long. I imagine, if I should trouble you with my fancies, I could give you an hypothesis would explain the deluge without half the difficulties, which seem to me to cumber this; but though I tell you, that I am not convinced of his doctrine, and have here sent you some of those doubts, which I had in reading of him, which is now almost two years ago; yet I must also assure you, that there are some chapters in him, that I cannot enough value, and the book is to be esteemed were it for those only[7]

932. James Tyrrell to Locke, London, 6 May [1687]

... I should be glad to hear you would resolve to print your papers:[1] or at least to communicate them to those you can trust to see how much of them is new; and fit for it: and now you have finisht that discourse I should be glad to hear whether you have done what you intended concerneing the Law of nature:[2] which you have so often promised to reveiw:[3]

[Your] discourse about Liberty of Conscience[4] would not doe amisse now to dispose peoples minds to passe it into a Law whenever the Parliament sits.[5] the thing gives so generall a satisfaction that more are displeased at the manner

---

[4] Genesis 1:21.   [5] Bursting.   [6] The waters.

[7] Tyrrell inferred that Locke meant the chapters on 'the providence of God, and the non-eternity of the world'.

[1] Presumably the *Essay*.

[2] The *Essays on the Law of Nature*, which Locke never published.   [3] Revise.

[4] 'Critical Notes' on Edward Stillingfleet's *Mischief of Separation* (1680) and *The Unreasonableness of Separation* (1681), written with Tyrrell's help in 1681, which Locke never published. Locke had, in 1685–6, drafted his *Letter Concerning Toleration*, which he would publish in 1689.

[5] James II worked hard to secure a pro-toleration parliament, but it never met before his overthrow.

of doeing it than at the thing it self.[6] so that I find few but the high Chur: E:[7] men highly displeased: but let the intent of those that doe it be as it will; I beleive whatever the chur: of England may loose the R.C.R.[8] will not gaine so much as they imagine more being likely to goe off to the Phanaticks[9] than to them, among the ordinary people, who can neither expect offices nor pensions by the change: and if so I think the R.C.R. (as Osborne sayes)[10] will onely change hearb John, for Coloquintida.[11] as for news I have not much to send you, onely to the great satisfaction of many, Judg Withins is put out,[12] and one Sir Rich: Allebone.[13] a R.C. of great integrity and ingenuity (as those say that know him) put in his roome and more such changes are dayly expected. the vicechancellour, of Cambridge[14] was suspended; and deprived this day by the commissioners Ecclesiasticall[15] ab Officio, et beneficio.[16] for refuseing to propose; and admit Father Francis a dominican Fryer[17] to the degree of Master of Arts in that university; the rest of the Doctors who likewise mannaged that affair[18] [or] signed the university plea, are to expect their doom but what that will be wee cannot yet tell. and now I am in talking of Universityes I will give you a short account of the state of Oxon because you have not bin a stranger to it. in Christ church tho there hath bin a R.C. Head allmost this half year:[19] yet I cannot hear of one conversion among the students. the old Hall in Canter: Quaderangle formerly the Bishops Woodhouse is now fiting up for a chappel, for the Deane.[20] yet are there not, (notwithstanding Mr: W:s great endeavours to turne people)[21] above 6 or 7 schollers besides himself who have declared themselves R.C. Mr. W. prints books at his new presse for his Religion, but they have had no very good success for one of them was answered as soon it came out;[22] and the other which is a kind of history of the Reformation has a very slight reception among the learned; being

---

[6] James's Declaration of Indulgence (Apr. 1687) was a prerogative edict suspending the laws which enforced religious uniformity, leaving Catholics and Protestant Dissenters free to worship unmolested. Paradoxically, toleration was the fruit of absolute monarchy; in 1689 it would be achieved by parliamentary statute.

[7] Church of England.   [8] Roman Catholic religion.

[9] Protestant Dissenters. i.e. toleration will benefit the Dissenters more than the Catholics.

[10] Francis Osborne, *Historical Memoirs* (1658).   [11] Change from a neutral taste to a bitter one.

[12] Sir Francis Wythens, a vicious Tory judge, much involved in the state trials of Whig conspirators.

[13] Sir Richard Allibone, judge; educated at Douai College in the Spanish Netherlands, as were many Catholic gentlemen.

[14] Dr John Peachell, Master of Magdalene College.

[15] The king's Commission for Ecclesiastical Affairs, created in 1686 to exercise control over the church and universities.

[16] From office and benefits.   [17] Alban Francis, a Benedictine monk.

[18] i.e. led the university's opposition to the king's command to award a degree to a papist. They included Isaac Newton.

[19] John Massey, a recent convert, Dean of Christ Church since Dec. 1686.

[20] Canterbury Quadrangle is part of Christ Church. Woodhouse: unidentified, but possibly Thomas Wood, master mason, who built the Ashmolean Museum, 1679–83.

[21] Obadiah Walker, Master of University College, Catholic convert. The king authorized him to establish a Catholic printing press in Oxford.

[22] Abraham Woodhead, *Two Discourses Concerning the Eucharist* (1687); answered by William Wake (future Archbishop of Canterbury), *A Discourse of the Holy Eucharist* (1687).

no more then a translation of Sanders and Gretsers storyes which have bin so long since confuted.[23] I doubt not but you have read Dr: B.s letters. which ar a patterne how a man should travell and what observations he should make. the book was forbid to be brought in, but it hath bin since printed here: and sells infinitely.[24] I forgot to tell you that Dr: Cl: the head of Maudlin Coll: in Oxon being dead[25] the King sent downe a mandamus[26] for one Mr: Farmour a new convert: a commoner Master of that house: but the Fellows refused to elect him but have bin so stout as notwithstanding to chuse one Mr: Hough chaplain to the Duke of O. for their President: my Lord Sund: has writ to them from the K. about it.[27] but their answere was that they could not chuse Mr: F. with a safe conscience being under an oath and haveing received the sacrament upon it to chuse none but a fit man, whereas this man was not so being a person of ill fame; and debauched life; and allso not of any of those foundations they are by their statutes to elect their President out of. I wish your cosens[28] affaires would suffer him to come over and see the face of things here for a month or two this summer; tho he returned againe at winter: he would find a strange alteration in mens humours: and need not doubt a favourable reception. . . .

951. Locke to William Charleton, Amsterdam, 2/12 August 1687

. . . I remember that a friend of mine one Mr Charleton[1] had by the use of tobaco in Snuff contracted at Monpelier a continuall head ach: which upon the forbearing of Snuff left him again. whether this at all concernes your present case I beseech you consider, and if fashon has prevaild upon you to doe your self harme, to quit it again. I with the more importunity presse this because I remember it was with great instance and violence I extorted that pleasure from you, which perhaps forgetfullnesse has sufferd you to return to again. I have already spoke to a friend of mine to get for you any raretys that he can light on in the East India fleet which is now here every day expected.

---

[23] Abraham Woodhead, *Church Government* (1687); Nicholas Sander (Saunders), *De Origine ac Progressu Schismatis Anglicani* (1585); Jakob Gretser, SJ, *Exercitationum theologicarum adversos haereticos* (1604). Burnet's *History of the Reformation* (1679) was a riposte to Sander.

[24] Gilbert Burnet, *Some Letters containing an Account of what seemed most Remarkable in Switzerland, Italy, &c* (1686). Addressed to Boyle, they dwelt on popery, tyranny, and persecution.

[25] Dr Henry Clerke.   [26] Royal instruction to make an appointment.

[27] Anthony Farmer (a disreputable Catholic); John Hough, a Protestant Fellow of the College (later Bishop of Oxford); James Butler, Duke of Ormonde (Chancellor of the University); Robert Spencer, Earl of Sunderland (Secretary of State). This defiance led the king to a full assault on the college. L973.

[28] This is Locke himself: Tyrrell is guarding his language.

[1] The recipient, Charleton, complained of severe headaches.

I the last weeke put into the hands of Mr Smith[2] a bookseller liveing at the Princes Armes[3] in Pauls Churchyard 26 Draughts[4] of the inhabitants of severall remote parts of the world espetially the East Indies they are marked thus .2.3.4.5.6.7.8.9.10.11.14.15.16.17.18.19.20.21.22.24.25.26.27.28.29.30. and the names of most of them writ on the backside with my hand, those whose names are not writ if you know them not I will get explaind here. the Brasilian Canibals (of which there are one or two) are easily known, but since there was not the name of the particular nation from which they were taken I would not adde them my self. For the excellency of the drawing I will not answer they being don by my boy[5] who hath faithfully enough represented the originals they were copyed from, soe that one may see the habits and com-plexion of the people which was the main end they were designd for and there-for you must excuse them if they be not excellent peices of painting. I also put into the hands of the said Mr Smith a litle box fild with the seeds and husks of Fœniculum Sinense.[6] the husks have a very fine aromaticall tast and are used by the Muscovites to be mixed with their Thè[7] as I have been told, which is not I imagin the most sotish thing they are guilty of, If you thinke the seeds will grow and you finde to spare I would be glad you would send two or three of them in my name to Jacob Bobert the gardener at the Physik garden in Oxford,[8] who may endeavour to raise plants from them he is a very honest fellow and will not be unwilling to furnish you with any curiositys of that kinde. . . .

973. James Tyrrell to Locke, [Oakley, Buckinghamshire?], 2 November [1687]

. . . I have nothing els worth writeing but a short account how things have gone lately at Maudlin College before the Commissioners,[1] whom the Ki: sent downe to visite that College: viz: the Bishop of Chester, the Lord Ch: Justice wright, and Baron Jenner:[2] when they came they summond the Fellows and President before them, and admonisht the latter to recede from the Goverment of the house; which he refuseing they expelld him;[3] then they asked all the Fellows severally whether they would admit the Bishop of

---

[2] Samuel Smith, a principal importer of foreign books into England.
[3] L268, n. 8.   [4] Drawings. A set in the British Library is apparently these.
[5] Sylvester Brownover, Locke's servant and secretary from 1678 to 1696.
[6] Fennel.   [7] Tea.   [8] Jacob Bobart the younger, professor of botany.

[1] For Ecclesiastical Affairs. The proceedings against Magdalen College for refusing to appoint the king's nominee for President occurred on 25 Oct. L932.
[2] Thomas Cartwright; Sir Robert Wright, Chief Justice of King's Bench; Sir Thomas Jenner, Baron of Exchequer.
[3] John Hough, the Protestant Fellow elected President in defiance of the king; he was restored at the Revolution.

Oxford[4] to be their head, which all of them refuseing except one Papist;[5] they admitted him themselves: by installing one of his chaplains,[6] and giveing him the Oathes by proxy; then they sent to Dr: Hough for the Keys of the Lodgings which he refuseing to deliver they sent for a smith and broke them open. and put the Bishops Proxy in possession; then they sent for all the Fellows againe and asked them whether they would submit to and obey the President which the King had set over them: which Dr: F.[7] (who was the first man asked:) utterly refused saying he neither would, nor could doe it with a safe Conscience; the rest of them signed a paper wherein they promised to submit to the Bishop [in] omnibus licitis, et honestis[8] according to the Stat[utes] of the house; which submission was taken; and they much commended for it: but Dr: F. upon the third admonition still refuseing had his name struck out of the booke [and] was ordered to depart the College within 14 dayes: against which proceedings as null, and unjust he read and gave in a Protestation, as allso Dr: Hough had done before both appealing to the King in his Courts. etc: so there were no more expelld at present for denying their authority than the President, Dr: F. and the under porter:[9] but on Friday morneing upon receiving fresh instructions; the former submission not being looked upon as full enough they were farther requir'd to signe an addresse to the King wherein they were to confesse and beg pardon for their passed contumacy and promise absolute obedience for the time to come: but instead of that when they came together they made a quite other sort of Addresse to the Commissioners where in they first assert that they are not conscious to themselves of haveing acted any thing contrary to their oathes; and the stat[utes] of the house; and therefore hope his Majesty will pardon them if they cannot render any more than a passive obedience[10] to his Majestyes commands. since they cannot looke upon the Bishop as their lawfull head or words to that effect: and desire the Commissioners to represent their case fairly to his Majesty, at which paper (being signed by all the Fellows theire, except 2. viz. Dr: Smyth,[11] and Charnock) they were very much displeased, and adjourned the Court 'till the 20th Instant: when it is to be feared they will come downe againe and proceed very severely against all that signed that paper: this is the summe of what hath bin done hitherto. Dr: F. is very chearfull under it; and many commend his carriage as much more plaine and above board than the rest; who meant the same thing tho they darst not speake it out. what will be the issue God knows but most wee fear a turneing out of most of the Fellows.[12] ...

---

[4] Samuel Parker, one of James's few Protestant Tory collaborators; he was nominated President by the king in place of Anthony Farmer. L932, n. 27.

[5] Robert Charnock, executed in 1696 as a Jacobite conspirator.   [6] William Wickens.

[7] Henry Fairfax, later Dean of Norwich.   [8] 'In all things licit and honest'.

[9] Robert Gardiner, for refusing to surrender the keys to the President's lodge.

[10] The political shibboleth of Tory royalism was 'passive obedience and non-resistance'. But, as is clear here, 'passive obedience' could mean civil disobedience or passive resistance, when kings issued commands contrary to conscience.

[11] Thomas Smith, later a Nonjuror (i.e. a refuser of the oaths to the new monarchs after the Revolution).

[12] The remaining Fellows were soon sacked and replaced by Catholics.

974. Joannes Grævius to Locke, Utrecht,
4/14 November 1687

... [W]hen I got back from Amsterdam last spring I had a talk with some friends about the business you know of.¹ They gave me to understand that a letter from Bentinck,² who is in the Prince's inner counsels, had been brought to the governor of this city, and later another from Dijkveld³ to the burgo-master,⁴ unless I am mistaken, in which they intimated that the person who was then acting as the king's envoy⁵ had complained at the palace in the king's name about you and certain others and had asked to be given power to arrest those whose names he had given and to send them to England. When this information was received here, they said, your friends began to fear that if the matter were pressed you might not eventually be able to escape the clutches of the man who had such designs on your safety in this place. For he had further mentioned the cities in which those whom, as he contended, the king wished to be handed over to him were living in concealment. Our friends, however, who told me of all this considered that we ought to wait for Dijkveld's arrival, so that we might hear his opinion from his own mouth. This was deferred for a month or two; but when at last Dijkveld came to see us again I spoke to him on your behalf, assuring him that any suspicion of offence that the king might have had had long been removed and cleared away through your friends, and that you were fully assured of this on reliable grounds and through trustworthy letters. He answered that he had no doubt that this was how matters stood, but that he thought it would be safest if we waited till Albeville came back,⁶ if he on his return did not renew those complaints or make any new move there could be no further risk and you might take up your abode where you wished. . . .

985. James Tyrrell to Locke, London, 14 December [1687]

... I hope you will come over next summer . . . for as things stand here you need not doubt of a good reception, and to be restored to your place¹ againe if you thinke it worth while to confine your self any more to a collegiat life. wee may expect a Parliament in the spring; and in the meane time they

---

¹ Locke's personal safety.

² Hans Willem Bentinck (later Earl of Portland), William of Orange's closest counsellor.

³ Everard van Weede, heer van Dijkveld, another of William's close aides.

⁴ Chief magistrate or mayor of the city.   ⁵ Bevil Skelton. L797, n. 16.

⁶ Ignatius White, Marquis of Albeville, English ambassador to the Netherlands.

¹ Locke's Studentship of Christ Church.

are new regulateing the Corporations;[2] and those who were turned out for Whigs, are now to be put in againe. your uncle Ad:[3] has bin offred to [be] Alderman; or Major[4] of his citty but hath refused it. if you will see upon what termes a man may be Justice of Peace or Deputy LeiuTenant[5] pray consult the London Gazette[6] of the 12th: Instant. I saw your noble Friend[7] lately who speaks very kindly of you, and I wish you were here whilst his interest lasts, for I fear it will not be long, for he has refused to propose the chuseing of such Members[8] as will take off the penall laws and test:[9] to the Gentlemen of his Countrey.[10] I am glad to hear from him; that you intend speedily to print your discourse, de intell:[11] I should be glad to know whether you will doe it there, or here: I hope either to come over with uncle A. or by my self for I will not stay long for him, and I would be at home againe before Midsummer. I have bin in Towne this month and goe away to day. Mr: B. is well and remembers his service to you: he has lately published a very ingenious treatise of fineall causes. how far to be admitted in Philosophy.[12] if you have a minde to it I will send it you . . .

1040. Lady Damaris Masham [née Cudworth] to Locke, [Oates], 7 April [1688]

. . . You are indeed in the Right to Beleeve That I do not Practice all the Rules of the Neighborhood; And that my Kitchen and Dairie, do not ingross All my Time. But how much you were so, if you Thought me Any Judge of the Essay you sent me[1] when I shall tell you I have made very little Improvment of that Kind, it will be needless to Say; I do not I confess think my self altogether Uncapable of Things of that Nature; And I am sure I have a Universal Love for All usefull Knowledge Beyond that Capacitie; But as I was Diverted from It when I was Young, first by the Commands of Others And Afterwards by that Weakness which Hapned in my Sight, The World through long Acquaintance begun almost to Claime All my Thoughts; And from my many Concerns now in It, Thinks to Justifie that Title; But as it is a True Bondage in my esteeme; and a very Ignoble One too; I assure you it is my Principle

---

[2] The king gerrymandered the personnel of borough corporations, purging Tories and Anglicans, and installing Catholics and Dissenters who were willing to co-operate in electing a parliament that would repeal the Penal Laws and Test Acts (see n. 9). A number of Whigs thrown out in the Tory purges of the early 1680s were now put in to office again.
[3] Dr David Thomas of Salisbury.   [4] Mayor.   [5] The senior county magistrates.
[6] The official government newspaper (and at this time virtually the only newspaper), founded 1665.
[7] The Earl of Pembroke.   [8] Of parliament.
[9] Pembroke was Lord Lieutenant of Wiltshire. The Penal Laws and Test Acts enforced Anglican worship and a monopoly of public office: the king purged those who were opposed to repeal.
[10] County.   [11] The *Essay*.
[12] Robert Boyle, *A Disquisition about the Final Causes of Natural Things* (1688).

[1] The *Abrégé*, a summary in French of the *Essay*.

Care and Business to Free my self from It;[2] But for one so much Ingag'd, and whose Time is so far spent, the Shorter Methods are Certainly the Best: Besides that being my self Cur'd of some sort of Scepticisme by arguments that However Solid in them selves have beene to me effectual, I think that I may much more Advantageously employ my Houres in Pursuing the End of these speculations than in indeavouring to Extricate those Difficulties that the Witts of Men have Intangled them with, Which being Needless to my self, can be no Part of my Obligations; who should not be likely to be in any Capacitie of Dispensing to Others: The Duty Certainly of those that Are. Religion is the Concernment of All Mankind; Philosophy as distinguish'd from It, onely of Those that have a freedome from the Affaires of the World; Which as They would Hinder the latter; May well Manag'd be Great Inforcements of the Former: And indeed the Pleasures of This life are so Triffling and Transitorie, And Its Cares so many and Bitter, That I think one must be very Miserable and Stupid, not to seeke Ones sattisfaction in some thing else; If one beleeves that it is to be found; . . . [Y]ou say It will become me to show you your mistakes: I confess I have a Desire to Know them my self (Because yours) if there be Any; And Accordingly as opportunitie Serves, shall employ better Judgment than my owne to find them out; which if to me unanswerable, You will give me leave I Know to Propose them from a second Hand. For my owne Part though I think of several things Confus'dly that I would say to you if you were in this Closet, I find them not well enough Deliberated to send so far: Though I should be glad more Clearely and fully to understand the Difference betweene you and some friends of Mine,[3] about that Principle thing, of the Souls Haveing no Actual knowledge;[4] Being not sure the Difference betweene You, is Really so great as it Seemes; Since by actual Knowledge They say that they meane not That there is a Number of Ideas flaring and shineing to the Animadversive Facultie like so many Torches; Or That there are Any Figures that are legibly writt there like the Astronomical Characters in an Almanack; But onely an Active Sagacitie in the Soul Whereby something being Hinted to Her she runs out into a More Cleare and large Conception; Her Condition being like that of a Sleeping Musician who dos not so much as Dreame of, Or has any representation of Any thing Musical in Him, till being Wak'd and Desir'd to Sing, Somebody repeating two or three Words of a Song to Him; He Sings it all Presently: And such are the Objects of sense to the Soul; which seemes to me Plainly to have a Facultie in Her above that of Sense Which is that that Judges of, and often Detects Impostures of it; As when the Atomick Philosophers[5] say that Heate and Cold Bitter and Sweet Red and Blew, are

---

[2] Damaris published her first book in 1696: *A Discourse Concerning the Love of God.*

[3] The Cambridge Platonists: what follows draws upon Henry More's *Antidote against Atheism* (1653) and Ralph Cudworth's *True Intellectual System of the Universe* (1678).

[4] Locke denied that there are innate ideas. He wrote that our mind begins as a 'tabula rasa', a blank tablet, prior to sense experience. (The famous phrase 'tabula rasa' occurs in the *Abrégé* but not in the *Essay*; in the latter he refers to 'white paper', II. i. 2.)

[5] Followers of Epicurus and Democritus.

not real Qualities in the Objects, onely our owne Fancies, These being not Intelligible Things: But Magnitude figure site Motion and Rest, into which They resolve them, We have not onely sensible Ideas of Passively impres'd from without, But also Intelligible Notions exerted from the Mind It self. Tho you seeme indeed to make them but the same thing to us; And under the Name of second Qualities to exclude All Account of the first more than that They are so.[6] But I beg your Pardon for this, which I did not intend; not Knowing distinctly enough my owne thoughts to undertake to tell them to Another; Which in a fitter Humour for It than Any I have beene in since I received your Book, are not much Inclin'd now to dwell long on these Matters; Haveing only regard to them so far as they may Weaken, or establish in the Minds of Any the foundations of Natural or Reveal'd Religion; I am not therefore Dissatisfy'd that Men (even those I most Esteeme) differ in these things as well as others Whilst They Agree in Those: And tho (so far as I can Judge) I do Think the Demonstration of a God from His Idea Conclusive,[7] Yet were there no Other but yours,[8] I should think it sufficient. Tho I can scarse think the Idea of Eternitie should be Form'd from That of Time repeated; Since no Succession but must once have beene all of it to Come but one moment; And there is no Imagining (I think) an Eternal Succession. But it is surely from what you say in that last Place, That nothing could ever have Come from Nothing; Or Any thing ever have beene if there once was nothing; From whence, One Cannot but Imagine the Necessarie Existence of Something; which is the same thing with Eternal Duration; which is not Properly, but onely Applicatively Successive; Containing in it Virtually all Successive Duration as the Channel of a River is always Present to the Water that Passes through it; or a Permanent Rock to the River that runs by it. For the 3 last Things about Revelation[9] I fancie I need not say that I am so far of your Mind; And think it Had beene Happy for the Christian World if everie body else had always beene so. . . .

1056. Locke to Lady Elizabeth Guise, Rotterdam, 11/21 June 1688

. . . I see by your Ladyships letter there are men touchy enough to be put into a heat by my litle treatise,[1] which I think has none in it. If they are soe

---

[6] Locke distinguished primary and secondary qualities (*Essay*, II. viii).

[7] The 'ontological argument', or *a priori* argument, for the existence of God as a logically necessary proposition.

[8] Locke denied the validity of the ontological argument and argued the existence of God from the necessity of there being an intelligent First or Uncaused Cause (*Essay*, IV. x).

[9] Locke discussed revelation in the *Essay*, IV. xviii.

[1] The *Abrégé*. She had written: 'I know not how far Emulation or a mistaken Zeal may prevaile over the minds of some, to Cavill with your philosophey: or question your religeon' (L1044).

concerned for truth and religion as becomes sober men, they will answer the end of its publication and shew me the mistakes in it. But if they are of those religious men, who when they can shew noe faults in his book can look into the heart of the author and there see flaws in the religion of him that writ it, though there be noe thing concerning religion in it, only because it is not suited to the systems they were taught I leave them to bethink themselves whether they are his disciples whose command it was Judg not.[2] Such gossiping talkers who supply the want of knowledg with a shew of zeale, and who if censure and tatle were reason and argument would certainly be very infallible I leave to their own good humor and charity, It haveing seldom been observed that any are forward to suspect or question others religion but those who want such a masque to cover some defect in their own. I have soe sincerely proposd truth to my self in all I have writ and doe soe much prefer it to my owne opinion that I shall think my self obleiged to any one who will shew me where I have missed it.

[2] i.e. disciples of Jesus. Matthew 7:1.

7

The Glorious Revolution, 1688–1689

In England the political crisis reached a climax in the summer of 1688. Having refused to read King James's edict of toleration (the Declaration of Indulgence) from their pulpits, the Archbishop of Canterbury and six other bishops were incarcerated in the Tower of London and tried for sedition. Their arrest was a stunning assault on the church and heralded a catastrophe for Protestantism. Furthermore, on 10 June, the way was opened for a continuing Catholic dynasty when the birth of the Prince of Wales diverted the succession from James's Protestant daughter, Mary, and her Dutch consort, William of Orange. James's fortunes, however, suffered a drastic reversal when the Seven Bishops were acquitted on 30 June. Shortly afterwards, Anne Grigg confides to Locke her belief that 'popery is spending itself and will soon expire by its extreme violence' (L1065). Encouraged by a number of leading politicians, William of Orange invaded England on 5 November. Deserted by the political elite, and fearful of assassination, James suffered mental collapse and fled to France. By Christmas William's army had occupied London (L1096). On 13 February 1689 the quasi-parliamentary Convention offered the crown jointly to William and Mary. In England, the Revolution was accomplished bloodlessly, though it would not be so in Ireland or Scotland.

At the invitation of Lord Mordaunt, one of William's officers, Locke agreed to accompany Mordaunt's flirtatious wife, Carey, on the ship bringing Princess Mary to England in February (L1100). Politically astute, Lady Mordaunt judges the effect of the Revolution on England's government as that of 'melting it down and mak[ing] all new', and hopes that Locke will produce a suitable 'scheme of government' (L1099). Before leaving, Locke sent Edward Clarke a letter that is today one of his most closely scrutinized, for it seems to hold a key to understanding what Locke intended when, a few months later, he published his *Two Treatises of Government* (L1102). He calls upon the Convention to debate 'fundamentals' and not 'incidentals', pronounces that the 'original constitution' has been 'invaded', speaks of 'restoring our ancient government', and urges a speedy settlement because France threatens Europe. Within days of his return to England, Locke was offered an ambassadorship, probably to the Elector of Brandenburg. Writing to Lord Mordaunt, he declines the offer, pleading ill-health (L1116). Recommending himself as a political adviser instead, he offers a paean of praise to William as England's 'deliverer' and 'redeemer'.

In truth, Locke wished to protect his time for private study, as he confesses to his friend, Phillip van Limborch, with whom he sustained a correspondence over many years (L1120, L1127). Limborch was a leader of the Arminian movement within the Dutch church, the Remonstrants, who rejected severe Calvinist predestinarianism. Limborch applauds the liberation of England from popery, but fears possible revivals of internecine rivalry among Protestant factions, especially in Scotland (L1101). As parliament began discussing religious toleration in March, Locke informs him of the widespread support for an inclusive, or 'Comprehensive', national church which did not insist upon those practices which were unacceptable to moderate Dissenters (L1120). For his part, Limborch hopes the religious settlement will 'afford to all an example of truly Christian toleration . . . under the two heads of Comprehension and Indulgence' (L1122). However, the Comprehension scheme soon collapsed in the face of Anglican rigidity, and while the Toleration Act allowed freedom of worship to dissenting Protestants outside the established church, the settlement was a blow to those who favoured their readmission to the church. Moreover, the Act continued to deny citizenship rights to non-Anglicans by excluding them from public office. Even though Locke doubted the viability of Comprehension schemes (L1182), he did not conceive of sectarian pluralism as the highest ideal. His *Epistola de Tolerantia* appeared in April 1689, followed later in the year by an English translation, *A Letter Concerning Toleration*. While seeking to conceal his authorship, Locke informs Limborch of the appearance of the new treatise (L1147). Limborch alludes to rumours circulating regarding authorship of the *Epistola*, which was soon available in three languages (L1158).

For many Tories, the Revolution involved a profound agony of conscience. Although they deplored James's Catholicism, they felt obligated by their oaths of allegiance to him. Those who refused to take the new oaths to William and Mary are called Nonjurors. A glimpse of one such troubled conscience occurs in a letter from Benjamin Furly (L1151), who tells of a Tory who had, like so many of their generation, imbibed the absolutist political doctrines of Sir Robert Filmer, whose *Patriarcha* was the target of attack in Locke's *Two Treatises*. Some Nonjurors, and some who took the new oath anyway, conspired to restore the deposed House of Stuart. These were the Jacobites, who sought to destabilize the Revolution regime for decades to come. Locke's future patron, the rising politician John Somers, urges government action to suppress Jacobite agitation (L1186).

If politics, religion, and philosophy bulk large in Locke's correspondence, by contrast he scarcely ever comments up on any art form. He lacked aesthetic sensibility. Apparently he did not attend plays, make music, or admire paintings (aside from their utility to capture likenesses). Poetry was a partial exception and in one letter he discusses classical and biblical prosody (L1069).

1065. Anne Grigg to Locke, [London], 22 June and 8 July [1688]

Tho my head and heart is very full of what now fils all Gazets,[1] I will as well as I can answer your kind caveling letter; The Book you sent me[2] is againe entertaining a Gentleman who has a world of Wit,[3] and who is so pleasd with what you write that I cannot obtaine of him to find the least fault, I have tried others but all are Obstenatly bent to commend it as much as Monsieur Capel,[4] who by the by told me that discoursing with Mr Boyle, the Noble Gentleman[5] complaind only of your being too Abstracted. The Deane of Canterbury[6] says this to me, in truth Mr Locks Book is a mervelous ingenious piece, it has no fault but that its writ in french, and this fault is the reason I send you no larger account of it, divers of my new and very learned friends being deprived of the pleasure of reading it. This lame Answer you must pardon, for till you think fit to make use of your own Country Language, I cannot speak more particularly. . . .

I durst not venture to utter what I every moment deplore and cannot but muz[7] on perpetually, nor am I alone in my raveries, Many hundred Thousands doe as I doe; Nor would you know England were you in it, all that you and I use to call worthy persons are full of affliction, and more inclin'd to vissit you than wish you here, Now are the spirits of the children of men tried, and for my comfort not one of those I did or doe love depart from the paths of righteousness and peace (tho extremly provoked) but such as cald the Bishops papist[8] are drudging slaves to father Peters.[9] . . .

I[10] have not a moments rest but whilst I sleepe so great and continued a Court attends the 7 Champions of whose conduct and diliverence[11] the worthy barer of this[12] will give you a large account, and by him I may without doing you mischief assure you that the very good Bishope of Ely[13] is your true friend speak often of you with great respect, what next is to be don with us I know not hitherto those arts which have bin us'd to root out the Church

---

[1] The Seven Bishops awaited trial for sedition; the Prince of Wales was born on 10 June.

[2] The *Abrégé*.

[3] Perhaps Anne's son William Grigg, an undergraduate at Jesus College, Cambridge.

[4] Jacques-Louis Cappel, theologian, Huguenot refugee.

[5] Noble: the Hon. Robert Boyle was son of the Earl of Cork.

[6] Dr John Tillotson, future Archbishop of Canterbury.

[7] Ponder, ruminate. Grigg now returns to the topic of the crisis of Protestantism.

[8] A gibe against the Dissenters who denounced 'prelacy' as popish: her point is that this was an empty charge since the bishops were now England's bastion against popery.

[9] Fr Edward Petre, a hated Jesuit and privy councillor; one of the king's chief Catholic advisers.

[10] A postscript, dated 8 July.

[11] To the king's dismay, the Seven Bishops were acquitted on 30 June.

[12] Edward, Mary, and Betty Clarke visited Locke in Holland.

[13] Dr Francis Turner, high Tory, one of the Seven Bishops.

and with her the Laws of England have by the goodness of God don much good, having served to demonstrat who are the men that keep innocence and fence us from Popery and Slavery, you need not be told how much business the present contests cut out for ingenious men, nor how all our thoughts are employ'd, dayly new papers come abroade and those of greatest spirit and use are said to be yours,[14] you are in a glorious spot of the world Keep you in it a while longer, I have faith enough to cheer my heart and to fancy strongly that popery is spending itself and will soon expire by its extreme violence ...

1069. Locke to Jean Le Clerc, Rotterdam, 20/30 July [1688]

I know not why you should excuse the slow sending the ninth tome of your Bibliotheque,[1] unless you have made to your self some law I know not of, and which I cannot suppose without a mighty increase of the obligation. Your discourse of the Hebrew Poetry I have red with mighty satisfaction, and am soe far from haveing any thing to say against your hypothesis that it seems to me as clear as any demonstration can be concerning such matters for soe I call such evident probabilitys as ariseing from the things them selves leave noe counterballance on the other side. I know not what cavils prejudice or party may raise against you, for some men who are devoted to a sect and not to Truth are never to be satisfied, and tis noe great matter whether they are or noe. If it were necessary to adde any thing to that full proof you have given of the Hebrew Verses being in *rhime*, I thinke one might say that the other by *measure*[2] is unnaturall and had never been in the world had not the variety of dialects, of the Greeks useing the same language in several distinct communitys, by their various placeing and formeing their words given occasion to it. The Romans who derived their language and learning from the Greeks were almost under a necessity to follow their way of Poetry too, but wanted soe much of the conveniencys of that language to doe it, that it was very late before poetry got any footing amongst them and then it was only Hexameters, which have the greatest latitude except their Dramatique Trimiters etc: which differ litle from prose, For Horace was the first as well as almost the last amongst the Romans that durst venture their tongue at Lyrick poetry. And he too with his great witt and command of expressions, was fain in many places to transgresse the rules of his language and with Gretian liberty use forain ways of speakeing to accomodate his words to the *measures* of the Greek verses he imitated. Besides these two languages I think there cannot be another produced wherein their way of versifying is not in *rhime*. For however you have Quoted the English for writeing verses without rhime,

---

[14] Rumours that Locke was publishing political papers at this time are not recorded elsewhere.

[1] Jean Le Clerc's learned journal, *Bibliothèque universelle* (1686–93).   [2] Metrical verse.

yet I know but one man that has don soe,[3] and he too one much versed in, and addicted to the Greek and Roman politer learning, whose admiration of their poetry put him as I imagin on that way of writeing. Some translations I thinke there may be too in that way of blanck verse, as we call them, but they are litle regarded and scarce thought different from prose. And we see as you your self have observed, that as soon as the Greeke language began to be out of vogue and use amongst the Romans rhimeing poetry came in also in their language, which as I said I think is the most naturall way of verses. Which the Greeks alone (who affected to be Originals in every thing) had the conveniency and boldnesse to transgresse[4] . . . About two months since I was told at Leers's[5] that P. Simons Hist: critique du N.T.[6] was in the presse and that it would be don about this time, but being last week at his shop I saw fower and twenty sheets of it, all that was then printed of threescore which they say it will amount to, soe that according to this reconing we may expect it will be published about fower months hence. . . .

1096. Dr Charles Goodall to Locke, London, 27 December 1688

I know you can be no stranger to the wonderfull successe which God Almighty hath given to the Prince of Orange in his late undertaking to deliver our miserable and distressed kingdoms from popery and slavery, which mercy we in England esteem no lesse then the Isralites deliverance from Ægypt by the hand of Moses, God grant that we and our posterity may live our mercies.[1]

I presume you have heard that the King went privately from Whitehall some few daies before the Prince came to St James's, with a design for France, but was stopped by some Fisher-men, and then return'd againe to whitehall on the Sunday in the Evening, but on the Tuesday (being the day the Prince came to London) he retired to Rochester, and is said to have left the kingdom last Sunday.[2] On Munday being the 24th. of this month, the Lords spiritual and temporal met at Westminster and pass'd the following Order.

---

[3] Milton, *Paradise Lost* (1667).

[4] Locke goes on to speculate on the usefulness, for establishing accurate scriptural texts, of knowing that Hebrew verse must have rhymed, and he encourages Le Clerc to 'goe on in reduceing the Psalmes into their Original rhimes'. More generally, however, Locke thought the pursuit of poetry a waste of time: *Education*, § 174.

[5] Reinier Leers, publisher in Rotterdam.

[6] Père Richard Simon, *Histoire critique . . . du Nouveau Testament* (1689; Eng. trans. 1689). His *Histoire critique du Vieux Testament* (1678; Eng. trans. 1682) was the most shocking contemporary contribution to scriptural hermeneutics; he denied Moses' authorship of the Pentateuch.

[1] William of Orange's invasion army landed in the West Country on 5 Nov.; James II massed his army on Salisbury Plain to do battle, but lost his nerve and withdrew. William entered London in mid-December.

[2] James II fled London on 12 Dec., but was captured by fishermen in Kent; he fled again and reached France on 25 Dec.

We the Lords Spirituall and Temporal assembled in this conjuncture do desire your Highness to take upon you the administration of publique affaires both civil and military and the disposal of the publique revenue for the preservation of our religion, our rights, liberties and properties and of the peace of the nation.

And that your Highness will take into your particular care the present condition of Ireland[3] and endeavour by the most speedie and effectuall means to prevent the dangers threatning that kingdom, all which we make our request to your Highness to undertake and exercise till the meeting of the intended convention[4] the 22th. of January next, in which we doubt not such propper methods will be taken as may conduce to the establishment of these things upon such sure and legal foundations that they may not be in danger of being again subverted.

yesterday the Knights, Citizens and Burgesses which were in town and served in any of the Parliaments that were held during the reign of K.Ch.2.[5] As likewise the Lord Mayor and Court of Aldermen of the City of London and 50 of the Common-Council of the same waited upon the Prince and concurred with the Lords in the foremention'd request.

Sir I hope that this news will encourage you to returne to London as soon as you can settle your affaires in Holland; . . .

1099. Carey Mordaunt, Viscountess Mordaunt, to Locke, The Hague, 21/31 January [1689]

Wher the impresions received from Mr Lock Liabel to tyme or decay: you might with some j'ustice acuse mee: but i fynd you nether kno your selfe: nor merite by suspecting: others should: or when thay doe: fancy them so slight: as to bee worne out in a months styme: no thay will grow and thrife haveing taken deepe route in a soile that is nott sandy though in a wman hart: i fear iff my Lord[1] seeses that expresion[2] he will revock is promis[3] you must give him Leave in his turne to bee jelous sence you wher because y did not wryt to you a Lese raison iff you heard his complants uppone that subject

---

[3] Ireland was in the hands of the Catholic Earl of Tyrconnel; James was to land there in March 1689 and to hold most of Ireland until defeated at the Battle of the Boyne on 1 July 1690.

[4] The Convention was a parliament in all but name: it could not properly be a parliament since there was now no monarch to issue writs of summons. The Convention was charged with establishing a Revolution settlement.

[5] i.e. all the MPs of any parliament that sat between 1660 and 1685. This *ad hoc* body lent authority to the request that William undertake the administration until a formal constitutional settlement was reached.

[1] Her husband, Charles, Viscount Mordaunt, an officer in William's invasion army.

[2] i.e. if he sees what I have just written.

[3] Revoke his promise to let Locke accompany Lady Mordaunt to England.

you will forgive mee and triomfe over a hussband: a common thing in your caise: i have beene very ille this fornight: the begining was: what is called the disease of one contrey: inpasience to bee ther: but ended yesterday with voilence as all great things doe but kings: ouers whent out: Lyke a farding candele:[4] and has given us by this convension[5] an occasion not of amending the goverment: but of melting itt downe and make all new: wich makes mee wish your ther to give them a wryt scame[6] of gorverment: having been infected by that great Man Lord i'asbury:[7] . . .

1100. Locke to Philippus van Limborch, Rotterdam, 26 January / 5 February 1689

This sudden departure of the Princess,[1] which was not expected so soon, upsets all my calculations. It also interferes with what I had resolved upon above all things, and which was a prime necessity for one on whom the greatest kindnesses had been heaped and who was not ungrateful, namely to visit you and my other friends at Amsterdam and say good-bye to you all in person.[2] I was in duty bound to do this much; but what moved me no less was my own keen desire to have the pleasure for a few days of meeting, seeing, and talking to the best of men and my greatest benefactors, and of a mutual embrace at parting. You cannot be unaware what a convenient opportunity this is for me to make the voyage in a light-hearted company among so many ships of war, now that the sea is everywhere infested by pirates. To tell the truth I am not in the least influenced by these things, nor would I be so ungrateful as to let myself be torn away from you by these advantages if I were not pressed against my will by a weightier reason. One of the English notables who set out from here for England with the Prince wrote to me recently asking me to accompany his wife, who is staying at The Hague, on her return home.[3] I readily undertook to do so, as it was my duty and a request not to be refused to the position of him who made it and to the claims of friendship, far less to the deserts of a most illustrious lady. But neither she nor I so much as dreamt of such an early departure. She and I both had in mind to go to

[4] i.e. James's kingship was snuffed out like a small candle.
[5] The Convention (L1096, n. 4).   [6] Right scheme.   [7] Shaftesbury.

[1] William of Orange's consort, Princess Mary, was urgently needed in London. The Convention met on 22 Jan./1 Feb. If the newborn Prince of Wales was disregarded (L3497, n. 2), Mary, as James's daughter, was next heir to the throne. It was not certain that the Whigs would succeed in crowning William. Mary's presence was necessary to placate those who wanted to preserve hereditary right. In the event, a unique joint monarchy of William and Mary was settled upon.
[2] Besides Limborch, Locke's principal friends in Amsterdam were Dr Pieter and Cornelia Guenellon, and Dr Egbertus and Maria Veen.
[3] Lord and Lady Mordaunt. L1099.

Amsterdam this week; but you know what has prevented this; the voyage to England is being unbelievably hurried on.[4] . . .

1101. Philippus van Limborch to Locke, Amsterdam, 27 January / 6 February 1689

. . . I congratulate you and ourselves that English affairs have been restored to a state which permits of your venturing to return thither without apprehension, and to see your own home once more. Truly no sane person can believe that so great and sudden a change in such a mighty kingdom can have come about without the especial direction of God. For my part, I acknowledge in this with gratitude the inexpressible loving-kindness of the Deity, in that he has in his mercy brought about the liberation of England as well as of our own country, under the auspices of the Prince of Orange, from the threat of bondage to the Papacy. May all Englishmen acknowledge this with grateful hearts, and by the exercise of mutual charity between those of differing opinions may they promote the noble enterprise of the Prince; for if Presbyterians and Episcopalians are minded to contend for predominance with the same bitterness as heretofore, what else will they effect but the ruin of this notable beginning? I fear the Scots with their zeal for their factious Covenant.[1] If, however, peace in the Church cannot be achieved amongst such determined adversaries, at least may so much restraint prevail amongst them all that each may willingly grant to another the liberty which he desires for himself, and that force be done to no man's conscience, of whatever persuasion he may be; for liberty is the right of all alike. So at length tempers will grow milder and will perhaps be prepared for closer bonds of peace. I hope that you may soon see this prosperous state of your native land. Since shortness of time does not permit of my bidding you good-bye in person, I will unfold myself to you in a few words. I account it no small part of my happiness that I am numbered among your friends. This betterment of your fortune the law of friendship leads me to feel as in a measure my own also. Therefore although I am not separated from you without sorrow I cannot but acquiesce in your situation, now that after long wanderings you are at last in old age to see your native land once more in peace and security. No length

---

[4] Delayed by bad weather, Locke and the royal party did not sail till 10/20 Feb. and reached England on 12/22 Feb.

[1] The English Presbyterians had abandoned their Civil War militancy and now sought reunion with the episcopalian Church of England. Militancy was more evident among the Scots. The Scottish Claim of Right of 1689 declared episcopacy an 'intolerable grievance': bishops were abolished, episcopalian ministers expelled, and a Presbyterian church established on the lines of the Covenant of 1638.

of time, 'whilst breath of life shall rule this frame',[2] will erase your memory from my heart; . . .

1102. Locke to Edward Clarke, [Rotterdam], 29 January / 8 February 1689

. . . I have seen the Princes letter to the convention,[1] which carys weight and wisdom in it. But men very much wonder here to heare of Committees of Priviledges of Greivances etc[2] as if this were a formall Parliament[3] and were not something of an other nature and had not businesse to doe of greater moment and consequence, sufficiently pointed out to them by the Princes letter. People are astonishd here to see them medle with any small matters and When the setlement of the nation upon the sure grounds of peace and security is put into their hands, which can noe way soe well be don as by restoreing our ancient government, the best possibly that ever was if taken and put togeather all of a peice in its originall constitution. If this has not been invaded men have don very ill to complain. and if it has, men must certainly be soe wise by feeling as to know where the frame has been put out of order or is amisse and for that now they have an oportunity offerd to finde remedys and set up a constitution that may be lasting. for the security of civill rights and the liberty and property of all the subjects of the nation. These are thoughts worthy such a convention as this, which if (as men suspect here) they thinke of them selves as a parlament and put them selves into the slow methods of proceeding usuall there in, and thinke of mending some faults peice meale or any thing lesse than the great frame of the government, they will let slip an oportunity which cannot even from things within last long. But if they consider forain affairs I wonder any of them can sleep, till they see the nation setled in a regular way of acting and puting it self in a posture of defence and support of the common interest of Europe. The spring comes on apace, and if we be, France will not be Idle.[4] And if France should prevaile with the Emperor for an accomodation (which is more than feard) I beseech you consider how much time you have to loose in England.[5] I mention not Ireland because that is in every bodys eye.[6] I writ some time since to J F.[7] suspecting you might

---

[2] Virgil, *Aeneid*, iv. 336.

[1] *His Highness the Prince of Orange his Letter to the Lords*, 22 Jan. It urged that 'no interruption may be given to a happy and lasting settlement', and reminded the Lords of the perilous situation facing Ireland and the Netherlands in the face of popery and France.

[2] The Convention met on 22 Jan.; not until the 28th did it turn to constitutional questions.

[3] L1096, n. 4.

[4] England declared war on France in May. William of Orange's overriding ambition was to use English power against France.

[5] The Austrian (Holy Roman) Emperor allied with England against France.

[6] L1096, n. 3.   [7] John Freke, lawyer, West Country Whig.

be out of town, concerning one point,[8] which if gaind will goe a great way to keep all right, I desired him to communicate it with you if you were not gon into the country. I could tell you severall other considerations I have, which I need not trouble you with who I am sure will thinke of the very same or better. I doe not perceive that you stood to be chosen any where, which when I see you I shall quarrell with you for not a litle, make not the like omission the next Election.[9] . . .

1116. Locke to Charles Mordaunt, Viscount Mordaunt, Whitehall, 21 February 1689

I cannot but in the highest degree be sensible of the great honour his Majestye has don me in those gratious intentions towards me which I have understood from your Lordship:[1] And it is the most touching displeasure I have ever received from that weak and broken constitution of my health which has soe long threatend my life, that it now affords me not a body suitable to my minde in soe desirable an occasion of serveing his Majestie. I make account every English man is bound in conscience and gratitude not to content himself with a bare slothfull and inactive loialty, where his purse his head or his hand may be of any use to this our great deliverer.[2] He has venturd and don too much for us to leave roome for indifferency or backwardnesse in any one who would avoid the reproach and contempt of all mankinde. And if with the great concernes of my Country and all Christendom I may be permitted to mix soe mean a consideration as my owne private thoughts I can truly say that the particular veneration I have for his person carys me beyond an ordinary zeale for his service. Besides this, my Lord, I am not soe ignorant as not to see the great advantages of what is proposd to me. There is honour in it enough to satisfie an ambition greater than mine, and a step to the makeing my fortune, which I could not have expected. These are temptations that would not suffer me easily to decline soe eminent a favour, as the other are obligations to a forward obedience in all things where there is hopes it may not be unusefull. But such is the misfortune of my circumstances, that I cannot accept the honour is designed me without rendring my self utterly unworthy of it. And however tempting it be I cannot answer to my self or the world my imbraceing a trust, which I may be in danger to betray even by my entring upon it. This I shall certainly be guilty of, if I doe not give your Lordship a true account of my

---

[8] Unidentified.

[9] In fact, Clarke stood for Taunton but was defeated; he entered parliament in 1690.

[1] The offer of an ambassadorship, probably to the Elector of Brandenburg.

[2] In the preface to the *Two Treatises* Locke called William 'our great restorer'.

self and what I foresee may be prejudiciall to his Majesties affairs. My Lord the post that is mentioned to me, is at this time if I mistake not one of the busyest and most important in all Europe, and therefor would require not only a man of common sense and good intentions, but one whom experience in the methods of such businesse has fitted with skill and dexterity to deale with not only the reasons of able but the more dangerous artifices of cunning men, that in such stations must be expected and masterd. But my Lord supposeing industry and good will would in time worke a man into some degree of capacity and fitnesse, what will they be able to doe with a body that hath not health and strength enough to comply with them? What shall a man doe in the necessity of application, and variety of attendance on businesse to be followed there, who sometimes after a litle motion has not breath to speake,[3] and cannot borrow an hower or two of watching from the night, without repaying it with a great wast of time the next day? Were this a Conjuncture wherein the affairs of Europe went smooth, or a litle mistake in management would not be soon felt, but that the diligence or change of the minister might timely enough recover it: I should perhaps thinke I might without being unpardonably faulty venture to try my strength, and make an experiment soe much to my advantage. But I have a quite other view of the state of things at present. And the urgency of affairs comes on soe quick, that there was never such need of succesfull diligence and hands capable of dispatch as now. The dilatory methods and slow proceedings, to say noe worse of what I cannot without indignation reflect on in some of my Country men at a season when there is not a moment of time lost without indangering the Protestant and English interest through out Europe, and which have already put things too far back, make me justly dread the thought that my weake constitution should in soe considerable a post any way clog his Majesties affairs. And I thinke it much better that I should be laid by to be forgotten forever than that they should at all suffer by my ambitiously forward undertakeing what my want of health or experience would not let me manage to the best advantage. For I must again tell your Lordship that however unable I might prove there will not in this Crisis be time to call me home and send an other. If I have reason to apprehend the cold air of the Country there is yet an other thing in it as inconsistent with my constitution and that is their warme drinking. I confesse obstinate refusall may breake pretty well through it. But that at best will be but to take more care of my own health than the Kings businesse. Tis noe small matter in such stations to be acceptable to the people one has to doe with in being able to accomodate ones self to their fashons and I imagin whatever I may doe there my self the knowing what others are doeing is at least one half of my businesse. and I know noe such rack in the world to draw out mens thoughts as a well managed Bottle. If therefor it were fit for me to advise in this case I should think it more for the Kings interest

---

[3] A reference to his asthma.

to send a man of equall parts that could drinke his share, than the soberest man in the Kingdom.

I beseech you my Lord to looke on this not as the discourse of a modest or lazy man but of one who has truly considerd himself and above all things wishes well to the designes which his Majestie has soe gloriously began for the redeeming England and with it all Europe. I wish for noe other happynesse in this world but to see it compleated and shall never be spareing of my mite where it may contribute any way to it, which I am confident your Lordship is sufficiently assured of, and therefor I beg leave to tell your Lordship that if there be any thing wherein I may flatter my self I have atteind any degree of capacity to serve his Majestie it is in some litle knowledg I perhaps may have in the constitutions of my country, the temper of my Country men and the divisions and interests amongst. whereby I perswade my self I may be more usefull to him at home, though I cannot but see that such an imployment would be of greater advantage to my self abroad would but my health consent to it. . . .

1120. Locke to Philippus van Limborch, London, 12 March 1689

. . . The truth is that since my return to my native land I have been much occupied: there is the converse with friends who come to see me or whom I must see; or the labour of seeking out my private effects, which are scattered in various places, and collecting them, for present purposes; or, if not some kind of entry upon the service of the state (if I may mention that service without boasting), at any rate my efforts, and justification of those efforts, to make sure that I shall not surrender my private leisure in exchange for public business; and worst of all, there is the bad effect on my health of the malign smoke of this city. All this has kept me so busy that I have hardly been left a moment of free time ever since I landed here. As soon as ever I stepped ashore, amongst the greetings of a crowd of people, I wrote hastily in my own tongue to Mr. Guenellon,[1] asking him to give my best wishes to you and the rest of my Amsterdam friends; for whatever joy and delight I found here told me that something had been left behind there which gave me no less pleasure in recollection than what I saw with my eyes here. Burnet[2] is designated bishop of Salisbury. The question of toleration has now been taken up in parliament[3]

---

[1] Pieter Guenellon, physician at the Amsterdam city hospital.

[2] Gilbert Burnet, who had been in exile, and sailed with William. He was William's principal propagandist.

[3] The Convention was declared a parliament on 23 Feb.

under a twofold title, namely Comprehension and Indulgence.[4] The former signifies extension of the boundaries of the Church, with a view to including greater numbers by the removal of part of the ceremonies. The latter signifies toleration of those who are either unwilling or unable to unite themselves to the Church of England on the terms offered to them. How lax or how strict these provisions are likely to be I hardly yet know; this at least is my impression, that the episcopal clergy are not very favourably inclined to these and other proposals that are now being mooted here; whether this is conducive to their own advantage or to that of the state is for their consideration. . . .

1122. Philippus van Limborch to Locke, Amsterdam, [2/12 April?], 1689

We learnt from your letter to Dr. Guenellon[1] of your safe landing in England, and if I had known how to address my letter to you correctly[2] I would at once have congratulated you on this happy event. For though it may be true that any place on earth is a brave man's fatherland,[3] and though you yourself have learnt by long observation and experience of the caprices of fortune to bear with any lot, yet I think that to attain at last after long wanderings a haven of rest in one's own country and amongst one's own kindred, especially when old age, a thing vexatious in itself, is coming upon one, is not to be counted among the least blessings of this life. Therefore I congratulate you heartily on your happiness, and I pray God that no civil commotions may disturb it, but that the realm of England may enjoy the peace it has longed for; may there be such moderation in its government as may protect all men alike; nor may it ever be accounted an offence in any man that he has stood by the laws of his fathers and has worshipped God according to the dictates of conscience. And indeed, I cannot but assure myself that there is in fact greater moderation in all things when I consider that *you* are entrusted with public affairs; for such I take to be your meaning when you say that you have made some sort of approach to the business of the state; which, it seems to me, is a modest way of signifying that you have been appointed to some political post. For my part, it is not so much you as your country that I congratulate, now that its business is in the hands of a man of such integrity of soul, such experience of worldly affairs, such learning, such wisdom approved by long use and in various emergencies, in fine, such moderation and moral probity

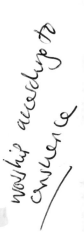

worship according to conscience

---

[4] The bills were introduced on 27 Feb. 'Comprehension' failed, and an act of 'Indulgence' or toleration became law in May. The Act of Toleration ended the 'Penal Laws' against Protestant Dissenting worship, but retained the 'Test Act' which excluded Dissenters from public office (L3161, n. 4).

[1] L1120, n. 1.
[2] Initially Locke lodged with Dr Charles Goodall; he moved to lodgings in Westminster in March.
[3] Ovid, *Fasti*, i. 493.

as we know and admire in you. And it is not only in political affairs but also in ecclesiastical that I hope for the same moderation; that the Church of England, to which the eyes of many churches in other places are directed as to one of distinction, may afford to all an example of truly Christian toleration, which is well represented under the two heads of Comprehension and Indulgence. God grant that, by embracing all who by the rule of the Gospel are manifestly not shut out from Heaven, it may give us the spectacle of a truly Catholic and Christian Church. But, to state the fact, when I consider more carefully the amount of prejudice that is commonly engendered in the minds of churchmen, particularly of prelates and those enjoying power and authority in the Church, by the decrees of the ancient Councils, and by the rash pronouncements of the earliest Doctors of the Church, whom the generality of theologians are wont to venerate, to the great prejudice of the truth, under the august title of Fathers,[4] I fear lest that Church of yours may find itself hedged about too narrowly. Popedom is a natural thing to all men, as Luther used to say in his time.[5] Since therefore it is able to recommend itself so plausibly to the multitude we can hardly expect that happiness in human affairs, that those who have the greater power by their votes should all shed their nature; yet I would not deny that recollection of the past might suggest saner counsels. If, however, Comprehension should prove too narrow, then wider Indulgence might offer a way of providing for the security of all, if those whom their conscience, whether wrongly or rightly informed, does not permit to join themselves to the Great Church were allowed to meet together by themselves without fear of punishment, and so to teach concerning God and so to worship Him as they believe to have been revealed to them in the Gospel. . . .

¶127. Locke to Philippus van Limborch, London, 12 April 1689

Yesterday the inauguration or, as they say, coronation of the king and queen was celebrated with very great splendour amid the acclamations of a vast concourse of people;[1] we believe that on the same day in Scotland they were both solemnly promulgated, or, as we usually say, proclaimed, as respectively king and queen of that kingdom; for it is confirmed by express messages that that throne was some days ago designated and decreed to our William and Mary by the estates of that realm.[2] Burnet is now bishop of Salisbury; he had his place in yesterday's solemnity; he preached before the king and queen, and did so in a manner that won general approval. I have no doubt that the sermon

[4] The Church Fathers, of the 'patristic age', are those of the first four cents. AD.
[5] Source unidentified.

[1] In Westminster Abbey.   [2] On 4 Apr. the Scottish Convention deposed King James.

is being published; I will send you a copy at the first opportunity.[3] . . . As to the establishment of toleration in our country I do not altogether despair, though it is proceeding very slowly, and you are quite right about the disposition of the prelates; still, I have hopes. I saw Burnet today; I told him you were preparing to write him a letter of congratulation as soon as you knew for certain that the bishop's crosier had been bestowed on him, and he was grateful for the information. The Scots are as keen in their aversion to episcopal governance as we are in holding to it, and they have put this first in their list of grievances.[4] All right-minded persons who favour sane and moderate counsels hope for some relaxation in the attitude of extremists on either side. Whether your friend Burnet is likely, as you feel sure, to be of the same mind at Salisbury as he was at Amsterdam[5] is a thing that some people are beginning to doubt; meanwhile let me tell you what happened when he had his first audience of the king after his consecration as bishop. The king noticed that Burnet's hat was wider than usual, and asked him what was the meaning of this enlargement of the brim; the bishop answered that it was the shape proper to his order; on which the king remarked 'I hope your hat will not work a change in your head'. . . . I see you are all very eager to know just what public post I have been appointed to; I can answer in a word, to none.[6] I have used my health as an excuse for avoiding an office which is honourable enough, and which I should undoubtedly seek if I were in the prime of life and in the enjoyment of my full powers;[7] as it is, my only concern now is for peace and quiet for myself and my country; one who is breaking up and putting his affairs in order should not rashly launch out into the open sea. I confess I am in somewhat better health now; my breathing is freer . . . Although I am not undertaking any public duties, yet public affairs and the private concerns of friends somehow keep me so busy that I am entirely torn away from books; at the moment a big auction sale of quite good books is being held here but I have not time even to go and see it; I hope that my old and longed-for leisure will soon be restored to me, so that I may return to the commonwealth of learning . . .

1147. Locke to Philippus van Limborch, London, 6 June 1689

No doubt you will have heard before this that Toleration has now at last been established by law in our country.[1] Not perhaps so wide in scope as might be wished for by you and those like you who are true Christians and free from

[3] Gilbert Burnet, *A Sermon Preached at the Coronation*; trans. into Dutch, French, and German.
[4] L1101, n. 1. [5] Burnet was in exile 1684–8.
[6] In May Locke accepted the minor office of Commissioner of Excise Appeals. [7] L1116.

[1] William gave the royal assent to the Act of Toleration on 24 May.

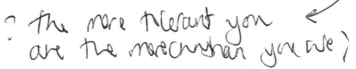

? the more tolerant you
are the more Christian you are?

ambition or envy. Still, it is something to have progressed so far. I hope that with these beginnings the foundations have been laid of that liberty and peace in which the church of Christ is one day to be established. None is entirely debarred from his own form of worship or made liable to penalties except the Romans, provided only that he is willing to take the oath of allegiance[2] and to renounce transubstantiation[3] and certain dogmas of the Roman church. In the case of the Quakers the oath has been dispensed with;[4] nor would the confession of faith which you will see mentioned in the law have been thrust upon them—a bad precedent—if certain of their number had not offered this confession,[5] an unwise step that is much regretted by many of the more judicious among them.

Thank you for the copies you sent me of the treatise on toleration and peace in the Church;[6] I duly received the bound ones, but the unbound have not yet reached me. I understand that some Englishman is just now at work on translating the pamphlet on Toleration.[7] I could wish that that opinion, which is calculated to foster peace and righteousness, might everywhere prevail. I am glad that the Acts of the Inquisition are now almost transcribed and I hope they will shortly appear; a useful and much-desired work.[8] . . .

1151. Benjamin Furly to Locke, Mortlake, Surrey, 10 June 1689

. . . I met with a scrupulous Cambridge schollar, that thought nothing, 'could discharge him of the oath of Allegiance that he had take to Ja: 2.[1] and his successors'. I had pleasant sport with him upon Sir R: Filmers maggot,[2] which he soon quitted, because he saw he could not make it bear to his purpose. And tho he were at every turn reduced ad non loqui,[3] he had the wit to hold fast the conclusion. Last night after our meeting was ended, I met with the

---

[2] The oath of allegiance, instituted after the Gunpowder Plot of 1605, required the king's subjects to renounce the pope's supremacy.

[3] The Catholic doctrine that the eucharistic elements of bread and wine are changed into the body and blood of Christ during the Mass, regarded by Protestants as idolatrous.

[4] Quakers refused to take formal oaths, because a person's mere word should be their bond. 'Let your yea be yea, and your nay, nay' (James 5:12).

[5] Amid allegations of their not being Christians, the Quakers feared being excluded from the Toleration Act, so they succumbed to accepting a creedal formula.

[6] Locke's own *Epistola de Tolerantia*, published alongside Samuel Strimesius's *Dissertatio Theologica de Pace Ecclesiastica* (*Dissertation on the Peace of the Church*) (1688).

[7] The translation of the *Epistola* (*A Letter Concerning Toleration*) by the Unitarian merchant William Popple was published in October.

[8] The 14th-cent. Inquisition of Toulouse, published in Limborch's *Historia Inquisitionis* (1692).

[1] King James II.

[2] Sir Robert Filmer, *Patriarcha, or the Natural Power of Kings* (written before the Civil War but publ. 1680); modern edn., ed. Johann Sommerville (1991). Maggot: whimsical notion.

[3] To silence.

like scruple in one of our folk,[4] who, when I thought I had fully convinc'd him, gravely told me I had more experience of these things than he, and had said much which he could not answer. But that I had not satisfyed his reason. I told him I could not help that at present there being no more time, but might perhaps another time. In the meanwhile I see not, that university learneing, nor inspiration,[5] does make all that pretend to it wise, or give them Common Sense. . . .

1158. Philippus van Limborch to Locke, Amsterdam, 8/18 July 1689

I am glad that toleration has gained a firm position in your country. The example of the Church of England is of great weight with the other Reformed churches, especially now that the Prince of Orange is on the throne, who they feel sure is by no means ill disposed towards the Presbyterians; they augur from this that he will use his royal authority to temper the excessive zeal of each of the parties. And, to be sure, it cannot be denied that if either of them were allowed to have its way it would probably tell the other to betake itself to some other part of the world. Accordingly if one alone is to enjoy the protection of king and parliament it will easily become strong enough to crush the other by its own power; the best rule is that all alike, in so far as they are all good citizens, should be allowed the rights of citizenship in equal measure, and that no one, so long as he does not offend against the laws of the state, should be denied what belongs to all alike by the law of nature.[1] If toleration should happen to be confined within narrower bounds, I hope that when England has had some taste of the prince's agreeable and equitable nature we may at last see the emergence of complete toleration, by which no man's conscience may be forced even in the smallest degree. The action of certain Quakers, as you justly remark, is ill advised; but perhaps they feared that unless they made that confession they might be excluded from the general benefit of protection;[2] it is now plain that superfluous precautions are sometimes harmful. I am glad that the treatise on Toleration is being translated into English.[3] Here it has been done into French by Mr. de Cene,[4] and I believe will soon be published; it has also been translated into Dutch, so that people will now

---

[4] Furly was a Quaker; Quakers called their religious assemblies 'meetings'; many Quakers, notably William Penn, had supported King James because of his tolerationist policy.

[5] Scholarly Anglicanism contrasted with mystical Quakerism.

[1] Protestant nonconformist worship was now legal, but under the Test Act (1673), Catholics and Dissenters remained excluded from public office.

[2] L1147, nn. 4, 5.   [3] L1147, n. 7.

[4] Charles Le Cène, refugee Huguenot minister. However, no independent French edition appeared until Voltaire's in 1764. A translation did appear in Locke, *Œuvres diverses* (1710).

soon be able to read it in four languages. I hope that the reading of it will not fail to bear fruit; and what pleases me especially is its translation into French, a tongue which is now generally familiar to all, even to great men and princes. People here believe that it was written by some Remonstrant,[5] because the positions which it defends agree with Remonstrant tenets. They do not, however, know anyone amongst the Remonstrants to whom they can attribute it. Others therefore suppose that, although the writer may not be living in Remonstrant circles, he is nevertheless imbued with Remonstrant teaching. For my part I congratulate myself that so scholarly a book, and one of such service to the common cause of Christianity, should be thought incapable of proceeding from anywhere else than the Remonstrant workshop. They have tried to find out from the printer the source from which he received it; but he says that he knows nothing about it: the pamphlet was sent him enclosed with a letter bearing no name or date. . . .

1182. Locke to Philippus van Limborch, London, 10 September 1689

The settlement of a certain measure of indulgence among us does not yet, however, result in a complete settlement of the differences between minds and parties, though with the granting of liberty those who differ from each other have been conducting themselves much more peaceably and moderately than I had expected. In the matter of comprehension there is already something on the anvil; the intention is that it should be submitted to the next session of parliament, which I believe will be soon.[1] What this measure is likely to effect, should it come into force, is not yet clear to me, nor can I feel any hope that ecclesiastical peace will be established in that way. Men will always differ on religious questions and rival parties will continue to quarrel and wage war on each other unless the establishment of equal liberty for all provides a bond of mutual charity by which all may be brought together into one body. Schomberg's campaign in Ireland is going forward well enough, and if God wills there can be little doubt of its success.[2] In the commonwealth of learning there is little or nothing going on, as everyone's attention is directed to politics. I desire to hear what the press is producing with you of any importance, but more to know how you and yours are. Here we expect the earl of

---

[5] The Arminian, anti-Calvinist, latitudinarian party in the Dutch church. The *Histoire des ouvrages* attributed the *Epistola* to the Dutch Remonstrant Jacques Bernard.

[1] Latitudinarian churchmen devised a scheme for Comprehension, but it was scotched by High Churchmen. For several years new Comprehension schemes were occasionally mooted, but they never succeeded. The Dissenters remained permanently separated from the Church of England.

[2] Marshall Frederick Schomberg commanded the campaign to defeat James II's regime in Ireland. L1096, n. 3.

Pembroke's return daily.[3] If this letter should reach you in time to permit of your buying a whole or half-pound of the best tea and sending it to Furly's servant at Rotterdam before the earl's departure, please do so. The box should be addressed to me, and Furly's servant should be told to take particular care to entrust it to Mr. Barker, the earl's secretary.[4] I should like the best tea, even if it should cost forty gulden[5] a pound. The only thing is to be quick about it, so that it may be brought into this country under the ambassador's protection, as I doubt if this would otherwise be permitted. I know you are a most experienced buyer of this herb, just as you have been its most eloquent panegyrist. . . .

1186. John Somers to Locke, Worcester, 25 September [1689]

. . . The Country, generaly speaking, is extremely well disposed in relation to the Government, but some few Clergymen who have not taken the Oaths[1] and some that have, and a very little party of such as pay them a blind obedience, use incredible diligence, by misconstructions of every thing, false stories, and spreading of libells to infect the people.[2] I wish heartily the freinds of the Government were encouragd to use the same diligence in supressing such doings, for tho they behave themselves with much malice, yet it is so very foolishly, that they ly as open as one could wish. I am making all possible hast to Town, and hope to learn from you all that I want by my long absence. Your former favours make mee bold to presume upon you, and your Judgement is such that I can depend upon your Instructions as the Rules for my behaviour.

[3] He was ambassador to the Netherlands.
[4] William Barker, later one of the first clerks of the Board of Trade.
[5] Gulden: guilders (Dutch currency).

[1] The Nonjurors, who refused the oath of allegiance to William and Mary.
[2] The Jacobites exploited growing complaints against heavy taxation, Dutch military occupation, King William's high-handedness, and mismanagement of war in France and Ireland.

8

Government and the Law of Nature, 1690–1692

Within a year of the Revolution, the three works on which Locke's subsequent fame chiefly rested were published: the *Essay Concerning Human Understanding* (which he dedicated to the Earl of Pembroke), the *Two Treatises of Government*, and the *Letter Concerning Toleration*. He put his name to the first, but he did not admit authorship of the *Two Treatises* or the *Letter* until shortly before his death.

From Oxford, James Tyrrell relays rumours regarding the authorship of these works, only to be rebuked by Locke for spreading gossip (L1312). Tyrrell's letters reveal the immediate impact of Locke's *Essay*, particularly among clerical conservatives who were worried that Locke's critique of innate ideas dissolved the law of nature by reducing morality to the customs and conventions of particular societies. Although Locke's later critics were to focus upon the doubtful Trinitarianism of the *Essay*, initial reactions concentrated upon the problem of how to sustain the moral law without a firm apprehension of divine rewards and punishments (L1266, L1301). The *Essay* certainly said very little about grounding the law of nature in God's scheme, revealed in scripture, and, as suspicions of 'Hobbism' began to appear, Tyrrell urges Locke to return to his former study of natural law (L1307). Defending himself from charges of moral scepticism, Locke insists on the need to distinguish between those aspects of the moral law which are discernible by the 'light of nature' and those ascertainable from divine revelation (L1309). Locke asserts that his purpose in writing the *Essay* was not to discuss the scriptural supports for the universal law of nature. Two years later, however, Tyrrell is still concerned about the need to defend natural law from sceptics and Epicureans (L1307).

More formal, printed reaction to Locke's writings soon appeared. The Quaker merchant Benjamin Furly was among those who kept Locke informed about tracts which challenged his views. Writing from Rotterdam, Furly not only reports an attack on the *Letter Concerning Toleration*, but also furnishes him with a summary of John Norris's Neoplatonist defence of innate ideas (L1325).

From 1691 onwards, Locke resided with Damaris Masham and her husband, Sir Francis, at Oates in Essex. Although he continued to lodge frequently in London, by 1692 he was sufficiently settled at Oates to collect together cherished books and possessions which had been dispersed into safe keeping when he went into exile (L1522). Edward Clarke's wayward son visited him at Oates and Locke advises the parents on his education (L1313, L1471). Clarke senior became an MP in 1690 and thereafter acted as Locke's voice in the House of Commons. After the Revolution, parliament sat every year, and Locke implies recognition of the emergence of a class of semi-professional politicians to whom affairs of state should be entrusted (L1326). Locke's own role increasingly became that of a political consultant. He advised a group of politicians who, from 1694, called themselves 'the College', and whose key members were Clarke, John Freke, and John Somers. Through them, Locke became involved in the ending of press censorship, and in fiscal and monetary reform. When parliamentary moves were afoot to reduce interest rates, Locke published *Some Considerations of the Consequences of the Lowering of Interest* in 1691 (L1439). Although he was aware that a reduction in interest was supported by capital-hungry merchants and indebted gentry, Locke argued that its effect would be to depress the economy by discouraging investors and reducing the amount of money available for borrowing. His main claim, however, was that statutory controls should not be used to interfere with the 'natural', or market, rate of interest. As a letter from Clarke illustrates, many of the arguments used in the House of Commons were indebted to ideas contained in Locke's tract (L1455). Locke's tract also had much to say on a wider economic front, about trade and taxation.

Locke's extant correspondence with Isaac Newton dates from 1690. In one letter included here, Newton provides Locke with an account of his experiment to investigate the relationship, in sense experience, between retinal shadows and the imagination (L1405). In another, Newton expresses doubts about an experimental method which Robert Boyle had claimed offered a successful formula for turning base metal into gold (L1519). Such discussions provide evidence of Newton's preoccupation with subjects such as alchemy and the apocalypse, which modern scholars have gradually come to terms with, though such topics have seemed antithetical to the proper concerns of the creator of modern physics.

Locke continued to receive supplications for advice on matters such as health and education. Fearing that she had contracted scrofula—the 'King's Evil'—Elizabeth Yonge asks him for medical advice (L1334). On another occasion, Locke advises Lord Mordaunt, now Earl of Monmouth, on his son's education, stressing good character and manners above bookish scholarship (L1252). To Mordaunt's wife, Carey, Locke sends an appeasing letter in response to her charge that he had not been paying her sufficient attention (L1397). To Benjamin Furly he sends consolation on the death of his wife (L1386). These are letters which evince Locke's epistolary suppleness.

1252. Locke to Charles Mordaunt, Earl of Monmouth, [London?], [February–March 1690?]

I must beg leave to own that I differ a little from your Lordship in what you propose;[1] your Lordship would have a thorough scholar, and I think it not much matter whether he be any great scholar or no; if he but understand Latin well, and have a general scheme of the sciences, I think that enough: but I would have him well-bred, well-tempered; a man that having been conversant with the world and amongst men, would have great application in observing the humour and genius of my Lord your son; and omit nothing that might help to form his mind, and dispose him to virtue, knowledge, and industry. This I look upon as the great business of a tutor;[2] this is putting life into his pupil, which when he has got, masters of all kinds are easily to be had; for when a young gentleman has got a relish of knowledge, the love and credit of doing well spurs him on; he will with or without teachers, make great advances in whatever he has a mind to. Mr. Newton[3] learned his mathematics only of himself; and another friend of mine, Greek (wherein he is very well skilled) without a master; though both these studies seem more to require the help of a tutor than almost any other.

1266. James Tyrrell to Locke, Oxford, 18 March [1690]

. . . I will let you know what, the good nature of some people of this place, have invented to disparage your booke:[1] a Freind told me the other day that he had it from one who pretends to be a great Judge of bookes: that you had taken all that was good in it; from[2] divers moderne French Authours. not only as to the notions but the manner of connexion of them; my answer againe was. that as long as I enjoyd your conversation in England: which was when the maine body of the booke was written:[3] to my knowledg you utterly refused to reade any bookes upon that subject: that you might not take any other mens notions: and that you have taken another course since that time I did not beleive: therefore that if you have fallen upon the notions of others, it was by a necessary traine of thoughts: since truth being but one thing hath commonly but one way to prove it: if you have any better defence than this

---

[1] For the education of Monmouth's son, John Mordaunt, aged about 9. He was later an MP and soldier, wounded at the Battle of Blenheim.
[2] Locke advocated household tutors rather than sending children to school. *Education*, §§ 88 ff.
[3] The earliest definite evidence of Locke's acquaintance with Isaac Newton dates from this time.

[1] The *Essay*. It was published in Dec. 1689.   [2] 'Descartes' is deleted in the manuscript.
[3] Perhaps referring to Locke's extended sojourns with Tyrrell at Oakley in 1681–2.

to make; pray let me know it; and I will make it for you; if you thinke it worth while: I pray likewise tell me what I shall say to those that make you here, the Authour of three new Treatises: the first a Treatise of Goverment. (which I writ to you about in my first)[4] the second of Toleration. (a pamphlet) and the third lesse than that of humane reason in Religion:[5] which they will need[s] have to be yours or els one of your disciples for the notions a[re] the same at the end. . . .

1301. James Tyrrell to Locke, Oakley, Buckinghamshire, 30 June [1690]

. . . [S]ince I came into the Countrey I have began again to read over your excellent Essay; with great satisfaction; and discourseing with some thinkeing men at Oxford,[1] not long since; I found them dissatisfyed with what you have sayed concerning the Law of nature, (or reason,) whereby wee distinguish moral good, from evil and vertue, from vice. for tho' I confesse in your third chap: p. 21.[2] you thinke they equally forsake the truth, who runing into the contrary extremes, either affirme an innate Law; or deny that there is a Law knowable by the light of nature; i.e. without the help of positive revelation. yet they thinke you have in your second Chap: p. 158. 159. 160.[3] destroyed this reasonable concession, and resolved all vertue and vice, and the Law by which it is establisht, out of a commonwealth, and abstracted from divine Revelation; into the praise, or dispraise that men give to certaine actions in several clubs or societyes, by which hypothesis. if Drunkennesse, and sodomy, and cruelty to Enemyes (for example) (which are not vices directly contrary to the peace of civil society) should be in any Countrey (as I thinke I can shew some examples of that kind: out of the Spanish and other relations of America)[4] thought praise worthy; and that those that could drinke

---

[4] L1225 (19 Dec. 1689): 'Here is lately come downe from London, a very solid, and rational treatise call'd of Government: in which Sir R. Filmers Principles are very well confuted: and since . . . some people doe me the favour to make me the authour of it I pray aske your Friend Mr. Churchill who prints it who is the Authour of it if it be not a secret; . . . I find he [the author] speakes of the authour of Patriarcha non Monarcha: with more respect than he deserves.' Locke praised Tyrrell's *Patriarcha non Monarcha* (1681) in *Two Treatises*, I, § 124. These two books, together with Algernon Sidney's *Discourses Concerning Government* were the three major assaults on Filmer.

[5] [William Popple], *A Discourse of Humane Reason* (1690), which urged that 'Liberty of Conscience, therefore, Universal, Impartial, Inviolable, is the true interest and great duty of Governor and People'.

[1] Unidentified. Early Oxford critics of the *Essay* include Thomas Creech (who preached a sermon against the Hobbesian ethics of the *Two Treatises* in 1695), and Sir George Mackenzie of Rosehaugh, known as 'Bloody Mackenzie' for his treatment of the Scottish Covenanters, now self-exiled in Oxford, who drafted a critique of the 'Hobbism' of the *Essay*.

[2] *Essay*, I. iii. 13.   [3] *Essay*, II. xxvii. 10–12 in the 1st edn.; latterly II. xxviii. 10–12.

[4] Perhaps the accounts by José de Acosta and Garcilaso de la Vega cited by Locke in *Two Treatises*, I, §§ 57, 153; II, §§ 14, 102.

most; or enjoy most boys and be most cruel (not only) should be counted the gallantest, and most vertuous, but allso be so indeed: and so would really become subjects of that which you call the philosophical Law of vertue, since it had all that you suppose was requisite thereunto, viz: the tacite and general consent of that whole nation where such wicked customes are establisht: and this you farther confirme by these words, p. 160. These three then, first the Law of God. secondly the Law of politick societyes. thirdly the Law of fashion, or private censure, are those to which men variously compare their actions:[5] which seems to come very near what is so much cryed out upon in Mr: Hobs; when he asserts that in the state of nature and out of a commonwealth, there is no moral good or evil: vertue, or vice but in respect of those persons, that practice i[t o]r thinke it so.[6] if you please to tell me what I shall say to those that [ma]ke this objection you will doe your self right . . .

1307. James Tyrrell to Locke, Oakley, Buckinghamshire, 27 July [1690]

. . . I am sorry any thing I sayed in my last should make you beleive[1] the conclusions which some had drawne from that passage in your booke should proceed from my self, for I did intend no more than to give you an account not of my owne but other mens censures: and therefore desired your meaneing of that place;[2] that I may know how to answere them, or any others upon occasion: Tho I must tell you as for the passage you quote in your vindication,[3] I tooke notice of it to them, when wee discoursed about it, but their answere was, that by a divine, Law, and a Law given by God to Mankind, and likewise a Law, whose only enforcements where the rewards, and punishments, of another life, you could meane no other than the divine, or reveald, Law given by Moses, and Reinforced by Jesus Christ with higher, rewards and greater punishments in the world to come, than were expressely promised, or denounced either by the Law of nature or that of Moses: I must confesse I could not tell positively what replye to make; because you doe not expressely tell us, where to find, this Law, unlesse in the SS.[4] and since it is likewise much doubted by some whether the Rewards and punishments you mention can be demonstrated as established by your divine Law, which I am satisfyed is the same with that which others call the Law of nature. tho I must freely tell you that you your self have bin in great part the occasion of this mistake;

---

[5] *Essay*, II. xxvii. 13 in the 1st edn.; latterly, II. xxviii. 13.   [6] Hobbes, *Leviathan*, ch. 15.

[1] Locke's response to L1301 is not extant.   [2] Passage. L1301, n. 3.
[3] *Essay*, II. xxvii. 7–8 in the 1st edn.; latterly II. xxviii. 7–8. In the 1st edn. Locke wrote: 'that God has given a Law to Mankind, I think there is nobody so brutish as to deny'.
[4] Scriptures.

since you there take no notice at all of Gods reveald will, or Law, given in the SS: which certainly were not intended only to discover Gospel mysteryes, but cheifly as a Rule whereby men might more plainly and easily know their duty towards God, and their neighbours, and Judge of the moral good and evil of their actions, than they could by the Law of nature or meer reason alone;[5] so that if some have mistooke your meaneing it was not out of ill will, but because you did not more clearly expresse what you meant by a divine Law: since it had bin easy for you to have added, in a Parenthesis, *which others call the Law of nature,*[6] or els to have allso expressely mentiond the reveald Law of God: as distinct from that, to have taken away all ambiguity; and so I should have advised you to have worded it, if I had had the honour of haveing it communicated to me before it had bin made publick. for in those notes you left in my hand, there is nothing sayed of these three Laws.[7] But now I am satisfyed of your meaneing I fully agree with you in your definition both of moral good, and evil, as allso of this divine, or natural Law; since did it not proceed from God as a Lawgiver I am satisfyed it could not properly be called a Law; and the not takeing God into this Hypothesis has bin the great reason of Mr: Hobs mistake that the Laws of nature are not properly Laws nor doe oblige mankind to their observation when out of a civil state, or commonwealth. but I conceive men for the most part lye under sufficient obligations to observe the Laws of nature from those natural rewards to Duty, and punishments for sin, which God hath by the natures of the things themselves appointed in this life; and where those fall short, that God will make it up in the life to come, as Dr: Cumberland hath very fully proved in his booke of the Laws of nature against Mr: Hobs.[8] and Dr: Parker as to the necessity of a future state hath more fully made out in his Demonstration of the Law of nature according to Mr: Cum: Principles.[9] and I could wish you would publish your owne thoughts upon this excellent; and material subject; since I know you have made long since a Treatise or Lectures upon the Law of nature which I could wish you would revise, and make publick, since I know none more able, than your self to doe it. and which would likewise make a second part to the former worke: and I have heard you say more than once that you intended it:[10] I have no more but if you doe not like that I should tell you what objections the world make against what you write I shall for the future be more reserved; . . .

---

[5] Arguably Locke took up this criticism in *The Reasonableness of Christianity* (1696), which suggests greater reliance on revelation.

[6] L1309, n. 5.   [7] Locke left a draft of the *Essay* with Tyrrell in 1683.

[8] Richard Cumberland, *De Legibus Naturae Disquisitio Philosophica* (1672), abridged by Tyrrell in *A Brief Disquisition of the Law of Nature* (1692).

[9] Samuel Parker, *A Demonstration of the Divine Authority of the Laws of Nature* (1681).

[10] L106, L932. Tyrrell's *Brief Disquisition* drew upon Locke's unpublished *Essays on the Law of Nature*.

1309. Locke to James Tyrrell, Oates, 4 August 1690

I see you or your freinds[1] are so far from understanding me yet rightly that I shall give you the trouble of a few lines to make my meaning clearer, if possible, than it is, though I am apt to thinke that to any unprejudiced Reader, who will consider what I there ought to say, and not what he will phansy I should say besides my purpose, it is as plain as any thing can well be—L.1. c 3. §. 13, where it was proper for me to speake my opinion of the Law of nature, I affirme in as direct words as can ordinarily be made use of to Expresse ones thoughts that there is a Law of Nature Knowable by the light of nature—Booke 2d: c.27. §. 7 and 8.,[2] where I have occasion to speake indefinetly of the divine law, 'tis objected I could meane none other But the divine revealed law, Exclusive of the law of nature and that for two reason. The first is because I call it a law given by God to mankinde—The law of nature then, in these mens opinions, had not God for its author, for if it had, he gave it to mankinde, and if he did I thinke it is no derogation to it to say he gave it to mankinde—I fear some body on the other side will from this very sentence argue that I could not meane the Mosaical or Evangelical law of God— I am sure they may with more reason, For neither of those, as I take it, was given to mankinde, which is a terme which in my sense includes all men. Tis plain the Mosaical laws was not given to mankinde, for it was 'Hear Ô Israel' and I never met yet with any one that said the laws of Moses was the laws of mankinde. And as for the revealed will of God in the New testament, which was a revelation made to the children of men 2000 Years after Moses law, and 4000 years after the Creation,[3] how that can be cald a law given to mankinde is hard to conceive, unlesse that men borne before the times of the Gospel were no part of mankinde, or the Gospel were [reveald] before it was reveald.

The other reason I finde in your Letter why I could not there meane the law of nature is because the divine law I there speake of has inforcements of rewards and punishments in another life—your Letter indeed says *whose only inforcements*; But *only* is of your putting in and not mine as you will perceive if you read that passage in my book again, and that I suppose would have as well Excluded the law of Moses as well as that of Nature, and I imagin the law of the Gospel too. But if those Gentlemen thinke that it is a denyall of that branch of the divine law which is cald the law of nature to speake of a divine law, whose inforcements are the rewards and punishments of another life which is as much as to say the law of nature has no such inforcements, And if they are of that opinion they cannot but be very sincere and Zealous stiklers for a divine law of Morality only upon rewards and punishments of this life 'tis easy to see what a kinde of Morality they intend to make of it. You tell me you could not tell me how to answer them. I am sorry for it not

---

[1] Answers L1307.   [2] Ch. xxviii in later editions.

[3] In *Annals of the World* (1658) Archbishop Ussher demonstrated that the world began in 4004 BC.

being able to see any difficulty. The reason you give in these words *I must confesse I could not tell possitively what reply to make because you do not Expressly tell us where to finde this law unlesse in the SS. And since it is likewise much doubted by some whether the rewards and punishments you mention can be demonstrated as established by your divine law.* This reason or reasons seems very admirable to me that I could not meane the law of nature *because I did not Expressly tell you where to finde this law unlesse in the SS.* I do not remember I any where tell you it is to be found in SS. cannot I tell you in matter of fact that some men many men do compare their actions to a divine law and thereby forme the Ideas of their Moral rectitude or pravity without telling where that law is to be found? Another thing that stumbles you is that it *is much doubted by some whether the rewards and punishments I mention can be demonstrated as established by my divine law.* Will nothing then passe with you in Religion or Morality but what you can demonstrate? If you are of so nice a stomach I am afraid If I should now Examine how much of your religion or Morality you could demonstrate how much you would have left, not but that I thinke that demonstration in those matters may be carried a great deale farther than it is But there are many perhaps millions of propositions in Mathematiques which are demonstrable which neither you nor I can demonstrate and which perhaps no man has yet demonstrated or will do before the end of the world. The probability of rewards and punishments in another life I should thinke might serve for an inforcement of the Divine law if that were the businesse in hand But in the present case demonstration of future rewards and punishments was no more my businesse than whether the Squaring of the circle could be demonstrated or no. But I know not how you would still have me besides my purpose and against all rules of method run out into a discourse of the divine law shew how and when it was promulgated to mankinde demonstrate its inforcement by rewards and punishments in another life in a place where I had nothing to do with all this and in a case where some mens bare supposition of such a law whether true or false servd my turne. 'Twas my businesse there to shew how men came by moral Ideas or Notions and that I thought they did by comparing their actions to a rule. The next thing I endeavour to shew is what rules men take to be the standards to which they compare their actions to frame moral Ideas and those I take to be the divine law, the Municipal[4] law and the law of reputation or fashon. If this be so in matter of fact I am in the right in all that I pretended and was proper in that place. If I am out in either of these propositions I must confesse I am in an error but cannot be accused for not haveing treated more amply of those rules in that place or enterd into a just disquisition of their nature force or obligation when if you will looke into the end of that chapter you will finde 'tis not of concernment to my purpose in that chapter whether they be as much as true or noe but only that they be considerd in the mindes of men as rules to which they compare their

---

[4] Civil.

actions and judg of their morality. But yet you thinke me guilty of other mens mistakes because I did not write plainer and I thinke they might have considerd better what I writ. I imagin what I was there to make out I have done very plainly And if readers will not allow so much attention to the books they read as to minde what the Author is upon and whether he directly pursues the argument in hand, they must blame themselves if they raise doubts and scruples to themselves where the Author gave no occasion for any. And if they be ill naturd as well as groundlesse objections one may suspect that they meant not over well to the Author or the argument they are so scrupulous about. You say that to shew what I meant I should after divine law have added in a parenthesis *which others call the law of nature* which had been so far from what I meant that it had been contrary to it For I meant the Divine law indeffinetly and in general how ever made known or supposd; and if ever any men referd their actions to the law of nature as to a Divine law 'twas plain I meant that if any judgd of their actions by the law of Moses or Jesus christ as by a divine law 'twas plain I meant that also.[5] Nay the Alcoran[6] of the Mahumetans and the Hanscrit[7] of the Bramins could not be in this case Excluded (though perhaps you or your freinds would have thought it more worth their censure if I had put them in and then I had lain open to I know not what interpretations) or any other supposd divine revelation whether true or false. For it being taken for a divine law it would have served men who made use of it and judgd of their actions by it to have given them notions of morality or Moral Ideas and that was all I was to shew. Indeed if you can tell of any other rule but 1°. Divine laws or the law of God 2°. Civil laws or the laws of the Magistrate 3°. the law of fashon and reputation where by men judg of the goodnesse of their actions I have then faild in giveing a full account whence men get their moral Ideas but that is all I can be accusd to have faild in here. For I did not designe here to treat of the grounds of true morality which is necessary to true and perfect happinesse and 'thad been impertinent if I had so designed: my businesse was only to shew whence men had moral Ideas and what they were and that I suppose is sufficiently don in that chapter.

1312. James Tyrrell to Locke, Rolleston, Staffordshire, 30 August [1690]

Had I not bin allwayes upon the remove for near this fortnight, I had sooner returned an answere to yours;[1] for I would not lye long under your mis-

---

[5] In the 2nd edn. Locke inserted a sentence before the passage quoted in L1307, n. 3: 'The Divine Law, whereby I mean, that Law which God has set to the actions of Men, whether promulgated to them by the light of nature, or the voice of Revelation'.

[6] Koran.   [7] Sanskrit. Locke seems to think it is a book, not a language.

[1] Answers L1309.

apprehension of me, concerneing what I spoke in private to Mr: P.[2] concerneing the booke. and therefore I shall first answere your encloseing paper[3] which
is of greater concernement to me than the letter it self, for whether I, or my
Freinds (as you are pleased to call them) have mistaken Mr: L. in a philosophical disquisition is of no great moment, and If I am in the wrong, am as
glad to be convinced of my mistake, as if I had allwayes bin in the right:
but whether or no Mr: L. doe rightly collect that Mr: T. hath not carryed
himself as becomes a Freind is a thing not of that indifference to him. and
therefore I shall endeavour to clear this mistake in the first place; for I did
not (I confesse) understand before, what it was I had concluded too quick:
and therefore I shall only represent the matter of fact, and then leave it to
your self either to excuse or condemne me. therefore in the first place I must
tell yow, that when I writ to you to know if you could informe me who was
the Authour of that booke.[4] you returned no answere at all, as I can shew you
by the letter it self, which I have still by me:[5] 'tis true in another[6] when I writ
you word that the People at Oxford had now found out a better Authour than
I, for it: viz: your self, your answere was to this effect, that since they would
not have you to be the Authour of a booke that you owned,[7] you did not thinke
it worth while to give them any satisfaction in those that you did not owne
at all:[8] but you farther sayed that you would convince me of their mistake
both about that, and another called humane reason (which they allso layed
to you)[9] when wee next met: so you may remember, that when I first waited
of you at your Lodging as soon as I came to Towne, I fell purposely in talk
of that booke,[10] and sayed that whoever had writ it, whether your self, or another,
I thought him very much in the right in most things: and that he agreed perfectly with my conceptions in Patriarcha non Mon: (which he had quoted)[11]
which I spoke on purpose that you might then take occasion to deny it if
I were mistaken, which since I found you did not, but rather declined, the
discourse, and turned it off to another subject; I must confesse I did then (as
I doe still) entertaine some suspicions of your being the Authour of it, as
I must doe till your pleased positively to averr the contrary: but for my
uttering this suspition to another, and not to your self; I must tell you I thought
it not good manners to urge you any farther upon that point: which if it 'twere
true, perhaps you had no mind I should know. but I assure you I never utterd
this suspition to any body but Mr: P. nor had I done it to him, but that I

---

[2] Probably Edward Pococke, junior, Student of Christ Church, a former pupil of Locke's. The topic here is not the *Essay*, but the authorship of the *Two Treatises*.

[3] Not extant. It evidently reproached Tyrrell for rumour-mongering about the authorship of the *Two Treatises*. L1266, n. 4.

[4] The *Two Treatises*.   [5] L1225 (L1266, n. 4).   [6] L1266.

[7] Probably referring to the charge that the *Essay* was derivative of 'French authors'. L1266, n. 2. Owned: acknowledged.

[8] Locke did not confess authorship of the *Two Treatises* or the *Letter Concerning Toleration* till the end of his life.

[9] L1266, n. 5.   [10] The *Two Treatises*.   [11] Cited rather than quoted. L1266, n. 4.

knew him to be a very good Freind of yours, and that would not doe you any prejudice by my discourse: but he might likewise have told you, that I then gave him some reasons why he might gather, that the booke was not yours; and then I then told him; that I was not confident of it (and therefore did not conclude etc) but only had such a suspition, for the reasons I have now given you, in which if I am mistaken, you must thanke your owne reservednesse. So that I hope when you consider better of it, you will find that you have no reason to take my uttering my private opinion ill, unlesse it be, because you will take it *amisse*, that is, not by the right handle; for Ile assure you whether you owne or disowne it; you shall never find that I publish this suspition to your prejudice, or ever speake so much againe of it. and if I sayed too much to him I beg your pardon. . . .

1313. Locke to Edward Clarke, Oates, 1 September 1690

. . . The inclosed from Monsieur[1] of your sons[2] proficiency not answering his expectation I hope is rather from his great care and concerne than any just cause of complaint and I am the more encouraged to hope soe because I finde he complains also of the litle progresse my wife[3] had made in French, which yet I found when she was in town was beyond what I could have expected. He names both childishnesse and obstinacy in your son, if it be the first though it be not now to be indulged, yet we are not to hope quite to cure it that must be the worke of age. But obstinacy is a dangerous point and must at any rate be masterd or else all will be spoild. I have writ to him soe and pressed him again to be sure to make himself obeyd. I know not whether Monsieurs temper be capable of that austerity and rigor which may be necessary. I must desire you to examine and looke to that and if there be any obstinacy in the case see it masterd. To dispose your son to it perhaps it may be enough to represent to him with a serious brow that it is absolutely your will that he should perfectly obey Mr Passebon and that if he make any difficulty to doe it, or that you finde he does not you will send him to schoole where he shall be hardly used, whipd often and be under your displeasure to boot. This said in few words and your countenance kept may perhaps be enough to produce all we desire if not you must both order Mr Passebon when he is obstinate to correct him severly and goe on in the correction till he finde him subdued or else you must see it don your self but it were better he did it by himself and if all this will not doe we must looke for a new Tutor rather than have your son spoild, though if this man can gain an authority over him perhaps we may not easily finde a better for I thinke him one of the best and honestest Frenchmen I have met with and let me tell you there is this good in his

---

[1] Passebon (forename unknown), tutor, Huguenot refugee.
[2] Edward Clarke junior, aged about 12.   [3] L809, n. 2. Betty was aged about 13.

temper that the lesse he is inclind to severity and the lesse he depends: on whiping the more pains he will take and if it can be brought to doe, the milder is certainly the better way. When I say your son must not be spoild we must not thinke that childishnesse or a neglect in him of his improvements is presently that, you must allow him to be a child and be like other children averse to study and carlesse of what is for his future advantage. But an obstinate pre-valency in haveing his will against the direction of his tutor or an habituall idlenesse must not be indulged and the later I am confident by the advances he makes it is not and the former I guesse consists more in a cunning elusion of Mr Passebons orders than an open refusall or opposition to them. I have writ something to Mr Passebon for a farther advance in his studys and I begin to thinke it time now to enter upon Latin which I advise Mr Passebon may be by reading the Latin Testament and explaining it in French . . .

1325. Benjamin Furly to Locke, Rotterdam, 16/26 October 1690

. . . I received from mr. Popple.[1] The Answer to the Letter of Toleration, whose Author is a Ninny, or he writes booty,[2] if the worthy Gentleman be known, I would gladly know his name.[3] I presume he printed it, at his own charges, the paper being so good, and the stuff so singular. With it I received the Ingenious reply to him,[4] in which he is as ingeniously corrected, as Sir R: F: in the Treatises of Goverment;[5] I wish he may be the better for it. I received besides Dr. Sherlocks Vindication of the Doctrine of the Trinity,[6] I hope the Noter upon the Athanasian Creed, will now pull in his hornes, or push them further out, and shew the contradictions he so confidently talks of.[7]

But what I expected more while my friend thought upon Dr. Sherlock, was, the account of his Conversion; for I suppose he has taken more care of his reputation than to leave the world to think it to be in expectation of a Bishoprick,[8] or to be the more capable of serving his Jure Divino masters:[9]

---

[1] William Popple, translator of the *Epistola de Tolerantia.*

[2] Play booty: to play a game with intention to lose.

[3] Jonas Proast, *The Argument of the Letter Concerning Toleration Answer'd* (1690). Proast was a High Church Oxford clergyman who waged a vehement paper war against Locke in defence of reli-gious coercion.

[4] Locke, *A Second Letter Concerning Toleration* (1690).

[5] Sir Robert Filmer. Furly implies knowledge of Locke's authorship of the *Two Treatises.*

[6] William Sherlock, *A Vindication of the Doctrine of the Trinity* (1690): a reply to the Unitarian Stephen Nye, *A Brief History of the Unitarians* (1687), and to the anonymous *Brief Notes on the Creed of St Athanasius* (n.d.).

[7] The Athanasian creed upholds the doctrine of the Trinity and the incarnation of God in Jesus Christ, against the Arian heresy, which tended toward Unitarianism.

[8] Sherlock was a Tory absolutist before the Revolution and in 1689 was at first a Nonjuror; then he took the oath of allegiance, and became Dean of St Paul's. His conversion was much discussed. Locke criticized his tract defending his volte-face, *The Case of the Allegiance due to Sovereign Powers* (1691): *Political Essays*, 313–17.

[9] 'Divine right masters': i.e. the Jacobites.

The next piece I received was mr. Norrises christian blessedness, and cursory reflexions upon your Essay Sir.[10]

And I hope by this time that you are sufficiently convinc'd that you had's good not have writ at all, if the understanding takes no notice of it self. That you are yet to tell the world what you mean by the word Idea. That there are Principles to which all mankind give an universall assent, because there are Propositions self evident. Tho all men assent not to them, till they think upon them, or are brought so to do. That there maybe truths imprinted upon the soule, tho she nor perceivs nor understands them; because the soule may have lost the view of many Ideas she once had, and yet has dormant in her memory, that is because she cant view and think upon all things at once. That as there is a certain time for thinking. or when children begin to think. so there is for such and such thoughts: and that (tho there are no innate Ideas propositions, or principles Imprinted upon any soule or mind) yet those which are not perceived till after a long time of thinking may as wel be innate, as any other perceivd long before.

That you have contradicted yourself, in denying that there is any practical truth universally received when this Proposition is (tho not perhaps universally received or thought on) as certain as any demonstration in Euclid, and as plain too—which you have assignd p: 274. sect. 18.[11] viz. That there is no injustice where there is no propriety. And because you own as incontestable principles, in morality, as in any other science. That Innate truths maybe deduced from Reason; and conclusions as wel Innate as propositions: tho indeed neither be so. That an Innate law (if there were any such) may as welbe transgressed, as a written and otherway known one. That 'tis not so easy a matter, as you imagind, to distinguish between innate, and other Impressions. Because Caiaphas could not distinguish his Inspired impression, from his own thoughts.[12]

Nay I hope by this time you are satisfyed that there are no mental impressions at all; and that al your labours lost, as well in shewing how the mind comes to have any thing impressd upon it, as that it has nothing so innately, tho your book (pray be not proud) be so excellent, that the Gentleman would not part with it for half a Vatican;[13] pray how much mony is that?

And finally I hope he has given you and the world, if not there, in his Reason and Religion; a clearer Idea, and account of the presentialness of his λόγος or Ideal world, what it is, and how we see in it all things.[14] . . .

---

[10] John Norris, *Christian Blessedness . . . To which are Added, Reflections upon a late Essay Concerning Human Understanding* (1690), which Furly proceeds skittishly to summarize. Norris was a Platonist and defended innate ideas, as being the intellect's participation in universal divine ideas.

[11] *Essay*, IV. iii. 18.   [12] John 11:51.   [13] The Vatican library.

[14] Norris: 'I account for the Mode of *Human Understanding . . .* by the Presentialness of the Divine [Logos] or Ideal World to our Souls, wherein we see and perceive all things'. Logos: word, reason. The influence of Malebranche is strong. L1622, n. 4.

1326. Locke to Edward Clarke, Oates, 17 October 1690

Things goeing soe easy soe smooth and soe right in your house,[1] I know you will excuse me that I went into the country to enjoy there an uninterrupted satisfaction and quiet in the contemplation of them. I hope they continue on in the same course since my comeing away, and the zeale and forwardnesse of you your selves makes it needlesse for us without dores[2] soe much as to thinke of the publique[3] which is the happyest state a country can be in, when those whose businesse it is, take such care of affairs that all others quietly and with resignation acquisce and thinke it superfluous and impertinent to medle or beat their heads about them. . . .

1334. Elizabeth Yonge to Locke, Escott, Devon, 3 November 1690

I could not with any confidence give you this trouble, especially at this time when soe many things of greater moment require your thoughts, and which indeed only deserve them, had I not by experience found you to be the most indulgent father,[1] and the most Obliging of all men; which encourages me to hope for your Pardon, and once more beg your advice, that has always been successfull to me, and which I am sure I vallue above all the worlds beside. the occasion of it is this, a bout a month since I perceived a little swelling in my left cheek, Just underneath the Jaw bone, and is now grown to the bignes of a small Walnut, it seems to be of a hard substance, and soe loose in the flesh that twill slip under my finger.[2] it is not at all sore, or tender, but I sometimes feel a little pain in it, but tis very little and is soon over, there is nothing of rednes appears but the flesh looks as it uses to doe, but it being in a place which is usual for swellings of the Kings-evil[3] it makes me the more concerned at it, tho I am willing to flatter my self its nothing of that nature, our Family having never been subject to it, and for my own particular have always been of a healthy constitution and never had any swelling of this nature before, and am at this time in other respects extreamly well. however I am a little causeous how I tamper with it for fear of the worst, therefore beg you to give me your opinion in it at your first leasure, whither a dissolving plaister will be proper, or inward medicins pray freely advise me what I ought

---

[1] The House of Commons, which met on 2 Oct. and proved remarkably compliant to the king's requests for troops, ships, and money.
[2] Those outside parliament.   [3] Public good, public affairs.

[1] Elizabeth was aged about 26.   [2] Perhaps goitre.
[3] Scrofula. It was traditionally cured by the royal touch: the ceremony was discontinued by William III, but briefly revived by Queen Anne.

to doe in this case, which I promis my self you will doe, it being so much your inclination to doe good, and having been always ready to oblige me, for which I am more indebted to you than I can express. besides pray remember your Daughter[4] is not yet past her preferment,[5] that moderate share of beauty which she posseses will be much eclips'd, and I believe will doe little execution for the future, noe Englishman will soe much as break their sheens[6] for her unless you help her to get rid of this blemish, but to be more serious, I shall look on it as a new Obligation upon me to esteem and honnour you, and as a fresh instance of your Friendship which I shall always cherish, and endevour to deserve in the best manner I am able. . . .

1386. Locke to Benjamin Furly, Oates, 28 April [1691]

Though I am very much concerned and troubled for your great losse,[1] yet your sorrow being of that kinde which time and not arguments is wont to cure, I know not whether I should say any thing to you to abate your grief, but that, it serveing to no purpose at all but makeing you thereby the more unfit to supply the losse of their mother to your remaining children, (who now more need your care, help, and comfort,) the sooner you get rid of it, the better it will be both for them and you. If you are convinced this is fit to be don, I need not make use to you of the common though yet reasonable topicks of consolation. I know you expect not to have the common and unalterable law of mortality which reaches the greatest, be dispensed with for your sake. Our friends and relations are but borrowed advantages lent us dureing pleasure, and must be given back when ever cald for; we receive them upon these termes, and why should we repine? or, if we doe, what profits it us? But I see my affection is runing me into reasoning, which you need not, and can thinke of without any suggestions of mine. I wonder not at the greatnesse of your grief, but I shall wonder if you let it prevaile on you; your thinkeing of retireing some whither from businesse was very naturall upon the first stroake of it, but here I must interpose to advise you the contrary. It is to give yourself up to all the ills that grief and melancholy can produce, which are some of the worst we suffer in this life: want of health, want of spirit, want of usefull thought, is the state of those who abandon themselves to griefs, whereof businesse is the best, the safest, and the quickest cure. . . . Keep in your imployment; increase it, and be as busy in it as you can now more than ever. This is best for you and for your children. And when your thoughts are a litle come to themselves and the discomposure over, then calmely

---

[4] Elizabeth herself.   [5] Eligibility for marriage. She married in 1692.   [6] Fall over themselves.

[1] Mrs Furly (Dorothy Grainge) had just died; their newborn baby had also died.

consider what will be the best way for you to dispose of them and yourself; but at present lay by none of your businesse, nor neglect it in the least. I know there is little roome for reasoning in the first disorder of grief; what that proposes is alone hearkend to. I must therfor desire you to trust me on this occasion. I am truly your friend, and love you; . . .

1397. Locke to [Carey Mordaunt, Countess of Monmouth], Oates, 12 June 1691

I litle expected two Ladys should confer notes about me to finde out whether I were not bestowing my self upon a third twas an honour which if ever I had been capable of I thought my self now past. But since your Ladyship who knows soe well the irresistible power of your sex concludes that neither philosophie the artificial nor age the natural fence against it is sufficiently armor of proof tis better to passe for a Jesuit or any thing rather than owne my self capable of noething but flat insensibility when your Ladyship thinks me worth the lookeing after. I will not therefor goe about to justifie my self against that accusation but conclude with my self that had the K of Fr but your Ladyships art in persecuteing[1] noe thing could stand him and he might by a sure and effectuall way make whom ever he pleased forward and willing slaves. the infinite worth that all the world acknowledges in your Ladyship and the infinite obligations I in particular have to you I thought left noe roome for any addition to the ties your Ladyship had upon me till I received the honour of your last letter where in I finde railery too and persecution in your hands when you please to make use of them that way are noe lesse effectuall to make one highly sensible of your favour and goodnesse than those which are cald real benefits. I shall always prefer that night I was misseing[2] in to the fairest of all my days since it hath drawn from your Ladyship those rebukes wherein you doe me the honour to use the names of Jealousy and freind. One who had the boldnesse to professe him self in love at first sight might perhaps not soe much wonder that your Ladyship should divert your self with one of them[3] at a time when there is litle other matter to be merry with But the other[4] is a title soe seriously weighty and glorious that if I were not before wholy devoted to your service this would ingage all the future care and service of my life to preserve it.[5] . . .

---

[1] A reference to Louis XIV's persecution of the Huguenots.
[2] 'Missing' replaces 'supposd to be lost'.   [3] Jealousy.   [4] Friend.
[5] During the summer Locke joined Lord and Lady Monmouth on a 'ramble' to Bath and Wiltshire. The letter closes with a piece of gossip: 'We had a story here of a Lady taken in bed, by her Lord with an other Lord.'

1405. Isaac Newton to Locke, Cambridge, 30 June 1691

... If the scheme you have laid of managing the Controulers place of the M.[1] will not give you the trouble of too large a letter, you will oblige me by it. I thank you heartily for your being so mindfull of me and ready to assist me with your interest. Concerning the *Ancient of days* Dan. 7, there seems to be a mistake either in my last letter or in your's because you wrote in your former letter that the Ancient of Days is Christ, and in my last I either did or should have asked how you knew that.[2] But these discourses may be done with more freedome at our next meeting. ...

The observation you mention in Mr Boyles book of colours[3] I once made upon my self with the hazzard of my eyes. The manner was this. I looked a very little while upon the sun in a looking-glass with my right eye and then turned my eyes into a dark corner of my chamber and winked to observe the impression made and the circles of colours which encompassed it and how they decayed by degrees and at last vanished. This I repeated a second and a third time. At the third time when the phantasm of light and colours about it were almost vanished, intending my phansy[4] upon them to see their last appearance I found to my amazement that they began to return and by little and little to become as lively and vivid as when I had newly looked upon the sun. But when I ceased to intend my phansy upon them they vanished again. After this I found that as often as I went into the dark and intended my mind upon them as when a man looks earnestly to see any thing which is difficult to be seen, I could make the phantasm return without looking any more upon the sun. And the oftener I made it return, the more easily I could make it return again. And at length by repeating this without looking any more upon the sun I made such an impression on my eye that if I looked upon the clouds or a book or any bright object I saw upon it a round bright spot of light like the sun. And which is still stranger, tho I looked upon the sun with my right eye only and not with my left, yet my phansy began to make the impression upon my left eye as well as upon my right. For if I shut my right eye and looked upon a book or the clouds with my left eye I could see the spectrum of the sun almost as plain as with my right eye, if I did but intend my phansy a little while upon it. For at first if I shut my right eye and looked with my left, the spectrum of the sun did not appear till I intended my phansy upon it; but by repeating this, appeared every time more easily. And now in a few hours time I had brought my eye to such a pass that I could look upon no

---

[1] Newton became Warden of the Mint in 1696.

[2] Newton tried to connect prophecies in the books of Daniel and Revelation. His *Observations upon the Prophecies of Daniel, and the Apocalypse of St John* appeared in 1733.

[3] *Experiments and Considerations touching Colours* (1664). Newton's experiment took place in about 1664.

[4] 'Intending my phancy': directing my imagination.

bright object with either eye but I saw the sun before me, so that I durst neither write nor read, but to recover the use of my eyes shut my self up in my
chamber made dark for three days together and used all means to divert my
imagination from the Sun. For if I thought upon him I presently saw his picture though I was in the dark. But by keeping in the dark and imploying my
mind about other things I began in three or four days to have some use of
my eyes again and by forbearing a few days longer to look upon bright objects
recovered them pretty well, though not so well but that for some months after
the spectrum of the sun began to return as often as I began to meditate upon
the phænomenon, even though I lay in bed at midnight with my curtains drawn.
But now I have been very well for many years, tho I am apt to think that if
I durst venture my eyes I could still make the phantasm return by the power
of my fansy. This story I tell you to let you understand that in the observation related by Mr Boyle, the man's phansy probably concurred with the impression made by the sun's light to produce that phantasm of the Sun which he
constantly saw in bright objects. And so your question about the cause of this
phantasm involves another about the power of phansy which I must confess
is too hard a knot for me to untye. To place this effect in a constant motion
is hard because the Sun ought then to appear perpetually. It seems rather to
consist in a disposition of the sensorium[5] to move the imagination strongly
and to be easily moved both by the imagination and by the light as often as
bright objects are looked upon. . . .

1439. Edward Clarke to Locke, London, 15 December 1691

Your letter of the 11th. with those inclosed for Mr. Pawling and Mr.
Churchill[1] came safe to mee, which I sealed and left them at theire Houses
they being both abroad[2] when I went to speake with them, And I will make
use of the first opportunity I can gett to take the Note of Him which Hee
Promised to give after this Edition touching the Copy etc,[3] I have given
Sir Francis[4] one and have disposed of 4. or 5.[5] more soe Advantagiousely in
the House,[6] That it is allready a doubt whither the Byll for Lowering the Interest
of money will ever bee read a second time or not, And all that have read
the Considerations are cleerely of opinion, the Arguments therein are abundantly suffitient to distroy that Byll and all future Attempts of the like Kind;[7]
I heare the whole Treatise generally much approved of and Commended, for

---

[5] The area of the brain that receives sense experience.

[1] Robert Pawling (L771, n. 8) and Awnsham Churchill, Locke's publisher.
[2] Away from home.
[3] Locke's authorial fee from Churchill for *Some Considerations of the Consequences of the Lowering of Interest,* newly published.
[4] Masham. [5] Copies of the tract. [6] House of Commons. [7] L1455.

the many usefull Notions therein touching *Money, Trade,* and *Taxing,* And there have been verie particular Inquieryes to Know the Author, And I must tell you that there have been many that have shrodely guessed at Him, And some I beleive there are, who mightily commend the ingenuity of the Author, yett I beleive will hardly forgive Him for some Parts of His Booke were Hee known;[8] . . .

1455. Edward Clarke to Locke, London, 23 January 1692

. . . This day the Byll for Reduceing the Interest of money to 5l. per Cent. Passed the House of Commons; severall Attempts wee had upon the first, second and third Reading of the Byll, to have thrown it out, wherein all imaginable Reasons were used to that End, In which Debates, I was not a little pleas'd, to heare all the Arguments used, that are contain'd in the Considerations upon Lowering the Interest of money,[1] whereby 'twas manifest to mee that the Greatest and best men in our House were obleiged to that Treatise for all the Arguments they used in those Debates, But I am satisfied if an Angell from Heaven had mannaged the Debate, the Votes would have been the same as now, For 'tis not Reason but a supposed Benifit to the Borrower that hath Passed the Byll, and I beleive 'tis that will carry it through the House of Lords likewise;[2] . . .

1471. Locke to Edward Clarke, Oates, 26 February 1692

I am satisfied about your son[1] that he wants not parts[2] soe that if he has not made all the progresse we could have desired I lay it wholy upon want of application, which as far as I can guesse is oweing, something to a saunteringnesse[3] that is in his temper; a good deale to an unsteadinesse of minde which is quickly tired with a bookeish attention which he takes noe great pleasure in; and a litle to something of my yonge master. I here mention not any particular aversion he had to Monsieur Passebon,[4] for I can discover noething of that. And I thinke all the quarrels he had with him was from a mixture of lazynesse and contempt and endeavour for mastery assisted possibly by the folly

---

[8] Locke admitted authorship when he republished it in 1696.

[1] Locke's tract: L1439.
[2] It lapsed in the Lords when parliament was prorogued.

[1] Edward Clarke junior, aged about 14, was staying with Locke at Oates.
[2] Qualities, talents.   [3] Dawdling (*Education*, §§ 123–7).
[4] A Huguenot tutor, recently dismissed (L1313).

and incouragement of servants, wherein he gaind his point and would noe doubt have a triall of skill with any other that shall succeed him. But yet though indulgeing to his ease tis like will make him weary and resty[5] with any other tutor espetially if he have hopes to tire him out, yet I looke upon it as very far from being unconquerable. For he does what I bid him and has sometimes since he has been here spent several hours in the day by himself and I suppose busy about what I set him. But to obtein this I think it necessary to keep a pretty cold and [constantly] severe countenance to him, and when at any time he neglects and makes excuses I shew him gravely and without passion that I see it to be an excuse which signifies noething but that he has had noe minde to doe it. And sometimes I chide him, but still gravely in few words and without any passion by which way of treatment I thinke he is better reconciled to his booke for he comes sometimes of himself to me to shew me what he hath don and to aske what he shall doe next though he has not all the Alacrity towards it I could wish. And I know not whether there be not some cuning in it for fear I should represent matters soe to you that I should incline you to send him to Westminster Schoole, of which and the discipline used there I have given him such a representation that I imagin he has noe great likeing to it[6]

I know the question you will be ready to aske me is But what will you have me doe with him? To which I answer I should be still of my first opinion of haveing a Tutor for him at home, But that there are two great Obstacles lye in the way. The one is that Madame[7] if I am not mightily mistaken is utterly averse to it. The other is Where shall we finde a man with discretion and steadynesse enough to manage him right, for he will require a constant attention and a due application to his temper

The next to this were some Frenchmans house where he might be taken in and looked after by the man him self

The last is a French schoole[8] where the master would have a particular eye to him and manage him with such a rain as his temper requires. But which of these three is easiest to be found I can not tell. A French man it must bee that he may not loose the French tongue or else perhaps I might advise you to Westminster or some other very severe schoole, where if he where whipd soundly whilst you are lookeing out an other fit Tutor for him he would perhaps be the more pliant and willing to learne at home afterwards. But for the reasons above mentiond I thinke not of that.

Whose ever hands he is put into, he must be sure to keepe a steady hand upon him for the bias lying on the lazy wayward side he will be ready to slip from him by all the artifices and excuses can be imagind all which he should constantly be beat out of by admiting noething but the thing don. And the

---

[5] Restive, indolent.
[6] Locke deplored the regime of beatings meted out to him at Westminster (*Education*, §§ 47–52).
[7] Mrs Mary Clarke.   [8] A Huguenot school in England.

first time any thing came in contest to be sure to correct him severely and repeat it on till his tutor perceived it had wrought upon his minde and setled the mastery. that once don and he was become pliant and submissive to orders with all his industry, then not to strain him too hard but give him such imployment, such tasks as his parts may with moderate industry dispatch. Prayseing him when he deserves it and findeing out ingenuous recreations for his vacant times but never leting him be saunteringly idle, but let play of some kinde or other and Exercise as Danceing, Fenseing etc⁹ or study take up all his time. If you can any where enquire out a man that will follow this method you will finde your son improve to your great satisfaction. and without this I fear he will have a great many unprofitable and uneasy hours and I wish he make not you have some uneasy ones too. . . .

1519. Isaac Newton to Locke, [Cambridge?], 2 August 1692

. . . I am glad you have all the 3 parts of the Recipe entire but before you go to work about it I desire you would consider these things. For it may perhaps save your time and expence.

This Recipe I take to be the thing for the sake of which Mr B.[1] procured the repeal of the Act of Parl. against Multipliers,[2] and therefore he had it then in his hands. In the margin of the Recipe was noted that the [Mercury] of the first work would grow hot with [Gold] and thence I gather that this Recipe was the foundation of what he published many years ago[3] about such [Mercuries] as would grow hot with [Gold] and therefore was then known to him, that is sixteen or 20 years ago at least. And yet in all this time I cannot find that he has either tried it himself or got it tried with success by any body els. For when I spake doubtingly about it, he confest that he had not seen it tried but added that a certain Gentleman was now about it and it succeeded very well so far as he had gone and that all the signes appeared so that I needed not doubt of it. This satisfied me that [Mercury] by this Recipe may be brought to change its colours and properties: but not that [Gold] may be multiplied thereby.

And I doubt it the more because I heard some years ago of a company who were upon this work in London, and after Mr B. had communicated this Recipe to me so that I knew it was the same with theirs, I enquired after them and learnt that that two of them were since forced to other means of living and

---

⁹ *Education*, §§ 196–8.

[1] Robert Boyle, who died in 1691. Locke was going through his papers.

[2] To multiply gold: alchemy, the turning of base metal into gold. A medieval law against alchemy was repealed in 1689.

[3] In the *Philosophical Transactions of the Royal Society* (1676): an experiment to mix mercury and gold filings into a hot paste.

a third who was the chief Artist was still at work but was run so far into debt that he had much ado to live, and by these circumstances I understood that these gentlemen could not make the thing succeed. When I told Mr. B. of these gentlemen, he acknowledged that the Recipe was gone about among several Chymists, and therefore I intend to to stay till I hear that it succeeds with some of them.

But besides if I would try this Recipe, I am satisfied that I could not. For Mr B. has reserved a part of it from my knowledge. I know more of it than he has told me, and by that and an expression or two which dropt from him I know that what he has told me is imperfect and useless without knowing more then I do. . . .

In diswading you from too hasty a trial of this Recipe I have forborn to say any thing against multiplication in general because you seem perswaded of it: tho there is one argument against it which I could never find an answer to, and which, if you will let me have your opinion about it, I will send you in my next.[4]

1522. James Tyrrell to Locke, Oxford, 9 August [1692]

I have deferred the answering your letter till now, that I could assure you that I have performed the effects of it, in sending away the rest of your things, which I could not doe sooner than last weeke, haveing not bin at okeley[1] to stay there till then, in above 2 monthes all things there haveing been very dirty, and unpleasant; but I have now put up, and sent you to Oxford these particulars following: first in the great pair of boxes are put all your paper bookes, which have no writeing in them; except 2, or 3 smaller ones which I have made use of, and will be answereable to you for. the other pair of boxes are sent up empty; because there were no small bookes left to fill them: all of that sort being either sent up allready, or els deliverd to Mr: Thomas;[2] with the rest of those physic bookes you orderd to be deliverd to him; and which filled allmost 3 ordinary boxes: and He, and I, have taken an exact Catalogue of them; which you will find put in the Japan Ennbassy[3] which is in your box with the lock, the Key of which Mr: Thomas hath likewise sent you in a letter to your self: or Mr: Pawling; wee were forced to have a new key made to it because my daughter had soe mislayed the old one before she went away, that it could not be found; but in that box you will find your 2 Carpets: with oglebyes 2 volumes of his Eng: Atlass[4] which I told you were borrowed by

---

[4] No further discussion is extant.

[1] Oakley, 10 mls. north-east of Oxford.   [2] William Thomas, son of Dr David Thomas.
[3] Arnoldus Montanus, *Atlas Japannensis* (1670).
[4] John Ogilby, *English Atlas* (1670–1), volumes on Africa and America.

Father and my son, as for your China Embassy[5] you may remember that being a weary of it you were pleased to give it me, but it shall still be as much at your service as if it were your owne; there is allso in that box Kettlewell of Christian obedience,[6] which my Sister had borrowed; and Bellonius;[7] with 4 small bookes of your collections which were before mislayd, and so omitted to be sent you: so that I have now nothing of yours in my hands, except those bookes I have borrowed of you; and which you have my note for; and besides an old Terrestriall Globe which would not goe into the box it was so full, and my son desires the use of it a little longer; I have allso your weather glasse[8] at Shotover,[9] which was too long to goe into any of the boxes, but tho' I have put quite new quicksilver[10] into it the old being so foul that it would not move right; yet you shall have it againe when ever you tell me it may be use full to you; and will bring it with me when I come up, next terme;[11] if you please so to order it: there is likewise a thin boxe, which I bought to keep all your Maps in apart from my owne; all which are carefully put up in it: so that you are to receive 4 boxes in all 3 of which are full: so haveing dispatcht this affair; I have nothing more to trouble you with at present;[12] but to know whether you have received the Dialogues which I orderd to be sent you as fast as they came out;[13] not for your instruction; but as a Testimony of my respect: I allso orderd my bookseller to send you my Treatise of the law of nature which I told you long since I had abridged out of Dr: Cumberlands latin treatise on that subject;[14] I hope you will have read it; and be able to give me your free censure of it next Time wee meet if not before; onely I desire you would make Syl:[15] correct the Errata (which are pretty many) before you read it: and I hope that this treatise may give the world sufficient satisfaction, or at least may els excite your self or some other thinking person, to give the world a better account of the Law of nature; and its obligation, than what hath bin allready performed: as allso to confute with better Reasons the Epicurean Principles of Mr: Hobs: for the doeing of which, I know no man more capeable than your self if you please to undertake it; and shall no more resent it than the publishing of the 2 Treatises of Goverment after Patriarcha non Monarcha;[16] since if truth can be better represented, and improved: by a greater hand: I shall not value if my small performances, serve for a foyle to set it off; since I have, (I thank

---

[5] Probably Jan Nieuhof, *L'Ambassade . . . vers l'empereur de la Chine* (1665); Eng. trans., *An Embassy . . . to China* (1669).

[6] John Kettlewell, *The Measures of Christian Obedience* (1681).

[7] Pierre Belon, *Les Observations de plusieurs singularitez* (1554).   [8] Barometer.

[9] Tyrrell's family home, 5 mls. east of Oxford.   [10] Mercury.

[11] Up to London in Michaelmas law term, October–November.

[12] In an earlier letter (L1420), Tyrrell mentions further items of Locke's: a cane chair, table linen, quilt, blanket, velvet cap, and telescope.

[13] Tyrrell, *Bibliotheca Politica* (in thirteen dialogues, 1692–4). The first is called 'Whether Monarchy be Jure Divino [by divine right]'. In L1477 Tyrrell told Locke, 'I suppose you will not trouble your self to read more than the preface, since, it being upon a subject, which either you or I have written on before you will not find any thing new in it'.

[14] L1307, n. 8.   [15] Sylvester Brownover, Locke's servant and secretary.   [16] L1266, n. 4.

God) learnt so far that Master Principle in Dr: Cumberlands booke, as to preferre the common good of mankind, before my owne Fame; and all the small reputation of an Authour: but perhaps I would have alterd somewhat in the Doctors definition of the Law of nature, in placeing it in the endeavour of the Common Good of rational Beings of which I suppose God to be the Head, had the notion bin owne: yet I suppose it may passe well enough with that explication the Authour hath given of it in the preface: however I hope you will not take amisse those passages I have added to this treatise out of your Excellent Essay[17] . . .

[17] *Essays on the Law of Nature.* L1307, n. 10.

9

Philosophy and Correction, 1692–1694

In 1692 William Molyneux won Locke's friendship, which continued until Molyneux's sudden death in 1698. Theirs is the most important philosophical exchange in Locke's correspondence, and Locke amended later editions of his *Essay* in response to Molyneux's criticisms. Molyneux was a Protestant Irishman, the leading light of the Dublin Philosophical Society, and an MP in the Irish parliament. He opens by insisting that Locke should write a treatise on ethics (L1530). At Locke's invitation, he turns to a critique of the *Essay* (L1538). He fastens upon a passage in the *Essay* that was to have an extraordinary influence upon Enlightenment material-ism, the suggestion concerning 'thinking matter'—the proposition that consciousness might inhere in matter (L1579). Molyneux next addresses a topic which had embroiled seventeenth-century philosophy and theology, that of free will and determinism. (It had formed the subject of a controversy in the 1650s between Thomas Hobbes and Bishop Bramhall.) Aware that the *Essay* was already being used in Trinity College, Dublin, Molyneux proposes that Locke write a textbook on logic. This sparks Locke's animus against scholasticism and the practice of disputation still current in the universities (L1592).

In relation to Locke's abiding preoccupation with the nature of sense experience, Molyneux poses a question regarding a blind man's capacity to connect what he has learned by touch with what he might see, were he to become sighted (L1609). Among modern philosophers and neuropsychologists this has become known as the Molyneux Problem, or Molyneux's Question. Molyneux next urges Locke to respond formally to the Cartesian philosopher, Nicolas Malebranche, who had denied that ideas in the immaterial mind could be produced by mechanistic collision with external bodies (L1622). Seeking to understand the incommensurable realms of mind and matter, Malebranche advanced a type of Neoplatonism by arguing that our ideas are occasioned by the divine mind. Hence Malebranche's famous dictum that 'we see all things in God'. Not wishing to introduce polemic into the *Essay*, Locke in due course produced two independent critiques of Malebranche. On another occasion, Molyneux discusses Locke's assertion in the *Essay* that personal identity lies in identity of consciousness rather than identity of substance. Locke poses a difficulty concerning the consciousness of drunkards, and answered his own conundrum by saying that this difficulty does not prevent the courts punishing people for what they do when drunk (L1693). Finally, having also subjected *Some Thoughts Concerning Education* to Molyneux's scrutiny, Locke denies Molyneux's allegation that he was unduly severe in prescribing techniques for correcting children; and he stresses the need to educate a child's preferences and desires (L1655).

During this period Locke engaged in the task of correcting the text of the *Two Treatises of Government*, appalled at the shoddy treatment meted out to the first and second editions by his publisher, Awnsham Churchill. Venting his vitriol against Churchill, Locke asks Clarke to copy out the errata in a fresh hand, in order to continue to conceal his authorship (L1690). To Clarke, Locke also gives vent to other grievances about the printing trade (L1586). The system of press censorship, established in the sixteenth century, continued until 1695. Locke's objection rested not only on a general principle of freedom of expression, but on hostility to the commercial monopolies exercised by the Stationers' Company. He was particularly angry at the damage done to classical scholarship through poor editions being sold at inflated prices. Such restrictions frustrated Locke's own attempts to publish a children's edition of Aesop's *Fables*.

In 1693 Locke encountered an Irishman, John Toland, who was embarking on a dazzling literary career (L1650). Later regarded as the most influential of the English deists, the young Toland assiduously attached himself to influential people, often causing them embarrassment. Locke's philosophy and theology was to become more suspect after Toland, in his *Christianity not Mysterious* (1696), dangerously extrapolated arguments from Locke's *Reasonableness of Christianity* (1695).

From William Popple Locke hears about the activities of the Dry Club, which met to discuss theology. Although its precise membership is uncertain, it apparently included Unitarians (L1567). The Christian churches were increasingly being disrupted by allegations by the orthodox that some members denied the doctrine of the Trinity. Such denials potentially opened the road to deism, for they entailed an assertion of the humanity rather than divinity of Jesus Christ, and placed an emphasis on Jesus as a moral teacher rather than as the sacrificial offering who atoned for the sins of humankind. Charges of Socinianism or Unitarianism were in due course levelled against Locke too.

Locke's relationship with Newton became difficult in 1693, the latter's wild accusations apparently stemming from a temporary mental breakdown (L1659, L1663). Locke's medical interests continued. He praises Sydenham's empirical methods of medical investigation, while doubting the worth of alternative approaches to physiology (L1593). Locke is asked by Clarke about the advisability of his pregnant wife drinking the mineral waters of Bath (L1647).

1530. William Molyneux to Locke, Dublin, 27 August 1692

... I was so ambitious of Making a Freindship with you, by presenting you One of My Trifles,[1] which I Orderd My Bookseller to lay before you under this Character, *As a Mean Testimony of the Great Respect I had for the Author of the Essay of Humane Understanding*. And since I find by Yours to Me, that My Ambition is not fallen short of its Designe; But that you are pleased to Incourage me by assuring Me that I have made great Advances of Freindship towards you; Give me leave to Imbrace the Favour with all Joy Imaginable. And that you may Judge of my Sincerity by my Open Heart, I wil plainly confess to you, that I have not in my Life read any Book with More Satisfaction, than your Essay; Insomuch that a Repeated perusal of it is still more pleasant to Me.

And I have indeavourd, with Great Success, to Recommend it to the Consideration of the Ingenious in this Place. Dr King Bishop of Derry, when he read it, made some slight Remarks on the formost parts of the Book;[2] but his Busines would not permit him to go through it all. what he did, rough as it was, he gave to me. and they are at your Commands, when you please.

One Thing I must needs insist on to you, which is, that you would think of Obleidging the World, with *a Treatise of Morals*, drawn up according to the Hints you frequently give in Your Essay, Of their Being Demonstrable according to the Mathematical Method.[3] This is Most Certainly True. But then the task must be undertaken only by so Clear and Distinct a Thinker as you are. This were an Attempt worthy your Consideration. And there is Nothing I should More ardently wish for, than to see it. And therefore, Good Sir, Let me Beg of you to turn your thoughts this way. and if so Young a Freindship as mine have any force; Let me prevail upon you.

Upon my Reading your Essay, I was so taken with it, that when I was in London in August 1690 I made enquiry amongst some of My Learned Freinds for any other of your Writings (if perhaps they knew any). I was recommended by some to *Two Discourses Concerning Government*, and a Little *Treatise Concerning Toleration*. there is neither of them Carrys your Name. and I wil not venture to ask, whether they are yours or Not. This only I think, No Name need be ashamed of Either. . . .

---

[1] *Dioptrica Nova* (1692). The dedication fulsomely praised Locke's *Essay*.
[2] William King, later Archbishop of Dublin. His remarks, later forwarded to Locke, were a partial defence of innate ideas.
[3] *Essay*, III. xi. 16; IV. iii. 18–20; IV. iv. 7–8; IV. xii. 8.

1538. Locke to William Molyneux, London, 20 September 1692

There being nothing that I think of so much value as the acquaintance and friendship of knowing and worthy men, you may easily guess how much I find my self obliged, I will not say by the offer of, but by the gift you have made me of yours.[1] . . . You must therefore expect to have me live with you hereafter, with all the liberty and assurance of a settled friendship. For meeting with but few men in the world whose acquaintance I find much reason to covet, I make more than ordinary haste into the familiarity of a rational enquirer after, and lover of truth, whenever I can light on any such. There are beauties of the mind, as well as of the body, that take and prevail at first sight; and wherever I have met with this, I have readily surrender'd my self, and have never yet been deceived in my expectation. Wonder not therefore, if having been thus wrought on, I begin to converse with you with as much freedom as if we had begun our acquaintance when you were in Holland;[2] and desire your advice and assistance about a second edition of my Essay,[3] the former being now dispersed. You have, I perceive, read it over so carefully, more than once, that I know no body I can more reasonably consult about the mistakes and defects of it. And I expect a great deal more from any objections you should make, who comprehend the whole design and compass of it, than from any one who has read but a part of it, or measures it, upon a slight reading, by his own prejudices. You will find, by my epistle to the reader, that I was not insensible of the fault I committed by being too long upon some points, and the repetitions, that by my way of writing of it, had got in, I let it pass with, but not without advice so to do. But now that my notions are got into the world, and have in some measure bustled through the opposition and difficulty they were like to meet with from the receiv'd opinion, and that prepossession which might hinder them from being understood upon a short proposal; I ask you whether it would not be better now to pare off, in a second edition, a great part of that which cannot but appear superfluous to an intelligent and attentive reader. If you are of that mind, I shall beg the favour of you to mark to me these passages which you would think fittest to be left out. If there be any thing wherein you think me mistaken, I beg you to deal freely with me, that either I may clear it up to you, or reform it in the next edition. For I flatter my self that I am so sincere a lover of truth, that it is very indifferent to me, so I am possess'd of it, whether it be by my own, or any other's discovery. For I count any parcel of this gold not the less to be valued, nor not the less enriching, because I wrought it not out of the mine my self. I think every one ought to contribute to the common stock; but to

[1] L1530, n. 1.   [2] Molyneux travelled in the Netherlands, France, and Germany in 1685.
[3] Which appeared in 1694.

have no other scruple or shyness about the receiving of truth but that he be not impos'd on, and take counterfeit, and what will not bear the touch, for genuine and real truth. I doubt not but, to one of your largeness of thought, that in the reading of my book you miss several things, that perhaps belong to my subject, and you would think belongs to the system: If in this part too you will communicate your thoughts, you will do me a favour. For though I will not so far flatter my self as to undertake to fill up the gaps which you may observe in it, yet it may be of use where mine is at a stand, to suggest to others matter of farther contemplation. This I often find, that what men by thinking have made clear to themselves, they are apt to think, that upon the first suggestion it should be so to others, and so let it go not sufficiently explained; not considering what may be very clear to themselves, may be very obscure to others. Your penetration and quickness hinders me from expecting from you many complaints of this kind. But if you have met with any thing, in your reading of my book, which at first sight you stuck at, I shall think it a sufficient reason, in the next edition, to amend it for the benefit of meaner readers.

The remarks of that learned gentleman you mention,[4] which you say you have in your hands, I shall receive as a favour from you.

Though by the view I had of moral ideas, whilst I was considering that subject, I thought I saw that morality might be demonstratively made out, yet whether I am able so to make it out is another question. Every one could not have demonstrated what Mr. Newton's book[5] hath shewn to be demonstrable: but to shew my readiness to obey your commands, I shall not decline the first leisure I can get to employ some thoughts that way; unless I find what I have said in my Essay shall have stir'd up some abler man to prevent me, and effectually do that service to the world.

We had here, the 8th instant, a very sensible earthquake, there being scarce an house, wherein it was not by some body or other felt. We have news of it at several places from Cologn, as far as Bristol. Whether it reach'd you I have not heard. If it did, I would be glad to know what was the exact time it was felt, if any body observed it. By the Queen's pendulum at Kensington, which the shake stop'd from going, it was 2 h. post m. At Whitehall, where I observed it, it was by my watch 2 h. 5 m. post m. Which supposing the Queen's pendulum went exact, and adding the æquation of that day,[6] it will fall near the time marked by my watch, or a little later. If there could be found people that in the whole extent of it did, by well adjusted clocks exactly observe the time, one might see whether it were all one shock, or proceeded gradually from one place to another. . . .

---

[4] William King.   [5] *Principia Mathematica* (1687).

[6] The equation of time is the difference between the time shown by a clock (mean time) and that shown by a sundial. Locke's watchmaker, Thomas Tompion, published tables showing the variation.

1567. William Popple to Locke, [London], 12 November 1692

However unconcerned your Retirement speaks you in respect of the present general noise of this place, yet I can not think you wholly disinteressed as to the Success of our more particular Undertaking. We have lately admitted two new Bretheren into our Club:[1] Mr Hedworth[2] and Mr Stevens:[3] both I think very Worthy Good Men, but of very different Characters. We have also chosen two others: Dr Foot[4] and Mr White:[5] but they are not yet come amongst us. The subjects we have been upon have been very important. The last was thus. It being supposed that God has given some General and Uniform Rule, or at least one same way of knowing his Will, though in never so different degrees, to all Mankinde, Q: 1. What that Rule is? 2. Of what weight or Authority that general Rule is in comparison with any other particular pretended or real Rule whatsoever? We dispatched the first, and are the next time to go upon the second head. But you must excuse me if I ad, that I do not tell you all this so much to satisfy your curiosity, as to excite you to come and see us. We fall naturally enough into Considerations of Weight: But you that know us, know how unequal our Shoulders are to such Burdens, and therefore I hope you will be so charitable as to let us have your assistance.

Another thing that I can not omit to tell you, though it be of a more public nature, is the most horrible breach of charity amongst the French Refugiez[6] here that ever was heard of. The Occasion was the death of Mr Mainbourg[7] (whose character I suppose you know.) Upon his death-bed being visited by some of the Zealous Orthodox Ministers, and prest by them to declare his opinion in some points that they suspected him to differ from them in, he frankly owned his own sentiments and endeavoured to maintain them with great calmness. But They out of their great Zeal endeavoured no less to terrify him with threats of damnation unless he changed his opinion and repented. Some few others more moderate visiting him also, discoursed with him more charitably, and prayed with him. He dyed in all respects like a Christian Philosopher. But after his death the Orthodox have made Enquiries into what past between him and the others, and upon meer suspicion without the least proof have suspended one from his Ministry; and complained to the Bishop of London of all:[8] But not being able to discover any thing that they could take hold of in those discourses with Mr Mainbourg they have

---

[1] The Dry Club: its rules in *Works*, x. 312–14. Members believed 'no person ought to be harmed in his body, name or goods for mere speculative opinions, or his external way of worship'.

[2] Probably Henry Hedworth, Unitarian clergyman.

[3] Probably William Stephens, Whig clergyman.

[4] Probably Daniel Foot, Presbyterian clergyman turned physician.

[5] Perhaps Jeremiah White, formerly one of Cromwell's chaplains.

[6] The word was first coined in English in 1685 and was, early on, as often spelled 'refugies' as 'refugees'.

[7] Théodore de Maimbourg, Huguenot convert from Catholicism.

[8] Dr Henry Compton. Some Huguenot ministers conformed to the Church of England.

animated the whole orthodox Herd, and set them upon Enquiring into any by-past conversation of these men that may be an argument of their Heterodoxy. The cry is Socinianism.[9] They have been assembled upon it in a perfect Court of Inquisition, to the number of fourscore Ministers, and are about making Formularies and Tests to choak all that have not so wide a Swallow as themselves. My Lord G—ay[10] too is at the Head of the Party, and has complained to the King of the Growth of this Heresy: And they say the King answer[ed] that he would not suffer any Socinians in his Dominions, but would have the Laws put in execution against them.[11] But what that may signify, or whether these things may tend, I undertake not to determin. Here inclosed I send you a Copy of some Errata that I have observed in the impression of the Letter for Toleration,[12] which I leave to your self to make what use of you think fit. . . .

1579. William Molyneux to Locke, Dublin, 22 December 1692

I now sit down to answer yours of September 20. concerning the second Edition of your Book, wherein you desire my Opinion and Advise. And after so long Consideration of the Matter, as between that and this, and Consulting some Ingenious Heads here about It; I can say but Little; Only that the same Judicious Hand, that first form'd it, is best able to reform it, where he sees Convenient. I never quarreld with a Book for being too Prolix, especially where the Prolixity is pleasant and tends to the Illustration of the Matter in hand, as I am sure yours always does. And after I received your Letter on this Subject, I communicated the Contents thereof to two very Ingenious Persons here,[1] and at the same time, I lent them your book desiring them to examine it strictly, and to find out, and Note whatever might be changed, added, or subtracted. And after a Diligent Perusal they agreed with Me in the same Conclusion, viz, that the Work in all its Parts was so wonderfully Curious,[2] and Instructive; that they would not venture to alter anything in it. But however, that I may in some measure answer your Expectations, I shall breifly note to you, what I conceive on this Subject.

[9] From Fausto Sozini (Faustus Socinus), 16th-cent. Italian anti-Trinitarian theologian.
[10] Henri de Massue, Marquis de Ruvigny, Earl of Galway, the leading Huguenot layman in England.
[11] The Toleration Act (1689) explicitly excluded anti-Trinitarians; but the wider state of the law on heresy was opaque.
[12] Locke, *A Third Letter for Toleration* (1692).

[1] Probably William King (L1530, n. 2) and St George Ashe, Provost of Trinity College, later Bishop of Cloyne, Clogher, and Derry.
[2] Careful, accurate.

And first, The Errata Typographica (besides those mentiond in the Table) are many and Great; These therefore, in your next Edition are [diligently] to be Corrected.

(Secondly) Pag. 270.[3] tis asserted that without a Particular Revelation we cannot be certain, that Matter cannot think, Or that Omnipotency may not indow Matter with a Power of Thinking. And Pag. 314. 315.[4] The Immateriallity of God is evinced from the Absolute Impossibility of Matters Thinking. These two Places I know have been stumbled at by some as not Consistent. To me indeed they appear, and are, very agreable; and I have clearly evinced their Consistency to those that have scrupled them. But I thought fitt to give you this Hint, that in your next Edition you may Prevent any such Doubt. My sense of these two Places is this, in the first tis said, that we cannot tell (without a Particular revelation to the Contrary) but an Almighty God can Make Matter think. in the other tis asserted that Unthinking Matter cannot be this Almighty God. The Next place I take Notice off as requiring some Farther Explication is Your Discourse about Mans Liberty and Necessity.[5] this Thread seems so wonderfully fine spun in your Book, that at last the Great Question of Liberty and Necessity[6] seems to Vanish. and herein you seem to make all Sins to proceed from our Understandings, or to be against Conscience; and not at all from the Depravity of our Wills. Now it seems harsh to say, that a Man shall be Damn'd, because he understands no better than he does. What you say concerning Genera and Species[7] is Unquestionably true, and yet it seems hard to assert, that there is no such sort of Creatures in Nature as Birds; for tho we may be Ignorant of the Particular Essense that makes a Bird to be a Bird, or that Determines and Distinguishes a Bird from a Beast, or the just Limits and boundarys between each; Yet we can no More doubt of a Sparrows being a Bird, and an Horses being a Beast, than we can of this Colour being Black and tother White, tho by Shades they may be made so Gradually to Vanish into each other, that we cannot tell where either Determines.

But all this I write more in Deference to your desires from me, than to satisfy my self that I have given you any material hints, or have offerd any Considerable Objection that is worth your Notice and Removal. Mr Norris's Unfortunate attempts on Your Book[8] sufficiently testify its Validity; and truly I think he trifles so egregiously, that he should forewarn all men how far they venture to Criticise on your Work. But this far after all I'll venture to intimate to you, that if you are for an other Work of this Kind, I should advise you to let this stand as it does; and your next should be of a Model wholy

---

[3] *Essay*, IV. iii. 6.   [4] *Essay*, IV. x. 10.

[5] *Essay*, II. xxi. 7–47; 7–73 in the 2nd edn., where, in § 71, Locke refers to the criticism of 'a very judicious Friend'.

[6] Hobbes and Bishop John Bramhall had had a controversy on this topic in the 1650s. The topic was connected, as here, with the theology of predestination.

[7] *Essay*, III. vi.   [8] L1325, n. 11.

New, and that is by Way of Logick, something accommodated to the Usual Forms, together with the Consideration of Extension, Solidity, Mobility, Thinking, Existence, Duration, Number, etc. and of the Mind of Man, and its Powers, as may make up a Compleat Body of what the Schooles call Logicks and Metaphisicks. This I am the More Inclinable to Advise on two Accounts; First because I have Lately seen Johannis Clerici Logica, Ontologia and Pneumatologia,[9] in all which He has little Extraordinary but what he Borrows from you; and in the Alteration he gives them he robbs them of their Native Beautys; which can only be preserved to them by the same Incomparable Art that first framed them. Secondly, I was the First that recommended and lent to the Reverend Provost of Our University Dr Ashe,[10] a most Learned and Ingenious Man, Your Essay, with which he was so wonderfully pleased and satisfyd, that he has Orderd it to be read by the Batchelors in the Colledge, and strictly examines them in their Progres therein. Now a Large Discourse in the way of a Logick would be much more taking in the Universitys, wherein Youths do not satisfy themselves to have the Breeding or Busines of the Place, unles they are ingaged in something that bears the name and Form of Logick.

This Sir is in Short what offers it self to me at present concerning your Work. There Remains only that I again put you in mind of the Second Member of your Division of Sciences, the Ars Practica or Ethicks;[11] you cannot Imagine what an earnest desire and Expectation I have raised in those that are acquainted with your Writings by the Hopes I have given them from your Promise of Indeavouring something on that subject. Good Sir Let me renew my request to you herein, for beleive me Sir twill be one of the Most useful and Glorious undertakings that can Imploy you. The Touches you give in many Places of your Book on this Subject are wonderfully Curious, and do largely testify your Great Abilitys that Way, and I am sure the Pravity of Mens Morals does mightily require the most Powerful Means to Reform them. Be as large as tis possible on this subject, and by all means let it be in English. He that Reads the 45 section in your 129 page[12] will be inflamed to read More of the same kind from the same Incomparable Pen. . . .

1586. Locke to Edward Clarke, Oates, 2 January 1693

I finde by your votes[1] of the 23 Dec that you have resolved to continue the Act for printing made in the 14th. Car. 2.[2] I wish you would have some care

---

[9] Jean Le Clerc, *Ontologia* (1692), dedicated to Locke. The first part, *Logica*, was dedicated to Boyle.
[10] Above, n. 1.　　[11] *Essay*, IV. xx. 3; 4th edn, IV. xxi. 3.
[12] *Essay*, II. xxi. 45; in later edns. § 70. 'Preference of Vice to Vertue a manifest wrong Judgment'.

[1] The printed *Votes of the House of Commons*.
[2] The Licensing Act (1662). The complaints in this letter recur in Locke's memoranda for repeal of the Licensing Act, 1694–5 (*Political Essays*, 329–39).

of Book buyers as well as all of Book sellers and the Company of Stationers who haveing got a Patent for all or most of the Ancient Latin Authors (by what right or pretence I know not)[3] claime the text to be their and soe will not suffer fairer and more correct Editions than any thing they print here or with new Comments to be imported without compounding[4] with them whereby these most usefull books are excessively dear to schollers and a monopoly is put into the hands of the company of ignorant and lazy stationers. Mr Smith a bookseller in Pauls Church yard[5] can give you a very fresh instance of this concerning the importation of a new fair correct Edition of Tully.[6] By this monopoly also of these ancient authors noe body here, that would publish any of them a new with comments or any other advantage can doe it without the leave of the learned judicious stationers, for if they will not print it themselves nor let any other be your labour about it never soe usefull and you have permission to print it from the ArchBishop and all the other Licencers[7] it is to noe purpose. If the company of Stationers soe please it must not be printed. An instance you have of this in Æsops fables. Pray talke with A Churchill concerning this[8] who I beleive will be able to shew you other great inconveniencys of that act and if they can possibly I wish they could be remedied. And particularly I thinke that clause where printing and importation of any books to which any have a right by Patent is prohibited should be at least thus far restraind, that it should be lawfull for any one to print or import any Latin booke whose author lived above a thousand year since. Pray talke with your members about it and I should imagin some of the Bishops too of your acquaintance should be for it, for it is a great oppression upon Schollers and what right can any one pretend to have to the writeings of one who lived a thousand years agoe, He that prints them best deserves best and should have the sale of them which our company of Stationers can by noe means pretend to. For if you examin it I beleive it will be found that those of the Classick authors which are of their publishing are the worst printed of any . . .

1592. Locke to William Molyneux, Oates, 20 January 1693

. . . Could I flatter my self so as to think I deserv'd all that you say of me in your obliging letter,[1] I should yet think you a better judge of what is to

---

[3] The Stationers Company was the London publishers' guild, which claimed a monopoly in the publication of classical texts.

[4] Coming to financial terms.   [5] Samuel Smith, who imported Locke's *Epistola de Tolerantia*.

[6] Cicero, *Opera Omnia* (1692), published at Leyden.

[7] Besides the official Licenser, the Archbishop of Canterbury and the Bishop of London were licensers, as were the Lord Chancellor, and university vice-chancellors.

[8] Locke began a Latin–English version of Aesop's *Fables* in 1691; his publisher, Awnsham Churchill, could not get it published until 1703.

[1] L1579.

be reform'd in my book than I my self. You have given the world proofs of your great penetration, and I have received great marks of your candor. . . . I confess, I thought some of the explications in my book, too long, though turn'd several ways, to make those abstract notions the easier sink into minds prejudiced in the ordinary way of education, and therefore I was of a mind to contract it. But finding you, and some other friends of mine, whom I consulted in the case, of a contrary opinion, and that you judge the redundancy in it a pardonable fault, I shall take very little pains to reform it.

I confess what I say, page 270, compar'd with p. 314, 315.[2] may, to an unwary reader, seem to contain a contradiction; but you, considering right, perceive that there is none. But it not being reasonable for me to expect that every body should read me with that judgment you do, and observe the design and foundation of what I say, rather than stick barely in the words, 'tis fit, as far as may be, that I accommodate my self to ordinary readers, and avoid the appearances of contradiction, even in their thoughts. P. 314. I suppose matter in its own natural state, void of thought, a supposition I concluded would not be deny'd me, or not hard to be prov'd if it should: and thence I infer'd, matter could not be the first eternal being. But page 270. I thought it no absurdity or contradiction to suppose, *That a thinking omnipotent being once granted, such a being might annex to some systems of matter, ordered in a way that he thought fit, a capacity of some degrees of sense and thinking.* To avoid this appearance of a contradiction in my two suppositions, and clear it up to less attentive readers, I intend in the second edition to alter it[3] . . .

I do not wonder to find you think my discourse about liberty[4] a little too fine spun, I had so much that thought of it my self, that I said the same thing of it to some of my friends before it was printed, and told them that upon that account I judg'd it best to leave it out, but they persuaded me to the contrary. When the connection of the parts of my subject brought me to the consideration of power, I had no design to meddle with the question of liberty, but barely pursued my thoughts in the contemplation of that power in man of choosing or prefering, which we call the will, as far as they would lead me without any the least byass to one side or other; or if there was any leaning in my mind, it was rather to the contrary side to that where I found my self at the end of my pursuit. But doubting that it bore a little too hard upon man's liberty, I shew'd it to a very ingenious but professed Arminian,[5] and desired him, after he had consider'd it, to tell me his objections if he had any, who frankly confessed he could carry it no farther. I confess, I think there might be something said, which with a great many men would pass for a satisfactory answer to your objection; but it not satisfying me, I neither put it into my book, nor shall now into my letter. If I have put any fallacy on my

[2] *Essay*, IV. iii. 6; IV. x. 10. On the possibility of thinking matter.
[3] Locke then gives his revised text, incorporated into the 2nd edn. in IV. iii. 6 and IV. x. 10.
[4] Liberty and necessity. L1579, n. 5.
[5] Jean Le Clerc, who reviewed the *Essay* in his *Bibliothèque universelle*, xvii (1690).

self in all that deduction, as it may be, and I have been ready to suspect it my self, you will do me a very acceptable kindness to shew it me that I may reform it. But if you will argue for or against liberty, from consequences, I will not undertake to answer you. For I own freely to you the weakness of my understanding, that though it be unquestionable that there is omnipotence and omniscience in God our maker, and I cannot have a clearer perception of any thing than that I am free, yet I cannot make freedom in man consistent with omnipotence and omniscience in God, though I am as fully perswaded of both as of any truths I most firmly assent to. And therefore I have long since given off the consideration of that question, resolving all into this short conclusion, That if it be possible for God to make a free agent, then man is free, though I see not the way of it.

In the objection you raise about species I fear you are fallen into the same difficulty I often found my self under when I was writing of that subject, where I was very apt to suppose distinct species I could talk of without names.[6] For pray, Sir, consider what it is you mean when you say, that *we can no more doubt of a sparrow's being a bird, and an horse's being a beast, than we can of this colour being black, and t'other white*, etc. but this, that the combination of simple ideas which the word bird stands for, is to be found in that particular thing we call a sparrow. And therefore I hope I have no where said, *there is no such sort of creatures in nature as birds*; if I have, it is both contrary to truth and to my opinion. This I do say, that there are real constitutions in things from whence these simple ideas flow, which we observ'd combined in them. And this I farther say, that there are real distinctions and differences in those real constitutions one from another; whereby they are distinguished one from another, whether we think of them or name them or no. But that that whereby we distinguish and rank particular substances into sorts or genera and species, are not those real essences or internal constitutions, but such combinations of simple ideas as we observe in them. This I design'd to shew in *l.* iii. *c.* 6. If, upon your perusal of that chapter again, you find any thing contrary to this, I beg the favour of you to mark it to me that I may correct it, for it is not what I think true. Some parts of that third book concerning words, though the thoughts were easy and clear enough, yet cost me more pains to express than all the rest of my Essay. And therefore I shall not much wonder if there be in some places of it obscurity and doubtfulness. It would be a great kindness from my readers to oblige me as you have done, by telling me any thing they find amiss; for the printed book being more for others use than my own, 'tis fit I should accomodate it to that as much as I can; which truly is my intention.

That which you propose of turning my Essay into a body of logick and metaphysicks, accomodated to the usual forms, though I thank you very kindly for it, and plainly see in it the care you have of the education of young

---

[6] *Essay*, III. vi.

scholars, which is a thing of no small moment, yet I fear I shall scarce find time to do it; you have cut out other work for me, more to my likeing and I think of more use.[7] Besides that, if they have in this book of mine what you think the matter of these two sciences, or what you will call them, I like the method it is in better than that of the schools, where I think 'tis no small prejudice to knowledge, that predicaments, predicables, etc. being universally in all their systems, come to be looked on as necessary principles or unquestionable parts of knowledge, just as they are set down there. If logick be the first thing to be taught young men, after grammar, as is the usual method, I think yet it should be nothing but proposition and syllogisme. But that being in order to their disputing excercises in the university, perhaps I may think those may be spared too. Disputing being but an ill (not to say the worst) way to knowledge.[8] I say this not as pretending to change or find fault with what publick allowance and establish'd practice has setled in universities, but to excuse my self to you, from whom I cannot allow my self to differ without telling you the true reasons of it. . . .

1593. Locke to Dr Thomas Molyneux, Oates, 20 January 1693

. . . The doctor, concerning whom you enquire of me,[1] had, I remember, when I liv'd in town and convers'd among the physicians there, a good reputation amongst those of his own faculty. I can say nothing of his late book of Fevers, having not read it my self, nor heard it spoke of by others: But I perfectly agree with you concerning general theories, that they are for the most part but a sort of waking dreams, with which when men have warm'd their own heads, they pass into unquestionable truths, and then the ignorant world must be set right by them. Tho' this be, as you rightly observe, beginning at the wrong end, when men lay the foundation in their own phansies, and then endeavour to sute the phænomena of diseases, and the cure of them, to those phansies. I wonder that, after the pattern Dr. Sydenham[2] has set them of a better way, men should return again to that romance way of physick. But I see it is easier and more natural for men to build castles in the air of their own, than to survey well those that are to be found standing. Nicely to observe the history of diseases in all their changes and circumstances, is a work of time, accurateness, attention, and judgment; and wherein if men, thro'

---

[7] Presumably the proposed treatise on ethics. L1530, L1579.

[8] Formal disputations continued to be a standard part of university pedagogy. L182, n. 15, L459, n. 14.

[1] Richard Morton, author of *De Morbis Acutis* (1692).

[2] Thomas Sydenham, the physician whom Locke most admired. In the *Essay* he saluted Boyle, Huygens, Newton, and Sydenham as the 'Master-Builders' in 'the Commonwealth of Learning'.

prepossession or oscitancy[3] mistake, they may be convinced of their error by unerring nature and matter of fact, which leaves less room for the subtlety and dispute of words, which serves very much instead of knowledge in the learned world, where methinks wit and invention has much the preference to truth. Upon such grounds as are the establish'd history of diseases hypotheses might with less danger be erected, which I think are so far useful, as they serve as an art of memory to direct the physician in particular cases, but not to be rely'd on as foundations of reasoning, or verities to be contended for; they being, I think I may say all of them, suppositions taken up gratis, and will so remain, till we can discover how the natural functions of the body are perform'd, and by what alteration of the humors or defects in the parts they are hinder'd or disorder'd. To which purpose I fear the Galenists four humors,[4] or the chymists sal, sulphur, and mercury,[5] or the late prevailing invention of acid and alcali,[6] or whatever hereafter shall be substituted to these with new applause, will upon examination be found to be but so many learned empty sounds, with no precise determinate signification. What we know of the works of nature, especially in the constitution of health, and the operations of our own bodies, is only by the sensible[7] effects, but not by any certainty we can have of the tools she uses, or the ways she works by. So that there is nothing left for a physician to do, but to observe well, and so by analogy argue to like cases, and thence make to himself rules of practice: and he that is this way most sagacious will, I imagine, make the best physician, tho' he should entertain distinct hypotheses concerning distinct species of diseases, subservient to this end, that were inconsistent one with another, they being made use of in those several sorts of diseases but as distinct arts of memory in those cases. And I the rather say this, that they might be rely'd on only as artificial helps to a physician, and not as philosophical truths to a naturalist.[8] But, Sir, I run too far, and must beg your pardon for talking so freely on a subject you understand so much better than I do. I hoped the way of treating diseases, which with so much approbation Dr. Sydenham had introduc'd into the world, would have beaten the other out, and turn'd men from visions and wrangling to observation and endeavouring after settl'd practices in more diseases, such as I think he has given us in some.[9] If my zeal for the saving mens lives and preserving their health (which is infinitely to be prefer'd to any speculations never so fine in physick) has carried me too far,

---

[3] Inattention.

[4] Galen: Greek physician whose ideas dominated Western medicine until Locke's era. Four humours: body fluids that were held to determine temperament: blood (sanguine), phlegm (phlegmatic), yellow bile (choleric), black bile (melancholic).

[5] The chemical theories of Paracelsus, 16th-cent. Swiss physician, alchemist, and scientist.

[6] Robert Boyle, 'Reflections upon the Hypothesis of Alcali and Acidum', in *Experiments* (1675).

[7] Observable by the senses.   [8] A student of natural science.

[9] Sydenham emphasized detailed clinical observation. His *Observationes Medicae* (1676) was a standard text for two centuries. He developed the use of quinine and opium, and advanced understanding of fevers and gout.

you will excuse it in one who wishes well to the practice of physick, tho' he meddles not with it. . . .

1609. William Molyneux to Locke, Dublin, 2 March 1693

. . . I wil conclude my tedious lines with a Jocose Problem,[1] that, upon Discourse with several concerning your Book and Notions, I have proposed to Diverse very Ingenious Men, and could hardly ever Meet with One that at first dash would give me the Answer to it, which I think true; till by hearing My Reasons they were Convinced. tis this. Suppose a Man born blind, and now adult, and taught by his Touch to Distinguish between a Cube and a Sphere (Suppose) of Ivory, nighly of the same Bignes, so as to tel, when he felt One and tother, Which is the Cube which the Sphære. Suppose then, the Cube and Sphære placed on a Table, and the Blind man to be made to see. Quære[2] whether by his sight, before he touchd them, he could now Distinguish and tel which is the Globe which the Cube. I answer, Not;[3] for tho he has obtaind the Experience of How a Globe, how a Cube affects his Touch. Yet he has not yet attaind the Experience, that what affects my Touch so or so, must affect my Sight so or so; or that a Protuberant Angle in the Cube that presd his hand unequally, shall appear to his Eye as it does in the Cube. But of this enough; perhaps you may find some place in your Essay, wherein you may not think it amis, to say something of this Problem. . . .

1622. William Molyneux to Locke, Dublin, 18 April 1693

I have lately received farther testimonys of your kindnes and Freindship to me in your Last of Mar. 28th. which brings withall the Welcome News of your having Committed your Work of Education to the Press:[1] than Which, I know not any thing that I ever expected with a more earnest desire. What my Brother told me relating to that Treatise, he had from your self in Holland.[2] But perhaps you might have forgot what pasd between you on that

---

[1] Locke incorporated Molyneux's Problem into the 2nd edn. of the *Essay*, II. ix. 8, quoting from this letter. Molyneux first posed it in a letter to the *Bibliothèque universelle* in 1688.

[2] Query: the question is.

[3] In the *Essay* Locke wrote: 'I agree with this thinking Gentleman whom I am proud to call my Friend, in his answer to this Problem; and am of opinion, that the Blind Man, at first sight, would not be able with certainty to say, which was the Globe, which the Cube'. The problem is taken up by the modern neuropsychologist Richard Gregory in *Eye and Brain* (5th edn., 1998). It was alluded to by Jonathan Swift in his account of the Academy of Lagado in *Gulliver's Travels*.

[1] *Some Thoughts Concerning Education* (1693).

[2] Dr Thomas Molyneux, who met Locke at Leiden in 1684.

Occasion. I perceive you fear, the novelty of some Notions therein may seem Extravagant; But if I may venture to judge of the Author, I fear no such thing from him. I doubt not, but the Work will be New and Peculiar, as his other Performances; And this 'tis that renders them estimable and Pleasant. He that travels the beaten Roads may chance indeed to have Company; but he that takes his Liberty, and manages it with Judgement, is the Man that makes useful Discoverys, and most beneficial to those that follow him. Had Columbus never ventur'd farther than his Predecessors, we had yet been Ignorant of a Vast Part of our Earth, preferable (as some say) to all the other three; And if none may be allowd to trye the Ocean of Philosophy farther than Our Ancestors, we shall have but little advancements or Discoverys made in the Mundus Intellectualis;[3] wherein I beleive there is much more unknown, than what we have yet found out.

I should very much approve of your Adding a Chapter in your Essay, concerning Malbranches Hypothesis.[4] As there are Enthusiasmes in Divinity, so there are in Philosophy; and as one proceeds from not Consulting, or misapprehending the Book of God; so the other from not reading and Considering the Book of Nature. I look upon Malbranches Notions, or rather Platos, in this particular perfectly unintelligible; And if you will Ingage in a Philosophick Controversy, you cannot do it with more advantage than in this matter. What you lay down concerning Our Ideas and Knowledge is founded and Confirmd by Experiment, and Observation, that any man may make in himself, or the Children he Converses with; wherein he may note the Gradual Steps that we make in Knowledge. But Plato's fancy has no foundation in Nature, but is meerly the Product of his Own brain. . . .

I know tis none of your Busines to ingage in Controversy, or remove Objections; save only such as seem immediately to strike at your Own Positions; and therefore I cannot insist upon what I am now going to mention to you; However I will give you the Hint, and Leave the Considerations thereof to your own Breast. The tenth Chapter of your fourth Book is a Most Exact Demonstration of the Existence of a God. But perhaps it might be more full, by an Addition against the Eternity of the World, and that all things have not been going on, in the same Manner, as we now see them, ab Æterno. I have known a Pack of Philosophical Atheists, that reley much on this Hypothesis; and even Hobbs himself does somewhere alledge (If I am not forgetful tis in his Book de Corpore in the Chapter de Universo)[5] that the same Arguments, which are brought against the Æternity of the World, may serve as wel against the Æternity of the Creatour of the World.

---

[3] The world of ideas.

[4] Nicolas Malebranche, French philosopher and theologian, author of *Recherche de la vérité* (*Search after Truth*) (1674). His notions were brought to Locke's attention by John Norris's book (L1325, nn. 10, 14). Locke wrote two critiques, not incorporated into the *Essay*: 'Remarks upon some of Mr Norris's books' and 'An examination of P. Malebranche's opinion of seeing all things in God' (*Works*, ix. 211–55; x. 247–59).

[5] Hobbes, *Elementorum philosophiae sectio prima de corpore* (1655), pt. iv, ch. 26, § 1.

1647. Edward Clarke to Locke, Chipley, Somerset, 2 August 1693

... Your Labours for the Publique are a Blessing to us all, and the Particular Honour you have done mee in the Publication of your thoughts concerning Education,[1] is never to bee suffitiently Acknowlidged; But haveing Return'd you my particular thankes upon that occasion in the last Letter I writt to you, I shall trouble you noe further on that subject at present; But begg leave to interrupt the Reviseing your Learned Essay touching humane understanding, which prevayles wonderfully amongst all the men of any sence and understanding that I converse with, with Acquainting you That I thinke my Wife is Breeding againe, I hope of another Boy, her Leggs often swell much, and shee has sometimes frequently the same payn on the lower part of the Right side of her Belly that wee have both formerly complayned to you of, and shee often makes that thick sort of water that you have heretofore seen; Shee is I Blesse God otherwise in perfect health, shee eates, drinks, sleepes, and Lookes well, but I would gladly know your thoughts upon the whole matter, whither Adviseable to drinke the Bath-water,[2] if shee bee desierouse of it, whilst shee is with Child, or what else you thinke proper; ...

[S]hee knows nothing of what I have writt, and perhapps I shall incurr her Displeasure by medling; Shee is full of vapours[3] as usuall when with Child, and soe the more difficult to bee pleased or satisfied, sometimes shee seemes to bee willing to goe to Bath, at other times that shee cannot bee content or satisfied to leave her Children here, and frequently askes if the Bath Waters may not bee dranke here at home with good successe, soe that I know not how to behave my selfe better, than to bee willing to goe thither, or to send for the Waters home as shall bee most adviseable, and shee shall bee most inclyn'd, beleiveing that if shee could bee content and quiet in her own mind, That would bee the best Physick to Her, and the greatest satisfaction to mee and all about Her, Pray write fully to Her, and perswade Her to bee a Philosopher if possible; and that shee may not suspect my haveing written to you, pray complayn a little of my Silence towards you, ...

1650. Benjamin Furly to Locke, Rotterdam, 9/19 August 1693

... I am heartily sorry for the delay in the book[1] for my Lord Pembrooke, which could not be got into England by the packet,[2] by reason of the great strictness of the Captains, who will take nothing: in so much, that by the great

---

[1] Published about July, dedicated to Clarke.   [2] Mineral waters of Bath.   [3] Nervous disorders.

[1] Jean Le Clerc's commentary on the book of Genesis.   [2] A ship carrying letters and passengers.

Authority of Monsieur Vander Poel the General Postmaster there, I could not get it passed that way; but received it back again yesterday, and have given it to the bearer hereof mr. John Toland,[3] who has a letter to you from monsieur Le clerc. I find him to be a free spirited ingenious man; that quitted the Papacy in Jameses time[4] when al men, of no principles were looking towards it, and having once cast off the yoak of Spirituall Authority, that great bugbear, and bane of ingenuity, he could never be perswaded to bow his neck to that yoak again, by whom soever claymed; this has rendred it somewhat difficult to him, to find a way of subsistence in the world, and made him ask my counsell in the case: I told him I know no way for him, but to find out some free ingenuous English Gentleman that might have occasion for a Tutor in his family, who would be as glad of the opportunity as himself, were my circumstances such, that I could entertain him, and he willing to abide with me, he should not be put to the trouble to seek further. But that being not so, I intreat you, Sir, to be assistant to him, wherein you can; not for my sake, but for his own worth; . . .

1655. Locke to William Molyneux, Oates, 23 August 1693

. . . I do not at all wonder that the affection of a kind father should startle at it at first reading,[1] and think it very severe that children should not be suffer'd to express their desires; for so you seem to understand me. And such a restraint, you fear, would be apt to moap[2] them, and hinder their diversion. But if you please to look upon the place,[3] and observe my drift, you will find that they should not be indulged, or complied with, in any thing their conceits have made a want to them, as necessary to be supplied. What you say, *that children, would be moap'd for want of diversion and recreation, or else we must have those about them study nothing all day, but how to find employment for them; and how this would rack the invention of any man living, you leave me to judge*, seems to intimate, as if you understood that children should do nothing but by the prescription of their parents or tutors, chalking out each action of the whole day in train to them. I hope my words express no such thing, for it is quite contrary to my sense, and I think would be useless tyranny in their governors, and certain ruin to the children. I am so much for recreation that I would, as much as possible, have all they do be made so. I think recreation as necessary to them as their food, and that nothing can

[3] Soon to be notorious for his deism and republicanism. He had been at Leiden since 1690.

[4] Toland was brought up a Catholic; he turned to the Presbyterians, who trained him for the ministry; now he was cutting adrift from them.

[1] The following is a discussion of 'Craving', in *Education*, §§ 101–2 in 1st edn.; §§ 106–7, much revised, in 3rd edn.

[2] To mope: to make spiritless or listless.   [3] Passage.

be recreation which does not delight. This, I think, I have so expressed, and when you have put that together, judge whether I would not have them have the greatest part of their time left to them, without restraint, to divert themselves any way they think best, so it be free from vitious actions, or such as may introduce vitious habits. And therefore if they should ask to play, it could be no more interpreted a want of fancy, than if they asked for victuals when hungry; though where the matter is well order'd, they will never need to do that. For when they have either done what their governor thinks enough in any application to what is usually made their business, or are perceiv'd to be tir'd with it, they should of course be dismissed to their innocent diversions, without ever being put to ask for it. So that I am for the full liberty of diversion, as much as you can be, and, upon a second perusal of my book, I do not doubt but you will find me so. But being allow'd that, as one of their natural wants, they should not yet be permitted to let loose their desires in importunities for what they fancy. Children are very apt to covet what they see those above them in age have or do, to have or do the like, especially if it be their elder brothers and sisters. Does one go abroad?[4] the other streight has a mind to it too. Has such an one new or fine cloaths, or play-things? they, if you once allow it them, will be impatient for the like, and think themselves ill dealt with if they have it not. This being indulged when they are little, grows up with their age, and with that enlarges it self to things of greater consequence, and has ruin'd more families than one in the world. This should be suppressed in its very first rise, and the desires you would not have encourag'd you should not permit to be spoken, which is the best way for them to silence them to themselves. Children should, by constant use, learn to be very modest in owning their desires, and careful not to ask any thing of their parents but what they have reason to think their parents will approve of. And a reprimand upon their ill bearing a refusal comes too late, the fault is committed and allow'd; and if you allow them to ask, you can scarce think it strange they should be troubl'd to be deny'd; so that you suffer them to engage themselves in the disorder, and then think the fittest time for a cure, and, I think, the surest and easiest way is prevention. For we must take the same nature to be in children, that is in grown men; and how often do we find men take ill to be deny'd what they would not have been concern'd for if they had not asked. But I shall not enlarge any farther in this, believing you and I shall agree in the matter; and indeed it is very hard, and almost impossible to give general rules of education, when there is scarce any one child, which, in some cases, should not be treated differently from another. All that we can do in general, is only to shew what parents and tutors should aim at, and leave to them the ordering of particular circumstances as the case shall require.

One thing give me leave to be importunate with you about: You say your son is not very strong; to make him strong, you must use him hardly, as I

---

[4] Outside, away from home.

have directed; but you must be sure to do it by very insensible degrees, and begin any hardship you would bring him to only in the spring. This is all the caution needs be used. I have an example of it in the house I live in, where the only son of a very tender mother[5] was almost destroy'd by a too tender keeping. He is now, by a contrary usage, come to bear wind and weather, and wet in his feet; and the cough which threatned him, under that warm and cautious management, has left him, and is now no longer his parents constant apprehension as it was.

I am of your mind as to short hand, I my self learn'd it since I was a man, but had forgot to put it in when I writ, as I have, I doubt not, overseen a thousand other things, which might have been said on this subject.[6] But it was only at first a short scheme for a friend, and is publish'd to excite others to treat it more fully.

I know not whether it would be useful to make a catalogue of authors to be read by a young man, or whether it could be done, unless one knew the child's temper, and what he was designed to.[7]

My Essay is now very near ready for another edition,[8] and upon review of my alterations, concerning what determines the will, in my cool thoughts I am apt to think them to be right, as far as my thoughts can reach in so nice a point, and in short is this. Liberty[9] is a power to act or not to act, accordingly as the mind directs. A power to direct the operative faculties to motion or rest in particular instances, is that which we call the will. That which in the train of our voluntary actions determines the will to any change of operation, is some present uneasiness, which is, or at least is always accompanyed with that of desire. Desire is always moved by evil to fly it; because a total freedom from pain always makes a necessary part of our happyness. But every good, nay every greater good, does not constantly move desire, because it may not make, or may not be taken to make any necessary part of our happiness; for all that we desire is only to be happy. But though this general desire of happiness operates constantly and invariably in us, yet the satisfaction of any particular desire can be suspended from determining the will to any subservient action, till we have maturely examin'd whether the particular apparent good we then desire make a part of our real happiness, or be consistent or inconsistent with it. The result of our judgment, upon examination, is what ultimately determines the man, who could not be free, if his will were determin'd by any thing but his own desire, guided by his own judgment. . . .

---

[5] Francis Cudworth Masham, aged about 7.

[6] A recommendation of shorthand was added in the 3rd edn., § 161. The first viable system of shorthand was invented early in the 17th cent.

[7] Recommended reading occurs in §§ 173–5 in the 1st edn., §§ 184–6 in the 3rd edn. Also L2320.

[8] The 2nd edn. of the *Essay* was published in 1694.

[9] The following summarizes II. xxi. 28–48 in the 2nd edn.

1659. Isaac Newton to Locke, The Bull, Shoreditch, London, 16 September 1693

Being of opinion that you endeavoured to embroil me with weomen[1] and by other means I was so much affected with it as that when one told me you were sickly and would not live I answered twere better if you were dead. I desire you to forgive me this uncharitableness. For I am now satisfied that what you have done is just and I beg your pardon for my having hard thoughts of you for it and for representing that you struck at the root of morality in a principle you laid down in your book of Ideas[2] and designed to pursue in another book and that I took you for a Hobbist.[3] I beg your pardon also for saying or thinking that there was a designe to sell me an office,[4] or to embroile me.

1663. Locke to Isaac Newton, Oates, 5 October 1693

I[1] have ben ever since I first knew you[2] so intirely and sincerly your friend and thought you soe much mine that I could not have beleived what you tell me of your self had I had it from anybody else. And though I cannot but be mightily troubled that you should have had soe many wrong and unjust thoughts of me yet next to the returne of good offices such as from a sincere good will I have ever done you I receive your acknowledgment of the contrary as the kindest thing you could have done me since it gives me hopes that I have not lost a freind I soe much valued. After what your letter expresses I shall not need to say anything to justifie my self to you: I shall always think your own reflection on my cariage both to you and all mankind will sufficiently doe that. Instead of that give me leave to assure you that I am more ready to forgive you than you can be to desire it and I doe it soe freely and fully that I wish for noe thing more than the oportunities to convince you that I truly love and esteem you and that I have still the same goodwill for you as if noe thing of this had happend. To confirme this to you more fully I should be glad to meet you any where and the rather because the conclusion of your letter[3] makes me apprehend it would not be wholy uselesse to you But whether you think it fit or not I leave wholy to you. I shall always be ready to serve you to my utmost in any way you shall like and shall only need your commands or permission to doe it.

---

[1] Most improbable. Newton was apparently mentally disturbed at this time. (This incident has inspired a novella by John Banville, *The Newton Letter* (1982).)

[2] *Essay*, I.   [3] Compare L1301, L1307.

[4] Newton's friends sought public employment for him; he became Warden of the Mint in 1696.

[1] Answers L1659.   [2] There is no definite evidence of their acquaintance before spring 1690.

[3] 'I am Your most humble and unfortunate servant'.

My book[4] is goeing to the presse for a second edition and though I can answer for the designe with which I writ it yet since you have soe oportunely given me notice of what you have said of it I should take it as a favour if you would point out to me the places that gave occasion to that censure that by explaining my self better I may avoid being mistaken by others, or unawares doeing the least prejudice to truth or virtue. I am sure you are soe much a friend to them both that were you none to me I could expect this from you . . .

1690. Locke to Edward Clarke, Oates, [12?] January 1694

He[1] has found all the rest right, *i.e.* all but what is wrong. Who doubts it, but what becomes of the wrong? To this add the list here enclosed, and he has well mended the matter. Whatever he promised this second time I am out of patience. If you please to give him a copy of the enclosed,[2] and keep the original by you, it is more than he deserves. I hope at the same time you will thank him for his great care and exactness. . . .

1 Ask him whether he thinks it will be for his credit to let it goe with soe many great faults as those he has now writ in the margent,[3] and to correct them only by seting them amongst the Errata

2 You may tell him 'tis a book of thought and requires consideration in the reader, which will be mightily disturbd if he must turne to the Errata for such as are more than literal or verbal faults in the book and if the Reader does not looke in the errata (which few readers are at the pains to doe) he will take it to be as in many places it is, as now printed, nonsense. And if any Reader be soe carefull as to correct his booke according to the errata, yet the paper of this second edition is soe bad that it will not bear writeing on it in the margent

3 Ask him whether the copy cost him dear, or any thing: and whether the profit of the booke will not bear the charges of reprinting above 8 leaves if there be occasion for more to make the Edition any way tolerable[4]

4 Whether he thinks he[5] that promised him *more when this is done* will ever send more to a man soe negligent in two editions, that to the omision of the corrections sent him of the first has added an hundred new ones in this second. That how ever he lays the blame on the printer the neglect will be imputed to him, and really is his, for if he had not carelessely given the

---

[4] The *Essay.*

[1] Awnsham Churchill, Locke's publisher. The following concerns corrections to the 2nd edn. of the *Two Treatises,* published in the spring.

[2] There were two enclosures, a list of errata (omitted here), and the following commentary.

[3] Margin.

[4] There are twelve cancels (replacement sheets) in the 2nd edn of the *Two Treatises.*   [5] Locke.

corrections, were sent him, to the printer. But had but taken care to have them writ into the book it self, the printer would not have omitted them. Or if he had lookd after it ever soe litle him self or had but a tolerable corrector Neither the former edition nor this espetialy had had soe many shamefull faults

5   What satisfaction or amends it will be to the Reader or Author that he will not imploy the printer again for the same Reason, they may think it best he, the bookseller,[6] should never be imploid again. Such a negligent Bookseller and printer may be laid aside togeather

6   That as to the Quæres[7] he has put to severall of the corrections you lately gave him, you have looked over those places again, and find that he that doubted whether they should be put in or noe understood not the Author as particularly that place p. 151 l. 17 is not sense unlesse printed thus: Heathens, Philosopher Aristotle, and[8] And therefor you are of opinion they ought all to be put in, except one which haveing your self some doubt about you have blotted out of his paper and another p. 120 which by the addition of a word omitted is made plainer[9]

7   That you have looked over the later sheets of the book printed since those he formerly shewd you, which are done with the same care as the former which appears by these additionall corrections you here give him

8   In fine, that whatever he made the world expect, this later is soe intolerable an edition that you leave it to him to doe what he will with it

1693. Locke to William Molyneux, Oates, 19 January 1694

... You doubt whether my answer be full in the case of the drunkard.[1] To try whether it be or no, we must consider what I am there doing. As I remember (for I have not that chapter here by me) I am there shewing that punishment is annexed to personality, and personality to consciousness: How then can a drunkard be punish'd for what he did, whereof he is not conscious? To this I answer, Human judicatures justly punish him, because the fact is proved against him; but want of consciousness cannot be proved for him. This you think not sufficient, but would have me add the common reason, that drunkenness being a crime, one crime cannot be alledged in excuse for another. This reason, how good soever, cannot, I think, be used by me, as not reaching

---

[6] Publisher: the term 'publisher' for a profession distinct from printing and bookselling did not yet exist. Locke described himself as the 'publisher' when he arranged publication of Boyle's *General History of the Air* (1692).

[7] Queries.

[8] *Two Treatises*, I, § 154. Churchill had printed: 'these Heathen Philosophers, Aristotle, and Poet Homer' instead of 'these Heathens, Philosopher Aristotle, and Poet Homer'.

[9] *Two Treatises*, I, § 122.

[1] In the *Essay*, II. xxvii. 22.

my case; for what has this to do with consciousness? nay, it is an argument against me, for if a man may be punish'd for any crime which he committed when drunk, whereof he is allow'd not to be conscious, it overturns my hypothesis. Your case of shooting a man by chance, when stealing a deer, being made capital, and the like, I allow to be just; but then, pray consider, it concerns not my argument; there being no doubt of consciousness in that case, but only shews, that any criminal action infects the consequences of it. But drunkenness has something peculiar in it when it destroys consciousness; and so the instances you bring justifie not the punishing of a drunken fact, that was totally and irrecoverably forgotten, which the reason that I give being sufficient to do, it well enough removed the objection, without entring into the true foundation of the thing, and shewing how far it was reasonable for humane justice to punish a crime of a drunkard, which he could be suppos'd not conscious of, which would have uselessly engag'd me in a very large discourse, and an impertinent[2] digression. For I ask you, if a man by intemperate drinking should get a fever, and in the frenzy of his disease (which lasted not perhaps above an hour) committed some crime, would you punish him for it? If you would not think this just, how can you think it just to punish him for any fact committed in a drunken frenzy, without a fever? Both had the same criminal cause, drunkenness, and both committed without consciousness. I shall not inlarge any farther into other particular instances, that might raise difficulties about the punishing or not punishing the crime of an unconscious drunken man, which would not easily be resolv'd without enquiring into the reason upon which humane justice ought to proceed in such cases, which was beyond my present business to do.[3] Thus, Sir, I have laid before you the reasons why I have let that passage go without any addition made to it. . . .

You write to me, as if ink had the same spell upon me, that mortar, as the Italians say,[4] has upon others, that when I had once got my fingers into it, I could never afterwards keep them out. I grant that methinks I see subjects enough which way ever I cast my eyes, that deserve to be otherwise handled, than I imagine they have been; but they require abler heads, and stronger bodies than I have, to manage them. Besides, when I reflect on what I have done, I wonder at my own bold folly, that has so far exposed me in this nice[5] and critical, as well as quicksighted and learned age. I say not this to excuse a lazy idleness, to which I intend to give up the rest of my few days. I think every one, according to what way providence has placed him in, is bound to labour for the publick good, as far as he is able, or else he has no right to eat. Under this obligation of doing something, I cannot have a stronger to determine me what I shall do, than what your desires shall engage me in. . . .

---

[2] Irrelevant.
[3] Later he added, 'I agree with you that drunkenness being a voluntary defect, want of consciousness ought not to be presum'd in favour of the drunkard' (L1744).
[4] 'A wise man never ought to put his finger into mortar'.   [5] Precise.

10

Civility and Superstition,
1694–1695

During the mid-1690s Locke was intensely preoccupied with new writing. In 1695 he published *The Reasonableness of Christianity*, which reduced Christianity to a few simple truths, grounded in a rational reading of scripture, and accenting virtue rather than dogma or ceremonial. The book was published anonymously. Locke tells Limborch about this project, allying it with the latter's *Theologia Christiana*, which was under attack from all sides (L1901). The extent of Locke's self-identification with Dutch Remonstrant theology, evident in his correspondence with Limborch and Le Clerc, is striking. He also commends Limborch's account of the medieval inquisition of Toulouse in *The History of the Inquisition*, which later became a popular text-book exposing Catholic persecution, when translated into English in 1732 (L1804). Limborch recounts his apparent success in dissuading a theologically erudite young woman from converting to Judaism. He had earlier engaged in public debate with a leading theologian among the distinguished Jewish community of Amsterdam (L1791). From Rotterdam, Benjamin Furly sends Locke a vituperation against 'hireling' priests and the intellectual bondage imposed by institutional churches upon their followers. Every church, Furly argues, reeks of 'Roman slavery' for they all use the weapon of 'heresy' to exact obedience (L1745). He voices the growing strain of anticlericalism in public discourse during the 1690s: the word 'priestcraft' came into fashion.

Locke continued to revise his *Essay* for successive editions—the second appeared in 1694, the third in 1695, and two chapters were added to the fourth in 1700. Still attending to his friends' opinions and suggestions, Locke provides Le Clerc with further clarification of his ideas on free will and determinism (L1798). Tyrrell echoes Molyneux's concerns about free will, consciousness, and personal identity (L1800). Locke consents to a proposal by an Oxford don, John Wynne, to produce a summary of the *Essay* for student use (L1846). The appearance of Wynne's *Abridgment* in 1696 encouraged the *Essay*'s use as a university textbook, though the orthodoxy of the *Essay* was still challenged. Locke also agrees to Molyneux's offer to arrange a Latin translation (L1887).

Locke began to receive letters from admiring strangers. A Staffordshire Dissenter deduces from Locke's rejection of innate ideas the implausibility of the conventional Christian doctrine of original sin. His remarks demonstrate the variety of heterodox ways in which the *Essay* could be interpreted (L1914). From a gentleman named James Hamilton, Locke receives praise for his *Thoughts Concerning Education* and a request for advice regarding a tutor for his children. He wanted to keep them out of the clutches of the clergy, who were wedded to divine right politics and intolerant religion (L1707). From his former pupil, later the third Earl of Shaftesbury, Locke receives an inflated and meandering letter. It evinces a Socratic insistence on the cultivation of virtue and sociability in preference to philosophical system-building or scientific discovery (L1794). Shaftesbury was later to attack Locke's moral philosophy as a 'selfish' system in his hugely popular collection of essays on benevolence and 'politeness', entitled *Characteristicks of Men, Manners, Opinions and Times* (1711).

After 1695 books no longer had to pass the press licensers, and printing was no longer confined to London and the two universities. The lapsing of censorship—the old Act had a time limitation—occurred when parliament was unable to agree upon new legislation. Edward Clarke and John Freke imply that censorship had come to be regarded as unacceptable, and that the bishops, sensing this, had changed tactics and now joined hands with the Stationers' Company. They based their continued defence of press controls on the ostensible protection of intellectual property rights, embodied in the copyrights of printers and authors (L1860). Meanwhile, to Clarke, Locke confides his opinion that the second edition of the *Two Treatises* was so sloppy that it should be sold off cheap 'amongst common readers' (L1728).

In 1694 the Bank of England was founded to manage government debt and help finance the expensive war against France. It bound a new rentier class to a financial interest in the stability of the Revolution regime. Despite his reservations that the Bank might damage the trade of towns outside London, Locke nevertheless invested in it and reproves Clarke for declining to become a director (L1768, L1849).

The Revolution regime received a shocking blow in December 1694 when Queen Mary died suddenly of smallpox. It deprived the crown of the semblance of hereditary right which the joint monarchy had enjoyed. That semblance would be restored at William's death in 1702, when Mary's younger sister Anne succeeded. Locke knew several members of Mary's entourage and a report of the queen's death comes to him from a lady of the royal bedchamber (L1834).

In the late seventeenth century, Bath rapidly became a popular resort for 'taking the waters'. Locke had recommended the waters for their medicinal value and Paul D'Aranda reports taking his advice to good effect (L1925). The cultivation of exotic fruits in England was another new fashion: Locke recommends the best aristocratic gardens for peaches, oranges, and grapes (L1768). To Hans Sloane, he comments on tumours and on the possibility of spontaneous generation (L1785).

1707. James Hamilton to Locke, London, 8 February 1694

The universall concurrence of very competent judges of the workes of the learned, in nameing you for the Author of *Some Thoughts Concerning Education*, hath occasioned my giveing you this trouble, to which I am not only prompted by the ingenious solid and practicable notions you have layde downe, as welle for the inculcateing and cherishing Moralitye in Youthe, as the improvement of theyr understandeing, but I am further incouraged by the generous and publicke spiritte which shines throughout your booke, and is very perticularly expressed in the midle of the second paragraph of the epistle dedicatorye to that booke;[1] give me therefore leave Sir thoe unfortunately a stranger to you, to desire your assistance without any further apologye in an affaire wherein the very first mistakes are attended with such pernicious consequences, as you have judiciously expressed. I have two sons the eldest whereof wille bee eight yeares olde next monthe, and the other six in August, neither of them can yette write which I doe not looke uppon as any greate matter as to losse of tyme, thoe I woulde not have deferred the eldests learneing it thus longe, but that hee hath hitherto been of a weakely constitution and hath a tendencye to growe awrye, which made mee aprehende the consequences of a constrain'd posture, thoe nowe hee gathers strengthe I intende hee shall begin to sette pen to paper next summer, and I have not through fondnesse lette him gette a habitte of idlenesse, for as soone as hee was capable of it I had him taught to reade in his mother tounge, and imediatly after frenche, in shorte Sir he can reade and speake both languages with almost an equall facilitye, and hee hath made a faire progresse in Geographye, and hath newely begunne Chronologye, which whilst hee is learneing hee shall perfect himselfe in what he hath alreadye learnt in Geographye by pointing to such places in the Maps as there wille bee occasion to mention; hee hath alsoe newely begunne to learne the frenche grammer, for hee hath hitherto learnt noe thing but by roate, which method I am likewise followeing as to his younger brother, whose parts wille I hope in tyme exerte themselves but hee is as yette very backwarde. I thought it proper to acquaint you with thus much of my children, and likewise that I intende for the future to observe your method, before I desired the favour of you to recommende to mee a proper person to bee theyr Tutor, if you knowe any such rightly qualiffyed to forme theyr mindes as to learneing, and moralitye, and wille bee chearefully contented with twentye poundes a yeare, and a wellecome to my owne table at dinner; his due instructing and constant attendance on my children is all I expect from him, but herein hee must bee very assiduous, for my fortune wille not admitte of my further encreaseing my familye, and I shalle have fulle

---

[1] 'I think it every Man's indispensable Duty to do all the Service he can to his Country.'

employement for the servants I alreadye have, soe that hee must even bee assisting to them in theyr dresseing themselves, which a discreete man wille not scruple at, thoe others more vainly punctilious maye object against this perticular, but suche persons would by noe meanes answer my endes, for besides what I have alreadye sayde I shoulde feare theyr infuseing mistaken notions in my children; I wille not trouble you with an account of the economye of my familye,[2] for I take it for granted there wille bee noe difficultye in conformeing to it, especially that noe orderly person wille thinke it muche to acquaint mee or my wife when any occasion of theyr owne maye calle them abroade; I have alreadye sayde soe muche that I would adde noe thinge more to it if London were my place of residence, but my liveing in Yorcke might perhaps bee an objection if I did not solve it with an assurance of alloweing the person I shall take for a tutor to my children three poundes to beare his charges up to towne, . . . ; neither neede hee question my using my utmost endeavours in doeing better for him when soe ever hee can putte mee in a waye, but I would not deceive any bodye, and my privatte waye of liveing wille not afforde many oppertunityes of that nature; I have indeede the presentation to a liveing,[3] when the incumbent dyes, worthe at least 150.[ll] per annum in Irelande, but thoe I am my selfe of the Churche of Englande, I am loathe to have my children tutor'd by any of the Clergye, for most of them have stille a hanckering after jure divino and passive obedience principles,[4] and are over tenacious as to indifferent ceremonyes,[5] and very fonde of nicetyes in religion, which are matters I would have none of my children trouble theyr heades about, but barre these tenets, I have noe repugnancye to an easye well humoured man of that coate. . . .

1728. Locke to Edward Clarke, Oates, 30 March [1694]

. . . The errata of the book you sent me[1] you will receíve on Monday by one that goes from hence. I have perused it a good way at your command and have put in only the grosse errata that make it unintelligible for the small ones are infinite. The use I think is to be made of this, is, since he[2] offers that he will if you think fit loose this edition, that he should sell this very cheap and then you may tell him you will at your leisure looke it over and correct it more exactly you haveing now left a great many faults in the pointing[3] that disturbs the sense, and then he may take care to have it printed correct in a

---

[2] i.e. the conduct and management of the household.
[3] The right to appoint a clergyman to a parish.
[4] The divine right doctrine of the Tory absolutists.   [5] 'Things indifferent': L108, n. 4.

[1] The *Two Treatises*, 2nd edn. L1730 is a list of errata, to be re-copied by another hand to hide Locke's authorship.
[2] The publisher, Awnsham Churchill.   [3] Punctuation.

fair character and good paper. But let him sel this at a very low rate: This will quickly rid him of this edition and not hinder the next though this be scatterd amongst common readers.

1745. Benjamin Furly to Locke, Rotterdam, 26 May / 5 June 1694

... I am of your mind, and experience has taught me, that it is no easy matter to get a society so free, as you and I would gladly see, and help propagate in the world: except it should consist of a very small and select number—

For the prejudice of Education lays in mens minds such an undue reverence for some things, and persons as is not easily overcome.

The Bugbear of Authority, Tradition, and the name of Church is so sacred with them, That few people dare call in question the Doctrines which holy church has taught for so many hundred years, or which their Learned and godly ministers have all along taught since the Reformation. What! say they, within themselvs, shall we dare to call in question what so many Ages, and so many learned men have determind?

People are afraid to examin, they dare not trust their own Judgments, their own eyes, their own sence. for fear of being deceived, seduced, deluded, and what not, which is a miserable estate. And differs not from that enslaved Estate of the people under the Romish church.

But that which is yet worse, and more to be lamented is that people are afraid to examine, lest their eyes should be opened to see, and be convinced of things that may break their rest, or peace, or oblige them to profess things, that may interfere with their Interest in the world, with their reputation amongst their Priests, and neighbours; And pass them for Hereticks, Schismaticks, and what not, conceited, troublesome spirits, that wilbe wiser than their neighbours, more knowing than all the great learned, and godly men of our party.

No, No, 'tis best, say they, to be quiet, and not to trouble ourselves to examine matters, our forefathers, our learned Teachers have examind things enough already.

These and such like snares keep men in slavery and bondage, and few men, but those that are endowed with a generous boldness, and courage, dare once examine matters.

I say not these things, dear Sir, for your sake, but for my childrens sake, who shall copy this Letter, that they may see how free their father was.

Had these considerations prevaild with Luther, Calvin, and those first reformers, who contradicted the Church, and feared not to examine the Doctrines she had establisht for so many hundreds of years, by her learned Bishops and Priests, Synods and Councils, and made no bones of Trampling all under foot, (notwithstanding the Authority of the church, that pretended not onely to learning and piety, but even to infallibility itself) which they found to be unreasonable and unscripturall

I say had such considerations of Authority, Tradition, church, learning, holyness, fear of being counted Hereticks, Schismaticks, or singular, troublesome, restless, nice heads, been able to discourage them, we had yet groaned under the Intollerable yoake of Romish slavery.

Are we escaped that, by their generous example, and shall we again bow our necks to the same pretences among their successors? Shall we put out our eyes to see with theirs? Surely no.

This makes me greedily grasp at all opportunities offered me to expose those two Words CHURCH, and HERETICK; as two of the most pernicious words that have for above 1000 years obtaind amongst mankind.

That of *Church*, to gain reputation to a company of Clerical Coxcombs, fooles, knaves, and slaves, who being so to their superior Ecclesiasticks would, by their lording it over Gods Heritage (or Clergy) that is the people, (which make the society of christians) make all men slaves to them, as if they alone were the church.

That of *Heretick*; to render odious, and run down, all honest, wel meaning, courageous, generous spirited men, that dare be so bold as to profess, and practise what they Judge to be their duty towards God, towards them selvs, and towards their neighbour, how contrary, and unpleasant soever it be to these church slaves and all their enslaved followers, who would make free men (if they could) bow their necks to their doctrines, decrees, orders, injunctions, and constitutions. . . .

1768. Locke to Edward Clarke, Oates, 6 August 1694

. . . I know not what you and your man John Barber[1] think of us travellers But if you continue to doubt of what I told you, you may goe to Mr Controlers at Winchington in Buckingham shire[2] and there have it verified to him that we eat there ripe Newington peaches the begining of July which they there had perfect ripe and good in June. we gathering and eating the last that was left. At my Lord Ferrers's[3] we eat the ripe Oranges and at the Earle of Chesterfeilds[4] the ripe grapes where also you may see oranges planted and thriveing in the ground. If John Barber will goe to these places he will perhaps see ways of ripening fruit and haveing it early which he has not thought on. These two last houses are in Darby shire and if he will take into his walke

---

[1] Clarke's gardener.
[2] Thomas, Lord Wharton, Comptroller of the Royal Household, at Upper Winchenden.
[3] Sir Robert Shirley, Lord Ferrers, at Shirley, Derbyshire.
[4] Philip Stanhope, Earl of Chesterfield, at Bretby, Derbyshire.

my Lord Mountagues[5] at Boughton in Northampton shire he will there find such a garden as he never yet saw in England. I am soe much Johns Friend that I wish he had seen all these places and some others I could name that soe he might not only out doe the Gardeners of the west but most others in England, for truly I met with what I could not expect though I was prepared with stories before hand

I cannot Imagin why you refuse to be one of the Directors of the bank.[6] I looke on it of noe small consequence to you and to England and therefor shall hope you will not persist in a refusall at least without consulting your friends who noe doubt will be ready to hear your reasons. . . .

1785. Locke to Dr Hans Sloane, Oates, 14 September 1694

It is very kindly and charitably done of you to send me some news from the commonwealth of letters into a place where I seldome meet with any thing beyond the observation of a scabby sheep or a lame horse. The great spleen you found in the woman you opend seems to be oweing as you rightly judg to the polypi[1] which sweld the sanguinary vessels since the other parts of the spleen were every way right. This is an observation very well worth recording and publishing and may give great light about tumors in the abdomen which are not always to be imputed to apostemes[2] or collections of peccant humors. Polypus's in the bloud vessels are found soe frequently that I think they would deserve to be treated of as a particular disease, If there were collections enough of their hystory and symptoms to build any theory on and lay a foundation for their cure. Pray when you doe me the favour to write to me again doe not forget to set downe the diameter of the bigest vessels you found in that spleen what part of an inch it was

The history of imperfect plants which you mention[3] will I guesse help much towards the perfecting that part of natural history. The notion of equivocal generation[4] I should quite lay aside as a groundlesse phansy if you could resolve me some instances that puzel me in that affair. One is the strange and new creatures that have been often found in the bodys of men and other animals, which could not be reduced to any species of animals in that country or else where from which they might derive their original. Another is the production of lice in any one who changes not though in a place and circumstances where there cannot be supposd to be any propogation by seed from other

---

[5] Ralph Montagu, Earl of Montagu, second husband of the Countess of Northumberland.
[6] The newly founded Bank of England.

[1] Polypus: blood clot; now, a tumour.   [2] Large deep-seated abscesses.
[3] Probably John Ray, *Historia Plantarum*, iii (1694).
[4] Spontaneous generation: the supposed development of living organisms without the agency of pre-existing organisms.

animals of that species. These and others that might be mentiond I think can hardly be accounted for by univocal generation[5] acc[o]rding to the ordinary philosophie. I hope the author in his account of submarine plants will not omitt to tell us how deep under water any of them are to be found, or whether they are any species of them are at any dept we can come at. For I am apt to suppose that the air hath something to doe with vegetation even under water, whether this will serve to discover any thing of it, or help us to guesse how far it descends in the body of the water I know not. This I conclude that there is noe thing constantly observable in nature, which will not always bring some light with it, and lead us farther into the knowledg of her ways of workeing. . . .

1791. Philippus van Limborch to Locke, [Amsterdam], [*c.*24 September / 4 October 1694]

. . . I have for some time wanted to write for you a careful account of my conversation with a girl who was doubtful and wavering about the truth of the Christian religion, and altogether inclined to Judaism. The matter is widely known throughout our country. To put it shortly, I have perceived in her such acuteness of mind, shrewdness of judgement, dexterity in argument, and indefatigable reading of various books, as well in theology as in philosophy, as can scarcely be believed. She is twenty-two years old; but with such maturity of judgement that she far surpasses men of riper years and exercised in the schools. She has yielded to my reasoning and has frankly acknowledged Jesus Christ as her Saviour. Three of the leading ministers of the Contraremonstrants' church[1] in this city, of which church she is a member, had already held several conversations with her, but without success. Nor was this surprising since they began the discussion with an affirmation of the dogma of the Holy Trinity, and indeed with passages drawn from the Old Testament; and what will surprise you more, they urged that the necessity of believing the dogma had been imposed on the Jews in the Old Testament. She easily parried all arguments of that kind. When I was summoned to her I adopted a very different procedure, in fact the same as that with which I assailed Don Balthasar:[2] that is, I first affirmed the truth of the New Testament history, and especially of the resurrection of Our Lord and the sending of the Holy Spirit, with arguments to which she frankly confessed that she could oppose nothing solid, and accordingly that she was persuaded by them. Next I proved that all

---

[5] Regular generation between male and female members of a species.

[1] The Calvinist (anti-Arminian or anti-Remonstrant) wing of the Dutch church.

[2] Balthasar Orobio de Castro, a Christian of Jewish descent, tortured by the Spanish Inquisition, settled in Amsterdam, converted to Judaism. Limborch debated Christianity with him: *De Veritate Religionis Christianae Amica Collatio cum Erudito Judaeo* (1687).

the prophecies in the Old Testament have their fulfilment in the history of the New Testament; this, as I had previously affirmed the truth of the Gospel, was not difficult for me. Now much more confirmed than before in the Christian religion, she discusses various matters with me from time to time. . . .

1794. Anthony Ashley Cooper, Lord Ashley, to Locke, St Giles, Dorset, 29 September 1694

. . . [T]he End to which my Studdyes, such as they are, have any leaning, or bent, is but to learn mee this one thing in short; how to Communicate every thing freely; how to bee more Sociable and more a Friend. how is itt possible that I should bee a Niggard here, and not impart all that I were able? Itt is not with mee as with an Empirick,[1] one that is studdying of Curiositys, raising of new Inventions that are to gain credit to the author, starting of new Notions that are to amuse the World and serve them for Divertion or for tryall of their Acuteness (which is all one as if it were some new Play, a Chess, or a Game of cards that were envented.) Itt is not in my case as with one of the men of new Systems, who are to build the credit of their own invented ones upon the ruine of the Ancienter and the discredit of those Learned Men that went before. Descartes, or Mr Hobbs, or any of their Improvers have the same reason to make a-doe, and bee Jealouse about their notions, and Discovery's, as they call them; as a practizing Apothecary or a mountebank has to bee Jealouse about the Compositions that are to goe by his name. for if itt bee not a Livelyhood is aim'd; 'tis a Reputation. and what I contend for Reputation in, I must necessarily envy another man's possession of.

But as for mee: could I make any of those admirable Discoverys, which were nothing worth but to bee commended for their Subtility; I would doe as Timon did (though out of a just contrary Principle) when he found Gold:[2] after I had by chance dugg upon itt and found what itt was; I would put the Clod over itt again, and say nothing of itt, but forgett itt if I could. for my part: I am so far from thinking that mankind need any new Discoverys, or that they lye in the dark and are unhappy for want of them; that I know not what wee could ask of God to know more than wee doe or easily may doe. the thing that I would ask of God should bee to make men live up to what they know; and that they might bee so wise as to desire to know no other things than what belong'd to 'em, and what lay plain before them; and to Know those, to PURPOSE: and that all other Affectation of Knowledg Hee would preserve us from, as from a Desease: in which sort of knowledg if wee excell'd ever so much; and were masters of all as far as wee coveted; Itt would not help us to bee one jott the Honester or Better Creatures. If there bee any one that knows

---

[1] Charlatan.   [2] Shakespeare, *Timon of Athens*, IV. iii.

not, or beleives not that all things in the Univers are done for the best, and
ever will goe on so, because conducted by the same Good Cause; If there bee
any one who knows nothing like this of God, or can think of him constantly
in this manner; and who cannot see that hee himself is a Rationall and Sociable
Creature by his nature, and has an End to which he should refer his slightest
actions; Such a one is indeed wanting of knowledg. But if this bee known
(as what is easyer to know?) there is not, then, one Studdy or Science that
signifys a rush, or that is not wors [than] Ignorance; which gives a Man no
help in the persuance of what he has learnt to bee his Duty; Assists him not
in the Government of the Irrationall and Brutall Part of himself; which
neither makes him more truly satisfy'd with what God does in the World (for
that is *Loving God*) nor more Sociable more Honest or more Just, by removing of those Passions which hee has allways to Struggle with, that he may preserve himself so. If there are any other Sciences that are worthy of Esteem;
they are what must relate to the wellbeing of Mankind in Societys: and on
that account a Button-maker is to bee esteem'd if hee improves his Art, and
adds some Conveniency to Life. but how the Founders of Metaphysicks, of
Rhetorick, of the Arts of Reasoning upon everything and never coming to an
end, of the Arts that lye in words, the Turns of them, and the Division that
may bee run upon them; how, I say, These Men came to bee preferr'd to
the Commonest Mechanicks, I cannot well tell. Anciently, These Notable
Inquisitive men, that were Curiouse in what signify'd nothing, were call'd by
a name that they thought themselves highly honour'd with, and aspir'd no
farther. They were calld *Sophists*: and never expected to bee treated in the style
of *Philosopher* or *Professours of Philosophy*. Who were True Philosophers
those Wise Men shew'd (for amongst them the Name came up) that were in
early times in Greece, whome the Fancy of People that succeeded put into a
certain number and call'd *Seven*,[3] though the number was far greater; of whome
not one but was signally remarkable for some Service to his Commonwealth;
who were all united in the Strictest Friendship and by good Offices and helps
one to another; and whose Studdy was that of knowing themselves, and learning how to bee serviceable to Others. When Socrates liv'd, itt was still thus.
for he made the Sophists know themselves, and keep their distance. but when
after his death, the Socratick Spirit sunk much; then began Philosophy and
Sophistry to bee better acquainted. but it was never known till more late days
that to Profess Philosophy, was not to Profess a Life: and that it might bee
said of one, that *Hee was a great Man in Philosophy*; whilst nobody thought
it to the purpose to ask *how did Hee Live? what Instances of his Fortitude,
Contempt of Interest, Patience etc:?*—What is Philosophy, then, if nothing of
this is in the case? What Signifys itt to know (if wee could know) what Elements
the Earth was made from; or how many Atomes went to make up the Round
Ball wee live upon; though wee knew itt to an Atome? What signifys itt to

---

[3] The Seven Wise Masters or Seven Sages (Plato, *Protagoras*, 343a).

know whether the Chaos was cast in Dr Burnet's mold or if God did itt a quite different way?[4] What if wee knew the Exact System of That and of our Frames; Should wee learn any more than this, that God did all things Wisely, and for the best? And are wee not allready satisfyd of this allready; or may bee assur'd of itt by the Thousandth part of what wee know and see? If wee should Discover anything that led us to Conceive what were Contrary to this; wee should have Learnt that which was wors than nothing. And Better than wee know allready, wee cannot Learn to know, for God cannot by any discovery, be conceiv'd to bee more wise, than perfectly so: and such itt [is] easy to conceive him to bee without knowing any more of the things of Nature than wee allready doe.

What I count True Learning, and all that wee can profitt by, is to know our selves; what it is that makes us Low, and Base, Stubborn against Reason, to be Corrupted and Drawn away from Vertue, of Different Tempers, Inconstant, and Inconsistent with ourselves; to know how to bee allways Friends with Providence though Death and many such Dreadfull Businesses come in the way; and to be Sociable and Good towards all men, though They turn Miscreants or are Injuriouse to us.

Whilst I can gett any thing that teaches this; Whilst I can search any Age or Language that can assist mee here; Whilst Such are Philosoppers, and Such Philosophy, whence I can Learn ought from, of this kind; there is no Labour, no Studdy, no Learning that I would not undertake. . . .

1798. Locke to Jean Le Clerc, [Oates?], 9 October 1694

Libertie.[1]

As to the determination of the Will we may take it under three considerations, 1 The ordinary and successive uneasinesses which take their turnes in the common course of our lives and these are what for the most part determine the will but with a power still of suspending. 2 Violent uneasinesse which the minde cannot resist nor away with. These constantly determin the will without any maner of suspension where there is any view of a possibility of their removeal. 3 A great number of litle and very indifferent actions which mix themselves with those of greater moment and fill up as it were the litle empty spaces of our time. In these the will may be said to determin it self without the preponderancy of good or evill or the motive of uneasinesse on either side. as whether a man should put on his right or left shoe first. whether he should fold a margent[2] or noe in the paper wherein he is goeing to write a letter to his friend, whether he should sit still or walke or scratch his head

---

[4] L779, L911.

[1] This discussion relates to the *Essay*, II. xxi. 31–47 (L1579, L1592, L1655).   [2] Margin.

whilst he is in a deep meditation. there are a thousand such actions as these which we doe every day, which are certainly voluntary and may be ascribed to the will determining it self, but there is soe litle thought preceds them because of the litle consequence that attends them that they are but as it were appendixes to the more weighty and more voluntary actions to which the minde is determind by some sensible uneasinesse and therefor in these the minde is determind to one or tother side not by the preferable or greater good it sees in either, but by the desire and necessity of dispatch, that it may not be hinderd in the pursuit of what is judgd of more moment by a lingring suspense between equall and indifferent things and a deliberation about trifles and in these the uneasinesse of delay is sufficient to determin and give the preference to one it matters not which side.

1800. James Tyrrell to Locke, London, [16?] October [1694]

... I have by the expence of but 2s: made my old edition as usefull to me as a new one,[1] by takeing the paines either to write in the margin all the shortest additions and to past[e] in the rest in their proper places, and by stitching up those sheets that cannot be so disposed of, and puting them at the end of the book: and indeed your concerne for those who had the first Edition is highly commendable, since otherwise it would not have bin half so value-able, and usefull as the new one in which you have added, and altered so many things so much for the better, as well as for the clearing of divers passages which before seemed too short, and obscure, as allso for the correcting of some things (in which (as you your self with great ingenuity acknowledge) you had not at first so well considered, especially in that great question wherein the freedome of our wills consists,[2] whereby you have as well avoyded the errours of Mr: Hobs and the old Fatalists[3] who denyed all freedome of will, as allso of such who supposed wee might will and doe every thing wee pleased.

But as for that Chapter, which you have writ concerning the Identity, and diversity of persons,[4] tho I must confesse it contains a great many new, and very usefull notions, yet give me leave to tell you; that by your makeing that concerne, or connexion of our present thoughts with those that precede, so as to repeat the Idea, of any past Action, with the same consciousnesse they had at first, and to tye them to the like Consciousnesse of present actions, as the sole thing that constitutes a personal Identity, and makes this person to be himself to himself, and to differ from another; does very much perplex me, for tho I cannot positively see where the fault lyes; yet this supposition will not onely make a mad or drunken man another person, from himself

---

[1] 1st and 2nd edns. of the *Essay.*   [2] There were new sections in II. xxi.
[3] Epicureans. Hobbes: L1579, n. 6.   [4] *Essay*, II. xxvii, a newly inserted chapter.

when sober; but allso will make those that quite forget, (as some have done) all that ever they did in their lives, tho' not to be different men, yet different persons from what they were an hour agone, and consequently they will be as many different persons, as they make different reflections upon themselves, or their owne actions, without any concerne of what is past, which seems very hard if not impossible to conceive, so much I thought fit to tell you as to this head, tho' there are some other things of lesser moment which seem allso exceptionable, which are too long to be mentioned here, and therefore shall reserve them till wee meet. . . .

1804. Locke to Philippus van Limborch, Oates, 26 October 1694

. . . I can scarcely say how much Pleasure and how much light I have obtained from your careful account of the Inquisition.[1] It is so written as an account should be written, where nothing is invented or embellished for ostentation or delight so as the more easily to deceive heedless readers, but everything is established and supported by the trustworthiness of authors and the evidence of documents; so much so that those who are most concerned to refute will not venture even to murmur. You have dragged that work of darkness and the hidden practices of execrable cruelty out of their dens into so clear a light that, should any vestiges of humanity remain among those henchmen of the Church, or rather of Antichrist, they would at last feel shame for so unrighteous and so fearful a tribunal, where all law, human and divine, and justice, are set at nought. If, however, these infamies—infamies that cannot be rebutted—do not move them, at least to the reformed and to those rescued from this cruellest prison may it give courage against such inhuman tyranny, under whatever semblance of religion or concord it again seeks to creep in. . . .

1834. Martha Lockhart to Locke, London, 5 January [1695]

There will need no excuse to you for not sooner writing nor doe I in the least question tho I have not h[e]ard from you but that I have had your pitty in the sad sceen[1] I have had my part in since I saw you. it has been indeed so far beyond description that I must not pretend to give you any perticuliar

---

[1] *Historia Inquisitionis* (1692); L1147, n. 8; Eng. trans., *The History of Persecution* (1736).

[1] The mourning for Queen Mary, who died on 28 Dec., aged 32.

acount at least till I have the good fortune too se you. So much in generall I cant forbear saying that the poor queen's small pox was I veryly belive of the worst sort that Could be seen and what severall of the phisitians say's in all ther practice they never meett with but on the other Side I could hartyly have wishet that Docttor Rattlif[2] had not made that fatall misstake of Calling it the Measles from Munday night till tusday night that from saying ther was noe danger it Came to the sad discovery of black spott's apearing in her face when the same Docttor Rattlife did asure uss she would be all over mortified[3] b[y] morning so that by this misstake some thirty hours was lost which tho the Case seemd desperate ther was so much strngth that I Cant tell if the Course was affterward's taken had been try'd in time, what effect's it might have produced the Kings greife on this occasion seem's proportiond to his loss which is the greatest man could make, and he has as deep a sence of it as can be imagin'd has thought of noe bussnes nor scarce seen any but my lord Portland[4] but the day he recev'd the adress from the parliement. thus wee have all made the greatest and most unexpected experiment of the vainity of all the world calls great in the loss of this good queen who from a very perfect state of health in the prime of her age the best regulated dyat without any maner of accident ether fright or surffet droped in to this desperate deseas and with the fewest Complaint's of ether paine or sikness in five days caryed off. it has been the greatest sermon on many account's I ever meett with and what I hope I shall never forget. . . .

1846. Locke to John Wynne, Oates, 8 February 1695

You cannot think it strange that I should be surprised at the receit of a letter,[1] of soe much civility to me. from a person I had not the honour to know; and of soe great commendation of my book, from a place where I thought it litle taken notice of.[2] And though the complements, you are pleased to bestow both on me and it, are above what belongs to either, yet I cannot but acknowledg myself sensibly obleiged by the kinde thoughts you are biased with in favour both of me and my essay. It haveing been begun by chance and continued with noe other designe but a free enquiry into that subject it would have been great vanity in me to publish it with hopes that what had been writ for the diversion of my idle hours should be made the serious businesse of studious men who knew how to imploy their time. Those who had leisure to throw away on speculations a litle out of the road I guessed

[2] John Radcliffe, founder of the Radcliffe Infirmary, Oxford.
[3] The period when the spots die away.
[4] Hans Willem Bentinck, Earl of Portland, King William's confidant.

[1] Wynne had written to propose that he prepare an abridgement of the *Essay*. [2] Oxford.

might perhaps looke into it. If by the credit and recommendation of those who like you enterteind it with a favourable opinion it be spread farther and got into the hands of men of letters and study it is more than I could expect for a treatise writ in a plain and popular stile, which haveing in it noething of the aire of learning nor soe much as the language of the schools[3] was litle suited to the use or relish of those who as teachers or learners applyd them selves to the mysterys of scholastique knowledg. But you I see are got above Fashion and Prejudice: And you must give me leave to have noe ordinary thoughts of a man, who by those two great opposers of all new offers at improvement will not suffer your self to be hinderd from contriveing how to make the way to reall knowledg more open and easy to those beginers who have set their faces that way. I should be very glad any thing in my book could be made usefull to that purpose. I agree with you that most of the larger ex-plications may be looked on as incidental to what you designe and soe may by one who would out of my booke make a systeme of the third part in my devision of science[4] be wholy passed by or but lightly touched: to which let me adde that those repetitions which for reasons then I let it goe with may be omitted and all the parts contracted into that forme and bignesse you propose. But in my litle health and lesse leisure considering that I have been soe long a stranger to systems and am utterly ignorant what would best suit those you designe it for, it is not for me to goe about it though what you have said would incline me to beleive it would not in any case be wholy lost labour. Tis not for noething I hope that this thought is fallen into the minde of one who is much abler to execute it. you I see are as much master of my notions as I my self and better able to put them togeather to the purpose you intend. I say not this to decline giveing my assistance if you in civility should think I can afford you any. The abstract[5] which was publishd in French in the Bibliotheque universelle of 1688 will neither in its size or designe answer the end you propose, but if the rough draught of it, which I think I have in English some where amongst my papers[6] be of any use to you, you may command it . . .

1849. Locke to John Freke and Edward Clarke, [Oates], 18 February [1695]

. . . My conclusion stands thus. The money in the Bank[1] is, and I conclude always will be, managed by London merchants, whereby it will come to pass

---

[3] Scholasticism.   [4] The theory of signs, words, and ideas: *Essay*, IV. xx. 4 (IV. xxi. 4 in 4th edn.).

[5] 'Extrait d'un livre . . . intitulé Essai Philosophique concernant L'Entendement': the same as the *Abrégé*. L1040, 1056, etc.

[6] Printed in Lord King, *The Life of John Locke* (1830), ii. 231–93.

[1] The newly founded Bank of England.

that they under under names[2] and their friends will be sooner and easier supplied for their occasions than others, whereby I am apt to think the greatest part of our trade will in a little while by secret combinations be got into a few hands, even by this monopoly of money. And I think it becomes the wisdom of the Parliament rather to consider how money might be better distributed into the country, and other ports, and trading parts of England, than to set up a corporation, and by law countenance its drawing all to London. For if you examine it I believe you will find trade in all the out ports mightily decayed: one cause whereof I looked on to be the banking trade (formerly) in London, which is now authorised by a law, and such an establishment of it as I fear will cost dear to England. And whatever good effects are boasted of now in the infancy of the corporation will not last long when they are a little grown up and know their own strength. . . .

1860. John Freke and Edward Clarke to Locke, [London], 14 March [1695]

The enclosed draught of a Bill for Regulating the Prees[1] has been approved by the Sollicitor[2] and severall other honest and able men who all agree that the Government is sufficiently secured by it and the Gentleman at the Great House[3] allows it to be a good provision, but yet the Court the Bishops and the Stationers Company take great exceptions to it for they all agree to say it is wanting as to the Securing of Property[4] when they are asked what they mean thereby they can none of them give any good answer and if they would all speak out they (every party) mean differently. The Court means that it would be allowd the power of Granting Patents.[5] The Stationers mean that they would have the regulation of property and disposall of it by making their Register[6] the Standard of it and the orders of their company to Controll and Govern that Standard. The Bishops mean I know not what but they Chime in with the other two because they think property a very popular word, which Licencer is not.

But there are many other objections against this Bill as that it leaves printers at Liberty to set up in any Town in England[7] And that there is noe care taken that new Notions in Phisick should not be publisht to prevent

---

[2] Presumably agents, intermediaries.

[1] i.e. for the renewal of press censorship. L1586; *Political Essays*, 329–39.

[2] Sir Thomas Trevor, solicitor-general.

[3] Lord Somers. 'Great House': Powis House, Lincoln's Inn Fields.   [4] Intellectual property.

[5] Patents of monopoly: exclusive rights to a particular product or market.

[6] All publications were supposed to be recorded in the Stationers' Company Register.

[7] Until 1695 printing was only permitted in London and the two universities. The growth of the provincial press was a major consequence of the lapse of the Licensing Act. L1978, n.9.

which the College of phisitians is very Industrious to press hard that all things relating to or concerning phisick should be brought to be perused by them before publisht lest some new Sidenham[8] should rise up and shew they kill by the rules of Art in other distempers besides the Small Pox and Fevor . . .

1887. Locke to William Molyneux, Oates, 26 April 1695

. . . I must beg you to believe, that my life would be much more pleasant and useful to me, if you were within my reach, that I might sometimes enjoy your conversation, and, upon twenty occasions, lay my thoughts before you, and have the advantage of your judgment. I cannot complain that I have not my share of friends of all ranks, and such, whose interest, assistance, affection, and opinions too, in fit cases, I can rely on. But methinks, for all this, there is one place vacant, that I know no body that would so well fill as your self. I want one near me to talk freely with, de quolibet ente;[1] to propose to, the extravagancies that rise in my mind; one with whom I would debate several doubts and questions, to see what was in them. Meditating by ones self is like digging in the mine; it often, perhaps, brings up maiden earth, which never came near the light before; but whether it contain any mettle in it, is never so well tryed as in conversation with a knowing judicious friend, who carries about him the true touch-stone, which is love of truth in a clear-thinking head. Men of parts and judgment the world usually gets hold of, and by a great mistake (that their abilities of mind are lost, if not employ'd in the pursuit of wealth or power) engages them in the ways of fortune and interest, which usually leave but little freedom or leisure of thought for pure disinterested truth. And such who give themselves up frankly, and in earnest, to the full latitude of real knowledge, are not every where to be met with. Wonder not, therefore, that I wish so much for you in my neighbourhood; . . .

The third edition of my Essay is already, or will be speedily in the press.[2] But what perhaps will seem stranger, and possibly please you better, an abridgment is now making (if it be not already done) by one of the university of Oxford,[3] for the use of young scholars, in the place of an ordinary system of logick. From the acquaintance I had of the temper of that place, I did not expect to have it get much footing there. But so it is, I some time since received a very civil letter from one wholly a stranger to me there, concerning such a design, and, by another from him since, I conclude it near done. He seems to be an ingenious man, and he writes sensibly about it; but I can say nothing of it till I see it, which he, of his own accord, has offer'd that I shall, wholly submitted to my opinion, and disposal of it. And thus, Sir,

---

[8] Thomas Sydenham, the celebrated physician.

[1] 'About anything in the world.'
[2] The 3rd edn. was published in 1695, the 4th in 1700.   [3] John Wynne. L1846.

possibly that which you once proposed[4] may be attained too, and I was pleased with the gentleman's design for your sake.

You are a strange[5] man, you oblige me very much by the care you take to have it well translated, and you thank me for complying with your offer.[6] In my last, as I remember, I told you the reason why it was so long before I writ, was an expectation of an answer from London, concerning something I had to communicate to you: It was in short this, I was willing to know what my bookseller[7] would give for a good latin copy; he told me, at last, twenty pounds. His delay was, because he would first have known what the translator demanded. But I forced him to make his proposal, and so I send it you, to make what use of it you please. He since writ me word, that a friend of his at Oxford would, in some time, be at leisure to do it, and would undertake it. I bid him excuse himself to him, for that it was in hands I approv'd of, and some part of it now actually done. For I hope the Essay (he was to shew you the next week after you writ to me last) pleased you. Think it not a complement, that I desire you to make what alterations you think fit. One thing particularly you will oblige me and the world in, and that is, in paring off some of the superfluous repetitions, which I left in for the sake of illiterate men, and the softer sex, not used to abstract notions and reasonings. But much of this reasoning will be out of doors in a latin translation. I refer all to your judgment, and so am secure it will be done as is best.

What I shall add concerning Enthusiasm, I guess, will very much agree with your thoughts, since yours jump so right with mine, about the place where it is to come in, I having designed it for *chap.* 18. *lib.* iv.[8] as a false principle of reasoning often made use of. But, to give an historical account of the various ravings men have embraced for religion, would, I fear, be besides my purpose, and be enough to make an huge volume.

My opinion of P. Malbranche[9] agrees perfectly with yours. What I have writ concerning seeing all things in God, would make a little treatise of it self. But I have not quite gone through it, for fear I should by somebody or other be tempted to print it. For I love not controversies, and have a personal kindness for the author.[10] When I have the happiness to see you, we will consider it together, and you shall dispose of it.

I think I shall make some other additions to be put into your latin translation, and particularly concerning the Connexion of Ideas, which has not, that I know, been hitherto consider'd and has, I guess, a greater influence upon our minds, than is usually taken notice of.[11] Thus, you see, I make you the confident of my reveries; . . .

---

[4] L1579.   [5] Exceptional, unusual.

[6] Molyneux's offer to arrange a Latin translation of the *Essay* by Ezekiel Burridge: *De Intellectu Humano* (1701).

[7] Awnsham Churchill.   [8] *Essay*, IV. xix in the 4th edn.

[9] Père Malebranche. L1622, n. 4.   [10] No personal connection is known.

[11] A new chapter, II. xxxiii, 'Of the Association of Ideas', appeared in the 4th edn.

1901. Locke to Philippus van Limborch, Oates, 10 May 1695

... Although I have heard no word of what you say about our Oxonians I would readily have believed it.[1] I commend you for disregarding your Kiel adversary[2] and esteem you so much the more for being flogged by others who differ among themselves, for that is usually what happens to sincere and incorrupt promoters of the truth. I must now thank you again for your *Theologia Christiana*, not because it has enriched [my] library with a volume but because it has enriched me with knowledge. For this winter, considering diligently wherein the Christian faith consists, I thought that it ought to be drawn from the very fountains of Holy Writ, the opinions and orthodoxies of sects and systems, whatever they may be, being set aside. From an intent and careful reading of the New Testament the conditions of the New Covenant and the teaching of the Gospel became clearer to me, as it seemed to me, than the noontide light, and I am fully convinced that a sincere reader of the Gospel cannot be in doubt as to what the Christian faith is. I therefore set down my thoughts on paper, thereby the better to survey, tranquilly and at leisure, the agreement of the parts with one another, their harmony, and the foundations on which they rested.[3] When everything in this creed of mine seemed everywhere sound and conformable to the word of God I thought that the theologians (that is, the Reformed) ought to be consulted, so that I might see what they thought about the faith. I went to Calvin,[4] Turrettini,[5] and others, who, I am compelled to admit, have treated that subject in such a way that I can by no means grasp what they say or what they mean; so discordant does everything in them seem to me with the sense and simplicity of the Gospel that I am unable to understand their writings, much less to reconcile them with Holy Writ. At last with better hopes I took in hand your *Theologia* and not without very great joy read book V, chapter VIII,[6] from which I perceived that one theologian was to be found for whom I am not a heretic. I have not yet obtained enough free time to go further with the reading of your book. Nothing could be more desirable for me than to see you and to read and to explain to you in person what I have composed, so that it might be subjected to your refined and incorruptible judgement. All this must be for your private ear, for I want my having treated this subject to be communicated to you alone....

---

[1] Some Oxonians sought to have Limborch's *Theologia Christiana* (1686) condemned out of hostility to the latitudinarian Archbishop of Canterbury John Tillotson, to whom Limborch had dedicated his *Historia Inquisitionis* (1692).

[2] Christophorus Franck, *Exercitationes Anti-Limborchianae* (1694).

[3] *The Reasonableness of Christianity*, published about August.

[4] *Institutes of the Christian Religion* (1536).

[5] François Turrettini, *Institutio Theologiae Elencticae* (1688–9).

[6] 'De Fide in Jesum Christum, ac primò de actu ejus antecedente, Scientiâ': 'On Faith in Jesus Christ; and firstly on the activity which precedes it, Knowledge'.

1914. Henry Hatrell to Locke, Newcastle, Staffordshire, 3 June 1695

... I enquire whether that common Phrase of having our souls and bodies our Natures and Faculties depraved by originall sin, and the bringing the habits and seeds of sin into the World be true or not, And herein the disproved Doctrine of Innate notions[1] gives me light, If the Soul have no Ideas connate but receives all from Sensation and Reflection, and if a Law cannot bind till knowne, and if Sin be a transgression of a knowne Law either in thought word or deed, and if Children before growne up to some maturity cannot understand the Law, I infer that all the thoughts and actions of Children whilst uncapable of knowing the Law are not sins. In the next place I think its plaine that Enjoyment of pleasure not referred to some Law is not sinfull in it self and I cannot think the Almighty hath made any Animall without desires to enjoy good or pleasure, and the contrary supposition would make odd work in the creation but to wave that, How should the naturall desire of pursuit and experience of pleasure be evill otherwise than as its done in instances or circumstances prohibited by some Law if Eating and drinking and the Embraces of the Bride and Groome be lawfull pleasures which I think no body questions. The Excess indeed may be reckoned a fault but that rather proves than overthroues the supposition. And I know no pleasure in the world but it may be lawfall or unlawfull in respect of the circumstances its accompanied with which shews its not evill in it self but in respect to a Law, that doth not so much forbid as regulate and limit the measures of it. But say Divines Originall Sin in the new Testament is called Flesh and Concupiscence etc. Can that be any thing els but the Inclination to pleasure that grows too strong and too unruly to be governed by the Law of God and that is not content to gratify it self in allowed ways but breakes all Rules and Bounds so that its not the thing but the manner that makes the fault, As for instance, A child loves apples. Who can say loving or eating apples with pleasure is Originall Sin or any sin, But when the Child understands that the Apples have an Owner, that the Owner will not part with them, That its Injustice to take any thing from the Owner without his consent, Then if the Child take and eat he transgresseth the Law, and the cause of his transgression is the unruliness of his Appetite, and this is sin, but I think not originall sin brought into the world with us, and if acts goe before habits, Habits cannot be brought into the world with us, acts taking their begining long after we come into the world, And how the body can be said to come defiled by sin into the world is altogether unintelligible to me and I think absurd in it self unless a Nature or Substance void of Reason can be said to be under the Government of Law which I cannot apprehend ...

[1] *Essay*, I.

1925. Paul D'Aranda to Locke, Bath, 15 July 1695

I was bold to give you the trouble of a few lines from Oxford, whence ariving here the 5th: instant I the next day began to drink the waters of the Bath, and have drank them every day since, Observing your advice in beginning with half a pint, and, finding that agree well with me, increasing every day, save one, as much, so that I to day drank two quarts and half a pint, the whole to greater benifit than my best hopes before durst promise me, all I have drank not onely staying with me, but also for the most part sitting easy on my stomack, and, especially when I ride immediately after drinking or drink while in the Crosse bath;[1] which I now therefore do every other day interchangeably, passing extraordinary well, all by Urine, and causing so good a disposition of Stomack, that as I want not appetite, so I have the advantage of well disgesting what I eat, and that so neer as it ought to be that I am as well after as before eating, almost allways wholly free from those sore pains in Stomack and back I have had so large a share of, indeed quite without any pain when I am enough master of my unruly pallat and greedy apetite to abstain from those sorts of dyet which experience has taught me will disagree with me, such as are bread and all things made of meal, fruit, herbs and roots and all liquors save these waters, warm milk at first milking and a little mum;[2] which last I by Dr Blackmore's[3] advice made tryal of, found agree with me drinking it warm'd, and believe has contributed much toward giving me an open body, which is that way now so well that I have dayly, about 5 of the Clock afternoon, sometimes by much, sometimes with little and oftener without any straining for it, good ease on the stool. the heat in my back which I felt on and about the edge of the shoulder blade bone I now seldome feel any thing of, never but when I have in eating or drinking sinn'd against knowledge of what I ought to do, and then but gently. I have been now two whole days without the least pain any where. I feel not any more, nor have not above twice since I began to drink the water felt, the least inclination to vomit. My rest by-night is better and much more refreshing as well as somewhat longer than it used to be; and whereas I have for many past months been forced to sit well nigh upright in Bed, I have now, without any inconvenience by it, lain two nights on bed with three pillows lesse than I used to have, so that my head's no more than ordinary raised by two pillows. and I have by degrees so diminish'd the quantity of Laudanum I used to take, that, instead of 20 drops in the Evening and sometimes more, and neer as much in the mornings, as I had for some time been forced to the use of, I have now for these three last nights taken no more than 12 drops each time at or some time before going to bed. . . .

---

[1] In Bath Street.   [2] A wheatmalt beer.
[3] Richard Blackmore, royal physician and poet. L2269.

11

Coinage and Commerce, 1695–1696

The greatest impact exerted by Locke on the everyday lives of his contemporaries arose from his advice during the recoinage crisis. By 1695 the currency was in disarray and a vigorous controversy arose over the best means of achieving a recoinage. Not only was there a shortage of coin to sustain everyday transactions, but also the credibility of coin had been eroded by the fraudulent practice of paring away the precious metal, known as 'clipping'. (Locke's own pocket was hit, for he complained that repayments on his loans, paid in clipped coins, were worth only a fraction of their proper amount.) It was agreed that a national recoinage was necessary, and that the new technology of milled coinage be implemented, but an argument arose about the best monetary system to use. William Lowndes, a treasury official, argued for a coinage whose face value would be greater than the market value of its silver content—anticipating the system of nominal valuation in modern coinage. This, he argued, would facilitate cash transactions without resulting in an inordinate drain on bullion stocks. To the contrary, Locke insisted that the face value of coins must equate with silver content value. After he had put his case in person, his model was adopted by the Lords Justices who governed England while King William was conducting military campaigns abroad. Locke's system proved beneficial to those who were owed money by the government—debts which were payable in new coin—but it harmed the poor who were exploited by money changers when they tried to dispose of old coin. The monetary economics of the Locke–Lowndes debate is complex and Locke's parliamentary friends of 'the College' urge him to publicize his position (L1974). During 1695 he published *Short Observations* and *Further Considerations on the coinage question*. Molyneux reports a discussion with the Lord Deputy of Ireland about Locke's tracts (L1984). Locke comments sardonically on the difficulty of getting reliable silver coinage into circulation in the face of the hoarders and clippers (L2016). He advises how to put an end to the circulation of clipped money. In a remarkable testimony to his grasp of the machinery of public opinion, he suggests that England will do what London does, and that London will do what is talked of in Richard's coffee house (L2060).

Locke's tracts caught the attention of a Bristol merchant, John Cary, who presents Locke with the mercantilist view that since the nation's wealth depended on its bullion stock, government policy should aim to achieve a favourable balance of trade, maximizing exports and minimizing imports of high value goods (L2000). Admiring Cary's *Essay on the State of England*, Locke agrees that country gentlemen should appreciate the importance of 'a right ordering of trade' (L2079). One aspect of Cary's tract particularly attracts Locke: the proposal that led the city of Bristol to secure legislation to reorganize its poor relief by creating a Corporation of the Poor. By combining several parishes into one unit it became viable to establish a workhouse for employing the able-bodied poor, who would thereby recoup their own expenses (L2084). Locke borrowed the idea in his *Essay on the Poor Law* (1678). In 1696 Locke was persuaded to accept significant public office as a member of the new Commission for Trade and Plantations (the Board of Trade) (L1978, L1981). Serving for four years, he engaged in issues of colonial policy for Ireland and the Americas, as well as the management of the poor law.

From Clarke and Freke, Locke receives a sarcastic account of parliamentary debates on another abortive printing bill intended to re-establish a system of censorship (L1978, L1981). They correctly predict that the bill would fail. In these reports the anxiety of churchmen about the spread of heretical books is palpable. Although Locke was himself soon accused of heresy, some contemporary readers interpreted his theology as a bulwark against irreligion. Anticipating eighteenth-century readings of Locke as a defender of Christianity, Popple writes admiringly of *The Reasonableness of Christianity* and encourages Locke to write more to combat the spread of deism and atheism (L2002). Among those critics of the *Essay* whom Locke took seriously enough to address was a Roman Catholic priest called John Sergeant. Sergeant wrote to him, taking issue with what he saw as the excessive empiricism of the *Essay*, and asserting that epistemic certainty requires principles of rational self-evidence (L2085).

To Molyneux, Locke sends a peculiarly revealing self-portrayal as friend, patriot, and intellectual, juxtaposing his service to the public good with the strains upon his health. Amid the welter of others' sophistry, propagandist distortion, and vainglorious quests after reputation, Locke depicts his own writings as an austere quest for the unvarnished truth. As in letters to other select friends, he makes a show of informality, unceremoniousness, and uncourtliness (L2059).

He continues to take delight in his friends' children. Elizabeth Duke is sixteen when she writes a vivid account of a coach journey from the West Country to London, telling of the beggars who 'minded' the coach overnight, the wearisome attentions of a male passenger, and the vulgarity of the wife of the mayor of Taunton (L2034).

1974. John Freke to Locke, [London], 5 December 1695

You needed not have been a sollicitor[1] had you been in Town and yet you would have been very serviceable to your Country in being here for There are very many gentlemen who would have sought to you to have been set right in their Notions what is fit to be done at this time with respect to the Coin. The Country Gentlemen[2] come up very raw in this matter and the Monyers are soe busie buzzing hard words and unintelligible cant in their heads and then threatening them with I know not what dreadfull Consequences that not onely the Country Gentlemen but even men that have been once right in their notions are (or for some private reasons seem to be) confounded. I will onely Instance in the Gentleman[3] whose visit you had not time to return and desired the Grave Squire[4] in a former letter to make your excuse to for that omission. You know when he and the Grave Squire met at your chamber last summer he seemed to understand the matter right but now he publickly talks otherwise and is full of fears of I know not what dangers may ensue if one could not with a clipt shilling pay a Coach man.[5] now I dare say had you been in Town you would have cured him of all his fears and made him a usefull instrument for the obtaining what is necessary to be done speedily if it be thought necessary that this Government should subsist three months longer.

However though with great difficulty The Commons in a Comittee of the whole House voted That the most effectuall way to prevent the mischiefs the Nation suffers by the Currency of Clipt mony is to recoin the same, but the Lords went further and voted that an Address be made to the King to Issue a proclamation to stop the currency of Clipt mony and have this day sent it down to the Commons for their Concurrence . . .

Though I have not had an oppertunity to speak with my Lord K[6] yet I dare give you licence for him to make the dedication as you desire[7] but let me entreat you earnestly to make what haste you can in p[er]fecting that work which the season calls soe earnestly for and the sooner it appears [the gr]eater will be its grace and usefullness. . . .

1978. John Freke and Edward Clarke to Locke, [London], 14 December 1695

I imagine that nobody will for the future say that the Government do's not take all the proper methodes for the incourgement of Trade that can be invented

---

[1] Advocate.   [2] Backbench MPs.   [3] Unidentified.   [4] A nickname for Edward Clarke.
[5] i.e. if clipped coins ceased to be legal tender.   [6] Lord Keeper Somers.
[7] Locke's *Further Considerations Concerning Raising the Value of Money* (1696) was dedicated to Somers.

since the House of Commons have given their approbation to the Resolutions taken by his Majesty[1] . . .

As to the powers that the House of Commons intend to give the Councill of Trade by Act of Parliament if they are necessary for the better execution of the Trust reposed in the Councill and such as could not be given by the King alone I believe the King and People will thank them for such an Act and promote the passing it: but if the Commons would Establish that Councill on such a foundation as is inconsistent with our Constitution[2] I believe they will hardly soe far agree amongst themselves as to make it pass their House and if they should the other two parts of the Legislature will scarce be brought to consent to make any breach in the orders of our Government And beside I believe they will get noe wise men (and of such this Councill ougt to consist or else twill be useless and perhaps dangerous) to accept of it. for to Execute a power inconsistent with the Fundamentalls of our Constitution is dangerous tho an Act of Parliament should Authorise it as Empsom and Dudleys Case[3] will convince any one that considers it

The House of Commons are to be upon the consideration of this same Councill of Trade again this day what they doe you shall be informd in a post script when I come to the Tavern[4] and receive a Report from the members. At presant I shall goe to another subject which I suppose may give you some Diversion and that is the Bill for Regulating the Press.[5]

The Grave Squire[6] is attacqued on all sides on account of that Bill the Bishops are Alarmd and by the AB of C[7] have treated with him that more Care might be taken of the Church and the truth on't is his Grace is soe reasonable and fair a man that he proposes litle but what will I believe be granted him and soe he will be contented though I doubt the rest of the Clergie as litle after the amendments he proposes as they are now. The Dissenters are likewise Alarmd and have Deputed one of their party to apply to the Squire and a time and place of meeting has been appointed between him and this Godly Deputy but the man of God was invited to a merry meeting together with his wife and soe faild the Squire who will therefore (I believe) be hardly brought to give him another Assignation. The Government is likewise Alarmd for fear of loosing the prerogative of granting other mens Labours and making mony by Giving a sole power to some to impose a kind of tax on others that is by enabling them to set what prices they please on books they can purchase a patent for the sole printing of.[8] But this grieveance to the Government is not the thing it complains of but a hundred petty objections are raised against the Bill as

---

[1] To create a Board of Trade.

[2] Some politicians proposed that the Board should be appointed by parliament; the king, Somers, and apparently Locke, wanted a Board chosen by the king.

[3] Sir Richard Empson and Edmund Dudley, executed in 1510 as scapegoats for Henry VII's financial oppressions.

[4] The postscript is addressed from 'Temple Tavern'.   [5] A further bill to that of March. L1860.

[6] Edward Clarke.   [7] The Archbishop of Canterbury, Thomas Tenison.   [8] L1860, n. 5.

that a printer may set up more presses than is fit and that Exeter Bristoll etc: are not places that need presses and that there is noe body in those Towns fit to Inspect them when the Bishops are at parliament.[9] And that noe body has power to strike out or alter any thing in a Book as it is printing and a great many other such objections they make all which would vanish if it would be agreed that old Grants of the Crown should be allowd and confirmd and thereby new ones acknowledged to be good. The universitys are also Alarmd and rail at the Bill but make noe other objection but that there is noe saving of their priviledges as was in the old Act and for that I believe it will be allowd them that it shall be added in the words of the Act by a saving without words of confirmation of their priviledges. The Kings printers are likewise Alarmd and perhaps they have reason but I believe twill be hard for them to get their Grants confirmed by parliament. The Common Printers likewise complain of the Bill and take exceptions against it for matters that are not containd in the Bill and soe doe the Booksellers and Stationers and especially the Company[10] whose great grieveance is that their property[11] is like to be limitted to certain number of years . . .

1981. John Freke and Edward Clarke to Locke, [London], 17 December 1695

. . . I have received the packet[1] and Letter which you sent away the 15th and my Lord[2] has read the Epistle and orderd me to strike out a whole line in one place and two words in another to avoid offence and with those corrections I have sent it and the rest of the papers (which I have perused and found noe need to Correct in any thing) to the press and Mr Churchill[3] promises me the whole shall be printed by the end of this week[4] and I have orderd him to give a book or two more in your name than you had set down in your list[5] and now the Comission for the Councill of Trade is past[6] I think he must be orderd to give one to every one of your Brother Comissioners but I hope you will be in Town soon enough to give those orders your self, for my Lord Keeper Comanded me to write earnestly to you to be here as soon as possibly you could and said the loss of a day by your absence at this time would be of consequence

The Comission appoints the Lord Chancellor or Lord Keeper Lord President Lord Privy Seal Lord Treasurer or first Comissioner of the Treasury

---

[9] L1860, n. 7.   [10] The Stationers Company.   [11] Copyright.

[1] Containing the manuscript of Locke's *Further Considerations Concerning . . . Money* (1696).
[2] Lord Keeper Somers, to whom the tract was dedicated.
[3] Awnsham Churchill, Locke's publisher.   [4] It was advertised in *The Post-Boy*, 28–31 Dec.
[5] Locke listed about 50 people to receive complimentary copies.
[6] In fact the Council did not sit until May 1696.

Lord High Admirall or first Comissioner of the Admiralty and the two principall Secretarys of State for the time being.[7] and

The Earls of Bridgewater and Stampford Sir Philip Meadhous, William Blathwait John Locke John Pollixfen and Samuell Clarke[8] or any 3 of them to meet in a place to be assignd them 1 To enquire into the State of the Trade of the Kingdom 2 How advanced or decayd and by what means 3 what Trades profitable what prejudiciall and by what methode advantageous Trades may be improved and hurtfull hinderd or made beneficiall 4 By what methodes Trade may be most effectually protected and secured in all its parts 5 By what means our manufactures may be improved and new and profitable ones introduced 6 How the poor may be set to work and made usefull.

They are also to Inform themselves 1° of the presant condition of the plantations[9] 2° How they may be improved 3 What Navall stores the plantations can furnish us with 4 What the Instructions to Governors are and how they may be amended 5 What persons are fit to be Governors Deputy Governors or other officers in the plantations 6 They are to examine the Acts of the Assemblys of the plantations transmitted hither 7 [They] are to hear complaints of oppressions and maleadministrations 8 They are to enquire into and take all the accounts of publique mony raised in the plantations and for these purposes They are empowerd to send for persons and papers and to examine upon oath and may call to their assistance the Attorney and Sollicitor Generall

And they are from time to time to make reports of their proceedings in writing under their hands or of 5 or more of them to his Majesty or the Councill.

I shall onely add that the Bill for New Coynage is come in and is as you desire or very near it and where it is not I hope it shall be amended to your content and as for the Bill about printing the severall different enemys it has will secure [u]s that there needs not many champions for the right in that case for their different interests will either hinder any Act from passing concerning printing or else make it a very good one. . . .

1984. William Molyneux to Locke, Dublin, 24 December 1695

. . . Your other of Nov. 20th. brought me a Paper,[1] which of all things I have ever seen on that subject, I most highly admire. You have therein reveald the

---

[7] These great officers were nominal members; the working members were to be as follows.

[8] John Egerton, Earl of Bridgewater; Thomas Grey, Earl of Stamford (not in fact a commissioner until 1699); Sir Philip Meadows, diplomat; William Blathwayt, secretary at war; John Pollexfen, merchant, writer on political economy; Samuel Clarke, Surveyor of the (Customs) Warehouse (not in fact made a commissioner). The initial commission also included Ford Grey, Earl of Tankerville; Abraham Hill, political economist; and John Methuen, diplomat.

[9] Colonies in the Americas.

[1] 'Answers sent to the Lords Justices' (Oct. 1695), a memorandum on money, coin, and bullion, the substance of which appeared in *Further Considerations*, published in December.

Whole Mystery of Mony, Exchange, Trade, etc. which have hitherto been wrap'd up in unintelligible Cant, I beleive partly out of Knavery, partly out of Ignorance. You gave me Liberty to make what Use of it I pleased; and therefore I ventur'd to give a Copy of it to His Excellency My Lord Deputy Capel,[2] rather than the Book of Interest and Coynage,[3] which I thought might be too long for his present perusal in his Multitude of Busines. But I can tell you, that your Admirable Perspicuity of Writing is so clearly different from all the World, and almost peculiar to your self; that in vain you expect to be conceald in any thing that comes from you. For I assure you in some Discourse I had with his Excellency no longer ago than yesterday concerning the Busines of Mony, He asked me (without any Occasion given him from Me) whether I had ever seen Mr Lockes Book of Interest etc. for he has formerly known (as I think I have told you) that I had the Happines of Your Acquaintance, I replyd to His Lordship that I had seen such a Book, but that it did not bear your Name in it. He answerd Me, The Printer presented it to him as yours, and besides (says he) All the World knows Mr Lockes Way of Writing, and if I may Gues, I believe that the Paper You gave me a few days ago came from Mr Locke; Pray did it not? I told his Excellency I was under some Obligation to Conceal the Author. That's enough (says he) I am sure tis his, and will put his Name to it, and lay it up amongst my Choysest Papers.[4] . . .

I herewith send you inclosed the Copy of a Letter from an Ingenious Man,[5] on the Problem which you have honourd with a Place in pag. 67. of your Essay.[6] You wil find thereby, that what I say of its puzling some Ingenious Men is true; and you wil easily discover by what false steps this Gentleman is lead into his Error. The Letter was communicated to me by the Party to whom it was writ, Dr Quail.[7] and the Writer of the Letter Mr Edw. Synge is the Author of a Little Book call'd the GENTLEMANS RELIGION, which Mr Churchil has printed, and I beleive vended it as Yours.[8] The Gentleman is on a Second Part which he wil shew me before he sends it to the Pres But this only between Our selves and the Bookseller, who has been lately informed of thu[s] much already. For tho the Book shew not [th]at Freedom of Thought as You or I perhaps may Expect, yet it shews enough to incense his own Herd against him, for there is little of Mystery or Enthusiastick[9] in it, and yet the Author is a Clergy Man. And you know that in a Writer on a Religious subject tis an high Offence even to be silent on those abstruse Points. The Clergy are not Dissatisfyd only with those that plainly Oppose them, but are inraged also

---

[2] Henry, Lord Capel, Lord Deputy of Ireland.

[3] *Some Considerations of the Consequences of the Lowering of Interest* (1691).

[4] Locke acknowledged authorship of *Some Considerations* when he republished it in 1696.

[5] Edward Synge, later Archbishop of Tuam.

[6] The 'Molyneux Problem': *Essay*, II. ix. 8. L1609. Synge disagreed with Molyneux's and Locke's conclusion.

[7] Francis Quayle, prebendary of Brigown, Cloyne.

[8] Synge, *A Gentleman's Religion* (1693). Sometimes attributed to Locke.

[9] L687, n. 4; L2340, n. 3.

even at those that omitt zealously to advance them, as we have had a late Instance in Him that writes against the Reasonablenes of Christianity.[10] . . .

2000. John Cary to Locke, Bristol, 11 January 1696

I have read your Answer to mr Loundes his Essay for the amendment of the Silver Coins[1] and I thinke the Nation obliged by the service you have done in handling a subject of that weight so fully; I know my private opinion will not adde a Mite to its valew, however I must give it this Character, that you have done it (as you doe all other things you write) with such clearnesse and strenght of Argument as if it had been the only thinge wheretoe you had bent your study; When Men undertake subjects whereof they have noe clear Notions, their bookes rather perplex the Reader than guide him to a right understanding of what they would seem to unriddle; he that desighnes to propose Methods to kepe our Mony at home must first consider what it is that causes it to be carryed abroad; in this I thinke you have hit the Marke; Its the Ballance of our Trade with Forreyn Countryes, not altering the standard of our Coin, which either encreases or lessens our Bullion at home, and then the next thinge is to consider how this Ballance may be brought of our side; when other Nations are brought into our depts[2] noe room is left for fetching away our Bullion, but on the contrary they must send us theirs; and this I judge cannot better be done than by encourageing our Manufactures, which will employ our people; The Wealth of England arises cheifely from the labour of its Inhabitants, which being added to our own Product, and alsoe to the forrein Materialls we Import, encreases their valew in those Markets whither we export them, and by how much we lessen the Importation of things already manufactured, and encrease that of the Primums[3] whereof they are made, soe much will the Ballance of our Trade alter every where in our Favour;

When the Publick Good of a Nation is the desighne of a Writer it armes him with some assurance, which hath emboldend me to present you with this little Tract, or Essay on Trade,[4] the worke of some leisure houres; all I shall say concerning it is, that 'twas wrote without partiall Respect to any one Trade more then another; if you shall thinke it worth your reading twill oblige me, . . .

---

[10] John Edwards, *Some Thoughts Concerning the Several Causes and Occasions of Atheism* (1695).

[1] William Lowndes (Treasury secretary), *A Report Containing an Essay for the Amendment of the Silver Coins* (1695); Locke, *Further Considerations*. L1974, L1981.

[2] Debts.   [3] Raw materials.

[4] *An Essay on the State of England, in Relation to its Trade, its Poor, and its Taxes* (1695). L2079, **n. 1**.

2002. William Popple to Locke, London, 16 January 1696

. . . Suffer me I beseech you to suggest to you some thoughts with which my own minde is at present deeply affected. The Reasonableness of Christianity (however Reasonable a Book it be) has I doubt had little Effect upon those that call themselves Deists in this Age. I dispute not how little they deserve that Title. The men I mean are such as deny all Immaterial Beings, though that dos not hinder them from talking of a God upon all occasions, but undoubtedly more for the sake of the Name than the Thing. Consequently to that, they make all Events necessary, and laugh not onely at Revealed but even Natural Religion. I say Religion: For they talk big of Virtue and Morality. But when they lay all the grounds of both Virtue and Morality onely in the good-nature of particular persons, or in the fear of the Magistrate's Rod, I fear their Superstructure will be very tottering. And what makes me fear this, is because I see plainly the Youth of this Age build all upon that Foundation. We are running from one Extream to another. Atheism, or, (if that word be too harsh), even Irreligion is a sad Sanctuary from the Mischiefs of Superstition.[1] Must we then needs lye under either the one or the other? Is there no Medium? Yes certainly there is. And these young Wits stand need of one to shew it them in a pure light, without any mixture of Clerical Fard,[2] which has now utterly disgusted them. Good Sir, pardon my liberty in hinting at these things to you. . . .

2016. Locke to John Freke and Edward Clarke, Oates, 14 February 1696

. . . I finde by the votes[1] (which the Gent who brings you this[2] brought hither with him) that the new Bank is to be a National Land Bank.[3] and that this and the Royal Bank[4] are soe opposed that noe body is to be a Sharer in both.[5] How a Land Bank shall supply the King with ready money I doe not well see.[6] And lesse why any body is shut out unless you are afraid there, that subscriptions and money will come in to fast and overlay the Exchequer. The

---

[1] It was an Enlightenment commonplace that an excessive reaction against superstition, popery, and clericalism was apt to drive people to deism or atheism.

[2] Face paint.

[1] The printed *Votes of the House of Commons.*   [2] Probably Sir Francis Masham.

[3] The Land Bank was a stillborn Tory rival to the recently founded Bank of England. It was authorized by Act of Parliament, despite Whig and Bank opposition, but flopped when it failed to be adequately subscribed.

[4] The Bank of England.   [5] Have shares in both.

[6] The Bank of England was founded to provide credit to the government, and thereby created the National Debt.

melting[7] which I hear busies them there is I confesse a laborious hot worke and for ought I see may last till they are weary of it. Methinks the silver does wisely not to come into England at this time where it is like to run a per-petuall circle of torment if it stay here. Into the fire it goes at the Exchequer and is noe sooner out but is committd to the tower[8] there to goe into the furnace again to be brought to Standard and then to size and then be pressed in the mill. Assoon as it get free out of the tower it is either lockd up in some Jaylors[9] chest from comeing abroad or if it peeps out tis ten to one but the thriveing company of Coiners and clippers put it again into the fire to be joynd with bad company.[10] and then to be hammerd and cut and so conveyd to the Exchequer to run the same Gantlet again. If it be not soe pray convince me of my mistake, and ease me of the trouble I am in for a poor Lady which we bookish men find the ancients had such a respect for that they called her *Regina Pecunia.*[11] . . .

2034. E. D. [Elizabeth Duke?] to Locke, [Sutton Scotney, Hampshire?], 10 March 1696

Don't you think I am more Constant than your frendship could hope or mine pretend to: I think it a great profe of it, amidst the fatigues of a west country journey, to give you thus an account of my insignificant self and travell's. we part'd from Hartly Row[1] at 3 this morning through a crowd of beggars who watch your Coach for allms, and will never leave it unbles't. hence a beaux in my Company took occasion of simile, bad me observe how wakefull those wreches wear for small Charity's; that he would doe the like in hopes of greater: and that my divine idea had so fill'd his sight, he Could not resolve to let sleep intrude for fear of shuting me out. I perceved he took pains to be thought uneasie, and I have more good maner's than to disapoint him. Mrs Mayoress of Taunton,[2] a she neighbour in the coach, has all the low, disagreable, familiarity of people of her Rank, she entertained us all the morn-ing with a sorry love business about her second husband, stuff so impertinent, I remember nothing of it. Beaux is very asiduous. I think none was ever so plagued with dying eyes, his are Continually in that posture, and my opposetes, that I am forced to take a good deall of pains to avoide 'em. The two other felow travellers, wear never so promoted before. and are much troubled ther

---

[7] Locke turns to the topic of silver bullion and coinage.
[8] The Royal Mint at the Tower of London.
[9] Newly minted coins were hoarded by speculators.
[10] Illicit coiners melted coins down in order to extract some of the silver content.
[11] 'Queen Cash': Horace, *Epistles*, I. vi. 37.

[1] Probably Hartley Wintney, Hampshire.
[2] In Somerset. Probably the wife of the Tory mayor, Thomas Towell.

journey is to last noe longer, and wish the 4 days[3] 4 monthes, I hope every jolt will squash ther gutts out, and give 'em enough on't but they are proof against any such disaster and hugely delighted with what they are pleased to Call riding in state. affter this rediculas acount you need not doubt but I am throughly mortified: the Trout's are just brought upon the table, which are the only good thing here. they look inviting, and won't stay for Cooling Compliements. . . .

2059. Locke to William Molyneux, Oates, [c.5 April] 1696

Though I have been very ill this winter, not without some apprehensions of my life, yet I am asham'd that either that or business, that has took up more of my time than my health could well allow, should keep me so long silent, to a man so kindly concern'd to hear from me. 'Twas more than once that I resolv'd on the next post, but still something or other came between; and I more readily yielded to delays, in hopes to hear something from you, concerning my answer to Mr. Lowndes.[1] If this be a fault in me, it is such an one that I am guilty of to no body but my friends. Perhaps the running from ceremony or punctuality towards those whom I look on as my sure friends, that is, my self, may sometimes carry me a little too far to the other side. But if you disapprove of it I shall only say, it is an ill effect of a very good cause; and beg you to believe, that I shall never be tardy in writing, speaking, or doing, whenever I shall think it may be of any moment to the least interest of yours.

The business of our money has so near brought us to ruin,[2] that, 'till the plot[3] broke out, it was every body's talk, every body's uneasiness. And because I had play'd the fool to print about it, there was scarce a post wherein somebody or other did not give me fresh trouble about it. But now the parliament has reduced guineas to two and twenty shillings a piece[4] after the 10th instant, and prohibited the receipt of clipp'd money after the 4th. of May next. The bill has passed both houses, and, I believe, will speedily receive the royal assent. Though I can never bethink[5] any pains or time of mine, in the service of my country, as far as I may be of any use, yet I must own to you, this, and the like subjects, are not those which I now relish, or that do, with most pleasure, employ my thoughts; and therefore shall not be sorry if I scape a very honourable employment, with a thousand pounds a year salary annex'd to it, to which the king was pleased to nominate me some time since.[6]

---

[3] A four-day journey suggests Exeter to London, about 170 mls.

[1] *Further Considerations Concerning Money.* L1974, L1981.
[2] By now there was a drastic shortage of coin, and public credit was near collapse.
[3] The Assassination Plot, by Jacobites to kill King William III.
[4] From 30 shillings. Guineas were gold coins.   [5] Grudge.   [6] Member of the Board of Trade.

May I have but quiet and leisure, and a competency of health to perfect some thoughts my mind is sometimes upon, I should desire no more for my self in this world, if one thing were added to it, viz. you in my neighbourhood. You cannot imagine how much I want such a friend within distance, with whom I could confer freely de quolibet ente,[7] and have his sense of my reveries, and his judgment to guide me.

I am asham'd to receive so many thanks for having done so little for a man who came recommended to me by you. I had so little opportunity to shew the civility I would have done to Mr. Burridge,[8] that I should not know how to excuse it to you or him, were not he himself a witness of the perpetual hurry I was in, all the time I was then in town. I doubt not at all of his performance in the translation of my book he has undertaken. He has understanding, and latin, much beyond those who usually medle with such works. And I am so well satisfyed, both of his ability, and your care, that the sending me a specimen I shall look on as more than needs. As to a treatise of morals,[9] I must own to you, that you are not the only persons (you and Mr. Burridge I mean) who have been for putting me upon it; neither have I wholly laid by the thoughts of it. Nay, I so far incline to comply with your desires, that I ever now and then lay by some materials for it, as they occasionally occur in the rovings of my mind. But when I consider, that a book of Offices,[10] as you call it, ought not to be slightly done, especially by me, after what I have said of that science in my Essay; and that *Nonumque prematur in annum*[11] is a rule more necessary to be observ'd in a subject of that consequence, than in any thing Horace speaks of; I am in doubt whether it would be prudent, in one of my age and health, not to mention other disabilities in me, to set about it. Did the world want a rule, I confess there could be no work so necessary, nor so commendable. But the Gospel contains so perfect a body of Ethicks, that reason may be excused from that enquiry, since she may find man's duty clearer and easier in revelation than in herself. Think not this the excuse of a lazy man, though it be, perhaps, of one, who having a sufficient rule for his actions, is content therewith, and thinks he may, perhaps, with more profit to himself, employ the little time and strength he has in other researches, wherein he finds himself more in the dark.

You put too great a value on my writings, by the design you own on Mr. Burridge, in reference to them. I am not to flatter my self, that because they have had the good luck to pass pretty well here amongst English readers, that therefore they will satisfie the learned world, and be fit to appear in the learned language. Mr. Wynne's abstract of my Essay is now published,[12] and

---

[7] 'About anything in the world'.

[8] Ezekiel Burridge, for undertaking a Latin translation of the *Essay* (L1887, n. 6).

[9] L1530, L1538.   [10] Duties, as in Cicero's *De Officiis* (*On Duties*).

[11] '(Put your parchment in the closet and) keep it back till the ninth year' (Horace, *Ars Poetica*, 388). A warning against hasty publication.

[12] L1846.

I have sent order to Mr Churchill to send you one of them. Thus far in answer to yours of the 14th. of March. I come now to that of the 24th. of December.

My Lord Deputy[13] and you did too great honour to the paper[14] I sent you, and to me, upon that account. I know too well the deficiency of my stile, to think it deserves the commendations you give it. That which makes my writings tolerable, if any thing, is only this, that I never write for any thing but truth, and never publish[15] any thing to others, which I am not fully persuaded of my self, and do not think that I understand. So that I never have need of false colours to set off the weak parts of an hypothesis, or of obscure expressions, or the assistance of artificial jargon, to cover an error of my system or party. Where I am ignorant (for what is our knowledge) I own it. And though I am not proud of my errors, yet I am always ready and glad to be convinced of any of them. I think there wants nothing but such a preference of truth to party, interest and vain glory, to make any body out-doe me in what you seem so much to admire. . . .

I see by Mr. S's answer[16] to that which was originally your question, how hard it is, for even ingenious men to free themselves from the anticipations of sense. The first step towards knowledge is to have clear and distinct ideas; which I have just reason every day more and more, to think few men ever have, or think themselves to want; which is one great cause of that infinite jargon and nonsense which so pesters the world. You have a good subject to work on; and therefore, pray let this be your chief care to fill your son's head[17] with clear and distinct ideas, and teach him, on all occasions, both by practice and rule, how to get them, and the necessity of it. This, together with a mind active, and set upon the attaining of reputation and truth, is the true principling of a young man. But to give him a reverence for our opinions, because we taught them, is not to make knowing men, but pratling parrots. I beg your pardon for this liberty; it is an expression of good will, and not the less so, because not within the precise forms of good breeding.

2060. Locke to John Freke and Edward Clarke, Oates, 6 April 1696

I am not a little glad that about the same time you were communicateing to me your opinion concerning the clippd money my thoughts fell in with your sense and I was explaining my self a little more fully to you on that subject. . . . And since you aske my opinion and would have me think of ways that

---

[13] Henry, Lord Capel, Lord Deputy of Ireland.   [14] L1984, n. 1.

[15] 'Publish' could still mean disseminating works in manuscript.

[16] Edward Synge, who had taken up the conundrum about the sensory perception of the blind. L1984, n. 6.

[17] Samuel Molyneux, aged 6, later a politician and astronomer.

may contribute to it[1] Thus I thinke:[2] first that London in all these matters of money gives a rule to all England, what is done there the rest will follow, and that therefor it should be begun in London. Secondly that as to the makeing it take in London, a good number of substantiall citizens who understand the matter and see the danger we are in of certain ruin if clippd money be not stopd, should agree togeather not to take any clipd money but as bullion for its weight, and should endeavour to bring in as many as they could into this necessary obedience to the law by joyning in a preparatory lawfull practise for the benefit of every body. you know how better to spread this in the town than I who am a stranger there. I will only name one a man of weight Mr Samuell Heathcote[3] he is the yonger brother but a very sensible man and I am satisfied will be industrious in it. And what too if you should as soon as it is seasonable begin to pay clippd money by weight[4] at Richards Coffee house,[5] the talke and example would spread. Thirdly to this purpose I am apt to thinke that it is of moment that those who practise it should besides scales have these species of our coin by them a peny two pence three pence a groat[6] and six pence besides bigger peices of our milled money against which to weigh the clippd. These I think much better than brasse weights, because every one knows not the value of those weights in silver and soe may suspect he has not the full allowance for his clippd money, but when he sees it weighed against money every one must presently be satisfied, and there is noe roome for scruple or debate on either side. These therefor are the materials should be got ready. Fowerthly when this is got into practise, it may not be amisse to spread the notice of it by the *Post-boy*[7] and such other printed papers, but in the wording of it I think that care should be taken to say that clippd money passes in London as Bullion by weight the word *Bullion* being put in to take off the notion that it passes as coin for that would be a violation of your law and open the flud gates again. Fifthly I think the Receits and payments of the Exchequer should be looked after and kept stanch[8] to the law. for if I am not misinformd they pay out coin which by the law, tis supposd should stop there. If the Exchequer gives it currency 'twill he hard labour to stop it any where else. Fifthley If the Bank of England could be brought to receive and give out clipped money as Bullion by weight it would be a mighty stroake towards it. Mr Heathcote is one of them. Sixthley The Goldsmiths must be watched for I feare you will have few or none of them on your side And therefor they must be exposd and laid open by publique talke, a Kings head club[9] would doe that.

---

[1] The prevention of circulation of clipped money.

[2] In Locke's private notebooks the phrase 'Thus I think' sometimes occurs, denoting a memorandum or essay recording his considered opinion.

[3] Wealthy Baltic merchant, brother of Sir Gilbert, director of the Bank of England.

[4] Rather than by nominal (face) value.

[5] Now 8 Fleet Street. Richard's (or Dick's) and the Grecian were favourite Whig coffee houses.

[6] A coin worth fourpence.   [7] A tri-weekly newspaper, 1695–1735.   [8] Staunch, firm.

[9] Probably the King's Head tavern, at the corner of Chancery Lane and Fleet Street.

and keepe them from opposeing the necessary and only means to save us. Those who acknowledg that they have been out of the way ever since they rejected this method might doe much towards the promoteing of it now, but how far these new converts are to be relied on you can better tell. . . .

2079. Locke to John Cary, Oates, 2 May 1696

I have read over your Essay of trade you did me the favour to send me and have found that satisfaction I expected.[1] It answers the Character I had of you and is the best discourse I ever read on that subject not only for the clearnesse of all that you deliver, and the undoubted evidence of most of it But for a reason that weighs with me more than both those and that is that sincere aime at the publick good and that disinteressed reasoning that appears to me in all your proposals; A thing that I have not been able to finde in those authors on the same argument which I have looked into. . . . You cannot employ your thoughts on a more necessary or usefull subject. The country Gent who is most concerned in a right ordering of Trade both in duty and interest is of all others the most remote from any true notions of it or sense of his stake in it. Tis high time somebody should awaken and informe him, that he may in his place looke a little after it. I know noe body soe able to doe it as you. I see noe party or interest you contend for but that of truth and your country. such a man carrys authority and evidence in what he says and those that will not take the pains to understand him throughly cannot refuse to believe him and therefor I hope the same reasons that first set you on worke will have force to make you goe on. . . .

2084. John Cary to Locke, London, 9 May 1696

I have yours 2d. Instant, with your Favourable opinion of my Essay on Trade, which was wrote without partiall Respect either to my selfe or anyone else; what I endeavoured was to set thinges in a true light, in opposition to those who I had observed in a former sessions to be continually perplexing the Parliament with notions fitted for their private Interests under the splendid name of the Publique Good; . . . There are some things I leave in the darke, as thinkeing them more proper to be spoken to in the House of Commons

---

[1] *An Essay on the State of England, in Relation to its Trade, its Poor, and its Taxes* (1695). Trans. into French, 1755, and Italian, 1764. It argued for the promotion of the American plantations, the protection of English wool textile manufacture, the confinement of the Irish textile industry to linen, and the employment of the poor. L2000.

than made the subject of a discourse, they might bringe me under the name of a Projector,[1] which I carefully endeavour to avoyd, I could say much on This, but I must then find fault with our Legislators, who to often examine thinges by the touchstone of their own Interest, and either throw them out, or coolely let them fall, as they answer that end; I wish That House were better fild with men of publique spirits than it is; our Taxes might be raysed with more Ease, our Trade better secured, and our Mony made to goe farther towards the use of the Warr, . . .

Inclosed I send you the proposalls I gave to the City of Bristoll for employing and maintaining their Poor, grounded on that part of my Essay, and alsoe the Act of Parliament past this Sessions; which hath met with such approbation, that tis generally desired for a president;[2] The other is a short Reply to a paper put into the House of Lords against passing a Bill sent them by the Commons,[3] which I thought would have been of great use to the Publique; The Managers had reprinted that part of my Essay which treated of the East India Trade, and delivered it to both Houses, wheretoe the Lynnendrapers raised Objections, to which this is a suddain Reply, made at the Request of the Manufacturers; I have fairly summed up their Arguments, . . .

2085. [John Sergeant] to Locke, 10 May 1696

After I had written and almost printed this Book I here send you,[1] (I mean all of it but the Preface and Appendix) I was favour'd by a Friend with a sight of your *Essay concerning Human Understanding*; to which, till then, my circumstances had made mee a Stranger. I will not disoblige your Modesty with giving you a full account of the high Esteem I had for it. I believe that, had I had the good fortune to have perus'd it thorowly ere I began to read these Lessons to a little Academy I had last Summer of a few, but choice, Witts, I had profited by the Lights it might have given mee; and, in case I had seen no reason to depart from my own sentiments, I should have shown my respects to you by making some incidentall Reflexions on diverse passages in it. But, the hast I was in, (the Printer having almost overtaken mee) did allow mee no more leasure than onely to take a cursory view of it here and there as it light. Yet that little I saw of it (*ex ungue Leonem*)[2] enabled mee to make

---

[1] A vogue term for financial and industrial schemers and quack inventors.

[2] Between 1696 and 1715 fifteen cities secured acts to establish Corporations of the Poor. They were generally dominated by Whigs and Dissenters. Bristol provided the model. President: precedent.

[3] A bill against wearing silks and calicoes imported from Persia and the East Indies; it failed. *The Linen Drapers' Answer* (1696): a plea for free trade. Cary, *A Reply to a Paper* (1696). Cary favoured a ban on imports of manufactured goods.

---

[1] *The Method to Science* (1696), a defence of syllogism and deductive knowledge.

[2] 'The lion (is known) by his claw': Erasmus, *Adages*, I. ix. 34.

a fair Estimate of the Whole. The most substantiall Difference between us (as far as I yet observe) is about the Necessity and Usefulnes of Identicall Propositions, on which I mainly build;[3] and to which (in my judgment) all Truths must either be reduc'd, or they will, if scann'd by Speculative and Acute Logicians, be left destitute of their Deepest and Firmest Ground. For, since you have so solidly confuted *Innate Ideas*, it must follow of course that Truths must be taken from the *Things without us*; and, consequently, must be *first built on*, and *finally resolved* into their *Metaphysicall Verity* or their *being what they are*, which is an Identicall Proposition, and can be nothing else: nor can we *speak* or *say* anything of their Natures or Essences *as such* (or staying there) or express them at all but by such an Identicall Speech, as upon triall you will find. Again, we must either come at last to Self-evidence, or no Dispute can ever come to an end; nor can any Propositions, but such as these, possibly lay any claim to Self-evidence, since all else can bear Explicating or the making them plainer, and clearer, which these cannot. These onely being Evident from themselves, or from the very Terms without the assistance of any other Light. I do grant, indeed, that they look at first sight, till attentive Reflexion comes to discover the Usefulnes of them, dry, Insignificant, and in a manner Foolish and Ridiculous. I grant too that there are many Principles exprest more handsomely and with a better grace, which seem to force every man, who has a good Mother-wit, to assent to them, without putting them into such an odd and nice form of words; but I must deny that there are any deserving the name of First Principles or Self-evident but because they do virtually include an Identicall; as I have exemplify'd in 'A Whole is more than a Part.' Besides, Sir, we have a Scepticall World to deal with, who will question even the verdict of our Senses and quarrell the meaning of every word, pretend it ambiguous and then distinguish it; and nothing can hamper such men but Identicalls, which put them past their Distinguishing. Add that all Truths consist in the Connexion of the Terms in the Proposition that expresses it; and the Terms of no Proposition are *self-connected* (to which we must either come at length or never make an end) but those of Identicall Propositions. But, I shall tire you with my insipid Speculations, and I fear my Book will weary you out of all Patience. I can onely say of it, that I am sure it goes to the bottome, and has as little of superficiall as the French have much of it. . . .

[3] Sergeant adduces logical maxims of identity and contradiction as the source of certainty, which go beyond empirical knowledge. Since Locke himself accepted the principle of self-evidence, he would be unlikely to disagree. But Sergeant, below, further proposes the (Aristotelian) criterion of 'Metaphysicall Verity', which Locke would think incoherent.

12

Reasonable Christianity, 1696–1697

The disturbing bifurcation of Locke's religious reputation was now becoming apparent. For his admirers, the *Essay* and the *Reasonableness* provided new foundations for
defending Christianity against irreligion, but for his enemies they were seedbeds of
atheism. In some circles the *Essay*'s rejection of innate ideas, which seemed shocking
when first published, now gained respectability. Following Robert Boyle's death in
1691, the Boyle Lectures became a prestigious series which espoused the new philosophical theology. Molyneux reports that Richard Bentley's Boyle Lectures against
atheism accepted the premiss that there is no innate knowledge of a deity (L2131).
However, in 1696, the single most important onslaught on the *Essay* appeared when
Bishop Stillingfleet accused Locke of anti-Trinitarian heresy. Locke found it necessary
to publish three replies to Stillingfleet and two vindications of the *Reasonableness*. The
suspicion of heresy in the *Reasonableness* meant that a sympathetic Irish bishop dared
not applaud the work openly (L2131). As with the *Essay*, it was what Locke did *not*
say that disturbed the orthodox. Elizabeth Berkeley reproves Locke for failing to give
due weight to the sacraments. She claims that Locke had a camp-following of people
'proud of every shadow of his authority to believe as little as they can' (L2109).
The Huguenot Pierre Coste worries that the *Reasonableness* said too little about
mankind's redemption through Christ's sacrifice on the cross (L2107). Coste, however, was an admirer who went to live at Oates to serve as Locke's literary assistant, and to whom Locke would owe his French readership, for he translated the
Essay, the *Reasonableness*, and *Education*. One of Locke's critics was the Tory cleric,
William Sherlock, who denounced the *Essay* for atheism in a London pulpit. Locke
and Molyneux share a contempt for Sherlock's politics and theology (L2202, L2221).

The attack that most stung Locke, and provoked the *Vindications* of the
Reasonableness, was John Edwards's *Brief Vindication of the Christian Faith*. This was
vicious vituperation, accusing Locke of atheism and Hobbism, and of being 'a lewd
declaimer' and 'perfidious scribbler'. The worst libel, which referred to the 'seraglio
at Oates', was tactfully removed by the printer, though Locke heard of it and was incan-
descent. Appalled that Cambridge University had given its imprimatur to Edwards's
book, he mauls the Master of Christ's College with his characteristic weapon of
savage sarcasm (L2319). In his *Second Vindication*, Locke included an admiring
epistle to Samuel Bold, a Dorset clergyman who had composed a tract in Locke's defence.
Bold, who in earlier years had been gaoled and ostracized because of his defence
of religious toleration, is elated that the great philosopher should take notice of a
country clergyman (L2232).

Locke's reputation was damaged by John Toland's manipulation of his ideas in the
notorious *Christianity not Mysterious*. Dublin was scandalized by Toland's outspoken
conversation in the coffee houses, and Molyneux acquaints Locke with news of his
subsequent condemnation (L2269, L2288). Locke indignantly distances himself from

Toland (L2277). Matthew Tindal, another devotee of Locke, and later a deist scarcely less notorious than Toland, offers Locke a treatise he has grounded in the *Letters Concerning Toleration* (L2173). Fear of accusations of heresy became palpable with the hanging for blasphemy in 1697 of an eighteen-year-old Scottish theology student, a case in which Locke took a close interest (L2207).

Describing himself as now 'a man of trade' to the young Esther Masham, Locke was initially an assiduous attender at the Board of Trade (L2124). He took advice from the textile manufacturer and philanthropist Thomas Firmin, and became an advocate of Firmin's device, the 'double wheel', for maximizing the productivity of spinners (L2241). He began to consider the Irish economy (L2131). This topic potentially put Locke on a collision course with his Irish friend Molyneux, though the crisis did not break until 1698. The policy of the English government, backed by the strong (especially West Country) woollen textile industry, was to protect English manufacture by forcing Ireland to concentrate on linen textiles instead of woollen ones. Molyneux provides Locke with information about the fragile Irish linen industry (L2131). The Locke–Molyneux correspondence continued to range over many topics. When Molyneux compares Sir Richard Blackmore's poetry to Milton's, and proposes that Blackmore write a philosophical poem, Locke responds by praising Blackmore's medical theories (L2277).

Fame made demands. An anonymous writer, encapsulating contemporary arguments for and against the naturalization of foreign immigrants, begs Locke to write a memorandum in favour of legislation for a general naturalization in time for the reading of a bill 'next Tuesday' (L2206).

Besides *Some Thoughts Concerning Education*, a significant source for our knowledge of Locke's advice on education is a letter to Carey Mordaunt for the improvement of her son, which offers a programme of reading in history, ethics, politics, and natural philosophy (L2320).

Locke had inherited a small estate from his father and had purchased land from his brother's widow, but he did not often return to Somerset and dealt with his tenants through agents. One letter provides an insight into the obligations which villagers carried in local communities, particularly the duty to undertake parish offices (L2299).

2107. Pierre Coste to Locke, Amsterdam,
[*c*.23 June / 13 July 1696]

I have just translated a little English book entitled *The Reasonableness of
Christianity* which I am taking the liberty of sending to you.[1] If you have not
read it in English, I believe that it will please you to see it in French. The
author's purpose is worthy of all sorts of praise since it goes as far as to silence
so many disputes which have been tearing apart Christianity for so long. It
has begun to be much talked about in these parts; and as is usual, it pleases
some and displeases others. Among those who share the views of the author,
there are some who are surprised that he has not explained more precisely
than he has done what should be understood by the term *Messiah*. The two
first pages of the book allow one to hope for something of the sort. Others
who never thought that the faith which Jesus Christ demands from his disciples was as simple as the author of this work claims to demonstrate, are
astonished to find nothing in the work about the death of Jesus Christ which
is so often mentioned in the Acts of the Apostles. The idea of *Sacrificer* that
the author of this pamphlet finds bound up in the office of the Messiah seemed
to oblige him to speak about this death. In truth, in order to avoid the end-
less controversies which the theologians have made about this topic, he should
not have determined the formal degree of necessity of this death with regard
to our redemption; this does not seem possible: but it seems that he was unable
to avoid speaking about it historically, as the Scriptures speak about it; when
they say, for example, like Jesus Christ (Matth. xxvi. 28) *that his blood was
shed for many for the remission of sins*. Although it is not for us to define up
to what point the death of Jesus Christ contributed to the forgiveness of sins,
it appears that one cannot avoid seeing in the Scriptures that his death contributed to something. And this is what one would have liked to find in this
work. I do not know if this is right. But I will say in accordance with some
very judicious persons whom I heard talking about this book, that the plan
that the author has made is very fine and he has completed it most satisfac-
torily. Perhaps he has left some gaps in his work, but I think that he had his
reasons for doing so. In the present state of religious controversies, there are
many things which one should of the greatest necessity keep silence upon so
as not to excite the passions of men, and not to lose the richness of things
which should of necessity be published. . . .

---

[1] *Que la religion chrétienne est très raisonnable* (1696).

2109. Elizabeth Berkeley to Locke, 13 July 1696

Having the good Fortune to read some of your excelent Books, I took in so great an opinion of the sincerity as well as great Judgment of their Author, (so far as my little knowledg made me capable of understanding them) that I was very unwilling to take as yours, some others; or if so, believe them liable to the objected defects, and errors. if I don't decieve my self I am not alltogether under the power of prejudice; and so I secure the Religion taught of God, am pretty indiferent what becomes of that which only derives from the Imagenations, and Intrests of men: further than the order peace and good government of the world is conscern'd; yet I confess, that as the Possitive or Arbitrary dutys of Christian Religion are very few and simple, so they apper to me, to be, at least a Natural, if not supernatural means of producing the effects generally imputed to them; therefore could not help being disquieted by hearing it as your Judgment, that there was no possitive obligation from scripture or Primitive[1] practice for the use of the sacraments[2]—I hoped in Conversation for a less observable way, of speaking my thoughts: I dare not say of knowing yours, having no reasonable pretence to such a favour; but mising that satisfaction, would not venture to inquire els where, both for fear of spreading a mistake, or having your thoughts misrepresented to my self; for except this is a truth usefull to be received, I am (so sensible of the allmost irresistable force of your Authority to be) very sorry it finds so powerfull a Patron; if it is inded your Judgment (tho I havn't found cause to make it mine, yet) won't condemn what I don't understand, I know truth is too sacred to be denyed, tho want of right dispositions to receive some truths, may render them unnecessary, if not dangerous, therefore innocently detain'd; but if in this you were misunderstood: in the whole, or part; were it not a presumption allmost too great for one so condescending[3] as Mr L— to forgive, I would desire him to be more cautious in speaking his thoughts, that his name ben't fixed to what is not his judgment; and recolect, he has observers, proud of every shadow of his Authority to beleive as little as they can; and others, to weaken the established rules to get more liberty for their own, which perhaps in time would be as imposing, if not end in confusion; I am sensible this letter requires a long apology, but that would be to make you suffer longer for my fault; the shortest and truest is, I fancy'd it might be of some use to an intrest 'tis every ones duty to serve, tho by it I exposs'd my self; I don't inded conclude Mr L—can't err, but am not at all disposed to beleive he dos, being conscious the just deference payed to your reasonings, makes it no slite inducement to doubt the truth of those opinions

---

[1] The word was used positively, referring to the 'primitive church', of the first four centuries AD.
[2] Apparently alluding to a discussion in *The Reasonableness of Christianity*.
[3] Gracious to inferiors.

you reject;—the uncertainty of life made the temptation of giving you this trouble successfull, . . .

2124. Locke to Esther Masham, London, 1 September 1696

Your Letter the last week after so long silence looks as if you had been bottleing up kindness for your Joannes which at last you have let run to the rejoycing of his heart more than if you had overflow'd to him in Sack[1] and Suger, or Cherry brandy. I was not a little dejected in being so long out of your thoughts as appeard to me by your no words which is a very ill sign in a prattle box of your age.[2] But in good sooth you have now made me amends, and if what you say be but true Joannes will perk up again, and will not give place to the finest powderd Spark[3] in the Town. I think you know my heart pretty well but you are a little mistaken about my head. Though it belongs now to a man of trade[4] and is thwack'd with Sea coal[5] and Fullers earth,[6] Lamp black[7] and hob nayles[8] and a thousand such considerable things, yet there is a room empty and cleare kept on purposse for the Lady, and if you did but see how you sit mistris there and command all the Ambergrease[9] and Pearles, all the fine Silks and Muslins which are in my Store house you would not complain of the overfilling of a place where you sit mistris. . . .

2131. William Molyneux to Locke, Dublin, 26 September 1696

. . . I do not wonder that your Essay is received in the Universitys,[1] I should indeed have wonderd with Indignation at the Contrary. Magna est Veritas et Prævalebit.[2] We may expect a Liberty of Philosophyzing in the Schooles, But that Your Doctrine should be so soon heard out of our Pulpits is what is much more remarkable. He that, even ten years ago, should have Preachd, that Idea Dei non est Innata,[3] Had certainly drawn on him the Character of an Atheist; Yet now we find Mr Bentley very large upon it in his Sermons at Mr Boyles

---

[1] A Spanish wine.   [2] About 20.   [3] Beau, gallant, dude.
[4] Referring to his membership of the Board of Trade.   [5] Ordinary coal, not charcoal.
[6] A silicate of alumina used in cleansing cloth.
[7] Lamp soot, from burning oil; used for pigment.
[8] A nail with a thick head, for horseshoes or work shoes.
[9] A secretion from sperm whales, used in cookery and medicine.

[1] Locke had expressed surprise that Oxford should take his *Essay* seriously. L1887.
[2] 'Great is the truth and it shall prevail'.   [3] 'The idea of God is not innate'.

Lectures, Serm. 1. p. 4. and serm. 3d. p. 5.[4] And Mr Whiston in his New-Theory of the Earth pag. 128.[5]

Mentioning these books minds me to Intimate to you, that these Ingenious Authors agree also exactly with you in a Passage you have in your *Thoughts of Education* pag. 337. 3d Edit. Sec. 192.[6] That the Phænomenon of Gravitation cannot be Accounted for by Meer Matter and Motion, but seems an Immediate Law of the Divine Will so ordering it.[7] And you conclude that Section thus—*Reserving to a fitter Oppertunity a fuller Explication of this Hypothesis, and the Application of it to all the Parts of the Deluge, and any Difficultys can be supposed in the History of the flood.* This seems to Imply that you have some thoughts of Writing on that subject; it would be a mighty satisfaction to me to know from you the certainty thereof. I should be very Glad also to hear what the Opinion of the Ingenious is concerning Mr Whistons Book.

As to the *Reasonablenes of Christianity*, I do not find but tis very wel approved off here amongst Candid unprejudiced Men that dare speak their thoughts; I'll tell you what a very Learned and Ingenious Prelate[8] said to me on that Occasion. I asked him whether he had read that Book, and how he liked it; He told me, very wel; and that if My Friend Mr Locke writ it, 'twas the best book he ever labourd at; But, says he, if I should be known to think so, I should have my Lawns[9] torn from my shoulders. But he knew my Opinion aforehand, and was therefore the freer to commit his secret thoughts in that matter to me.

I am very sorry I can give you no better an Account of the Linen Manufactures of late years set up in Ireland than what follows.

About the Year 1692 (I think) One Monsieur du Pin[10] came to Dublin from England; and here, by the King and Qs Letter, and Patents thereon, he sett up a Royal Corporation for Carrying on the Linnen Manufacture in Ireland. into this Corporation Many of the Nobility and Gentry were admitted, More for their Countenance and Favour to the Project, than for any great help could be expected either from their Purses or Heads to carry on the Work. Du Pin himself was nominated Under-Governour, and a great Bustle was Made about the Busines, Many Meetings were held, and considerable Sums advanced to forward the Work, and the Members promised themselves Prodigious Gains, and this Expectation prevaild so far (by what artifices I cannot tell) as to raise the Value of each Share to 40 or 50 pounds, tho but 5 pounds was paid by each Member at first for every Share he had. At length Artificers began to be set at Work, and some Parcels of Cloath were made, when on a sudden there hapned some Controversy between the Corporation here in Ireland, and such

---

[4] Richard Bentley, classical scholar, later Master of Trinity College, Cambridge. *The Folly and Unreasonableness of Atheism* (1692). L2221, n. 1.

[5] William Whiston, later successor in Newton's Cambridge chair, but latterly expelled for heresy. *A New Theory of the Earth* (1696), dedicated to Newton.

[6] § 180 in 1st and 2nd edns.   [7] Newton's hypothesis concerning action at a distance.

[8] Probably Bishop William King.   [9] Lawn sleeves: a bishop's gown.

[10] Nicholas Dupin, a linen promoter in all three kingdoms.

an other Corporation established in England, by London-undertakers, and in which Du Pin was also a Cheif Member. Much time was spent in Managing this Dispute, and the Work began in the Mean time to flag and the Price of the Shares to Lower mightily.

But some little time before this Controversy hapned, some Private Gentlemen and Merchants, on their own Stock, without the Authority of an Incorporating Patent, set up a Linnen-Manufacture at Drogheda which Promised, and thrive very wel at first; And the Corporation of Dublin[11] perceiving this began to quarrel with them also, and would never let them alone till they embodied with them; These Quarrels and Controversys (the Particulars whereof I can give you no Account of, for I was not ingaged amongst them, and I can get no one that was who can give any tollerable Account of them) I say they grew so high, and Du Pin began to play such Tricks, that all were discouraged, and withdrew as fast as they Could. So that now all is blown up; and nothing of this kind is Carried on, but by such as out of their own private purses set up Looms and bleaching Yards. We have many of these in Many Parts of Ireland; and I beleive no Country in the World is better adapted for it, especially the North. I have as Good Diaper[12] made by some of My Tenants nigh Armagh as can come to a Table, and all other Cloath for Househould Uses.

As to the Law for incouraging the Linnen Manufacture tis this. In the 17 and 18th of Char. 2.[13] there was an Act of Parliament made Obleidging all Landlords and Tenants to sow such a Certain Proportion of their Holdings with Flax under a Great Penalty on both on failure; and impowring the Sherifs to Leavy 20 pounds in each of their Respective Countys to be Distributed at the Quarter sessions yearly to the Three persons who should bring in the Three best Webs of Linen-Cloath of such a length and breadth, 10 [pounds] to the first, 6 to the second, and 4 to the third. This whilst it lasted was a great incouragement to the Country [people] to strive to outdo each other, and it produced excellent Cloath all over the Kingdom; but then it was but Temporary, only for 20 years from passing the Act, and is now expired. But that part of the Act ordaining Landlords and Tenants to Sow Flax is Perpetual; and I can give no Reason why tis not executed; Only this I can say, that the Transgression is so Universal, and the Forfeiture thereon to the King is so severe; that if it were Inquired into I beleive all the Estates in Ireland would be forfeited to his Majesty. So that now the Multitude of Sinners is their security. This Statute you will find amongst the Irish Acts 17 and 18 Ch. 2. Chap. 9.

England most certainly will never let us thrive by the Wollen trade, This is their Darling Mistris, and they are jealous of any Rival. But I see not, that we interfere with them in the least by the Linnen trade, so that That is yet left open to us to grow rich by, if it were well Establishd and managed. But by

---

[11] The linen corporation.   [12] Table cloth.   [13] 1666.

What Means this should be, truly I dare not venture to give my thoughts. There is no Country has better land or Water for Flax and Hemp; and I do veryly beleive the Navy may be provided here with Sayling and Cordage Cheaper by far than in England. Our Land is Cheaper, Victuals for Workmen is Cheaper, and Labour is Cheaper, together with the other Necessarys for Artificers. . . .

2173. Dr Matthew Tindal to Locke, 10 January 1697

I should be very ungrateful, considering I have got more tru and useful knowlege by your writings than by all the books I ever read besides, if I did not take this opportunity of giving you my sincere acknowlegements; and as a token of that great respect I have for you, I have sent you this Essay,[1] in which I can not pretend to say anything new on the subject of Toleration: For I am very sensible its as impossible to add to what the Author of the letters concerning that subject has said on it, as it is to defend Persecution. but least I should persecute you with a long letter I shall subscribe myself with all respect imaginable, Sir, Your most obedient, humble servant

2202. Locke to William Molyneux,
Oates, 22 February 1697

. . . [Y]ou are pleased out of kindness to me, to rejoyce in yours of September 26.[1] that my notions have had the good luck to be vented from the pulpit, and particularly by Mr. Bentley, yet that matter goes not so clear as you imagine. For a man of no small name, as you know Dr. Sherlock[2] is, has been pleased to declare against my doctrine of no innate ideas, from the pulpit in the Temple, and, as I have been told, charged it with little less than atheism. Though the Doctor be a great man, yet that would not much fright me, because I am told, that he is not always obstinate against opinions which he has condemned more publickly, than in an harangue to a sundays auditory. But that 'tis possible he may be firm here, because 'tis also said, he never quits his aversion to any tenent[3] he has once declared against, 'till change of times bringing change of interest, and fashionable opinions open his eyes and his heart, and then he

---

[1] *An Essay Concerning the Power of the Magistrate, and the Rights of Mankind, in Matters of Religion* (1697), an adroit mixture of Lockean tolerationism and Hobbesian Erastianism.

[1] L2131.

[2] William Sherlock, Master of the Temple, the Inns of Court Chapel. L1325, n. 6. His critique of the *Essay* was published in *A Discourse concerning the Happiness of Good Men* (1704).

[3] Tenet.

kindly embraces what before deserved his aversion and censure.[4] My book crept into the world about six or seven years ago, without any opposition, and has since passed amongst some for useful, and, the least favourable, for innocent. But, as it seems to me, it is agreed by some men that it should no longer do so. Something, I know not what, is at last spyed out in it, that is like to be troublesome, and therefore it must be an ill book, and be treated accordingly. 'Tis not that I know any thing in particular, but some things that have hapned at the same time together, seem to me to suggest this: what it will produce, time will shew. But, as you say in that kind letter, *magna est veritas et prevalebit;*[5] that keeps me at perfect ease in this, and whatever I write; for as soon as I shall discover it not to be truth, my hand shall be the forwardest to throw it in the fire.

You desire to know what the opinion of the ingenious is, concerning Mr. Whiston's book.[6] I have not heard any one of my acquaintance speak of it, but with great commendation, as I think it deserves. And truly, I think he is more to be admired, that he has lay'd down an hypothesis, whereby he has explain'd so many wonderful, and, before, unexplicable things in the great changes of this globe, than that some of them should not go easily down with some men, when the whole was entirely new to all. He is one of those sort of writers that I always fancy should be most esteem'd and encourag'd. I am always for the builders who bring some addition to our knowledge, or, at least, some new thing to our thoughts. The finders of faults, the confuters and pullers down, do but only erect a barren and useless triumph upon human ignorance, but advance us nothing in the acquisition of truth. Of all the motto's I ever met with, this, writ over a water-work at Cleve, best pleased me, *Natura omnes fecit judices paucos artifices.*[7]

I thank you for the account you gave me of your linen manufacture. Private knavery, I perceive, does there as well as here destroy all publick good works, and forbid the hope of any advantages by them, where nature plentifully offers what industry would improve, were it but rightly directed, and duly cherished. The corruption of the age gives me so ill a prospect of any success in designs of this kind, never so well laid, that I am not sorry my ill health gives me so just a reason to desire to be eased of the employment I am in.[8] . . .

2206. Anonymous to Locke, [London?], [*c.*23 February 1697]

What hath been done allready by you to serve your Country, hath not only testified your honourable love to it and mankinde; but by the good success

---

[4] A sly dig at Sherlock's belated conversion to the Revolution. L1325, n. 9; L2221.
[5] L2131, n. 2. Locke had expressed surprise that Oxford should take his *Essay* seriously. L1887.
[6] L2131, n. 5.   [7] 'Nature made all men critics but few craftsmen.'
[8] In January Locke asked to resign from the Board of Trade; he was dissuaded.

of your services it plainly appeare's, none was soe capeable. But since the sinews of warr and strength of a Kingdome is not only money; but people; perfect therefore your noble designements for good and by your successfull pen encourage the multiplication of the latter, as you have preserved the former, by makeing the way reasonable to an Act of generall naturalization.[1] And since there may be as many mistaken Objections about this as the coyne, I have reason to believe they will be as easily reconciled as soon as you have given your judgment to your Country in this affaire. There are three sorts of Opponents, the one for fear it should make England to[o] powerfull and happy, which you have mett with before; the common obstructers of all good to this nation, whose principalls when unmasked will make their Arguments of noe force.[2] One other who for fear of Schism in a greater Multitude, will rest themselves contented with what are allready converted, nay unconverted, instead of walking about doeing good and preaching and converting all nations; for these their owne arguments will answere their objections and cover them with shame.[3] But then for the third sorte, their objections may seem more sensible and moveing, I mean the Merchant, tradeing, handicraft and labouring people of this Kingdome, who will say that this Act will lett in such of other nations, who will outtrade underworke underlive and eat the bread (not menconing their delicacies) out of their mouthes to their utter ruine; to these it may be truly said that the Lawes of England allready without any other naturalization lett in All Alien friends who may by merchandize trade or other lawfull wayes acquire and get any treasure or goods personall whatsoever and may maintaine any action for the same as our natives; which is the only ill consequence, if any, in a generall naturalization, but indeed this is an evill only for want of a naturalization; for such strangers comeing here, Leech like, suck our vitall riches till they are full, and then must drop of into their owne Countries to lay their treasure out, being uncapeable of purchaseing or layeing it out here (a great loss to this Kingdome). In short wee have all the effects of a Naturalization allready that are complained of by some, tho without reason or consideration, for the interest of England, as well as trade, is consumption of our product and what a vast Item in that account is made when each stranger[4] one with the other spend of our product 10l. per annum by computation; which is repaid from abroad when such person is exercised in some trade or exportable comodity which being sent abroad brings in to support that expence with an overplus and consequently makes his trade and labour parte of our treasure. What advantage hath accrewed to this nation allready by the many profitable arts and foreigne wayes of trade taught us by such strangers, may bee seen in many instances in fact true. About 30. or 40. yeares since an Eminent Clothier in the West of England[5] sent for severall Dutch people to

---

[1] A bill was defeated on 2 Mar. [2] Jacobites.
[3] High Churchmen, fearful of immigrants of different religions.
[4] Foreigner. [5] Possibly Christopher Cooke of Wilton (Wiltshire).

worke with him, by whome he learn't the best and cheapest way of spinning and makeing fine woollen Cloth, which hath propagated that sort of manufacture to the greatest perfection in the world and even to this day hath preserved and advanced that trade with us. Wee have of later times by the many strangers comeing here gotten the perfect manufactory knowledge and insight into the arts and trade of Holland, Spane and France etca, before unknown to us, the particulars whereof are to[o] universall to be here [inserted]; for which formerly wee exported vast treasure, which is now (in respect of that) not only kept at home; but by the exportation of such manufactures wee have great returnes from abroad which bring the ballance of trade on our side. Wee have many foreigne farmers in Lincolnshire[6] and other Countyes and traders in London and elsewhere who make the best tenants and payments of rents, but our lawes preventing leases to be granted to such deprieve our native Landlords of such advantages. but then as to the rich foregners, they and their treasure are locked out, they can't purchase here, tho our owners want money and our lands new masters. A thousand pounds layed out in land etca. by a foreigner is soe much clear gaines to the English nation for our Subjects money that might be layed out on the same purchase will not be exported but layed out in profitable trade manufacture and new improvements; was our Country as Holland open to the reception of such, the pulse of our government would be enlivened by new accessions of vitall treasure instead of being exhausted. Who would live in a continent continually exposed to warr and the insults of an Ambitious neighbouring prince and the more unjust arbitrary power of their owne, when he may be secure in his liberty and estate in a free country defended from such cares by that sea which convey the treasure of the world to it. the most happy scituation for universall trade and commerce; by this the inhabitants of our Isle att their owne election may be neighbours to or farther removed from the rest of the world as the occation of trade or warr require. The deer Leaps and avenues of a well contrived Parke for the benefit of its Master for multiplication and preservation of the heard, are made inviteing and easey to let in but difficult to let out, and such is the case of that Kingdome truly in its owne interest, and when its otherwise the motion is retrograde and unnaturall, such as are the polities of tyrants by banishments to compleat their arbitrary power; which could not be soe easily effected with the multitude. And for the Objection that numbers of Enemys may be sent over to subvert our Government, like the bowells of the Trojan horse; This is but of one single example and of as single force, for its hoped the Nation will not be soe intoxicated, but will have such qualifications in the naturalization by such Oath registry[7] etca. as for that purpose shall be thought meet to prevent such new guests from haveing any hand in the government till wee are assured they are good members thereof, and

---

[6] Dutch settlers in the newly drained fens of Cambridgeshire and Lincolnshire.
[7] Oaths of allegiance, registration of aliens.

certainly wee must have a greater proportion of friends than enemys come over being in amity with all most all the world, except one Kingdome, whereof good parte of the natives are in our interest by the bonds of gratitude, being socoured from the tyranny of their prince.[8] farthermore such foreigners soe transplanted here in 10 or 20 yeares would become good Englishmen and lovers of their protection in this Country perhaps more than many of our owne natives, and better enured to their duty of Obedience, by their property secured and their enlargement from a more severe subjection. What evill hath Holland and other states and free Countries received by its multitude of strangers? What strength what benefit and what treasure? What poverty and weakness hath ensued to Kingdomes and Empires by severe lawes and arbitrary power dispeopling them, whereby they have been exposed to the insults of a much less well peopled state made equall in their strength by their multitude to vast dominions History both auntient and moderne will evince. Nay our owne seas could not secure us was it not for our Navall force supplying the defect of people to garde our Coasts which would be more sensibly defitient were wee in a Continent secured only by the common boundaries and barriers of Kingdomes. But to conclude this tedious letter, was England in proportion as well peopled as Holland it would be invincible and its treasure inexhaustible, it would be the mart of the world and the ballance of peace and warr would be then intirely ours. Sir, . . . its hoped your penn will fully and speedily enlarge on this subject to perfect soe glorious a designe[9] . . .

2207. [James Johnstoun?] to [Locke], London, 27 February 1697

You have enclosed[1] (to satisfie your curiosity) the evidence against Aikenhead[2] and two of his Petitions. If the process come you shall have it or it shall be left where you shall order. The flying post[3] bore that he had not retracted till the day of Execution which you see is false.

The first act of parliament in Scotland against Blasphemy is act 21 parl: 1 sess: 1 Ch: 2d. anno 1661. which has two articles, By the first *railling upon or cursing God, or any of the persons of the Trinity is punishable with death*, these are the words, and here retracting availeth nothing. The next article is, that *denying God, or any of the persons of the Trinity and obstinatly continueing therein is punishable with death.*

---

[8] The Huguenots of France.

[9] In fact Locke had drafted a paper on this topic in 1693 (*Political Essays*, 322–6).

[1] The documents are in Locke's papers and were printed in Cobbett's *Complete Collection of State Trials* (1812), xiii, cols. 917–40.

[2] Thomas Aikenhead, aged about 18, hanged for heresy in Edinburgh on 8 Jan.

[3] The *Flying Post*, Scottish newspaper, founded 1695.

The next act is the 11th. of Tweeddal's[4] Session of Parliament two years agoe, and was obtained by trick and surprise. It ratifies the former act and adds, that *whether by writing or discourse To deny, impugne, querrell, argue, or reason against the being of God or any of the persons of the Trinity, or the authority of the Scriptures, or a providence is for the first fault punishable with imprisonment till they retract in sackcloth in the Church. For the second with imprisonment and a years Rent till as in the first case. and for the third, they are to die as obstinat blasphemers*; so that retracting after the third fault signifys nothing.

It's plain Aikenhead must have died by the first act, since it was his first fault as he himself pleads in his petition, and that he did retract which delivers him from the second article of the first act. Now the words of the first article being *railing* and *cursing*, no evidence except that of Mr Mungo Craigs[5] (in which he is said to have called Christ an imposture) seems to answer the meaning of those words, and as to this Craig Aikenhead in his speech in which he owns other things, denies his evidence and no doubt he is the decoy who gave him the books and made him speak as he did, and whose name is not put in the copy of the petition to the Justiciary sent to you, because the writer would spare Craig.

The age of the witnesses is observable[6] and that none of them pretend, nor is it laid in the Indictment that Aikenhead made it his bussines to seduce any man. Laws long in dessuetude should be gently put in Execution and the first example made of one in circumstances that deserve no compassion, whereas here ther is youth, Levity, docility, and no designe upon others.[7]

2221. William Molyneux to Locke, Dublin, 16 March 1697

... Both Whiston and Bentley are positive against the Idea of God being Innate.[1] and I had rather reley on them (if I would reley on any Man) than on Dr Sherlock;[2] Tis true the Latter has a great name; but that, I am sure, weighs not with You or Me. besides, you rightly observe, the Doctor is no Obstinate Heretick, but may veer about when an other Opinion comes in Fashion, for some men alter their Notions as they do their Cloaths in Complyance to the Mode. I have heard of a Master of the Temple[3] who during the siege of Limerick writ over hither to a certain Prelate to be sure to let him know by the first Oppertunity when ever it came to be surrendred. which was done accordingly,

[4] John Hay, Marquis of Tweeddale, High Commissioner.

[5] Mungo Craig, *A Satyr against Atheistical Deism* (1696); *A Lye is no Scandal* (1697).

[6] Young students, Aikenhead's associates.

[7] This letter has in the past been misattributed to Locke himself and taken as direct evidence of his own opinion.

[1] William Whiston, *A New Theory of the Earth* (1696); Richard Bentley, *The Folly and Unreasonableness of Atheism* (1692), the first series of Boyle Lectures. L2131.

[2] L2202, n. 2.   [3] Sherlock himself.

and Immediately the Good Doctors Eyes were opened and he plainly saw the Oaths to King Wil, and Q. Mary were not only expedient but Lawful and Our Duty.[4] A Good Roaring Train of Artillery is not only the Ratio Ultima Regum,[5] but of other men besides.

I fancy, I pretty wel gues what it is that some men find Mischeivous in your Essay. Tis opening the Eyes of the Ignorant, and rectifying the Methods of Reasoning, which perhaps may undermine some received Errors, and so abridge the Empire of Darknes, wherein tho the Subjects wander deplorably yet the Rulers have their Profit and Advantage. But tis ridiculous in any man to say in general your book is Dangerous; Let any fair Contender for Truth sit down and shew wherein tis Erroneous. Dangerous is a Word of an uncertain signification; every one Uses it in his Own Sense. A Papist shall say tis Dangerous at Rome because perhaps it agrees not so wel with Transubstantiation;[6] and a Lutheran, because his Consubstantiation[7] is in hazard; but neither consider whether Transubst. or Consubst. be True or False. but taking it for Granted that they are true or at least gainfull, whatever hitts not with it, or is against it, must be Dangerous. . . .

I am hartily glad to understand that you have taken notice of what the Bishop of Worcester says relating to your Book.[8] I have been in Discourse here with an Ingenious Man upon what the Bishop alledges, and the Gentleman observed that the Bishop does not so Directly object against your Notions as Erroneous, but as misused by Others, and Particularly by the Author of Christianity not Mysterious.[9] but I think this no very just Observation; the Bishop directly Opposes your Doctrine, tho, tis true, he does it on the Occasion of the foresaid Book. I am told the Author of that Discourse is of this Country, and that his Name is Toland, . . .

2232. Samuel Bold to [Locke], Steeple, Dorset, 26 March 1697

I have now read your very Rational, exact, and ful Answer[1] to mr Edwards's books.[2] which very much confirms me in my perswasion of your pious

---

[4] The lifting of the siege of Limerick in Oct. 1691 marked the completion of the reconquest of Ireland from the Jacobites. Molyneux's chronology is confused. Sherlock took the oaths in Aug. 1690, just after the Battle of the Boyne. L1325, n. 8.

[5] 'Ratio ultima regum': 'The ultimate argument of kings'. The phrase is associated with Cardinal Richelieu, and was apparently a motto engraved on French cannon.

[6] The doctrine that the eucharistic elements of bread and wine are changed into the body and blood of Christ during the Mass.

[7] The doctrine that the body and blood of Christ are present as well as the eucharistic elements.

[8] Edward Stillingfleet, *A Discourse in Vindication of the Trinity* (1696), which accused Locke of Socinianism; Locke, *A Letter* (to Stillingfleet) (1697).

[9] John Toland, *Christianity not Mysterious* (1696).

[1] *A Second Vindication of the Reasonableness of Christianity* (1697).

[2] John Edwards, Fellow of St John's College, Cambridge. *Some Thoughts Concerning the Several Causes and Occasions of Atheism* (1695); *Socinianism Unmask'd* (1696); *A Brief Vindication of the Fundamental Articles of the Christian Faith* (1697); *The Socinian Creed* (1697).

Design, and most Judicious procedure in your most excellent Treatise The Reasonableness of Christianity etc. You have pinn'd matters so closely on mr Edwards, and set forth the Truths you before published in such a clear light, and given such a perfect Demonstration of them, if mr Edwards do not publickly acknowledge his faults, and set his seal to what you have so fully prooved, I shal be hard put to it, to maintain the Charitable opinion of Him, I have hitherto striven to entertain. We are certified of a very eminent Prophet, that He had such passions as other men had.[3] But I cannot but bewail the Clergy, that they so ordinarily suffer (if not provoke) their passions to transport and carry them to greater Indecencies, than the rest of mankind commonly do. As if it were their priviledge to set no bounds to themselves, but were to exceed the generality in their faults and Intemperancies to as great a degree, as they conceit their Office doth raise them above the vulgar. How deplorable is our case, when those who are peculiarly engaged to study the Christian Religion, do make it their busyness, rather to give the world proofs of the Raging Furious Spirit of a Party, than of the meek and charitable spirit of that Holy and Good Religion they are obliged to instruct people in? You have bin treated very Injuriously, and with detestable Disingenuity. I am glad to finde you resent[4] It so calmly, and with a temper so becoming a sincere Disciple and follower of your Meek and patient Lord, And that you have made so good a use of your Adversaries base, and unworthy Conduct, as to take occasion from It, to contribute the most, that I think any man hath done to set the world right, and bring people to be Judicious and good Christians.... You have given a more satisfactory account of the Covenant of Grace, than I ever mett with in any books on that Subject. You have directed us all, to the true and right way of pressing people to read and study the Holy Scriptures.[5] I am entirely beholden to you, for helping me to observe and improve the Divine wisdom in our Saviours Conduct, to the resolving of several doubts, which must have retained much strength, without the Light you have given for the removing of them. You have fixed (I think) on the only proper and effectual method to convince and bring the Deists to espouse Christianity.[6] They are generally (as far as I can guess) persons of good parts, and if they wil but approve themselves Honest, I apprehend you have done them, as wel as Christianity it self, the greatest and best service it is possible for man to do them. Sir, I thank you most heartily for your charitable and kind Acceptance of my mean papers, and for the great Honour you have done me, in condescending to take notice of me, in your publishing your further thoughts upon the subject treated of, And that you have bin pleased to acquaint the publick, as wel as me with the True History of the birth of your Reasonableness of Christianity as delivered in the Scriptures, and your design in publishing It, by so particular and obliging an Address to me.[7] I wish your

---

[3] Elijah: James 5:17. [4] Receive. [5] In the opening paragraph of the *Reasonableness*.
[6] The stated purpose of the *Reasonableness*.
[7] The preface to the *Second Vindication* includes a complimentary epistle to Bold.

expressing so great Respect to me, who have lain under an Ill eye, ever since I appeared against Persecution,[8] may not prove some prejudice to your most excellent Book. Had I known you would have stooped so low as to vindicate my sermon and Animadversions against mr Edwards's Postscript (for which singular favour I return you my most solemn thanks) I would not have troubled the publick with my Insignificant Reply to Him,[9] . . .

2241. [Thomas Firmin?] to [Locke?], [8 or 9 April 1697?]

I Received yours and had answered it soner but that I was willing at the same time to give you an account of the fate of our bill in parliament for the lutestring company[1] which yesterday passed the house of Lords with som small amendments at the desire of the smuglers that appeared in great numbers against it and they good men ought to be incoraged. We Expect this bill will be greatly to the Advantage of the company which of late have suffered so much by bringing in french goods[2] and makeing other in Spitle feilds[3] that for 8 months past we have sold little or nothing, a little time will show the effect . . .[4]

. . . booth linen and woolen. but I have seen one of each sort to goe with boath hands which if people could be brot to is the finest way of spining in the world.[5] I would not advise you to put your country people upon Spining flax they will earne much more in spining wool, my poor people spin 800 yards of yarn for 1d and they are but few that can earne 6d a day tho they work 16 howers. I have made 700 peces of cloth in about 18 months time at 5l a pece one with a nother, and 4 parts in 5 have been paid to the poor . . .

2269. William Molyneux to Locke, Dublin, 27 May 1697

The Hints you are pleased so friendly to communicate to me in yours of the 3d Inst. concerning Mr T.[1] are fresh marks of your Kindnes, and Confidence in me; and they perfectly agree with the Apprehensions I had conceived of

---

[8] Bold had been imprisoned briefly for his *Sermon against Persecution* (1682).

[9] Bold, *A Short Discourse of the True Knowledge of Christ Jesus* (1697).

[1] The Royal Lustring Company bill imposed penalties on imported silks. Locke invested in the company. Lustring or lutestring was a high quality silk fabric.

[2] There was widespread objection to French imports, now that war with France was suspended.

[3] Spitalfields in East London was predominantly a community of immigrant Huguenot silkweavers.

[4] Only the top half of this letter survives.

[5] The double spinning wheel, invented by or for Firmin. Locke advocated it to the Board of Trade and refers to it in a draft of his *Essay on the Poor Law*, 1697 (*Political Essays*, 192).

[1] John Toland, who had now arrived in Ireland. Locke had warned Molyneux against him.

that Gentleman. Truly to be free, and without Reserve to you, I do not think His management since he came into this Citty has been so prudent; He has raised against him the Clamours of all Partys; and this not so much by his Difference in Opinion, as by his Unseasonable Way of Discoursing, propagating, and Maintaining it. Coffee-houses and Publick Tables are not proper Places for serious Discourses relating to the Most Important Truths. But when also a Tincture of Vanity appears in the Whole Course of a Mans Conversation, it disgusts many that may otherwise have a due Value for his Parts and Learning. I have known a Gentleman in this town that was a Most strict Socinian, and thought as much out of the Common road as any man, and was also known so to do; but then his Behaviour and Discourse was attended with so much Modesty, Goodnes, and Prudence, that I never heard him publickly Censur'd or Clamourd against, neither was any man in Danger of Censure by receiving his Visits or keeping him Company. I am very loath to tell you how far tis otherwise with Mr T. in this place; but I am perswaded it may be for his advantage that you know it, and that you friendly Admonish him of it, for his conduct hereafter. I do not think that any man can be Dispensed with to Dissemble the Truth, and full perswasion of his Mind in Religious Truths, when duly called to it, and upon fitting Occasions. but I think prudence may guide us in the Choise of proper Oppertunitys, that we may not run our selves against rocks to no purpose, and inflame Men against us unnecessarily. Mr T. also takes here a great Liberty on all occasions to vouch your Patronage and Friendship, which makes many that rail at him, rail also at You. I beleive you will not approve of this, as far as I am able to Judge by your shaking him off in your Letter to the Bishop of Worcester.[2] But after all this, I look upon Mr T. as a very ingenious Man, and I should be very Glad of any Oppertunity of Doing him service, to which I think my self indispensibly bound by your recommendation. One thing more I had almost forgott to intimate to you; that all here are mightily at a Losse in Guessing what might be the Occasion of Mr T. coming at this time into Ireland. He is known to be of no Fortune or Imploy, and yet is observed to have a subsistance; but from whence it comes no one Can tell certainly. These things joynd with his great forwardnes in appearing Publick makes people surmise a thousand Fancys. If you could give me light into these matters, as far as it may help me in my own Conduct, I should be much obleidged to you. . . .

Mr Churchil Favourd me with the Present of Sir R. Blackmores K. Arthur. I had Pr. Arthur before,[3] and read it with Admiration, which is not at all Lessend by this second Peice. All Our English Poets (except Milton) have been meer Ballad-makers in Comparison to him. upon the Publication of his first Poem, I intimated to him, through mr Churchils hands, how excellently I thought

---

[2] *A Letter to the Bishop of Worcester* (Edward Stillingfleet) (1697).

[3] Sir Richard Blackmore, royal physician, and poet. *Prince Arthur* (1695) and *King Arthur* (1697): Williamite epic poems.

he might Perform a Philosophick Poem from many touches he gave in his Pr. Arth. particularly from Mopas's Song.[4] And I perceive by his preface to K. Arth. he has had the like Intimation[s] from others, but rejects them as being an Enemy to all Philosophick Hypotheses. Were I acquainted with Sir R. Blackmore I could assure him (and if you be so I beseech you to tell him) that I am as little an Admirer of Hypotheses as any Man, and never proposed that thought to him with a Designe that a Philosophick Poem should run on such a strain. A Natural History of the Great and Admirable Phænomena of the Universe is a subject, I think, may afford sublime Thoughts in a Poem. and so far, and no farther, would I desire a Poem to Extend.[5] . . .

2277. Locke to William Molyneux, Oates, 15 June 1697

. . . As to the gentleman,[1] to whom you think my friendly admonishments may be of advantage for his conduct hereafter, I must tell you, that he is a man to whom I never writ in my life, and, I think, I shall not now begin. And, as to his conduct, 'tis what I never so much as spoke to him of. That is a liberty to be only taken with friends and intimates, for whose conduct one is mightily concerned, and in whose affairs one interesses himself. I cannot but wish well to all men of parts and learning, and be ready to afford them all the civilities, and good offices in my power. But there must be other qualities to bring me to a friendship, and unite me in those stricter tyes of concern. For I put a great deal of difference between those whom I thus receive into my heart and affection, and those whom I receive into my chamber, and do not treat there with a perfect strangeness. I perceive you think your self under some obligation of peculiar respect to that person upon the account of my recommendation to you; but certainly this comes from nothing but your over-great tenderness to oblige me. For, if I did recommend him, you will find it was only as a man of parts and learning for his age, but without any intention that that should be of any other consequence, or lead you any farther, than the other qualities you should find in him, should recommend him to you. And therefore, whatsoever you shall, or shall not do for him, I shall no way interest my self in. I know, of your own self, you are a good friend to those who deserve it of you; and for those that do not, I shall never blame your neglect of them. The occasion of his coming into Ireland now, I guess to be the hopes of some employment, now upon this change of hands

---

[4] *Prince Arthur*, IV: Mopas, Arthur's bard, describes how 'the great Eternal Mind' impresses ordered 'Perfection' upon the 'chaos' of brute matter.

[5] Blackmore later obliged in *Creation, A Philosophical Poem, Demonstrating the Existence and Providence of God* (1712). Philosophic poems celebrating the deity's grand design in the order of nature were an Enlightenment fashion.

[1] John Toland. This letter answers L2269.

there.[2] I tell you, *I guess*, for he himself never told me any thing of it, nor so much as acquainted me with his intentions of going to Ireland, how much soever *he vouches my patronage and friendship*, as you are pleased to phrase it. And as to his subsistence, from whence that comes, I cannot tell. I should not have wasted so much of my conversation, with you, on this subject, had you not told me it would oblige you to give you light in these matters, which I have done, as a friend to a friend, with a greater freedom than I should allow my self to talk to another.

I shall, when I see Sir R. Blackmore, discourse him as you desire. There is, I with pleasure find, a strange harmony throughout, between your thoughts and mine. I have always thought, that laying down, and building upon hypotheses, has been one of the great hindrances of natural knowledge; and I see your notions agree with mine in it. And, though I have a great value for Sir R. Blackmore, on several accounts, yet there is nothing has given me a greater esteem of him, than what he says about hypotheses in medicine, in his preface to K. Arthur, which is an argument to me that he understands the right method of practising physick; and it gives me great hopes he will improve it, since he keeps in the only way it is capable to be improved in; and has so publickly declared against the more easie, fashionable, and pleasing way of an hypothesis, which, I think, has done more to hinder the true art of physick, which is the curing of diseases, than all other things put together; by making it learned, specious, and talkative, but ineffective to its great end, the health of mankind; as was visible in the practice of physick, in the hands of the illiterate Americans; and the learned physicians, that went thither out of Europe, stored with their hypotheses, borrowed from natural philosophy, which made them indeed great men, and admir'd in the schools, but, in curing diseases, the poor Americans, who had scaped those splendid clogs, clearly out-went them. You cannot imagin how far a little observation, carefully made, by a man not tyed up to the four humours; or sal, sulphur and mercury; or to acid and alcali,[3] which has of late prevailed, will carry a man in the curing of diseases, though very stubborn and dangerous, and that with very little and common things, and almost no medicines at all. . . .

2288. William Molyneux to Locke, Dublin, 20 July 1697

. . . I am obleidged to you for the Confidence you put in me by communicating your Thoughts concerning Mr T.[1] more freely than you would do to every One. He has had his Opposers here; as you will find by a Book, which I have sent to you[2] by a Gentlemans Servant to be left for you at your

---

² Perhaps referring to John Methuen's appointment as Lord Chancellor of Ireland.
³ L1593, nn. 4–6.

¹ John Toland. This letter answers L2277.
² Peter Browne, *A Letter in Answer to a Book Entituled, Christianity not Mysterious* (1697).

Lodging. wherein you will meet a Passage relating to your self; which tho with decency, yet I fear will not redound much to the Authors Advantage; for with very great Assurance (a usual companion of Ignorance) he undertakes to *demonstrate* the Immateriality of the Soul, and to shew the falsity of your Argumentation wherein you assert that we have no proof; but that God may communicate a Power of Thinking to a Certain system of Matter.[3] But this is all but Assertion and Promise; we are so unhappy as yet to want this *Demonstration* from this Author; and I fear we shall ever want it from him and I beleive you will be of my Opinion when you read his Book. The Author is my Acquaintance, but two things I shall never forgive in his Book; The One is the Foul language and Opprobrious Names he Gives Mr Toland; The other is, upon several Occasions calling in the Aid of the Civil Magistrate, and delivering Mr Toland up to secular Punishment. This indeed is a killing Argument, but some will be apt to say, that where the strength of his Reason faild him, there he flys to the strength of the Sword. And this minds me of a Busines that was very surprising to many, even several Prelates, in this Place, The Presentment of some Pernicious Books and their Authors by the Grand Jury of Middlesex.[4] this is lookd upon as a Matter of Dangerous Consequence, to make Our Civil Courts judges of Religious Doctrines; and no one knows upon a Change of affairs, whose turn it may be next to be Condemned. But the Example has been followd in our Count[r]y and Mr [Toland], And his book have been presented here, by a Grand Jury, Not one of Which (I am perswaded) ever read One Leaf in Christianity not Mysterious. Let the Sorbone[5] for ever now be silent, a Learned Grand Jury directed by as Learned a Judge does the busines much better. the Dissenters here were the chief Promoters of this Matter; but when I asked one of them, What if a Violent Church of England Jury should present Mr Baxters Books[6] as pernicious and condemn them to the flames by the Common EXECUTIONER;[7] He was sensible of the Error, and said he wishd it had never been done. . . .

2299. Edward Clarke to Locke, Wells, Somerset, 14 August 1697

. . . I can now informe you, That I spent a greate deale of time with your new tenant Francis Carpenter, and had greate Difficulty to gett Him

---

[3] The 'thinking matter' hypothesis (*Essay*, IV. iii. 6).

[4] On 17 May. Grand juries were assemblies of citizens which gave preliminary consideration to indictments, and voiced the grievances of the county. The books condemned were: Toland, *Christianity not Mysterious*; Locke, *The Reasonableness of Christianity*; (William Stephens?), *A Lady's Religion* (1697), sometimes attributed to Locke; Francis Atterbury, *A Letter to a Convocation Man* (1696).

[5] The university at Paris: implying a Popish inquisition.

[6] Richard Baxter, doyen among Presbyterian authors, convicted of sedition in 1685.

[7] Books condemned by parliament or the courts were publicly burned. In September the Irish House of Commons condemned Toland's book to be burned, and Toland retreated to England.

under Covenants to doe the Offices of Overseer of the Poore, Constable, Tythingman,[1] Surveyor of the High-Wayes, and other Personall offices, which, by reason of That Tenement hee now is, or shall hereafter bee Lyable to,[2] and the rather for that Hee is this verie yeare made Overseer of the Poore, Which, if you had payd for, would have cost the better part of five pounds;[3] The Church and Poore Rates Hee positively refused to pay, or allow any part towards it, I did all I could to have brought Him up to Discharge those Payments, But I could not prevayle, Indeed His obstinacy was such in that poynt, That by my insisting soe much on it, I had like to have lost your Tenant quite; Upon the whole matter, Being satisfied, there is a much greater Advance made by Him, in the Rent, and by the Covenants for Repayres of the House, out-houses, Gates, Barrs, and Fences, And by doeing the Personall-Offices belonging to the Tenement at his own Costs and Charges, than would have been Consented by any other Person whatsoever, I concluded with Him and Hee has Sealed a Counterpart with a Bond for performance of Covenants . . .

2319. Locke to Dr John Covel, London, 29 September 1697

I am told the Booksellers in Cambridg have made bolder than they should with the booke you will herewith receive, by pasting a paper over the Authors Epistle to the Bookseller.[1] Tis pitty soe excellent a treatise as this is should loose the authority and recommendation your name gives to it.[2] I therefor send you one with all its ornaments displaid, as our shops here afford them: And you will doe well to Keep it safe, that posterity may know, as well as this present age, who lent his helping hand to usher into the world soe cleanly a peice of divinity, and such a just model of manageing of controversie in Religion, to be a pattern for the youth in his own Colledg, and in the rest of the Universitie to imitate. This is all at present, till I have a fitter oportunity to talke with you about what the dull stationer here made bold to strike out notwithstanding it had the warrant of your *Imprimatur*. Tis not that I pretend to be interested in the Controversie wherein Mr Edwards is a party: but hearing he had named me in the title of his booke I thought my self concerned to read

---

[1] Sometimes another name for a parish constable; sometimes a deputy. Literally, an officer for ten households.

[2] Parish offices were annual appointments, sometimes elected, sometimes, as here in Pensford, falling by rotation among the householders, a practice called houserow.

[3] The costs incident upon declining to hold an office.

[1] John Edwards, *A Brief Vindication of the Fundamental Articles of the Christian Faith* (1697), the epistle to which contained libels against Locke, including the reference to the 'seraglio at Oates'.

[2] The book contained the Covel's imprimatur.

it: And haveing perused it I think it will not misbecome our old acquaintance[3] to doe you this right. . . .

2320. Locke to Carey Mordaunt, Countess of Peterborough, [Oates?], [September/October 1697?]

In[1] obedience to your Ladyships commands I take the libertie to present you in writeing with some part of what you had the patience to hear me discourse in your presence the last time I had the honour to wait upon you. I have always thought that to direct a yonge gentlemans studys right it is absolutely necessary to know what course of life either by the distinction of his quality or fortune or by the choise and determination of his parents he is designed to. The want of a due regard to this is often the cause that a great part of his time is painfully thrown away in studys and exercises wholy besides his purpose whilst others of absolute use and necessity are wholy overseen and neglected

My Lord Mordants[2] birth without any more adoe tells every one what he is to be in the world and directs us to consider what may conduce to make him an accomplished and great man in his country. But your Ladyships enquiry being now barely in reference to the choise and conduct of his studys twill be besides the present businesse to medle with anything but bookes and learning

My Lord is goeing now to a place[3] where he may have masters and Tutors of all kindes and in all the arts and sciences. The first thing therefor to be considerd when and how far a man should use a Tutor and to that I thinke the same answer should be given as to one that askes how long a child should be guided by leading strings and to that every one will readily say till he can goe alone. When a man knows the termes sees the method and has got an entrance into any of the sciences, twill be time then to depend upon himself relye upon his own understanding and exercise his own faculties which is the only way to improvement and mastery. Only where the studys are in themselves knotty and hard there the Tutors help is longer usefull and to be left of[f] by degrees reserveing that assistance only for difficult cases

---

[3] They were acquainted in Holland when Covel was chaplain to Princess Mary. Covel was dismissed in 1685 on suspicion of plotting to abduct Mary on behalf of the English government. In drafting this letter, Locke thought better of including a threatening allusion to that incident: 'I may chance to write relateing to some transactions at the Hague . . . nor shall a word of it be kept from the world'. Locke was acquainted with William III's brilliant secret service agent, Abel Tasien d'Alonne.

[1] This letter is closely related to 'Some Thoughts Concerning Reading and Study for a Gentleman' (1703); *Political Essays*, 348–55, 376–80), and *Education*, esp. §§ 182–6.

[2] Carey's son, John Mordaunt, aged about 16. L1252, n. 1.

[3] Utrecht, with a tutor called Marx, who closely followed Locke's advice.

History is esteemd one of the most necessary studys for a gentleman and in it self one of the most entertaining and most easy, And soe it is and therefor should be begun with. But to profit by it a yonge gentleman will at first seting out have need of a guide. If not to explain some difficulties in the language, yet to make him remarke the particular Beautys and excellencys of the Author he reads and teach him to observe the most important things in it Relateing to a mans private conduct in common life, or to the turns of state in publick affairs

To this purpose I think it would be most advisable for my Lord M to begin with Livys history which is the great repository of the Roman Antiquities, as well as the best history of that state.[4] In the reading of this author I thinke it would be usefull to him that somebody should explain all the Roman Customs as any expressions in the course of the history give occasion to take notice of them. Other critical expositions where with men versed in that sort of learning use to abound I thinke my Lord neither needs nor ought to be troubled with. Yonge persons of quality should have none of their time wasted in studys which will be of noe use to them when men. They must have time allowd them for diversion and recreation, these are as necessary as study, and what can be spared from health and diversion should be all imploid only in necessary and to them usefull parts of knowledg. To the explication therefor of the customs and manners of the Romans as they occur in Livie it would be well to joyn the Turns of State and the causes upon which they depended. This is fit to Remarke to a yonge Nobleman and make him take notice of in his Reading

The great end of such historys as Livy is to give an account of the Actions of men as embodied in societie and soe is the true foundation of politicks. But the flourishing or decays of commonwealths depending not barely on the present time, or what is don within themselves, but most commonly on remote and precedent constitutions and events and a train of concurrent actions amongst their neighbours as well as themselves. The order of time is absolutely necessary to a due knowledg and improvement of history, as the order of sentences in an author is necessary to be kept to, to make any sense out of what he says.

To Chronoligie Geographie too should be added for the right use and understanding of history. The scene of the action contributes always to the memory of it, and is very often soe necessary to a clear conception of the fact, that it cannot distinctly be comprehended without it

Though Chronologie and Geographie be both of them usefull to History, yet a very nice and criticall knowledg of either of them is not at all necessary noe not soe much as convenient for a yonge Gentleman. The knowing the figure of the earth, The meridian, Æquator Tropicks Polar Circles and Poles and thereby longitude and latitude by the figures placed on the sides of

---

[4] Livy, *History of Rome.*

particular maps is enough to begin with and a little of this every day just before he begins to read Livy will quickly lead him to the knowledg and use of Maps and then he has as much Geographie as need be taught him. If he has aminde to be more exact in this knowledg being thus far enterd he will be able to goe on well enough of himself, and whether for thus much he will need any printed systeme or noe I know not but leave it to his Tutor

When he is perfect in the use of Maps which he should always have before him when he reads history it will be time enough to enter upon Chronologie and there without troubleing him with the several accounts of years and months that have been used in the world I thinke it is enough to make him conceive the Julian Period, and then setle in his minde the several great Epochs that are most remarkeable in History. as Particularly the Creation of the world,[5] The Olympiads, The building of Rome, the birth of our Saviour, and the Hegira.[6] and to make him remember in what year of the Julian period each of these Epochs began. For this the explication of some small part of Strauchii Breviarium Temporum and Helvicus's Chronologie will be enough.[7] and every time he comes to a lecture in a Latin Historion to aske him in what year of the Julian Period Rome was built. in a Greeke historion, in what year of the Julian period the first Olympiad was and soe of the rest. For the only way to setle the memory of any number in any ones head is often to repeat it.

With the reading of History I thinke the study of Morality should be joynd, I mean not the Ethicks of the Schools fitted to dispute, but such as Tully in his Offices.[8] Puffendorf De officio hominis et Civis et de Jure Naturali et Gentium[9] and Aristotle[10] and above all the New Testament teaches, wherein a man may learne how to live. which is the businesse of Ethicks, and not how to difine distinguish and dispute about the names of virtues and vices.

True politicks I looke on as a Part of Moral Philosophie which is noething but the art of conducting men right in societie and supporting a communitie amongst its neighbours. Wherein Aristotle[11] may be best to begin with, and then afterwards if he pleases he may discend to more moderne writers of Government either as to the foundations and forms of politick societies, or the art of ruleing them.[12]

With these he may after some little time joyn a course of Natural philosophie Chymistry or which I should rather choose to begin with Anatomie

---

[5] 4004 BC. L1309, n. 3.

[6] The flight of Mohammed from Mecca, AD 622, from which is dated the Muslim era.

[7] Aegidius Strauch (Strauchius), *Breviarium Chronologicum* (1686); Christophe Helwig (Helvicus), *Theatrum Historicum sive Chronologiae systema novum* (1609).

[8] Cicero, *De officiis* (*On Duties*).

[9] Samuel Pufendorf, *De Officio Hominis et Civis* (*On the Duty of Man and Citizen*) (1673); *De Jure Naturae et Gentium* (*On the Law of Nature and Nations*) (1672).

[10] *Nicomachean Ethics.*   [11] *Politics.*

[12] In 'Some Thoughts', Locke specifies the works of Richard Hooker, Samuel Pufendorf, Algernon Sidney, and the obscure Peter Paxton, together with his own *Two Treatises* (*Political Essays*, 377).

because that consists only in seeing the figure texture and situation of the parts and some little matter about their use. For I thinke in all the sciences the easiest should always be began with, which are those that lye nearest the senses. and from thence by degrees to proceed to those that are more [abstract] and lie wholy in thought.

This Madam I thinke is enough to begin with. . . .

13

Divinity and Ireland, 1697–1698

Locke's asthma gradually became more oppressive. He found it increasingly difficult to cope with the London smog, though he still managed the journey to most meetings of the Board of Trade. Even in rural Essex he was forced to sit inactively by the fireside and he tells Molyneux that he does not think he has long to live (L2376). When the king asks him to undertake another political office, perhaps that of secretary of state, he declines, pleading ill-health and lack of experience in handling people who are used to the public stage (L2384).

Having earlier written a substantial memorandum for the Board of Trade on the reform of the poor law, he was disappointed that his ideas did not come to legislative fruition. To Edward Clarke he again recommends the more effective employment of the able-bodied poor (L2398). Locke's reputation as a public policy adviser was nationally known, quite independently of the fame of his philosophical writings. An unsolicited appeal for his support for a naturalization bill was noted earlier. A Derbyshire clergyman now asks him to support a bill for clarifying the law on tithes (L2451). The economic support of the clergy by the payment of tithes remained fundamental to the Church of England's economy until the nineteenth century. Although zealous high churchmen argued for the 'divine right' of tithes, tithe disputes were a perennial source of friction and litigation, tithe-payers having financial and sometimes conscientious objections to paying. The letter to Locke illuminates the agrarian tithe problem, and shows that tithes were still often calculated as an actual proportion of the harvest and not commuted to cash payments.

In Amsterdam, Limborch discussed Locke's letters with a number of public officials, professional men, and clergy, who were absorbed in theological speculation. One topic they raised was the adequacy of proofs of the 'unity of God', that is to say, arguments from reason (as opposed to biblical revelation) that there is one god only, and not a plurality of gods, as the heathens believed. Locke takes up the matter (L2340, L2395, L2413, L2443, L2498). Arguably the topic has no connection with the doctrine of the Trinity, which theologians almost universally allowed to be a truth known only from revelation, but some commentators have taken Locke's remarks to be indicative of his anti-Trinitarianism. Limborch thought that some parts of Locke's initial response would make no headway with his Cartesian friends, and so Locke adjusts his presentation (L2413). Locke continues to express his objection to Cartesian notions of disembodied thought, for he did not think Descartes had demonstrated the immateriality of thinking substance. He also sorts all Christians into the evangelical, who ground their religion on 'proofs and reason', and the papistical, who rely on infallible dogma (L2498). He expresses his dismay that his *Essay*, a book of philosophical speculation, should belatedly become the object of clerical animus (L2340). Locke settled his earlier disagreement with the Master of Christ's College, Cambridge, John Covel, over the university's imprimatur upon John Edwards's libellous attack. Covel had speedily apologized, but Locke elicits a revised version of the apology with a view to its publication (L2481).

From about 1694 Locke began to befriend a cousin of his, Peter King, an aspiring lawyer who rose to be Lord Chancellor, the son of a Presbyterian grocer of Exeter. King was to become Locke's literary executor, and the bulk of Locke's private papers passed down through King's descendants. In 1698 Locke was ready to exert his influence to secure for King a call to the bar. He found that Lord Chief Justice Treby had already made a recommendation, and Locke thanks him for bestowing his patronage (L2440). This was the making of King, who soon acquired a considerable legal reputation, and by 1701 was an MP.

Molyneux tells Locke of the publication of his *Case of Ireland* (1698), reporting that he has grounded it upon Locke's theory of consent in the *Two Treatises* (L2422). The immediate provocation for the book was England's policy of protecting its own woollen industry by ruthlessly banning Irish competition. Molyneux asserted that Ireland was an independent kingdom, not a colony bound by the legislation of English parliaments. English Whigs condemned his tract as an affront to the sovereignty of the imperial parliament and as a misreading of Locke. Locke himself avoids recording an opinion, penning some evasive remarks in which he refuses to commit himself (L2414). The *Case of Ireland* became a foundational text for eighteenth-century Irish nationalism and exerted an influence upon American arguments for independence.

Locke hoped for an opportunity to talk with Molyneux in person 'before I go out of this world', but it was Molyneux who departed this world first. Locke's cherished correspondence with his friend came to an abrupt end that autumn when Molyneux died of kidney stones at the age of forty-two. Ezekiel Burridge describes Molyneux's last days, and Locke sends commiserations to Molyneux's brother, Thomas (L2495, L2500).

2340. Locke to Philippus van Limborch, [Oates?], 29 October 1697

If my name has come to be known by the erudite men with whom you some-times converse, and if they deign to speak of my writings in the conversations which you have with them, it is a favour for which I am entirely indebted to you. The good opinion which you have of a person whom you are kind enough to honour with your friendship has made them well disposed towards me. I would like my *Essay concerning Understanding* to be written in a language which these excellent men can understand, for by their fine and sincere judgement of my work, I could solidly count on what is right and wrong and on what might be tolerable.[1] It is seven years since this book was published. The first and the second edition had the good fortune to be generally well received: but the last has not had this same advantage. After a silence of five or six years people are starting to find all number of faults which have not been noticed previously; and what is most curious is their claim to find matter for religious controversy[2] in this work where my intention was merely to treat questions of pure philosophical speculation. I had resolved to make various additions, of which I have already composed some quite ample ones, and which should have [appeared] in their place in the fourth edition which the bookseller is preparing to make, and I would willingly have satisfied your wish or that of any of your friends by [inserting] the proofs of the unity of God which occur to me.[3] For I am inclined to believe that the unity of God can be as clearly demonstrated as his existence; and that it can be established on proofs which will give no cause for doubt. But I am a lover of peace, and there are people in the world who so love bawling and groundless quarrels,[4] that I doubt whether I should furnish them with new subjects for dispute.

The comments which you tell me that learned men have made on the *Reasonableness of Christianity* etc are surely most just, and it is true that several readers were shocked by certain thoughts which are found at the start of this book which do not accord at all with commonly received doctrines. But on this point I must refer these gentlemen to the two defences which the author has made of his work. For as he published this little book, as he says himself, principally in order to convince those who have their doubts about the Christian religion, it appears that he has been forced to deal with these matters despite himself, for in order to make his book useful [against] deists, he could not be entirely silent about these articles, which they are [confronted]

---

[1] Pierre Coste's French translation of the *Essay* appeared in 1700.   [2] L2202.

[3] The 4th edn. included new chapters 'Of the Association of Ideas' and 'Of Enthusiasm'. On the unity of God see L2395, L2443.

[4] Locke's postscript complains of 'the cassocked tribe of theologians' ('gens theologorum togata').

with as soon as they wish to embark on an examination of the Christian religion.

2376. Locke to William Molyneux, Oates, 10 January 1698

... Business kept me in town longer than was convenient for my health: all the day from my rising was commonly spent in that, and when I came home at night my shortness of breath and panting for want of it made me ordinarily so uneasy, that I had no heart to do any thing; so that the usual diversion of my vacant hours forsook me, and reading it self was a burden to me. In this estate I linger'd along in town to December, till I betook my self to my wonted refuge in the more favourable air and retirement of this place. That gave me presently relief, against the constant oppression of my lungs, whilst I sit still: But I find such a weakness of them still remain, that if I stir ever so little I am immediately out of breath, and the very dressing or undressing me is a labour that I am fain to rest after to recover my breath; and I have not been once out of the house since I came last hither. I wish nevertheless that you were here with me to see how well I am: For you would find, that, sitting by the fire's side, I could bear my part in discoursing, laughing, and being merry with you, as well as ever I could in my life. If you were here (and if wishes of more than one could bring you, you would be here to day) you would find three or four in the parlour after dinner, whom you would say pass'd their afternoons as agreeably and as jocundly as any people you have this good while met with. Do not therefore figure to your self that I am languishing away my last hours under an unsociable despondency and the weight of my infirmity. 'Tis true I do not count upon years of life to come, but I thank God I have not many uneasy hours here in the four and twenty; and if I can have the wit to keep my self out of the stifling air of London, I see no reason but by the grace of God I may get over this winter, and that terrible enemy of mine may use me no worse than the last did, which as severe and as long as it was let me yet see another summer. . . .

When I see a man, disinterested as you are, a lover of truth as I know you to be, and one that has clearness and coherence enough of thought to make long mathematical, i.e. sure deductions, pronounce of J. H. and J. S.'s books that they are unintelligible to you;[1] I do not presently condemn my self of pride, prejudice, or a perfect want of understanding, for laying aside those Authors, because I can find neither sense or coherence in them. If I could think that discourses and arguments to the understanding were like the several sorts of cates[2] to different palates and stomachs, some nauseous and

---

[1] James Hodges, *The Present State of England, as to Coin* (1697); John Sergeant, *Solid Philosophy Asserted* (1697); both against Locke.

[2] Delicacies.

destructive to one, which are pleasant and restorative to another; I should no more think of books and study, and should think my time better imploy'd at push-pin[3] than in reading or writing. But I am convinced of the contrary: I know there is truth opposite to falshood, that it may be found if people will, and is worth the seeking, and is not only the most valuable, but the pleasantest thing in the world. And therefore I am no more troubled and disturb'd with all the dust that is raised against it, than I should be to see from the top of an high steeple, where I had clear air and sunshine, a company of great boys or little boys (for 'tis all one) throw up dust in the air, which reach'd not me, but fell down in their own eyes. . . .

It will not be at all necessary to say any thing to you concerning the linen bill,[4] . . . I think it a shame, that whilst Ireland is so capable to produce flax and hemp, and able to nourish the poor at so cheap a rate, and consequently to have their labour upon so easy terms, that so much mony should go yearly out of the king's dominions, to enrich foreigners, for those materials and the manufactures made out of them, when his people of Ireland, by the advantage of their soil, situation, and plenty, might have every penny of it, if that business were but once put into a right way. . . . The short is, I mightily have it upon my heart to get the linen manufacture established in a flourishing way in your country. I am sufficiently sensible of the advantages it will be to you, and shall be doubly rejoyced in the success of it, if I should be so happy that you and I could be instrumental in it, and have the chief hand in forming any thing that might conduce to it. Imploy your thoughts therefore I beseech you about it, and be assured, what help I can give to it here shall be as readily and as carefully imploy'd, as if you and I alone were to reap all the profit of it. . . .

2384. Locke to Sir John Somers, Baron Somers, [Oates], 28 January 1698

Sunday in the evening after waiting on the King[1] I was to wait upon your Lordship, it being as I understood him his Majesties pleasure that I should doe soe before I returnd hither. my misfortune in missing your Lordship then I hoped to repaire by an early diligence[2] the next morning. But the night that came between destroid that purpose and me almost with it. For when I was laid in my bed my breath faild me. I was fain to sit up right in my bed where I continued in this posture a good part of the night with hopes that my

---

[3] A children's game; hence trivial or childish pursuits. (The word later occurs in Jeremy Bentham's well-known remark that 'push-pin is of equal value with poetry'.)

[4] The bill to encourage the Irish linen industry lapsed in December.

[1] At Kensington.   [2] Stagecoach.

shortnesse of breath would abate and my lungs grow soe good naturd, as to let me lie down to get a little sleep wherof I had great need. But my breath constantly faileing me as often as I laid upon my pillow at three I got up and soe sat by the fire till morning. My [case] being brought to this extremitie There was noe roome for any other thought but to get out of town immediately. For after the two precedent nights without any rest I concluded the agonies I labourd under soe long in the second of them would hardly faile to be sure death the third If I staid in town. As bad weather therefor as it was I was forced early on Monday morning to seeke for a passage and by good luck found an empty Cambridg coach just seting out which brought me hither.

His Majestie was soe favourable as to propose the imployment your Lordship mentiond.[3] But the true knowledg of my owne weake state of health made me beg his Majestie to bethinke of some fitter person and one more able to serve him in that important post, to which I added my want of experience for such a businesse. That your Lordship may not thinke this an expression barely of modestie I crave leave to explaine it to your Lordship and though there in I discover my weakenesse. My temper, always shie of a crowd and strangers, has made my acquaintance few and my conversation too narrow and particular to get the skill of dealeing with men in their various humours and drawing out their secrets.[4] Whether this was a fault or noe in a man that designed noe bustle in the world I know not this I am sure it will let your Lordship see that I am too much a novice in the world for the imployment proposed

Though we are soe odly placed here that we have noe ordinary conveyance for our letters from Monday till Friday yet this delay has not fallen out much amisse. The King was graciously pleased to order me to goe into the Country to take care of my health. These 4 or 5 days here have given me a proof to what a low state my lungs are now brought and how little they can beare the least shock. I can lie down again indeed in my bed and take my rest, but bateing[5] that I finde the impression of these two days in London soe heavie upon me still, that the least motion puts me out of breath and I am under a constant uneasienesse even when I sit still. which extends farther than the painfulnesse of breathing and makes me listlesse to every thing soe that methinks the writeing this letter has been a great performance.

My Lord I should not trouble you with an account of the prevailing decays of an old pair of lungs were it not my duty to take care his Majestie should [not] be disappointed and therefor that he lay any expectation on that which to my great misfortune every way I finde would certainly faile him, and I must beg your Lordship for the interest of the publick to prevaile with his Majestie

---

[3] What post the king offered is unknown.

[4] The draft letter has many alterations. Here, for instance, Locke deleted: 'But for man that animal *incertum varium multiplex* [uncertain, inconstant, and complex] as Tully [Cicero] calls him I have as much avoided as I could, reduceing my conversation to a few of the best . . . when I am in town I doe not goe once in three months to a Coffee house and never seek company'.

[5] Excepting.

to thinke on somebody else, since I doe not only fear but am sure my broken health will never permit me to accept the great honour his Majestie meant me.

2395. Locke to Philippus van Limborch, Oates, 21 February 1698

. . . The[1] question is How the Unitie of god can be proved? Or in other words How it can be proved that there is but one god? To resolve this question it is necessary before we come to the proofs of the unitie of god to know what it is is meant by the name God

The usual and as I thinke true Notion those who acknowledg a Deitie have of him is this. That he is an infinite eternal incorporeal being perfectly perfect From which Idea of god it seems very easie to me to make out his unitie. For a most perfect or perfectly perfect being can be but one Because a perfectly perfect being cannot want any of those attributes perfections or degrees of perfection which it is better to have than to be without for then he would want soe much of being perfectly perfect As for example to have power is greater perfection than to have none; to have more power is a greater perfection than to have lesse and to have all power (which is to be omnipotent) is a greater perfection, than not to have all power But two omnipotents are inconsistent. Because it must be suppos'd that it is necessary for one to will what the other wills; and then he of the two whose will is necessarily determind by the will of the other, is not free: and soe wants that perfection; it being better to be free than under the determination of an others will. If they are not both under the necessity of willing always the same thing, then one may will the doeing of that, which the other may will should not be done, and then the will of the one must prevail over the will of the other, and then he of the two, whose power is not able to second his will, is not omnipotent. for he cannot doe soe much as the other, and then one of them is not omnipotent and soe there are not nor can be two omnipotents and consequently not two gods. By the same steps of perfection we come to know that god is omniscient But in an estate on a supposition that where there are distinct beings with distinct powers and distinct wills, it is an imperfection not to be able to conceale his thoughts. But if either of these can conceale his thoughts from the other, that other is not omniscient, for he not only comes short of knowing all that is knowable, but comes short of knowing what an other knows.

The same may be said of Gods omnipresence it is better to be every where in the infinite extent of space than to be shut out from any part of it. for if he be shut out from any place he can neither operate there nor know what is doeing there and soe is neither omnipotent nor omniscient.

---

[1] Locke's English draft; a French version was sent to Limborch.

If to avoid the foresaid arguments it be said that these two (or two hundred thousand) gods (for by the same reason there can be two there may be two millions for there can be noe reason to limit their number) have all perfectly exactly the same power, the same knowledg, the same will, and exist equaly in the same individual place, this is only to multiply sounds, but in reality to reduce the supposd plurality only to one. for to suppose two intelligent beings, that perpetualy know will and act the same thing, and have not a seperate existence, is in words to suppose a plurality, but in realty to make but one. For to be inseperably united in understanding will action and place is to be as much united as any intelligent being can be united to its self, and to suppose that where there is such an union there can be two beings is to suppose a division without a division and a thing divided from its self

Let[2] us consider his omnipresence a little farther god is infinitely omnipresent, which he must be unlesse he be shut up in some little corner of space we know not why, nor how nor by whome nor where (I say little corner for any parcel of space compared to infinite space is very little). Now if god be infinitely omnipresent it seems to me to come near a demonstration that there can be but one. Wherever god is (let his nature or being or substance be what it will) there certainly is some real, nay the most real of all beings. Let us therefor suppose this reall being in any one physicall point of space, I thinke it is demonstration that an other reall being of the same kinde cannot be in the same individual point of space, for then they would be but one. For where there is noe difference in kinde nor distance in place that can be but one being. Nor let this way of argueing be thought to reach body alone and the parts of matter: It will be found to hold in that which is the remotest from it, I meane pure space. For two physical points of space can noe more be brought into one, than two physical attoms of matter can be brought into one. For if they could, then all space might be brought into one physical point, which is as impossible as that all matter should be brought into one attome.

I who know not what the substance of matter is, doe much lesse know what the substance of god is. But some thing I know it is, and must exclude where it is all other substances (could there be any such) of the same kind. if therefor god be immense and omnipresent it is to me evident beyond doubt that there is and can be but one god. . . .

2398. Locke to Edward Clarke, Oates, 25 February 1698

. . . My time is all divided between my bed and the chimney-corner, for not being able to walk for want of breath upon the least stirring, I am a prisoner

---

[2] L2413 includes a (French) revised version of this letter, with the material from here onward omitted, at Limborch's suggestion.

not only to the house, but almost to my chair, so that never did anybody so truly lead a sedentary life as I do. . . .

I writ some time since to Mr. Popple to give you a copy of my project about the better relief and employment of the poor[1] since our Board thought not fit to make use of it, that now the House was upon that consideration you might make use of it, [if] it should suggest to you anything that you might think useful in the case. It is a matter that requires every Englishman's best thoughts; for there is not any one thing that I know upon the right regulation whereof the prosperity of his country more depends. And whilst I have any breath left I shall always be an Englishman.

2413. Locke to Philippus van Limborch, Oates, 4 April 1698

. . . Since Mr. H[1] is so thoroughly devoted to the Cartesian philosophy Mr. Le Clerc and you were certainly right in warning me. If the Cartesians are to be understood concerning Spirit, that it is Thought [*Cogitatio*] and not a thinking substance, they certainly assert God in words [and] annul Him in deed. For Thought is an action that does not exist of itself but is an action of some substance. But this dispute is not between you and me, and will certainly not be between Mr. H and me; therefore, as you have advised, I have now omitted that argument from omnipresence[2] which I believe is the only *a priori* argument by which the unity of the Godhead can be demonstrated. I do not wonder therefore that one so thoroughly imbued with those principles is seeking what he will always seek in vain, an argument that so ill-founded a philosophy never will or can provide. You have therefore done very well in not allowing me to become involved in Cartesian disputations and subtleties.

As to your other warning, that about the term 'incorporeal': I have not altered it: first, because there is no need for me to suspect that I have to do with a Cartesian; secondly, because, if I recognized that Mr. H is a Cartesian, the term 'incorporeal' or 'immaterial' would not on that account have to be omitted from the definition of God since whoever wants to think rightly about God ought to remove all matter or corporeity from Him. 'Thought' certainly does not do this, whatever the men devoted to Descartes's opinions suppose to the contrary. But enough of this; I do not want to detain you with philosophical speculations when you are better employed. . . .

---

[1] *An Essay on the Poor Law* (1697); Locke's scheme was rejected by the Board of Trade and not pursued in parliament (L2084; *Political Essays*, 182–98).

[1] Johannes Hudde, burgomaster (chief magistrate) of Amsterdam, who raised the question of the uniqueness of God with Limborch and Le Clerc.

[2] L2395, n. 2.

2414. Locke to William Molyneux, Oates, 6 April 1698

... The thing I above all things long for is to see, and embrace, and have some discourse with you before I go out of this world. I meet with so few capable of truth, or worthy of a free conversation, such as becomes lovers of truth, that you cannot think it strange if I wish for some time with you for the exposing, sifting, and rectifying of my thoughts. If they have gone any thing farther in the discovery of truth than what I have already published, it must be by your encouragement that I must go on to finish some things that I have already begun, and with you I hop'd to discourse my other yet crude and imperfect thoughts, in which if there were anything useful to mankind, if they were open'd and deposited with you, I know them safe lodg'd for the advantage of truth some time or other. For I am in doubt whether it be fit for me to trouble the press with any new matter;[1] or if I did, I look on my life as so near worn out, that it would be folly to hope to finish any thing of moment in the small remainder of it. I hoped therefore, as I said, to have seen you, and unravel'd to you that which lying in the lump unexplicated in my mind, I scarce yet know what it is my self; for I have often had experience, that a man cannot well judge of his own notions, till either by setting them down in paper, or in discoursing them to a friend, he has drawn them out, and as it were spread them fairly before himself. ...

Amongst other things I would be glad to talk with you about before I die, is that which you suggest at the bottom of the first page of your letter.[2] I am mightily concern'd for the place[3] meant in the question you say you will ask the author of the treatise you mention, and wish extremely well to it; and would be very glad to be inform'd by you what would be best for it, and debate with you the ways to compose it. But this cannot be done by letters, the subject is of too great extent, the views too large, and the particulars too many to be so manag'd. Come therefore your self, and come as well prepar'd in that matter as you can. But if you talk with others on that point there, mention not me to any body on that subject; only let you and I try what good we can do for those whom we wish well to. Great things have sometimes been brought about from small beginnings well laid together. ...

---

[1] Locke had completed his long second *Reply* to Stillingfleet, and he also had the manuscript of *The Conduct of the Understanding* on hand. He did not publish any further books in his lifetime.

[2] In L2407 (15 Mar.) Molyneux wrote: the English parliament 'bear very hard upon us in Ireland; How justly they can bind us without our *Consent* and *Representatives*, I leave to the *Author* of the *Two Treatises of Government* to Consider'. Molyneux pursued the theme in print in his *Case of Ireland*, where he cites the 'incomparable' *Two Treatises*, 'said to be written by my excellent friend, John Locke'.

[3] Passage. If Molyneux and Locke had a particular passage of the *Two Treatises* in mind, it is perhaps § 140, which Molyneux paraphrased in the *Case*.

2422. William Molyneux to Locke, Dublin, 19 April 1698

... My Dear Friend, Must therefore know, that the Consideration of what I mentiond in my last from the Incomparable Author of the Treatise etc.[1] has moved me to put pen to paper, and Commit some thoughts of mine on that Subject to the Pres in a small octavo Intitled *The Case of Irelands being Bound by Acts of Parliament in England Stated.* This you'll say is a Nice subject, but I think I have treated it with that Caution and Submission, that It cannot justly give any offence;[2] insomuch that I scruple not to put my Name to it, and, by Advice of some good Friends here, have presumed to dedicate it to his Majesty. I have Orderd some of them to Mr. Churchil to be presented to you, and some of your Friends, and they are now upon the Road towards you. I have been very free in giving you my Thoughts on your Peices, I should be extreamly obleidged to you for the like freedom on your side upon mine.[3] I cannot pretend this to be an Accomplisd Performance, it was done in hast, and intended to overtake the Proceedings at Westminster,[4] but it comes too late for that, What effect it may possibly have in time to come, God and the Wise Council of England only knows, but were it again under my Hands I could considerably amend, and add to it. But till I either see how the Parliament at Westminster is pleasd to take it, or till I see them Risen, I do not think it adviseable for me to go on tother side the Water. Tho I am not apprehensive of any Mischeif from them, Yet God only knows what Resentments Captious Men may take on such Occasions.[5] ...

2440. Locke to [Sir George Treby], Oates, 17 May 1698

The obligations I receive from your Lordship always prevent[1] my requests: And your favours to me have this peculiar increase of value that they cost me not soe much as the asking. I had a designe when you passed through our neighbourhood the last Assizes[2] not only to have kept up the priviledg you allow me of stoping you on the high way; But also to have made a petition to you

---

[1] Locke's *Two Treatises*. L2414, n. 2.

[2] It gave a great deal of offence in England, and embarrassed the Irish government too.

[3] There are no recorded comments by Locke on Molyneux's *Case of Ireland*, but English Whig authors declared Molyneux to have misapplied Locke's arguments.

[4] Molyneux wished to avert tough English legislation to force the Irish to abandon wool exports in favour of a linen industry.

[5] In June the English parliament condemned the book as being 'of dangerous consequence to the crown and people of England' by denying the dependence of Ireland on 'the imperial crown of this realm'.

[1] Anticipate, precede.　　[2] At Chelmsford, Essex, in March.

on the behalf of my Cosin King³ a student of the Middle Temple. But my health that confined me then within dores, robd me of that oportunity, as well as hinderd me from the honour of waiting on you when I was last in town. The time now appro[ac]hing for a call to the Bar I intended to be a sollicitor to you for a favou[ra]ble recommendation of him to the Benchers: But I find My Lord I am again prevented. My Cosin sends me word of the great favours he has al[re]dy received from you on this occasion beyond what he could expect or des[erve.] Though the testimonys he has given of himself make me hope you will [not] have cause to repent this extraordinary marke of honour to him or think it w[as m]isplaced on a worthlesse subject: Yet my Lord give me leave to put [in for] a share in the obligation; and to enjoy the pleasure of acknowl[edging] this new favour, which the nearest Kinsman I have in the world re[ceiving] the benefit of, I cannot but think my self to have a title to thank you for. The multiplying of bonds to those to whose worth one is tied by esteem and inclination is I think a pardonable ambition. . . .

2443. Locke to Philippus Van Limborch, Oates, 21 May 1698

. . . Had I by the question [that] was first proposd to me perceived as I doe now what this gentle man¹ of deep thought aimes at I should not have sent the answer that I did. But one much shorter because more in the order of nature and reason where in every thing stands in its best light.

I thinke it is unquestionably evident to any one who will but reflect on himself that there hath been from eternity an intelligent being I imagin it is as evident to any thinkeing man that there is also an infinite being. Now I say there can be but one infinite being, and that infinite being must also be the eternall being because what is infinite must have been soe from eternity for noe additions made in time can make any thing to be infinite which is not soe in and from it self from all eternity it being the nature of infinite that noe thing can be taken from it noe thing added to it, soe that it can neither be seperated into or made up of more than one. This I take to be a proof a priori that the eternall independent being is but one to which if we adde the Idea of all possible perfection we have then the Idea of god Eternall infinite omnisficient² and omnipresent.

If this any way agrees with the Judicious gent's notions I shall be extremly satisfied, if not I shall take it for a very great favour if he please to communicate to me his proof which I shall either keep secret to my self or communicate as received from him as he shall please to appoint.

---

³ Peter King, Locke's cousin, called to the bar on Treby's recommendation.

¹ Johannes Hudde, burgomaster (chief magistrate) of Amsterdam. L2413.

² Apparently an accidental conflation of 'omniscient' and 'omnific' (all-creating).

2451. John Tatam to Locke, Sutton-on-the-Hill, Derbyshire, 3 June 1698

Your known abilities to advice, as well as opportunities and Interest to promote and procure redress of publick Grieveances, and that noble and generous spirit which shines in all those your writings that I have had the Advantage and happiness to peruse, and hath engaged you (if am not very much misinformed) to do very extraordinary Kindnesses for some of your Antagonists,[1] encourage me, an utter stranger to your person, so far to presume upon your Candour and Generosity as to entreat you to use your best Interest for an Act of Parliament to prevent those frequent vexatious Lawsuits as well as private Quarrels about the manner of setting out the tenth or tith[2] of hay and corn; for notwithstanding the statutes of the 27. of Hen: 8. and the 32d of Hen: 8. and the 2. of Ed. 6.[3] do oblige all persons to set out their tiths after such way and manner as hath been usual and Customary in the Parishes and Places where the tiths arise, yet it is so difficult to prove what is the Custom of a Place (most antient records of such customs having been lost in the unhappy Civil wars) that those Statutes tho plain and full enough to an honest mind, are far otherwise to Lawyers and troublesome persons: Who tho it hath been the usual Custom of a Parish for the tith of hay to have been set out time beyond memory when it is fully made and cured (and the oldest persons living not able to give above 10 or 20 instances and it may be only of the tith of 2 or 3 acres that hath been set out in grass so soon as cut and made into handcocks)[4] yet some Lawyers will have those few peevish instances to destroy the Custom, whilst others are of another opinion; and there are not wanting too many troublesom persons (having indeed an aversion from paying any tiths at all and loving according to the proverb, to pinch on the Parsons side) who take advantage from these different Judgements and the uncertain Determination of the Law, and set out the tith, which ought to be of hay, in grass so soon as cut and made into small cocks, and when they have so set out the tith, do spread about their own nine parts after such a manner that the owner of the tith's cannot possibly so much as come to and much less spread about and cure his said tyth grass (for tis no other, tho I meet with no law but what is for tith hay which is grass made and cured) till the owner of the nine parts hath fully made and cured them, by which peevish doings the tith is made little worth nay frequently so spoiled that it is not worth carrying away, which yet it must be, least the owner of the ground bring his Action for the injurie it does his Aftergrass. Thus also tho it hath been the usual custom of a Parish to set out the tith of corn in shocks,[5] yet some cross people will throw out the said tith of corn in sheaves unbound to the great trouble of the owner of the said tith and no

---

[1] Presumably protagonists is meant. [2] Tithe (and so on below).
[3] 1535, 1540, 1548. [4] Small piles of hay. [5] Propped-up groups of sheaves.

less prejudice to the tith it self; That it is difficult to prove what is the customary way of tithing in any Parish is plain because the records of those customs are generally lost, and I conceive it is utterly unfit that those who pay tiths should be witnesses about the manner of paying them because they are parties; and I am well informed that an Impropriator[6] in a late tryal about the Custom of setting out the tith of corn brought several witnesses, some of them 60 or 70 or more years old, who swore it had been the Custom of that place ever since they could remember to set out the tith of corn in shocks, and on the other hand the person who disputed the Custom with the Impropriator produced as many or more witnesses who swore quite contrary viz: that it was the Custom ever since they could remember till about 6 or 7 years ago for the tith of corn to be thrown out into the furrows in sheaves unbound; Now that there were persons perjured in this cause is manifest, and whether it is ended yet or ever will be I cannot say: I could give several other instances of the like Nature, but these I beleive will satisfie you that it is highly requisite for the way and manner of setting out the tith of hay and corn to be positively ascertained by a plain Act of Parliament which I humbly and earnestly entreat you to procure and perhaps a short act to the following purpose might do the business viz: 'That all persons whatever shall so order and manage, make and cure the tenth part of their Corn and hay for the respective Impropriators, Rectors, Vicars, Curates or any other persons to whom the said tiths do belong, as they do order and manage, make and cure their own nine parts.[7] . . .

2481. Dr John Covel to Locke, Christ's College, Cambridge, 2 August 1698

You[1] might indeed be very justly offended at me when you saw my name to the *Imprimatur* of Mr Edwards his late book; and I must confesse that I am as much asham'd of it my self. But when I have inform'd You of the whole matter of fact, I hope you will rather pity my Misfortune, than count me guilty of the least disrespect to you. Mr Edwards is of my own year in the University, and I have known him a long time, though not so well as I know him now. He meeting me one day in the publick street, told me that he was going to the presse with a little book, which he had shew'd to the Vicechancellor[2] and the Professor,[3] and that they had licenc't it to be printed;

---

[6] A lay owner of ecclesiastical revenues.

[7] Tatam adds further clauses for policing tithe corn and hay obligations.

[1] An answer to L2319, written on 2 Aug. 1698, but backdated to 4 Oct. 1697. Covel's original draft answer was now revised to Locke's satisfaction.

[2] Henry James, President of Queens' College.   [3] John Beaumont, regius professor of divinity.

and he ask't me to give him leave to adde my name also. I told him, if they had read and approved of his book, he might, if he pleased, make use of my name and so we parted. Now I do solemnly assure you that I never saw the book till long after it was printed, neither did I know the least syllable of its contents, or that you were in any manner concern'd, much lesse that you were so ill treated in it. I appeal to Mr Lock himself and every body else with whome I have been so long acquainted, whether they ever found in my Nature or Behaviour any rude or uncivil conversation, or that I ever approved of it in others; for I declare to all the world, that in all discourses (whether they be by word or pen) I do think good Manners as absolutely necessary as good Reasoning. And therefore I hope you will believe, that if I had been in the least conscious of your unhandsome usage in that Piece, I would not have so much injur'd my self or you, or so farre violated the common bonds of Freindship betwixt us, as to have approved of it. This I must humbly offer as my Vindication to the world, and as my just Excuse to your self.

2495. Ezekiel Burridge to Locke, Dublin, 13 October 1698

I am oblig'd to give you the trouble (as I may well call it) of a letter; 'tis what was given me in charge by a dying friend. Last night your good friend Mr Molyneux was bury'd. his death was very suddain and surprizeing. On Saturday he was very brisk in the house of commons till near 3 of the clock: between 5 and 6 he sent for me to sit with him, he was then very well, whilest I was with him he complaind of his old pain, (which he told me he gave you an account of in England) the next day he vomited a great quantity of bloud, and a great quantity afterwards came from him downwards. by Sunday night he was brought so low, that he himself and all his friends about him thought he wou'd not live out that night; however he continu'd alive (but with the flame so faint and weak that it cou'd only be just call'd life) till 3 of the clock on tuesday morning. Since his death, according to his own desire, he has been open'd; in each of his kidneys there were two stones found, the largest, in his left kidney was bigger than a large nutmeg, the other 3 were much of a size: in each of the kidneys there was one of the stones seated within the flesh of the kidney. The vessell which, by his streining to vomit, 'tis suppos'd, broke in his stomach, and immediatly occasion'd his death, they cou'd not discover.

At the time that his bloud ran lowest, when with pain and difficulty, he gave his last advice to his son, he remember'd you; And desir'd me as soon as he was dead to write you an account of his death, and bid me tell you *that as he liv'd, so he dy'd with a very great honour, and esteem for you.* These were his words; and this complaysance[1] in a dying man did not seem strange to

---

[1] Obligingness, civility.

me, who was so well acquainted with him, who knew the excellent spirit of the man; the great regard he had to vertue and learning, and the singular value he set on you: This every one knew who knew him.

I had the happiness of being very intimatly acquainted with him, and do fear I shall not again on this side my grave have the happiness of being intimate with such another friend. he was a great lover of justice, of vertue, of learning, and of mankind. . . .

2498. Locke to Philippus Van Limborch, London, 4 and 18 October 1698

. . . I[1] do not at all understand the Cartesians' way of talking that I find in your letter. For what infinite thought means completely escapes me. For I can by no means persuade myself that thought exists of itself, but only that a thinking thing or substance does so, and it is of that that it can be affirmed that it is either finite or infinite. Those who are wont to speak otherwise seem to me to comprise in so uncertain an expression something, I know not what, that is obscure or fraudulent, and to wrap everything in darkness or at least not to venture to express clearly and distinctly what they think, favouring too much a hypothesis that is not entirely sound. But more of this perhaps at some other time when there is greater leisure. . . .

I declare war on no one on account of difference of opinions, myself an ignorant and fallible manikin.[2] I am an Evangelical Christian, not a Papist. . . .

Learn in a few words what I mean when I say that I am an Evangelical or, if you prefer, an Orthodox Christian, not a Papist. Among those who profess the name of Christians I recognize only two classes, Evangelicals and Papists: the latter those who, as if infallible, arrogate to themselves dominion over the consciences of others; the former those who, seeking truth alone, desire themselves and others to be convinced of it only by proofs and reasons; they are gentle to the errors of others, being not unmindful of their own weakness; forgiving human frailty and ignorance, and seeking forgiveness in turn. . . .

2500. Locke to Dr Thomas Molyneux, Oates, 27 October 1698

Death has with a violent hand hastily snatch'd from you a dear brother. I doubt not but on this occasion you need all the consolation can be given to one

---

[1] Continues the discussion in L2413.   [2] Dwarf, small person.

unexpectedly bereft of so worthy and near a relation. Whatever inclination I may have to alleviate your sorrow, I bear too great a share in the loss, and am too sensibly touch'd with it my self to be in a condition to discourse you on this subject, or do any thing but mingle my tears with yours. I have lost in your brother, not only an ingenious and learned acquaintance, that all the world esteem'd; but an intimate and sincere friend, whom I truly lov'd, and by whom I was truly loved; and what a loss that is, those only can be sensible who know how valuable and how scarce a true friend is, and how far to be prefer'd to all other sorts of treasure. He has left a son[1] who I know was dear to him, and deserv'd to be so as much as was possible for one of his age. I cannot think my self wholly incapacitated from paying some of the affection and service was due from me to my dear friend as long as he has a child or a brother in the world. If therefore there be any thing at this distance wherein I in my little sphere may be able to serve your nephew or you, I beg you by the memory of our deceased friend to let me know it, . . .

---

[1] Samuel Molyneux, aged 9, later an astronomer and politician.

14

Manners and Americans, 1699–1701

The 1690s witnessed a 'moral revolution'. The demand of the Restoration church for compulsory Anglican worship gave way to the demand of the Revolution church for compulsory moral discipline. It was exacted by the Societies for the Reformation of Manners, which secured prosecutions for drunkenness, fornication, and sabbath-breaking. Locke identified himself with this movement for the 'reformation of manners' in his *Third Letter for Toleration* (1692) and now does so again (L2846, L2932).

Locke became increasingly interested in scriptural hermeneutics and the major project of his last years was his *Paraphrase and Notes on the Epistles of St Paul*. His letters include minute examinations of biblical passages, together with attempts to articulate an adequate methodology for interpreting scripture. This bore fruit in his 'Essay for the Understanding of St Paul's Epistles', prefaced to the *Paraphrase* (L2590).

After publication of the fourth edition in 1700, discussion of the *Essay* occurs less frequently in the correspondence. Nevertheless, he was grateful to Samuel Bold for his continued support, and presents Bold with a disquisition on the unbiased pursuit of truth, and ridiculing 'servile submission' to dead patriarchs and to current intellectual fashions (L2590). In Amsterdam, Limborch continues to worry away at the problem of free will, especially since it was central to the theological dispute dividing his own Arminian party from the Calvinist predestinarians. Locke explains his understanding of free will, and reflects on Calvinist intolerance, while praising Limborch's biography of the early Arminian leader, Episcopius (L2925, L2935).

As a member of the Board of Trade Locke handled a large amount of North American business. One signal intervention was his assistance in removing Governor Andros of Virginia, formerly James II's governor of New England, who was in dispute with James Blair, president of the College of William and Mary. Blair reports gratefully on the benefits of Andros's sacking, and asks for further leverage to quell Andros's continuing vengeful influence (L2545). The governor of New York, the Earl of Bellomont, vents his frustration at the lack of support from Whitehall and at the corrupt administration he has inherited. He needs warships to combat piracy (he had just seized Captain Kidd), money to pay his troops, and competent lawyers (L2614). William Popple reports on the government's attempt to pacify the native Americans (L2714).

Although Locke resigned from the Board in 1700, he continued to show a keen interest in parliamentary politics. The war against France had been suspended in 1697 and the Whigs pressed for an urgent resumption of hostilities. Furly warns Locke of Europe's crisis, and in the newspapers Locke reads of the forces being massed by Louis XIV across the Channel (L2832). Locke was appalled that parliament reacted feebly to the threat of invasion. He advises his cousin Peter King, newly elected to parliament, how to act, and rebukes him for according greater importance to getting legal fees than to his presence in the House of Commons (L2855, L2874). By now, King was acting as Locke's financial manager, receiving instructions regarding investments (L2643, L2849). Locke's *Two Treatises* has often been characterized as a philosophical defence of capitalism. Be that as it may, Locke is the first of the canonical political philosophers to trade in a capitalist stock market, for that market was just emerging.

Among Locke's new correspondents was Jean-Baptiste du Bos, who was later attacked by Montesquieu for his advocacy of French absolutism. His relationship with Locke, however, was confined to exchanges of news from the 'republic of letters' (L2673, L2748). Du Bos refers to the bitter quarrel among Catholics over the 'Chinese rites'. The Jesuits in China were willing to blend Catholic with local rituals, but their enemies thought that this was a betrayal of Christianity's unique claims.

Retaining his interest in scientific matters, Locke submits a proposal to the Royal Society for calendrical reform. The Gregorian calendar had begun to be introduced in continental Europe in 1582 but the Julian calendar remained in use in England. Before 1700 England was ten days behind the Continent, after 1700 eleven days. Not until 1752 was England's calendar brought into line, by omitting eleven days. Locke's more gradual solution was to omit leap years for the next forty-four years (L2640).

Now that the children of Locke's friends were approaching adulthood he was called upon to provide career advice. The youngest of all his correspondents was Damaris Masham's thirteen-year-old son Francis, destined for the law, who recounts a visit to an assize court (L2613). Benjamin Furly debates the problem of placing his bookish fifteen-year-old, which leads to a sally against the worthless wrangling of the learned professions and the oppressive gibberish of churchmen, and in turn to an account of a pious minister who raped young girls (L2754). Locke advises that Arent's bookishness should be encouraged by his being placed with a leading Rotterdam publisher (L2932). From young men—and their parents—anxious for advancement in the church, the law, or the civil service, Locke received many supplications to use his influence. Anne Grigg begs a decent country vicarage for her son (L2692). Among others who sought guidance is a trainee Presbyterian minister who has doubts about the divinity of Christ (L2775).

2545. James Blair to Locke, Virginia, 8 February 1699

The tranquillity we begin to enjoy in this Countrey by the happy change of our Governour,[1] and Government is so great that I who have the happines to know by whose means these blessings were procured have all the reason in the world to take all occasions of expressing my gratitude for them, and to pray to God to reward those noble publick souls[2] that bestow so many of their thoughts, in contriving the relief of the oppressed, and the happines of mankind. Dear Sir think not that I speak this from any other principle or design I have, but only from a sense how much this whole Countrey in generall and my self in particular are beholding to yow for the thoughts you was pleased to bestow on our late unhappy circumstances, and the methods you contrived to relieve us.[3] You are to look for your reward from a better hand. only give me leave to say that I think no sort of good works are preferable to these, that have such an universall good influence on whole Countreys to make all the people happy. This Countrey is so barren of action that it affords nothing to satisfy your curiosity. Our new Governour Coll. Nicholson is very heartily welcomed to this place. Sir Edmund Andros is gone home mighty angry not only for the loss of such a good Government but for being succeeded by such a person, whom of all others he had the least kindnes for. I doubt not if he or his great friend at your board[4] can get him to be put into any post wherein he can reach this Countrey we shall feel the effects of his resentment and revenge to the utmost of his pouer: of which he has given us some proof at parting. For there being a vacancy in the Councill[5] by the death of Coll. Christopher Wormley[6] (after they had the news here that Coll. Nicholson had the Government) he filled this place with one Mr Dudley Diggs, a factor[7] of Mr Jeoffrey Jeoffreys,[8] a man that had no sort of merit to recommend him to that honour, but that he had signalized himself by his publick enmity to our Colledge[9] to that degree that being Executor to one Coll. Cole his father in law who left 50 pound to our College, he could never be prevailed with to pay the money but suffered himself to be sued for it, and by severall tricks of law (which was no hard matter to do in the late government) has hitherto shifted off the payment. In the prosecution of that suit there was one remarkable saying of his which recommended him much

---

[1] Sir Edmund Andros, governor of Virginia, 1692–8, was replaced by Francis Nicholson.

[2] The Board of Trade.

[3] Locke's memorandum on the grievances of Virginia is printed in *Western Political Quarterly*, xxii (1969), 742–58.

[4] William Blathwayt, MP, secretary-at-war, member of the Board of Trade.   [5] Of Virginia.

[6] Wormeley had command of the lower Potomac River against 'the Indian enemy'.

[7] Agent.   [8] Jeffrey Jeffreys, MP, London merchant.

[9] William and Mary College, of which Blair was president, founded in 1693, in the town that took the name of Williamsburg in 1699.

to Sir Edmund Andros's favour. I desire a Reference, says he, that I may have time to prepare my defence, otherwise not only I but the whole Countrey may be *cheated* of their money. This was so gross an aspersion thrown on a Society of the honestest men in the Countrey, and in so publick an Audience that it is thought nothing could have endeared him more to Sir Edmund. For our Colleges sake I would beg that such a man as this may be kept out of the Councill, as he is at present out of it, not having been nominated in the Governours Instructions.[10] We are now upon severall good designs, which as they come to be formed I will not fail to give you an account of. . . .

2590. Locke to Samuel Bold, Oates, 16 May 1699

. . . I promise myself, that to all those who are willing to open their Eyes, and enlarge their Minds to a true Knowledge of Things, this little Treatise of yours will be greatly acceptable and useful.[1] And for those, that will shut their Eyes for fear they should see farther than others have seen before them, or rather for fear they should use them, and not blindly and lazily follow the Sayings of others, what can be done to them? They are be let alone to join in the Cry of the Herd they have placed themselves in, and to take that for Applause, which is nothing but the Noise that of Course they make to one another, which Way ever they are going; so that the Greatness of it is no manner of Proof that they are in the right. I say not this, because it is a Discourse wherein you favour any Opinions of mine (for I take Care not to be deceived by the Reasonings of my Friends) but say it from those, who are Strangers to you, and who own themselves to have received Light and Conviction from the Clearness and Closeness of your Reasonings, and that in a Matter at first Sight very abstruse, and remote from ordinary Conceptions.

There is nothing that would more rejoice me, than to have you for my Neighbour. The Advantage that you promise yourself from mine, I should receive from your Conversation. The impartial Lovers and Seekers of Truth are a great deal fewer than one could wish or imagine. It is a rare Thing to find any one to whom one may communicate one's Thoughts freely, and from whom one may expect a careful Examination and impartial Judgment of them. To be learned in the Lump by other Men's Thoughts, and to be in the right by saying after others, is the much easier and quieter Way: But how a rational Man, that should enquire and know for himself, can content himself with a Faith or Religion taken upon Trust, or with such a servile Submission of his Understanding, as to admit all, and nothing else but what Fashion makes passable among Men, is to me astonishing. I do not wonder you should have, in

---

[10] Digges's appointment to the Council was confirmed.

[1] Bold, *Some Considerations on the Principal Objections against Mr. Lock's Essay* (1699).

many Points, different Apprehensions from what you meet with in Authors; with a free Mind, that unbiassedly pursues Truth, it cannot be otherwise. First, All Authors did not write unbiassedly for Truth Sake. Secondly, There are scarce any two Men, that have perfectly the same Views of the same Thing, till they come with Attention, and perhaps mutual Assistance to examine it. A Consideration that makes Conversation with the Living, a Thing much more desirable and useful, than consulting the Dead; would the Living but be inquisitive after Truth, apply their Thoughts with Attention to the gaining of it, and be indifferent where it was found, so they could but find it.

The first Requisite to the profiting by Books, is not to judge of Opinions by the Authority of the Writers. None have the Right of dictating but God himself, and that because he is Truth itself. All others have a Right to be followed as far as I, *i.e.* as far as the Evidence of what they say convinces; and of that my own Understanding alone must be Judge for me, and nothing else. If we made our own Eyes our Guides, and admitted or rejected Opinions only by the Evidence of Reason, we should neither embrace or refuse any Tenet, because we find it published by another, of what Name or Character soever he was.

You say you lose many Things because they slip from you: I have had Experience of that myself, but for that my Lord Bacon[2] has provided a sure Remedy. For as I remember, he advises somewhere, never to go without Pen and Ink, or something to write with; and to be sure not to neglect to write down all Thoughts of Moment that come into the Mind. I must own I have omitted it often, and have often repented it. The Thoughts that come unsought, and as it were dropt into the Mind, are commonly the most valuable of any we have, and therefore should be secured, because they seldom return again. You say also, that you lose many Things, because your Thoughts are not steady, and strong enough to pursue them to a just Issue. Give me Leave to think, that herein you mistake yourself and your own Abilities. Write down your Thoughts upon any Subject as far as you have at any Time pursued them, and then go on again some other Time when you find your Mind disposed to it, and so till you have carried them as far as you can, and you will be convinced, that, if you have lost any, it has not been for want of Strength of Mind to bring them to an Issue; but for want of Memory to retain a long Train of Reasonings, which the Mind having once beat out, is loth to be at the Pains to go over again; and so your Connection and Train having slip'd the Memory, the Pursuit stops, and the Reasoning is neglected before it comes to the last Conclusion. If you have not tryed it, you cannot imagine the Difference there is in studying with and without a Pen in your Hand. Your Ideas, if the Connections of them that you have traced be set down, so that without the Pains of recollecting them in your Memory you can take an easy View of them again, will lead you farther than you can expect. Try, and tell me if it is not

---

[2] Francis Bacon, the lawyer, essayist, and philosopher. Source unidentified.

so. I say not this that I should not be glad to have any Conversation upon whatever Points you shall imploy your Thoughts about. Propose what you have of this kind freely, and do not suspect that it will interfere with my Affairs. . . .

What you say about Critics and Critical Interpretations, particularly of the Scriptures, is not only in my Opinion true, but of great use to be observed in reading learned Commentators, who not seldom make it their Business to shew in what Sense a Word has been used by other Authors; whereas the proper Business of a Commentator, is to shew in what Sense it was used by the Author in that Place, which in the Scripture we have Reason to conclude was most commonly in the ordinary vulgar Sense of the Word or Phrase known in that Time, because the Books were written, as you rightly observe, and adapted to the People. If Criticks had observed this, we should have in their Writings less Ostentation and more Truth, and a great deal of Darkness now spread on the Scriptures had been avoided. I have a late Proof of this myself, who have lately found in some Passages of Scripture a Sense quite different from what I understood them in before, or from what I found in Commentators;[3] and yet it appears so clear to me, that when I see you next, I shall dare to appeal to you in it. But I read the Word of God without Prepossession or Biass, and come to it with a Resolution to take my Sense from it, and not with a Design to bring it to the Sense of my System. How much that has made Men wind and twist and pull the Text in all the several Sects of Christians, I need not tell you. I design to take my Religion from the Scripture, and then, whether it suits, or suits not any other Denomination, I am not much concerned: For I think, at the last Day, it will not be enquired, whether I was of the Church of England or Geneva, but, whether I sought or embraced Truth in the Love of it. . . .

2613. Francis Cudworth Masham to Locke, Oates, 21 August 1699

. . . Sir according to your desire, I will tell you as well as I can, what I saw at the assises.[1] When we were within a mile of Burntwood,[2] we mett the High Sheriff, comeing to meet my Lord chief Justice Trebie;[3] then we went back with him, and mett the Judge, who came on horseback. The next day I went upon the bench, which was very full, and heard the Judges speech, which I liked very well; he praised the King and answered all the objections that might be made against him. He said that idleness was in great measure the cause of

---

[3] Locke may by now have been engaged on his *Paraphrase and Notes on the Epistles of St Paul.*

[1] Twice a year judges travelled on circuit, holding courts of assize to hear criminal cases too serious to be dealt with by county magistrates.

[2] Brentwood, Essex.   [3] Sir George Treby.

the robberies that were done; and that no body was born to live idlely, tho' all do not work with their hands, yet they must study with their minds the good of their country in their several places; and also many other things which I liked a great deal better than the trials which were tiresome. I thought it was a very noble office to be a Judge, but not a very easie one. I think it is a very serious thing to condemn people to death. I saw some burnt in the hand, and some in the cheek. I thought it very moveing to see the poore prisoners when they were condemned fall down upon their knees beging pardon or transportation.[4] When my Lord gave sentence he said, since you have lived as the Theif who was crucified with our blessed Saviour I hope you will repent like him at your deaths. . . .

2614. Richard Coote, Earl of Bellomont, to Locke, Boston, Massachusetts, 7 September 1699

I hope you were present at the board,[1] when my Letters by the two Last Conveyances were read. that of the 13th. of last April about the Indian affairs;[2] that of the 17th ditto about Naval stores;[3] that of the 27th. ditto about Calling the assembly of N.york, and their Continuing the Revenue;[4] that of the 3d. of may about Bradish a Pyrate[5] and his Crew taken; that of the 13th. ditto about the Courts of Justice Ceasing at N.york,[6] and about the trade of that province; that of the 15th. ditto Containing my answer to the Lords of the Council of Trade's Letters of the 25th. of October the 5th. of Jan: and 2d. of feb: 98. that of the 8th. of Last July about my seizing and Committing Captain Kidd[7] to gaol. and that of the 22th. July giving an account of the affairs of N.york, and the acts of assembly pass'd there the last session and sent with my said Letter of the 22th. of July; among which acts there is one that breaks some of Colonel Fletcher's[8] extravagant Grants of Lands in that province, and one of his Grants which that act breaks, was to the Church of N.york; and

---

[4] The death sentence was sometimes commuted to transportation to the plantations in the West Indies.

[1] Board of Trade.

[2] The letter contained a long account of negotiations, in rivalry with the French, for the loyalty of the Five Nations (L2714, n. 3). It mentions a native American called Decinisorre, 'a brave fighting fellow that has done the French much mischief'.

[3] The troops stationed at New York were badly short of provisions.

[4] Another long account, concerning violent party strife in elections to the New York Assembly, between the Leislerites and Jacobites. Jacob Leisler had led New York's rebellion against James II in 1689. The Jacobites objected to levying customs revenues, calling them 'a badge of slavery', and moved that the word 'happy' be deleted from a motion concerning 'the late happy Revolution'.

[5] Joseph Bradish, hanged in 1700.

[6] Bellomont had complained that the lawyers were incompetent and Jacobitical.

[7] William Kidd, the pirate, hanged in 1701.

[8] Benjamin Fletcher, governor of New York, 1692–7, whom Bellomont regarded as corrupt.

the Parson who is a great knave[9] has stirr'd up some of the Clergy French and Dutch to Join with him to write home and Complain to the Bishop of London.[10] another Letter of mine of the 26. of July to your Lordships of the Council of Trade gives an exact account of all goods and treasure taken with Kidd, and of my taking the Concurrence of the Council here in that matter, and our ordering the said goods and treasure into the hands of five trusty persons. this Course I took, because I would lye under no sort of suspicion of unfair dealing; and though the greatest part of the treasure was discover'd and seiz'd by my own vigilance; I would not so much as see it, but order'd it into the hands of those persons; where all that's found is to lye till the King's pleasure be known, for so the orders of the Lords Justices of England and of Mr. Secretary Vernon do appoint.[11]

Pyrates do so Increase in these plantations that they will destroy the trade of England especially that to the E. Indies, if a speedy remedy be not taken to suppresse 'em. we have had two or three new Pyrate ships on these Coasts lately, they rob our trading ships of the stoutest and likelyest of their men and of all their provisions (because they know provisions are Carried from hence and N.york and Pensylvania to the Western Islands)[12] and then they declare themselves bound for Madagascar and the Red Sea. we have a Pyrate ship of force now at this time on the Coast that robbs all our ships. and because nothing but ships of war Can secure us and destroy them, the Lords of the Admiralty are pleas'd not to allow us a single ship. you will see what I propose to your board by this Conveyance in my Letters of the 24th. of aug: about the affairs of N.York; in that of the 28th. ditto, about those of this Province; and in that of the 1st. of this moneth about the affairs of N. Hampshire. I do in all my letters (or almost all) Complain of the want of means of Checking piracy; viz: two good ships of war here and N.york whereof one to be a 4th. rate ship: for a 5th. rate will not be a match for some of these pyrates; and this pyrate now on the Coast has 24. guns and a 110 Choice men, and a 5th. rate man of war has but 95 men: therefore I am of opinion this pyrate would take a 5th. rate should they Ingage in fight. a 4th. rate ship here then, and a 5th. rate at N.york is one of my three postulata: the next is two honest good lawyers to be Judges at N.York and an able honest Attorney Generall, for the present one[13] is a right Scot, Cunning, but as false as hell and Corrupt, and besides, no lawyer. he being the only Council for the King, by his means we loose all Pyrates we take, and all the seizures of unlawfull ships and goods. he was formerly a rank bitter Jacobite, and I see no signs of his Conversion. all the rest of the pettyfoggers[14] in that province are the greatest rogues and Jacobites in nature, and debauch the principles and affections of the people from the Government, besides the mischief they do them in their estates by

---

[9] Godfrey Dellius, minister at Albany.
[10] Henry Compton. There were no bishops in America and jurisdiction lay with the Bishop of London.
[11] James Vernon, Secretary of State. [12] Presumably the Caribbean Islands.
[13] James Graham. [14] A derogatory term for lawyers.

their sinister practice of the law. The third and last of my postulata, is the recruiting and well paying the four Companies[15] in the province of N.york, which are at present barbarously us'd by the treasury and pay-office. if these three things are granted me, I will make these provinces flourish, and at the same time be much more usefull and subservient to England than they ever have been. I am every day more and more Convinc'd of the vast advantage these Plantations are to England, and of the Improvement that might be made of that advantage by the honest Care of the severall Governors. if our Navigation be a thing valuable to England, then Certainly these plantations must be allow'd to Contribute to that the most that Can be. then again the furnishing the King with masts for his ships of war, and the Navy and all the shipping of England with Naval stores as pitch tar etc: which my Letter of the 17th. of Last april to your board treats of, and which I undertake therein to furnish from the province of N.york at Cheaper rates than they are at this time sold in England that are brought from Sweden and Denmark. I am so sure of performing this thing of Naval stores, that I will loose my head if I do not perform it. and when I do it, I thinke I may without vanity pretend to do as great and valuable service to England as ever was done by a subject. I desire you will please to be at the pains of reading all those Letters I have mention'd to have writ to your board, and that you will make use of that great and generall Influence you have on all the Ministers, to excite them to support and assist me vigorously and effectually. if all the rest of the Ministers were as Industrious and vigilant in businesse as your board, England would quickly be made happy and great. with a 4th. rate and 5th. rate ships, I will undertake to root out piracy from all North America, viz: from the Eastermost bounds of the Province of Mayne, to the southermost point of South Carolina which is the whole extent of the English territory on this Continent, and about 400 leagues[16] in Length, provided the Governors of the other Plantations will but be honest, and will Co-operate with me. I Cannot doubt of your favour, and ready Compliance with the request I have made you, because it tends to the service of England, . . .

2640. Locke to Dr Hans Sloane, Oates, 2 December 1699

Since you command me I here send you what I proposed above a twelvemonth since for the reforming of our year,[1] before the addition of another day increase the error and make us, if we goe on in our old way, differ the next year eleven days from those who have a more rectified Calendar.[2] The remedie

---

[15] Of soldiers. They were two years in arrears of pay.   [16] A league is 3 nautical miles.

[1] i.e. the calendar. The paper is not extant.

[2] The Julian calendar was ten days behind the Gregorian in the 17th cent. and eleven days in the 18th. Most of Catholic Europe had introduced the Gregorian calendar in the 16th cent.

which I offer is that the intercalar day should be omitted the next year and soe the ten next leap years following by which easy way we should in 44 years insensibly return to the right, and from thence forwards goe on according to the new stile. This I call an easy way because it would be without any pre-judice or disturbance to any ones civill rights, which by the loping off of ten or eleven days at once in any one year might perhaps receive inconveniencies the only objection that ever I heard made against rectifying our account.[3] I need not say any thing to you how inexcusable it is, that in soe learned an age as this, and in a country wherein astronomie is caried to an higher pitch than ever it was in the world, an error of this kinde should be sufferd to goe on, an error which every body sees, and ownes to have growing inconveniencies in it: I shall rather choose to wish that when this reformation is made the begining of the year with us might be reduced from 25th of March to the first of January.[4] that we might herein agree with our neigbours and the rest of the Christian world.

Now I am writeing give me leave to say one word more though on a subject very different. The storys I have heard of the performances of the Strong man now in London would be beyond beleif were there not soe many witnesses of it.[5] I think they deserve to be communicated to the present age and recorded to posterity. And therefor I think you cannot omit to give him a place in your transactions. his country age stature bignesse make weight, and the several proofs he has given of his strength, which may be a subject of speculation and enquiry to the philosophical world.

I took the liberty to send you just before I left the town the last edition of my Essay. I doe not intend you shall have it gratis. There are two new Chapters in it of the *association of Ideas* and an other of *Enthusiasme* these two I expect you should read and give me your opinion frankly upon.[6] . . .

2643. Locke to Peter King, Oates, 4 December 1699

I have £1000 lyeing dead by me. I would desire you to consult with your Cosin Freke[1] to know of him what is the best way of turning money to advantage

---

[3] The implication for civil rights was in respect of taxes, rents, and other annual obligations, should the year be foreshortened. There were riots in 1752 when the calendar was changed and eleven days were 'stolen'.

[4] The convention was also changed in 1752. 25 Mar., Lady Day, was the year's end for many financial transactions; taken with the eleven-day Gregorian shift, this explains why the end of the modern British tax year falls on 5 Apr.

[5] William Joy, 'the English Samson', who performed feats at the Duke's Theatre; he later became a smuggler.

[6] II. xxxiii and IV. xix, added to the 4th edn. (1700).

[1] John Freke was a stock-jobber (the name then for a stockbroker) and, through King, was Locke's financial adviser; he is not the same man as John Freke, the politician.

now. I would not have you tell him it is mine. I am advised to buy Tallys² on the Land tax or on Wines Vinegar and Tobacco which I am told the Bank will discount at any time. pray informe your self. For I would dispose of my money thus only till I could get some good land security where I might lodg it safe for some considerable time and for such I desire you to looke out, for I have £1600 that I would soe place, but whether upon one or more mortgages is to me indifferent, soe that if you should light on one at first but of £200 I would not have you refuse it because it was soe small. Mr Churchill writes me word that he has paid you my bill. Upon second thoughts I guesse it is £20 more than you will need, For you will now at Christmas receive £2 per cent from the East India company for the annuity.³ I mention not this that your haveing £20 in your hands of mine will breake any squares,⁴ for I had rather you should have too much than too little, But to minde you of the 2 per cent, that you may not forget it at the next payment . . .

2673. Jean-Baptiste Du Bos to Locke, Paris, 14/24 February [1700]

. . . The Abbé Boileau, brother of Despreaux,¹ has just published a book which he calls *Historia flagellantium* in 12°. In it he makes plain that the use of this monastic discipline is very recent in the church and bad for the health when it is applied to the back: it is even worse if it is applied to the backside owing to the violent temptations which result from it. The book by Meibomius² is greatly cited, and thus the monks have done their best, to have it banned, but their attempts have been useless. . . .

A dancing master has had the idea of noting down the steps and figures of dances as is done for the tones and movement of a musical air. He has just published his system which he calls choregraphie.³ . . .

One of my friends who is working on the kingdom's march or the history of our frontier wishes to have information on the titles⁴ which the English once took away from France and which are preserved in the Tower. He has asked me to enquire whether a man sent expressly to England on his command would be permitted to see these titles and to copy whatever he found to be historic and useful to his project. I thought that I could not do better

---

² What today would be called 'gilts', gilt-edged stock: an investment in government loans secured against taxation (in Locke's time, either land or excise taxes). Tallies were, literally, wooden sticks, notched to keep account.
³ Dividend payments on company stock.   ⁴ Will do any harm.

¹ Abbé Jacques Boileau, brother of the poet Nicolas Boileau Despréaux.
² J. H. Meibom, *De Flagrorum Usu in Re Veneria* (*The Sexual Use of Flagellation*) (1643).
³ Rauol Auger Feuillet, *Choregraphie* (1700); Eng. trans., *The Art of Dancing* (1706).
⁴ Documents, charters.

than to address myself to you, Monsieur, since you are the friend of My lord Chancellor,[5] so that I might know whether their wish might be granted.[6] . . .

A month ago a Jesuit gave us an account of the Marianes islands,[7] which is the name he gives to the Larrons islands because her majesty the queen mother of Spain, Marianne of Austria, founded missions there. There are few things of curiosity in this book except for the discovery of a number of islands which are to the south of the Larron islands. The rest is but devotion and miracles. According to the author these islands produce nothing which is useful to commerce and their fathers are directed only by the zeal of the house of God, however it is clear from this book that from time to time they send vessels loaded at Agua pulco.[8]

2692. Anne Grigg to Locke, Oxford, 19 March [1700]

I am but just out of a scurvey fever that made my Oxford friends fear that it would quickly end my life; And no sooner is my danger over than the cares of this world return, not that I am over solicitous for the old Woman, but having receiv'd a leter from my son which tenderly gives me a new concerne for him,[1] I cannot but impart it to you who are most likely to make it significant to him; he informes me that to mend his smal fellowship he is tempted to accept of a Country living of 25£ a yeare,[2] I have answer'd him, that considering the expence of Orders etc besides the fatigue of cold and hot journeys, as well as the labour of his Brains and Lungs, that the good managment of his present College life will agree better with him. This advice I conclude he will take; Now if I have don ill pray Sir reprove me; and yet punish me no other ways for this fault than by remembering the young man when it comes within your reach to set him more at his Ease; hitherto he has found me as liberall to him as I could, and being sensible that he cannot without inconveniencing a Mother who loves him intirely, expect the usuall suplys during my life;[3] he seemes dispirited with the straitness of his fortune; Elce he would not be so very willing to be thus humbly prefer'd. I conffess I am vaine enough to think he deserves better, And considering that from an Enfant he has bin in your favour, I will not dispare of succeeding by your recomendation of him to those who have it in their power to oblige you. There are variety of

[5] Somers.   [6] Locke advised an application to the Historiographer Royal, Thomas Rymer.

[7] Charles le Gobien, *Histoire des isles Marianes nouvellement converties à la religion chrestienne* (1700). The Ladrones or Marianas Islands, in the Pacific.

[8] Acapulco, Mexico.

[1] William Grigg, Fellow of Jesus College, Cambridge, later Master of Clare College.

[2] Contemporaries reckoned that £50 p.a. was the decent minimum for a parish minister.

[3] She was a widow with a lifetime interest in her husband's estate. Thomas Grigg, rector of St Andrew Undershaft, London, died in 1670, aged about 32.

Donitives and little Dignitys in my Lord Chancelors guift[4] which Ambitious men disdaine, and ar below his Lordships favorits which are often granted at the request of persons Esteem'd by great men, And why may I not hope this way to prevail? there being few whose intrest exceeds yours; I aime at nothing that looks above my Sons Education and deserts. Tho divers by a lucky word mount high who mirit very litle; I say not this to reproach your friend-ship for as inconsiderable as I am, I have prevail'd for greater things for others than I now would be glad of for my own good son, and yet I cannot accuse myself for want of kindness for him, and I assure you I am far from fancy-ing that you will decline proper ways of setting honest W G more at his Ease, who to endeare him to you is so very like his excellent father in Temper and Mind, tho he falls short of his preferments (when he was many yeares younger than this son) who I hope will live longer; And waite with modesty and patience for what we wish him. Pardon deare Brother this solicitude of mine, and think how naturall it is for a parent to desire a setlement for an only Child, where I may give my helping hand to the fixing him happyly, fancy your old friend setting a Parsonage house in a good Aire in Order, stitching for the poor and making them wellcome to her without giving offence to her richer neighbours, and the Country Parson zealous in doing his duty, then think it possible that Mr Grigg and his mother may be such, and how plesant it will be to you to come and find us happyer than the generality of those who make a greater flutter. . . .

2714. William Popple to Locke, Whitehall, 19 April 1700

. . . The three inclosed Copies of our Minutes shew you what this Board are now doing.[1] The ground of this Conspiracy of the Indians which you will finde there mentioned arises wholly from an Artifice of the French. It seems the Commissioners who came over to treat here in winter $169\frac{8}{9}$ agreed with our Commissioners that letters should be writ by the French King to the Governor of Canada,[2] and by his Majesty to the E: of Bellomont, about dis-arming the Indians on both sides, upon pretence of keeping them in peace, and with certain conditions to be agreed on between those Governors: Which letters were writ accordingly. But instead of concerting any thing with the E of Bellomont thereupon, who also on his side not thinking fit to do any thing in it did not propose any thing about it to the Governor of Canada, the French

---

[4] Clerical livings in the crown's gift were allocated by the Lord Chancellor, currently Somers; Locke had briefly served as clerical patronage secretary in 1672–3, when Shaftesbury was Lord Chancellor.

[1] Popple was secretary of the Board of Trade. For the topics in this letter see L2614.

[2] Hector Callières, successor to the better-known Comte de Frontenac, who had fought the British and the native Americans during the 1690s.

have industriously spread Reports through the five Nations[3] and all the rest of those Indians that the Earle of Bellomont was designing to take away their Arms in order to the utter extirpation of them. This Belief instill'd into them by the French Missionaries (whom they call the Governor of Canada's cunning men[4]) has put them into such a rage that they are all of them, from the Eastermost parts of New England to the Westermost of our New-York Indians, enter'd actually into a combination against the English on that Continent: And God knows what Mischief they may have already done. However the preventing or remedying of any such Mischief has been the subject of this dayes Deliberation, upon which I am now to draw up a Representation: But what it will be I can give very little guess till the Board shall have agreed upon the Draught of it. Presents for our Indians; One hundred Recruits, and Clothes for the four Companies;[5] A Sod fort[6] in the Onondage Country; And a Credit for the E: of Bellomont to draw a limited sum upon the Treasury here; are some of the Heads.[7] . . .

2748. Jean-Baptiste Du Bos to Locke, Paris, 17/28 July [1700]

. . . Monsieur Perrault has given us his second volume of illustrious Frenchmen containing fifty such men, which is as many as were in the first volume.[1] You will have heard at the time that he was obliged[2] to remove Monsieur Arnaud[3] and Monsieur Pascal[4] from his first volume. I gave him some advice on this occasion which he has benefited from, which was that he should include Protestants in his volume to show that it is not a vehicle of orthodoxy. He has found a place in the second volume for Blondel[5] Bochard[6] [and] Joseph Scaliger,[7] as well as several Protestant military men and he has replaced Monsieur Pascal and Monsieur Arnauld in the first volume. . . .

---

[3] The Iroquois: a confederation of native Americans (the Cajugas, Mohawks, Oneidas, Onondagas, and Senecas), formed supposedly by Hiawatha in 1570.

[4] Magicians.   [5] Of English troops.   [6] Defensive earthworks.

[7] Events in Canada provided the theme for John Dennis's play *Liberty Asserted* (1704), in which a virtuous Iroquois chief persuades the French governor to denounce French tyranny, declare independence, and ally with the English. The Preface says the play is aimed 'to make men in love with liberty' and invokes Locke's name.

[1] Charles Perrault, *Les Hommes illustres qui ont paru en France pendant ce siecle* (1700; 1st vol., 1696).

[2] By the Jesuits.

[3] Antoine Arnauld, philosopher, theologian, mathematician: leader of the Jansenists, and hence regarded as heretical.

[4] Blaise Pascal, philosopher, theologian, mathematician, inventor; also a Jansenist.

[5] David Blondel, Huguenot theologian, settled in Amsterdam 1650, suspected of Arminianism.

[6] Samuel Bochart, Huguenot theologian.

[7] Joseph Justus Scaliger, classicist, historian, famed for his prodigious erudition.

The quarrel between the Jesuits and the French missionaries in China on the cult of Confucius and the honours paid to the dead is immensely heated here and every day pamphlets are published by both sides in which people do their utmost to present their adversaries as odious and to make the public believe that the tolerance of one side for the Chinese ceremonies is an effect of their indifference for Christianity and that the zeal of the others is caused purely by their jealousy. *tantoene animis Coelestibus irae.*[8] The Sorbonne is to intervene in this quarrel and will examine a proposition in the letter by the p[ère] Le Comte, that the Chinese preserved the true religion until the time of Jesus Christ.[9]

A book is being sold here by a well known author but to which Monsieur de Saint Evremont[10] has not contributed any more than you or I and yet it has this title *Saint Evremontiana* or good words and thoughts of Monsieur de Saint Evremont.[11] Such audaciousness is the cause of many reflections on what might have happened before the invention of printing and when books were not yet as common as they are. Probably in a century this book will pass for one by St Evremont. It will appear from its date and from the journals that it was printed during the lifetime of the person whose name it bears and as it were also bears his mark. It is true that Monsieur de St Evremont will disclaim it but this disavowal will be contained in some letters to his friends which will perish and the book will survive. . . .

2754. Benjamin Furly to Locke, Rotterdam, 9/20 August 1700

. . . My son John[1] I have placed at Norwich to learn the manufacture of that place,[2] and serve for a factor,[3] when his time is out, to such of my acquaintance here, and in Amsterdam, as have their goods from thence, which if he behave himself soberly, as I hope he will, wilbe of great advantage to him. . . .

Where to place Arent[4] in England I am yet uncertain, Very willingly would I have him under your good Ey and instruction, could a place be found in the village near you, and if it might be that he might be your Amanuensis: as being well assured it would be advantageous to him in his studyes: For tho, for reasons I have sub rosa[5] acquainted him with, I cannot promise my self, nor him, that he shall for the future be bred to his studyes alone, yet I would

---

[8] 'Can heavenly minds such high resentment show?' (Virgil, *Aeneid*, i. 11).

[9] Louis Daniel le Comte, SJ, *Nouveaux memoires sur l'état present de la Chine* (1696); Eng. trans., *Memoirs and Observations made on a Late Journey through the Empire of China* (1697).

[10] Charles de Saint-Evremond, critic, freethinker, satirist, Epicurean; he fled France and settled in England, 1661.

[11] Carlo Cotolendi, *Saint-Evremoniana* (1700).

[1] His second son, aged about 17.   [2] Principally worsted weaving, the 'new draperies'.

[3] Agent, middleman.   [4] His third son, aged 15.   [5] Privately.

not have him lose, but increase what he has. His whole bent would be, if it might be, that way, but I tell him 'tis so hazardous to rely upon that, alone, for a comfortable, moderate subsistence in the world, merely by literature,[6] that he must think upon some other imploy. His heart is so intent upon books and learning, that he would have me place him with mr. Leers,[7] His choice is not ill. But Leers is furnisht at present, so that what to do with him, I know not, but he is but 15 years and a half old yet, so may spend a year and half yet in his studyes. In this Cuntry to breed him to a Doctor, is to expose him to penury, almost, and not much better for a Lawyer, for many years, except a young man very much excels indeed, and has very good friends to recommend and help him forward. And for the other Learned craft and Craftsmen, you know, I cannot possibly have bred him to have any tolerable reverence for it or them, I mean the art of wrangling about words that most what signify nothing; about which the great High-Waymen of the Church, do ram and damn one another, whose work it is to rob men of their civil and spirituall libertyes, and to pick out their eyes that they may follow them blindfold: From whom and their Artifices Libera nos Domine.[8] . . .

I have not bred my children, to the learning of any their Gibberish Articles, but onely to understand and practice that Religion, which Jesus christ [taught], whom I instruct them to be the Saviour of all men, and not of one party, sect or kirk alone, which is most plain and easy, that is to love and honour God above all, and their neighbour as themselvs, to walk humbly, act righteously towards all, and to shew mercy, and practice charity where it is needed: and to have nothing to do with any of the wrangling Crew, heaps[9] or sects, because they all arrogate themselvs the glorious name of the church of Christ: nor to join with any of them, as such, against all the rest, Till they shall meet with a society of men, that shalbe able to prove their title by those signs that Christ said should attend his true church in the world. . . .

'Twil I fancy not be irksome to you, to relate a very remarkable thing happend here last week, about a broad-Phylactery-man,[10] a Deacon of the kirk, forsooth, and father, or Governour of that house of charity of this town, nigh the port, that leads to the dwelling of our friend the Burgermaster[11]—This man was composed of nothing but religious gravity, long and lowd prayers, an exemplary starcht conversation, a painted sepulcher[12] without, but of a most lewd, and vile deportment behind the curtain, who, having sworn to watch over the yong orphans of the house, that no lewdness, nor wantonness be practisd betwixt the lads and lasses; forced two of them, and by threats and treats brought others to satisfy his goatish lust: till at last he so treated a girl (ni fallor)[13] of 14 years old, that the child could not with ease sit, who being askt the reason of her uneasyness, told it to an ancient woman of the house; so inquiry was privatly made whether others were not so handled by him,

---

[6] Humanistic (rather than practical) learning.   [7] Reinier Leers, publisher in Rotterdam.
[8] 'Lord deliver us.'   [9] Companies.   [10] An ostentious displayer of religiosity, a hypocrite.
[11] Unidentified.   [12] Matthew 23:27.   [13] 'Unless I am mistaken.'

and he so watcht that he was seen to act his villany. Complaint was made to our Ballju,[14] the thing became a publick talk, He was advisd to pack him away if guilty, But instead of that he scornd it vaunted of his Innocency, said that the godly must go thro' ill, as well as good report, and the righteous be bold as a yong lyon. At length the Ballju (a brave man) cites him up, layes attestations before him, produces witnesses, confronts them together. The Parsons espouse his cause, cry shame that eare should be given to such malicious persons, to the staying the reputation of so holy a man, say that more defference was to be given to his obtestation[15] of the name of god in his own compurgation,[16] than to such persons, who were become his enemys for the severe discipline he practisd among them—So that the Judges let him go 2 or 3 times till the Ballju grew earnest, and got him detaynd. And at last told him it was the utmost impudence to outbrazen such evidence. And that he must bring him to the Torture, giving him time to bethink himself, and ordring him to his chamber, but before he went out, he acknowledged all; begging for pardon; But finding none, (as the custome here is) he was brought into the open street, there to confess his crimes, during which time his heart so faild him, that he was fain to be sustain'd by 2 men from falling. Yet, by the converse of his ghostly fathers,[17] and som of their disciples, he recoverd so much his spirits, and courage, and assurance of his election and salvation, that no man was ever seen, they say, to dy so unconcernd, to the admiration of all that had se[en] him 3 days before: his crimes are now so extenuated, and holyness so highly cryed up, that the Judges are by some reflected upon, as having gone to, if not beyond, the rigour of the Law in beheading him, of which they being aware, before they would condemn him they consulted the ablest lawyers in the hague, who unanimously said they must condemn him to dye. . . .

2775. John Hardy to Locke, Shrewsbury, 17 September 1700

The great distance there is betwixt your self and Me, had for ever discouraged Me from troubling You with My Impertinencyes, had I not flatter'd My Self Into the Opinion, that your large Soul would make the distance less, since (perhaps) you would not think it out of your Sphere to help even the Poorest Searcher for Truth; Truth, which is almost lost in terms of Art and unintelligible vaine Janglings of words; what should such as I do In this great Confusion! did not now and Then a Clear Reasonablenesse of Christianity Appear. Pardon Me Sir if I venture to Consult you to have My Scruples Solv'd, who have so often found satisfaction In Many points by your Works.

---

[14] Baljuw: bailiff, magistrate. [15] Witnessing. [16] Vindication. [17] Fellow ministers.

It has been a Grand Controversie (You are not ignorant) even since the first Ages of our Religion whether Christ (for certain the Son of God by Extraordinary Birth and by having the Sperit dwelling Bodily In him) is properly God from all Eternity:[1] I have endeavour'd to search the Scriptures, but can find litle In favour of the Affirmative at first sight, what ever wonder's other Men's quickness can Espy, in litle Phrases, and some flights of Pious Men. But the truth is, I could never yet rightly see, how the first Ch: of John[2] Can be Expounded without forcing, to please those who have opposed the Deity of Our Lord, . . . Can the earn'st Desires of an Unsatisfyed Mind prevail with You, to give Me Your Thoughts of as much of that Ch[apter]: as you thinke difficult. . . .

I have lately seen a Piece, admir'd by all Moderate Men, The Irenicum Magnum,[3] But Virtus laudatur et Alget,[4] som fear (as our Historians of Learning)[5] that ther's a snake in the Grass.[6] other's Cry it down as wholly Heterodox. But other's admire the Authors Great, and Noble design, Grounded upon such Convincing Reasons; but they say It's impracticable. And indeed I've spent some thoughts upon it, and am affraid that such things the world Cannot bear. For, suppose a Minister of the Ch: of E. should offer to set up for a Scripturalist,[7] the Poor Gentleman would quicly be humbled by Church discipline. And if any of our Presbyte[rian] way should offer, all his brethren would certainly snarl at him, and thus would his Pious design vanish. Honoured Sir, if you are the Authour, as Most believe,[8] I should be glad to understand, How you think such Methods may be put in practice. For aiming at that Publick office of the Ministry (for which I am now pre-pairing) I would willingly be furnish'd with all the requisites to keep my Conscience pure and undefiled before God in that station, and not onely Talk but act as much as possible; I'm sure you know the world and the Great Trade of Priestcraft[9] (in fashion in every church) better, than to think that ever they will throw away all their narrow notions of Man-made-Divinity, and silly scandals by which they offend one another, and receive instead of it true and free Reasonable Religion. . . .

---

[1] A reference to Arianism, which denied the complete divinity of Christ and hence his eternity in God. Often associated with Socinianism and Unitarianism.

[2] John 1:1 and 1:14: 'In the beginning was the Word, and the Word was with God, and the Word was God'; 'And the Word was made flesh, and dwelt among us'.

[3] Anon., *Irenicum Magnum: The Gospel Terms of Communion Stated* (1700): a scheme for 'Comprehension', the reuniting of Protestants, particularly Anglicans and Presbyterians.

[4] 'Virtue is praised and left to shiver'. Varied from Juvenal, *Satires*, i. 74.

[5] *History of the Works of the Learned*, a review journal (1699–1712).   [6] Lurking danger.

[7] An advocate of Comprehension.

[8] It is striking that a scheme for Anglican–Presbyterian Comprehension should be attributed to Locke.

[9] This new word appears to have been coined by James Harrington in 1657. It was given prominence by the opening line of John Dryden's *Absalom and Achitophel* (1681) ('In pious times, e'r Priest-craft did begin'), and became fashionable in the 1690s. It first appears in Locke's correspondence in a letter from Popple to Locke, 18 May 1693 (L1630).

2832. Benjamin Furly to Locke, [Rotterdam?],
[*c.*26 December 1700 / 6 January 1701]

... I am informd ... that his Majesty has dissolved this Parliament.[1]

God send him another that will take care of the Protestant interest, and the cause of universall liberty as men and christians, for now, if ever, there is need of vigourous and unanimous councils, amongst all that are heartily concerned for Liberty, against Priestcraft.

I know nothing that can tend to the stopping of that overflowing deluge, with which all Europe seems now, more than ever, threatned, but a hearty conjuction, and union betwixt these two nations, upon a Nationall bottome,[2] this may prove a basis for a further alliance that may give check to that design which france seems to have, of extirpating heresy, that he[3] may have the Glorious Title of Restorer of the Churches unity, and treader down of her enemies.

And yet when alls done, they will have difficulty enough, except God sends a spirit of Jealousy, and division betwixt the Spaniards and the French.[4] ...

2846. Locke to [Richard King], Oates, 20 January [1701]

... I thank you for the printed Paper you sent me,[1] and am very glad to see such a Spirit rais'd, for the Support and Enlargement of Religion. Protestants, I think, are as much concern'd now as ever, to be vigorous in their joint Endeavours, for the Maintenance of the Reformation. I wish all that call themselves so, may be prevail'd with by those whom your Paper intimates, to imitate the Zeal, and persue the Principles of those great and pious Men, who were instrumental to bring us out of Roman Darkness and Bondage. I heartily pray for good Success on all such Endeavours.

If I may guess at the Intention of the Society, by the only Man you let me know of it, I may be confident that the Glory of God, and the Propagation of True Religion is the only Aim of it. May God eminently prosper all Endeavours that way, and increase the number of those who seriously lay it to heart. ...

---

[1] Parliament was dissolved on 19 Dec.; the next parliament met in February.

[2] England and the Netherlands. There was a fleeting proposal for a formal union in 1689.

[3] Louis XIV.

[4] The War of the Spanish Succession began in 1702, England and her allies fighting to prevent Louis uniting the thrones of France and Spain.

[1] Perhaps Thomas Bray, *A Short Account of the Several Kinds of Society, set up of late years for the promoting of God's worship, for the reformation of manners, and for the propagation of Christian knowledge* (1700). Locke's letter may refer specifically to the founding of the Society for the Promotion of Christian Knowledge in 1699.

2849. Locke to Peter King, Oates, 24 January [1701]

I thank you for your pains and concerne in my business. Had I foreseen your being chosen Parliament man[1] I had taken quite other measures. Whether you shall put the money into Bank bills or East India bonds[2] I leave it to you to doe just as you would doe with your own only I would have it soe as I might have it at command to buy again when it is sunk to the lowest which I am apt to think will not bee till tis seen not only what resolutions will be taken about peace or warr[3] but also about the two companyes themselves[4] in this parliament. For I beleive it may be suspected that this parliament will not be much friends to the New Company and soe may perhaps shake it. I never loved stock jobing[5] and therefor sold not with any such view. But now I am out, though I intend to buy again, yet I would stay till it is at worst, as I beleive you would advise me, and therefore I desire you to mention in your letters how the rate goes, and when you write anything that requires a quick answer direct it to be left at Mr Harisons at the Crown in Harlow.[6] The list also of the Parliament members will as it grows compleat be able to give you some guesse at the temper of the house which I should be glad to know as also what the College[7] thinks. One thing only give me leave to caution you of, that is that I would not have you let any one know that this is my money or that when you purchase again it is for me. What views I had that made me, when I gave you order to sell out, not like to be in, I shall hereafter at more leisure explain to you. . . .

2855. Locke to Peter King, Oates, 31 January [1701]

. . . Your staying in town the next vacation I look upon as resolvd and the reasons I finde for it in your own lettre now that I have time to read them a little more deliberately I think sufficient to determin you should, though I say noe thing at all. Though every time I think of it I am more and more confirmd in the opinion that it is absolutely necessary in all respects whether I consider the publique or your own private concernes neither of which are indifferent to me. Tis my private thought that the Parliament will scarce sit even soe much as to choose a speaker before the end of the terme.[1] But when ever he is chosen tis of noe small consequence which side carys it, if there be

---

[1] For Beeralston, Devon.   [2] The Bank of England and East India Company.

[3] War against France was suspended in 1697 and resumed in 1702.

[4] The rival East India Companies; the new (Whig) company was founded in 1698; the old in 1600.

[5] Speculative dealing in stocks and shares.   [6] Innkeeper and postal agent.

[7] Locke's parliamentary associates, chiefly Edward Clarke and John Freke.

[1] Robert Harley was chosen Speaker on 10 Feb.; the law term ended on the 12th.

two nominated or at least in view, as tis ten to one there will be espetialy in a Parliament chosen with soe much strugle.[2] Haveing given all the help possibly you can in this which is usualy a leading point shewing the strength of the partys, My next advice to you is not to speak at all in the house for some time, what ever fair oportunity you may seem to have.[3] But though you keep your mouth shut I doubt not but you will have your eyes open to see the temper and observe the motions of the house and diligently to remarke the skil of management, and carefully watch the first and secret beginings of things and their tendencys, and endeavour if there be danger in them to crush them in the Egg. You will say what can you doe who are not to speak? Tis true I would not have you speake to the house, but you may communicate your light or apprehensions to some honest speaker who may make use of it. For there have always been very able members who never speake, who yet by their penetration and foresight have this way donne as much service as any within those walls. And here by you will more recommend your self when people shal observe soe much modesty joynd with your parts[4] and judgment, than if you should seem forward, though you spoke well. But let the man you communicate to be not only well intentioned but a man of Judgment. Methinks I take too much upon me in these directions. I have only this to say in my excuse, that you desird it more than once and I advise you noething which I would not doe my self were I in your place. I should have much more to say to you were you here, But it being fitter for discourse and debate than for lettre I hope I may see you here e're long Sir Francis[5] haveing already proposed to me your stealeing down sometimes with him on a Saturday and returning monday. The Votes[6] you offer me will be very acceptable if I [mistake] not the members have more than one copy gratis and for sometime at least dureing this busy season I would be glad you would send me every post the three news papers viz *Postman Post boy*, and *Flying post*.[7] But when you begin to send them you will doe me a kindeness to stop Mr Churchil from sending me any more of them. For he sends them now but it is by the Butcher and they come very uncertainly. . . .

2874. Locke to Peter King, Oates, 3 March 1701

. . . I imagin by what you say of the Circuit[1] that you have not your self read the Pamphlet[2] you gave to Mr Coste. Pray read it and then tell me whether

[2] The general election was bitterly fought and the new Commons was finely balanced.
[3] King was entering parliament for the first time.   [4] Qualities, talents.
[5] Masham, MP for Essex.   [6] The printed *Votes of the House of Commons.*
[7] *Post Man* (1694–1730); *Post Boy* (1695–1735); *Flying Post* (1695–1731); all tri-weekly Whig papers.

[1] Assize circuit (L2613, n. 1).
[2] Presumably on the French threat: perhaps George Stepney's *An Essay upon the Present Interest of England* (1701).

you can think of being a week togeather absent from your trust in Parliament till you see the main points setled and the Kingdom in a posture of defence against the ruin that threatens it. The reason why I pressed you to stay in town was to give the world a testimony how much you preferd the publick to your private interest and how true you were to any trust you undertook, this is noe small character nor of small advantage to a man comeing into the world. Besides I thought it noe good husbandry for a man to get a fee or two and loose Westminster hall.[3] For I assure you Westminster hall is at stake, and I wonder how any one of the house can sleep till he sees England in a better state of defence, and how he can talke of any thing else till that is donne. I mind you of it again. pray read that pamphlet presently.[4] . . .

2925. Locke to Philippus van Limborch, Oates, 21 May 1701

. . . I hold it a great honour for me that you value my lucubrations[1] so highly as to be willing to bestow your good hours on reading them through, and I am glad that they have not displeased you who are a lover of truth. When I say, bk. II, ch. xxi, § 24,[2] that liberty consists in a power to act and not to act, I by no means restrict this to external actions only, as is evident from §§ 8, 38, and other places in that chapter. On this, then, we are agreed. But when you say that 'whatever a man wills is considered by him to be agreeable' I fear that you are confusing Will with Desire, as I see is done by most of those who treat this subject, not without great damage to truth or at least to perspicuity. I grant that Desire is directed to the agreeable, but Will is directed only to our actions and terminates there. But since Will rarely acts unless Desire leads, they are therefore generally taken to be one and the same act, whereas they are perfectly distinct from one another. §§ 30, 40. For Longing [*Cupido*] is a passion moved by an absent good; Volition on the other hand is an act of the will or of the mind [*anima*] exercising command over the operative powers of a man. Unless these two operations of the soul, viz. that whereby it longs for [*cupit*] something and that whereby it determines or commands that something must be done, are properly distinguished, nothing, it seems to me, can be clearly established about the human will; and therefore I hope that you will forgive me for wishing to warn you about that way of speaking, since you do not disagree with me at all about the main thing. It is not surprising that I should differ from your writers[3] in the use of the word 'Indifferency' since in writing about these things I have neither followed other men's opinions nor so much as consulted any writings at all, but have set forth in the most

---

[3] Where Parliament sat.   [4] At once.

[1] In the *Essay*. Limborch had to rely on the French and Latin translations of the *Essay*.
[2] 'Of Power': §§ 22–4: 'In respect of Willing a Man is not free.'
[3] The Remonstrants (L1158, n. 5).

suitable words in my power what the things themselves have taught me, so far as they could be compassed by investigation and meditation. There will then be no arguing between us about the use of terms, provided that we agree about the thing itself. Although, to speak freely, that antecedent 'indifferency' of a man, by which he is supposed, before the determination or decree of the will, to have liberty to determine himself to one or other of opposites, seems to me not to have any bearing at all on the question of liberty, because liberty consists solely in a power to act or not to act according to the determination of the will. Moreover to argue as to whether a man, before the last judgement of the understanding, has liberty to determine himself to one or other of opposites seems to me to be arguing about nothing at all or about an impossibility. For who would ask, or what does it avail to ask, whether a man can determine himself to one or other of opposites when he is in a state in which he is altogether unable to determine himself? For before the judgement of the understanding he is altogether unable to determine himself, and so it is idle to inquire whether in that state he has liberty to determine himself to one or other alternative when he is altogether unable to determine himself to either. And therefore all those disputes that are carried on about liberty to determine oneself to one or other alternative before the judgement of the understanding seem to me (forgive me for saying so) in no respect to pertain to the question of liberty: which should not and cannot even be supposed in a state in which it is manifest that a man as a free agent cannot act, since liberty, as I have said, consists solely in the power to act or not to act consequent on, and according to, the determination of the will. But so it often happens. The fervour of disputants and partisan zeal spread cloud and darkness over things clear in themselves, while everywhere one tries to entangle another in snares that he has sought out, and to involve him in a absurdities. . . .

2932. Locke to Benjamin Furly, Oates, 30 May 1701

. . . You ask me one of the hardest questions I know when you ask me how you should dispose of your son Arent.[1] The like has been demanded of me by persons of several conditions, and I have seldom found my self able to propose any thing that I could fully satisfie my self in. This when I examin into the causes of it I impute to the great corrupsition and dissoluteness which has overspread this part of the world and of late years got into all ranks and professions of men. and seems to me the certain forerunner of that ruin confusion and disorder which seems to threaten all Europe. Without a stop to the overflowing of vice, and a reformation into better manners tis easy to

---

[1] Aged 16 (L2754, n. 4).

see the several communities in this part of the world will very hardly be able
to subsi[s]t. for vertue is the very strength and cement of Societie without
which it cannot stand. Such reformations have seldom if ever been brought
about in the world without great and publick calamities. Old as well as
yonger boys are seldom amended without scourging. and noe thing but over-
turnings bring depraved [hearts] from fashionable and growing immoralitys.
But hold I see my apprehensions (for fear is the common doteage of old men)
have caried me away from the subject I was upon, and I wish we were
togeather to debate particulars the better to come to a resolution about your
son. I have talked with him more than once since the receit of your letter. I
find as I imagind before that he has an inclination to learning and knowledg
and wants not capacity for it. But since speculations of the head will not fill
an empty stomach, his study if he makes study his business must be applied
to some particular calling that may afford a lively hood as well as information. Divinity he has noe mind to and therefor of that I shall say noe thing.
Law in England enough to bring a man to the bar and pleading is very
chargable to get and requires his being of one of the Inns of Court and at last
all that learning when gotten is of noe use or improvement any where but in
England. The under trade of Solicitors and Atturnys has soe many temptations to corruption both in the attainment and practise that I cannot imagin
you should ever have a thought that way. The law you speak of that some
have advised he should study for a year I imagin is the civil law or that of
Holland. But the studying of law for a year in order to any other calling is
what I cannot understand or that he should study law for any thing else but
to be a Lawyer. but what state that is in on that side the water I am ignorant
and soe can say noe thing. Physick[2] is the freest of all studys and is not tied
to any particular place a good physitian being welcome every where. But against
that you have made an objection which I cannot answer, and your son Arent
an other as hard to be over come which is a natural aversion in him to see
soars bloudletting and other such unpleasing objects as often occur in the
practise of physick, this at first was his objection to me and some instances
he gave of such an antipathie in himself as I think may be hard to conquer
and at least will clog his progress in this study, Though after we had discoursed
togeather he told me he thought that might be no hindrance But the reason
of that I found to be that if he studys physick England must be his residence,
and there he ownes he had rather be than in Holland But besides his and your
objection which are both [strong] against the study of physick I have an other
thing to adde which is that if I mistake not the practise of physick is goeing
to decay apace in England. Besides that I beleive the faculty is overstockd and
there be many amongst us that make a hard shift to live. Upon the whole
therefor I think his first was his most natural and the best choise. For to a
bookseller[3] the languages he has will be usefull, and the calling it self will afford

---

[2] Medicine.   [3] Publisher, as much as bookseller.

him books which he has a love for, and oportunitys to improve his know-ledg. I think his first choise of a calling not only right but the place also I mean Rotterdam under your eye, and the man Leers if his temper be as good as his skil in that trade seems to be.[4] Holland certainly is much better for that trade than England where they print Latin and French in aboundance and fill all Europe with books of all kinds from their presses, and as I hear men from small beginings quickly grow if they have skill and care into great trade stock and credit. Our booksellers for the most part are but a company of pittiful pedlers, few of them get anything, but by their dear and ill printing they have shut themselves out from sending any of their commoditys into forain parts and have noe commerce with the rest of the world. Thus you have what appears reasonable to me upon this matter . . .

2935. Locke to Philippus van Limborch, Oates, 1 June 1701

. . . I have read through the life of Episcopius[1] with very great pleasure. The narrative pleases, what was done thoroughly displeases. I truly grieve that the Reformed[2] so quickly imitated the Pontifician[3] ways of which they com-plained so bitterly. But it is pleasing to know what one cannot praise when it is known. I seem to see the Inquisition, which in the Roman Church grew more slowly, here started and almost brought to perfection as it were by a single effort. I do not know whether God will now chastise these hostilities of Protestants among themselves, and their mutual persecutions. This at least I believe: that the self-seeking dissensions of theologians, and their longing to lord it over their brothers in their turn, have anew exposed the reformed world to being overwhelmed by its old enemies and have brought it into such great danger. May God Almighty avert the omen and not punish with Catholic persecution spirits so prone to persecute. . . .

---

[4] Reinier Leers, publisher in Rotterdam. Pierre Bayle once worked for him.

[1] Van Limborch, *Historia vitae S. Episcopii* (1701). Simon Biscop (Episcopius), Dutch theologian, Arminius's successor, condemned for deviation from Calvinist predestinarianism by the Synod of Dort, 1618.
[2] Calvinists.   [3] Roman Catholic, papist.

15

Politics Revived, 1701–1703

The affair of the Kentish Petition in 1701 sparked a revival of the 'rage of party' and shaped the political discourse of the ensuing decade. The petitioners, probably prompted by the Whig leadership, asserted that the House of Commons should 'have regard to the voice of the people'. Their aim was to push the Commons towards renewing war against France. The ensuing furore provoked Daniel Defoe's *Original Power of the Collective Body of the People*, often said to be Lockean, and—if he was the author—Lord Somers's *Jura Populi Anglicani*, which cited Locke's *Two Treatises*. Outraged Tories, who now abandoned their pre-Revolution commitment to monarchical absolutism, took their stand on the sovereignty of parliament against the sovereignty of the people (L3095).

One of the most important interpreters of the *Two Treatises* to eighteenth-century audiences was Jean Barbeyrac, who made abundant use of it in footnotes to his edition of Pufendorf's *Law of Nature and Nations*. He regarded the *Two Treatises* as an essay in natural jurisprudence built upon, but taking issue with, Grotius and Pufendorf. Barbeyrac informs Locke that he is at work on his edition (L3232). Locke meanwhile responds to requests to lay out a scheme of reading on the subjects of politics and ethics. For Samuel Bold he wrote 'Thoughts Concerning Reading and Study for a Gentleman', and to Richard King he writes along similar lines (L3328). As well as suggesting texts in political theory by authors such as Aristotle, Cicero, Hooker, Grotius, and Pufendorf, Locke recommends his own *Two Treatises* as the best book concerning property. He also urges a mastery of English constitutional history, as well as of the sermons of the latitudinarian divines. King thanks Locke, praising him as 'the perfect Socrates of the age' (L3346).

Locke was deeply immersed in biblical analysis, surrounded by the accumulated erudition of the previous half-century of hermeneutic effort: the polyglots, variorums, commentaries, paraphrases, and 'harmonies' of scripture. He gives Richard King advice as to which reference books are best (L3339). Most of his correspondence with Newton was on these themes. He showed him drafts of his commentary on St Paul's epistles, although he continues to find his relationship with Newton precarious (L3275).

From his early years Locke took opportunities to receive travellers' reports on the flora and fauna, and manners and mores, of distant lands. His namesake, John Lock, was an East India Company merchant, the most far-flung of his correspondents. He wrote from Surat in India and Amoy in China, letters which took ten and twelve months to reach Locke (L3046, L3136). Lock provides an intricate account of commodities, prices, and profits in the trade between India and China, and of the Mogul emperor Aurangzib. The Highlands of Scotland were scarcely less exotic, and Locke hears of folkloric investigations in the Western Isles (L3018).

Locke retained one minor office, membership of the Commission of Appeals in Excise. When the commission was renewed at the accession of Queen Anne, all officeholders were required to take several oaths (L3161). The ubiquity of political oath-taking may shed light on Locke's remarks in the *Two Treatises* about what constitutes 'explicit consent' to a regime.

Locke's powers of advocacy were sought by a Fellow of the Royal College of Physicians (L3045). The physicians were locked in conflict with the Society of Apothecaries, whom they regarded as encroaching on their professional monopoly of diagnosis and prescription. The quarrel was complicated by the emergence of a rebellious group within the College, frustrated by the College's restrictive practices. Locke's correspondent assumes that Locke will side with the College's establishment.

Requests for patronage continued to flow. A judge's widow, Lady Eyre, whose eldest son was an MP and the second a clergymen, seeks a civil service position for the third (L3081). A politician's widow, Lady Calverley, believing herself to be dying of breast cancer, entreats Locke for a position for a young acquaintance (L3222).

A new admirer was a Catholic playwright turned philosopher, Catharine Trotter (later Cockburn). In 1702 she published a defence of Locke's *Essay* against the charge of materialism. Elizabeth Berkeley brings her to Locke's attention (L3153), and Locke sends Trotter a grateful letter (L3234).

Among the letters concerning Locke's little estate at Pensford, one is especially telling (L3310). It instructs his agent to send in the bailiff to tenants whose rents are seriously in arrears, but also to spend twenty shillings at Christmas on bread for the 'honest and industrious' poor of the village.

Locke was not given to biographical writing, but he responded when asked for an account of the Arabist Edward Pococke, whom he had known at Christ Church. This memoir is his most sustained attempt at a character portrait (L3321). In his covering letter he remarks, 'I have not known a fitter person than he, to be preserved as an example, and proposed to the imitation of men of letters'. Locke meanwhile contemplates his own decay, striving to hold at bay the 'sullenness' and 'mystick' disengagement of old age (L3198).

3018. Andrew Fletcher to Locke, Saltoun, Scotland, 14 October 1701

He who delivers this to you, is Mr Martin the author of the little book concerning St Kilda:[1] He comes up fraughted,[2] with new curiositys of the kind; to wit, materials for a natural and moral history of the rest of wersterne isles of Scotland.[3] Among other things you will be mightyly pleased with his account concerning that which is called the Second, but more properly the first or prophetick sight;[4] as well as smell, and hearing. Their is so little encouragement for such a man herre, that if he can meete with any in England, he thincks of staying their or going further abroad. I belive he may be very proper for what he pretends, the waiting upon some young Gentleman, eather at the university, or abroad: for he is a very sober man, of good temper, and conduct. He will communicate to you all he knows, tho I thinck to no body else, least he might come to see some things in print, befor he himself had published them. Sir I was very glad of the occasion, to recommend him to you, knowing how much delight you take in new discoverys about natural things; and that you are no less pleased to have an opportunity of doing good. . . .

3045. Dr Robert Pitt to Locke, [London], 22 November 1701

I apprehend, that you will be fully acquainted with the circumstance of our Affairs,[1] when I assure you, that all the Squabbles among the members of the College (against their new statutes, officers, punishments, as of one in 7 or 8 Years) have no other foundation, [than] that that Anti College Party recommended themselves to the Apothecarys favour and Interest and consequently to the Publick, by obliging them in betraying the Profession to their incroachments for the present profitt. I confess, the greater part of the

---

[1] Martin Martin, *A Late Voyage to St Kilda* (1698), part of Sir Robert Sibbald's scheme for a systematic description of Scotland.

[2] Freighted.

[3] *A Description of the Western Islands of Scotland, containing a full account of the situation, extent, soils, product . . . the ancient and modern government, religion and customs . . . methods to improve trade* (1703). Samuel Johnson and James Boswell took it with them on their tour of the Hebrides in 1773.

[4] 'A Particular Account of the Second Sight, or Faculty of Foreseeing Things to Come, by Way of Vision', in *A Description*. There was extensive contemporary interest in Second Sight, evinced especially in Robert Kirk's *The Secret Commonwealth* (1691).

---

[1] The Royal College of Physicians, which put its case in its quarrel with the Apothecaries in *The Present State of Physick* (1701) and *The Necessity of the Dispensary* (1701). The College was also divided within itself.

Nob[ility] and Gentry etc. has been prevail'd on by so many Ap[othecaries] and one half almost of the College to the prejudice of the Society. About 20 Phys[icians] of the Town have lately defy'd the College, when invited into its Fellowship. The pretence was the support of the University licence per totam Angliam;[2] the true design to declare on the Apothecary's side. This Cause came to tryal before my Lord Cheif Justice Holt[3] this week: who declar'd in the College Favour, that every Practicer of the Town is oblig'd to the College Examination and Licence. The City begins to be sensible of the true state of the Case; and very many of the best Families, as well as many thousands of the meaner, have experienc'd, that many diseases are cur'd with few medicines, that ours are beyond exception, and that no profitt will ever be made on that Part. They observ, that even from the Poor, the Apothecary has greater profitt, than the Faculty[4] from the Rich: That 90 in 100£ (of which bills we have had in the City very many lately) were the fees to the Ap. when the Phys. probably had 8 or 10 in his Fees. Those Expressions in the Papers can only be excus'd from the great provocations some time since given, by Lampoons, and the basest Characters industriously spread on every Member of the Dispensary:[5] when nothing had been publish't but the first book of the transaction before the Committee of Aldermen. Besides, you are sensible of the humour of the Age, that a Contest of this Nature cannot be manag'd without coming in a little time to these Extremities. We are publishing an Account of the value and price of all the Medicines; leav it to the Publick to determine the profitt to be allow'd, and do only demand, that the Ap. be separately consider'd for his trouble of Attendance. Upon these Terms, we are satisfy'd, the People will apply for advice to the Physician, who has no end to interfere with the Cure of his Patient. I desire the favour of your Opinion, if you can recollect any thing, which may assist the most generous Design of this Age. We shall, as in Consultation, readily close with a Proposal supported with your Reasons. You will, as the General, judge better, being out of the Fray and your Orders will be as readily observ'd. . . .

3046. John Lock to Locke, Amoy, China, 23 November 1701

. . . I esteem it a Priviledge given mee to write you from the remotest Parts my fortune Leads mee to, and should make use of it much oftener if my education and Imployments, which has bin from the School, with Merchants and Merchandizing, were able to furnish mee with such discoveries as has escaped the notice of those who have made it their peculiar business to search

---

[2] 'In all England': the College claimed control of medical practice within 7 mls. of London; some university graduates claimed they were licensed to practice anywhere in England.
[3] Sir John Holt.   [4] The physicians.
[5] The College opened a dispensary in 1697 or 1698, for the sick poor, and to counter the apothecaries by creating its own supply of drugs.

into the Pollicy, Religion, Goverment, and the products of these Forreigne countryes, which is difficult for mee to doe that goe noe deaper than a Sea Port,
and am conversant constantly with people of my owne profession and the
greatest part of my Time imploy'd in the disposeal of what I bring, and pro-
cureing effects proper for another market, but since I write to a person of soe
great worth and soe well acquainted, how mankind coms to gather all their
knowledge of these things, I shall not seek for further matter to troble you
with than what I find in my dayly imployment

I come from Surat[1] in the Service of his Excellency Sir William Norris[2] his
Majesties Embassador to the Great Mogull[3] and Sir Nicholas Wait[4] his Consull
at Surat, with a ship of the Natives burthen 400 Tons, sailed by an English
Comander and Officers, and Laschars[5] or blackfellows, their wages and hyre
of the Ship for 12 months with the Bottomry of what mony was advanced
for her outsett will amount to 25731 Rupees which is 64 Rupees per Ton,
A Europe Ship of that Burthen for 12 months, at the usual Demorage[6] the
Companies pay is £9 Stg. per Ton at 27 Pence per Rupee, is Rupees 80 per
Ton, soe that there is Lost by imploying a Europe Ship 16 Rupees or 36 Shillings
in every Ton.

The Goods I brought from Surat were Putchuck,[7] Olibanum.[8] Mirh,
Cominseed,[9] Cotton, and Pearle, all which renders good Proffit, especially
Cotton sold for above 100 per Cent. but being very bulky noe great value can
bee brought of it, and Pearle gives 30 per Cent if bought well, for the most
part $\frac{2}{3}$ of the Ships Stock is in Dollars[10] or other Silver.

Comodities proper for Surat, are Copper as much as can bee procured,
formerly Quicksilver[11] and Vermillion, but now not demanded, Sugar, Sugar
Candy, Tutenegue,[12] Camphire,[13] China Ware, and Gold, which last when
it is at touch for touch,[14] and 100 waters,[15] that is full fine, 1 Tale[16] of Gold is
worth just 10 Tale of Dollar Silver, but usually there is allow'd 3 or 4 waters,
according to the demand for it.

At our first arrival wee agree with the Hoppo or Custom Master for the
Ships Messurage,[17] which with Presents, houserent, and Linguister[18] hyre,
for the Ship I come in will come to 1500 Tale[19] or £500 Stg. and to purchase
the foregoing Comodities, are obliged to trust the Merchants with most of
our Mony and Goods and often are very dillatory in our dispatch, tho am
now in hopes to Leave this Port in 3 or 4 days

---

[1] In Gujarat on the west coast of India.
[2] Envoy to India to seek trading privileges for the New East India Company.
[3] Aurangzib.   [4] Waite, New East India Company agent.   [5] Lascars: Indian sailors.
[6] Demurrage: presumably here meaning the rate paid for the period of the voyage.
[7] A root used for medicine and joss-sticks.   [8] Frankincense.   [9] Cumin.
[10] Spanish silver dollar, the medium of international exchange in China.
[11] Mercury.   [12] Tutenag: an alloy of copper, zinc, and nickel.   [13] Camphor.
[14] Touch: a test for the quality of gold or silver by rubbing it on a touchstone.
[15] Of the best lustre or quality; as in the phrase 'the first water'.   [16] Tael: Chinese ounce.
[17] Measurage: duty payable on cargo.   [18] Interpreter.   [19] Tael: Chinese currency.

The Trade from Surat to China is at Present the most proffitable, and by a modest Computation beleive may cleer 55 per Cent. for my Imployers[20] which will bee neer £7000 Stg. when am engaged in any other Voyage I shall take the freedom I doe now to give you a short Account of it, presuming what is Proffitable to private Merchants here, is an encrease of Riches to the Nation, which being so, you that are one of the Protectors of our Comerce, and Love to nourish the Least branches of it, will not bee displeased with what may bee offerd, . . .

3081. Lady Martha Eyre to Locke, [Newhouse, Wiltshire?], 31 January [1702]

[W]ere you not a most generus friend I should not thus persecute you by giving you a freesh troble that nothing less can Excuse.—had you ben in town I had wayted one you, to have beged your advise in Relation to my youngest Son,[1] breed a Merchant and whose Time[2] unhappily Expiered when nothing was to be dun in the way he was designed for.—some Commissioners of the Customes, were pleased to say he was so fite for Employment with them, or in the Treashury, Navye Offece or Admiralty, that were he but known he could not want it,[3]—and a Great Merchant the other day Reproved mee, for not geting him Recommended to my Lord high Admiral,[4] asuring mee I need not fiend out a pertickular thing to aske, he having a general knowledge that would Capacittate him for most; he has bin Eight years in Holand and Mr Chitty with whom he served his Aprentisship served the Navye Office with Considerable Storess,—and has by a letter given him an advantagus Charector; I am no good beger; but was not longe Resolveing who to Adress too for the favor of having him Named to my Lord,[5] but with an unacount-able asurance beg it off you as the worthyest hand to goe by,—O be not weary of oblidging Sir your very graitfull hum: ser

3095. Peter King to Locke, London, [17] February [1702]

This day was expected to be the greatest day of this parliament, the busyness thereof being to consider the rights and libertys of the house of Commons,[1]

---

[20] The New East India Company.

[1] Kingsmill Eyre, later secretary of Chelsea Hospital. [2] Apprenticeship.
[3] Could not fail to get it. [4] The Earl of Pembroke. [5] Pembroke.

[1] In relation to the challenge made by the Kentish Petitioners on behalf of the people.

mr Finch[2] moved for it, and he proposed the first question, which was assented to without any division, as were likewise two others, which were

1. That to assert the house of Commons was not the representative of all the people of England was subversive of the Constitution of the house of Commons[3]
2. The same as to asserting that the house of Commons had not power to imprison others besides their members.[4]
3. The same as to libels against the house of Commons

A fourth Question propos'd was th[at . . .] Ref[lec]ting on the house of Commons and praying a dissolution of the parliament were tending to sedition etc that was oppos'd with Courage and heat, so that the Gentlemen who were for it moved to leave out the latter words about praying the dissolution of the parliament, upon which a motion was made to leave the chair,[5] and thereupon the Speaker[6] took the chair and adjourn'd, by which means all the busyness of the Committee is fallen to the ground, and is as if it never were; which is a very great mortification to some people, tho, not to Your most affectionate Cosin and Servant.[7]

3136. John Lock to Locke, Surat, India, 28 April 1702

. . . Aureng Zeeb the Present Emperor as I am inform'd by his Excellency Sir William Norris Baronet, now on his return for Europe.[1] is neer Ninety Six years of Age,[2] and a Man of Great Temporance, worn out rather by Age than any Violent diseases, drinks noe Wine, nor makes use of Women to doe his constitution harm, neither eats or wears any apparrill, but what is the produce of a smale maintenance which he had when [he] Lead the Lyfe of a Priest or Facquir[3] before he usurpt the Throne, which he gott by the Pollicy and assistance of his Sister,[4] put four of his Brothers to death or made away with them, and confin'd his Father[5] about 6 years in Prison where he died,

---

[2] Heneage Finch, extreme Tory MP.

[3] The exact words were: 'That to assert that the house of commons is not the only representatives of the commons of England, tends to the subversion of the rights and privileges of the house of commons, and the fundamental constitution of the government of this kingdom.'

[4] The Commons had imprisoned the Kentish Petitioners.

[5] i.e. for the House to come out of Committee, the Committee not being chaired by the Speaker.

[6] Sir Robert Harley.

[7] In L3101 Locke responds that he is glad the day 'went off . . . soe well'. The episode implies a populist reading of the *Two Treatises*: i.e. that parliament is subordinate to the constituent power of the people.

[1] L3046, n. 2; he died from dysentery on the voyage home.

[2] Aurangzib was born in 1618 and died in 1707.　　[3] Fakir: ascetic.

[4] Raushan-Ara.　　[5] Shah Jahán.

he has reign'd neer 46 years and Govern'd his Kingdom with great wisdom, appoints Eunuchs to bee in the most private appartments of his Umbrahs[6] that nothing is don but what is knowne to him even in their secret retirements with their Women, has Harcarrars[7] or newswriters in all his Provinces, and neer his Ministers to write him all manner of informations, nor will suffer them to Visit one another to prevent Cabals. which his good intelligence has often Prevented. My Lord Embassador has the 10 first years written in Persian, but the Emperour will not permit the History of his Reign to be carry'd on any further, his Excellency has also his Picture which his Lordship promist mee if he had an Opertunity to shew it you before he deliver'd it the King, he would do me that favour, and also gratifye your Curious inquiries into the Actions and manners of these People.

There are four Sons which will all make their Pretentions to the Crowne after his decease, and those that have the greatest force have the neerest title to the throne, but some are of one Opinion, and others of the contrary, but as yett not knowne who will bee the Successor to soe wise a Prince, and tis thought he will dye peaceably and fall Like a Leaf from a Tree, when the Force of Nature has quite forsaken him.

We have Braminees[8] of Several Casts here, but never had any acquaintance with any they not understanding our Language nor wee theres, but since you are pleas'd to point out to mee what may bee both usefull and pleasant, I shall this Season when the Ships are gon make some Search after those that are most Likely to furnish mee with some knowledge of their Religion, and Morals and the Laws of their Country. . . .

3153. Elizabeth Burnet [née Berkeley] to Locke, Salisbury, 20 June 1702

Haveing lately read a book[1] writ in answer to some objections made some time ago to your most excelent Essay, and according to that litle judgment I have thinking it tho not worthy of its subject yet comendably performed, I thought you might not be ill pleased to know a litle more of its Author than you might as yet be informed of; her Father[2] for I suppose you know 'tis a Female writter, was a Capatin of a ship in K Jeames time and dyed about the time of the revolution; I think he was a scoch man, as her Mother[3] is a scoch women, who aplying her self to the Bishop[4] in hopes to gett some old arear, I came to that litle acquantance I have which is seeing her Daughter three or four times. they were left in mean curcumstances, and I know not by what

---

[6] Omrah: lord, grandee.   [7] Hircarras: spies, messengers.   [8] Brahmins.

[1] Catharine Trotter, *A Defence of the Essay of Human Understanding* (1702).   [2] David Trotter.
[3] Sarah Ballenden.   [4] Elizabeth's husband, Bishop Gilbert Burnet of Salisbury.

misfortune of ill compeny both the writter of the late book and her sister turned papist and are so I think at this time, your Champion is unmaried,[5] and having as you see a more then comon genius write three plays,[6] partly to gratefy her humer that was studious, but more I beleeve to help her too live, that sort of writing where it takes being the most profitable; but as you will allow by her late litle book, 'tis great pety her studys are not better directed, and I can't but admier that one of such clear thoughts can be of a relegion that puts such schacles on the exercies of thought and reason, if by any accident you see her, or think it fit to take farther notice by writing to her[7] I wish you could be an instrument to free her from those erors, she would perhaps pay more difference to you than to any other, which would be not only a kindness in its self, but make her more capable of the asistence and incouragment of her Frinds; she knows not at all that I have informed you of her, but since by accident I knew this, I thought it might not be amis to let you know; . . .

3161. Locke to Peter King, Oates, 7 July 1702

. . . I have an account from Mr Tilson[1] that our Commission is passed, soe that I think it convenient, (Pray tell me if be not necessar) to take the Oathes[2] at Chelmsford at the Sessions[3] there next week. I aske you also whither the certificate which is to be signed by the parson and Churchwardens where I take the Sacrament[4] ought not to be on stampd paper.[5] If soe pray send me one in your Thursday nights packet and direct your letter to Mr Harrisons at the Crown in Harlow[6] that soe I may be sure of it Friday morning, and write by that post whether it be not necessary to take the Oathes now, this being the next quarter-sessions after the passeing the Commission. And if the forme of the Certificat of the parson and churchwardens be prescribed by the Act of parliament pray send me also that forme, for we have not the Act here

---

[5] Catherine Trotter returned to Anglicanism in 1707 and married a clergyman, Patrick Cockburn in 1708.

[6] *Agnes de Castro* (1695) (the author was aged 16); *The Fatal Friendship* (1698); *Love at a Loss* (1700). (The 1695–6 season saw the highest proportion ever of new plays on the London stage written by women.)

[7] L3234.

[1] Christopher Tilson, secretary to the Commissioners for Appeals in Excise.

[2] Oaths of Supremacy, Allegiance, and Abjuration. Under the Abjuration Act (1701) citizens were required to abjure the Jacobite Pretender's claim. Pretender: L3497, n. 2.

[3] County magistrates' quarter-sessions. Chelmsford was 15 mls. from Oates.

[4] Under the Test Act (1673), which was designed to exclude Catholics and Dissenters from office, officeholders must receive the Anglican sacrament of the eucharist within three months of appointment and secure a certificate of proof. Dissenters were legally admitted to office only in 1828, though they had evaded the requirement in practice; Catholics in 1829.

[5] Paper bearing a government revenue stamp: a tax was imposed on legal documents.

[6] Innkeeper and postal agent.

and if I faile in any circumstance I shall be disappointed and loose my labour if that be the worst [of it]. . . .

3198. Locke to Benjamin Furly, Oates, 12 October 1702

. . . All the action is on your side the water, and dayly furnishes matter:[1] We here make noe noise, and I am too far out of the way (which I am not sorry for) to hear any thing that does not. And whither it be society[2] or dull old age, or any thing else, I have noe curiosity to be prying, or to acquaint my self with the bias or bent of affairs, only I shall always be glad to hear of publick events that tend to the prosperity and preservation of my country, and the security of Europe. I promised my self much satisfaction in your company here this sommer, and 'tas been a great disappointment to me to miss it. Besides the joy it would have been to me to see You again I flatter my self we could have passed some days togeather not unpleasantly, though news and politiques had been excluded out of our conversation. I think my self upon the brink of an other world, and being ready to leave those shuflings which have generaly too broad a mixture of folly and corruption, should not dispair with you to find matters more suited to the thoughts of a rational creature to entertein us. Doe not think now that I am grown either a Stoick or a Mystick. I can laugh as heartily as ever, and be in pain for the publick as much as you. I am not grown into a sulleness that puts off humanity, noe nor mirth neither. come and trye. But I have laid by the simplicity of troubleing my head about things that I cannot give the least turn to one way or t'other. I rather choose to imploy my thoughts about some thing that may better my self, and perhaps some few other such simple fellows as I am. You may easily conclude this written in a chimny corner in some obscure hole out of the way of the busy men of this world. And I think not the worse of it for being so: And I pray heartily it may continue soe as long as I live. I live in fear of the Bustlers, and would not have them come near me. Such quiet fellows as you are, that come without drum and trumpet, with whom one can talke upon equall termes, and receive some benifet by their company I should be glad to have in my neighbourhood, or to see some times though they came from totherside the water. Though I have noe thing to say to you nor send to you but my hearty good wishes, which are far from news to you, yet I am you see got into a veyn of talking, and know not how long I should run on in it, did not my arm stop my hand. I have of late soe great a pain in my arm when I write, that I am often fain to give off. But tis not strange that my frail tenement has decays in it, tis rather to be wonderd that it hath lasted soe long. . . .

---

[1] War was renewed in May. The Duke of Marlborough was waging a successful campaign between the Meuse and the Rhine.
[2] Satiety.

3222. Lady Mary Calverley to Locke, 28 November [1702]

I am obliged to make use of a Secretary, my breast at present being so
painfull that my writeing hand is disabled. they have pronounc'd it a Cancer,[1]
so that I am afraid I shall never again have the pleasure to salute you with
my own pen.

I have a boon to beg of you, before I leave this life, I dont question a kind
return from you, haveing had all my life time such proofs of your freindship;
It is this that you would please to write a billet to my Lord Peterborough,[2]
and direct it to me in Soho square, in favour of Mr Banbary, an honest
parsons son,[3] though but five and twenty has been some years set up Bookbinder. but the world has so frown'd upon him, that he has been forc'd to
leave of his trade and is now destitute of all helps. What this unfortunate man
petitions, is that my Lord would have the Goodness to take him along with
him to the Westindies.[4] he writes readily and well, and hopes by that
qualification to be serviceable to my Lord. and if No Ensigns or other place
be to be dispos'd of, he would throw himself under my Lords protection
hopeing by his diligence to recommend himself to his Lordship, and in the
mean time desires onely necessaries for life; such acts as these must recommend us in the next world . . .

3232. Jean Barbeyrac to Locke, Berlin,
27 December 1702 / 6 January 1703

I have never felt such a great honour, nor such great pleasure, as when I received
your reply.[1] It would have been much for me if you had deigned only to excuse
me the liberty which I took in writing to you; but generous persons, like
you, do not oblige by half measures, they are not content until they have
liberally spread their favours. I have a happy experience of it in the goodnesses
which you shower upon me to such a point that I am confused by it. As to
the praises which it pleased you to make of me, I do not dare flatter myself
that they are true. I consider them to be a kindly and ingenious ruse, which
you use to encourage a person in whom you think you see some disposition
to seek the truth, and to follow its lights. I am all too aware of the smallness
of my genius, and *quàm mihi sit curta supellex,*[2] to draw any consequence from

---

[1] Yet she lived until *c.*1716.   [2] Formerly Lord Mordaunt.

[3] Perhaps son of Cyprian Banbury, rector of Woolsthorpe, Lincolnshire.

[4] In fact Peterborough declined the command of an expedition to Jamaica.

[1] Barbeyrac had written to Locke with a question about the concept of simple ideas in the *Essay.*
Locke recorded the query and his own response in a footnote to II. xv. 9 in the 5th edn.

[2] 'How poorly equipped I am' (Persius, *Satires,* iv. 52).

your generosity in my own favour, if only it is that I have had the happiness to find myself of that number to which you have had occasion to make sensible the effects of your generosity. I will put all your goodness to good use, Monsieur, by attempting to make myself worthy of your beneficence, and by taking a part of the praise which you give me, although I find no foundation for it in myself.

After this, Monsieur, I am infinitely obliged to you for the explanations which you were kind enough to send to me on some parts of your book. I am entirely satisfied with them. I will take the liberty of proposing my doubts to you, as soon as one occurs to me which is capable of perplexing me, since you invite me to do so so obligingly. But by all appearances, I will not often give you this trouble, since, the more one reflects on your work, the more the light which gleams in all its parts disperses the clouds caused by the novelty, the depth, and the abstraction of your ideas.

. . . I am working at present on a translation, and I base the greatest part of its success on the advantageous approbation which you gave to the original in your treatise on *Education*.[3] It is the book *de Jure Naturae et Gentium*, by the Baron Pufendorf.[4] I will not fail to show the value of the judgement which you have made on this book in a preface, by placing it before Grotius' *De Jure Belli et Pacis*.[5] I will ask Monsieur Coste to send you the plan I am working on, and I hope that you will honour me with your good opinions, as you did upon the manner of learning your English Language. Otherwise, Monsieur, I should find that I returned your generosity badly, if I refused your kind offer to send me an English Bible and a dictionary; especially since I am in a country where these sorts of books are not to be found. I have indicated to Monsieur Coste the means whereby he may send them to me. With this recourse, and the method which you prescribed to me, I hope one day to be able to know perfectly all the beauty of your works, when I am capable of reading them in their original language. . . .

3234. Locke to Catharine Trotter, Oates, 30 December 1702

There was nothing more public, than the obligation I received from you,[1] nor any thing more concealed, than the person I was obliged to.[2] This is a generosity above the strain of this groveling age, and like that of superior spirits, who assist without shewing themselves. I used my best endeavours to

---

[3] *Education*, § 186; see also *Political Essays*, 352; L2320.
[4] *On the Law of Nature and Nations* (1672). Barbeyrac's translation was published at Amsterdam in 1706; Basil Kennett's English edition in 1717.
[5] *On the Laws of War and Peace* (1625).

[1] Catharine Trotter, *A Defence of the Essay of Human Understanding* (1702).
[2] She had tried to conceal her authorship.

draw from you, by your Bookseller,[3] the confession of your name, the want whereof made me, that I could, whilst you kept yourself under that reserve, no more address myself directly to you with good manners, than I could without rudeness have pulled off your mask by force, in a place where you were resolved to conceal yourself. Had not this been so, the bearer hereof[4] had not the first time have come to you, without a letter from me, to acknowledge the favour you had done me. You not affording me an opportunity for that, I designed to make you some small acknowledgement, in a way, that chance had opened to me, without your consent. But this gentleman transgressed my order in two main points of it. The one was, in delaying it so long: The other was, in naming me to you, and talking of matters, which he had no commission from me to mention. What he deserves from you for it, must be left to your mercy. For I cannot in earnest be angry with him for procuring me, without any guilt of mine, an opportunity to own you for my protectress, which is the greatest honour my Essay could have procured me. Give me leave therefore to assure you, that as the rest of the world take notice of the strength and clearness of your reasoning, so I cannot but be extremely sensible, that it was employed in my defence. You have herein not only vanquished my adversary,[5] but reduced me also absolutely under your power, and left no desires more strong in me, than those of meeting with some opportunity, to assure you, with what respect and submission I am,

> Madam,
> Your most humble, and most obedient servant

3275. Locke to Peter King, Oates, 30 April 1703

...I am puzzeld in a little affair, and must beg your assistance for the clearing of it. Mr Newton in Autumn last made me a visit here. I shewd him my Essay upon the Corinthians[1] with which he seemd very well pleased, but had not time, staying but one night, to looke it all over. But promisd me if I would send it him he would carefully peruse it, and send me his observations and opinion. I sent it him before Christmas, but hearing no thing from him I about a month or six weeks since writ to him, as the inclosed tells you with the remaining part of this story. when you have read it and sealed it I desire you to deliver it at your convenience. He lives in German Street[2] four or five doors west of Mrs Lockharts.[3] you must not goe on a Wednesday for that is his day of being at the tower.[4] The reason why I desire you to deliver it to

---

[3] John Nutt and William Turner.   [4] Peter King.
[5] Thomas Burnet, *Remarks upon An Essay* (1697); *Second Remarks* (1697); *Third Remarks* (1699).

[1] Part of a *Paraphrase and Notes on the Epistles of St Paul*.   [2] Jermyn Street.
[3] Martha Lockhart.   [4] Tower of London: Newton was Master of the Mint, housed there.

him your self, is that I would fain discover what is the reason of his so long silence. I have several reasons to think him truly my friend, but he is a nice[5] man to deale with, and a little too apt to raise in himself suspitions where there is no ground. Therefore when you talke to him of my papers and of his opinion of them pray doe it with all the tenderness in the world, but talke soe to him of them, as to discover if you can, why he kept them soe long and was so silent. But this you must doe without askeing why he did soe, or discovering in the least that you are desirous to know. You will doe well to acquaint him that you intend to see me at Whitson tide, and shall be glad to bring a letter to me from him or any thing else he will please to send. This perhaps may quicken him and make him dispatch those papers if he has not done it already. It may a little let you into the freer discourse with him if you let him know that when you have been here with me you have seen me busy on them (and the Romans too, if he mentions them too, for that I told him I was upon when he was here), and have had a sight of some part of what I was doeing. Mr Newton is really a very valuable man not onely for his wonderfull skill in Mathematicks but in divinity too and his great knowledg in the Scriptures where in I know few his equals. And therefore pray manage this whole matter so as not onely to preserve me in his good opinion but to increase me in it, and be sure to press him to noe thing but what he is forward of himself to doe . . .

3310. Locke to Cornelius Lyde, Oates, 28 June 1703

I here with send you by my Cosin King an account of arears of rent that were due to me at our Lady day last was twelve month according to the account you sent me the 15th of August last. I have also sent you a warrant for distraining on Mary Cooke[1] if she has not paid you before it comes to your hands. I beleive Pensford is not without a Baylif in it, he perhaps will be fitest to execute it. You must tell my Cosin King whom you think fitest to direct it to, that it may be donne accordingly. Eight year is too long to let a rent run in arear, upon promise from time to time of payment which is never donne. I am resolvd to stay noe longer

I desire also that the arear may be got in from William Gullock and that he may be sufferd noe longer to be behindhand. If he will not pay by fair means I shall take a shorter way than to aske and solicit from time to time

---

[5] Over-particular.

[1] A widow; her son George Horwood was approached. Peter King reported later that 'Horwood is very poor, but being frighted, hath promised to pay the Mony at Pensford fair, which if he doth not, mr Lyde will distrain' (L3367, 4 Nov.).

to noe purpose which tends to noe thing but with a great deale of trouble to loose the money at last[2]

Hanny also has a long time promised to pay some, if he gives me fair words and does noe thing I can looke on it as noe other but an intention to deceive me and to laugh at me. He were therefore best shew an honest mind and pay some least it cost him dearer.[3]

I have desired my Cosin King to present Mrs Lyde your wife with a piece of plate from me which I desire her to accept

I not writeing to you last winter near the time I know not whether the poor of Pensford had the bread that I usualy give them about Christmas. That it may not hereafter be forgotten I desire that you would as long as you doe me the favour to receive my rent there, every year about Christmas lay out twenty shillings in bread to be distributed to the poor of Pensford espetialy to those that are old and cannot worke and those who have a numerous familye of small children whom they cannot well maintain. still prefering the honest and industrious to those that are or have been lazy and vitious:[4] and this I desire you to doe every year whether I mention it again to you hereafter or noe. . . .

3321. Locke to [Humphry Smith], Oates, 23 July 1703

I have so great a Veneration for the Memory of that Excellent Man,[1] whose Life you tell me you are writing,[2] that when I set my self to recollect what Memoirs I can (in answer to your Desire) furnish you with; I am asham'd I have so little, in particular, to say on a Subject that afforded so much. For I conclude you so well acquainted with his Learning and Virtue, that I suppose it would be superfluous to trouble you on those Heads. However, give me leave not to be wholly silent upon this Occasion: So extraordinary an Example, in so degenerate an Age, deserves for the Rarity, and I was going to say, for the Incredibility of it, the Attestation of all that knew him, and consider'd his Worth. The Christian World is a Witness of his great Learning; that, the Works he publish'd would not suffer to be conceal'd: nor could his Devotion and Piety lie hid, and be unobserv'd in a College where his

---

[2] Later: 'Gullock hath paid 14s. towards the arrears, and promises to pay the rest in a little time'; but he too is 'verry Poore' (L3367, 4 Nov.).

[3] Something was extracted from Joseph Hanny, likewise 'very poore'.

[4] See Locke's *Essay on the Poor Law* (1697): *Political Essays*, 182–98.

[1] Edward Pocock, Arabist, who studied at Corpus Christi College, was latterly a canon of Christ Church, professor of Arabic, then of Hebrew. A hugely erudite scholar of Middle Eastern languages.

[2] Smith did not publish a biography. Extracts from Locke's letter appeared in Leonard Twells's 'Life' prefixed to Pocock's *Theological Works* (1740).

constant and regular assisting at the Cathedral Service,[3] never interrupted by sharpness of Weather, and scarce restrain'd by down-right want of Health; shew'd the Temper and Disposition of his Mind. But his other Virtues and excellent Qualities, had so strong and close a covering of Modesty and unaffected Humility, that tho they shone the brighter to those who had the Opportunities to be more intimately acquainted with him, and Eyes to discern and distinguish Solidity from Shew, and esteem Virtue that sought not Reputation; yet they were the less taken notice and talk'd of by the Generality of those to whom he was not wholly unknown. Not that he was at all close and reserv'd, but on the contrary, the readiest to communicate to any one that consulted him. Indeed he was not forward to talk, nor ever would be the leading Man in the Discourse, tho it were on a Subject that he understood better than any of the Company; and would often content himself to sit still and hear others debate, in matters which he himself was more a Master of. He had often the Silence of a Learner, where he had the Knowledg of a Master: And that not with a Design, as is often, that the Ignorance any one betray'd, might give him the Opportunity to display his own Knowledg with the more Lustre and Advantage, to their Shame; or censure them when they were gone. For these Arts of Triumph and Ostentation, frequently practis'd by Men of Skill and Ability, were utterly unknown to him; 'twas very seldom that he contradicted any one: or if it were necessary at any time to inform any one better, who was in a Mistake, it was in so soft and gentle a manner, that it had nothing of the Air of Dispute or Correction, and seem'd to have little of Opposition in it. I never heard him say any thing that put any one that was present the least out of Countenance; nor ever censure, or so much as speak diminishingly of any one that was absent. He was a Man of no irregular Appetites; if he indulg'd any one too much, it was that of Study, which his Wife[4] would often complain of (and, I think, not without Reason) that a due Consideration of his Age and Health could not make him abate. Tho he was a Man of the greatest Temperance in himself, and the farthest from Ostentation and Vanity in his way of Living; yet he was of a liberal Mind, and given to Hospitality: which, considering the Smallness of his Preferments, and the numerous Family of Children he had to provide for, might be thought to have out-done those who made more Noise and Shew. His Name, which was in great Esteem beyond Sea, and that deservedly, drew on him Visits from all Foreigners of Learning, who came to Oxford to see that University. They never fail'd to be highly satisfy'd with his great Knowledg and Civility, which was not always without Expence. Tho at the Restoration of King Charles, when Preferment rain'd down upon some Mens Heads, his Merits were so overlook'd, or forgotten, that he was barely restor'd to what was his before,[5] without

---

[3] The chapel at Christ Church is also the cathedral of Oxford diocese.
[4] Mary Burdet of West Worldham, Hampshire. They had six sons and three daughters.
[5] He had been ejected from his canonry by the Republic in 1649.

receiving any new Preferment then, or at any time after; yet I never heard him take any the least Notice of it, or make the least Complaint in a Case that would have grated sorely on some Mens Patience, and have fill'd their Mouths with Murmuring, and their Lives with Discontent. But he was always unaffectedly chearful; no Marks of any thing that lay heavy at his Heart for his being neglected, ever broke from him. He was so far from having any Displeasure lie conceal'd there, that whenever any Expressions of Dissatisfaction for what they thought hard Usage broke from others in his Presence, he always diverted the Discourse: And if it were any body with whom he thought he might take that liberty, he silenc'd it with visible Marks of Dislike.

Tho he was not, as I said, a forward, much less an assuming Talker; yet he was the farthest in the World from sullen or morose. He would talk very freely, and very well of all parts of Learning, besides that wherein he was known to excel. But this was not all; he could discourse very well of other things. He was not unacquainted with the World, tho he made no shew of it. His backwardness to meddle in other People's matters, or to enter into Debates, where Names and Persons were brought upon the Stage, and Judgments and Censures were hardly avoided; conceal'd his Abilities in matters of Business and Conduct from most People. But yet I can truly say, that I knew not any one in that University, whom I would more willingly consult in any Affair that requir'd Consideration, nor whose Opinion I thought better worth the hearing than his, if he could be drawn to enter into it, and give his Advice.

Tho in Company he never us'd himself, nor willingly heard from others, any personal Reflections on other Men, tho set off with a Sharpness that usually tickles, and by most Men is mistaken for the best, if not the only seasoning of pleasant Conversation; yet he would often bear his part in innocent Mirth, and by some apposite and diverting Story, continue and heighten the Good-Humour.[6] . . .

I know not whether you find amongst the Papers of his, that are, as you say, put into your Hands, any Arabick Proverbs, translated by him. He has told me that he had a Collection of 3000, as I remember; and that they were, for the most part, very good. He had, as he intimated, some thoughts of Translating them, and adding some more, where they were necessary to clear any Obscurities; but whether he ever did any thing in it before he died, I have not heard. But to return to what I can call to mind, and recover of him.

I do not remember, that in all my Conversation with him, I ever saw him once angry, or to be so far provok'd, as to change Colour or Countenance, or Tone of Voice. Displeasing Accidents and Actions would sometimes occur; there is no help for that: But nothing of that kind moved him, that I saw, to any passionate Words; much less to Chiding or Clamour. His Life appear'd to me, one constant Calm. How great his Patience was in his long

---

[6] There follows a tedious anecdote involving a college porter's beard.

and dangerous Lameness,[7] (wherein there were very terrible and painful Operations) you have, no doubt, learnt from others. I happen'd to be absent from Oxford most of that time; but I have heard, and believe it, that it was suitable to the other parts of his Life. To conclude, I can say of him, what few Men can say of any Friend of theirs, nor I of any other of my Acquaintance; that I do not remember I ever saw in him any one Action that I did, or could in my own Mind blame, or thought amiss in him. . . .

3328. Locke to [Richard King], Oates, 25 August 1703

. . . You ask me, *What is the shortest and surest way for a young Gentleman to attain a true Knowledg of the Christian Religion, in the full and just Extent of it?* for so I understand your Question: if I have mistaken it, you must set me right. And to this I have a short and plain Answer: Let him study the Holy Scripture, especially the New Testament. Therein are contain'd the Words of Eternal Life. It has God for its Author; Salvation for its End; and Truth, without any mixture of Error, for its Matter. So that it is a wonder to me, how any one professing Christianity, that would seriously set himself to know his Religion, should be in doubt where to imploy his Search, and lay out his Pains for his Information; when he knows a Book, wherein it is all contain'd, pure and entire; and whither, at last, every one must have recourse, to verify that of it, which he finds any where else.

Your other Question, which I think I may call two or three, will require a larger Answer. As to Morality, which, I take it, is the first in those things you enquire after; that is best to be found in the Book that I have already commended to [you]. But because you may perhaps think, that the better to observe those Rules, a little warning may not be inconvenient, and some Method of ranging them be useful for the Memory; I recommend to you the *Whole Duty of Man*,[1] as a methodical System: and if you desire a larger View of the Parts of Morality, I know not where you will find them so well and distinctly explain'd, and so strongly inforc'd, as in the Practical Divines of the Church of England. The Sermons of Dr. Barrow,[2] Archbishop Tillotson,[3] and Dr. Whitchcot,[4] are Masterpieces in this kind; not to name abundance of others, who excel on that Subject. If you have a mind to see how far Human Reason advanc'd in the Discovery of Morality, you will have a good Specimen of it in Tully's *Offices*:[5] unless you have a mind to look farther back into the Source,

---

[7] As a result of an illness in 1663.

[1] Anon. (1658), probably by Richard Allestree. The most popular devotional manual of the age.
[2] Isaac Barrow, Newton's predecessor as Lucasian professor of mathematics at Cambridge.
[3] John Tillotson, Archbishop of Canterbury, 1691–4, whose sermons were greatly revered in the 18th cent.
[4] Benjamin Whichcote, Cambridge Platonist, provost of King's College, Cambridge.
[5] Cicero, *De officiis* (*On Duties*).

from whence He drew his Rules; and then you must consult Aristotle, and the other Greek Philosophers.

Tho Prudence be reckon'd among the Cardinal Virtues, yet I do not remember any profess'd Treatise of Morality; where it is treated in its full Extent, and with that Accuracy that it ought. For which possibly this may be a Reason, That every imprudent Action does not make a Man culpable *in foro Conscientiæ*.[6] The Business of Morality I look upon to be the avoiding of Crimes; of Prudence, Inconveniences; the foundation whereof lies in knowing Men and Manners. History teaches this best, next to Experience; which is the only effectual way to get a Knowledg of the World. As to the Rules of Prudence, in the Conduct of Common Life, tho there be several that have imploy'd their Pens therein; yet those Writers have their Eyes so fix'd on Convenience, that they sometimes lose the Sight of Virtue, and do not take care to keep themselves always clear from the Borders of Dishonesty, while they are tracing out what they take to be, sometimes, the securest way to Success: most of those that I have seen on this Subject having, as it seem'd to me, something of this Defect. So that I know none that I can confidently recommend to your young Gentleman, but the Son of Syrac.[7]

To compleat a Man in the Practice of Human Offices,[8] (for to that tend your Enquiries) there is one thing more requir'd; which tho it be ordinarily consider'd, as distinct from both Virtue and Prudence, yet I think it so nearly ally'd to them, that he will scarce keep himself from Slips in both, who is without it. That which I mean, is Good-breeding. The School for a young Gentleman to learn it in, is, the Conversation of those who are well-bred.

As to the last part of your Enquiry, which is after Books that will give an insight into the Constitution of the Government, and real Interest of his Country: To proceed orderly in this, I think the Foundation should be laid, in inquiring into the Ground and Nature of Civil Society; and how it is form'd into different Models of Government; and what are the several Species of it. Aristotle is allow'd a Master in this Science, and few enter upon the Consideration of Government, without reading his *Politicks*. Hereunto should be added, true Notions of Laws in general, and Propriety,[9] the subject Matter about which Laws are made. He that would acquaint himself with the former of these, should thorowly study the judicious Hooker's first Book of *Ecclesiastical Polity*.[10] And Propriety, I have no where found more clearly explain'd than in a Book intituled, *Two Treatises of Government*. But not to load your young Gentleman with too many Books on this Subject, which requires more Meditation than Reading; give me leave to recommend to him Puffendorf's little Treatise, *De Officio Hominis et Civis*.[11]

To get an insight into the particular Constitution of the Government of his own Country, will require a little more Reading; unless he will content

---

[6] 'In the court of conscience'.   [7] The Wisdom of Jesus (Ecclesiasticus).   [8] Duties.
[9] Property.   [10] Richard Hooker, *Of the Laws of Ecclesiastical Polity* (1593).
[11] Samuel Pufendorf, *On the Duty of Man and Citizen* (1673).

himself with such a superficial Knowledg of it, as is contain'd in Chamberlain's *State of England*,[12] or Smith *De Republicâ Anglicanâ*.[13] Your Enquiry manifestly looks farther than that; and to attain such a Knowledg of it, as becomes a Gentleman of England to have, to the Purposes that you mention, I think he should read our antient Lawyers; such as Bracton,[14] Fleta,[15] the *Mirror of Justice*,[16] etc. which our Cousin King can better direct you to, than I; joining with them, the History of England under the Normans, and so continuing it down quite to our Times; reading it always in those Authors, who liv'd nearest those Times: their Names you will find, and Characters often, in Mr. Tyrrel's *History of England*.[17] To which, if there be added, a serious Consideration of the Laws made in each Reign, and how far any of them, influenc'd the Constitution; all these together, will give him a full Insight into what you desire.

As to the Interest of any Country, that, 'tis manifest, lies in its Prosperity and Security. Plenty of well-imploy'd People, and Riches within, and good Alliances abroad, make its Strength. But the ways of attaining these, comprehend all the Arts of Peace and War; the Management of Trade; the Imployment of the Poor; and all those other things that belong to the Administration of the Publick: which are so many, so various, and so changeable, according to the mutable State of Men, and Things in this World; that 'tis not strange, if a very small part of this consists in Book-Learning. He that would know it, must have his Eyes open upon the present State of Affairs; and from thence take his Measures, of what is Good, or Prejudicial, to the Interest of his Country.

You see how ready I am to obey your Commands, tho in Matters wherein I am sensible of my own Ignorance. I am so little acquainted with Books, especially on these Subjects relating to Politicks, that you must forgive me, if perhaps I have not nam'd to you the best in every kind. And you must take it as a Mark of my Readiness to serve you, that I have ventur'd so far out of what lay in my way of Reading, in the Days that I had leisure to converse with Books. The Knowledg of the Bible, and the Business of his Calling, is enough for an ordinary Man; a Gentleman ought to go farther.[18] . . .

3339. Locke to [Richard King], Oates, 27 September 1703

I am sorry to find, that the Question which was the most material, and my Mind was most upon, was answer'd so little to your Satisfaction, that you are

---

[12] Edward Chamberlain, *Angliae Notitia*, a political cyclopedia published periodically from 1669.

[13] Sir Thomas Smith, *De Republica Anglorum* (1583).

[14] Henry de Bracton, *De Legibus et Consuetudinibus Angliae* (*On the Laws and Customs of England*) (13th cent.; printed 1569).

[15] Anonymous, *Fleta, seu Commentarius juris Anglicani* (c.1290; printed 1647); a summary of Bracton.

[16] Andrew Horne, *The Mirror of Justices* (1646).

[17] James Tyrrell, *General History of England* (1697–1700).

[18] Compare *Education*, §§ 182–6; 'Some Thoughts Concerning Reading and Study for a Gentleman', in *Political Essays*, 348–55, 376–80; L2320.

fain to ask it again. Since therefore you ask me a second time, *What is the best Method to study Religion?* I must ask you, what Religion you mean? For if it be, as I understood you before, the Christian Religion in its full Extent and Purity, I can make you no other answer but what I did, viz. That the only way to attain a certain Knowledg of that, is, the Study of the S. Scripture. And my Reason is, because the Christian Religion is a Revelation from God Almighty, which is contain'd in the Bible; and so all the Knowledg we can have of it, must be deriv'd from thence. But if you ask, which is the best way to get the Knowledg of the Romish, Lutheran, or Reformed Religion, of this or that particular Church, etc. each whereof entitles it self to be the true Christian Religion, with some kind of Exclusion or Diminution to the rest; That will not be hard to tell you. But then it is plain, that the Books that best teach you any one of these, do most remove you from all the rest; and in this way of studying, you pitch upon one as the right, before you know it to be so: whereas that Choice should be the Result of your Study of the Christian Religion, in the Sacred Scriptures. And the Method I have propos'd, would, I presume, bring you the surest way to that Church, which, I imagine, you already think most conformable to the Word of God. I find, the Letter you last honour'd me with, contains a new Question, and that a very material one, viz. *What is the best way of Interpreting the Sacred Scripture?* Taking Interpreting to mean Understanding, I think the best way for understanding the Scripture, or the New Testament (for of that the Question will here be, in the first place) is to read it assiduously and diligently; and, if it can be, in the Original: I do not mean, to read every day some certain number of Chapters, as is usual; but to read it so, as to study and consider, and not leave till you are satisfy'd, that you have got the true meaning. To this purpose, it will be necessary to take the Assistance of Interpreters and Commentators; such as are those call'd the Criticks,[1] and Pool's *Synopsis Criticorum;*[2] Dr. Hammond on the New Testament,[3] and Dr. Whitby,[4] etc. I should not think it convenient to multiply Books of this kind, were there any one that I could direct you to, that was infallible. But you will not think it strange, if I tell you, that after all, you must make use of your own Judgment, when you consider, that it is, and always will be, impossible to find an Expositor, whom you can blind-fold rely upon, and cannot be mistaken in following. Such a Resignation as that, is due to the Holy Scriptures alone; which were dictated by the infallible Spirit of God. Such Writings also as Mr. Mede's[5] and Dr. Lightfoot's,[6] are very much conducing to lead us into a true Sense of the Sacred Scriptures. As to the Method of reading them, Order requires, that the Four Evangelists should,

---

[1] *Critici Sacri,* ed. John Pearson *et al.* (9 vols., 1660).

[2] Matthew Poole, *Synopsis Criticorum* (4 vols., 1669–75).

[3] Henry Hammond, *A Paraphrase and Annotations upon all the Books of the New Testament* (1653).

[4] Daniel Whitby, *Paraphrase and Commentary on the New Testament* (1703).

[5] Joseph Mede, *Works* (1644).

[6] John Lightfoot, *Horae Hebraicae et Talmudicae . . . in Acta Apostolorum* (1679).

in the first place, be well study'd and thorowly understood. They all treating of the same Subject, do give great light to one another; and, I think, may, with greatest Advantage, be read in Harmony. To this purpose, Monsieur Le Clerc's,[7] or Mr. Whistons' Harmony of the four Evangelists[8] will be of Use, and save a great deal of Time and Trouble in turning the Bible. They are now both in English, and Mr. Le Clerc's has a Paraphrase. But if you would read the Evangelists in the Original, Mr. Le Clerc's Edition of his Harmony in Greek and Latin will be best.[9] If you find, that by this Method, you advance in the Knowledg of the Gospel; when you have laid a Foundation there to your Satisfaction, it will not be hard to add, what may help you forwards in the Study of other parts of the New Testament. . . .

3346. Richard King to Locke, Exeter, 9 October [1703]

The method you propose[1] for the right understanding of the S[acred] Scriptures I am very well satisfyed is the best. To read Them daily with close application of mind and with sincere intention of heart to make Them the Rule of Life, I am sure is that simple and honest way to attain the true sense of them, which their great Author will never fail to bless. To turn over many Commentators will rather distract than enlighten; but to use none is too much to rely upon our own understanding, and will make us guilty of willful ignorance whilst we depend alone upon our own knowlege. since therefor it is necessary to take the assistance of some Interpreters; such as are least bigotted to a Party will be most likely to give the fairest Interpretation. and such as are generally esteemed the best of every party will sett before our eyes the sense of all Parties, whereby we may have a view of their several opinions and be the better able to exercise our judgements concerning what is true; which, in the scripture Phrase, is to try all things, and to hold fast what is good.[2] Amongst the Commentators which you have not named I esteem no one more for Integrity and candour, great Learning, witt and judgement than Erasmus, whom our first Reformers highly respected. The comparing of Editions is another way to come to the true meaning of the Text; but the best of all (as you advise) is to read the several Gospels in Harmony; which indeed is to make the S[acred] Scripture a comment upon it self.

Now Sir I must heartily thank you for the extraordinary favour you have done me by answering all the Questions my importunate desire to be informed by you did move me to ask you, . . . [T]he experience of many years

---

[7] Jean Le Clerc, *Epistolae Criticae, et Ecclesiasticae* (1700).

[8] William Whiston, *A Short View of the Chronology of the Old Testament, and of the Harmony of the Four Evangelists* (1702).

[9] *Harmonia Evangelica* (1699).

[1] L3339.   [2] 1 Thessalonians. 5:21.

and the knowledge of men and things have made you the perfect Socrates of the Age. and to you I come with the same intention of mind as the young Gentlemen of Greece went to that great man, or the young Romans to Cato Major,[3] to be instructed in those things that would make them wise and happy. and what they sought after from them I know is to be obtained from you, Cui sunt

> Compositum jus, fasque animi, sanctique recessus
> Mentis, et incoctum generoso pectus honesto.[4]

---

[3] Cato the Elder (Cato the Censor), statesman and man of letters.

[4] 'Who have at heart an ordered sense of justice and right, sacred retreats of the mind, and a breast imbued with noble integrity' (Persius, *Satires*, ii. 73–4).

16

Recessional, 1703–1704

Locke's last recorded visit to London was in May 1702. He ventured out little and spent many hours in the chimney seat at Oates. In these last years he was shielded from his adversaries, and from direct confrontation with the vociferous world of political and philosophical controversy, by men of letters acting as protectors, who provided synopses of new publications, wrote ripostes, made book purchases, or took dictation. The most insistent of his young admirers was Anthony Collins, later notorious for his *Discourse of Freethinking* (1713)—a neologism to which he gave currency. Collins may have initiated a correspondence with Locke with a view to posthumous publication, and it is possible that Locke knowingly connived. Locke's letters to Collins are self-conscious disquisitions on the pursuit of truth, the nature of friendship, and the cultivation of those unceremonious manners so much favoured in the 'polite' new century (L3361). One of Collins's tasks was to arrange for Locke's books to be bound. A bookbinder's close cropping of the margins of his Greek New Testament provokes from Locke a denunciation of every branch of the book trade (L3556).

Another new ally was John Shute, later Viscount Barrington, who rose higher in public office than any other contemporary Dissenter. He alerts Locke to the Occasional Conformity controversy, the last political debate that engaged his attention (L3394). Although Locke did not directly address the issue, it provides a context for his unfinished *Fourth Letter for Toleration* (1704). Shute asks Locke to defend the 'Occasional Conformists', those Dissenters who qualified themselves for office by taking the Anglican sacrament just once, as the law required, but who otherwise, even ostentatiously, continued to attend their Nonconformist chapels. They were under threat from Tory attempts to outlaw the practice. To vindicate the Dissenters' cause Shute made use of Locke's *Letter Concerning Toleration* in his *The Rights of Protestant Dissenters* (1704–5).

Locke was apprised of the crisis looming in Scotland. Whereas the English Act of Settlement of 1701 gave statutory force to the Protestant Hanoverian succession, no equivalent act had been passed by the Scottish parliament. During 1703–4 this constitutional hiatus was exploited by an array of anti-English forces, including Jacobites, Presbyterians, and quasi-republicans such as Andrew Fletcher, who sought to extract political and economic concessions from England. Concessions were granted, but by 1707 the outcome—surprising given the circumstances of 1703–4—was the Act of Union with England, which brought an end to the Scottish parliament for nearly three centuries. The Presbyterian Whig James Johnstoun recounts the uncovering of a Jacobite conspiracy and, so he hoped, the impending resolution of the succession crisis at the hands of the Marquis of Tweeddale's newly empowered party, of which he was a conspicuous member (L3497). In fact Tweeddale's project failed, and more energetic English intervention was needed to bring about the Union.

Evidence of the unsteady reputation of Locke's *Essay* made a final appearance in 1703. Several heads of Oxford colleges attempted to have it banned, though others warned of the folly of such a move. Efforts at suppression seem to have failed; indeed the *Essay* rapidly became a textbook. Locke offers a wry comment on the Oxford condemnation (L3483), and a further account of the affair comes from his old friend, James Tyrrell (L3511).

When he first came to Oates, Locke kept a daily record of the weather. He used a 'thermoscope' made by the celebrated instrument-maker Thomas Tompion. He sent his register to Hans Sloane and recommends that the Royal Society promote a national network of weather stations (L3489). The great storm that struck England on 26 November 1703—not equalled until 1987—occasions an anxious letter from Elizabeth Clarke, reporting that Bishop Kidder and his wife had been killed (L3400). A merchant is keen to disclose the discovery of a means to measure longitude at sea accurately, vital for international navigation (L3499). There were to be several such 'discoveries' before the palm went to John Harrison some decades later.

Locke did not live to make use of his last luxury: a chaise for outings, which he instructs to be built after the fashion of Queen Anne's (L3542). However, he did preside over a last convivial feast among the Mashams to celebrate the marriage of Peter King and Anne Seys. His orders for provisions tells much about the luxury foods of the early eighteenth century (L3627).

Locke died at Oates on 28 October 1704, shortly after listening to Damaris Masham reading from the Psalms. His final letter provides his executor, Peter King, with instructions additional to his will, concerning his unpublished writings, and arrangements for the well-being of Damaris's son, Francis, who received a large legacy (L3647). To Anthony Collins he leaves instructions in a letter notable for its desire to protect mother and son from the patriarchal expectations of the husband and father (L3648). In a codicil to his will Locke finally acknowledged 'all the Books whereof I am the Author which have been publishd without my name on them': the three letters on toleration; *The Reasonableness of Christianity* and its two *Vindications*; and the *Two Treatises of Government*, 'whereof Mr Churchill has published severall editions but all very uncorrect'.

3361. Locke to Anthony Collins, Oates, 29 October 1703

... Think that I am as much pleased with your company, as much obleiged by your conversation as you are by mine, and you set me at rest and I am the most satisfied man in the world. You complain of a great many defects and that very complaint is the highest recommendation I could desire to make me love and esteem you and desire your freindship. And if I were now seting out in the world I should think it my great [happyness] to have such a companion as you who had a true relish of truth, would in earnest seeke it with me, from whom I might receive it undisguisd, and to whom I might communicate what I thought true freely. Beleive it my good Friend to Love truth for truths sake is the principal part of humane perfection in this world and the seed plot of all other virtues, and if I mistake not you have as much of it as ever I met with in any body. What then is there wanting to make you equall to the best, and a freind for any one to be proud of? Would you have me take upon me because I have the start of you in the number of years and be supercilious conceited for haveing in a long ramble traveld some countreys which a yonge voyager has not yet had time to see, and from whence one may be sure he will bring larger collections of Solid Knowledg? In good earnest Sir when I consider how much of my life has been trifled away in beaten tracts where I vampd on with others onely to follow those that went before us I cannot but think I have just as much reason to be proud, as if I had travelled all England and (if you will) France too, onely to acquaint my self with the roads and be able to tell how the high ways lye wherein those of equipage and even the herd too travel. Now me thinks (and these are often old mens dreams) I see openings to truth, and direct paths leading to it wherein a little industry and application would setle ones mind with satisfaction even in those matters which you mention and leave noe darkeness or doubt even to the most scrupulous. But this is at the end of my day when my sun is seting. And though the prospect it has given me be what I would not for any thing be without, there is so much irresistible truth beauty and consistency in it, yet it is for one of your age, I think I ought to say, for you your self to set about it as a worke you would put into order and obleige the world with. You see whether my just thoughts of you have led me. and that I shall have no quarrel with you if you will cease to set me as you doe on the higher ground; and to think that I have not as much pleasure and satisfaction from your company as you have from mine. If I were able to live in your neighbour hood in town I should quickly convince you of that, and you scape being haunted by me onely by being out of my reach. A little better acquaintanc will let you see that in the communication of truth between those who receive it in the Love of it, he that answers is no less obleiged than he that asks the question: and therefore you owe me not those mighty thanks you send me for haveing the good luck to say something that pleased you. If it were good seed I am sure it was sown in good grownd and may expect a great increase. . . .

3394. John Shute to Locke, London, 30 November 1703

. . . I confess I vallue my self as much more for being Mr Lockes Favorit, than for being that of a Prince's, as the bounds of his strong sense exceed those of the others Empire. I say this with the more justice Sir, since you have done that in your Province, which they have but attempted in Theirs. You alone have vindicated the Rights and Dignitys of human nature, and have restor'd Liberty to Mens Consciences from the Tyranny of human Laws and their own Passions, Whilest they how well soever supported by Leagues and Alliances, have barely contented themselves with maintaining the freedom of their own Countrys from some degrees of foreign force.

You must not wonder then Sir, that a parcell of People desirous of Liberty and threatned with hardships; Defenceless and Expos'd but Secure in a Pen which has baffled the boldest Champion of Slavery,[1] and expos'd the Sophistry of a more Refind Scheme of Persecution,[2] shou'd fly to You for Protection: and beg of You once more to reasume your pen, and vindicate the Liberty of Ocasionall Communion[3] from the Objections of a last Week's Author:[4] who is but a Second to two other Adversarys, over whom you have had a glorious triumph. Forgive me Sir for saying you have done all this, since I say it, because I think no other capable to have done it. Take then Sir an honor reserv'd for you, and dont deny a Body of People your Aid, who make it their Suit, because they know there's none so Capable to manage it to the Silencing and the Shame of their Enemys. . . .

3400. Elizabeth Clarke to Locke, Chipley,
Somerset, 4 December 1703

. . . My perticular inquiry is at present, how You, and the rest of the family[1] escaped the Most Dreadfull Storm that perhaps was ever known in England;

---

[1] Sir Robert Filmer, against whom the *Two Treatises* was written.

[2] Jonas Proast, against whom the second and third *Letters Concerning Toleration* were written. L1325, n. 3.

[3] Occasional Conformity was the practice whereby Dissenters qualified themselves for public office by taking the Anglican sacrament just the requisite once (L3161, n. 4). Shute sent Locke a copy of his *Interest of England Consider'd in Respect of Protestants Dissenting from the Establish'd Church. With some thoughts about Occasional Conformity* (1702)

[4] Sir Humphry Mackworth, *Peace at Home* (1703). Mackworth was a champion of 'the Church Party', or Tories, who planned to outlaw occasional conformity.

[1] Household, at Oates. L620, n. 4.

I hope Well, but indeed the Sad Storys I daily hear, of the Destruction it has Made on Person's, as well as Churches, Houses, Trees, Mow's, etc. I owne it makes Me Shake to thinke what are become of My Distant friends, from whom I cannot hear as yet, amongst which number You are not the Least of My Concern. The Damage Done in this Country[2] is very great, and of the number of Those that have Lost their Lives, The Bishopp and his Lady (of Bath and Wells)[3] are two. May you have escaped this danger, And May You never be Molested by any, . . .

3483. Locke to Anthony Collins, Oates, 6 March 1704

Were you of Oxenford it self, bred under those sharp heads which were for damning my book,[1] because of its discourageing the staple commodity of the place, which in my time was called hogshearing,[2] (which is, as I hear, given out for the cause of their decree) you could not bee a more subtil disputant than you are. You doe everything that I desire of you with the [utmost] care and concerne: and because I understand and accept it so, you contend that you are the party obleiged. This I think requires some of the most refined logique to make good, and if you will have me beleive it I think you must forbid me too to read my own book, and obleige me to take to my help more learned and scholastick notions. But the mischeif is I am too old to goe to school again, and too resty[3] now to study arts,[4] how ever authorised or wherever taught, to impose upon my own understanding. . . .

3489. Locke to Dr Hans Sloane, Oates, 15 March 1704

I herewith send you the copy of my register of the weather to the end of the year 1692. If you find it worth your acceptance (for it is bare matter of fact) my man[1] shall if you desire it goe on to transcribe it and when he has done an other year I will send it you. If you think it fit to be published in your *philosophical transactions*[2] tis fit I explain a litle to you some things in the table for the better understanding of it

[2] County.

[3] Richard Kidder, killed in the episcopal palace. It was, said the Jacobites, divine vengeance for his occupying the see of a deposed Nonjuring bishop.

[1] L3511.   [2] Disputation.   [3] Restive.   [4] The Scholastic curriculum.

[1] Locke's servant, William Shaw.

[2] It was published in 1705. Locke's earlier weather record, published in Robert Boyle's *General History of the Air* (1692), was apparently the first systematic register of the weather.

I have often thought that if such a register as this or one that were better contrived with the help of some instruments that for exactness might be added, were kept in every county in *England* and so constantly published many things relateing to the air winds health fruitfulness etc might by a sagatious man be collected from them, and several rules and observations concerning the extent of winds and rain etc be in time established to the great advantage of man kinde. Whether you will think it worth the Royal Societies consideration and promotion I leave it to you. From this solitary one there is little to be collected. The pains is so little that I indulged my curiosity when it cost me the writeing not so much as a line a day For though besid[es] the ordinary observation which I set down commonly every morning, There seldom happend any rain snow or other remarkable change which I did not set down but as you see a few letters and figures doe it, such as it is I send it you and if it may be of any use to any one I shall be glad. . . .

3497. James Johnstoun to Locke, London, 23 March 1704

. . . I am mighty glad to hear that there is ground to hope, we shall have one year more of you. . . . [My health] is dayly better, but in order to what I know not; if it be to inable me to help to recover the almost irrecoverable state of affairs in Scotland, I shall value it the more, but it is my lott never to be called for, till matters be desperate;[1] In short I have a new argument that the p.p. of wales is not a Stewart,[2] for he is luckier than they use to be; for this winter our friends, his enemies here have done him more service as to his pretensions in Scotland than his enemies could ever have done.[3] The whole proceedings about the Scotch plott[4] and the addresse to the Q. to settle the succession there[5] with Atwoods ridiculous book[6] and such other Incidents one would thinck were all directed by the Court of St Germains[7] to hinder the settling of it; for it is equally true that the Lords are heartily and sincerely for the settling of it and that nothing can hinder it more than what they have done, so God

---

[1] Johnstoun was bitter at his dismissal as Scottish Secretary of State in 1696; he was now poised to return to office as part of the Marquis of Tweeddale's 'squadrone volante' party.

[2] 'Pretended Prince of Wales': James Stuart, the Old Pretender, son of James II, called James III and VIII by Jacobites. Johnstoun alludes to the widespread belief that the prince, born in 1688, was an imposter, introduced to the queen's bedroom in a warming pan.

[3] The newly fallen chief minister in Scotland, James Douglas, Duke of Queensberry, had alienated several magnates, pushing them towards Jacobitism, by denouncing them as Jacobite traitors on the strength of false accusations by Lord Lovat.

[4] The Jacobite pseudo-conspiracy by Simon Fraser, Lord Lovat.

[5] The English House of Lords pressed Queen Anne for a settlement in Scotland.

[6] William Atwood, *The Superiority and Direct Dominion of the Imperial Crown of England over the Crown and Kingdom of Scotland* (1704), an assertion of English sovereignty over Scotland. Johnstoun means that such claims merely provoke Scottish hostility.

[7] The Jacobite court at St Germain-en-Laye near Paris.

in his providence plays (ludit) with humane affairs says Grotius having observed that the dutch in their wars had least successe, when they had most hopes of it[8]—To break off from such a malancholy subject I hope you still read books to divert you and therefor pray get the True-Tom double[9] (I know not hou to send you it) it is written by some unknown pen, which rises far above the most part of writers both for stile and thought: and so entertaining that My Lady Masham and you will owe me a great dale of pleasure when you read it. . . .

3499. John Sowter to Locke, London, 25 March 1704

You may please to remember I had some discourse with you as you sate for your picture to Mr Dahl;[1] and afterward at your Lodgings about the Manufacture of Copper etc:[2] But I could not from soe smale an Acquaintance presume to trouble you with this, and obtaine the favour of an Answer, And therefore desired My Good freind Mr King[3] to introduce me, which is the bussines of the enclosed.

The Occassion of this Sir is, That a very studious thoughtfull, freind of mine[4] about 100 miles from London is soe very positive that he has found out the Longitude soe as to be usefull to Navigation; that I cann noe longer refuse him my assistance, in first enforming my self and then him, If there be not severall Donations[5] in England and else where allready setled, or promised to be given to him or them that shall first discover the Longitude soe as to be of use to Navigators etc: And if soe how to take such Measures as may secure the rewards; I know Sir you cann if your time will permit, answer me hereto, and I doubt not but you will, with your first leasure.

I would advise my freind for secureing the rewards, to make the discovery to a Second able skillfull person that should first examine into the truth of his pretensions; and if they were found good to let this second person share the reward a quarter or a third, This my freind is willing to doe, to such a person as your self, but he dare not trust (as he saies) any but my Lord Pembroke or Mr. Lock. . . .

---

[8] Hugo Grotius, Dutch jurist. Source unidentified.

[9] Anon., *The True Tom Double: or, an Account of Dr Davenant's Late Conduct and Writings* (1704), an attack on Charles Davenant's opposition to Tory attempts to legislate against Occasional Conformity (L3394, n. 3). Hitherto Davenant had been a scourge of the Whigs, especially in his *True Picture of a Modern Whig* (1701).

[1] Michael Dahl, Swedish portrait painter who settled in London in 1689. Dahl's picture of Locke was done in 1696 and hangs in the National Portrait Gallery.

[2] Perhaps a scheme for copper coinage.   [3] Peter King.

[4] Unidentified. Several impractical schemes were mooted at this time.

[5] Prizes. A reward was established by parliament in 1714 and eventually awarded to John Harrison. L253.

3511. [James Tyrrell] to Locke, [Oakley, Buckinghamshire?], [c.17 April 1704]

... [T]he best Information wee can give you concerning the forbiding the reading of your Essay[1] is as follows: that in the begining of November last there was a meeting of the Heads of Houses[2] then in Town. The [process for] certain I cannot tell it not being registred or any publick Act, onely it was there proposd by Dr: Mill[3] and seconded by Dr: Maunder[4] that there was a great decay of Logical Exercises in the university, which could not be attributed to any thing so much as the new Philosophy which was too much read; and in particular your Book and Le Clercs Philosophy,[5] against which it was offred that a Programma[6] should [be] publishd forbiding all Tutors to read them to their Pupils: this was like at first to have passed: till it was opposed by some others there present and particularly by Dr: Dunstar,[7] who not onely vindicated your book, but sayd that he thought the making the Programma would do more harm than good, first by making too much noise abroad as if the University went about to forbid the reading of all Philosophy save that of Aristotle next that he thought that instead of the end proposd it would make yong men more desirous to buy and read those books when they were once forbid than they were before: then at another meeting their Resolution upon the whole was, that upon Dr: Edwards's proposeal,[8] they agreed instead of a Programma that all Heads houses should give The Tutors private Instructions not to read those Books to their Pupils, and to prevent their doing it by themselves as much as lay in their power: and yet I do [no]t find after all that any such thing has bin put in Execution in those Colledges in which I have any acquaintance, as par[ti]cularly in university, Maudlins, New Colledg and Jesus, all which have Heads that are sufficiently for the High Charch Party:[9] so that I beleive they finding it like to have little Effect they have thought fit to let it drop: and besides this there are to my knowledg several of that Party who having read your book themselves do not onely very much approve of it but allso encourage their Pupils after they have done with their Logick, as particularly Mr: Sacheverel of Maudlins[10] as I am [told] by one of was, not to mention Mr. Percyval the son of your old Acquaintance, who when he was of Christ Church (being lately gone into Ireland)[11] not only read your book himself but encouraged his Pupils

---

[1] In Oxford University.   [2] Colleges.   [3] John Mill, Principal of St Edmund Hall.

[4] Roger Mander, Master of Balliol College.   [5] Le Clerc, *Logica* and *Ontologia* (1692).

[6] A public notice issued by the University authorities.

[7] Thomas Dunster, Warden of Wadham College.

[8] Jonathan Edwards, Principal of Jesus College.

[9] Arthur Charlett, Master of University College; Thomas Bayly, President of Magdalen College; Thomas Braithwaite, Warden of New College; Edwards of Jesus.

[10] Henry Sacheverell, Fellow of Magdalen, later notorious as a High Church preacher, impeached by the Whigs in 1710.

[11] William Percival, Archdeacon of Cashel, Student of Christ Church, son of George Percival, Locke's contemporary at Christ Church.

to do it. and now you will be best able by what wee have written what seems best for you to do in the affair about the books you writ to me you once intended to bestow:[12]

3542. Locke to Anthony Collins, Oates, 25 May 1704

When you come to my age you will know that with us old fellows *Convenient* always carrys it before *ornamental* And I would have as much of the free air when I goe abroad[1] in it[2] as is possible. Only I ask whether those which fall back soe as to give as free a prospect behind as before be as easily managed and brought over you again in case of need (as in a shower) as one that fals back upon two standing corner pillars? and next whether that which fals back so well, does when it is drawn up over you, come so far over your head when it is erected as to shelter it from the dew without shutting you up from the free open air? For I think sometimes in the evening of a warm day to sit abroad in it to take the fresco, but would have a canopy over my head to keep the dew off. If this be soe I am plainly and without balanceing for that which falls flatest. One question more and I have done. Pray what place is there for a footman in any of them? Most of my time being spent in siting I desier special care may be taken in makeing the seat broad enough and the two cushions soft plump and thick enough. You know I have a great likeing to be Canonical[3] but I little thought that you of all others was the man to make me soe. I shall love it the better for your sake and wish that Canonical were ready that you might have the hanseling[4] of it hither speedily. Collonel Masham[5] will be in town to the end of this month and if you goe that way may be heard of at the Gant Coffee house by St James's gate.[6] I tell you this because he perfectly knows the fashion of the Chaises that the Queen hunts in and the man that makes them . . .

3556. Locke to Anthony Collins, Oates, 9 June 1704

. . . However you thought fit to prepare me for being disappointed in the binding my Greek Testament, there is noe thing in it that offends me but

[12] Locke gave copies of his books to the Bodleian Library.

[1] For a ride, on an outing.   [2] The chaise or light carriage which Locke was having built.
[3] Like a priest or bishop.   [4] Inaugurating.
[5] Samuel Masham, son of Sir Francis, soldier, equerry to Princess Anne's consort, Prince George of Denmark.
[6] Gaunt Coffee-house, St James's Street.

the runing of his pareing knife too deep into the margent,[1] a knaveish and intolerable fault in all our English Bookbinders. Books seem to me to be pestilent things, and infect all that trade in them, i e all but one sort of men, with something very perverse and brutal. Printers. Binders, Sellers and others that make a trade and gain out of them have universally so odde a turne and corruption of mind that they have a way of dealeing peculiar to them selves, and not conformed to the good of Society, and that general fairness that cements man kind. Whether it be that these instruments of truth and knowledg will not bear being subjected to any thing but those noble ends, without revengeing them selves on those who medle with them to any other purpose, and prostitute them to mean and misbecomeing designes I will not enquire. The matter of fact I think you will find true, and there we will leave it, to those who sully them selves with printers ink. till they wholy expunge all the candor that nature gives, and become the worst sort of Black cattle. . . .

3627. Locke to Peter King, Oates, 16 September 1704

. . . [T]hings,[1] . . . which you must not forget nor omit viz

4 Dried neats[2] tongues

12 Partredges that are fresh and will bear the cariage and keep a day after they are here, for tis to noe purpose to bring down stinking things of good name that will stink and must be thrown away after all the trouble one has been about them, as I was lately served. Therefor if you cannot light upon partredges that are very fresh bring but 6

4 Pheasants the same I said of the partredges I say of the pheasants the full number if fresh else onely half

4 Turkey poults ready larded if they be not out of season

4 Fresh Aburn[3] Rabets if they are to be got

Plovers or woodcocks or snipes or whatever else is good to be got at the poulterers except ordinary tame foule

12 Chichester Male Lobsters if they can be got alive if not 6 dead ones that are sweet

2 Large Crabs that are fresh

Crawfish and prawns if they are to be got

A double Barrell of the best right Colchester Oysters if they are fresh come in

Not knowing whether you have any body better to get these things for you I have by this post writ to Mr Gray to find you out as soon as he receives my

---

[1] Close cropping of the margin.

[1] For a feast at Oates to celebrate the marriage of Peter King and Anne Seys.

[2] Ox.   [3] Auburn.

letter and offer you his service to get such things as you shall direct him. He was bread up in my old Lord Shaftesburys Kitchin and was my Lady Dowagers[4] Cooke and Caterer. I got him to be messenger to the Council of Trade and Plantations and have often imploid him when I have had occasion in matters of this nature wherein I have found him very diligent and usefull to me and therefor I send him to you at this pinch to be made use of in geting the things I write for if you have nobody that you can better depend upon. If you imploy John Gray you must furnish him with money to goe to market

I desire you also to lay out between twenty and thirty shillings in dried sweet meats[5] of several kinds such as some woman skilfull in those maters shall choose as fit and fashionable (excepting Orange and Lemon pils[6] candied of which we are provided). Let them be good of the kind and doe not be spareing in the cost but rather exceed thirty shillings. These drie sweet meats must each sort be put up in a paper by it self and then all the papers put up in a box together, I mention this because for want of this care some that my Lady lately sent for were quite spoiled. . . .

Pray let there be a pound of Pistachios, and some China Oranges if there be any fresh come in . . .

One thing more let me mind you of. All these things that I send for should I think be put in a little hamper and packd with care and the hamper put up before the coach if possible, for if it be put behind and there be no servant that rides behind or followes the coach on horse back you will be in danger to have it cutt of[7] (as some of our neighbours have been lately served) unless it be extremly fast tied on and somebody in the coach constantly look out after it espetially rideing through the town or any of the towns by the way

3647. Locke to Peter King, Oates, 4 and 25 October 1704

That you will faithfully Execute all that You finde in my Will I cannot doubt my Dear Cosin. Nor can I lesse depend upon your following my directions and complying with my desires in things not fit to be put into so solemn and publique a writeing

You will find amongst my papers several subjects proposed to my thoughts, which are very little more than extempory views, layd down in suddain and imperfect draughts, which though intended to be revised and farther looked into afterwards, yet by the intervention of business, or preferable enquiries happend to be thrust aside and so lay neglected and sometimes quite forgotten. Some of them indeed light upon me at such a time of leisure and in such a temper of mind that I laid them not wholy by upon the first interruption, but took them in hand again as occasion served, and went on in pursuance

---

[4] Margaret Spencer, third wife of the first Earl of Shaftesbury.
[5] Sugary confectionary.   [6] Peels.   [7] i.e. stolen.

of my first designe till I had satisfied my self in the enquiry I at first proposed. of this kind is

1° My discourse of *Seeing all things in god*[1] which though upon examination it appears to me and I think I have shewn to be a very groundless opinion, and thereupon have been pressed by some freinds (who have seen and thought what I have writ upon it to be a sufficient confutation of it) to make it publique. yet I could never consent to print it Both because I am noe freind to controversie and also because it is an opinion that spreads not and is like to die of it self or at least to doe noe great harm. I therefore think it best that it should not be published. But yet I doe not absolutely forbid it. If you and others of my judicious freinds should find occasion for it hereafter

2° You are not a stranger to a little discourse I writ about *miracles* on occasion of Mr Fleetwoods book on that subject and an anonymous answer published to it.[2] A learned friend or two as well as your self that have seen it were mightily for publishing of it. If upon serious consideration you and some other of my judicious freinds think it may be of use to the Christian Religion, and not unseasonable at this time, and fit for the publique, For it being writ for my own satisfaction I never went beyond the first draught, you may doe with it as you think good.

3° *The Conduct of the understanding*[3] I have allways thought ever since it first came into my mind to be a subject very well worth consideration, though I know not how, it seems to me for any thing that I have met with to have been almost wholy neglected: what I have done in it is very far from a just treatise. All that I have done has been, as any miscariage in that point has accidentaly come into my minde, to set it downe, with those remedies for it that I could think of. This method though it makes not that hast to the end which one would wish, is yet perhaps the onely one can be followed in the case, it being here as in physick impossible for a physitian to describe a disease or seek remedies for it till he comes to meet with it. But those particulars that have occurd to me and I have set down being as I guess sufficient to make men see some faults in the conduct of their understandings, and suspect there may be others you may also doe with as you think fit. For they may perhaps serve to excite others to enquire farther into it, and treat of it more fully than I have done. But the heads and chapters must be reduced into order.

4 ... some papers inscribd *Physica*[4] ...

5° Those who have seen what I have done upon some of St Pauls Epistles[5] are all very desirous it should be printed, perswadeing themselves it will be

---

[1] 'An Examination of P. Malebranche's Opinion of Seeing all Things in God', *Works*, ix. 211–55. L1622, n. 4.

[2] 'A Discourse of Miracles', *Works*, ix. 256–65; William Fleetwood, *An Essay upon Miracles* (1701); Benjamin Hoadly, *Letter to Mr Fleetwood* (1702).

[3] *The Conduct of the Understanding.*   [4] Unidentified.

[5] *A Paraphrase and Notes upon the Epistles of St Paul's.*

of great use to religion in giveing the true sense of those Epistles and therein a quite other view of the doctrine of Christianity than what is to be found in the expositions of Commentators, or the systems of divinity espoused in the several churches and sects of Christians. This enquiry into the sense of St Pauls Epistles was began by me for my own private instruction, not in favour of any opinion I already had, but in search of what St Paul taught. Wherein I used the same indifferency that I should have done in searching the meaning of any other author whose sense I had a mind to know nor have been lead into that which I have given by any prejudices of my owne but by what, upon the best judgment I could make, I took to be his. This, if ever it be published must be my excuse for whatever may appear a novelty, or dissonant from the interpretation of other Commentators. I have neither out of choise forsaken them any where, nor given my self up blindly to any ones authority. St Paul I have made my guide as much as possible, and concludeing him to be as I every where find him a rational pertinent arguer his sense is not so liable to be mistaken as some have imagined. That I have every where endeavourd to follow impartialy every where and if it shall be judgd usefull to the Christian religion am not unwilling what I have donne on St Pauls Epistles should be published but in this method That after the Galatians the 1 to the Corinthians. The 2d to the Corinthians. To the Romans and to the Ephesians. Each of which Epistles in this order should not till after 3 months from the publication of the former[6] and as much later as you shall see occasion be conveyd to Mr Churchil to be printed as that to the Galatians is. Accordingly you will find them sealed up seperately ready to be sent in their order when you find it seasonable. If Mr Churchill prints them tis well if not you may take your own measures[7]

I know not whether you will find any other papers of mine worth the keeping. I am sure there are none that look towards printing

You will find two or three sheets of Memoires,[8] they were writ at the request of a Person you will easilye guess to preserve the memory of some facts which he thought he might some time or other have use of. I had gon on farther if my time and health would have permitted. What there is of them pray deliver to him.

You will find a little packet sealed up and directed to Mr Newton to whom pray let them be delivered, with a brass ruler made by Butterfeild[9] in Paris which I have given to Mr Newton.

You were present when Mr Clarke begd my hone[10] and I gave it him. Pray let it be delivered to him. These are not fit things to be put into a Will. . . .

Remember it is my earnest request to you to take care of Sir Francis's yongest son Francis Cudworth Masham in all his concernes as if he were your brother.

---

[6] The five parts were published separately from 1705 to 1707, then in a collected edition.
[7] In a deleted passage Locke recommended that Samuel Bold correct the proofs.
[8] 'Memoirs relating to the Life of Anthony first Earl of Shaftesbury', *Works*, ix. 266–84.
[9] Michael Butterfield, scientific instrument-maker.   [10] Smooth stone for sharpening.

He has never failed to pay me all the respect and doe me all the good offices he was capable of performeing with all manner of Cheerfulness and delight in it so that I cannot acknowledg it too much and therefore must desire you and leave it as a charge upon you to help me to doe it when I am gon. Take care to make him a good, an honest and an usefull man. I have left my directions with him to follow your advice and rules to him and I know he will doe it for he never refused to doe what I told him was fit. If he had been my owne sone he could not have been more carefull to please and observe me

I wish you all manner of prosperity in this world and the everlasting happyness of the world to come. That I loved you I think you are convinced. God send us a happy meeting in the resurrection of the Just. Adieu

JOHN LOCKE

You[11] will find what I have done upon St Pauls Epistles tied up in several bundles and directed to Mr Churchil in the order they should be conveyd to him. The distance of time I leave to your judgment. I have not sealed them because my seales comeing to your hands you may doe that when it is time and may perhaps have occasion to open and look into them before they goe out of your hands, which when they doe conceale your self and let it not be known they come from you. If my Paraphrase and notes on the Ephesians are not wholy transcribed before I dye (as I fear they will not. For however earnestly I have pressed it again and again I have not been able to prevaile with *Will*:[12] to dispatch the two first Chapters in three months) you must get it to be transcribed out of my filed papers after I am dead, that so it may be in a condition to be printed. *Will* after all will I think be the fitest to transcribe them because he can read my hand and knows my way of writing with the use of the references

If by any backwardness you shall find (which I doe not suspect) in Mr Churchill, you should have any apprehension that the preface[13] might be lost in his hands, pray consider whether you will think it worth while to take a copy of it in short hand before you let it goe out of your keeping, there being noe other copy of it but that first and foul draught which is directed to Mr Churchill

My will is left sealed up in my Lady Mashams hands

In the assigneing to the Trustees[14] the Three thousand pounds given them in my will for the use of my Lady Masham and Frank, I would have you let them have any of those securitys which my Lady Masham and the two other Trustees shall like best upon your giveing them a particular account of those securitys. I wish you happyness. Adieu

---

[11] Postscript dated 25 Oct.   [12] Locke's servant, William Shaw.
[13] 'An Essay for the Understanding of St Paul's Epistles', prefaced to *A Paraphrase and Notes*.
[14] Anthony Collins, Peter King, Awnsham Churchill.

3648. Locke to Anthony Collins, Oates, 23 August 1704; to be delivered after his death

By my will you will see that I had some kindness for Frank Masham[1] And I knew no better way to take care of him than to put him and what I designed for him into your hands and management. The knowledg I have of your vertue of all kinds secures the trust which by your permission I have placed in you. And the peculiar esteem and love I have observed in the yonge man for you will dispose him to be ruled and influenced by you, so that of that I need say nothing. But there is one thing which It is necessary for me to recommend to your especial care and memory. And that is that when the Legacy, which I have given you Trustees[2] for the use of him and his mother, comes to be put into your hands, whether you take it in money or any other securities, a morgage which I have of Sir Francis in the name of my Cosin King and Mr Churchill should be no part of it. I know the family and foresee what inconveniencies and disorders it will produce if Sir Francis should be under any such obligations to his wife or children. which I think so carefully to be avoided, that if decency had not forbidden it I should have put it into my will it self. The money I have given you in trust for my Lady and her son I would have always placed in such hands where they may at any time freely call for it without scruple or offence; and if there be need, sue for it. Fathers and husbands usualy exspect other treatment and are disobleiged when such relations demand their due. Heads of familyes must be forborne till they please, and if a wife or a child uses importunitie or the assistance of the law to get from them, what they have their hand and seal for, the father complains of disrespect and injury, a breach of affection is made where it should be studiously avoided; and the foolish world usualy joyns in with their censures to widen and keep open the breach. To prevent this I think there should be noe such transactions as borrowing or lending between such persons or securities passed from a father to a son but in cases that are absolutely necessary. In all other cases where it is at a mans choise to put out his money upon security as he thinks fit, let him take such security as he can upon any occasion make use of, and let the hand and seale he has for his money be of such a man as he can without restraint produce and urge upon him when there is need, to what purpose else is hand and seale? If I use them not I have not my owne when I need it; and if I use them I loose my quiet and reputation and perhaps my father. But I have dwelt too long upon this matter, the fatall consequences I have seen of such things in the disturbance of familyes and the ill effects it has had, has made me very carefull to prevent it In one that I wish well to. May you live long and happy in the enjoyment of health, freedom, content and all those [blesseings] which providence has bestowed on

---

[1] Francis Cudworth Masham, Damaris's only son.
[2] Anthony Collins, Peter King, Awnsham Churchill.

you and your virtue intitles you to. I know you loved me liveing, and will preserve my memory now I am dead, All the use to be made of it is that this life is a scene of vanity that soon passes away and affords no solid satisfaction but in the consciousness of doeing well and in the hopes of an other life. This is what I can say upon experience and what you will find when you come to make up the account. Adieu.

Biographical register of correspondents

The figures in parentheses after a person's life dates record the letters which are included in this volume. *DNB* denotes an entry in the *Dictionary of National Biography*. Members of Parliament in the period 1660–90 have entries in B. D. Henning (ed.), *The House of Commons, 1660–1690* (3 vols., History of Parliament Trust, London, 1983). All colleges are in Oxford unless otherwise stated. FRS stands for Fellow of the Royal Society; MD for Doctor of Medicine; and DD for Doctor of Divinity. Of the 93 correspondents listed here, 17 were MPs, 12 were Anglican clergy, 13 were lawyers, 8 were physicians, 10 were merchants, 19 were women, 13 were Fellows of the Royal Society, 3 were Dissenters, 3 were Huguenots, 4 were Catholics, and 4 were adolescents. Some of these categories of course overlap.

Alford, Lady Anne (*c.*1619–93) (171). Daughter of Clement Corbet, civil lawyer, and widow of Sir Edward Alford of Offington, Sussex. Her son was Locke's pupil.

Alford, John (1645–91) (200). Educated at Christ Church, where he was Locke's pupil. Tory MP, Midhurst, 1679, and Bramber (Sussex), 1689–90.

Ashley, see Cooper.

Aubrey, John (1626–97) (268). Antiquary, topographer, folklorist, biographer. Educated at Trinity College and Middle Temple. FRS, 1663. Wrote *Brief Lives* of his contemporaries. A friend of Hobbes. See Michael Hunter, *John Aubrey and the Realm of Learning* (London, 1975). *DNB*.

Banks, Sir John (1627–99) (352). Wealthy merchant. Tory MP, Maidstone, Rochester, etc. (Kent), 1654–59, 1678–98. Baronet, 1661. FRS, 1668. See D. C. Coleman, *Sir John Banks* (London, 1963). *DNB*.

Barbeyrac, Jean (1674–1744) (3232). French (Huguenot) jurist, who lived in Berlin, 1697–1710. Known chiefly as the translator and annotator (1712) of Pufendorf's *De Jure Naturae et Gentium* (1672), the notes to which cite Locke extensively. An English translation, *Of the Law of Nature and Nations*, appeared in 1717.

Barrington, see Shute.

Bellomont, see Coote.

Berkeley, Elizabeth (Mrs Burnet) (1661–1709) (2109, 3153). Author of *A Method of Devotion* (1709). Daughter of Sir Richard Blake. Lived at The Hague, 1684–9. Married, first, Robert Berkeley of Spetchley, Worcestershire, 1678; second, Gilbert Burnet, Bishop of Salisbury, 1699. *DNB*.

Blair, James (1656–1743) (2545). Scottish episcopalian clergyman. Missionary to Virginia, 1685. Founder of William and Mary College, Virginia, 1692. *DNB*.

Bold, Samuel (1649–1737) (2232, 2590). Anglican clergyman and author. Rector of Steeple, Dorset, 1682–1737. Fined and jailed for preaching against religious persecution in 1682. Wrote tracts defending Locke's *Essay* against John Edwards. Visited Locke at Oates. *DNB*.

Bonville, John (692). Pewterer in Houndsditch, London. A cousin of Locke.

Boyle, Robert (1627–91) (175, 197, 335, 478). Chemist and natural philosopher. Son of the first Earl of Cork. Set up a laboratory in Oxford in the 1650s. A founder of the Royal Society. Investigated air, vacuums, combustion, and respiration. Dedicated *Memoirs for the Natural History of the Human Blood* (1683–4) to Locke. Boyle Lectures founded by his will. Locke prepared his *General History of the Air* (1692) for publication. See James R. Jacob, *Robert Boyle and the English Revolution* (New York, 1977). *DNB*.

Briolay de Beaupreau, René de (1629–71) (250). Abbot of SS Serge et Bacchus, Angers, France.

Burnet, see Berkeley.

Burridge, Ezekiel (*c*.1661–1707) (2495). Irish lawyer and scholar. Studied at Trinity College, Dublin. Published a Latin translation of Locke's *Essay* (1701).

Calverley, Lady Mary (d. *c*.1716) (3222). Of Soho Square, London. Daughter of Sir Henry Thompson, Whig MP and friend of Andrew Marvell. Widow of Sir Henry Calverley, Whig MP, who died in exile in 1684. Hostess of 'debates about the truth of the Bible and the Christian religion', between Anthony Collins, Samuel Clarke, Matthew Tindal, and William Whiston, *c*.1710.

Cary, John (d. 1720?) (2000, 2079, 2084). West India sugar merchant. Son of a vicar of Bristol. Reformed poor relief in Bristol. Wrote tracts on commerce and currency. His *Vindication* (1698) against Molyneux's *Case of Ireland* cited Locke's *Two Treatises*. *DNB*.

Charleton (or **Courten**), **William** (1642–1702) (951). A keen collector of coins, medals, and natural history specimens. Locke met him in France in 1675. *DNB*.

Clarke, Edward (*c*.1651–1710) (771, 776, 801, 886, 1102, 1313, 1326, 1439, 1455, 1471, 1586, 1647, 1690, 1728, 1768, 1849, 1860, 1978, 1981, 2016, 2060, 2299, 2398). Whig lawyer and politician, of Chipley, near Taunton, Somerset. Educated at Wadham College and Inner Temple. Trustee to the Shaftesbury family. Arrested during the Monmouth Rebellion, 1685. MP, Taunton, 1690–1710. Auditor-General to Queen Mary II. Leading member of 'the College', the political group around Lord Somers; and 'the Row', Locke's West Country friends (Clarke, Duke, Freke, Yonge). Dedicatee of Locke's *Some Thoughts Concerning Education* (1693). *DNB*.

Clarke, Elizabeth (b. *c*.1677) (3400). 'Betty'. Eldest daughter of Edward and Mary Clarke. Locke doted on her and styled her his 'wife'.

Clarke, Mary (d. 1706) (809). Apparently related to Locke. Niece of John Strachey and wife of Edward Clarke. Ran the Chipley household during her husband's absences in London. Locke took a deep interest in their children, of which there were eleven, eight surviving infancy.

Cockburn, see Trotter.

Colleton, Sir Peter (1635–94) (275, 279). One of the Proprietors of Carolina. Also engaged in Bahamas, Hudson's Bay and Africa Companies. Second baronet, 1667. FRS, 1677. Whig MP, Bossiney (Devon), 1681, 1689–94.

Collins, Anthony (1676–1729) (3361, 3483, 3542, 3556, 3648). Deist. Educated at Eton and King's College, Cambridge. Shocked the orthodox by his *Discourse of Freethinking* (1713). Friend of Locke, 1703–4. See J. O'Higgins, *Anthony Collins* (The Hague, 1970). *DNB*.

Cooper, Sir Anthony Ashley, Lord Ashley, first Earl of Shaftesbury (1621–83) (297, 561, 620). Of Wimborne St Giles, Dorset. Educated at Exeter College and Lincoln's Inn. Royalist, then turned Parliamentarian, in the Civil War. MP, 1640–61, usually for Wiltshire. Sat in Oliver Cromwell's council of state and Charles II's privy council. Chancellor of the Exchequer, 1661–72; Lord Chancellor, 1672–73. Barony, 1661; earldom, 1672. A leader of the Whig opposition, 1675–82. Charged with treason, 1682. Fled to Amsterdam. Achitophel in John Dryden's anti-Whig poem, *Absalom and Achitophel*. Locke's patron and employer, 1667–82. FRS, 1663. See K. H. D. Haley, *The First Earl of Shaftesbury* (Oxford, 1968). *DNB*.

Cooper, Anthony Ashley, Lord Ashley (later third Earl of Shaftesbury) (1671–1713) (1794). Moral philosopher. Whig MP, Poole (Dorset), 1695–8. Inherited earldom, 1699. Essays on morality and civility collected as *Characteristicks of Men, Manners, Opinions, Times* (1711). Locke supervised his early education. See Lawrence E. Klein, *Shaftesbury and the Culture of Politeness* (Cambridge, 1994). *DNB*.

Coote, Richard, Earl of Bellomont (*c*.1655–1701) (2614). Inherited Irish peerage, 1683. Captain in William of Orange's invasion army, 1688–9. Created Earl of Bellomont (Ireland), 1689. Whig MP, Droitwich (Worcestershire), 1689–95. Treasurer to Queen Mary II, 1688–94. Sent as governor to New England, 1695, to suppress piracy. Commissioned, but later arrested, the famous pirate Captain Kidd. *DNB*.

Coste, Pierre (1668–1747) (2107). Translator into French of several of Locke's works. Born near Nîmes. Educated at Geneva and Leiden. Huguenot minister. Settled in Amsterdam, then in England with Locke, as tutor in the Masham household. FRS, 1742. *DNB*.

Courten, see Charleton.

Covel, John (1638–1722) (2319, 2481). Educated at Christ's College, Cambridge; Fellow, 1659–82. DD, 1679. Chaplain at Constantinople. Travelled in the Middle East and Italy. Chaplain to Princess Mary at The Hague, 1681–5, until dismissed. Master of Christ's College, 1688–1722; twice vice-chancellor of Cambridge University. Locke met him in Paris in 1678. *DNB*.

Cudworth, Charles (d. 1684) (765). East India Company agent in Bengal, India, 1683–4. Brother of Damaris.

Cudworth, Damaris (Lady Masham) (1659–1708) (687, 696, 699, 779, 805, 837, 896, 1040). Writer of philosophical theology. Educated by her father, Ralph Cudworth, Cambridge Platonist, master of Christ's College, Cambridge. Married Sir Francis Masham, later a Whig MP, in 1685. She had one son, Francis Cudworth Masham. She probably met Locke in 1681. He lived in her home at Oates from 1691 until his death. Author of *A Discourse Concerning the Love of God* (1695), against John Norris and Mary Astell, which Norris took to be by Locke; and *Occasional Thoughts in Reference to a Virtuous or Christian Life* (1705). *DNB*.

D'Aranda, Paul (1652–1712) (1925). Merchant. Son and grandson of Huguenot ministers at Southampton. Became a Justice of the Peace in Kent.

Du Bos, Jean-Baptiste (1670–1742) (2673, 2748). French author and diplomat. Educated at the Sorbonne. Awarded an abbacy, 1723. His *Histoire critique* (1734) argued for the descent of the French monarchy from the Roman *imperium*; it was criticized by Montesquieu. A friend of Toinard and Pierre Bayle. See Robert Shackleton, *Montesquieu* (Oxford, 1961).

Duke, Elizabeth (2034). L2034 is signed 'E.D.', who is probably Elizabeth (b. 1679), daughter of Isabella and Richard Duke.

Duke, Isabella (1650–1705) (854). Sister of Sir Walter Yonge. Wife of Richard Duke, Presbyterian gentleman of Otterton, Devon. Member of 'the Row': the Clarke–Duke–Freke–Yonge circle.

Edwards, Sarah (64). An unidentified West Country woman.

Evelegh, Anne (83). Lived in Oxford with Elinor Parry when Locke was at Christ Church. Daughter of John Evelegh, Dean of Ross (Ireland). Married Benjamin Cross, of Chester, precentor of Cloyne (Ireland).

Eyre, Lady Martha (d. 1728) (3081). Widow of Sir Samuel (1633–98), a judge, whom Locke knew from at least 1676.

Firmin, Thomas (1632–97) (2241). Wealthy mercer of Lombard Street. London's principal philanthropist. Friend of Tillotson and other clergymen, yet also a supporter of unitarians. He established a workhouse for the poor. *DNB.*

Fletcher, Andrew (1655–1716) (3018). Scottish republican and patriot. Participant in Monmouth's Rebellion, 1685. MP in Scottish parliament active against Anglo-Scottish Union, 1703–7; today a hero of the Scottish National Party. See his *Political Works*, ed. John Robertson (Cambridge, 1997). *DNB.*

Freke, John (*c.*1652–1714) (1849, 1860, 1974, 1978, 1981, 2016, 2060: all but one jointly with Edward Clarke). Whig barrister from Dorset. Educated at Wadham College and Middle Temple. Arrested during the Monmouth Rebellion, 1685. Member of 'the College'.

Furly, Benjamin (1636–1714) (1151, 1325, 1386, 1650, 1745, 2754, 2832, 2932, 3198). Quaker merchant, settled in Rotterdam *c.*1660, son of a mayor of Colchester. His home and library were a refuge for English political and religious fugitives. Probably met Locke in 1683. See W. I. Hull, *Benjamin Furly and Quakerism in Rotterdam* (Swarthmore, PA, 1941). *DNB.*

Godolphin, William (1634–96) (60, 66). Diplomat. Educated at Westminster School and Christ Church. Schoolfriend of Locke. Cousin of Francis Godolphin, to whom Hobbes dedicated *Leviathan.* Doctor of Civil Laws, 1663. FRS, 1664. MP, Camelford (Cornwall), 1665–78. Knighted, 1668. Ambassador to Spain, 1671–8. Converted to Catholicism, 1671. *DNB.*

Goodall, Charles (1642–1712) (1096). Physician. Educated at Emmanuel College, Cambridge, and Leiden. MD, 1670. President of the Royal College of Physicians, 1708–12. Friend of Sydenham and Sloane. Locke lodged with him on his return from exile, 1689. *DNB.*

Grævius, Joannes (1632–1703) (974). Professor of politics, history, and rhetoric, at Utrecht from 1667. He published an edition of Cicero's letters.

Grenville, Denis (1637–1703) (327, 328, 374, 426). Anglican clergyman. Son of the Royalist Sir Bevil Grenville. Educated at Exeter College. DD, 1671. Dean of Durham, 1684–91. Denounced the Revolution, fled to France, and died in exile. Jacobite 'Archbishop of York'. See *The Remains of Denis Granville* (Surtees Society, 2 vols., 1861–5). *DNB.*

Grigg, Anne (or **Anna**) (1065, 2692). Wife of Thomas Grigg (*c.*1638–66), minister in London, who was perhaps related to Locke's aunt, also called Anne Grigg.

Guise, Lady Elizabeth (1056). Sister of Scrope Howe, Baron Howe. Wife of Sir John Guise (*c.*1654–95), Whig MP, Gloucestershire, 1679–81, 1689–95; colonel in William of Orange's invasion army.

Hamilton, James (1707). The signatory of L1707 is likely to have been the James Hamilton who became sixth Earl of Abercorn in 1701 (1661–1734). He took part in the defence of Derry against the Jacobites, 1689. Privy councillor in Anne's reign and after. *DNB.*

Hardy, John (2775). Presbyterian minister. Attended a Dissenting academy in Shrewsbury. Conformed to Anglicanism, *c.*1727.

Hatrell, Henry (1914). Dissenting attorney of Newcastle-under-Lyme, Staffordshire. Governor of a grammar school for the poor.

Herbert, Thomas, eighth Earl of Pembroke (1656–1733) (797, 828). Educated at Christ Church. Succeeded to the earldom, 1683. Lord Lieutenant of Wiltshire. Helped suppress the Monmouth Rebellion, 1685. President of the Royal Society, 1689–90. Moderate Tory politician. Held several high offices after 1689. Patron of Locke and dedicatee of the *Essay*. *DNB*.

Hoskins, John (*c.*1640–1717) (528). The Earl of Shaftesbury's solicitor. Educated at Christ Church.

Huntington, Robert (1637–1701) (253). Oriental scholar. Educated at Merton College; Fellow. DD, 1683. Chaplain at Aleppo (Syria), 1671–81. Travelled in the Middle East. Provost of Trinity College, Dublin, 1683–92. Bishop of Raphoe (Ireland), 1701. Pupil of Edward Pococke. See G. J. Toomer, *Eastern Wisdom and Learning* (Oxford, 1996). *DNB*.

Johnston, James (1655–1737) (2207, 3497). Assisted William of Orange's invasion. Secretary of State for Scotland, 1692–6. Scottish MP. Cousin of Gilbert Burnet. *DNB*.

King, Peter (later first **Baron Ockham**) (1669–1734) (2643, 2849, 2855, 2874, 3095, 3161, 3275, 3627, 3647). Lawyer. Locke's cousin, protégé, and executor. Whig MP, Beeralston (Devon), from 1701. Knighted, 1708. Privy councillor, 1715. Peerage, 1725. Lord Chancellor, 1725–33. Wrote theological tracts. *DNB*.

King, Richard (b. *c.*1671) (2846, 3328, 3339, 3346). Anglican clergyman. Educated at Exeter College. Vicar of Rockbeare, Devon, 1713–18.

Le Clerc, Jean (1657–1736) (1069, 1798). Scholar, theologian, journalist. Calvinist minister. Educated at Geneva. Settled in Amsterdam, 1683. Professor of philosophy in the Remonstrant college. Dedicated *Ontologia* (1692) to Locke. Editor of learned periodicals, especially the *Bibliothèque universelle*, in which Locke published reviews and the 'Extrait' (*Abrégé*) of the *Essay* (1686–8); and of its successor the *Bibliothèque choisie*, which reviewed Locke's works. Friend of Limborch. See Annie Barnes, *Jean Le Clerc et la République des Lettres* (Paris, 1938); S. A. Golden, *Jean Le Clerc* (New York, 1972).

Limborch, Philippus van (1633–1712) (1100, 1101, 1120, 1122, 1127, 1147, 1158, 1182, 1791, 1804, 1901, 2340, 2395, 2413, 2443, 2498, 2925, 2935). Leading Dutch Remonstrant (Arminian) theologian. Professor of theology, Amsterdam, from 1668. His chief work was *Theologia Christiana* (1686). Locke met him in 1684. Probable dedicatee of the *Epistola de Tolerantia* (the Latin version of *The Letter Concerning Toleration*).

Lock, John (d. 1746) (3046, 3136). Turkey merchant. Agent for the East India Company in the Middle and Far East. Knighted, 1717.

Locke, John, senior (1606–61) (29, 30, 59, 91, 110). Locke's father. Minor gentleman and attorney of Pensford, Somerset. Clerk to the Somerset Justices of the Peace. Captain of horse in the Parliamentary army in the Civil War. Client of Alexander Popham.

Lockhart, Martha (1834). Lady of the Bedchamber to Queen Mary II. Daughter of Sir William Lockhart, soldier and diplomat. Distant cousin of Sir Francis Masham.

Lyde, Cornelius (*c.*1640–1717) (3310). Acted as Locke's steward for his Somerset estate.

Mapletoft, John (1631–1721) (360, 417). Physician and clergyman. Educated at Westminster School and Trinity College, Cambridge; Fellow. Tutor to the eleventh Earl of Northumberland. MD, 1667. FRS, 1676. Gresham professor of physic, 1675–9. Then ordained. Minister in London and Ipswich. DD, 1690. *DNB*.

Masham, Damaris, see Cudworth.

Masham, Esther (*c*.1675–1722) (2124). Daughter of Sir Francis Masham by his first marriage. Lived at Oates from 1685.

Masham, Francis Cudworth (1686–1731) (2613). Only child of Damaris. Inherited wealth from Locke. Barrister. Master in Chancery, 1726.

Molyneux, Thomas (1661–1733) (1593, 2500). Irish physician. Educated at Trinity College, Dublin, and Leiden. MD, 1687. FRS, 1686. President, Irish College of Physicians, 1702 and later. Baronet, 1730. Brother of William. *DNB*.

Molyneux, William (1656–98) (1530, 1538, 1579, 1592, 1609, 1622, 1655, 1693, 1887, 1984, 2059, 2131, 2202, 2221, 2269, 2277, 2288, 2376, 2414, 2422). Irish philosopher and politician. Educated at Trinity College, Dublin, and Middle Temple. Founder of the Dublin Philosophical Society, 1683. FRS, 1686. Fled Jacobite Ireland, 1689. MP, Dublin University, 1692, 1695. Praised Locke in *Dioptrica Nova* (1692), which won Locke's friendship. His *The Case of Ireland* (1698) asserted the legislative independence of Ireland. See J. G. Simms, *William Molyneux of Dublin, 1656–1698* (Dublin, 1982). *DNB*.

Monmouth, see Mordaunt.

Mordaunt, Carey, Viscountess Mordaunt, Countess of Monmouth, Countess of Peterborough (*c*.1658–1709) (1099, 1397, 2320). Daughter of Sir Alexander Frazer, physician to Charles II. Lady of the Bedchamber in Charles II's court. She had an affair with Charles Mordaunt, became pregnant, and married him *c*.1678. Friend of Locke from at least 1688.

Mordaunt, Charles, second Viscount Mordaunt, Earl of Monmouth, third Earl of Peterborough (1658–1735) (1116, 1252). Admiral, general, diplomat, courtier. Officer in William of Orange's invasion army. Privy councillorship and peerage, 1689. Inherited earldom, 1697. General in Spain, 1705. An important patron of Locke in the early 1690s. *DNB*.

Newton, Isaac (1642–1727) (1405, 1519, 1659, 1663). Mathematician and natural philosopher. Fellow of Trinity College, Cambridge. Lucasian Professor of Mathematics, 1669. FRS, 1672; president, 1703–27. Made advances in calculus, optics, astronomy, and gravitational theory. *Principia Mathematica* published in 1687. Whig MP, Cambridge University, 1689–90, 1701–2. Warden, then Master, of the Mint, 1696–1727. Knighted, 1705. Earliest known connection with Locke, 1690. See Richard R. Westfall, *The Life of Isaac Newton* (Cambridge, 1993). *DNB*.

Parry, Elinor (1640?–90) (72). The recipient of L72, 'PE', is probably Elinor Parry, with whom Locke appears to have fallen in love at Oxford. Daughter of Edward Parry, Bishop of Killaloe (Ireland). Married Richard Hawkshaw of Dublin, *c*.1670. Fled Jacobite Ireland, 1689, and sought Locke's help. Sister of John.

Parry, John (*c*.1634–77) (219). Anglican clergyman. Educated at Trinity College, Dublin, and Jesus College; Fellow. Dean of Christ Church, Dublin, 1666; Bishop of Ossory, 1672. Brother of Elinor. *DNB*.

Pembroke, see Herbert.

Peterborough, see Mordaunt.

Pitt, Robert (1653–1713) (3045). Physician. Fellow of Wadham College, 1674. MD, 1682. FRS, 1682. Physician, St Bartholomew's Hospital, 1698–1707. Polemicist for the Royal College of Physicians. *DNB*.

Popham, Alexander (*c*.1605–69) (96). Gentleman of Somerset. Locke's first patron. Educated at Balliol College. MP in most parliaments, 1640–69, variously for Bath, Minehead, and Wiltshire. Soldier in the Parliamentary army in the Civil War.

Member of the council of state, 1649–52, 1660. Presbyterian royalist at the Restoration.

Popple, William (1638–1708) (1567, 2002, 2714). Wine merchant at Bordeaux, c.1670–88; then settled in London. Nephew of Andrew Marvell. Published *A Rational Catechism* (1687). Translator of Locke's *Epistola de Tolerantia*. Secretary of the Board of Trade, 1696–1707. Friend of Locke from at least 1689. *DNB*.

Sergeant, John (1622–1707) (2085). Roman Catholic priest, theologian, philosopher. Acquainted with Locke in Oxford, 1682. His *Solid Philosophy Asserted* (1697) attacked the *Essay*. Locke annotated his copy of it. *DNB*.

Shaftesbury, see Cooper.

Shute, John (later **Viscount Barrington**) (1678–1734) (3394). Lawyer, theologian, polemicist for the Dissenters. Educated at Utrecht. Went with Defoe to Scotland to seek Presbyterian support for the Treaty of Union with England. Whig MP, Berwick-upon-Tweed, 1715–23. Adopted surname Barrington, 1709. Irish peerage, 1720. The highest ranking Presbyterian in public office. Cited Locke in *The Rights of Protestant Dissenters* (1704–5). *DNB*.

Sloane, Hans (1660–1753) (1785, 2640, 3489). Physician, naturalist. Educated at Paris and Montpellier. Friend of Sydenham. MD, 1683. FRS, 1685; secretary, 1693–1712; president, 1727–41. President of the Royal College of Physicians, 1719–35. Baronet, 1716. Founded Chelsea Physic Garden, 1721. See Arthur MacGregor (ed.), *Sir Hans Sloane: Collector, Scientist, Antiquary, Founding Father of the British Museum* (London, 1994). *DNB*.

Smith, Humfry (b. c.1655) (3321). Educated at The Queen's College. Vicar of Dartmouth, Devon, 1685–1709. Collected materials for a life of the Arabist, Edward Pococke.

Somers, Sir John, Baron (1651–1716) (1186, 2384). Whig barrister and politician, one of the Whig 'Junto' in power, 1693–1700. Educated at Trinity College. MP, Worcester, 1689–93. Helped draft Declaration of Rights. Knighted, 1689; peerage, 1697. Lord Keeper, 1693–97; Lord Chancellor, 1697–1700. FRS, 1698. Patron of Locke; not apparently acquainted before 1689. Supported by 'the College', Locke's allies in parliament. Probable author of *Jura Populi Anglicani* (1701), which cited Locke's *Two Treatises*. Dedicatee of Locke's *Further Considerations* on coinage (1696). See William L. Sachse, *Lord Somers* (Manchester, 1975). *DNB*.

Sowter, John (3499). Merchant, perhaps a goldsmith, of Exeter.

Strachey, John (1634–75) (163, 177, 182, 226, 261, 264). Barrister, of Sutton Court, near Pensford, Somerset. Educated at Lincoln College. Childhood friend of, and apparently related to, Locke.

Stubbe, Henry (1632–76) (75). Author and physician. Educated at Westminster School and Christ Church; Student (expelled, 1659). Friend and admirer of Hobbes. Author of *An Essay in Defence of the Good Old Cause* (1659). See James R. Jacob, *Henry Stubbe, Radical Protestantism and the Early Enlightenment* (Cambridge, 1983). *DNB*.

Sydenham, Thomas (1624–89) (295, 337). Physician. Educated at Magdalen Hall. Fought in the Parliamentary army in the Civil War. Fellow of All Souls. Studied medicine at Montpellier. Investigated smallpox and other epidemic diseases; encouraged the use of laudanum. See Kenneth Dewhurst, *Dr Thomas Sydenham* (London, 1966). *DNB*.

Tatam, John (d. 1733) (2451). Anglican clergyman. Educated at Cambridge. Vicar of Sutton-on-the-Hill, Derbyshire, 1689–1733.

Tindal, Matthew (1657–1733) (2173). Deist. Educated at Exeter College. Fellow of All Souls, 1678–1733. Doctor of Civil Laws, 1685. His *Rights of the Christian Church* (1706) angered high churchmen. *Christianity as Old as Creation* (1730) was the coping stone of the deist movement. His tracts of the 1690s were influenced by Locke's *Two Treatises* and *Letters on Toleration*. *DNB*.

Toinard (Thoynard), Nicolas (1628–1706) (394, 475, 605). French natural philosopher and theologian, resident at Paris and Orleans. Travelled widely in western Europe. Strove to compile a harmony of the four gospels (published 1707). Investigated astronomy and mechanics. Locke met him about 1677.

Towerson, Gabriel (*c*.1635–97) (106, 108, 118). Clergyman and theological writer. Educated at The Queen's College; Fellow of All Souls. Rector of Welwyn, Hertfordshire, 1662–97. DD, 1678. Almost certainly the dedicatee of Locke's *First Tract on Government*. His *Explication of the Decalogue* (1676) carried forward discussions with Locke on the law of nature. *DNB*.

Treby, Sir George (*c*.1644–1700) (2440). Judge, politician. Whig MP, Plympton (Devon), 1677–92. Investigated the Popish Plot allegations, 1678. Recorder of London, 1680–3, 1688–92. Knighted, 1681. Counsel for the Seven Bishops arrested by James II, 1688. Solicitor-general, then attorney-general, 1689–92; lord chief justice, 1692–1700. Promoted the Bill of Rights, 1689. An ally of Somers. *DNB*.

Trotter, Catharine (1679–1749) (3234). Roman Catholic dramatist and philosopher. Dedicated *A Defence of the Essay* (1702) to Locke. Converted to Anglicanism, 1707. Married Patrick Cockburn, a clergyman, 1708. See *Works* (with Life) (2 vols., London, 1751, repr. London, 1992). *DNB*.

Tyrrell, James (1642–1718) (842, 911, 932, 973, 985, 1266, 1301, 1307, 1309, 1312, 1522, 1800, 3511). Whig lawyer and political and historical writer. Educated at The Queen's College. Deputy-lieutenant of Buckinghamshire. Author of *Patriarcha non Monarcha* (1681) against Filmer's absolutism; and *Bibliotheca Politica* (1692–94), which publicized the *Two Treatises*. Met Locke in 1658. Hosted Locke at Oakley in 1681, where he assisted the writing of a tolerationist tract against Stillingfleet. *DNB*.

Walls, George (*c*.1645–1727) (459). Anglican clergyman. Educated at Westminster School and Christ Church. DD, 1694. Chaplain at Hamburg, 1682–9. Prebendary of Worcester, 1694–1727; of St Paul's, 1695–1727.

Westrowe, Thomas (81, 82). Educated at Christ Church (matriculated, 1657), and Inner Temple. L81 and L82 are assumed to be written to him.

Woodward, Henry (*fl.* 1666–86) (305). Surgeon and explorer in North America.

Wynne, John (*c*.1665–1743) (1846). Anglican clergyman. Educated at Jesus College; Fellow. Chaplain to the Earl of Pembroke. Professor of Divinity, Oxford, 1705–15. Principal of Jesus College, 1712–20. Bishop of St Asaph, 1715–27; of Bath and Wells, 1727–43. DD, 1706. His *Abridgement of Locke's Essay* (1696) was dedicated to Locke. *DNB*.

Yonge, Elizabeth (b. 1663) (1334). Sister of Sir Walter Yonge (1653–1731), Whig gentleman and MP, of Escott, Devon, and of Isabella Duke. Married Bartholomew Beale, 1692.

Bibliography

Locke's writings

Paperback editions of Locke's main works are available:

A Letter Concerning Toleration, ed. James H. Tully (Indianapolis, IN, 1983).
An Essay Concerning Human Understanding, ed. Peter H. Nidditch (Oxford, 1979); or, abridged by John W. Yolton (London, 1976); or, abridged by Kenneth P. Winkler (Indianapolis, IN, 1996).
Political Essays, ed. Mark Goldie (Cambridge, 1997).
Political Writings, ed. David Wootton (London, 1993).
Writings on Religion, ed. Victor Nuovo (Oxford, 2002).
Some Thoughts Concerning Education, ed. John W. and Jean S. Yolton (Oxford, 1999); or (with *Of the Conduct of the Understanding*), ed. Ruth W. Grant and Nathan Tarcov (Indianapolis, IN, 1996).
Two Treatises of Government, ed. Peter Laslett (Cambridge, 1960, student edition 1988); or, ed. Mark Goldie (London, 1993).

The Clarendon Edition of the Works of John Locke (Oxford University Press) will ultimately include most of Locke's writings. So far, besides the correspondence, the following volumes have appeared, starting in 1975:

An Essay Concerning Human Understanding, ed. Peter H. Nidditch (1975; pb 1979).
A Paraphrase and Notes on the Epistles of St Paul to the Galatians, 1 and 2 Corinthians, Romans, Ephesians, ed. Arthur W. Wainright (2 vols., 1987).
Some Thoughts Concerning Education, ed. John W. Yolton and Jean S. Yolton (1989; pb 1999).
Drafts for the Essay Concerning Human Understanding, and Other Philosophical Writings, ed. Peter H. Nidditch and G. A. J. Rogers (vol. 1, 1990).
Locke on Money, ed. Patrick Hyde Kelly (2 vols., 1991).
The Reasonableness of Christianity, ed. John C. Higgins-Biddle (1999).

Locke's French journals are printed in John Lough (ed.), *Locke's Travels in France, 1675–1679* (Cambridge, 1953).

Biographies and bibliographies

Cranston's is the standard modern biography. The bibliography of writings about Locke is kept up to date by Roland Hall in the annual issues of the *Locke Studies* (for information: www.luc.edu/depts/philosophy/LockeStudies) and by John C. Attig at www.libraries.psu.edu/iasweb/locke.

ATTIG, J. C., *The Works of John Locke: A Comprehensive Bibliography* (Westport, CT, 1985).
FOX BOURNE, H. R., *The Life of John Locke* (2 vols., London, 1876).
CRANSTON, MAURICE, *John Locke: A Biography* (Oxford, 1957; repr. 1985).

DEWHURST, KENNETH, *John Locke, Physician and Philosopher* (London, 1963).

HALL, ROLAND, AND WOODHOUSE, ROGER, *Eighty Years of Locke Scholarship* (Edinburgh, 1983).

HARRISON, JOHN, AND LASLETT, PETER, *The Library of John Locke* (Oxford, 1965; 2nd edn. 1971).

KING, PETER, *The Life of John Locke* (London, 1829; 2 vols., 1830).

LONG, PHILIP, *A Summary Catalogue of the Lovelace Collection of the Papers of John Locke in the Bodleian Library* (Oxford, 1959).

YOLTON, JEAN S., *John Locke: A Descriptive Bibliography* (Bristol, 1998).

Books about Locke's thought

AARON, R. I., *John Locke* (Oxford, 1937; 3rd edn., 1971).

ALEXANDER, PETER, *Ideas, Qualities and Corpuscles* (Cambridge, 1985).

ARNEIL, BARBARA, *John Locke and America* (Oxford, 1996).

ASHCRAFT, RICHARD, *Revolutionary Politics and Locke's 'Two Treatises of Government'* (Princeton, NJ, 1986).

—— *Locke's Two Treatises of Government* (London, 1987).

—— (ed.), *John Locke: Critical Assessments* (4 vols., London, 1991).

AYERS, MICHAEL, *Locke* (2 vols., London, 1991).

CHAPPELL, VERE (ed.), *The Cambridge Companion to Locke* (Cambridge, 1994).

DUNN, JOHN, *The Political Thought of John Locke* (Cambridge, 1969).

—— *Locke* (Oxford, 1984).

FRANKLIN, J. H., *John Locke and the Theory of Sovereignty* (Cambridge, 1978).

GRANT, RUTH, *John Locke's Liberalism* (Chicago, 1987).

HARRIS, IAN, *The Mind of John Locke* (Cambridge, 1994).

HORTON, JOHN, AND MENDUS, SUSAN (eds.), *John Locke: 'A Letter Concerning Toleration' in Focus* (London, 1991).

JOLLEY, NICHOLAS, *Leibniz and Locke* (Oxford, 1984).

LLOYD THOMAS, D. A., *Locke on Government* (London, 1995).

KRAMER, MATTHEW, *John Locke and the Origins of Private Property* (Cambridge, 1997).

MACPHERSON, C. B., *The Political Theory of Possessive Individualism* (Oxford, 1962).

MARSHALL, JOHN, *John Locke: Resistance, Religion, and Responsibility* (Cambridge, 1994).

MONTUORI, MARIO, *John Locke on Toleration and the Unity of God* (Amsterdam, 1983).

ROGERS, G. A. J., (ed.), *Locke's Philosophy: Content and Context* (Oxford, 1994).

SCHOULS, PETER A., *Reasoned Freedom: John Locke and Enlightenment* (Ithaca, NY, 1992).

SIMMONS, A. JOHN, *The Lockean Theory of Rights* (Princeton, 1992).

—— *On the Edge of Anarchy: Locke, Consent, and the Limits of Society* (Princeton, 1993).

SPELLMAN, W. M., *John Locke and the Problem of Depravity* (Oxford, 1988).

—— *John Locke* (London, 1997).

TARCOV, NATHAN, *Locke's Education for Liberty* (Chicago, 1984).

TULLY, JAMES, *A Discourse on Property: John Locke and his Adversaries* (Cambridge, 1980).

—— *An Approach to Political Philosophy: John Locke in Contexts* (Cambridge, 1993).

VERNON, RICHARD, *The Career of Toleration: John Locke, Jonas Proast, and After* (Montreal, 1997).

WOOD, NEAL, *The Politics of Locke's Philosophy* (Berkeley, 1983).

YOLTON, JOHN W., (ed.), *John Locke: Problems and Perspectives* (Cambridge, 1969).

YOLTON, JOHN W., *A Locke Dictionary* (Oxford, 1993).

The background to Locke's political ideas

ARMITAGE, DAVID, *The Ideological Origins of the British Empire* (Cambridge, 2000).

BURNS, J. H., AND GOLDIE, MARK (eds.), *The Cambridge History of Political Thought, 1450–1700* (Cambridge, 1991).

HAAKONSSEN, KNUD, *Natural Law and Moral Philosophy from Grotius to the Scottish Enlightenment* (Cambridge, 1996).

KENYON, J. P., *Revolution Principles: The Politics of Party, 1689–1720* (Cambridge, 1977).

PATEMAN, CAROLE, *The Sexual Contract* (Cambridge, 1988).

PHILLIPSON, NICHOLAS, AND SKINNER, QUENTIN (eds.), *Political Discourse in Early Modern Britain* (Cambridge, 1993).

POCOCK, J. G. A., *The Ancient Constitution and the Feudal Law* (Cambridge, 1957; 2nd edn. 1987).

—— *Virtue, Commerce and History* (Cambridge, 1985).

—— et al. (eds.), *The Varieties of British Political Thought, 1500–1800* (Cambridge, 1993).

SKINNER, QUENTIN, *The Foundations of Modern Political Thought* (2 vols., Cambridge, 1978).

SMITH, HILDA L. (ed.), *Women Writers and the Early Modern British Political Tradition* (Cambridge, 1998).

TUCK, RICHARD, *Natural Rights Theories* (Cambridge, 1979).

WALDRON, JEREMY, *The Right to Private Property* (Oxford, 1988).

Locke's influence and his critics

AARSLEFF, HANS, *From Locke to Saussure* (London, 1982).

BOYD, WILLIAM, *From Locke to Montessori* (London, 1914).

FLIEGELMAN, J., *Prodigals and Pilgrims: The American Revolution against Patriarchal Authority, 1750–1800* (Cambridge, 1982).

FOX, C., *Locke and the Scriblerians: Identity and Consciousness in Early Eighteeenth-Century Britain* (Berkeley, CA, 1988).

HUTCHINSON, R., *Locke in France, 1688–1734* (Oxford, 1991).

GOLDIE, MARK (ed.), *The Reception of Locke's Politics* (6 vols., London, 1999).

MACLEAN, K., *John Locke and English Literature of the Eighteenth Century* (New Haven, CT, 1936).

PICKERING, S. G., *John Locke and Children's Books in Eighteenth-Century England* (Knoxville, TN, 1981).

ROGERS, G. A. J. (ed.), *Locke's Enlightenment: Aspects of the Origin, Nature, and Impact of his Philosophy* (Hildesheim, 1998).

SELL, A. P. F., *John Locke and the Eighteenth-Century Divines* (Cardiff, 1997).

YOLTON, JOHN W., *John Locke and the Way of Ideas* (Oxford, 1956).

—— *Thinking Matter: Materialism in Eighteenth-Century Britain* (Minneapolis, 1983).

—— *Locke and French Materialism* (Oxford, 1991).

YOUNG, B. W., *Religion and Enlightenment in Eighteenth-Century England: Theological Debate from Locke to Burke* (Oxford, 1998).

There are entries on Locke's philosophical contemporaries, including some of his little known critics and admirers, in Edward Craig (ed.), *The Routledge Encyclopedia of Philosophy* (10 vols., London, 1998); and in Andrew Pyle (ed.), *The Dictionary of Seventeenth-Century British Philosophers* (2 vols., Bristol, 2000). See also: Daniel Garber and Michael Ayers (eds.), *The Cambridge History of Seventeenth-Century Philosophy* (2 vols., Cambridge, 1998). For scientists see: C. C. Gillespie (ed.), *Dictionary of Scientific Biography* (16 vols., New York, 1970–80).

Other topics

Agriculture: JOAN THIRSK (ed.), *The Agrarian History of England and Wales*, vol. 5: *1640–1750* (Cambridge, 1984).

Alchemy: BETTY JO TEETER DOBBS, *The Foundations of Newton's Alchemy* (Cambridge, 1975).

America: RICHARD MIDDLETON, *Colonial America: A History, 1585–1776* (2nd edn., Oxford, 1996).

Americans, Native: KAREN ORDAHL KUPPERMAN (ed.), *America in European Consciousness, 1493–1750* (Chapel Hill, NC, and London, 1995).

Anglicanism: JOHN SPURR, *The Restoration Church of England, 1646–1689* (New Haven and London, 1991).

Anticlericalism: J. A. I. CHAMPION, *The Pillars of Priestcraft Shaken: The Church of England and its Enemies, 1660–1730* (Cambridge, 1992).

Aristocracy: J. V. BECKETT, *The Aristocracy in England, 1660–1714* (Oxford, 1986).

Astronomy: JOHN NORTH, *The Fontana History of Astronomy and Cosmology* (London, 1995).

Atheism: MICHAEL HUNTER AND DAVID WOOTTON (eds.), *Atheism from the Reformation to the Enlightenment* (Oxford, 1992).

Banking: ERIC KERRIDGE, *Trade and Banking in Early Modern England* (Manchester, 1988).

Bath: R. S. NEALE, *Bath, 1680–1850: A Social History* (London, 1981).

Biblical chronology: FRANK E. MANUEL, *Isaac Newton, Historian* (Cambridge, 1963).

Book trade: MARJORIE PLANT, *The English Book Trade* (London, 1939; 2nd edn., 1965).

Boyle Lectures: M. C. JACOB, *The Newtonians and the English Revolution, 1689–1720* (Hassocks, Sussex, 1976).

Britain and Europe: JONATHAN SCOTT, *England's Troubles* (Cambridge, 2000).

Calendars: ROBERT POOLE, *Time's Alteration: Calendar Reform in Early Modern England* (London, 1998).

Cambridge: JOHN GASCOIGNE, *Cambridge in the Age of Enlightenment* (Cambridge, 1989).

Cambridge Platonists: RICHARD KROLL, RICHARD ASHCRAFT, AND PEREZ ZAGORIN (eds.), *Philosophy, Science, and Religion in England, 1640–1700* (Cambridge, 1992).

Censorship: F. S. SIEBERT, *Freedom of the Press in England, 1476–1776* (Urbana, IL, 1952).

Charles II: RONALD HUTTON, *Charles the Second* (Oxford, 1989).

Childbirth: ADRIAN WILSON, *The Making of Man-Midwifery: Childbirth in England, 1660–1770* (London, 1995).

Children: LINDA A. POLLOCK, *Forgotten Children: Parent–Child Relations from 1500 to 1900* (Cambridge, 1983).

Clocks: D. S. LANDES, *Revolution in Time: Clocks and the Making of the Modern World* (Cambridge, MA, 1983).

Coffee houses: BRYAN LILLYWHITE, *London Coffee Houses* (London, 1963).

Consumption: LORNA WEATHERILL, *Consumer Behaviour and Material Culture in Britain, 1660–1760* (London, 1988).

Dissenters: M. R. WATTS, *The Dissenters: From the Reformation to the French Revolution* (Oxford, 1978).

Dissenting literature: N. H. KEEBLE, *The Literary Culture of Nonconformity in Later Seventeenth-Century England* (Leicester, 1987).

Dublin: K. T. HOPPEN, *The Common Scientist in the Seventeenth-Century: The Dublin Philosophical Society* (London, 1970).

Dutch Republic: JONATHAN I. ISRAEL, *The Dutch Republic: Its Rise, Greatness, and Fall, 1471–1806* (Oxford, 1995).

Earth, theories of the: ROY PORTER, *The Making of Geology: Earth Sciences in Britain, 1660–1815* (Cambridge, 1977).

East India Company: K. N. CHAUDHURI, *The Trading World of Asia and the English East India Company, 1660–1760* (Cambridge, 1978).

Economic thought: WILLIAM LETWIN, *The Origins of Scientific Economics: English Economic Thought, 1660–1776* (London, 1963).

Economy: D. C. COLEMAN, *The Economy of England, 1450–1750* (London, 1977).

Education: ROSEMARY O'DAY, *Education and Society, 1500–1800* (London, 1982).

Empire: NICHOLAS CANNY (ed.), *The Origins of Empire: British Overseas Enterprise to the Close of the Seventeenth Century* (Oxford, 1998).

England: JULIAN HOPPIT, *A Land of Liberty? England 1689–1727* (Oxford, 2000).

Englishness: PAUL LANGFORD, *Englishness Identified: Manners and Character 1650–1850* (Oxford, 2000).

Enlightenment: JONATHAN I. ISRAEL, *Radical Enlightenment: Philosophy and the Making of Modernity, 1650–1750* (Oxford, 2001).

Enthusiasm: S. I. TUCKER, *Enthusiasm: A Study in Semantic Change* (Cambridge, 1972).

Feminism: HILDA L. SMITH, *Reason's Disciples: Seventeenth-Century English Feminists* (Urbana, IL, 1982).

Filmer: SIR ROBERT FILMER, *Patriarcha and Other Writings*, ed. Johann P. Sommerville (Cambridge, 1991).

Finance: P. G. M. DICKSON, *The Financial Revolution in England* (London, 1967).

France: ROBIN BRIGGS, *Early Modern France, 1560–1715* (2nd edn., Oxford, 1998).

French thought: NANNERL O. KEOHANE, *Philosophy and the State in France: The Renaissance to the Enlightenment* (Princeton, NJ, 1980).

Gardens: TOM WILLIAMSON, *Polite Landscapes: Gardens and Society in Eighteenth-Century England* (Stroud, 1995).

Gentry: FELICITY HEAL AND CLIVE HOLMES, *The Gentry in England and Wales, 1500–1700* (Basingstoke, 1994).

Germany: MICHAEL HUGHES, *Early Modern Germany, 1477–1806* (Basingstoke, 1992).

Glorious Revolution: JONATHAN I. ISRAEL (ed.), *The Anglo-Dutch Moment: Essays on the Glorious Revolution and its World Impact* (Cambridge, 1991).

Hobbism: SAMUEL I. MINTZ, *The Hunting of Leviathan* (Cambridge, 1962).

Huguenots: ROBIN D. GWYNN, *Huguenot Heritage* (London, 1985).

Invention: CHRISTINE MACLEOD, *Inventing the Industrial Revolution: The English Patent System, 1660–1800* (Cambridge, 1988).

Ireland: T. W. MOODY, F. X. MARTIN, AND F. J. BYRNE (eds.), *Early Modern Ireland, 1534–1691* (A New History of Ireland, vol. 3; Oxford, 1976).

Jacobitism: PAUL MONOD, *Jacobitism and the English People, 1688–1788* (Cambridge, 1989).

James II: JOHN MILLER, *James II: A Study in Kingship* (Hove, 1978).

Judaism: JONATHAN I. ISRAEL, *European Jewry in the Age of Mercantilism, 1550–1750* (Oxford, 1989).

Lawyers: WILFRED PREST (ed.), *Lawyers in Early Modern Europe and America* (London, 1981).

Letter writing: SUSAN E. WHYMAN, *Sociability and Power in Late Stuart England: The Cultural Worlds of the Verneys, 1660–1720* (Oxford, 1999).

Literacy: DAVID CRESSY, *Literacy and the Social Order: Reading and Writing in Tudor and Stuart England* (Cambridge, 1980).

Literature: STEVEN N. ZWICKER (ed.), *The Cambridge Companion to English Literature, 1650–1740* (Cambridge, 1998).

Local government: ANTHONY FLETCHER, *Reform in the Provinces: The Government of Stuart England* (New Haven and London, 1986).

London: STEPHEN INWOOD, *A History of London* (London, 1998).

Longitude: WILLIAM J. H. ANDREWES (ed.), *The Quest for Longitude* (Cambridge, MA, 1996).

Marriage: LAWRENCE STONE, *The Family, Sex, and Marriage in England, 1500–1800* (London, 1977).

Medicine: ROY PORTER AND DOROTHY PORTER, *In Sickness and in Health: The British Experience, 1650–1850* (London, 1988).

Molyneux problem: MARJOLEIN DEGENAAR, *Molyneux's Problem* (Dordrecht, 1996).

Monmouth Rebellion: ROBIN CLIFTON, *The Last Popular Rebellion* (London, 1984).

Naturalization: DANIEL STATT, *Foreigners and Englishmen: The Controversy over Immigration and Population, 1660–1760* (Newark, DE, 1995).

Navy: JOHN EHRMAN, *The Navy in the War of William III, 1689–1697* (Cambridge, 1953).

Oxford: NICHOLAS TYACKE (ed.), *Seventeenth-Century Oxford* (History of the University of Oxford, vol. 4, Oxford, 1997).

Orientalism: EDWARD SAID, *Orientalism* (London, 1978).

Pirates: KRIS E. LANE, *Pillaging the Empire: Piracy in the Americas, 1500–1750* (Armonk, NY, and London, 1998).

Politeness: LAWRENCE E. KLEIN, *Shaftesbury and the Culture of Politeness* (Cambridge, 1994).

Politics: Tim Harris, *Politics under the Later Stuarts, 1660–1714* (London, 1993).

Poverty: PAUL SLACK, *From Reformation to Improvement: Public Welfare in Early Modern England* (Oxford, 1999).

Print culture: ADRIAN JOHNS, *The Nature of the Book: Print and Knowledge in the Making* (Chicago, 1998).

Professions: GEOFFREY HOLMES, *Augustan England: Professions, State, and Society, 1680–1730* (London, 1982).

Publishing: JOHN FEATHER, *A History of British Publishing* (London, 1988).

Quakers: ADRIAN DAVIES, *The Quakers in English Society, 1655–1725* (Oxford, 2000).

Reformation of manners: TONY CLAYDON, *William III and the Godly Revolution* (Cambridge, 1996).

Republic of letters: ANNE GOLDGAR, *Impolite Learning: Conduct and Community in the Republic of Letters, 1680–1750* (New Haven and London, 1995).

Religion, popular: KEITH THOMAS, *Religion and the Decline of Magic* (London, 1971).

Recoinage: MING-HSUN LI, *The Great Recoinage of 1696 to 1699* (London, 1963).

Roman Catholicism: JOHN MILLER, *Popery and Politics in England, 1660–1688* (Cambridge, 1983).

Royal touch: MARC BLOCH, *The Royal Touch* (London, 1973).

Science: MICHAEL HUNTER, *Science and Society in Restoration England* (Cambridge, 1981).

Scientific instruments: J. A. BENNETT, *The Divided Circle: A History of Instruments for Astronomy, Navigation and Surveying* (Oxford, 1987).

Scotland: JOHN ROBERTSON (ed.), *A Union for Empire: Political Thought and the British Union of 1707* (Cambridge, 1995).

Second Sight: MICHAEL HUNTER (ed.), *The Occult Laboratory: Magic, Science and Second Sight in Late Seventeenth-Century Scotland* (Woodbridge, Suffolk, 2001).

Sermons: LORI ANNE FERRELL AND PETER MCCULLOUGH (eds.), *The English Sermon Revised: Religion, Literature and History, 1600–1750* (Manchester, 2000).

Society: KEITH WRIGHTSON, *English Society, 1580–1680* (London, 1982).

State, growth of the: JOHN BREWER, *The Sinews of Power: War and the English State, 1688–1783* (London, 1989).

Three Kingdoms: BRENDAN BRADSHAW AND JOHN MORRILL (eds.), *The British Problem, c.1534–1707* (London, 1996).

Toleration: O. P. GRELL et al. (eds.), *From Persecution to Toleration: The Glorious Revolution and Religion in England* (Oxford, 1991).

Toland: ROBERT E. SULLIVAN, *John Toland and the Deist Controversy* (Cambridge, MA, 1982).

Towns: PETER BORSAY, *The English Urban Renaissance: Culture and Society in the Provincial Towns, 1660–1770* (Oxford, 1989).

Travel: JOHN STOYE, *English Travellers Abroad, 1604–1667* (London, 1952).

Weather: VLADIMIR JANKOVIC, *Reading the Skies: A Cultural History of English Weather, 1650–1820* (Manchester, 2000).

Wife sales: S. P. MENEFEE, *Wives for Sale* (Oxford, 1981).

William III: S. B. BAXTER, *William III* (London, 1966).

Women: SARA MENDELSON AND PATRICIA CRAWFORD, *Women in Early Modern England, 1550–1720* (Oxford, 1998).

Checklist of letters selected

This checklist identifies the 244 letters which have been included in this volume. The numeration follows that given in de Beer's edition of the complete correspondence.

29, 30, 59, 60, 64, 66, 72, 75, 81, 82, 83, 91, 96, 106, 108, 110, 118, 163, 171, 175, 177, 182, 197, 200, 219, 226, 250, 253, 261, 264, 268, 275, 279, 295, 297, 305, 310, 327, 328, 335, 337, 352, 360, 374, 394, 417, 426, 459, 475, 478, 528, 561, 605, 620, 687, 692, 696, 699, 765, 771, 776, 779, 797, 801, 805, 809, 828, 837, 842, 854, 886, 896, 911, 932, 951, 973, 974, 985, 1040, 1056, 1065, 1069, 1096, 1099, 1100, 1101, 1102, 1116, 1120, 1122, 1127, 1147, 1151, 1158, 1182, 1186, 1252, 1266, 1301, 1307, 1309, 1312, 1313, 1325, 1326, 1334, 1386, 1397, 1405, 1439, 1455, 1471, 1519, 1522, 1530, 1538, 1567, 1579, 1586, 1592, 1593, 1609, 1622, 1647, 1650, 1655, 1659, 1663, 1690, 1693, 1707, 1728, 1745, 1768, 1785, 1791, 1794, 1798, 1800, 1804, 1834, 1846, 1849, 1860, 1887, 1901, 1914, 1925, 1974, 1978, 1981, 1984, 2000, 2002, 2016, 2034, 2059, 2060, 2079, 2084, 2085, 2107, 2109, 2124, 2131, 2173, 2202, 2206, 2207, 2221, 2232, 2241, 2269, 2277, 2288, 2299, 2319, 2320, 2340, 2376, 2384, 2395, 2398, 2413, 2414, 2422, 2440, 2443, 2451, 2481, 2495, 2498, 2500, 2545, 2590, 2613, 2614, 2640, 2643, 2673, 2692, 2714, 2748, 2754, 2775, 2832, 2846, 2849, 2855, 2874, 2925, 2932, 2935, 3018, 3045, 3046, 3081, 3095, 3136, 3153, 3161, 3198, 3222, 3232, 3234, 3275, 3310, 3321, 3328, 3339, 3346, 3361, 3394, 3400, 3483, 3489, 3497, 3499, 3511, 3542, 3556, 3627, 3647, 3648.

Index

All but the principal classical authors are gathered under 'classical allusions/authors'. Books of the Bible are gathered under 'scriptural citations'. Foods (e.g. oysters, pistachios) are gathered under 'foodstuffs'. Primary goods (e.g. ambergris, tobacco) are gathered under 'trade, raw materials' or 'plants, fruits and trees'. Illnesses (e.g. smallpox) and treatments (e.g. bloodletting, laudanum) are gathered under 'health'. Chemistry, mathematics, etc. are gathered under 'science'. Under some of these heads, space constraints prevent full itemising. Other extensive headings include 'exercise, games and sport', 'industry', 'passions/emotions', 'medicine/medical profession', 'vices', 'virtues'. The Biographical Register has not been indexed, and the chapter headnotes only lightly so.